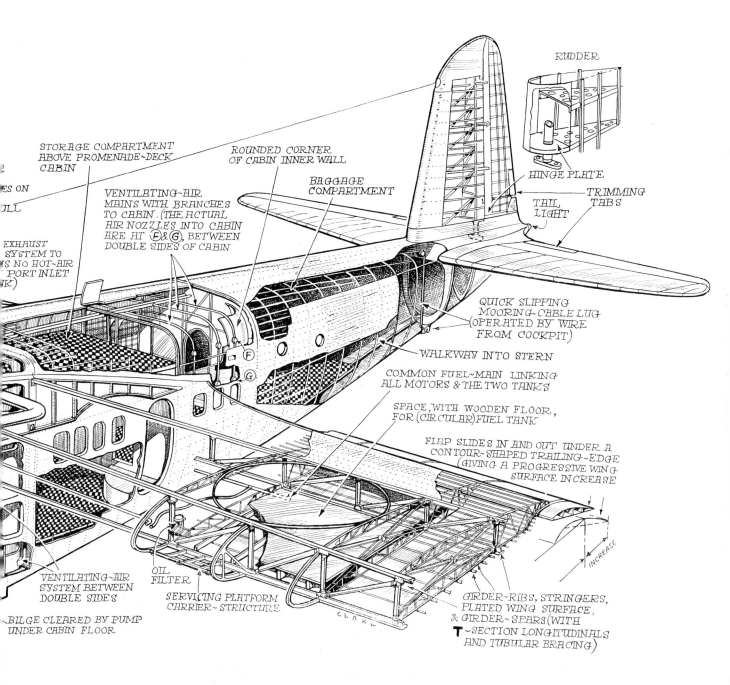

STORAGE COMPARTMENT
ABOVE PROMENADE~DECK
CABIN

ROUNDED CORNER
OF CABIN INNER WALL

RUDDER

BAGGAGE
COMPARTMENT

...ES ON
...LL

VENTILATING~AIR
MAINS WITH BRANCHES
TO CABIN. (THE ACTUAL
AIR NOZZLES INTO CABIN
ARE AT Ⓕ & Ⓖ, BETWEEN
DOUBLE SIDES OF CABIN

HINGE PLATE

TRIMMING
TABS

TAIL
LIGHT

...EXHAUST
...S SYSTEM TO
...S NO HOT~AIR
...PORT INLET
...K)

Ⓕ
Ⓖ

QUICK SLIPPING
MOORING~CABLE LUG
(OPERATED BY WIRE
FROM COCKPIT)

WALKWAY INTO STERN

COMMON FUEL~MAIN LINKING
ALL MOTORS & THE TWO TANKS

SPACE, WITH WOODEN FLOOR,
FOR (CIRCULAR) FUEL TANK

FLAP SLIDES IN AND OUT UNDER A
CONTOUR~SHAPED TRAILING~EDGE
(GIVING A PROGRESSIVE WING~
SURFACE INCREASE

INCREASE

INCREASE

VENTILATING~AIR
SYSTEM BETWEEN
DOUBLE SIDES

OIL
FILTER

SERVICING PLATFORM
CARRIER~STRUCTURE

CLARK

GIRDER~RIBS, STRINGERS,
PLATED WING SURFACE,
& GIRDER~SPARS (WITH
T~SECTION LONGITUDINALS
AND TUBULAR BRACING)

BILGE CLEARED BY PUMP
UNDER CABIN FLOOR

ALL FLOORS CONVENTIONALLY
RENDERED "CHECKY"
FOR CLARITY

(STARBOARD DOOR FOR MAILS)
(ACCUMULATORS & HATCHWAY
UP FROM GALLEY)
(AILERON CONTROL~RUNS &
OPENING INTO CENTRE~SECTION)

—

ADVENTUROUS EMPIRES

ADVENTUROUS EMPIRES

The Story of the Short Empire Flying-boats

PHILLIP E. SIMS

Airlife
England

Copyright © 2000 Phillip E. Sims

First published in the UK in 2000
by Airlife Publishing Ltd

British Library Cataloguing-in-Publication Data
 A catalogue record for this book
 is available from the British Library

ISBN 1 84037 130 7

Typeset by Servis Filmsetting Ltd, Manchester
Printed in England by Butler & Tanner Ltd., London and Frome.

Airlife Publishing Ltd
101 Longden Road, Shrewsbury, SY3 9EB, England
E-mail: airlife@airlifebooks.com
Website: www.airlifebooks.com

Dedicated to the spirits of all those who made this story.

Acknowledgements

The sources for *Adventurous Empires* are many and varied. In addition to the large number of books and periodicals consulted, over one hundred and fifty people have provided photographs and documents or written accounts of their contribution to this history. They have all given freely of their time and for that I am most thankful.

To credit some by name always leaves others unnamed and it is to the many unnamed people that I offer my first thanks.

With regard to the named, in no particular order, I wish to acknowledge the assistance of Mr Clive Richards, Royal Air Force Museum; Mrs Jean Buckberry, Mr Tim Pierce and staff at the Library of the Royal Air Force College Cranwell; Mr Ernest Aldis of the QANTAS Historical Collection; Sqn Ldr P. A. Harrison (RNZAF), Mr B. R. Anderson, and Mr Paul Sheehan, the three of whom assisted with the New Zealand escapades. Of those who were there, thanks to Mr Jack Chinery, Mr Kevin Corr, Mr Rowland Doyle, Mr Bob McNamara, Mr R. E. Moss, Mr A. T. Mears, Mr Gordon F. Staples. There are few flying-boat pilots left with us today but I feel honoured to have met or talked with Dundas K. Bednall, Captain Gerald H. Easton, Johnny Hackett, Vic Hodgkinson, Wg Cdr Lywood, DFC, RAF (Retd), Captain John Pascoe, Captain 'Taffy' Powell and Captain Dick Reid. Other crew members were the Radio Officers Mr Alan Finch and Mr G. 'Paddy' Cussans; the cabin staff, Mr Pat McKenny and Mr Cyril Thornes. My sincere appreciation to 'Bill' Morgan's family for granting access to Bill's archive. Help was also given by relatives: Mrs Helen Musson, Mrs Rosemary Madge, Mrs Una M. Hartle, Mr A. J. Brown, Mrs Ruth Harvey, Mrs K. Lawford, Mrs P. Inggs, Mrs Peggy Lewis, Mrs Gladys Woods and Dr C. J. Rose. Further information was forthcoming from engineers and traffic officers. The information provided by Mr Hugh Gordon, Mr Don Munro, Mr Alf Cowling, Mr Peter Newnham, Mr L. E. Turnill, Mr S. R. 'Bill' Peek, MBE, Mr Geoff Pett and Mr A. H. 'Steve' Stephen has been invaluable. Finally, there are the historians, researchers and enthusiasts: Mr Harry H. Pusey, Mr Richard P. Bateson, Mr Scott Bigby, Mr Dave Duxbury, Mr J. Evans, Mr Ray Gasparich, Mr J. Meaden, Mr H. Rolfe, Mr W. Waters, Mr R. A. R. Wilson, Mr Hugh J. Yea and Mr Brian Waterland, your articles, contacts, information and assistance is appreciated.

All the foregoing have assisted, many in no small part, but Brian Cassidy, author of *Flying Empires*, Edwin Cheetham, 'my photographer', and John Ellingworth, 'proof reader', have been a great source of inspiration and have sweated their efforts into this work. Further acknowledgement is given to Cobham plc, Darryl Robinson, R. T. Jackson, Whites Aviation Photos, Lufthansa, © Times Newspapers Limited (1936–1938), Quadrant Picture Library/Flight International, © IPC Magazines Ltd 1999 and Richard Drewe.

It was whilst reading Harald Penrose's account of *Corsair*, that I came across the name Hugh Gordon. After six or seven years we met and at the risk of ruining our relationship, I asked Hugh to write the foreword for *Adventurous Empires*. It was his action in the Congo that kindled my obsessive interest in the Empire Flying-Boats and I feel his foreword completes the circle.

When I met Johnny Hackett, he said I would meet many interesting people whilst researching this story. Sadly Johnny is with us no more but his words rang true. Many of the people I met have become friends. Alas, some have passed on, but I hope their spirits will live in this tale, along with the spirits of all those who made this story.

Foreword

The entry into service of the Empire flying-boats in 1937 was without doubt a milestone in the history of civil aviation. Commissioned by Imperial Airways, they opened the air routes of the British Empire, connecting England with the Dominions, and in so doing, fulfilled the dream of Lord Thompson of Cardington seven years earlier when, as Secretary of State for Air in the Labour Government of the time he sincerely believed that this was the role for the airships then being built. This was a dream that ended for him in the early hours of the morning of 5 October 1930 when he perished in the ill-fated airship R.101, which crashed in northern France on its maiden voyage to India. This was a disaster which shocked the nation, ending the British airship programme and, consequently, prospects of an Empire air service. And so it remained until the arrival of the Empire flying-boats.

These new aircraft would be a great advance on the existing Short biplanes, namely the Calcuttas and the later Kents, already in service with Imperial Airways operating across the Mediterranean between Brindisi and Alexandria. They were to be monoplanes with a much improved performance and, in addition to carrying passengers in exceptional comfort, were designed to carry freight and mail.

Under what was to be known as the Empire Airmail Scheme, first-class Royal Mail was to be carried at one and a half pence per ounce, the normal UK rate at that time. It should be remembered that there were two hundred and forty pence to the pound Sterling in those days. Not surprisingly, public imagination was fired at the prospect.

Political uncertainty prevailed in England in the early thirties; Germany was rearming but our armaments expansion programme had yet to begin. Industry, in this country, was in the doldrums, so for Short Bros of Rochester, the order to design and build twenty-eight flying-boats was a cause of great excitement, not only to the firm but to the whole of the surrounding Medway towns whose fortunes, to a large extent, depended on Short Bros for trade. I served my apprenticeship with this famous company and well remember the elation felt throughout the offices and works when the contract was announced.

I remember, too, air passengers' reactions to their first flight in one of these fine aircraft; their apprehension on the journey in the launch down Southampton Water from the docks and approaching this impressive craft at its moorings and the gasp of surprise on stepping aboard, at its vast interior. This was air travel with a difference and was to remain so until shortly after the war ended and the concrete runway was here to stay. It was then that travelling by air to the far corners of the Empire was to lose its magic.

Phillip Sims describes in great detail a part of aviation history which, until now, has been neglected. I applaud him for his dedication and enterprise. I am only sorry he was born too late to have journeyed with me in those magnificent flying machines, in the golden years of aviation.

Hugh Gordon
Halstock

Contents

INTRODUCTION   *11*

CHAPTER ONE **SETTING THE SCENE**

EARLY DAYS   *12*
Fabre & Benoist – AT&T – The Atlantic, Wellman, Hamel, J. C. Porte, USN Curtiss, Short Shamrock,
Brackley, Alcock & Brown.

GOVERNMENT POLICY   *13*
Sir Frederick Sykes – The Weir Committee – The 1920 Air Conference.

THE RAF AND CAIRO TO BAGHDAD   *14*
The Royal Air Force commences a service.

CONCEPTION OF IMPERIAL AIRWAYS   *14*
Sir Sefton Brancker – Sir Samuel Hoare – Hambling – Imperial Airways conceived.

BIRTH OF IMPERIAL AIRWAYS   *16*
The equipment – The pilots' 'strike' – Brackley – The management.

COBHAM'S EMPIRE AIR-ROUTE SURVEYS   *17*
Brancker and Cobham - Airships - Further Cobham surveys – 20,000 miles around Africa – Short
Valetta.

TO INDIA   *18*
Imperial order the D.H.66 – The Minister of State for Air, Sir Samuel Hoare, to India.

FORGING TO THE EDGE OF EMPIRE   *19*
To and across India – Trouble through Europe – Persian government prevarication – India – Through
Africa – Loss of Short Calcutta City of Khartoum *– Battles nearer home.*

CHAPTER TWO **THE RAISON D'ÊTRE**

BEFORE THE EMPIRE AIRMAIL SCHEME   *22*
Early airmail – Kingsford Smith saves the day – Airmail to Australia.

EMPIRE AIRMAIL SCHEME   *23*
The germ of an idea – Geddes presents his plan – Brackley to Australia in Armstrong Whitworth
Atalanta Astraea *– EAMS announced.*

THE FIRST DECADE   *23*
Macpherson Robertson Air Race – Imperial complacent – The Empire Airmail gains support – Short
Bros – The Imperial Flying-Boat.

CONSTRUCTION OF THE SHORT BROS EMPIRE 'BOAT   *26*
A description of the S.23 airframe – The Rochester works – Personnel – Royal visit.

EARLY FLIGHTS   *34*
Launch and flight of Canopus *– Loss of* Scipio *–* Caledonia *launched and certificated –*
Demonstrations and scheduled service.

CHAPTER THREE **CHANGE AND PROGRESS**

CHANGES AFOOT   *38*
The amalgamation of the independents into British Airways - Twelfth AGM.

ROUTES, SURVEYS AND SCHEDULES   *38*
Canopus, *the first schedule – Christmas 1936 airmail – 'Castor oiled' – African survey – Towards the*
antipodes – Kallang, the new Singapore – QEA enters the stage – Fysh/Brackley survey – Australian
impasse – Survey to Singapore.

EARLY DAYS | 48
Training – Building experience – Passenger comforts.

CHAPTER FOUR A WORTHY AIRLINE

THE LOSSES OF 1937 | 58
Loss of Capricornus, Courtier *and* Cygnus.

THE NORTH ATLANTIC | 69
Early studies, brave attempts – Political manoeuvres – Aeronautical answers – Gentlemen's Agreement – Trial crossings of Caledonia *and* Cambria.

UNREST – IMPERIAL DIFFICULTIES | 80
Empire Airmail Scheme – 1937 Turbulent times – Death of Geddes – Perkins and the Cadman Committee.

THE EMPIRE AIRMAIL SCHEME MATURES | 82
Christmas 1937 – Services are expanded and accelerated – Londonderry's letters – Christmas 1938.

REORGANIZATION | 87
Cadman Report – Arrival of Reith.

HOME BASE | 89
Hythe, a temporary arrangement – Langstone harbour.

MAINTENANCE | 92
Beaching – Turnaround – Night staging posts – Daily servicing – Engine starting.

CHAPTER FIVE ALTERNATIVE DEVELOPMENTS

DEVELOPMENTS ELSEWHERE | 97
Italy – France – Germany – America and Pan Am.

MAIA AND *MERCURY,* 'THE PICK-A-BACK 'PLANE' | 99
Early flights – The Atlantic – South Africa – The war and the end of composite.

CHAPTER SIX EASTWARD AND SOUTHWARD

THE MIDDLE EAST AND INDIA | 112
Ceres in India – Corio in the Persian Gulf – Calpurnia at Habbaniyah – Centurion in Calcutta – Calypso at Bahrain.

CAMBRIA FORCE-LANDS | 114
The rescue of Brigadier-General Lewin – Alcock and the forced landing of Cambria.

CORSAIR | 118
The forced landing of Corsair *– Salvaged.*

THE LOSS OF *CHALLENGER* | 132
Mozambique, 1 May 1939.

CHAPTER SEVEN BERMUDA AND THE ATLANTIC CONQUERED

BERMUDA | 136
The forced landing of Calypso *–* Cavalier, *Bermuda and the Atlantic miracle.*

AIR-TO-AIR REFUELLING AND THE ATLANTIC | 145
Early trials – Cobham joins research – Cobham to India – 'C-class' system works – Pan Am looks at the Atlantic – 'The Gentlemen's Agreement' laid to rest – The Clippers cross - 'G-class', and others – Cabot, Caribou, Connemara and Clyde equipped – Harrows to Botwood – Perseus trial – Pan Am and the Boeing 314 mail service – Connemara trials and loss – The S.30 system, final demonstration – Cabot's and Caribou's crossings of summer '39 – Impressed.

CHAPTER EIGHT TO AUSTRALIA AND BEYOND | 159
QANTAS receive the 'boats – Camilla to Singapore – Challenger and the Darwin débâcle – From a journalist's viewpoint – EAMS, Australia to England – Salvage of Coorong – Damage to Capella.

CHAPTER NINE REITH | 167
British Overseas Airways Corporation – Reith leaves.

CHAPTER TEN TASMAN EMPIRE AIRWAYS LIMITED (TEAL) 169
Kingsford Smith's Tasman dream – Tri-national talks – 1937 the Centaurus *flight – Samoan Clipper – Recruiting for TEAL – Delivery of* Australia *–* Aotearoa *–* Awarua *in Imperial colours –* Aotearoa *to New Zealand – Training and survey –* Awarua *to New Zealand – Inauguration.*

CHAPTER ELEVEN IMPERIAL AT WAR

ENGLAND 1940 183
The reserve routes – The Phoney War – Fall of France – Cabot, Caribou *and* Norway *–* Cathay *to France and Sikorsky – The Horseshoe conceived –* Clare *and* Clyde *to America.*

CORDELIA, CLIO AND THE 'G' 'BOATS 190
Cordelia *and* Clio *impressed into the RAF – RAF service of the 'G-class' 'boats.*

THE HORSESHOE ROUTE 191
Horseshoe activated – Clyde *and the Free French –* Cassiopeia, Corinthian *and* Cooee *– Loss of* Clyde *–* Habbaniyah *–* Coorong *and* Cambria *at Suda – Across Africa to Lagos –* Aqaba *– Japanese influence in India – Loss of* Cassiopeia *–* Cordelia's *dash to the Horseshoe – Captain Alger rescues Catalina crew – The loss of* Clare *– 'G-class' and Lake Kogella – Lock and the loss of* Golden Horn *– Some passengers and freight –* Reid, Cameronian *and* The City of Canton *– Peace looms.*

THE POOLE–FOYNES SHUTTLE 206
The Poole–Foynes shuttle – Victory in Europe.

CHAPTER TWELVE THE FAR EAST AND AUSTRALIA 209
RAAF commandeers Centaurus, Calypso, *and others – Special to Manila – The Phases – 7 December 1941 – RAAF early 'C-class' operations – Loss of* Corio *– Fall of Singapore – Darwin attacked – Tjilatjap shuttle –* Circe *lost –* Coogee *– 3 March, Broome – Loss of* Corinthian *– New Guinea and many rescues –* Calypso *and* Camilla *are lost –* Clifton *and* Coolangatta *follow –* Coriolanus *the sole survivor.*

CHAPTER THIRTEEN NEW ZEALAND AT WAR 225
Military use of TEAL 'boats – New Zealand hastens Awarua *–* Awarua *despatched –* Awarua *and surface raiders* Orion *and* Komet *–* Turakina *sunk –* Rangitane *sunk – Chief of Air Staff's Inquiry – Standing orders – Militarization of the 'boats, bombs, guns and radar – Liaison with No. 11 Sqn RAAF – January '42* Awarua *to Honolulu with Nash – Covert mission – Engine problems – Hamilton Standard propellers – No more specials – 1947 final beaching – After the Empires.*

CHAPTER FOURTEEN END OF EMPIRE 239
BOAC in turmoil – Empire seadrome again – 'There was a great future' but the 'C-class' scrapped – Land planes! – The Princess – Postscript from Mayo.

BIBLIOGRAPHY 248

APPENDICES
  1 The Imperial Airways/BOAC S.23 Flying-Boats 249
  2 The QANTAS Empire Airways S.23 Flying-Boats 250
  3 The Imperial Airways/BOAC S.30 Flying-Boats 250
  4 The Tasman Empire Airways Limited Flying-Boats 250
  5 Short S.33 Flying-Boats 251
  6 Short Composite S.20 *Maia* and S.21 *Mercury* 251
  7 Short S.26 'G-class' Flying-Boats 251
  8 Maps
     Africa 252
     Europe and the Mediterranean 253
     The North Atlantic 253
     The Indian Ocean 254
     South-east Asia, Australasia and Oceania 254

INDEX 255

Introduction

'No pictorial representation gives an idea of the size of the Empire 'Boat. To say that the inside is 17 feet from bottom of hull to top of wing does not bring home its capacity. The vastness of the craft becomes more obvious when you wander around a smoking room as large as any modern flat and rather higher than some, and then hear a member of the crew walking above you on the upper deck. Then consider that there are three more cabins, two of them even bigger and both longer, and they are being pushed through the air at up to 200 mph - and you begin to see what Shorts have achieved. Yet this boat, and another twenty-seven, was built without there ever having been a prototype.'

With these words, in October 1936, Thurstan James of *The Aeroplane* informed the British public about the Empire Flying-Boat. These same words were quoted by Harald Penrose in *Ominous Skies*, part of his History of British Aviation. It was in *Ominous Skies* that I read of Hugh Gordon and his achievement salvaging the flying-boat *Corsair*. She was forced down in the Congo, repaired, only to be crashed on take-off, and rebuilt again before finally joining the newly formed British Overseas Airways Corporation. Entrapped by the romance, perseverance and adventure of that tale, I embarked upon the search for the wonderful truth that lay behind Short Bros' flying-boat.

This is a story from a bygone age, recalling the most successful flying-boat airliner ever built. Designed to a specification for Imperial Airways, then Britain's national airline, it carried passengers and, more importantly, mail throughout the British Empire. In an age devoid of instant electronic communications but offering luxurious travel for the privileged few, every journey was an adventure, shared by passengers and crew. During the war, several of the 'boats were impressed into military service, seeing action in Europe and the Far East. The Empire Flying-Boat marked the watershed between the pioneering services of ponderous leviathans like the Handley Page H.P.42s and the grace and efficiency of the Lockheed Constellation and other American 'craft which dominated the post-war years.

Foremost, this is the tale of the realization of a dream and the efforts of those who made it possible. Alas the world moved on, at a pace probably accelerated by the Second World War, and the flying-boat was forced from the air routes. No more will *Adventurous Empires* grace the skies.

To capture the attitudes and perceptions of the day, contemporary units of measurement and place names are used. Although this may be the first publication laying out the career of the Empire Flying-Boats, some areas remain obscured by the mist of time. Just what was Captain Harrington doing in Bulgaria before September 1939 and were the crew fired upon? The tale of Harrington and others may now be lost for all time but perhaps this book will assist in bringing some remaining adventures to light.

Phillip E. Sims
Oakham
Rutland

CHAPTER ONE

Setting the Scene

*C*amilla lay, back broken, under the gaze of Port Moresby's Basilisk Lighthouse. The spray and sounds of the crash subsided, whilst the cries of those remaining in the flying-boat rent the tropical, storm-laden dusk. In the sinking cockpit, Aubrey Koch struggled to free himself from the captain's seat and the torrent of warm sea that was rapidly engulfing him. Stricken, *Camilla* began to settle. Captain Koch unbuckled his straps and felt his way forward, across the instrument panel, up and out of the shattered windscreen. His lungs struggled to retain his last vestige of breath, as he struck upwards towards the fading light. Almost twenty of the Australians and Americans aboard had survived the impact of the crash landing and the crushing force of the cargo, which, released from its failed restraints, surged forward into the servicemen. Limbs were broken and bodies torn, in those last seconds of movement.

The pilot broke the surface. This time the Japanese fighters were not circling overhead. He gasped at the air, still heavy with the fumes of what little petrol had remained. Spluttering, he called out for his crew, 'Peak – Barley – Phillips!' They could not answer. Koch swam around the wing, almost awash, and approached the rear door, intent upon releasing the life-raft, which had not deployed. In the half-open doorway, someone stood. Close by survivors were scrambling from the 'push-out' windows. Koch stretched out his hand to be pulled aboard. It was met by a kick from the doorway, as bodies fled the sinking flying-boat. Again he tried to climb aboard and again he was forcefully prevented.

He swam across to the port float and scrambled up onto the wing: he would enter the cabin via the top escape hatch and free the life-raft. Now in the cool night air, Koch felt the warm, sticky trickle that came from his torn right elbow. A survivor applied a field dressing, then Koch slipped into unconsciousness and slithered off the hull. Doused, he came round and clambered back upon the wing. *Camilla* lurched and, slowly, she sank into the depths of the Coral Sea.

Koch and three others were cast into the night. The rescue launch approached . . . and sped past. They swam. The Basilisk light seemed to move away from them. Koch, determined to survive this flying-boat crash, as he had his last, swam on defiantly. His mind wandered to those hectic December and January days just over a year ago, to his early days with QANTAS, to the routes that stretched all the way back to England and the mighty Empire Flying-Boats that had united the Commonwealth.

The truth that lies behind the romantic myths of the flying-boats is a wondrous tale of politics, dreams, engineering triumphs and the people who brought it all to life. To see the Empire Flying-Boats in perspective, it is necessary, briefly, to look back to the remnants of a distant world before the Great War.

EARLY DAYS
Fabre & Benoist – AT&T – The Atlantic, Wellman, Hamel, J. C. Porte, USN Curtiss, Short Shamrock, Brackley, Alcock & Brown.

The first take-off from water was achieved by a Frenchman, Henri Fabre, on 28 March 1910 at La Mede harbour, near Marseilles. The flying-boat had been born. Across the border, in Germany, the world's first commercial passenger air service was being offered by an airship company. Between 1910 and 1914 the company carried 35,000 fare-paying passengers between various German cities. The two dreams were joined when the first scheduled use of a heavier-than-air craft was made in Florida. A twenty-two-mile route from St Petersburg to Tampa was operated by the Benoist Company and they flew the first schedule on 1 January 1914. Four months and 1,024 passengers later, the service ceased.

Other pioneers of waterborne craft were Glenn Curtiss in America, Short brothers in England and several German manufacturers. With the end of the First World War, a number of aircraft companies started passenger air services, using crudely converted ex-military aircraft. Passengers flew in open cockpits and were provided with heavy clothing to keep the cold and wet at bay.

Britain's first airline, Aircraft Transport and Travel (AT&T) Limited, had been registered in London in October 1916 and operated from the RAF training camp at Hounslow, now part of Heathrow. The commencement of scheduled services, however, had to wait until the war's end. Meanwhile, the Royal Air Force provided air transport from London to Paris for Government officials attending the Versailles Peace Conference. The following year, on 29 March 1920, Customs Facilities were transferred to the south London site at Croydon, previously known as Waddon. Another year on, 31 March 1921, Croydon became the official London

Airport and remained so for the next two decades.

Similar services were starting up all around the world.

To the west, the siren of the Atlantic Ocean had been heard some years previous, and although she failed to lure one Walter Wellman to a watery grave, the costly attempts to traverse the Atlantic started in earnest before the First World War. Wellman, probably more inspired than prepared, departed Atlantic City on 15 October 1910 in his dirigible *America*. This first attempted air crossing of the North Atlantic ended forty-eight hours later. Happily, the crew of five and their dog were rescued by the British steamer SS *Trent*. There were, however, two serious attempts at the Atlantic before war broke out. Gustav Hamel had managed private backing and commissioned Martinsyde to build a 'plane, and J. C. Porte received assistance from an American millionaire to cross in a Curtiss flying-boat. The early death of Hamel and the outbreak of war curtailed these attempts.

Rapid developments in aviation spawned by the war brought forth more serious attempts to cross the Atlantic. A United States Navy expedition, flying Curtiss NC-1, NC-3 and NC-4 'boats, attempted the crossing eastward. They routed by way of Newfoundland, the Azores, Lisbon and finally Plymouth. This amazing feat of navigation was in fact a feat of surface support. They were aided by sixty-eight United States Navy destroyers, one stationed every fifty miles along the route. Using radio, smoke and pyrotechnics the United States Navy provided navigational assistance. Although NC-1 and NC-3 force-landed safely, NC-4, *Liberty*, arrived in England on 31 May 1919, having left Newfoundland a fortnight beforehand.

At this stage, the Short Brothers made their appearance, as entrants in the *Daily Mail* £10,000 non-stop transatlantic crossing challenge. They offered the Short Shirl, a single-engined biplane torpedo bomber. Shorts intended to fly their aircraft, which had a range of 3,200 miles, westwards from Ireland. Another Shirl, flown by Shorts' test pilot, John Lankester Parker, accompanied the 'Atlantic Shirl', now christened *Shamrock*. They left Rochester to position for the attempt but tragedy struck when *Shamrock*'s engine failed and she came down in the Irish Sea off Anglesey. Although there were no fatalities, the attempt was cancelled. Meanwhile, Handley Page were preparing their V/1500 4-engined biplane 'Berlin' bomber, with one Major Brackley at the controls, for their attempt from Newfoundland. However, less than a month after the US Navy crossing, the *Daily Mail* prize went to Alcock and Brown who, on 14 and 15 June 1919, made the first non-stop crossing of the Atlantic in a Vickers Vimy biplane.

GOVERNMENT POLICY
Sir Fredrick Sykes – The Weir Committee – The 1920 Air Conference.

Before the First World War, civil aviation was unregulated and during the war prohibited. Following the Armistice, civil aviation came under the jurisdiction of the Air Ministry, who, so it appeared, were primarily concerned with military aviation.

In February 1919, the Air Ministry appointed Sir Fredrick Sykes as Controller-General, Civil Aviation. He saw that it was his duty to:

'… try to extend the air supremacy which we [Great Britain] *have gained in the war to civil flying.'*

He gave Major-General Ernest Swinton, who was to become a leading protagonist in the field of civil aviation, the post of Controller of Information. The ban on civil flying was lifted on 1 May 1919. This delay, following the Armistice, allowed time for the creation of the Civil Aviation Department of the Air Ministry and the passage through Parliament of the Air Navigation Act, but permitted continental competitors to steal a march on British efforts. The Act may have ensured the future safety of British skies but it did not release funds for Sykes's pursuance of those aspects he felt important to the future of Imperial air travel, namely blind-flying, night landing and the development and promotion of commercial flying-boats.

The Government's policy towards civil aviation was, at the time, summed up by Winston Churchill, the Secretary of State for Air:

'I do not myself believe that it is the business of Government to carry civil aviation forward by means of great expenditure of public money. … The best thing we [the Government] *can do is to make sure that we do not get in the way of it* [civil aviation].'

Accordingly, the Weir Advisory Committee on Civil Aviation was established, to 'advise and report to the Secretary of State for Air on the best methods of organising Imperial air routes'. The Committee believed a demonstration route ought be made operative as soon as possible. The chosen route was Cairo, that 'Clapham Junction of the air', to Karachi. Cairo to Cape Town could follow. As these routes crossed vast tracts of the British Empire, there would be no problem with overflight clearances. The Committee recommended that the service should be operated by a State-aided private enterprise, with meteorological forecasting, radio facilities and airport services being provided at public expense. The Committee also recognized the importance of carrying mail as a lucrative cargo. They estimated that, if air travel was used, the travelling time from London to Bombay could be cut from fourteen to seven days.

Although Weir's recommendations were implemented, Churchill asked the Committee to consider what Government measures should be taken to develop civil aviation – 'bearing in mind the need for the utmost economy'.

By March 1920, the Weir Committee was of the opinion that civil aviation needed State aid. However, gravely threatening Weir's proposals and doing little other than reiterating his views of the previous year,

Churchill stated:

'Civil aviation must fly by itself; the Government cannot possibly hold it up in the air.'

Despite Churchill's statement, Weir managed to persuade Churchill to endorse the recommended subsidies, but on 15 June 1920, the Treasury published their report upon the Weir Committee. The tone was most unsupportive and a bitterly disappointed Weir pleaded emotively that the Cabinet should go to Croydon and witness the air operations:

'The whole thing is full of romance and practical possibilities. The service may be irregular, many of the arrangements very crude, but quite definitely the work is started and is being done ... a new era in communications is being opened up. This has all been done in eighteen months. Think what might be done with some help in the next two years.'

In October 1920, during the opening address of an 'Air Conference' sponsored by the Air Ministry, Sykes expressed the opinion that:

'... the nation which is strongest in air traffic will be the strongest in the aerial warfare of the future.'

The Conference closed, calling upon the Government to 'decide definitely' that first-class internal mail should travel by air on selected routes. There was to be no action on airmail until 1934.

THE RAF AND CAIRO TO BAGHDAD
The Royal Air Force commences a service.

It was a coincidence, that part of Weir's recommended Cairo to Karachi route was opened up to support the United Kingdom's policing of Iraq. On 23 June 1921, the RAF began a mail service from Cairo to Baghdad; this service was to continue until commercial schedules replaced it in January 1927.

It was proposed to fly the route throughout the year and in all weathers, as it was envisaged that it would be of good training value to the RAF. However, the desert between Jerusalem and the Euphrates, although crossed by ancient caravans, was considered a great natural barrier. It was decided to ease navigation by providing a path for the pilots to follow. Although originally the route was to be blazed by craters blown into the desert's surface, it was soon noticed that, in most places, tyre tracks left by the reconnaissance vehicles were adequately visible from the air. Where necessary, the track was heightened by a ploughed furrow. In the event of a force-landing, the aircraft would be able to land next to the track. Hopefully, within a few hours the crew would be found, before dehydration overwhelmed them. Additionally, emergency landing fields, each identified by a letter or number marked onto the sands, were sited every fifteen to twenty miles. Despite non-stop re-marking of the track, it was not always easily seen from the air, especially after the rains, in dust storms or simply against the constant desert glare. If the pilot lost sight of the track for a moment he would, invariably, have to fly a zig-zag in search of the track.

Every flight was an adventure in itself, fraught with danger. RAF pilot Roderick Hill, flying a Vickers Vernon, recorded such a journey. It was during his third trip that he suffered engine trouble and force-landed in the desert. There, working through the night, he and his crew managed to repair the engine and next morning they were airborne again. They had not been aloft long before they were subjected to a vicious battering from turbulence. The Vernon was flung a thousand feet up and down at a time. Hill took a pounding at the controls but suffered no more than the aircraft. A terrible, frightening vibration started to shake the plane and, above the roar of the slipstream and the growl of the starboard engine, the port engine, with much banging and screeching of metal, shook itself to pieces. On the remaining engine, Hill executed a forced landing next to a 2,000-year-old Roman fort. Soon, they had rigged up a wireless aerial and, hand cranking the generator in the heat of the day, managed to send a distress message. Cairo, Baghdad and Amman acknowledged them. The following afternoon, another Vernon landed next to the fort to rescue, not them, but the mail which had to be hurried on. Left alone, awaiting overland help and repairs, Hill and his crew summoned all their courage and explored the eerie Roman fort. Creeping fearfully among the partly ruined rooms, they found several skeletons, one of which had been decapitated. Needless to say, they did not venture back to the fort.

Eventually, just before dusk on the second day, a convoy was seen approaching them from the horizon, an armoured car and two desert vehicles. The following day, after a more comfortable night, spares were flown in by three aircraft. Again, working through the night, they replaced the engine and by mid-morning on the third day they were ready to fly out.

Such was the way of flights across the Empire in the early 1920s.

CONCEPTION OF IMPERIAL AIRWAYS
Sir Sefton Brancker – Sir Samuel Hoare – Hambling – Imperial Airways conceived.

Sykes remained Controller-General of Civil Aviation until April 1922, when he was replaced by Sir Sefton Brancker, a pilot of meagre ability, but an outstanding organizer. Brancker was a driving force behind British civil aviation.

His Air Minister wrote of him:

'Brancker had the faults of his great qualities. He was a superb propagandist, and when he wrote or spoke in public, his enthusiasm swept away the words of caution in his official briefs.'

Sir Sefton Brancker served until his death in the R.101 disaster; he was irreplaceable.

In October 1922, the Bonar Law Conservative Government appointed Sir Samuel Hoare as Secretary of State for Air. Brancker briefed him well, and Sir Samuel rapidly appreciated the complexities of his new Ministry and, as an imperialist:

> '... saw in the creation of air routes the chance of uniting the scattered countries of the Empire and Commonwealth.'

He was greatly impressed by the advances made in Australia by the budding Queensland and Northern Territories Aerial Service Company, QANTAS, operated by three ex-servicemen, Fergus McMaster, Pat McGuinness and Hudson Fysh. Equally impressive were the bold and skilful Australian pilots, Ross Smith and Bert Hinkler. Hoare held this enterprise as an example of what was possible with a little foresight and investment.

Hoare was aware that a suspicious Treasury coupled with an ill-informed and dubious public were not ideal progenitors of civil aviation. The airlines, without security of income, relying only upon sporadic Government doles, could not be expected to plan ahead or make long-term investments. Of this Hoare said:

> 'The Treasury did not believe in Civil Aviation and strongly objected to long-term commitments to companies that were obviously in financial difficulties.... It seemed to me that the best way to convert the critics was to invite two or three well known businessmen to look at the problem from a practical angle, and to give to me their conclusions with least possible delay.'

For that, Hoare formed the Hambling Committee, and within a month they were able to report. Hambling's findings reminded the Government that they had, effectively, abandoned the principle of competition the previous October, when they had finally granted subsidies. Airlines were unwilling to risk expansion when operating only Government-allotted routes. Hambling proposed that a monopoly company, with some board members nominated by the Government, should be formed. The recommendations were accepted by the Cabinet and announced with the Air Estimates of 1923–24.

Bonar Law resigned as Prime Minister in May and Baldwin became the nation's leader. He knew nothing of aviation but:

> 'The romantic streak in his complex character had reacted to the wide horizons and undiscovered opportunities of the air.'

Hoare was offered a seat in the Cabinet. The importance of aviation was at last being recognized but, despite Cabinet approval for Hoare's air-transport plan, Hoare identified a further obstacle in the way of air progress – the public ignorance of everything to do with aviation. Matters were not helped by an unfavourable press that, as late as 1924, were noting that the grass at Croydon was cut by a horse-drawn mower and off-duty pilots used to rough shoot on the aerodrome and its surrounds. In an attempt to make the public more air-minded, Hoare regularly travelled by air to demonstrate its practicality.

Hoare experienced difficulty promoting his proposed monopoly airline, formed from Daimler Airways with Colonel Searle and Woods Humphery, Handley Page Transport, Instone Airline and British Marine Air Navigation. After much bargaining, the rival groups and the Government came together. Each airline brought its own strengths: Daimler style, Handley Page great technical ability, and Instone, a flair for publicity. Samuel Instone had once flown grouse across to Paris for the lunch of Lord Londonderry, the Parliamentary Under Secretary of State for Air. Also, Instone's was the first airline to introduce blue serge uniforms with brass buttons which, since 1922, have become de rigueur for airline pilots.

Hoare offered Sir Eric Campbell Geddes the chairmanship of the proposed airline. Geddes was then Managing Director of the Dunlop Rubber Company. To his earlier career in politics and commerce he had brought his massive physique, clean-cut, clean-shaven appearance, coupled with a forceful personality. With quickness and vigour he had tackled the country's problems. He was an expert on transport, especially railways, had been First Lord of the Admiralty 1917–18, Minister of Transport 1919–21 and had headed the amalgamation of the railways. He was best known, or feared, as the politician who had wielded the 'Geddes Axe', when he chaired the 1922 Inquiry into National Expenditure. He was to become a most competent Chairman of Imperial Airways. Geddes accepted the appointment on condition that Sir John George Beharrell, also at Dunlop, could accompany him.

Beharrell was a tactful Yorkshireman of Hebraic appearance. He had been financial adviser to Geddes at Dunlop and was to hold a similar post at Imperial. Initially a railways man, during the First World War he became first Assistant Director-General Transportation, France, and later Assistant Inspector-General Transportation all Theatres of War. He achieved the rank of Lieutenant-Colonel, was awarded the DSO in 1917 and was knighted in 1919. Periods at the Admiralty, as Director of Statistics, and the Ministry of Transport were followed by attachment to the Geddes Committee on National Expenditure.

A contract was signed on 3 November 1923 and thus a monopoly civil air transport company, privately financed but Government backed was formed. It was intended to call the new organization British Air Transport Service, but Woods Humphery observed the initials spelt BATS, and he suggested Imperial Air Transport Ltd. The Imperial Air Transport Company, later changed to Imperial Airways, was founded with £1 million capital and a further £1 million over the next ten years. All the pilots and aircraft were to be British. This all-British equipment policy would lead to criticism in future years. Contrary to Hambling's recommendation, the pilots would be part of the Royal Air Force Reserve and the Government could commandeer all aircraft if necessary.

BIRTH OF IMPERIAL AIRWAYS
The equipment – The pilots' 'strike' – Brackley – The management.

Hambling's recommendation and Hoare's plan became reality on 1 April 1924. The main independents, Handley Page Transport, Instone, Daimler and British Marine, combined their assorted aircraft to become Imperial Airways. The new Imperial Airways fleet comprised a selection of Handley Page O/400 derivatives, a number of de Havilland aircraft and two examples of each of Vickers' and Supermarine's handiwork: a total of sixteen aircraft with an overall seating capacity of about 120. With the exception of the Ensigns and the 'C-class' 'boats, some dozen years later, Imperial Airways never ordered its aircraft in large numbers. They were to pay high prices for hand-built 'craft.

The independent airlines brought their pilots who promptly went on strike. The facts and grievances were in dispute. The pilots stated Imperial Airways, now the sole employer of civil pilots in the United Kingdom, had not offered them contracts and wished to impose upon them lower pay and poorer conditions of service. The offer that Imperial was said to have made, a small retainer and further payment by the mile flown, would penalize those flying slower aircraft. Additionally, termination of employment would be at one day's notice. The pilots, somewhat aggrieved, formed a union affiliated to the Trade Union Congress and refused to fly. To seek a solution, and at the request of the pilots, Imperial Airways called in Major Brackley as intermediary. Brackley is one of several figures around which this story revolves.

Major Herbert George Brackley ('Brackles') had been a Royal Naval Air Service squadron commander before becoming Chief Pilot to Handley Page. Although part of Handley Page's unsuccessful transatlantic attempt, 'Brackles' had overseen the London to Paris schedules and worked alongside G. E. Woods Humphery, now appointed Imperial Airways General Manager. Brackley found himself in a difficult position, having been a colleague of Woods Humphery at Handley Page. There, following an accident, a misunderstanding between

17 March 1925, (L to R) Mr Alan Cobham, his mechanic Arthur B. Elliott and Air Vice-Marshal Sir Sefton Brancker, Director of Civil Aviation, after their successful flight to India and return. The flight enabled Sir Sefton to survey the possibilities of an Empire Air Service.
(Photograph courtesy of Cobham plc)

Woods Humphery and the pilots occurred and Brackley had been called in to represent the pilots, with whom he later sided. Although Woods Humphery had been a Royal Flying Corps Major, the General Manager of Handley Page Transport and the Manager of Daimler Airways, some said he lacked the credibility required of the General Manager of Imperial Airways. It was said he contributed to the root cause of the current pilots' strike. There was even a story that on one occasion he had found a man lounging in the waiting room. Believing him to be a pilot, Woods Humphery peremptorily dismissed him, only to discover he was a passenger awaiting a delayed flight. Despite the delicate state of affairs, Brackley accepted the offer to arbitrate. The dispute was resolved and Imperial services, delayed until 26 April, commenced. In the opinion of the pilots, they had not been on strike; they had simply refused to accept the jobs on the terms offered.

COBHAM'S EMPIRE AIR-ROUTE SURVEYS
Brancker and Cobham – Airships – Further Cobham surveys – 20,000 miles around Africa – Short Valetta.

Following its 1924 beginnings, Imperial Airways financed a survey flight to India and Burma. They engaged Alan Cobham, Britain's most enthusiastic aviation pioneer, to take on this venture. He, in turn, persuaded the Director of Civil Aviation, Sir Sefton Brancker, to accompany him and his engineer, Arthur B. Elliott. Cobham's aircraft was the D.H.50, G-EBFO. Brancker was bound for India, to discuss future airship operations, and he accepted that this flight with Cobham would be prestigious to both British and Empire aviation. The journey started on 10 November 1924 and by 17 March 1925, when they arrived back in England, they had flown 18,000 miles in 210 flying hours.

Many experts argued the advantages of lighter-than-air craft and cited the German experience of operating large airships. The British planned to operate airships to India and across the Atlantic. To those ends, mooring masts and hangars were constructed at Ismailia, Karachi and Montreal. Whilst the Director of Civil Aviation was discussing the forthcoming airship operations with the Indian authorities, the Air Ministry broadly followed the plans in the Burney Airship Scheme and oversaw the construction of the two ill-fated British airships, R.100 and R.101. However, airship operations were still five years away and, in the meantime, a heavier-than-air option was required, hence Imperial Airways sponsored Cobham's survey flights.

Looking into the future, although R.101's disastrous maiden flight to India, in October 1930, and the resultant scrapping of R.100 would officially put paid to British airship hopes, the British lighter-than-air dream would continue to glimmer. As late as April 1937, the airship lobby was heartened by the shipping lines' forecasts of trade being lost to the German Zeppelins. As a result of these dismal predictions, the British Zeppelin Syndicate would be formed with a view to operating two Zeppelins across the Atlantic. The R.100-series

mooring facilities, which were to remain in existence at Cardington and Montreal for some years to come, would be used. Supporters of the argument would hark back to eight years of German transatlantic passenger operations which were yet to experience one occurrence of air sickness.

However, Lakehurst, New Jersey, awaited the airship!

On 6 May 1937, thirty-five people perished when the *Hindenburg*, the world's largest airship, burst into flames at Lakehurst, whilst mooring at the end of her first crossing for the season. Few bodies were identified, so fiercely did the hydrogen and light alloy burn, and six people were never accounted for. Of the thirty-six passengers and sixty-one crew, eleven passengers and twenty crew were incinerated or declared missing. Some of the survivors suffered horrific injuries and one of the ground crew succumbed to burns he sustained during the catastrophe. He, and three others, died from their injuries after the holocaust.

But, in 1925, the end of the airship lay ahead.

After Cobham and Brancker's return to England, in March 1925, Brancker recommended that Imperial Airways should commence an England to India service by taking over the RAF's already well-proved Cairo to Baghdad sector. Meanwhile, Cobham's aircraft was prepared for a 'hot and high' survey flight to South Africa. A more powerful engine, the 385 hp Armstrong Siddeley Jaguar, was installed, and between 16 November 1925 and 17 February 1926 Cobham, Elliott and Gaumont cameraman B. W. G. Emmott flew from Croydon to the Cape. They covered 6,000 miles and arrived back at Croydon on 13 March 1926.

Not everybody was in favour of the airship for long-distance travel. Many favoured the seaplane or flying-boat, which, they argued, would be safer in the event of a forced landing. Additionally, or so it was believed, there would be no requirement to construct expensive aerodromes. Seaplane supporters continued, that once more powerful engines had been developed, the problems of getting airborne with a worthwhile payload would have been solved.

Cobham supported this view and, almost immediately after the South Africa flight, he had the D.H.50 fitted with a pair of Short Bros floats and readied for an epic survey flight to Australia. Cobham, in his open cockpit, and radio-operator-cum-engineer, Arthur Elliott, crammed into the small cabin, lifted from the River Medway on 30 June 1926.

Cobham soon discovered the difficulties of operating a float-plane off unknown and flowing waters. Once alighted and having switched off the engine, a float-plane is at the mercy of the wind and currents and can soon drift into buoys or jetties. Not only that, it is not the strongest of craft. It was necessary to get help when mooring, and much to Cobham's annoyance, since shared by many an Englishman, he discovered that foreign river-folk did not understand English, even when shouted loudly.

At the end of the first week, tragedy struck; whilst

caught in a sandstorm over southern Iraq he descended low over the marsh reed beds. A violent explosion was heard to come from the cabin. He shouted to Elliott, to inquire what was happening, but could hear nothing because of the engine's roar. Cobham was passed a note from Elliott, 'A petrol pipe has burst. I am bleeding a pot of blood.' With grim determination Cobham continued to Basra, where he coerced the natives into helping him lift Elliott from the cabin. He had been shot by a Marsh Arab. Sadly, Elliott died in hospital at Basra.

A Royal Air Force mechanic, Sergeant Ward, volunteered to crew for the remainder of the flight. Cobham found the flight most exhausting. Poor weather, especially torrential rain, changes of climate and changes of time zone all combined to tax even the strongest of travellers. The final hazard was the six-hour crossing of the hostile Timor Sea, the longest expanse of water on the proposed Empire route. On 5 August 1926, Cobham landed at Darwin and eventually arrived in Melbourne on 15 August. Finally, on 1 October, having flown for 320 hours over seventy-eight days, he alighted upon the Thames at Westminster. On the following day, Sir Samuel Hoare announced King George V's award of a knighthood for Cobham.

A year later, 17 November 1927, Cobham commenced his round-Africa survey. A Short Singapore was provided by the RAF and financial support came from Sir Charles (later Lord) Wakefield. Cobham's crew of five included his wife and a cinematographer. They routed across France and the Mediterranean to Alexandria and then up the Nile to Lake Victoria. They continued south to the coast at Beira. From Beira, they continued clockwise, hugging the coast of Africa and on to Gibraltar. They were dogged by misfortune and on several occasions almost lost the 'boat. Cobham's gritted and cussed determination brought them back to England on 4 June 1928 after a momentous 20,000-mile journey.

On 22 July 1931, in the Short S.11 Valetta float-plane, Cobham departed Rochester for Lake Kivu, to the west of Lake Victoria. The route was selected for its diversity and would be a true test of future flying-boat operations. For this flight, in addition to a cinematographer, Cobham was accompanied by a Marconi wireless operator. After a most successful flight, they returned to Rochester on 31 August. These flights by Cobham, and others by Imperial themselves, paved the way for the eventual Empire, or 'Red Route', routes across the globe. However, it was necessary to encourage the public to travel by air. Such motivation was to be given by Air Minister Hoare.

TO INDIA
Imperial order the D.H.66 – The Minister of State for Air, Sir Samuel Hoare, to India.

Belatedly, in November 1925, Imperial Airways and the British Government agreed that the Cairo to Basra route should be civilianized and extended to Karachi. The route would cross the hostile wildernesses of Egypt, Palestine, Transjordan, Iraq and Persia before passing Baluchistan destined for Karachi. Imperial placed an order for five land planes in order to maintain a fortnightly freight and mail schedule over the route. In response, de Havilland designed the biplane, three-engined D.H.66. The pilot and navigator were located in an open cockpit, whilst the engineer and wireless operator enjoyed the comforts of a small cabin. The passenger cabin could accommodate fourteen, but usually only seven passengers were carried, as the extra payload was required for the mails. The aircraft had an endurance of five hours and it was hoped that by having three engines, forced landings would be kept to a minimum. At that time in Europe, Imperial Airways averaged a forced landing once in every seven flights.

A competition in the *Meccano Magazine* called for a name for the new D.H.66. Mr E. F. Hope-Jones, of Eton College, claimed the honour of having his suggestion selected, *Hercules*.

The first Hercules left Croydon for Cairo on 20 December 1926. On 27 December, a more prestigious flight rose from Croydon's frosty grass. This flight carried the Minister of State for Air, Sir Samuel Hoare, and he was bound for Karachi. As the Parliamentary Christmas recess was the only time he could absent himself, he was forced to fly through the dangers and uncertainties of a European winter to face the diplomatic uncertainties of negotiating permission to overfly Persia. Such approval was not forthcoming and stops on the southern coast of Persia were made without official approval. Many of his friends and colleagues, the Prime Minister included, attempted to dissuade him. Never before had a Cabinet Minister contemplated such a long air-journey. To compound the concern of others, Sir Samuel was adamant that Lady Maude, his wife, should accompany him. She wished to prove that flying was not an adventure reserved for men.

The Hoares' fellow passengers were Christopher Bullock (Hoare's Principal Private Secretary) and Sir Geoffrey Salmond (AOC India). The responsibility of aircraft commander rested with F. L. Barnard until they reached Aboukir (Alexandria), where C. F. Wolley Dod took command. Throughout the voyage, Squadron Leader E. L. Johnston acted as the navigator and Mr Hatchett was the wireless operator. Bristol provided a Mr Mayer to service the engines, and an official photographer, B. W. G. Emmott, was also carried.

Sir Samuel was trying to convince a sceptical British public that flying was an ordinary affair and quite safe. Lady Maude, on the other hand, was faced with more decorous problems: a complete yet practical and lightweight wardrobe. Although she travelled without her maid, she still needed to appear smart at the end of each exhausting day's flying. At night, appropriate dress was required for the many official functions Lord and Lady Hoare were to attend *en route*. For all this she was allowed only a pair of cases. Lady Maude applied great ingenuity to meet the challenge. To contain her make-up and toiletries, she used aluminium containers instead of the finest chinas and glass to which she was more accustomed. For their India stay, they did of course send luggage ahead by sea.

The flight itself would not be without discomfort. In the air, they would be confronted by heat and cold, sun and rain. In addition, only the minimum of comforts would be found at the refuelling stops. In the event, the most useful clothes turned out to be wellington boots, for the muddy aerodromes, and a dressing gown, that Lady Maude was able to wear on the aeroplane. She took two outfits, one a suit made from a new stockinet material worn with a crêpe de Chine jumper, and the other, a woollen jumper and tweed skirt. Over these she could wear leather or fur coats, accompanied by a felt hat. For evenings, the obligatory black evening dress was worn.

With the preparations, including the making of wills, complete, Sir Samuel and Lady Maude boarded the aircraft. Should they be forced down into the Mediterranean, they carried the latest life-preserving jackets and six Royal Navy destroyers had steamed into the area. The first leg was horrendous, the most appalling of storms lashing the bucking aircraft with sleet and snow. Cold, airsick and miserable the group disembarked at Dijon, during refuelling. From then on they flew two 300-mile legs a day, landing for lunch and refuelling around noon. At every stop speeches were made and banquets attended. Basra was reached at the end of the first gruelling week.

Leaving the comfort and security of the route previously blazed by the RAF, they flew on eastward, across the top of the Persian Gulf, bound for India. Their second night out from Basra was spent at Jask. Here, the only form of transport to convey them from the strip to the telegraph station, where they were accommodated, was camel. Their departure from Jask was even more uncomfortable. They were immediately ensnared by a violent dust storm. In an attempt to put back down at Jask, Wolley Dod descended over what he thought was the sea. By the narrowest of margins they missed striking a party of Persian caravanners trekking along the coast. They did, however, finally land safely and the remainder of the day was spent at the telegraph station waiting out the storm.

Of that day's flight, Lady Maude said, 'We were much too interested to be frightened.'

The following day they clambered up to 10,000 feet in an effort to fly above the dust storm and on to Karachi. After eleven adventure-filled days the Hoares arrived in Karachi, on 6 January 1927. Here they received a congratulatory telegram from the King. Continuing to Delhi, on 8 January, the Viceroy's wife christened the D.H.66, *City of Delhi*. The flight was inaugural in name only. Whilst the Hoares had flown to India, the more plebeian fare-payer had to catch a succession of cars, buses, Mediterranean liners and trains to make the same journey across Europe to Cairo and beyond. As of yet, there were no seaplanes capable of carrying a useful load across the Mediterranean, and the European governments squabbled about overflying rights and routes. The Hoares returned to Cairo by air and then took boat and train to England, arriving back on 17 February 1927.

Following Hoare's return, Neville Chamberlain said:

'There is no doubt that your demonstration has impressed forcibly upon the public the immense progress in safety and reliability of air travel and you have done a great service to aviation, and incidentally the Government.'

FORGING TO THE EDGE OF EMPIRE
To and across India – Trouble through Europe – Persian government prevarication – India – Through Africa – Loss of Short Calcutta City of Khartoum – Battles nearer home.

In 1927, the erection of radio masts, the construction of aerodromes and the provision of facilities for meteorological and air traffic services for the routes to South Africa and India were well under way. By 1933, radio stations had been established every 250 miles along the routes.

Although the route to India had been proved in 1927 by the Hoare flight, Persian government prevarication delayed the schedule two years. Eventually, on 30 March 1929, the weekly carriage of commercial passengers and mail to Karachi commenced. The journey took seven days; departure from Croydon was by Armstrong Whitworth Argosy. At Basle, passengers boarded a train for Genoa, as permission to overfly Italy had not been granted and it was thought unsafe to cross the Alps by air. Moreover, France, in dispute with Italy, would not allow direct flights to Italian aerodromes. Once back in the air, the trans-Mediterranean route was Genoa, Rome, Naples, Corfu, Athens, Suda Bay (later Mirabella) Crete, Tobruk and Alexandria. On this sector, Imperial operated their five Short S.8 Calcuttas, a three-engined biplane flying-boat, capable of carrying fifteen passengers and evolved from the military Short Singapore.

No sooner had this route been established, than the Italians, wanting a share of the Genoa to Alexandria revenue, withdrew Imperial's authorization to operate from Italian ports. From 31 October 1929, Imperial's passengers joined the flying-boat at Salonika, Greece, rather than Genoa. Although for the first two journeys passengers were able to fly by Argosy through Germany and Austria to Salonika, winter weather curtailed further flights. For the remainder of the winter, passengers went from Paris to Salonika by train. The Italians also withdrew permission for Imperial to stage through Tobruk, Libya being under Italian colonial rule. Faced with too great a distance for the Calcuttas to fly direct from Crete to Alexandria, Imperial Airways selected Mersa Matruh, Egypt, as a refuelling stop, but its moorings were unsheltered. Many options were examined and it was finally decided to build a scaled-up, four-engined Calcutta – the Kent. Three S.17 Kents were built for Imperial Airways, as were two land plane versions, L.17s. The Kents were christened *Scipio* (G-ABFA), *Sylvanus* (G-ABFB) and *Satyrus* (G-ABFC). The L.17s, described by some as the most unpleasant aircraft ever built, were christened *Scylla* (G-ACJJ) and *Syrinx*

Pictured here possibly at Crete, the Calcutta *was the mainstay of Imperial Airways' flying-boat fleet from the late 1920s until the arrival of the Empire 'boats. G-AATZ* City of Salonika, *later* City of Swanage, *was finally scrapped at Hamble in 1939. (Turnill)*

(G-ACJK). As the Kents became available, the Italians relented and allowed Imperial Airways to operate through Genoa and Brindisi. On 16 May 1931, the first Kent left Genoa eastbound. From October 1931, passengers boarded at Brindisi, having just spent two and a half days on the train from Paris.

At Alexandria, the air passengers boarded another train, this time to Cairo. There, they were transferred to the D.H.66. From Egypt, the route went east via Gaza, across Transjordan, to Iraq, Persia and India. Perversely, Persian prevarication delayed the opening of the Basra to Karachi sector, which routed along the northern coast of the Persian Gulf. Apparently, in 1925, the German Junkers company had established a flying school at Teheran and was now hoping to operate a tri-weekly service to Baghdad. This did not find favour with the RAF, and the British Government did not condone the Junkers' operation. In retaliation, the Persian Government, under pressure from Junkers, withdrew their assent for Britain to fly the recently negotiated north coast route. The withdrawal did not come to light until Hoare's inauguratory flight of January 1927.

Although partial reconciliation was achieved in 1929, when Persia allowed an international air corridor to India, Britain's relations with Persia continued to be difficult and the British Government longed to be rid of overflying the country. Matters worsened in 1931 when the Persian Government advised Imperial Airways that a new inland route, crossing the mountains, had been decided upon. Imperial thought this route to be unsafe and secretly negotiated a route with the sheikhs on the southern side of the Gulf. A wireless station and aerodrome were established at Bahrein and, in October 1932,

the Northern Arabia Persian Gulf Route was opened. Bahrein and Sharjah were used as refuelling stops. Imperial Airways would have preferred to operate flying-boats over this sector but suitable harbours were difficult to find and, as yet, they lacked suitable 'boats.

The route was extended to Delhi on the last day of December 1929, but flight across India was not possible until 1933. The route to India had been established for parcels, not people, and although the new Kents and Handley Page H.P.42s made travelling more comfortable, political problems prevailed. In order to keep the mail moving, the Delhi Flying Club came to Imperial's aid and flew the mail from Karachi to Delhi. The Indian Government wanted to be involved both in the operation of the Empire routes and the establishment of commercial flying on the subcontinent. Regretfully, negotiations were bungled by the British delegate, Lord Chetwynd, who, amongst other things, was reported as saying, 'Who'd ever fly with an Indian?' Despite the bigoted British attitude, the Indian Government arranged a service between Karachi and Delhi by chartering crews and aeroplanes from Imperial Airways. The Indian Government further surveyed the route as far as Rangoon, but the Depression ceased further funding. The Indian authorities seemed uncooperative towards Imperial Airways and thwarted Imperial's ambitions to forge the route on to Singapore and Australia. This caused annoyance in Great Britain, as the Indians appeared to be allowing France and the Netherlands to operate through India without hindrance. This impasse was finally settled by the formation of Indian Trans-Continental Airways, owned jointly by Imperial Airways and the Indian Government. In

July 1933, the route was extended to Calcutta and in September to Rangoon. Singapore was reached on 9 December 1933.

For Africa, an Argosy carrying the mail for Kenya and Tanganyika departed Croydon, on 28 February 1931. As with the route to India, the Alexandria to Cairo sector was by rail. A mixture of Argosies, Calcuttas and D.H.66s was employed across the dark African continent. The 1931 Christmas mail for South Africa left the United Kingdom on 9 December and arrived in Cape Town on 21 December. This was the start of an eleven-day, weekly service to Cape Town; the first scheduled aircraft left on 20 January 1932 and passengers were carried from the 27 April.

Despite these apparent improvements, passenger flying remained unpopular. In 1932, only 75 fare-paying passengers had been taken to India; in 1933 the total was little better. Although the service was used by the Civil Service, Army and oil companies, it was generally seen as a stunt rather than an accepted form of travel. Commercially, there was strong competition from the French and Dutch.

The amount of fuel reserve carried in aircraft had yet to be regulated and, on occasions, passengers could find themselves subject to unscheduled refuelling stops in the desert, or worse. On 4 March 1933, Captain V. G. Wilson was forced to put down the Kent, *Satyrus*, twenty miles short of Piraeus. He had been attempting Alexandria to Athens non-stop and simply ran out of fuel. Even closer to home, unscheduled landings on the English south coast were not unknown. Once established on the 'Empire' route beyond Europe there were definite risks to be encountered. Engine failure could mean a forced landing in bandit-invested deserts and it was not unknown for the odd pot-shot to be taken at passing airliners.

In November 1935, whilst moored at Brindisi, *Sylvanus* was destroyed by an Italian arsonist. Possibly as a result of the loss of the longer-range Kent, the Short Calcutta, *City of Khartoum*, was put on to the Crete–Alexandria sector. On New Year's Eve 1935, she made a forced alighting short of Alexandria, with the loss of twelve lives. Yet again Captain V. G. Wilson was the commander and yet again his aircraft simply ran out of fuel. All three engines stopped simultaneously as the flying-boat was at a height of 600 feet, commencing its descent into Alexandria. Wilson was forced onto the sea, outside the harbour. Although normal contact was made with the water, the 'boat was swamped by heavy swell and gradually settled down, the tail and part of the starboard wing remaining above the surface. It seems the crew and passengers survived the forced alighting, but only the captain and two others were picked up by HMS *Brilliant*. They had clung to the wreckage for two hours before spending another three hours in the water awaiting rescue.

The Inspector of Accidents, Major Cooper, accepted that Wilson was unaware of recently changed carburettor settings. By mistake, the carburettor main jets, rather than the idle jets, had been opened, following verbal instructions. The change of settings raised the rate of consumption from about 82 to about 89 gallons an hour. Endurance would have been reduced from 5 hours 45 minutes to 5 hours 20 minutes. Moreover, a fault in one or both of the petrol gauges, caused by fuel venting, could have been a contributory factor leading the pilot to believe 25 gallons of petrol remained in the tank, which was in fact empty. Following the accident, there was a delay in forming a rescue party. It seems that although the patrol boat at the flare-path reported the disappearance of the flying-boat, the full urgency of the message had lost its impact by the time it had been received ashore. The Inspector concluded that the sudden and complete loss of engine power at low altitude created an extremely difficult situation where a successful forced landing, in darkness, was unlikely. To his great credit, Captain Wilson achieved all that could be expected of him in the circumstances. In all probability, the loss of life would have been reduced if there had been efficient communication between the flare-path and the shore base. This and other accidents would pave the way for stringent safety-regulation in the airline industry.

European operations were not without frustration and chaos. Routes were constantly amended, depending upon the time of year, the weather and the various levels of reciprocity of overflying rights between Great Britain and the other European nations. As stated, passengers had to cross the Alps and Italy by train, initially re-boarding the flying-boat at Genoa but later at Brindisi. Possibly, as it was cheaper to transport passengers across Europe by train rather than aeroplane, this arrangement may have had some financial support. The Empire Air Route was not a totality. It was almost non-existent over Europe. Despite overstretch and under-funding, Imperial Airways managed to survive. They had only 32 aircraft compared with 269 for France and 177 for Germany. Imperial Airways had only 32 pilots (one for each aircraft) compared with France's 135 and Germany's 160. Even Italy's airlines were double that of Great Britain. The British naturally flew a correspondingly lower mileage. Of the half million air miles flown weekly by the major European airlines, Imperial Airways flew a mere 35,000.

Imperial Airways soon discovered that Government interference went hand in hand with Government subsidies. Although driven out of Europe by the continental opposition, the airline maintained its arrogant complacency towards the Empire routes. Additionally, it became embroiled in British foreign policy whilst contesting the Opposition Party in Westminster and the Civil Service in its fight for commercial survival.

CHAPTER TWO

The Raison D'Être

BEFORE THE EMPIRE AIRMAIL SCHEME
Early airmail – Kingsford Smith saves the day – Airmail to Australia.

On 18 February 1911, Henri Pequet, piloting a Humber biplane, flew the world's first 'heavier-than-air' airmail. He covered a distance of about five miles from Allahabad to Naini Junction, India. Four days later, he started a regular service to coincide with the Universal Postal Exhibition being held in Allahabad. In England, during the late summer of that same year, the first official United Kingdom airmail service was flown. British-born Gustav Hamel, in his Blériot XI, carried official papers from Hendon to the King's residence at Windsor. Overseas, to support the British 'Air Policing Role' in Iraq, the Royal Air Force started a Cairo to Baghdad airmail service on 23 June 1921.

The first truly commercial, long-range airmail service started as part of the London to India schedule of 1929, and, within two years, surcharged airmail and fare-paying passengers were leaving Croydon for the Empire. On 28 February 1931, Imperial Airways inaugurated a London to Central Africa service, carrying passengers to Khartoum and mail alone on to Lake Victoria. Encouraged by the African service, the Government and the Post Office announced arrangements for two experimental mail flights to Australia. The first was to be made on 4 April, three days after the announcement, and the second on the 25th. The flights, between London and Sydney, would be an extension of the London to Delhi service and a combined operation by Imperial Airways, Australian National Airways (ANA) and Queensland and Northern Territory Aerial Services (QANTAS). It was not without difficulty.

The Armstrong Whitworth Argosy *City of Coventry* (G-AAEJ) departed Croydon on the appointed day and arrived at Karachi on the 16th. There, the 15,000 pieces of mail were transferred to the five-year-old D.H.66 *City of Cairo* (G-EBMW), which had been fitted with long-range fuel tanks. She was commanded by Captains Roger Mollard and Jimmy Alger; a flight engineer and a wireless operator completed the crew. On 19 April, Alger commanded the leg out of Rambang, Indonesia. As they struggled against strong headwinds over Timor, to their alarm, a fuel leak was discovered. Beneath them – jungle – it seemed there was nowhere to put down for temporary repairs. In the distance they saw the town of

Kupang and a large green area was spotted, the racecourse. Gentlemen to the last, they decided to land upon a stretch of grass next to the turf. An approach was made, but the green and exceedingly tall grass hid large and jagged boulders. The inevitable happened and the undercarriage was ripped off. Having extricated themselves, the unscathed crew rescued the mail, which for the next six days remained in the custody of the Dutch postal authorities.

It had been envisaged that the mail would reach Australia by air in half the time normally taken to transport it by sea. Alas, for the moment, it was in Timor. Although QANTAS had a contract with Imperial Airways to collect the mail from Darwin and then fly it down the central Queensland route to Brisbane, they were without an aircraft of sufficient range to reach Timor and rescue the mail. Charles Kingsford Smith and Charles Ulm were waiting at Brisbane to fly the mail onwards to Australia's southern cities. Grasping the opportunity, Kingsford Smith flew his Fokker Tri-motor *Southern Cross* up to Kupang and rescued the mail from a dejected Mollard and Alger. He sped back to Darwin, giving Mollard a lift, and handed the mail on to QANTAS, on 25 April. He then turned around with the westbound mail and flew it as far as Akyab, Burma. There it was handed to Imperial Airways to continue its passage to England in the Hercules *City of Karachi* (G-AARY). The mail arrived back in England nineteen days later; the disastrous eastbound leg had taken twenty-four days.

Mollard, meanwhile, on instructions from Imperial, purchased a D.H.66 from West Australia Airways, *City of Cape Town* (G-AUJQ) (once in the possession of Imperial, she was reregistered G-ABMT). Making the most of Imperial's misfortune, *Southern Cross* waited in Akyab for the eastbound second flight, which had left Croydon on 25 April carrying 5,000 items of mail. The post was duly collected and delivered to QANTAS in Darwin. Mollard was now ready in Australia to fly the second westbound load directly to Karachi, where the scheduled service would be joined. The east- and westbound legs of the second experimental flights were done in eighteen and sixteen days respectively but the shadow of Timor hung over the whole operation and it was to be two years before the experiment was repeated by the British.

An all-Australian service was flown during

Christmas and New Year 1931 by Kingsford Smith and G. U. 'Scotty' Allan. 'Scotty', in an Australian National Airways Avro Ten, started the service from Hobart on 19 November 1931. Unfortunately his aircraft was severely damaged on 26 November, at Alor Star, Malaya. Yet again, the mail was rescued by Charles Kingsford Smith. This time he flew it all the way to England and arrived on 16 December.

The Australians were not the only people flying this route. The Dutch were operating a scheduled mail and passenger service from Amsterdam to Batavia (Jakarta). These flights were quietly ignored by Imperial Airways. However, Imperial Airways were making some headway. In the New Year of 1932 they extended their central Africa mail service to Cape Town. The first departure from Croydon was on 20 January, whilst the first Cape Town northbound aircraft left on 27 January.

EMPIRE AIRMAIL SCHEME
The germ of an idea – Geddes presents his plan – Brackley to Australia in Armstrong Whitworth Atalanta Astraea *– EAMS announced.*

In 1924, with the inception of Imperial Airways, an all-up airmail service (no surcharge) had been proposed. Although it was argued that as the Post Office and Imperial Airways were both Government backed, the Post Office ought to be duty bound to ensure that as much trade as possible, airmail, was generated and transported by Imperial Airways. However, a more sceptical view was adopted and the proposal foundered in 1927.

In early 1931, Great Britain, and Imperial Airways in particular, were lagging behind France, Germany and Italy in passenger miles flown. Imperial was renowned for its sedate services. It was thought that Imperial Airways had reached its limit of expansion if only passengers and surcharged airmail were carried; additional revenue needed to be generated. Exactly who conceived the idea of an Empire Airmail Scheme is debatable but the company secretary, Mr S. A. Dismore, has been credited with the idea. In essence, all first-class mail to Commonwealth countries and the Empire would travel, without surcharge, by air. Dismore put the idea to Woods Humphery, Imperial's Managing Director, and whilst Woods Humphery and Geddes were on a tour of prospective South African routes, they formulated the basis of the scheme. The pilot of their H.P.42 was Captain Griffith 'Taffy' Powell. Once in South Africa, they completed their business before returning to England on the SS *Caernarvon Castle*. However, as they bade farewell to their H.P.42, Griffith Powell sought a private word with Woods Humphery. Captain Powell asked if he might have permission to marry. It was granted along with a piece of advice. Griffith Powell was advised to seek a transfer to flying-boats – that was where the future lay, according to Woods Humphery.

On board SS *Caernarvon Castle*, they completed their plans and worked to produce a convincing argument that would placate the General Post Office, thus allowing Imperial to carry the Royal Mail, without surcharge,

by air throughout the Empire.

In March 1933, Geddes presented the Cabinet with a memorandum:

'Imperial Airways has conclusively demonstrated its reliability and dependability already, and the board has every confidence in its ability to carry a vastly increased volume of Empire letter mail. The Board therefore invites H M Government to investigate, in conjunction with Imperial Airways, the carriage by air of letter mail in bulk on the London-Cape Town and London-Australia routes in the next four or five years to come, on revised rates of conveyance to be negotiated.'

On 29 May 1933, a month-long survey from London to Melbourne was flown by Brackley and Captain Prendergast in an Armstrong Whitworth Atalanta, *Astrea* (G-ABTL). Regular London to Melbourne flights were achieved by extending the London–Karachi service. The route reached Rangoon in September 1933 and Singapore the following December. A year later, on 8 December 1934, a weekly schedule for mail to Australia was established. Passengers followed in April 1935. Thereafter, a single passage on the twelve-and-a-half-day, 12,754-mile journey could be purchased for £195.

The route was operated by Imperial Airways alone as far as Karachi, and Imperial Airways and Indian Trans-Continental Airways to Singapore. Finally, the leg down to Brisbane was flown by QANTAS Empire Airways, a joint QANTAS/Imperial Airways venture, formed on 18 January 1935.

THE FIRST DECADE
Macpherson Robertson Air Race – Imperial complacent – The Empire Airmail gains support – Short Bros – The Imperial Flying-Boat.

In the early 1920s, it was commented:

'As aircraft grow larger the question of landing space will become more and more prominent… The flying-boat can increase in size to any limit commensurate with efficiency, and there will always be room to alight without laying waste land possessing other and greater uses.'

By the close of 1934, Imperial Airways had been operating for a decade, but despite the scheduling of the weekly service to Australia, celebrations were muted. The Macpherson Robertson, Mildenhall to Melbourne, Race, two months earlier, perhaps the most influential air race of all time, had shown that the modern, all-metal, low-winged monoplane, with retractable undercarriage, was the way ahead. That being said, the race was won by the wooden de Havilland D.H.88 Comet racer. More significant, however, were the second and third places taken by the Douglas DC-2 and the Boeing 247, both all-metal, twin-engined, monoplane airliners with retractable undercarriages.

Following the race, and despite an English victory, Imperial Airways was still being criticized for retaining its slow and obsolescent fleet. Considering Geddes' complacent address to that year's shareholders' meeting, criticism may have been justified:

'You cannot expect commercial undertakings to emulate an air race. I would counsel you, my friends and shareholders, not to run away with the idea that speed was all important. We have the record of Imperial Airways going on its steady, non-spectacular course, and that is soundest and best in the end.'

In the three years intervening since their visit to South Africa, Geddes and Woods Humphery had gained political support for their Empire Airmail Scheme. On 20 December 1934, Sir Philip Sassoon, Parliamentary Under-Secretary of State for Air, announced that, from 1937, Imperial Airways would carry all first-class mail for the Empire without surcharge, the Government having agreed to subsidize first-class airmail and pay Imperial Airways an economic rate for its carriage. Sassoon suggested a schedule of just over two days to India and East Africa, four days to the Cape and Singapore and seven days to Australia. Moreover, new aircraft would be required to sustain a flying rate of four or five flights per week to India, three per week to Singapore and East Africa and two per week to South Africa and Australia.

Sassoon's announcement generated rumours of a fleet of new aircraft for Imperial Airways, and designs for a new transatlantic aircraft abounded. In anticipation of the Empire Airmail Scheme, Major R. H. Mayo, Imperial Airways' Technical Adviser, was ready with the specification that would eventually lead Shorts to build the 'C-class' flying-boat.

There were three Short brothers: Horace Leonard, 1872 to 1917; Albert Eustace, 1875 to 1932 and Hugh Oswald 'The Kid', 1883 to 1969. (Hugh Oswald resigned in January 1943 when the company was nationalized.) Short Bros started as balloon builders, with a workshop under a London railway arch, around 1906. They remained innovationists, an early example of their foresight being in 1908, when Oswald decided the end of ballooning was nigh. By 1909 they had obtained a licence to build six Wright Flyers. Short Bros created the first factory in Britain devoted to the making of aircraft. In 1912, the Short 'Pusher' became the first aircraft to take off from a moving ship. Short Bros continued their association with water and during the First World War built aircraft for the Royal Navy. A Shorts' aircraft was the first to have folding wings. Through the 1920s and into the '30s, they concentrated their efforts on building a number of float-planes and flying-boats which relied heavily upon metal construction. Early problems of corrosion and electrolytic reaction were soon dealt with, and aluminium hulls, some with stainless steel bottoms, were built.

They invested in research facilities, building one of the few hull-testing tanks in the country. However, it was not aircraft production that kept the company solvent but large contracts for bus and coach bodies.

Barges were also built. In the early '20s, Oswald Short proudly informed C. G. Grey, outspoken editor of *The Aeroplane* magazine, that Shorts 'now' employed more men than they did during the Great War. Shorts turned their workforce to many projects in order to remain in being, though not all were successful. Their attempt to build bus ticket machines was a failure as the men were inexperienced at working to the fine tolerances required and the rejection rate among the ticket machines was unacceptable.

Although vehicle body construction continued for many years, the 1930s saw an upturn in the aircraft industry and orders from the RAF and Imperial Airways guaranteed Shorts' survival.

Shorts' designer, Arthur Gouge, was aware of Air Minister Sassoon's specification calling for an improved 'Kent-class' flying-boat, capable of carrying 24 passengers and half a ton of mail, at 150 mph, over 800 miles. Gouge was also aware of the RAF specification (R.2/33 – issued November 1933) for a four-engined flying-boat of similar performance to the Sarafand, but smaller. Imperial Airways was expected to order two prototypes and the RAF one. Gouge noted similarities in the two specifications and produced a common design. At the close of June 1934, to meet the 'Kent-class' specification, Short Bros tendered to Imperial the Short S.23. They received an 'instruction to proceed' in late January 1935. First delivery was to be April 1936. A large design staff was employed and the first metal must have been cut by early summer 1935.

Facts do not support the legend stating that whilst viewing the competitors of the Macpherson Robertson Race, in October 1934, Gouge, Lankester Parker (chief test pilot) and Oswald Short were impressed by the clean lines of the KLM DC-2 that Parmentier and Moll were to fly. So influenced, the myth purports, that Gouge decided a clean monoplane could meet the RAF's and Imperial's requirements. Similarly, Gouge's presence at Igor Sikorsky's Royal Aeronautical Society lecture on the Sikorsky S.42, in November 1934, should be seen as little more than professional curiosity on Gouge's part.

Concurrent with the S.23 'C-class' and their subsequent derivatives (S.30 and S.33), Shorts were designing and constructing the S.20/21 composite, *Maia* and *Mercury* (Chapter 5) and the S.26 'G-class' 'boats. Whilst not strictly correct, all these 'boats are generically termed Empire Flying-Boats and mention of their gestation must be made.

In 1932, Short Bros built a large six-engined biplane flying-boat, the S.14 Sarafand, in response to specification R.6/28. One of the Ministry of Aviation Experimental Establishment's (MAEE Felixstowe) criteria for the Sarafand type was an ability to be airborne within 60 seconds in still air, from calm water. The 72,000 lb Sarafand could just achieve this with a wing loading of 21 lb/sq ft. Bearing in mind the R.2/33's sister craft, the Empire 'Boat, proposed a wing loading of 27 lb/sq ft, doubts were expressed as to the R.2/33's ability to meet the take-off criteria. Some form of

In the Rochester factory the new Sunderlands and the last of the Singapore IIIs were constructed alongside the Empire 'Boats. Here, Champion *is under construction.* (Short Bros plc)

take-off assistance might be required. Proposals had already been submitted for the construction of catapult ships, capable of launching aircraft of weights up to 80,000 lb. Furthermore, if these catapults were made available in peacetime, a flying-boat of simple construction, having to operate off water only at light weights, could be built to carry a considerable transatlantic payload. Short Bros were invited to tender to Specification 35/36 calling for a catapult-launched flying-boat. Meanwhile, Imperial Airways, possibly conscious of the next generation of giant flying-boats being developed in America, asked Short Bros to consider an enlarged 'Empire type', capable of carrying a useful payload across the Atlantic without recourse to refuelling. Shorts commenced preliminary studies of the S.26 for Imperial and the S.27 catapult 'boat.

Imperial Airways were impressed greatly with the design of the S.23 Empire 'Boat and by the end of May 1935 had ordered 14 'off the drawing board' and on 2 September 1935 increased the order to 28. In September, Imperial also ordered three of the larger S.26s, which

were designated 'G-class'. The RAF ordered the R.2/33 – Sunderland, of which eventually 721 were built. Shorts wanted to build a 'C-class' prototype, but Imperial Airways was in dire need of a modern craft as demand for air travel was rapidly exceeding its capacity. At a unit cost of £41,000, it was the largest order Imperial Airways ever made, a gamble that gave great returns. The order was under the manufacturer's reference of S.23, an official name not being bestowed, but the Imperial Airways' designation 'C-class' was accepted. Despite Imperial's later official terminology 'Imperial Flying-Boats', the 'craft were more widely known as 'C-class' or Empire Flying-Boats.

The Armstrong Whitworth Ensign and de Havilland Albatross, both land planes, soon followed, but they were not as successful as the 'C-class'. The flying-boat was already an accepted mode of air travel and there were many voices in its favour, amongst them Brackley, now Superintendent of Imperial Airways, who extolled the 'boat's capacious hull and the ability to operate from any sheltered piece of water along the Empire Route.

CONSTRUCTION OF THE SHORT BROS EMPIRE 'BOAT

A description of the S.23 airframe – The Rochester works – Personnel – Royal visit.

S.23 construction commenced at Rochester in 1935. Considering the experience gained with the shoulder-mounted monoplanes, Scion and Knuckleduster, there seemed no structural reasons why a large, clean monoplane could not be built. However, a more refined wing root was desired and certain structural challenges had to be faced. Lankester Parker observed that the twin-engined Scion handled well, and similar excellence was expected from the four-engined Scion Senior, which was to be powered by Pobjoy engines. The Pobjoys were half the linear diameter of the Bristol Pegasus, the preferred engines for the new flying-boat, and it seemed logical to base the overall layout of the new 'boat on the Scion Senior, with the linear measurements doubled.

The proposed wing loading would be much higher than that of current biplanes and Gouge invented a fully retractable trailing-edge flap, 'the Gouge Flap'. This allowed the lift coefficient to be increased by 30% and

the landing speed reduced by 12 mph, but with little increase in drag. Meticulous tank testing allowed the beam of the hull to be 18 inches narrower than the 11 ft 6 in dictated by standard calculations. The hull thus had vertical sides from chine to wing root and no flares or tumblehome. This gave a minimum of drag-inducing frontal area for a maximum of internal volume. Drag was further reduced by flush counter-sinking all the rivets in the Alclad skin. The successfully redesigned wing root gave a simple wing attachment with a taller than usual fuselage. Space was thus available for two decks, and this partly compensated for the relatively narrow body.

The wing section was similar to the Göttingen 436, as used in the Knuckleduster and Scion. The 'Gouge' flaps were borne on rollers and ran on a circular-arc track; they were driven by screw-jacks, powered by a hull-mounted electric motor. The ailerons were fabric covered, Frise type, and the mass-balanced rudder and elevator were similarly covered. Tailplane and fin were constructed in a way similar to the wing and they were butted onto stub surfaces which were built into the rear

The flight-deck was not sound-proofed, the windscreen leaked and the Exactor hydraulic controls continually seeped oil onto the wooden flight-deck flooring. (Lufthansa)

fuselage. The trailing edges of all control surfaces were fitted with trim tabs, those on the ailerons being fixed.

The 'boat was constructed with a double deck. The upper deck, or flight-deck, ran forward from the wing spar. It incorporated dual flying controls, the radio equipment, which included a small, two-stroke generator, and space for a flight clerk's desk, ship's papers and mail stowage. The captain and first officer, seated side-by-side, each had a spectacle-type control wheel. Before them was an excellent view over the curved coaming. Between them was the quadrant, housing throttles, mixture controls, pitch controls and fuel cut-offs. In the centre of the instrument panel were the autopilot controls, above which were the engine starter buttons and the ignition switches. Instruments in front of the captain were primarily for blind-flying, and facing the first officer were some engine instruments and a limited blind-flying panel. On the starboard wall, but immediately behind the first officer, were the engine temperature gauges. Within the starboard wing root, but accessible from the flight-deck, was the drift sight. At the rear of the flight-deck, on the aft bulkhead were the fuel gauges, the controls for the engine cooling gills and the primer pumps for engine starting. Between the pilots, there was a small roof panel which housed the controls for the rudder trim and flap selection and the tail line release. Above the first officer was an observation hatch. The first officer was expected to take regular readings of the fuel gauges on the rear bulkhead and adjust the engine cooling gills as required. Much of his time would have been spent walking the length of the flight-deck. The captain had to suffer some discomforts as well. The controls for the Sperry autopilot were on the port side and these tended to leak oil onto the captain's left leg.

The flight-deck, looking aft from the pilots' position. The wireless operator sat on the port side, behind the captain, and faced aft, looking upon the two wireless sets. To his right, upon the floor, was the temperamental petrol-driven auxiliary generator. Behind the wireless sets was the flight-deck mail-storage area and to starboard was the passage aft to the cooling gills, electrical control panel and the wing-root drift sight. (Short Bros plc)

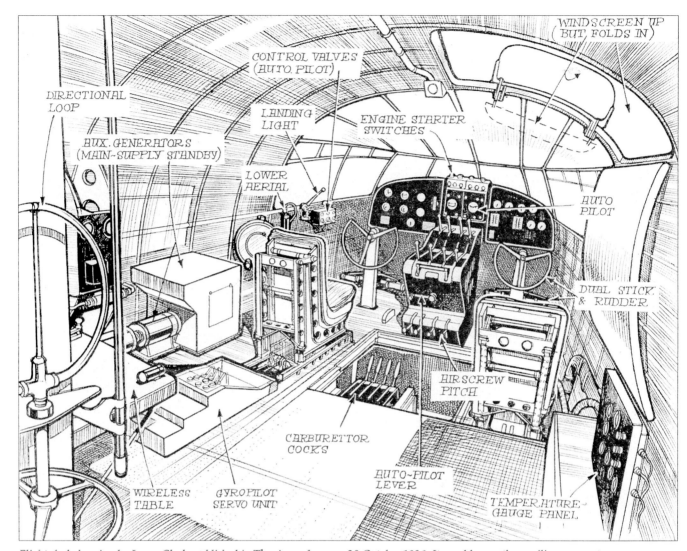

DIRECTIONAL
LOOP

CONTROL VALVES
(AUTO. PILOT)

LANDING
LIGHT

ENGINE STARTER
SWITCHES

WINDSCREEN UP
(BUT FOLDS IN)

AUX. GENERATORS
(MAIN-SUPPLY STANDBY)

LOWER
AERIAL

AUTO
PILOT

DUAL STICK
& RUDDER

AIRSCREW
PITCH

CARBURETTOR
COCKS

AUTO-PILOT
LEVER

WIRELESS
TABLE

GYROPILOT
SERVO UNIT

TEMPERATURE-
GAUGE PANEL

Flight-deck drawing by James Clark, published in The Aeroplane *on 28 October 1936. It would seem the auxiliary generators were removed during the war. Access to the bow compartment was via the hatch between the airscrew pitch levers and the carburettor cocks. The observation hatch above the first officer was only used when the 'boat was on the surface.* (James Clark, The Aeroplane)

When it rained, both pilots got wet. On either side of the cupola, sun blinds were fitted, but ahead, the pilots had to suffer the glare. The seat cushions could become a little hard. The flight-deck had a wooden floor which became oil-soaked after years of leaking autopilots and bleeding Exactor engine controls.

The wireless operator sat behind the captain and faced aft, looking at his Marconi radio installation. The small standby generator was to port, between the captain and the wireless operator. It was mounted tight against the port wall and enshrouded in a fireproof box. Aft from the wireless operator was a mail storage area, which occupied the remainder of the length of the flight-deck and half its width. Fitted against the wall of the mail stowage area, on the aircraft's centre line was the retractable direction-finding (DF) loop aerial. Also close to the centre line but at the rear of the flight-deck was a hatch up to the flat topside of the flying-boat. In this way access to the wings for refuelling and inspection was obtained. Directly below this hatch was another leading into the galley area below. A tube alloy ladder extended from the top hatch down into the galley.

The starboard wall of the flight-deck housed the electrical control panel, in front of the wing root, with the batteries adjacently positioned upon the floor. Forward of the electrical control panel was the mail stowage hatch. On the floor, between the pilots' seats, was a small hatch that allowed direct access into the mooring compartment, and behind this hatch cover was the autopilot gyro unit. Separate navigation and engineering officers were not carried as those duties were the responsibility of the first officer.

Behind the untrimmed and poorly soundproofed flight-deck, the wings abutted the fuselage. Within the fuselage wing box was space for additional mail stowage, but in the long-range 'boats, this space would be taken up with additional fuel tanks. The aft portion of the wing box, above the promenade cabin, was used to store bedding. Access to the bedding locker was via high-level hatches at the forward end of the rear cabin.

Over the forthcoming years there were minor changes to cockpit layout.

On the lower deck were compartments for mooring equipment, the galley, toilets, four passenger cabins and a baggage and freight compartment. At the nose of the flying-boat, below the flight-deck, was the mooring

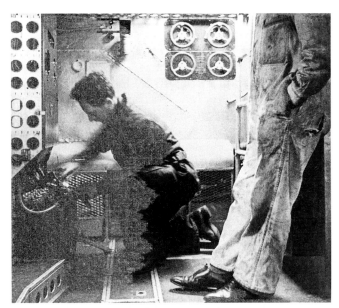

The 'Nife' batteries were stowed at the rear of the starboard wall of the flight-deck. Light is flooding in from the open top-access hatch. The four wheels upon the bulkhead control the engine-cooling gills. (Peek)

wireless operator to stand upon, it being his duty to attend to mooring. Just below this hatch was a retractable mooring bollard and below that, just above the waterline, was the towing eye. At the rear of the compartment was the ladder up to the flight-deck and a door into the forward cabin.

The forward cabin, originally referred to as the smoking compartment, was rectangular and seated seven. Aft, on the port wall, was the forward entrance door. The lobby area around this door was curtained off from the main body of the cabin. Forward of the door were three inward-facing seats. Opposite them, across a stowable, lightweight meal table, were two inward-facing seats. On the aft wall of the forward cabin, to starboard, was a pair of forward-facing seats, with an associated table and a wonderfully large rectangular window to starboard.

Movement aft from the port side entrance door took one down a 'central' (slightly offset to port) corridor, where on the port side were two toilets and to starboard was the galley or pantry. The upper deck could be reached by a ladder from the steward's pantry. The central corridor opened out into the midships or spar cabin, so called as it lay between the main fuselage bulkhead frames which supported the front and rear wing spars. Mounted on the bulkhead were an altimeter and a clock. In the spar cabin, three passengers could be accommodated by day, but for night flights all the seats could be converted into bunks, a fourth bunk being housed in the ceiling.

compartment. Here were stowed the drogues, to assist surface manoeuvring, and the anchor. Recessed into the port side was a retractable landing light which the captain could steer from his position. On the top of the 'boat's nose was the top-hinged, inwardly opening mooring hatch, below which was a small step for the

The bow compartment hatch hinged upwards and inwards. The mooring line was attached to the retractable mooring bollard. It was the wireless operator's responsibility to pick up the mooring and stream the drogues as instructed by the captain's whistle. (Baldwin and Bigby)

Steward's pantry. Hot meals were brought aboard in Thermos flasks and could be loaded through the pantry window. The steward was solely responsible for preparing the meals and cleaning up afterwards.

Continuing aft down the 'central' corridor, a small step led to the famed promenade deck. This cabin, behind the main spar bulkhead, seated eight during the day, in four pairs, and at night could sleep four. The seats were fitted to the starboard side of the offset corridor, leaving ample space for passengers to admire the panorama below through the four large windows to port. As an aid to comfort, an elbow rail was fitted

below these windows.

A step up led to the rear door, on the port side, and another step up found the rear cabin with seats for six. The top of the forward bulkhead of the rear cabin was fitted with hatches giving access to a bedding locker over the promenade deck. The back of the rear cabin was in line with the aft step. Behind the rear cabin was the main freight hold, access to which could be gained through a central bulkhead door or the two-piece hatch in the starboard side.

The 'boats were powered by four Bristol Pegasus XC, 9-cylinder air-cooled radial engines of 920 hp. These were nacelle mounted in long-chord, monocoque cowls, faired into the leading edge of the wing. Engine cooling was controlled by gills, which could be adjusted from the rear of the flight deck by means of a hand-rotated 'quick thread actuator' shaft. Throttle and pitch manipulation was by way of Exactor hydraulic controls. The engines drove three-bladed de Havilland variable-pitch (coarse and fine) propellers. Sections of the leading edge of the wing hinged down to act as servicing platforms.

Although the wing-tip floats were of standard design, incorporating watertight compartments and bilge pumps, the method of mounting was ingenious. Similar to the Knuckleduster installation, the floats were mounted on wire-braced struts. A low-weight, low-drag, central link allowed the floats to rock fore and aft, thus reducing the shock loading that would have

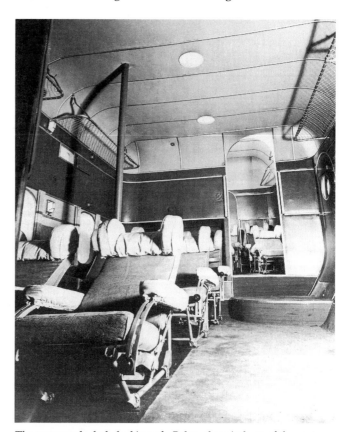

The spar-cabin sleeping berths were never used on scheduled flights. Full night-flying facilities did not become available, and, once airborne, the 'boats flexed so much that the bunk bed supports and stays would not locate into the aircraft fittings. (Imperial Airways via R. T. Jackson)

The promenade deck, looking aft. Below the windows of the port side of the promenade deck an elbow rail was fitted. The rear passenger door is on the step, between the promenade and aft cabin. The reclining chairs were made by Rumbolds. (Imperial Airways via R. T. Jackson)

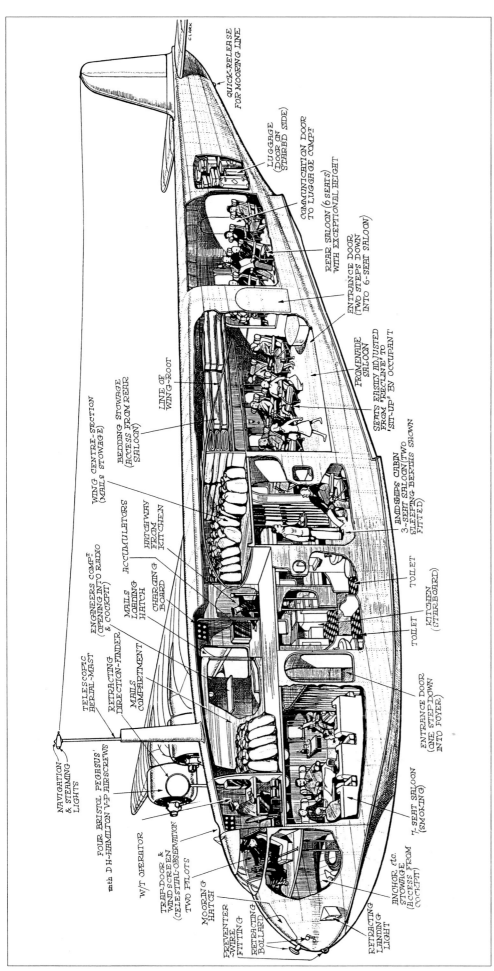

QUICK-RELEASE
FOR MOORING LINE

LUGGAGE
(DOOR ON
STARB'D SIDE)

COMMUNICATION DOOR
TO LUGGAGE COMP'T

REAR SALOON (6 SEATS)

ENTRANCE DOOR
(TWO STEPS DOWN
INTO 6-SEAT SALOON)

PROMENADE
SALOON

SEATS EASILY ADJUSTED
FROM 'RECLINE' TO
'SIT-UP' BY OCCUPANT

AMIDSHIPS CABIN
3-SEAT SALOON (TWO
SLEEPING BERTHS SHOWN
FITTED)

LINE OF
WING-ROOT

BEDDING STOWAGE
(ACCESS FROM REAR
SALOON)

WING CENTRE-SECTION
(MAIL STOWAGE)

ENGINEERS COMP'T
(OPENING INTO RADIO
& COCKPIT)

ACCUMULATORS

MAILS
LOADING
HATCH

HATCHWAY
FROM KITCHEN

CHARGING
BOARD

TELESCOPIC
AERIAL MAST

RETRACTING
DIRECTION-FINDER

MAILS
COMPARTMENT

TOILET

KITCHEN
(STARBOARD)

7-SEAT SALOON
(SMOKING)

ENTRANCE DOOR
(ONE STEP DOWN
INTO FOYER)

ANCHOR, etc.
STOWAGE
(ACCESS FROM
COCKPIT)

MOORING
HATCH

PREVENTER
-WIRE
FITTING

RETRACTING
BOLLARD

RETRACTING
LANDING
LIGHT

TRAP-DOOR &
WIND SCREEN
(CELESTIAL-OBSERVATION)

TWO PILOTS

W/T OPERATOR

FOUR BRISTOL PEGASUS
with D.H.-HAMILTON V-P AIRSCREWS

NAVIGATION
& STEAMING
LIGHTS

Cutaway by James Clark, in The Aeroplane, 4 March 1936. This diagram, most likely based upon a mock-up which was built beneath the canteen at the Rochester works, typifies Clark's style. He was not averse to a little distortion of true perspective, if technical clarity was improved. Early in the boat's career, the seven-seat smoking saloon beneath the flight-deck, was converted to use for mail stowage and as the flight clerk's office. Passenger capacity was reduced. The flight-deck trap-door and windscreen were not used for celestial observation. (James Clark, The Aeroplane)

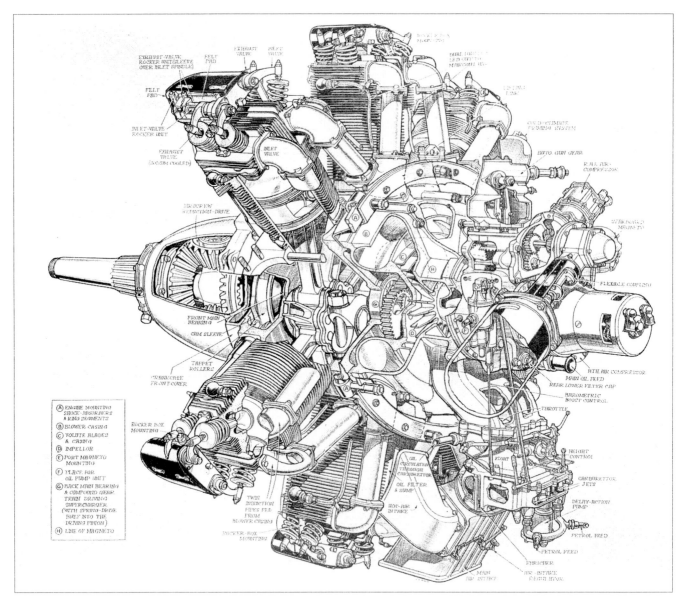

The Bristol Pegasus engine, as depicted by James Clark, in The Aeroplane, 4 November 1936. Although succeeding the Jupiter, the Pegasus was thought by many to be not as good as its predecessor. Engines were overhauled after 250 hours. Engine failures were not rare, and being devoid of feathering propellers and fire extinguishers they were all the more hazardous.
(James Clark, The Aeroplane)

The inboard installation of the Pegasus engine showing the three-bladed de Havilland variable-pitch (coarse and fine) propellers. The upper-surface flush exhaust ports were later modified and fitted with short stubs. The leading edge of the wing is darkened by the application of 'Kilfrost' a granular, sticky, blue substance which delayed the onset of airframe icing. It was also applied to the floats and the tail surfaces. (Peek)

otherwise been transferred to the wing. Nevertheless, later 'boats adopted a simpler and more reliable ridged mounting for their floats. To cater for the various climates in which the 'boats would operate, self-tensioning control cables, which allowed for thermal expansion, were used.

Fuel was carried in two 326-gallon, drum-shaped, light alloy tanks, located between the engines, fitted with cruciform internal baffles. In order to prevent chafing, the tanks rested upon plywood floors and were installed through cutouts in the top surface. Refuelling could be achieved either 'over the top', via filler caps in the individual tanks, or by a single-point, pressurized refuelling system, this point being on the starboard fuselage side, beneath the wing, just to the rear of the galley. The flying-boat's overall finish was of natural metal; all unclad aluminium parts were anodised before assembly.

The dimensions of the 'C-class' 'boats were:

Span:	114 ft	34.75 m
Length:	88 ft	26.84 m
Height:	31 ft 9¾ in	
Wing area:	1,500 sq ft	139.35 sq m
Tare (empty):	23,500 lb	(10,670 kg)
load:	8,000 lb	(3,629 kg)
AUW:	40,500 lb	(18,380 kg)

The basic performance figures of the 'C-class' 'boats were:

Max level speed:	174 kt	(322 kmph)	200 mph
Max cruise:	142 kt	(264 kmph)	164 mph
Rate of climb	950 ft per min		290 m per min
Ceiling:	20,000 ft		6100 m
Range:	660–703 miles		1,245–1,300 km
Endurance:	4.5 hours		

Construction of the 'boats presented Shorts with some formidable challenges. They lacked suitable machine tools for some of the operations, and because of rearmament, there was a shortage of skilled labour. Unskilled boys were employed as dolly holders to work inside the flush-riveted airframes. To quote Oswald Short:

'Credit is due to this unskilled labour, but more credit is due to those very skilled foremen, leading hands, and first-class workmen who with ever watchful eye and much patience directed energy lacking experience to such effect that there were few blemishes to detect in the workmanship even in the first machine.'

Oswald, the remaining Short brother, was appreciated by his workforce. He was a little reclusive but nevertheless would go upon the shop floor and inspect the machine tools for cleanliness. Apprentices in charge of machine cleaning were suitably rewarded for their troubles. Gordon Staples was once given ten shillings for having a clean machine. Oswald's nephew, Horace's son Francis, was also a director and tended the financial aspects of the company, but his dedication to the business could be described as not absolute.

More a visionary was Arthur Gouge the designer. Although slighted by a squint, he was a most unassuming person, possessing an undoubted reputation amongst the Shorts staff. He joined Short Bros in 1915, as a mechanic on a bench, and was soon promoted to chargehand. He took his Bachelor of Science degree at London University and was appointed Chief Designer in 1926, rising to General Manager in 1929 and Vice-Chairman in 1939. For many years Gouge was obsessed with the idea of a giant flying-boat. In 1943, he joined Saunders-Roe and assisted in designing the Princess. Sadly, she was not the ultimate fulfilment of his dream.

The Short Brothers' business and Gouge's designs were moulded into commercial flying-boats by Works Director Alfred E. Bibby. He had risen from a humble work bench to become a capable and formidable 'hirer and firer' of men. Although his strengths may not have been technical, he maintained a constant awareness as to events upon the shop floor and had a habit of visiting the works at night, letting himself in, much to the surprise of the watchmen. He was the driving force behind the tight production schedules, and if necessary would fire men on the spot. He did, however, have a gentler side and put great energy into arranging the annual Masonic children's party and acted as the children's entertainer. But at work, rough men settled their

The Short team: Front row (L to R): W. C. Jackson, Assistant Chief Designer; J. H. Wood; A. Gouge, General Manager and Chief Designer; H. O. Short; Chairman; Francis Short; A. E. Bibby; C. P. T. Lipscombe, Assistant Chief Designer; and John Lankester Parker; Test Pilot. Back row (L to R): Quittenden; Wyborn; Coppins; Lawson; Watson; Boorman; Clarke; Shepherd; Dyer; Smart;Parkes, Chief Draughtsman; Newton; Newnham, Foreman-in-charge; Drury and Cozens. (Flight, 1936)

On 14 March 1939, Their Majesties King George VI and Queen Elizabeth visited Short Bros at Rochester. Mr Piper demonstrated the milling machine which was used to produce the main spars. Oswald Short looks on. (Central Press photograph)

differences with fair, bare-knuckled fights. Of all this Bibby said:

> 'The difficulties of a Works Manager in producing these machines is nothing to the joy he experiences in pushing one out of the doors, down the slipway, and seeing it take off on its first flight.'

Just as Bibby ruled the factory floor, George Wadhams's word was law upon the Medway. He, along with generations before him, was a Freeman of the River Medway. Wadhams had been brought up upon the river and understood every nuance of her winds, tides and currents. His skill and empathy with the Medway were unreal. Lankester Parker trusted and respected him greatly and would follow his every instruction to the letter. Wadhams could rush his boat headlong at a flying-boat, seemingly miss it by inches yet take the mooring line from the pilot's hand. Similarly, he could be seen drifting with the wind and tide, almost oblivious to the eighteen-ton 'boat at the end of his line, as he moved the Empire 'Boats between moorings.

'Doesn't he know how much it has cost to build?' a white-knuckled Oswald Short was often heard to say.

Ne'er a boat had a mishap at Wadhams's hand.

On 14 March 1939, Rochester was graced with a visit from Their Majesties King George VI and Queen Elizabeth. They were met by Oswald Short and Councillor C. S. Knight, the Mayor of Rochester, and Mrs Short presented Her Majesty with a bouquet. During the course of their rain-swept visit, they viewed the partially completed interior of *Australia* and saw Mr Piper operate the famed milling machine, the only one long enough to machine the spar sections.

EARLY FLIGHTS
Launch and flight of Canopus – *Loss of* Scipio – Caledonia *launched and certificated – Demonstrations and scheduled service.*

Canopus, lacking her interior fittings, was gingerly towed from the hangar, rolled down the open slipway and secured, on 1 July 1936. Registered G-ADHL (Construction Number S.795), she was the first S.23 and did much of the initial test-flying. Whilst secured on the slipway by hawsers, initial engine runs were carried out. The morning tide of 2 July saw *Canopus* launched and moored at her buoy. Further inspections were completed and she was declared fit to fly. The following morning, Friday, the press speculated that flight-testing would commence by the middle of July. Notwithstanding press speculation, the first flight was planned for Saturday, the fourth, but that was not to be.

Shorts' factory was planning to close at noon on Friday, it being the workers' sports day, and, in preparation for the first flight on Saturday, Lankester Parker had agreed to carry out fast taxi tests that afternoon. The taxi tests went well, and the wind was favourable, so Lankester Parker elected to make the maiden flight. No sooner were the four Pegasus engines opened than *Canopus* was aloft. The flight lasted fourteen minutes and, until they attempted to alight back on the Medway, had been uneventful. The electrically driven flaps failed to run out to their full extent. However, the slightly

Allegedly the first flight of Canopus. *Lankester Parker made a 14-minute flight on the afternoon of Friday 3 July 1936: there were few onlookers. The official first flight took place on Saturday 4 July.* Canopus *was airborne within 17 seconds. (Short Bros plc)*

longer landing run went unnoticed by the few onlookers present.

The 'official' first flight took place on Saturday 4 July 1936. After a take-off run of seventeen seconds, *Canopus*, at a weight of 37,140 lb, climbed steadily towards Gillingham Reach – a precaution in case an emergency landing was required. Lankester Parker returned over Rochester Castle and the works, put *Canopus* into a steep climbing starboard turn and sped down the Medway valley. Moments later, he swept down before the assembled work force. This was the pre-arranged signal to Oswald Short and Gouge, who thankfully lit a cigarette, that all was well. The graceful *Canopus* was climbed gently, before being turned into wind for alighting. As speed was reduced, the flaps were selected. Yet again they failed to run out correctly. Yet again few of the spectators or aviation press noticed this second alighting, at less than the ideal flap setting. When Parker stepped ashore, in hushed tones he assured Short, 'Nothing wrong'.

Although *Canopus* was the first 'C-class' flying-boat and the initial trial flights were performed with her as 'prototype', *Caledonia* was the 'boat used for Certificate of Airworthiness (CofA) evaluation by the Marine Aircraft Experimental Establishment (MAEE) at Felixstowe.

Trial flights commenced on 6 July, when *Canopus*

flew for an hour. On 8 July, engine tests were flown, but two days later she suffered an engine failure after take-off. Fortunately, Lankester Parker was able to complete a safe circuit and touchdown. The trials paused for a few days. Then, instrument position error checks at various altitudes were carried out on 13 July and, during a one-hour flight, speed trials were completed on the 19th. On 30 July, *Canopus* was returned to No. 3 Shop for modifications to her rudder, elevators and flaps.

A month later, she emerged but still without her complete interior trim. She was relaunched and delivered to Imperial Airways on Monday 7 September 1936. That night, a gale struck southern England and southerly and south-westerly winds lashed the Medway. *Canopus* rode the storm. Events were driving Imperial Airways to introduce *Canopus* into early service. Along with *Caledonia*, which was about to be launched, it was hoped to impress both these 'boats into trans-Mediterranean service to replace the lost Kent, *Scipio*.

Scipio, G-ABFA, one of the two remaining Kent flying-boats, crashed on 22 August 1936. *Scipio* was *en route* from Alexandria to Athens when she crashed whilst alighting at Mirabella Bay, Crete. Although the approach was made in turbulent conditions, with many down-currents, poor crew co-operation may have exacerbated the accident. Captain A. S. Wilcockson, who was relatively inexperienced, judged the approach poorly, but conditions were difficult and Mirabella was known to be treacherous. Wilcockson later stated he thought he had detailed Wireless Officer Birkenshore to set the tailplane trim. Birkenshore had either not heard the instruction or had turned the trim wheel the wrong way, thus rendering the flying-boat increasingly nose heavy as it neared the water. Struggling against the down-draughts from the surrounding hills, Wilcockson applied a surge of power, just before touchdown. This burst of power from the high-mounted engines, coupled with the nose-down trim, caused the aircraft to pitch into the sea. Mr T. A. C. Forbes, Indian Police (Retired), and Lieutenant R. G. Wilson-Dickson, Royal Tank Corps, perished in the crash. Of the five passengers rescued, Mr J. N. Draft was seriously injured but First Officer Long and Steward Hemming were uninjured. The survivors were quickly transferred onto the Imperial Airways' Motor Yacht-cum-depot-ship *Imperia* and treated by local doctors.

On 9 September, at Rochester, following the gales, *Caledonia* was wheeled onto the slipway. Two days later and after engine runs, she was launched onto the morning's rising tide. *Caledonia* and her sister ship, *Cambria*, were built as long-range 'boats. Their centre-section mail stowage space was occupied by two fuel tanks and two additional tanks were fitted in each wing. Their fuel capacity was 2,330 gallons as opposed to 652 gallons for the standard S.23. The all-up weight was increased to 45,000 lb and the range expected was 2,865 nm. Apart from crew accommodation in the centre cabin and one toilet, *Caledonia* too was untrimmed. For the maiden flight, Lankester Parker had her loaded to 35,000 lb. A light, westerly wind blew on the morning of 11 September, and after easy handling on the water, *Caledonia* was briskly airborne. Following the flight, she was considered ready for heavyweight trials and that evening was loaded with sandbags in preparation for the morrow's trial. During the next few days, several flights, totalling over three hours, were made at maximum weight. *Canopus* too carried out full-load trials and on 9 September she was aloft after a run of only twenty-one seconds. Thence, back to the upholsterers for her interior fittings and more sound proofing.

The public were being kept informed of progress and on 12 September *The Times* wrote:

> '*Meanwhile,* Canopus, *the first of the series, was nearly ready for acceptance trials at Imperial Airways. The work that was being done this afternoon, when two privileged visitors were lowered aboard, consisted of finishing touches like fitting of the electric light switches over every berth and the installing of the last items in the pantry and lavatories. Everything else had been done. The four saloons were lined in soft green, the windows were curtained with material equally soothing in texture, colour and design and the fittings for converting the saloons into sleeping cabins are in place. The chairs for daytime are not yet in position but when the tests are over the fixing of these will take only an hour. The impression of ample space one has gained in previous inspections of the unfinished boat is strengthened now that it is ready for passengers. No aeroplane yet built has given that same sense of freedom to move and breathe. Every saloon has a breadth and height in excess of the best that rail or road transport can offer. The twenty-four passengers that fly by day and the sixteen that fly through the night will have cause to bless the scheme which decrees that there shall be big mail loads for the boats to carry. A ton of mails may be carried aft of the saloon where the hull begins to taper and more than twice that load may be carried in the mail compartment on the upper deck amidships. The forward part of the deck in the* Canopus *is fully occupied with the gear of control, navigation and communication. The instruments and the apparatus, from the loop aerial of the directional wireless to the artificial horizon and the switch for the landing lights, the levers, dials and levels, makes the pilots' compartment a mass of complications and foreshadows the day when the big aeroplanes, such as will certainly be built for ocean crossings, will need an engine room separate from the bridge. For the present, the* Canopus *is the model of what an efficient, luxurious flying-boat should be and gives every promise of surviving the owners' trial with credit.'*

No sooner had *The Times* commented, 'It was a rare occurrence indeed that such a large aircraft was ready for certification trials so soon after the first flight', than *Caledonia* was delivered to MAEE, Felixstowe for the CofA trials on 15 September. Three days later, *Canopus* emerged from the workshop, fully fitted out.

At Felixstowe, up until the end of September, Lankester Parker and Squadron Leader Martin shared the test flying. Two take-offs and alightings at an overload weight of 45,000 lb were included. Squadron Leader Martin passed the aircraft and on the first of October, Lankester Parker set the newly certificated *Caledonia* back upon the Medway.

Despite Imperial Airways' satisfaction with *Canopus*, the airline could not depart for Genoa, and the trans-Mediterranean service, until the type certification administration had been completed. The time was, however, well spent in demonstration and training flights. Between the 1st and the 10th of October, Brackley flew *Canopus* nine times. On the first, he and Lankester Parker made a maximum-weight landing, and the following day, a dusk alighting was made. After two days' training, Brackley was awarded his 'C-class' type rating.

On 5 and 6 October a number of VIP familiarization flights were made. Amongst the official passengers were the Air Minister, Lord Swinton, and Chief of the Air Staff, Sir Edward Ellington, with their respective entourages. Brackley and Captain Bailey piloted them. Lankester Parker had the honour of flying Sir Eric Geddes, Sir John Reith, then Director-General of the BBC, Sir Samuel Hoare, First Sea Lord, and the Board of the Admiralty. During these flights, the Sperry Autopilot was tested.

Brackley flew again on the 7th, this time for an hour,

and made several take-offs and alightings using various flap settings. Fuel-consumption trials were flown by Lankester Parker on the 9th and then assorted minor faults were rectified.

Finally, on 20 October 1936, after *Canopus* had had a twenty-minute check flight, Lankester Parker formally handed over *Canopus,* the first of the Imperial Flying-Boats, to Brackley. Brackley made two further flights and then, during the afternoon of 22 October, following type certification gained by *Caledonia* earlier that day, *Canopus* departed for Genoa.

Halcyon days had dawned.

On the morning of *Canopus'* departure, the British public were advised the 'boat was capable of 200 mph … the fastest of its class in the world. Also, fuel con-sumption and performance was better than expected. The MAEE pundits had been astonished by the take-off performance during the trials and Chief Technical Officer, Harry M. Garner, suggested Gouge might like to make further refinements. The Rochester team carried out many hours of hydrodynamic trials in the water tank and although it was too late to incorporate their findings in the S.23, the vertical knife-edge stern post at the rear of the planing bottom of the Sunderland, and subsequent 'boats, was a result of that work. The impressive take-off performance of the S.23 finally silenced those dubious as to the Sunderland's ability and consequently the catapult-assisted S.27 project was abandoned.

CHAPTER THREE

Change and Progress

CHANGES AFOOT
The amalgamation of the independents into British Airways – Twelfth AGM.

During the early 1930s, the financial institutions, Whitehall Securities, and the bankers, Erlangers, invested in the embryonic independent airlines. The Hon. Clive Pearson, Manager of Whitehall Securities, bought into Saunders-Roe and Spartan Airways in 1931. Erlangers also supported the entrepreneurial ex-coach operator and founder of Hillman Airways, Edward Hillman. Hillman, Spartan, United and a few smaller lines merged on 30 September 1935, forming the bedrock upon which British Airways (pre-war) and later British Overseas Airways Corporation (BOAC) were to be built.

The conglomeration of independents became Allied British Airways Ltd but a month later the company was retitled British Airways. They were soon awarded Government mail contracts and subsidies; services started, from Heston, on 17 February 1936. One clause of the British Airways' contract specified that all aircraft should be capable of 200 mph. Due to rearmament, no suitable home-produced aircraft were available so British Airways purchased Lockheed Electras and Lockheed 14s.

The twelfth Annual General Meeting of Imperial Airways took place at the Hotel Victoria, Northumberland Avenue, on 10 November 1936. Sir George Beharrell deputized for the sick Sir Eric Geddes and announced that in 1935, civil aviation had expanded. Moreover, the 1936 Air Estimates included £75,000 for transatlantic aircraft bases, £20,000 for Imperial Airways' experimental flights and £18,000 for the Bermuda to New York service. Against this background, Sir George presented his report. He said that Imperial Airways expected to be granted New York landing rights soon and arrangements had been made with Pan American Airways (Pan Am) for the development of mutually co-operative services. Once wireless stations and meteorology facilities had been prepared, transatlantic trial flights would commence. Two 'boats, *Caledonia* and *Cambria,* were being prepared for long-range Empire and Atlantic routes. Development of the Mayo composite was progressing, as was flight-refuelling, which showed great promise. However, it was recognized that only one of these range-extending techniques would eventually be employed. In the Atlantic, facilities were completed for *Cavalier*'s Bermuda to New York service, and as soon as the United States' permit to operate was issued, the inauguratory date would be announced. Sir George continued that Durban had been chosen as the southern extremity of the Empire route; certain political difficulties had to be overcome before they could continue to Johannesburg and Cape Town. In the meantime, flights from Durban to Cape Town would be flown by the South African state service, South Africa Airways, and Imperial Airways would cease operating between Johannesburg and Cape Town.

To supply a human element to his report, Sir George read the following unsolicited letter from a passenger:

> '*Sir,*
> *As a passenger in* Canopus *last Saturday, I desire to express my appreciation of magnificent performance and the courtesy with which I was treated. It was certainly the most memorable and one of the most delightful days of my life.*'

ROUTES, SURVEYS AND SCHEDULES
Canopus, *the first schedule – Christmas 1936 airmail – 'Castor oiled' – African survey – Towards the antipodes – Kallang, the new Singapore – QEA enters the stage – Fysh/Brackley survey – Australian impasse – Survey to Singapore.*

An airline's routes were, to a great extent, dictated by the capability of its aircraft. As aviation advanced, the scheduled route structure was not far behind and many pioneering flights were sponsored by airlines and governments searching for new routes. With the airlines becoming more soundly established, the emphasis on the survey flights changed from record breaking to feasibility study. Once a route had been surveyed and accepted, *en route* support facilities had to be constructed and local services arranged. Then, the route could be proved. Following Cobham's 1931 survey flight to Goma, on Lake Kivu (west of Lake Victoria), over three years elapsed before, on 8 December 1934, the route became part of the Imperial Airways' scheduled structure. Even then, it was only seen as a spur off the service to Karachi. Much of the later route proving for the Empire Routes was done by *Satyrus,* the then remaining Kent 'boat.

The intention to make first commercial use of the Empire 'Boats on the Cairo to East Africa route, during 1936, was thwarted by late delivery. It became apparent that it would be the end of 1936 before the 'boats were available for any route. Matters worsened with the loss of the Kent 'boat, *Scipio*, and it became imperative to introduce the 'C-class' 'boats on the Mediterranean service, Brindisi to Alexandria.

With the first of their new flying-boats in their possession, Imperial Airways were hoping for a new and improved service. Cruising speeds of the 'boats were 30 mph higher than those of existing land planes, and day and night flights were contemplated. Certification trials were complete and *Canopus* now had to earn her keep.

Canopus departed Rochester at 14:35 on 22 October. She was crewed by Brackley, Captain Bailey, First Officer Long, Wireless Operators Bell and Vallett, Flight Clerk Adam and Engineers Crowson and Hards. The flight to Alexandria, the Mediterranean terminus, should have taken two days but bad weather plagued them. They night-stopped at Caudebec, on the Seine near Rouen, and poor weather forced them to remain there the following day. Brackley was unable to continue to Macon on the Saturday, because of fog in the Rhône Valley, so he routed instead through Bordeaux and eventually arrived at Marseilles on 25 October. Having refuelled, they continued to Lake Bracciano and finally Brindisi, where they night-stopped. Whilst at Brindisi, the Italian Director-General of Civil Aviation and the President of the Italian state airline were invited aboard *Canopus*.

On 26 October, *Canopus*, with Captain Bailey in command, left Brindisi for Alexandria on a proving flight. All was not well. Shortly after departure a radio call was received: *Canopus* had struck stormy weather and was returning. Safely clear of the weather, she alighted back at Brindisi at four o'clock that afternoon. The proving flight was delayed yet another day. Once the eastbound proving flight had been flown, the first scheduled flight of an Empire Flying-Boat was from Alexandria to Brindisi on 30 October. Refuelling stops were made at Mirabella and Athens and the flight took seven hours and twenty minutes, as compared to the Kents' time of thirteen hours. On board was mail which had left Brisbane on 21 October. The first eastbound schedule was flown on 2 November.

Whilst *Canopus* plied the Mediterranean between Brindisi, Athens and Alexandria, other 'boats began to trickle from the Rochester works. *Centaurus*, G-ADUT, the third 'boat, was launched at the end of October. Ten days later, she was being displayed to the press, upon the rain-lashed Medway. Lightly loaded, *Centaurus* easily negotiated one of the Medway bends and the crosswind during her 21-second take-off run. Those reporters on board commented upon the quietness of the take-off.

Canopus departed Rochester at 14:35 on 22 October 1936, bound for the Mediterranean. She was crewed (L to R) by Mr Crowson, engineer; Mr Vallett, Marconi wireless operator; Major H. G. Brackley, DSO DSC, Air Superintendent of Imperial Airways; Mr Hards, engineer; Mr W. Bell, Imperial Airways wireless operator; Mr C. E. Adam, flight clerk; First Officer S. G. Long and Captain F. J. Bailey. The flight and subsequent entry into service were plagued by poor weather. (The Aeroplane, 28 October 1936)

They missed the 'sharp bullet-like thuds as the hull slapped through even the smallest of waves.' Similarly, 'Those in the smoking compartment with their backs to the window, did not know the boat had touched the water' when the 'calm but steep approach over Rochester Bridge resulted in soft but certain contact with the river.' Moreover, 'Those taking their rest in the sleeping compartment were only aware of the landing as the boat gently rocked when it had lost way, as the man in the bow position picked up the mooring.' During the flight an engine was intentionally shutdown; the change of note went unnoticed by the reporters. 'An air of great comfort' abounded.

Caledonia, which had returned from MAEE on 1 October, and been diverted from her intended task – the Atlantic – was used by Brackley to award type ratings to Imperial's pilots. Thereafter, on 4 December, she was the first 'boat to be delivered to Hythe when Captains Cumming and Richardson ferried her in from Rochester.

Although the Empire Airmail Scheme had yet to be started, Empire 'Boats, *Caledonia* included, were pressed into service delivering the Christmas 1936 airmail. On 13 December 1936, Captain Cumming, in *Caledonia*, left for India carrying five and a half tons of mail. They returned on the 18th with a similar load. On the same day, *Centaurus*, with Captains Egglesfield and Alcock, left Hythe with mail for Egypt and earned a subsidy of £22,500 for Imperial. Use of the 'C-class' was not before time, since Armstrong Whitworth Atalantas, as well as Kents, were being lost. Atalanta *Athena* (G-ABTK) had been destroyed by fire at Willingdon Airport Delhi on 29 September. The Indian Postmaster, however, had reported, the following day, that the mails for the Dutch East Indies, Australia and New Zealand had been saved intact and were being sent on.

In the meantime, the long-range 'boat, *Caledonia*, set records. On 18 December, Captains Cumming, Powell and Wilcockson, with First Officer 'Geordie' Garner, departed Hythe at 11:00 and night-stopped at

The Armstrong Whitworth Atalanta Athena *(G-ABTK) was destroyed by fire at Willingdon Airport Delhi on 29 September 1936. The mails for the Dutch East Indies, Australia and New Zealand were saved intact and sent on. (Hartle)*

Marignane. The following morning they departed for Alexandria, eleven and a quarter hours away, carrying mail for Egypt and India. Three days later, *Caledonia* flew the return trans-Mediterranean flight to Marseilles, 1,700 miles, in eleven and a half hours. After stopping the night of 21/22 December at Marseilles, they crossed France to Southampton in four hours ten minutes, arriving at noon. Flying time for the complete return journey had been less than 32 hours.

As the Christmas mail rush drew to a close, the Postmaster-General announced the Christmas airmails had been the heaviest yet dispatched from England. About ten tons of mail had been sent to Africa, India, Malaya and Australia. That was about half as much again as the previous year.

The story of the Atlantic and the Bermuda service is told elsewhere in this book (Chapters 4 & 7) but for the moment suffice to say by default, *Cavalier*, G-ADUU, was allotted to the Bermuda to New York route. Hurriedly she was launched, test flown, fitted with long-range tanks and then dismantled. The dismembered flying-boat was shipped to Bermuda for re-erection. *Cavalier* arrived in Bermuda on 30 December 1936. The last S.23 to be launched in 1936 was *Castor*, G-ADUW; she graced the Medway on 15 December.

As additional Empire 'Boats entered service, route expansion gathered pace. Brindisi–Alexandria was extended to Marseilles–Alexandria on 4 January 1937, the first 'boat on this schedule being the recently launched *Castor*, with Powell and First Officer A. Gordon Store at the helm. Over 12 and 13 January, as a trial, Captain Egglesfield flew *Centaurus* from Alexandria to Southampton. He refuelled at Marseilles, following a night stop at Brindisi. *Centaurus* carried eight passengers and a ton of mail. An outward flight from Southampton was made on 16 January by *Centaurus*.

The first scheduled Empire 'Boat departure from Southampton should have taken place on 6 February 1937. Captain Jimmy Alger was to take *Castor* to Alexandria. The remainder of his crew were First Officer Gordon Store, Wireless Operator Albert Lowe, the unfortunate Bill Claridge acted as Steward and Bill Morgan was Flight Clerk. The 'boat was loaded with ten passengers, a ton of mail and five large cases of bullion. Although the departure was delayed slightly by the MV *Hotspur II*, the master of which ignored appeals from Imperial's launches to move away, *Castor* slipped at 11:40. All had been made fast below. She was airborne within minutes and circled whilst a cameraman in a Percival Gull attempted to snap her image. Unleashed, *Castor* sped on her way to France but within ten minutes she was back on her mooring.

Captain Alger explained the plugs on the port-outer had oiled up and he had been forced to turn back. He expected to be airborne within the hour. The plug change took longer than anticipated. Marseilles could not be reached in daylight. The passengers were booked back into the Lawn Hotel at Hythe and the police were called to guard the bullion. Departure the following day was thwarted by rough water. Soaked, the crew returned to the hotel.

Finally they were away at 07:20 on 8 February but bad weather in the Rhône valley and at Marseilles forced them to make an unscheduled stop for fuel at Hourtin. It took Alger three hours to refuel using four-gallon petrol cans but, fortuitously meanwhile, the Marseilles weather improved. They gained Marseilles that night but the passage of the all-important mail was now two days behind schedule. It was probable Imperial would lose the airmail subsidy, which was only paid if the mail arrived on time. Alger decided they would make up time with quick turnarounds and over-flight of staging posts wherever possible. Finally, an 'illegal' alighting at night, amongst the Fleet at Alexandria, brought the mail back within schedule. It had been an inauspicious start to the all-air mail service to Australia. Previously, mail had been flown to Paris, taken by rail to Brindisi and then on by air.

The press had made great play of headlines referring to 'Castor Oiled' and generally derided the service. However, once it was learnt Alger had got the mail to Egypt on time, the delayed start and the determined passage was seen more as a demonstration of responsibility.

The return flight was just as notable. Out of Brindisi they circled Mount Vesuvius before turning north to Rome. Once out of Marseilles they were informed there was fog on Southampton Water so they night-stopped at Macon. Amongst the passengers was the new Line Manager, Mr Charlie Cross, returning from Egypt. Mr Cross achieved the sobriquet 'Slack-arse Charlie' by virtue of his ill-fitting trousers. As fog was still being reported in the Channel, he told Flight Clerk Morgan to get the passengers and freight onto a train. This was duly done. Morgan was supposed to follow, with the mail, in a subsequent train. As it was, Alger decided to press on and after a 'hairy' flight they made Southampton despite the fog. This allowed Bill Morgan ample time to get up to Waterloo to meet the boat-train, his passengers and the new Line Manager.

Once six 'boats became available, two 'boats a week were scheduled. From the beginning of March, the schedule was further increased to four flights a week. If Shorts were able to maintain a delivery rate of two per month, it was expected that Imperial would replace the Handley Page H.P.42s on the Cairo to Great Lakes route by early March 1937. Moreover, by 1 April, with nine 'boats in service, the new coastal route to South Africa would be open. A lot hinged upon whether the H.P.42s on the Cairo to Great Lakes sector were replaced before those operating from Paris to Brindisi. Alas, at the end of May, plans were thrown into disarray with the loss of H.P.42, *Hengist*, in a hangar fire in the airship shed at Karachi. A workman had mistakenly fitted an incorrectly coloured oxygen bottle to the compressed-air

Hengist, G-AAXE, was delivered in December 1931 as a H.P.42W (western) but was converted to E (eastern) standard in 1935. The Jupiter engines were fitted with a compressed-air starter system. On 31 May 1937, in the old airship hangar at Karachi, someone connected an oxygen bottle to the starter system. Hengist was destroyed in the resultant fire. (Hartle)

engine-starting system. *Hengist* was destroyed in the resultant explosion.

In preparation for what was looking more like a June than an April service to South Africa, survey flights were flown. These flights complemented the experience already gained by the three-engined Short Calcuttas on the 'old' Cairo to Great Lakes sector. The new route would extend beyond Victoria Nyanza, on the Great Lakes, to Naivasha, a lake adjacent to Nairobi, and from there to the coast at Mombasa. Between Cairo and Nairobi the 'boats would fly from lakes and rivers. At the coast, the route would continue southward to Dar-es-Salaam, Lindi, Portuguese East Africa and eventually – Durban.

By adopting a coastal route, the high ground, which had been a hazard on the earlier overland trek by land planes, would be avoided. Avoidance was imperative if, as hoped for, the schedule was to continue throughout the night and during bad weather. Navigational accuracy was increased by the establishment of a chain of twenty-one 'Marconi Adcock' short-wave radio direction-finding sites, between Cairo and Durban. This navigational facility would be essential for future night operations. Beforehand, aircraft had taken bearings from the established medium-wave stations, situated at the various landing-fields, but medium-wave stations were subject to interference at night and during electrical storms.

In March and April of 1937, the Kent 'boat, *Satyrus*, surveyed part of the central/southern Africa route. Several of Imperial's more experienced captains took part, including 'Tich' Attwood, 23 March to 14 April, L. A. Egglesfield from 1 to 14 April and 'John' Alcock, 11 to 23 July. The remainder of the crew was made up from First Officers Rotherham and Murray, Wireless Operator Challis and Engineer Cullen.

After departing Alexandria, *Satyrus* called at Cairo, Luxor, Wadi Halfa, Kareima and, for two days, Khartoum. They continued to Kosti, Malakal, Bor, Laropi and Butiaba, on Lake Albert, and thence to Kampala and Kisumu. During the survey, *Satyrus* encountered few difficulties and the ground organization was recorded as well founded. Some improvement to the facilities had already been attempted and a jetty had been built at Khartoum. Often more substantial works were required or occasionally it was necessary to secure an alternative landing site. Much of the route had already been surveyed by surface parties, using time-honoured weighted lines or modern echo-sounding equipment to plumb the alighting areas. Egglesfield's survey was planned to coincide with the period the Nile would be at its lowest. Despite the reassurances received that the water at Juba was of sufficient depth, it was no surprise to discover that the Juba Nile had

In April/May 1937, Captain Egglestone surveyed the route to Durban with Cambria, *the first Empire 'Boat over Africa. He departed Durban on 4 June.* Cambria, *moored here at Salisbury Island, lacks windows – a standard fit on many survey flights. (Baldwin and Bigby)*

silted-up, and a new 'riverdrome' at Laropi, near Nemuli, some ninety miles away, was selected.

The altitude of landing sites could also be a problem as, at height, aircraft engines produce less power. Nairobi is 5,000 feet above sea level and the 'C-class', as with all aircraft of the day, had little reserves of power to cater for the unexpected. To worsen matters, Lake Naivasha – Nairobi's selected lake – was another 1,000 feet higher. To compound matters it was believed that weather conditions upon the lake, particularly visibility and cloud base, were not always suitable for flying operations. These and other factors had to be examined on *Satyrus's* survey flight.

Egglestone repeated the survey in *Cambria* and departed Southampton on 26 April, at the beginning of a 20,000-mile survey of African routes. In early May, *Cambria*, the first Empire 'Boat over Africa, flew up the Nile to Khartoum. She arrived in Durban on 22 May and tied up at temporary moorings north of Salisbury Island. Shore facilities were not complete and there was some disagreement as to the siting of the moorings, as the resident operators with their knowledge of local weather disagreed with Imperial's staff. *Cambria* left Durban on 4 June, leaving the ground support operation in place and ready for scheduled flights.

On 15 May, the 'boats entered service on the route to South Africa. Initially, the schedule terminated at Kisumu, and *Capella* was the first to serve that route, arriving on 29 May. In contrast, signifying the end of the land planes, which had been in service for the previous five years, Captain 'On Time Dudley' Travers piloted the Armstrong Whitworth XV Atalanta *Amalthea* (G-ABTG) out of Rand Airport, Johannesburg on 7 June 1937 – the last land plane Imperial Airways scheduled out of Africa.

The opening of the new coastal route, south of Mombasa, was delayed for a few weeks as permission from the Portugese East African authorities had not been immediately forthcoming. Finally, *Canopus* departed Hythe for Durban, on 2 June 1937. She arrived six days later having completed the first through scheduled flight. *Canopus* was joined on the route by *Centaurus* and Captain Bailey at the end of the month. Once the mail reached Durban, it was distributed by aircraft of the Union of South Africa.

To the east, a similar story was unfolding. Between 6 and 9 September, *Ceres* surveyed the route from Alexandria to Karachi, via Lake Habbaniyah and Sharjah. She operated out of the Dead Sea, the Sea of Galilee having been refused on religious grounds. In contrast, Iraq approved the use of Lake Habbaniyah, fifty miles west of Baghdad, as it was considered a more suitable alighting place than Basra, where the poorly charted Euphrates and Tigris met. There, the rivers suffered large seasonal level changes and were prone to silting. The fairways were moved according to the season and operations were invariably hazardous. Also, use of Lake Habbaniyah removed the necessity of the long desert crossing from the Mediterranean to the Persian Gulf. Meanwhile, at Margil, Basra, a combined

Dar-es-Salaam, in former German East Africa, presented the flying-boat passenger with a curious mix of European architecture and African flora. (Author)

Ceres taxies into the Congella basin, Durban. During the war, Ceres *was destroyed in a hangar fire. Just as* Connemara *was destroyed on the surface by fire, so was* Ceres. *In both instances there was one fatality, both named Mr Vincent. (Author, via Cameron)*

land and sea aerodrome was being built and the lake-side facilities at Habbaniyah were being improved. It was hoped Habbaniyah and Margil would be complete before the opening of the Empire 'Boat route to Australia in 1938.

On 25 March 1938, King Ghazi opened the new Shatt-el-Arab aerodrome at Margil. Situated about a mile up river from the main wharves at Basra, the aerodrome had exceptionally clear approaches and the sheltered waters gave fine moorings. Night-landing facilities to the American 'A1' standard were fitted. Included was a revolving flashing beacon, which in normal conditions was visible out to ninety-five miles. A neon beacon was also fitted, as were three banks of three million candle power lamps, to floodlight the aerodrome. The river-side Shatt-el-Arab Hotel had fifty bedrooms, a restaurant seating seventy, a swimming pool and tennis courts.

From Iraq, the route blazed eastward across India, first calling at Karachi. Assistance was forthcoming from the Indian authorities, who agreed to help construct the bases. India already operated land planes of Trans-India Airlines along with those of Imperial Airways. At Hyderabad Sind, on the River Indus, it was proposed to establish an emergency alighting fairway, and although not on the main trans-India route, Lake Tikra was chosen to service Bombay. The first regular night halt was made upon the holy lake at Raj Samand. Next, Udaipur, Madho Shear in Gwalior and on to the Parichha Reservoir, Jhansi. From there, to Allahabad

and the confluence of the rivers Jumna and Ganges. The last call in India was made at Calcutta, at the mouth of the River Hooghly. Calcutta was a difficult alighting as the Akra Reach was narrow and the spans of the Willingdon Bridge dominated the approach. It is said that on one occasion Captain D. C. T. Bennett (to become AVM 'Pathfinder' Bennett) flew under the bridge. Throughout India, operations were hazarded by changes of water level and currents brought about by the monsoon.

In mid-November 1937, it was reported that the Air Ministry and the Burmese authorities were surveying an air route across Burma between India and French Indo-China. Chittagong, Akyab, Rangoon, Moulmein, Mergui, and Victoria Point were all possible landing sites.

At the tip of the Malay peninsula, the crossroads, city-port of Singapore was building a brand-new sea and land plane aerodrome. (In contrast, we in England continued to squabble over the site for our purpose-built base, Langstone harbour or elsewhere.) In the early thirties, reclamation work started upon the 1,000-yard-wide, malarial, mangrove swamp, at Kallang, to the south-east of Singapore city. Ten hours a day, at eight-minute intervals, for four years, trains brought earth to fill the swamp from a small hill four miles away. The site had been chosen as it was close to the city-centre Post Office, easily accessible to land and water and for many years considered prime for reclamation as a health

Corio *lifting from the Shatt-el-Arab aerodrome at Margil, about a mile upstream from the main wharves at Basra. Night-landing facilities included a revolving flashing beacon, visible out to ninety-five miles. The riverside hotel had fifty bedrooms, a swimming pool and tennis courts.* (RAF Museum 5851–8)

measure. A further twenty acres of swamp-land adjacent to the airport were later reclaimed in an attempt to finally rid the area of malarial mosquitos. A large, domed, circular grass airfield, sloping upwards at 1 in 160 towards the centre and bounded by a high wall, was constructed. To its south were the sheltered waters of the Singapore Roads. For the flying-boats, there was a 1 in 15 slipway leading from the glare-reducing, green concrete apron and a loading wharf. The alighting area was 600 feet wide, a mile long and surrounded by a boom which excluded floating debris. At night, the area was edged by lights at 300-foot intervals. On the landward side of the grass, stood the three-storeyed, flat-roofed, terminal building, with its central cylindrical control tower. Atop the tower was a neon beacon that flashed 'S' for Singapore. Two large hangars and associated offices flanked the approach road to the terminal building.

Although opened officially in June 1937, the £4.5 million airport had been in use for some months. The driving force behind this project was not Imperial Airways but ex-Governor Mr Cecil Clemanti. He, with foresight and perseverance, ensured the most modern civil airport in the eastern Empire was completed. Sir Thomas Shenton Thomas, Governor of the Straits Settlements, officiated at the opening ceremony on 12 June. His arrival in an Imperial Airways aircraft from RAF Seletar (previously the civil airport for Singapore) and the opening ceremony were witnessed by the many thousands crowded onto Kallang.

Whilst Imperial Airways forged eastward during the

1930s, the Australians, in the form of QANTAS, were pioneering their way westward. Following the trial mail-flights of 1931, and the efforts of Kingsford Smith to salvage the disaster they almost became, a regular air-mail and passenger service between the United Kingdom and Australia eventually became reality.

A service to Australia would require the combined resources of Imperial Airways, Indian Trans-Continental Airways and the Australians. Imperial Airways and QANTAS formed QANTAS Empire Airways Ltd (QEA), in January 1934. Imperial and QANTAS later agreed that QEA would be responsible for the route from Singapore to Sydney. Crews would slip at Singapore but the 'boats would fly the complete route. In April 1934, QEA was contracted to fly mail from Brisbane to Singapore. The first mail was dispatched in a D.H.86 by the Duke of Gloucester, on 10 December. On 13 April 1935, a passenger service to Australia, using a variety of aircraft, and the odd train, commenced. It took 12½ days to complete the almost 13,000-mile journey. In contrast, an ocean liner could make the passage in 30 days. Following the introduction of the Empire 'Boats, it was hoped Sydney would be reached in 9½ days – 7 days once night flights started.

Although QANTAS had sided with Imperial Airways and formed QEA, the Australian Government had yet to commit themselves to flying-boats and QANTAS doubted their commercial viability. Nevertheless, Hudson Fysh joined Brackley in a survey flight from Singapore to Sydney. The RAF provided a Short Singapore III and crew. Brackley headed the

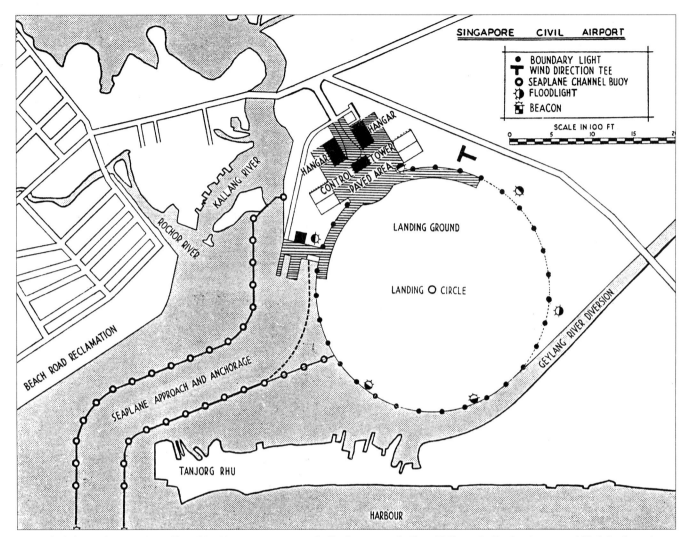

Persia had the seadrome at Margil, and in Singapore a purpose-built airport was built at Kallang: in England, we squabbled. Reclamation work had started in the early 1930s to the south-east of Singapore city, the site being close to the Post Office and easily accessible. On the landward side of the grass aerodrome stood the terminal building, with its central control tower, topped with a neon beacon. Two large hangars flanked the approach road to the terminal building. (Wonders of World Aviation, *originally courtesy of General Electric Company Ltd*)

expedition and Flight Lieutenant 'Rick' Riccard commanded the aircraft. Sergeant Pilot Elder (soon to join Imperial Airways) acted as navigator. The radio operator was Aircraftman Warren and the engineer, Corporal Fairweather. Some portent was read into the fact that a Flying Officer Thunder also accompanied them. In all, there were ten souls on board.

The survey commenced with a false start on 7 May 1936. After Air Commodore Smith had seen them off, they had flown barely a hundred miles, when the starboard forward engine failed. They returned to Singapore and 205 Sqn. The engine was changed and departure on 8 May was successful. They flew south to Klabat Bay, that fine stretch of sheltered water on Banka Island. There, the Chinese Shell Agent and the Head of the Dutch Colonial Service tendered to their needs. Accommodation was lacking and the crew slept aboard their flying-boat. Fysh described the experience as being, 'Still strange enough to appeal as romantic.'

A dawn take-off was followed an hour later by iced orange juice, fried eggs and bacon, bread and butter, and large mugs of tea. There then followed the long

oversea leg to the port of Surabaya, Java. They rested for two days in the hills, overlooking the hot and torrid port.

From Surabaya they flew eastward along the jewelled chain of islands. Bali, with its conical lava-scarred peaks, was admired and the curious volcanic formations of Sumbawa Island were studied with awe – a veritable Devil's inferno. They alighted within the sheltered waters of Bima. The flight from Bima to Kupang took them over the almost uninhabited isle of Komodo. 'The Eastern Archipelago Pilot' noted the presence of 'a peculiar creature, sometimes called the Komodo dragon … attacks the numerous wild horses and sometimes even man.'

Kupang was reached with a few hours of light remaining. The town, an odd mix of old Portugal and Dutch, gave witness to its colonial past. That evening, Brackley and his team watched the celebrations of Passer Malam, or night fair. They were entertained by the *Dance of the Meos*, the rajas' bodyguard of old.

From the mystique of the orient to the reality of Darwin – the back door to Australia. After a night in the

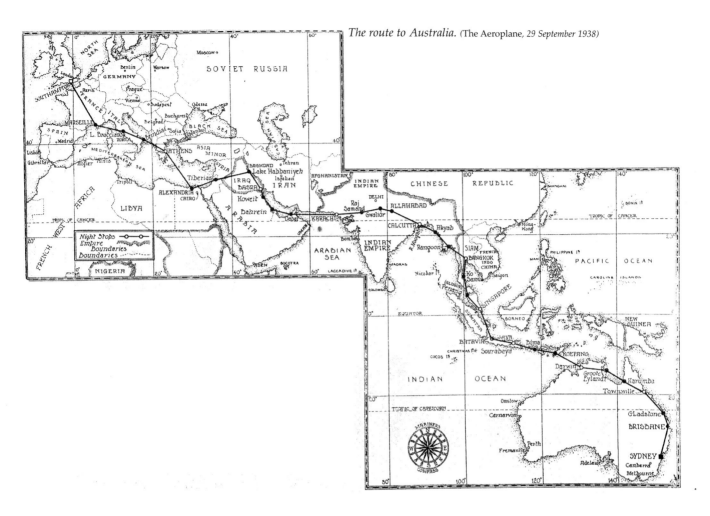

The route to Australia. (The Aeroplane, 29 September 1938)

Victoria Hotel, they were joined by Mr A. R. McComb, Controller of Ground Services, Civil Aviation Department and Squadron Leader A. G. Hempel RAAF. They crossed the 300 miles of Arnhem Land and alighted on the Roper River, Gulf of Carpentaria. Having gone ashore and surveyed the area, they continued to Mornington and Denham Island. Such was the uncharted nature of the gulf, that Denham Island was not shown upon their map. All the while, beneath them they could see vast numbers of fish in the crystal waters. They spent the night at the Mission as guests of the Reverend Wilson, who, according to Fysh, was 'doing great work amongst the natives and half-caste children, who were mostly sent to them from the mainland'.

Take-off from Mornington required them to cross the bar. As they taxied, they felt the 'boat drag and lurch over the shallows. Once free from the sandbanks they were faced with a three-foot swell, the remnants of the previous night's blow, and during the take-off run they shipped 'green water' over the lower wings. They crossed the base of the Cape York Peninsula and followed the coast to the south. Overnight stops were made at Bowen, Gladstone and Brisbane *en route* for Sydney.

Brackley and his RAF crew returned to Singapore. Fysh considered 'a pioneering trip had been completed with full satisfaction over more or less uncharted waters.'

On 3 September 1936, Great Britain, Australia and New Zealand met to discuss the extension of the Empire Airmail Scheme that would connect them. The Air Ministry was represented by former Deputy Director of Civil Aviation, Mr F. G. L. Bertram, recalled from retirement. The Australians were not particularly enthusiastic about the use of the forthcoming Empire Flying-Boats. There was already an adequate land plane service to the United Kingdom and it was with land planes that Australia's internal future lay. Why should they go to the expense of developing additional flying-boat services and the necessary supporting infrastructure? On 28 January 1937, the Australian Prime Minister, Mr Lyons, announced that the British Government understood the Australian view. The British accepted a stipulation allowing Australia to withdraw from the scheme if, during the first two years, they had reason to be dissatisfied with the use of flying-boats on the Singapore to Sydney sector. It was also agreed that Australia would control that sector. The agreement would run for fifteen years. The British did, however, take a firm stand as to the Tasman route. They declared that a service to New Zealand would take place whether or not Australia participated.

The planned commencement in 1938 of the Empire Airmail Scheme to Australia was announced in Canberra on 17 September 1937. The Commonwealth would arrange for the construction of flying-boat bases in the Dutch East Indies – the Singapore to Darwin sector. The British and Dutch had already agreed to use sites at Klabat Bay, Batavia, Surabaya, Bima and Kupang. However, the location of the Australian bases had yet to be finalized. Site selection was not easy; Groote Island and Normanton (Karumba), on either coast of the Gulf of Carpentaria, were initially favoured. From Normanton it was proposed to route overland 400 miles to Townsville and from there, down the coast, to Sydney. Notwithstanding the decision of the Imperial Conference, which found favour with Imperial and its flying-boats, there were still those who believed that a land plane service would be preferable. Amongst the criticisms were the large tidal ranges in some locations, the vulnerability of the seadrome at Darwin to hostile naval bombardment and the difficulties of land transport in the sparsely populated Darwin area.

Finally, a route was chosen, even if the funding was not forthcoming. Ignoring the disadvantages, Darwin, long thought of as 'the hole in Australia's back fence', was selected as the gateway to Australia. From Darwin, the route turned east across Arnhem Land and coasted out at Port Roper, then across the Gulf of Carpentaria to Normanton. Another land crossing, and another 400 miles across the Cape York Peninsula to Townsville. From then on, the route hugged the east coast to Bowen, Gladstone, Brisbane and Sydney.

During the last quarter of 1937, delays in the commencement of a passenger service were already evident and passenger flights seemed unlikely until the bases were constructed. Delay was caused by disagreement between the British and Australian Governments over the proposed cost. The estimate obtained, £300,000, was far in excess of the budgeted £200,000 which had been voted by the Australian and British Governments. Although the British had said that they would make up any shortfall, they were not expecting to find such a gross underestimation confronting them.

Efforts to resolve the matter and get the route operating were being made. Australia's Premier Lyons told his Parliament at the end of November that the Commonwealth was making every effort to instigate the Empire Service. In particular, the feasibility of erecting temporary facilities in north-west Australia was being examined with a view to commencing a service in the New Year. Already QEA had agreed to provide temporary fuelling facilities if the Commonwealth provided radio and meteorological services. Imperial Airways allowed the political discourse to continue and meanwhile, in October 1937, a second survey flight from Alexandria to Singapore was flown using *Satyrus*. On 29 October, she arrived in Singapore and finally returned to Hythe for scrapping in June 1938.

The survey was soon followed up by *Cordelia*, which had been taken out of Southampton by Dudley Travers and flown, as a scheduled service, to Karachi. From there, on 15 November, Captain Egglesfield took command for the first Karachi to Singapore survey flight by 'C-class'. Gordon Store was first officer and A. J. Coster the radio operator. The other crew members were Flight Clerk Boughton, Steward Moore and Mr Green, the engineer. *Cordelia* arrived in Singapore on 21 November

and the alighting, abeam Tanjong Rhu, was witnessed by Sir Shenton and Lady Thomas, Marshal of the Royal Air Force and Government Director of Imperial Airways, Sir John Salmond and Air Vice-Marshal Tedder, Air Officer Commanding RAF Far East. Later, two flights were made carrying dignitaries, airline representatives and serving officers of the RAF. A public inspection was allowed on the afternoon of 22 November.

Cordelia departed Singapore on 23 November and Sir John Salmond, continuing his tour of inspection, was aboard. Whilst passing through Rangoon, a demonstration flight was flown for officials. Sir John disembarked at Karachi and a week later continued in *Cygnus*.

Meanwhile, *Cordelia* completed her flight without incident and returned to Southampton on 30 November. On this homeward flight she picked up the schedule at Karachi and carried mail from Australia and New Zealand in addition to her one passenger.

EARLY DAYS
Training – Building experience – Passenger comforts.

With the introduction of the Imperial Flying-Boat, as Imperial Airways first wished to call them, the airline was presented with a shortage of suitably qualified pilots. Imperial had operated their Calcuttas and Kents with barely a dozen qualified pilots. By summer 1937, as part of their planned expansion, the number of pilots was almost doubled to 190. From that total, only 69 were flying-boat pilots: insufficient for the fleet of some thirty-odd 'boats on order. It had been Imperial Airways' past policy to train their pilots in the skills of navigation, ground engineering and wireless operation. This, as Brackley propounded during a lecture to the Royal Aero Club, resulted in 'a fully educated airman with the

The fuel tank, viewed from the wing root, with the leading edge to the right. Each wing of the S.23 carried a single fuel tank, sited between the engines. Access to the wing could be gained via the bedding locker, to the rear of the flight-deck. High above the Mediterranean, in June 1937, Supernumerary First Officer Reid crawled behind the fuel tank to plug an oil leak in Castor's *port-outer engine. (Peek)*

knowledge and status befitting an officer.'

Many of Imperial's land plane pilots, Griffith Powell included, converted to flying-boats. QEA took advantage of the training facilities and in late May 1937, Captains Brain, Gurney and Crowther arrived in England to convert onto Empire 'Boats. A contract for conversion training was let to the School of Air Services Training Ltd at Hamble. Trainee pilots first learnt basic seamanship on small sailing dinghies. They were then taught marine navigation, the use of Admiralty charts, handling skills – picking up anchorages and manoeuvring close to jetties – and the tying of knots and bends. In the air, they started flying in the small Cutty Sark amphibian, a difficult aircraft to fly accurately, thus a fine test for the over-confident. Air Services Training had purchased three Cutty Sarks (G-ACDP, G-ACDR and G-AETI). They were powered by 140 hp Armstrong-Siddeley Genet Major radial engines. Following the Cutty Sarks, pilots graduated to the larger three-engined Rangoon, the militarized Calcutta. (Air Services Training had taken delivery of an ex-203 Sqn Rangoon – S1433 – in 1935/6.) By the end of the three-month course they had flown 12 hours in Cutty Sark and 20 hours in the Rangoon. There were also many 'C-class' flights, as supernumerary officers, to be made as part of the training.

Supernumerary First Officer Reid found himself acting above and beyond the normal call of duty. Reid was under the command of Captain Burgess in *Castor* when, on 2 June 1937, between Rome and Marseilles, an oil leak from the port-outer nacelle was noticed. Each nacelle carried an oil tank behind the engine. The engine could not be shut down, as the propellers did not feather, and a forced landing seemed the only way to avert an engine seizure. There was no oil contents gauge and a loss of oil pressure would be the first indication of an empty tank. Prompt decisive action was required. It was possible to see into the wing root from the rear of the flight deck but entry into the bowels of the wing was hazardous and called for great dexterity amongst the stringers and bracing wires. Notwithstanding the difficulties, First Officer Reid crawled into the port wing. Somehow he passed the inner engine and circumvented the fuel tank. He located the cause of the leak: a rivet had 'popped' and oil spouted from the hole. With great difficulty he was passed the ice pick and a tea towel from the cocktail bar. With these he plugged the hole, and the engine, and possibly the aircraft, was saved. He remained in that most uncomfortable, hot, noisy, position until they alighted at Marseilles. A more permanent repair was effected and they continued to Southampton.

Once at home, Burgess drafted his post-voyage report on notepaper from the Hotel Cecil, Alexandria. In his report Burgess gave Reid credit for his deed and called for the 'boats to be fitted with oil contents gauges and supplied with a tool kit and essential spares.

In the main, commanders were drawn from the H.P.42 and Atalanta fleets. The pilots brought some of their old habits with them. It was noted that H.P.42 pilots tended to make steep, full-flap glide approaches,

finishing with a final turn at low altitude. This would cause a rapid loss of height on finals. Fear of a heavy touchdown would cause the pilot to flare excessively and, as a consequence, the touchdown, albeit with level wings, was tail down, heavy and with the 'boat drifting. On the other hand, Atalanta pilots chose to make straight-in, shallow, powered approaches with little flap. They would touch down fast and flat, and run a considerable distance before stopping.

Night alightings could be challenging. There was a reluctance to use flap, but this led to higher touchdown speeds and a tendency to overshoot. To circumvent the overshoot, power would be reduced and the glide angle steepened. Impact with the water was usually firmer and earlier than anticipated. It was recommended that approaches at night be flown from 500 feet, at 100 mph with a little power and half to three-quarters flap. A rate of descent of 300 or 400 feet per minute would be experienced. In this condition the 'boat sat level and could be flown into the sea. This same method was also recommended for alighting in 'glassy-calm' conditions.

Through early 1937, the pilots and ground crews built up operating experience which would soon be put to the test on the forthcoming route from Cairo to the Great Lakes and onwards to Mombasa and Durban. Although night-flying was being taught, it would be a few months before night schedules were flown, as the company believed in allowing ample time for the pilots to become fully night proficient. Moreover, the 'boats had only recently been granted a Certificate of Airworthiness for flight at night.

The main differences experienced by flying-boat pilots as compared with their terrestrial brethren were neatly summed up at the time:

> 'Land pilots, who had never had to park the aeroplane amongst cars, coaches and lorries, were being trained to handle their flying-boat amongst native canoes, Arab dhows and ocean liners. Pilots learnt the vagaries of water landing and how the many variables could effect their landing: wind, current, swell and tides. They are taught to taxi across the currents, whilst engines were warmed, and to steady the boat with a drogue at every turn.'

International regulations demanded that any aircraft proceeding more than 600 miles off-shore must carry a licensed First-Class Navigator. The qualification became a prerequisite for promotion to captain. As Imperial Airways had only fourteen so qualified navigators, it was decided that pilots holding Second-Class Navigator's licence were to attain the standard of First-Class Navigator. A school, Pilots Training Ltd, was established at Croydon and courses, eight or nine months long, were held. Following the course, candidates sat the appropriate Air Ministry examinations.

As just one type of aircraft was being operated down the route, it was possible to station all the aircrews at home base, Hythe. Similarly, the old practice of allocating a particular aircraft to a particular captain ceased.

Karachi, India. The first officer checks around from his observation port, whilst the captain towers over the wireless operator who is attempting to pick up the mooring on the first pass. The inboard engines are stopped, and the 'boat is manoeuvred using the outboards and the drogues, which the wireless operator has already deployed. (Hartle)

The flying-boats were now capable of proceeding along the route with far less rest than their crews, and the practice of 'slipping' crews was introduced. With rest days taken into account, it would take a crew about eighteen days to make the round trip to Singapore. On return they would have eight to ten days 'off', but during this time reports had to be written and test flights flown.

Boarding, or more importantly crossing the water to the 'boat, would always be a problem at other than specially constructed flying-boat stations. The elements were no respecter of position. Even Woods Humphery came to grief, when he visited Hythe in the spring of 1937 to inspect the 'boats. There was an extraordinarily low tide and his launch was unable to return to the quay at the Supermarine sheds. For some hours he had to be content with drifting steadily down the river awaiting the rising tide.

Following the Empire 'Boats' introduction into service, in November 1936, the public were made more aware of their splendour. The 'boats are best remembered for the exquisite service they provided. Much of the success of the passenger service was due to the administrations of the flight clerk. The flight clerk, carried in addition to the steward, had his own desk towards the rear of the flight-deck and was responsible for making each 'boat a self-contained unit as far as ship's papers were concerned. His duties included the preparation of load and trim sheets, completion of passenger lists, customs health and immigration procedures, the handling of freight consignments and the custody of crew and passenger inoculation and vaccination certificates.

The flight clerk's position on the rear of the flight-deck was not ideal. In flight, he was poorly placed to be available to his passengers and his papers tended to blow about. Once afloat, he and his paraphernalia were in the way of those loading mail, refuelling and servicing the 'boat. From mid-1937 onwards, the flight clerk was moved below the flight-deck into the forward, formerly smoking, compartment. Also about this time, the flight clerk's title was changed to purser. In his new location, the purser's desk was positioned in the rear starboard corner of the forward cabin, facing aft, abutting bulkhead. Because of the added demand for airmail, the remainder of the forward cabin was used as an additional hold and the aft cabin was then designated as the smoking cabin. The overall passenger complement was reduced to seventeen. To the port of the purser's desk was a ladder up to the flight-deck, terminating behind the pilots. Those aircraft built after mid-1937 were constructed with this modification incorporated.

Imperial Airways adopted a staid and conservative approach towards the employment of females. They maintained strongly the opinion that their kind of flying required the stewardship of a man. As Imperial saw it, '… this curious hybrid nursemaid-cum-waitress was not the best way of putting the passengers at their ease.' Moreover, Imperial Airways believed men worked harder than women. They declared:

'Our aerial stewards are men of a new calling. They had to be since much was expected of them. In less than an hour a couple of flying stewards can serve six courses, with wines, to between thirty and forty people.'

According to one satisfied customer, a well respected member of the American aviation press, who had recently flown to Paris:

'The English air traveller demands four things: comfort, tobacco, drink, food. Imperial Airways provides all four with superlative flying services, not only on the Paris run but also on the Empire Boats. As we took off from Croydon, the stewards handed round wine lists, everybody ignored them and ordered Scotch and soda or bottles of ale. Wines are only for banquets or foreigners but what helped most was the sight of the sun, the first glimpse in two weeks. By this time, hardy Britons were eating consomme Julien, fricassee of chicken, roast fillet of veal, ham and egg salad and cheese – gorgonzola, cheddar or cheshire. The stewards moved about with the grace and speed of panthers; the only thing that I saw in England that moved faster were Spitfires and Hurricanes. In slightly less than an hour and a half everyone had been filled up with something, the dishes and glasses all whisked away, nearly everyone was smoking and we were gliding down to Le Bourget. I was sorry to get out; it had been like sitting in a comfortable friendly club. It is the English genius for being human and understanding with air travellers that makes Imperial Airways one of the best liked services in the world. This is not only my impression, several other travellers, mostly Americans, also thought the same way.'

Food was not cooked in flight but brought aboard in Thermos flasks. Coke ovens, with the coke removed before flight, had been used on the short European legs flown by land planes, and a steam oven was experimentally fitted to *Champion*. The menus are all the more sumptuous if consideration is given to the difficulties of buying, and keeping fresh, provisions on tropical routes. A typical luncheon menu – Imperial Airways did not proffer 'lunch' – as served on *Challenger* was:

Iced Melon
Roast Chicken
York Ham
Veal Gelatine
Tomatoes, Asparagus Tips
Fruit Salad and Cream
Cheshire, Cheddar and Cream Cheeses with 'Toast Imperial'
Biscuits, Crystallised Fruit, Coffee, Liqueurs and Brandy.

Dinner seemed to have more than a passing resemblance to luncheon:

Pate de Foie Gras or Grapefruit
Roast Chicken
Ox Tongue
York Ham
Russian or Green Salad
Peaches and sauce Melba
Golden Figs
Cheshire, Camembert and Kraft Cheese 'Toast Imperial'
Biscuits, Dessert and Coffee.

After several days the menu may have become tedious. Although in-flight entertainment was not as today, the 'boats carried a respectable wine list upon which was found the intriguingly named 'Airway Cocktail'. The most enjoyable entertainment found on the Empire Flying-Boat was – to look out of the window. The 'boats rarely flew above eight or nine thousand feet – they were unpressurised – and they often flew lower, much lower. Captain Bennett described part of the African route:

'There was interest all along the line, particularly south of Khartoum. We often used to fly low over the herds of wild elephants or give the passengers a view of a charging rhino, or the lope of cantering giraffes. One of the most popular sights was the river just below the Murchison Falls; the area teemed with countless hippos. Also along the route was the story-book-shape outline of Mount Kilimanjaro.'

Such sights could be enjoyed from the Empire 'Boat's well-known promenade cabin, which was fitted with a panoramic window and an elbow rail. For those tired of the view, there was, at first in the bows, a smoking cabin. Although panoramic windows and elbow rails have vanished from modern airliners, one aspect of passenger comfort owes its origins to Imperial Airways – the cabin passenger chair.

Imperial Airways were justifiably proud of their cabin chair. They patented it as the 'Imperial Airways Adjustable Chair'. Its esteem was such that it soon

Kilimanjaro is over 19,000 feet high. At light weights the Empires could clamber up to 20,000 feet but they were unpressurized and devoid of an oxygen system. Passenger-carrying flights rarely ventured above 10,000 feet. However, on occasions it was necessary to go higher: stewards fainted and passengers got very cold. (Brown)

Murchison Falls, at the northern end of Lake Albert (Uganda), were a regular spectacle for the passengers. The waters teemed with hippos and crocodiles. (Baldwin and Bigby)

A herd of wildebeest is startled by the passing flying-boat. (Stephen)

This is Cameronian *and the houseboat* Mayflower *at Cairo. Throughout the career of the Empire 'Boats, a number of houseboats were employed throughout the route as overnight passenger accommodation. (RAF Museum 5851–17)*

The Richard King, *originally purchased as a discarded hulk in Durban, was moored at Mozambique. At great expense, accommodation, plumbing and superior fittings were installed. The houseboat was powered by a vast array of batteries, which were charged during the day, before the arrival of flying-boat passengers. (Rose)*

A passenger looks over Mosuril Bay. (Author)

spread beyond Imperial and was manufactured under licence by Accles and Pollock and later, in Germany, by Junkers. In 1937, the chair was described thus:

'By the touch of a lever – operated without raising from your seat, you can adjust these wonderful chairs from a sit up lunch table position to a reclining afternoon nap position – by far the most luxurious chair in the world an exclusive to Imperial Airways.'

The chairs were made by Rumbolds and the cushions, which doubled up as life-jackets, were made by

Ceres in collision with Tanjor. *Accidents did sometimes happen.* Ceres *was presumably attempting to nose into the houseboat.* (Author)

Ceres *damaged.* (Author)

David Mosely and Sons Ltd. The 'cushion-cum-lifebelt' was demonstrated to the press after a flight in *Capella*, early in June 1937. Captain Satchwell and First Officer Shakespear flew the 'boat during the bumpy jaunt around Southampton Water. Once alighted, a volunteer, complete with hat and cigar, donned the life-jacket in a few seconds and then calmly stepped into Southampton Water. His cigar was extinguished.

In flight, traditions of the highest order were maintained. On King George VI's Coronation, 12 May 1937, Captain Powell came down amongst his passengers on *Courtier*'s promenade deck and proposed a loyal toast. Meanwhile, as with the passengers on *Castor* and *Cassiopeia*, they listened to the Coronation Service being broadcast from London.

All this service at moderate cost: London to Egypt in two days for £40 single, to India in five days – £85, to Australia in twelve days for £116 and to South Africa in eight days – £125. The fares included meals, overnight hotel accommodation and tips. There were no extras; travelling in an Empire Flying-Boat was travelling in a veritable flying hotel, being served restaurant meals in spacious saloons.

It was airline policy to lodge passengers at only the more select hotels during night stops. As a proviso, the hotels had to be managed by European staff. In Athens the Grande Bretagne was frequented and in Singapore – where else but Somerset Maugham's beloved Raffles. Where hotels were not available, the airline went to great lengths to find suitable accommodation. When refuelling at Mirabella, Crete, passengers were entertained to tea aboard the Imperial Airways' yacht *Imperia*, which was moored there expressly for that purpose and to act as the wireless ship. On the Nile, at Cairo, there were the sumptuous houseboats *Mayflower* and *Agamemnon*.

Another ship, the *Richard King*, was moored at Mozambique in the late thirties. Before that time, passengers and crew were accommodated in the station staff's quarters. To rid themselves of the inconvenience of consistently moving out of their accommodation, the staff built themselves a small annexe in the grounds. The *Richard King* (nicknamed Wretched Thing) could accommodate 30 guests. It had been purchased as a discarded hulk in Durban and, at great expense, the accommodation superstructure was built atop. Once complete, it was towed up to Mozambique. The fittings were, in their day, most superior and all the rooms were equipped with electric lights, fans and plumbing for hot and cold running water. The public rooms, which were furnished to Imperial's usual fine taste, included a lounge, dining room and a bar. Behind the scenes was a fully equipped kitchen with refrigeration facilities. All this was electrically powered by vast banks of batteries which, once the passengers had departed, were charged by a raucous generator.

As the lure of Empire air travel spread, the public was given hints and advice on how to travel. The following charming piece, very much from a bygone age, advises the lady traveller on how to journey by air to the corners of the Empire. It is a far cry from Lady Maude in the Hercules:

Flying in Comfort – Suggestions for
the Woman Passenger.
From a Correspondent – The Times *15 June 1938.*

'Many women who are going by airliner for the first time are a little doubtful about what they should take with them. They want to anticipate any little extras and they would like to know how to compile their wardrobe.

A surprising number of them imagine that they can take little else than the clothes that they stand up in, that they survive on light snacks in the air, waiting for the airliner to land to enjoy a proper meal. They imagine that they must board an airliner muffled in scarves and coats and armed with rugs to keep warm at high altitudes, that they will end a journey feeling cramped and stiff from sitting too long in a confined space. Some people have even been known to arrive at the aerodrome with a flying helmet to keep out the noise and cold. All

these ideas are erroneous.

There is no need to wrap yourself up. All aeroplanes are heated and air conditioned. If you feel the need for a rug, rugs are provided – and, on the Empire routes, foot muffs also.

Promenade Deck
These airliners are so spacious that there is plenty of room for passengers to walk about; the Empire 'boats have a promenade deck. And there is no need to worry about noise, for the walls are insulated, allowing conversation to be carried out at a normal voice.

If the ears should get that 'full' feeling, as it is sometimes when climbing high mountains, this can be stopped by swallowing hard, or yawning several times, or holding the nose and blowing with the mouth closed. The time consecutively spent in the air is never more than a few hours.

No special clothes are needed on the European routes, but it is worth noting that the free luggage allowance on these routes is 33 lb. Every kilo, 2.2 lb in excess, is charged for, the rate being according to the distance. To keep within the 33 lb free luggage allowance to Europe take a suitcase weighing about six and a half pounds and measuring about 26 inches by 15 inches by 7½ inches.

Clothes to Take
In that suitcase you can pack all the following things – sufficient for the average woman's holiday: two evening frocks, one short evening wrap, one light suit, one cocktail outfit, three silk cool afternoon frocks, four silk night dresses, four camiknickers, one dressing gown, six pairs of silk stockings, two pairs of Clarks, one pair evening shoes, two pairs walking shoes, one pair of mules, a complete toilet set, a bathing suit and a cap.

On the Empire route to Egypt, Africa, India, Singapore and Australia a slightly different basis of weighing in applies to luggage. Fares here are based upon the transport weight of 221 lb, this includes the weight of

Ladies taking tea. This was the service that Imperial Airways wished to portray. (IA/BOAC)

the passenger and their baggage. If a passenger weighs more than 187 lb however an allowance of 33 lb of baggage free of charge is made irrespective of the passenger's weight.

A Useful Trunk
Suitcases designed to meet air regulations on Empire routes may be bought at many stores. Particularly successful is a specially designed wardrobe trunk that weighs 22 lb. It has an attractive appearance of rawhide, a space for dresses to hang, compartments for underclothing, accessories and shoes.

You can pack into this suitcase all the following clothes giving preference to dresses of crease resistant material and hats which can be rolled up: one lightweight flannel suit, two evening dresses, two washing silk frocks, two dinner frocks, one cashmere pullover, one cashmere cardigan, one lisle thread jumper, two washing foulard silk shirts, a bathing costume, a cap, two scarves, an evening bag, three pairs of gloves (one for evenings), sun shade, dressing gown, three night dresses, two chemise and knicker sets, two pair camiknickers, two slips, six pairs of stockings, two light corsets, four hats, two pairs of evening shoes, two pairs of court shoes, a pair of beach shoes, a pair of slippers.

For the Tropics
The articles you need at night stops should if possible be restricted to one suitcase which will be available in your room at the hotel each night. Any other baggage is not available on the voyage and will not be accessible during the journey except by special arrangement with the flight clerk. A topee or sun helmet is desirable if you are going to move about at stops in the tropics but it is better to buy this locally. Dark glasses are provided for passengers on the liner. The longest Empire air journey takes only nine and a half days all the way to Australia.

To amuse you during the flight there are jigsaw puzzles, crossword puzzles, playing cards, board games, and annotated route maps which help you to trace your way across the earth geographically and historically.

Children Who Fly
So many young folk travel by air that special provision has been made for them with toys and children's books and magazines. And special children's foods can be supplied provided due notice is given. This service applies also to passengers on special diets, vegetarians or people who must have different foods because of religious beliefs.

It is well to remember that alcohol expands at high altitude and for this reason it is advisable to see that your fountain pen is not full before boarding the aeroplane. Ink contains a high percentage of alcohol. For the same reason all face lotions should be carried in screw top bottles.

The Pyramids. Scenes like these, from around the world, were presented to the promenade deck windows. (Author)

Flying used once to be an adventure. Today it is just a comfortable and quick way to reach a fixed destination.'

Much was made of the S.23's 200 mph cruise but the truth lay nearer 145 mph. It seems that airspeed indicators may have been fitted in the passenger cabins of early 'C-class' 'boats but the instruments had to be removed as the public could see that 200 mph was never achieved in service.

Flying may not have been quite as comfortable as advertised. The air entering the cabin could be heated by a steam- (or hotwater-) filled heat-exchanger in the starboard wing root. The steam (or hot water) was produced in an exhaust muff fitted to the starboard-inner engine. It was not a particularly efficient system and few crews could get it to operate correctly. Passengers often complained of the cold, and blankets and foot mufflers were provided. Cruising altitude could be uncomfortable as the 'boats were neither pressurized nor fitted with an oxygen system but they could clamber up to 15,000 feet plus, 20,000-odd when empty. Such discomfort-producing altitudes seemed to have been accepted by passengers, although the crew, steward and flight clerk in particular would have found moving around the aircraft exhausting. Hugh Gordon recalls that on one occasion he found the steward collapsed at the foot of his ladder in the pantry.

Passenger comfort had reached new standards but flying could still be a hazardous business.

CHAPTER FOUR

A Worthy Airline

THE LOSSES OF 1937
Loss of Capricornus, Courtier *and* Cygnus.

The loss of *Capricornus* says much about past attitudes to accidents and their investigation. Although an inquiry was convened, and it may have employed the finest minds then available, certain of their assumptions have, following recent research, been found to be incorrect. Some practices and procedures of yesteryear may seem incredible today, but in 1937 the airline industry was still learning its trade. The indisputable facts behind the loss of *Capricornus* follow.

Imperial Airways' Empire Flying-Boats had been operating across France for only six weeks when, on 24 March 1937, *Capricornus* struck a French hillside, twelve miles south-west of Macon. She was on her maiden scheduled flight, from Hythe to Marseilles, having been launched only ten days earlier. Until the morning of the crash, *Capricornus* had logged just seven and a half

hours. Captain A. S. 'Jock' Paterson was in command and Gareth E. Klein acted as his first officer. The remainder of the crew were Wireless Operator J. L. Cooper, Flight Clerk D. R. O'Brien and Steward F. A. E. Jeffcoate. They were charged with one passenger, Miss B. M. Coates, a load of bullion and the first Australia-bound airmail scheduled to be carried all the way by flying-boat. Just over two and a half hours after lifting from Southampton Water, *Capricornus* lay broken upon a 2,500-feet-high, fir-tree-covered hill, in the Beaujolais mountains. Wireless Operator Cooper was the only survivor of the crash.

Contemporary accounts of the accident, including those published in *Flight* and *The Aeroplane*, erroneously gave *Capricornus*'s destination as Macon. Published accounts, then and since, have concentrated upon reports that the flying-boat was lost in snowstorms, taking on ice and attempting a precautionary alighting. Wireless messages stating they were completely lost and frantically requesting their position were widely

Imperial Airways' Empire Flying-Boats had barely commenced operations when Capricornus *struck a French hillside on her maiden scheduled flight. Captain Paterson, First Officer Klein, Flight Clerk O'Brien and Steward Jeffcoate, along with the sole passenger, Miss B. M. Coates, perished. Only Wireless Operator Cooper survived.*

reported. The drama was heightened by accounts of French radio operators at Lyons muttering 'Poor devils!' at the moment of impact. These misleading and sensational press reports have, over the years, become the accepted account of the accident. Even after the inquiry, in which it was established that *Capricornus* was making for Marseilles, Imperial Airways appear to have done nothing to right the incorrect and misleading reports.

As for the wreckage, the inquiry found *Capricornus* had struck the crest of a hill, 12 miles south-west of Macon, at Le Craouge near Ouroux. The debris trail was spread over about 250 metres and orientated in a south-easterly direction. The 'boat struck in a near level-flight attitude and bounced. During the initial impact and rebound, the port float and numbers one, two and three engines were shed. The comparatively intact remainder of the aircraft came to rest on the edge of a wood and several fir trees penetrated the starboard wing, as far as the rear spar. Beneath a line drawn from the top of the windscreen to below the rear port door, *Capricornus* was a mass of crumpled wreckage. The rear passenger and freight compartments, along with the tail section, appeared complete, as did the starboard-outer engine

and floatless port wing. It is evident from the propeller of the starboard-outer engine and a severed prop found in the wreckage trail that the engines were throttled back at the moment of impact.

The left-hand side of *Capricornus* had broken open upon impact and Wireless Operator Cooper, sitting in his rearward-facing seat, had been thrown clear, sustaining only a broken arm. Cooper struggled valiantly and made his way through two miles of snowstorms to a farm, from where aid was summoned. Sadly, First Officer Klein and Steward Jeffcoate had died instantly and Captain Paterson died shortly after rescue arrived. Flight Clerk O'Brien succumbed to his injuries in the farm of La Fôret, soon after rescue, and Miss Coates failed to regain consciousness and died in hospital at Macon.

Shorts dispatched a salvage party under the command of Hugh Gordon to dismantle the wreck and clear the site. The bodies were attended to by the local butcher and placed in a temporary mortuary. The secret consignment of gold bullion, possibly destined for Indian royalty and supposedly worth £10,000, was secured along with the mail. The gold was in unmarked boxes

The fuselage of Capricornus *split open. Pieces of the pilots' centre console are recognizable on the left-hand side of the photograph. The contents of the bedding locker dominate the foreground.* (Newnham)

and thus attracted no attention from the locals. That was until officials from England questioned Hugh Gordon. The conversation was overheard and from then on the gold had to be guarded. A funeral service for the five victims was held on the morning of 28 March in the village of Ouroux. Afterwards, the coffins were returned to England by way of Boulogne.

Much later, during the 1939–45 war, Cooper served in the RAF, was captured, escaped through Switzerland and rejoined the fight. But it was after the war that fate finally caught up with Jimmy Cooper. Cooper returned to flying-boats and married in 1949. Before he could depart with his bride on honeymoon, he was asked to act as relief radio officer on a DC-3 flight to Malta. At Malta the aircraft crashed, Cooper being the only fatality.

The French technical inquiry commissioned to investigate the loss of *Capricornus* sat on 26 March. The evidence presented included extracts from the radio logs of *Capricornus* and the French wireless stations, an extract from *Capricornus's* navigational log, the engine tachograph readings and the testimony of Wireless Operator Cooper.

Meanwhile, in England and before the inquiry sat, lurid accounts referring to unsubstantiated wireless messages from *Capricornus* and ill-informed supposition were being published in a Southampton newspaper:

'14:08 – Snowstorm. Give us our position.
14:12 – Completely lost. Give position. Can see nothing.
Ice beginning to form on wings.'

The newspaper continued:

'Six minutes before the crash the pilot requested the Bron aerodrome at Lyon to give him his position, so that it is evident that the terrible weather had driven the pilot off course.'

The French authorities convened an inquiry, which focused upon two aspects of the accident, the navigational error and the fatal descent through cloud. The inquiry made only a brief reference as to why *Capricornus* was 75 miles east of track. They concluded the crew had made a navigational mistake and miscalculated the upper wind. The inquiry did not produce any meteorological evidence to support that premise.

With regard to the descent, the inquiry examined carburettor icing, airframe icing, instrument icing and human error. Although the meteorological conditions made icing possible, it was, however, thought unlikely that *Capricornus* had been so afflicted. They stated that carburettor icing was probably not affecting the engines as the carburettor air-intake was not set to the 'hot' position and the tachographs showed no rpm irregularities due to icing. They concluded airframe icing was not affecting the 'boat, as power had not been increased to counter the additional weight. Moreover, Cooper had no recollection of the propellers slinging ice onto the fuselage, and the crew could have always looked out to see if ice was accruing upon the wings and floats. The

inquiry did recognize the possibility of frozen flight instruments. Just as the airframe was not equipped with an anti-icing system, neither were the air-intakes for the flight instruments heated. Furthermore, the inquiry acknowledged that should the instrument air-intakes become blocked with ice, it was possible that a descent of the aircraft would not be correctly registered on the flight instruments. Finally, the inquiry examined the temptation that Captain Paterson may have faced in wishing to get beneath the snow showers, which had characterized the crossing. They concentrated upon the fact that *Capricornus* had, at 14:08, been given a bearing from Lyons, indicating they were approaching the Saône Valley. They discussed the desire Captain Paterson might have had to descend into the valley and continue to Marseilles at low altitude, beneath the weather. A gentle descent into the Saône Valley seemed a logical course of action. However, such a course of action would be fatally flawed, as Paterson would be making his descent without having first fixed his position.

Although the inquiry was unable to reject completely the icing hypothesis, they felt strongly that *Capricornus* had been in a voluntary descent at impact. They noted that at 13:23 *Capricornus* had declared its altitude to be 2,000 metres, whereas at 13:00 it had declared 2,400 metres. This statement cannot be supported by the radio logs. *Capricornus* did not make a 13:00 broadcast. Moreover, the 13:23 message from the radio and navigation logs of *Capricornus* show an altitude of 8,000 feet – 2,400 metres – and it is only in the French logs that the altitude is shown as 2,000 metres. Perhaps Cooper's message was misheard, he was having radio troubles, or perhaps a mistake in translation or conversion was made. What is not in doubt is that at 13:52 *Capricornus* stated it was descending through cloud. This message was not acknowledged. Contrarily, the tachographs showed, at 13:52, the engines to be at cruise rpm.

As stated, the inquiry considered the descent to be intentional. In support, newspapers reported that the residents of Ouroux saw an overflying aircraft, and it is possible Paterson caught a glimpse of the ground at that same moment and throttled back, in order to descend further. Cooper recalled that a few minutes before impact he sensed they were descending. This is borne out by the tachographs which, for the two minutes preceding impact, showed a reduction in rpm from 2,000 to 1,500. More convincing is the rearward bend of the propeller blades. This indicates the propellers were not producing thrust at the moment of impact. It was noted that the first officer's altimeter read 3,500 feet and not 2,500 feet, the altitude of the crash site. The inquiry thought this misreading was a result of crash damage.

Imperial Airways and the French inquiry seemed content with a hypothesis that explained some aspects of the accident yet left many questions unaddressed. The unexplained loss of the aircraft and the deaths of five people would have done little to instil public confidence in Imperial Airways' new fleet of Empire

Flying-Boats. Deeper investigation, possibly establishing the aircraft was far off track and perhaps bringing the competence and professionalism of the crew into question, might not have been in the airline's best interests.

Although we shall never know exactly what occurred upon the flight deck of *Capricornus* on 24 March 1937, the accident deserves re-examination, if only to establish some of the facts.

Imperial Airways' Empire 'Boats had been operating upon this route for only six weeks, and Paterson and Klein, both experienced men albeit not on Empire 'Boats, were making their first flight as a crew. They had previously made the return flight from Southampton to Alexandria as supernumerary crew with Captains Alcock and Stacey. Both Paterson and Klein had gained most of their recent experience flying out of Cairo; moreover, Klein had spent most of his RAF career flying in the Middle East. It is unlikely that either of them was well versed in flying through European winter weather, and the winter weather of late March 1937 was particularly severe.

Imperial Airways established two routes across eastern France. Route One was almost direct to Marseilles whereas Route Two called at Macon, for fuel or passengers as required. Choice of route was the captain's prerogative and was usually dependent upon weather. Both routes set heading from above the Nab Tower (east of the Isle of Wight) and crossed the English Channel. Route One maintained a south-easterly track (153 degrees) until about 150 miles north of Marseilles and Route Two was direct (136 degrees) to Macon. Air Traffic Control, such as it was, divided airspace into sectors. Each sector had its own control agency and several subordinate radio stations, but all the control agencies and subordinate radio stations shared the same wireless frequency. Although the range of those early radios was limited, adjacent sectors could overhear and follow the progress of aircraft in adjoining sectors. Communication was by morse (Wireless Telegraphy, WT), and an international code system, using groups of three letters (the Q-code), had been devised and could be used to pass most aeronautical messages.

Navigation was primarily by dead reckoning, backed up by visual fixes and radio bearings. It was possible to obtain a radio fix from the sector control agency. The sector agency would collate bearings received from its subordinate radio stations and, using triangulation, plot the aircraft's position, which was then passed to the aircraft.

Even before *Capricornus* was boarded, Captain Paterson is reported to have expressed reservations

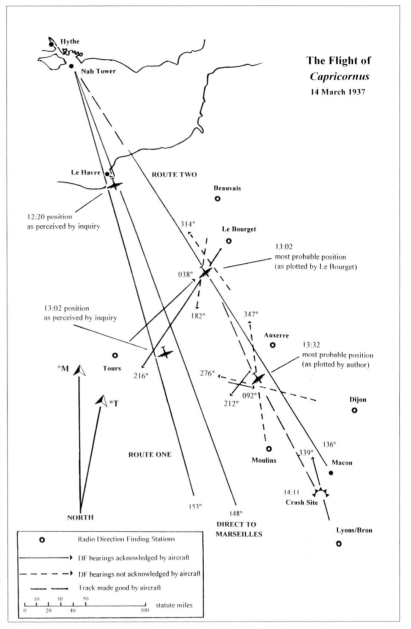

The flight of Capricornus. *The accident enquiry attributed a crucial navigational oversight by the crew to a stronger than calculated wind. Fact and history do not substantiate the findings. Although a plausible explanation of* Capricornus's *fatal position is given by the Author, it is difficult to understand what drove them to descend into the hillside. (Author)*

about making the flight in such poor weather. However, the Line Manager, Mr 'Slack Arse Charlie' Cross, impressed upon Paterson the importance of the occasion and reminded him of his duty towards Imperial Airways and the Royal Mail.

Capricornus departed Southampton Water at 11:30, crossed the Nab Tower at 11:40 and set heading 148 degrees. Portsmouth was signalled that they were airborne and destined for Marseilles. At 12:17 a time check was obtained and at 12:20 *Capricornus* reported to Portsmouth she had crossed the French coast. At 12:23 contact was established with Le Bourget, the next sector control agency. At 12:30 Paterson broadcast his 12:20 position as 108 miles (statute) 148 degrees but failed to state from exactly where the bearing was taken. Paterson reported his destination as Marseilles and his groundspeed as 168 mph. During the next half-hour, various *en route* weather reports were received, all of them indicating low cloud, poor visibility and showers. The contemporary weather observations are supported by archive information.

At around 12:55, Captain Paterson went below to converse with Miss Coates, the sole passenger. She was a clergyman's daughter from Folkestone and was travelling to visit her brother, whom she had not seen for many years as he lived in South Africa. It was ironic that Miss Coates had a fear of the sea and considered it safer to journey by air.

At 13:02 Cooper obtained a bearing of 216 degrees (True) from Le Bourget. Cooper's request for a bearing from Le Bourget was also heard by Tours, Beauvais and Auxerre. They in turn relayed bearings to Le Bourget for onward transmission to *Capricornus*. Although *Capricornus* acknowledged receipt of bearings from Tours, 038 degrees (T), and Le Bourget, 216 degrees (T), the radio logs do not show conclusive acknowledgement of the bearings from Auxerre and Beauvais (314 degrees (T) and 182 degrees (T) respectively). On board *Capricornus*, the Tours bearing simply reinforced the cross-track information obtained from Le Bourget. The bearings from Beauvais and Auxerre appear not to have been acted upon.

Despite having received the cross-track bearings, Klein delayed broadcasting *Capricornus*'s 13:02 position until 13:23. Moreover, notwithstanding that Le Bourget later plotted the bearings to give *Capricornus*'s 13:02 position as Hythe 133 degrees (T) 220 miles (statute), Klein broadcast his position as Hythe 148 degrees 220 miles (almost 50 miles south-west of his actual position).

At 13:32, *Capricornus* received bearings of 092 degrees (T) and 212 degrees (T) from Tours and Auxerre respectively. Meanwhile, Wireless Operator Cooper was having some difficulties with his radio equipment and he changed from the trailing aerial to the shorter-range fixed aerial. Although it could be argued that the cross-track bearing from Auxerre did make some sense, the two-position line fix, available from the Auxerre and Tours bearings, placed *Capricornus* some 50 miles east of track. Possibly as a result of this apparent anomaly, the Captain was summoned back to the flight-deck. Some twenty minutes later (13:52), *Capricornus* announced she was descending.

At 14:08 *Capricornus* requested a true bearing from Lyons. At 14:10 the bearing, 339 degrees (T), was acknowledged and Lyons were informed that *Capricornus* was destined for Marseilles. The bearing placed them to the north-west of Lyons, and they should have been to the west. At 14:11 another bearing from Lyons was requested. The reply, 340 degrees (T), was not received, for *Capricornus* had crashed. Although during the previous hour *Capricornus* did, on two occasions, state she was flying in snow showers, at no time did she ask for her position, declare herself to be lost or state she was taking on ice. Possibly, the misleading

nature of the press accounts was due to a lack of technical understanding upon the part of the journalists and difficulties with translation.

The author reappraised the radio logs and examined the French inquiry's report in an attempt to formulate a hypothesis that truly explained the accident. Invariably the perceived facts failed to provide a satisfactory explanation. However, once the terminology used and some of the assumptions made by the inquiry were examined, a plausible hypothesis revealed itself. With the evidence available, including archive meteorological information, it is possible to plot *Capricornus*'s path from Southampton Water to Macon.

Capricornus broadcast two position reports. They both reported a bearing of 148 degrees, and Hythe was specified as the origin of one of these bearings. It was assumed by the inquiry that these bearings from Hythe were relative to True North. Such positions, when plotted, indicate *Capricornus* to be roughly following Route One, to Marseilles. It cannot, however, be denied that plots of the French radio bearings show *Capricornus* followed, approximately, the direct track to Macon, Route Two. But *Capricornus* repeatedly declared her destination as Marseilles and there was no need for her to route to Macon. There must have been a reason why *Capricornus* was apparently following Route Two whilst the crew thought they were routing to Marseilles, Route One. The difference between the two tracks is seventeen degrees.

Had variation (the difference between True and Magnetic north – then 12 degrees west) not been applied, *Capricornus*, steered by reference to a magnetic compass, would have tracked to the east of her intended route. Moreover, if Paterson was following neither route but had decided to fly direct to Marseilles, his required track would have been 148 degrees True. If Paterson then headed 148 degrees Magnetic, having failed to apply variation, his resultant track would approximately follow Route Two. (In fact, the difference between the tracks from Nab Tower to Marseilles and from Nab Tower to the crash site is just over 12 degrees!) As unlikely as this error may at first seem, it should be noted the crew and airline were inexperienced at flying this route, neither pilot held an 'A'-class Navigator's certificate nor had they obtained much experience of above-cloud navigation during their previous careers. In the RAF, Klein would have received little formal training in navigation. Paterson had previously been an engineer and had qualified as first officer five years beforehand. He then spent one year flying the London–Paris route before being posted to Cairo. It had been in the clear skies of the Middle East that Paterson and Klein had gained most of their flying experience. At that time, in the Middle East magnetic variation was near zero and it may well have been practice to ignore variation.

Having miscalculated their outbound heading and, coincidentally, set off in the direction of Macon, they then misidentified their landfall as their view of the French coast was obscured by cloud. (This is confirmed by the Le Havre weather.) Matters were compounded by Paterson's failure to establish he was on track by use of a radio back-bearing from Portsmouth or a bearing from one of the French stations ahead. The only directional information available to him was his heading, 148 degrees. The 148 degrees referred to in his positions was not his True bearing from Hythe but his uncorrected magnetic heading.

The inquiry understood the 12:20 position to be coasting in to the south of Le Havre, 108 miles from Nab Tower. *Capricornus* declared her ground speed, up until 12:20, as 168 mph, a little high, especially as the climbing speed was around 105 mph. Moreover, the ground speed between Nab Tower and the radio bearing position at 13:02 was only 150 mph. However, if they coasted in north-east of Le Havre, a shorter cross-Channel distance, but thought they were south-west of Le Havre, that would explain the apparently contradictory high ground speed. When climb performance is taken into account, a landfall to the north-east of Le Havre at just before 12:20 is possible. It has been assumed that the 12:20 position is coasting in, but they requested a time check at 12:17; perhaps that was when they crossed the coast.

Capricornus continued on her south-easterly heading and at 12:55 (or thereabouts) Paterson went below to converse with Miss Coates. Klein and Cooper remained on the flight deck. The 13:02 bearings from Le Bourget and Tours were from well either side of track and give no indication that the track made good was incorrect. They did, however, give a good cross-track cut, albeit indicating further along track than they had flown. Unfortunately, they were already working with an excessive ground speed, hence the indication of better than expected progress made sense. If the bearings from Beauvais and Auxerre were received, they may have been considered erroneous as they did not support Klein's perceived position.

At 13:23, *Capricornus* reported her 13:02 position to Le Bourget. Again it was assumed (by the inquiry) that 148 degrees was a True bearing from Hythe, hence the apparent discrepancy in position. Thirty minutes after the previous fix, another series of bearings was obtained, this time from Tours and Auxerre. Although the Auxerre bearing could have made some sense had they been on a direct track to Marseilles, the Tours bearing lay in an unexpected direction. There is no evidence to support that the bearings from Moulins and Dijon, passed to Tours, were relayed to *Capricornus*.

It must have been at this time that doubt first appeared in Klein's mind. One position line was dubious, and should he have plotted the two-position line fix available from Tours and Auxerre, he would have found *Capricornus* about 50 miles east of a direct track to Marseilles. Klein asked Cooper to summon the Captain back to the flight deck. There is no record of the pilots' conversation and because of the engine noise Cooper would have been unable to overhear what the pilots said.

One can assume that Paterson checked the navigation log, but no changes of heading or requests for bearings were made. Perhaps Paterson realised their error and understood they had been heading towards Macon all the time. Although at 13:52 they announced their descent, the tachographs did not record a significant reduction of engine rpm. Perhaps the descent did not occur as intended. Nevertheless, the aircraft did descend. If descent from 8,000 feet commenced at 13:52 until impact with the 2,500-foot hill at 14:11, the rate of descent would have been just over 200 feet per minute. Such a rate of descent should have registered upon the flight instruments.

From his hospital bed, Cooper told Reuters they thought themselves to be in the Saône Valley (near Macon). For this to be true and for them to have set off on a direct track to Marseilles they must have made a navigational error which they now realised. If they were approaching Lyons from the north-north-west, it would have been comparatively safe for them to lose some of their height. The first officer's altimeter, a Smiths AV 567 Static altimeter, was recovered from the wreckage. It indicated 3,500 feet and the inquiry concluded this erroneous indication had been caused by the crash. The Smiths AV 567 Static altimeter could not be adjusted to compensate for varying atmospheric pressure: the instrument assumed a standard atmospheric pressure of 1013.2 millibars. The atmospheric pressure at Lyons Bron was 1011 ± 1 millibars. It was up to the pilots to obtain an actual atmospheric pressure and apply the correction required (in this case minus 70 feet). If instrument icing had been encountered during the descent, it is possible the altimeter would lag, or over-read, during the descent. Perhaps it was reading 3,500 feet at the moment of impact.

The final moments of the flight are conjecture but ...

Paterson realised his navigational error and, seeking a visual fix, commenced a slow descent. Unfortunately, the first officer's altimeter was suffering a partial blockage due to icing. The indication lagged behind the true height. Meanwhile, should they be unable to fix their position visually, Paterson decided to home onto Lyons and then establish himself outbound for Marseilles. At 14:08 they obtained a bearing from Lyons. Before requesting a second bearing (14:11), they overflew Ouroux, and through a gap in the clouds they saw the ground. As recalled by Cooper and confirmed by the tachographs, they reduced power and descended to 3,500 feet, as indicated on the over-reading altimeter. Believing the ground was still 1,000 feet beneath them, they struck the gently rising hillside.

Regardless of the cause of the accident, Paterson's absence from the flight deck can have hardly eased Klein and Cooper's task in navigating the craft in a safe manner. Once Paterson had returned to the flight deck, their overall lack of expertise and experience in radio navigation and instrument flying may well have turned against them.

On 21 April 1937, *Courtier* was launched, and within a week she was in service crossing the Mediterranean, under the command of Griffith Powell. Recent research

The flying-boats could not climb above the weather and were thus prone to the poorly understood phenomenon of engine and airframe icing. The dark areas on the leading edges of the floats, wings and tail fin is 'Kilfrost', an anti-ice paste. Cassiopeia *is fitted with spinners, most likely as part of a trial of propeller de-icing systems. (Peek)*

has shown that Royal occasions were not always what they seemed. On 30 April 1937, the Duke of Kent opened the new Headquarters for the Civil Aviation Department of the Air Ministry, in [sic] Ariel House, the former offices of the Marconi company. During the proceedings, Air Minister Lord Swinton used the new short-wave radio-telephone to speak with Captain Wilcockson who, at the time, was flying over London in *Caledonia*. Beforehand, the Duke was offered the chance to send a wireless telegraphy message on the long-range communication equipment to *Courtier* as she crossed the Mediterranean 170 miles north of Alexandria. The message, or so it was reported, was sent at 12:10 and a reply was received sixteen minutes later. The commander, speaking on behalf of the officers and passengers, thanked the Duke for his message and wished him good luck. He reported that *Courtier* was cruising at 6,000 feet and was flying in good weather.

That is not quite true; *Courtier* was unable to receive the message from the Duke but sent a pre-arranged reply at the duly allotted time.

Records were being broken and individual flights reported. On 23 May, *Cassiopeia* was running late on her return from Egypt. To make up time, Captain Bennett decided to fly Alexandria to Southampton in a day,

despite there being no night-alighting facilities at Southampton. They carried fourteen passengers and the ubiquitous ton and a half of mail. Satchwell was first officer. With an early start and grumbling passengers they battled through strong head-winds across the Mediterranean to Athens. Rushing refuelling and local formalities they kept on, speeding through Bracciano and on to Marignane. As they left Marseilles, Bennett thought they had been beaten, but as a favourable tail-wind was forecast, he pressed on. By the time they were half-way across France, the passengers were encouraging him and he had to give them progress reports every quarter of an hour. Even that was not enough and the stewards were forced to give a running commentary. They made Southampton with twenty minutes of daylight to spare but missed the last train to London. Imperial Airways arranged cars for those passengers needing to reach town that night and the remainder recovered from the journey in hotels.

Some 'boats seemed unlucky. Several months after the 'Castor-oiled' incident, *Castor* was being taxied from her mooring to the embarkation raft. A gust of wind took her from Captain Alger and she struck the yacht *Neptune*, causing considerable damage to her tailplane and ailerons. It was 22 May 1937 and *Castor* should have

Castor being repaired at Lake Bracciano, near Rome, probably September/October 1937. Short Bros despatched teams of craftsmen to repair damaged 'boats throughout Imperial Airways' route structure. (Newnham)

Peter Newnham next to Castor's *new float, probably September/October 1937.* (Newnham)

been departing with the one-thousandth Empire 'Boat passenger. The passengers, Commander Alger and crew transferred to *Cygnus*. *Castor* was off line for about a week.

Barely back on line, it was whilst returning from Alexandria that Supernumerary First Officer Reid wormed his way into the wing to plug the oil leak. *Castor* arrived back in Southampton on 2 June and three or four days later Captain Powell took her back to Alex'. Whilst routing from Alexandria to Athens and passing Mirabella, the starboard-inner engine failed. The following is extracted from Griffith Powell's hand-written log:

Flight Log 8.6.37 <u>CASTOR</u> *Alex – Athens*
06.30   *Airborne S/C* [set course] *325*
09.10   *After normal cruising into headwind 700 feet 110 knots aircraft filled with smoke and or exhaust fumes. Sent broadcast signal standby for 'Urgency' message. Very severe vibration causing all instruments unreadable – got progressively worse our aircraft losing height. S.I.* [starboard-inner] *failed as a result.*
09.30   *Crete coast at Yanishares.*
09.50   *Landed first available area Mirabella bay owing danger structural failure.*
10.30   *Made Poro Bay under escort and own power.*

On 11 June, *Courtier* arrived from Alexandria, *en route* to Hythe, following a survey flight to Durban, flown by Captain Alcock.

11.6.37   *Lifting tackle and engine arrive by 'Courtier'. Failed engine literally fell out when dismantling started. After, piece of local boiler plate bolted on front of nacelle (An artistic engineer painted a V engine on it). Owing London fears of structural damage no answer my request home ferry and idea was that 'Imperia' should tow to Mersa Matruh but this lost realism when barometer fell sharply. I decided to go on 3 engines.*
12.6.37   *Trusting inspection OK by G/E* [Ground Engineer] *McMeeking I decided to go.*
03.04   *Left Poro Bay at first light to get in and out of Athens before London aware. Slight swerving take-off at Poro owing restricted area no trouble elsewhere.*
05.46   *Left Athens for Rome by-passing Brindisi on basis that if I could get to Rome without being stopped London would let me proceed. Which is what happened.*
12.02   *Left Rome.*
15.30   *Airborne from Marseilles.*
19.49   *Landed Hythe.*
Completing Crete – Southampton in the day on 3 engines.

As expected Hythe very pleased but message from London to see M.D. [Managing Director] *following morning. The flush of success had faded and I was not sure what I was about to receive. It was both thanks and*

Launched in the April and destroyed in the October of 1937, Courtier is credited with the first night arrival at Durban. However, the Empire 'Boats did not fly through the night but regularly made pre-dawn departures and evening landings: the mail had to be kept moving. (Baldwin and Bigby)

a homily about what might have happened. With M.D. was M. Lamplugh the underwriter of British Aviation Insurance who was more than grateful for saving him a lot of money. The beginning of a long friendship.'

Powell's log gave notes of another engine failure, this time on take-off:

'I had another case of engine failure and losing the prop on take-off from Hythe but the vibration and engine seizure were momentary and the prop sheared off and went ahead of me before falling away. I was back on the water and into the raft within minutes – no trouble but it underlined the problem of no feathering facilities although in this case the warning was minimal.'

Summer led to autumn and *Courtier* flew the route to Kisumu and Durban several times. One flight terminated with a night arrival at Durban. On 1 October 1937, however, returning from Africa, *Courtier* became victim of the phenomenon 'glassy calm' and crashed on alighting at Phaleron Bay, Athens.

In conditions of flat calm, especially over clear water, it is difficult for pilots of descending aircraft to judge their height. This is all the more difficult when a continuous layer of untextured cloud blends with the horizon. There is a tendency to either round out too high, stall and fall into the sea or flare too late and simply fly into the water.

Courtier was under the command of Captain E. Poole, a relatively inexperienced flying-boat pilot. They were flying a supplementary, unscheduled service and carried no mail or freight. At half-past ten, they arrived over Phaleron Bay, having departed Alexandria earlier that morning. The wind was calm and a little mist hung under the expanse of high cloud. The sea shimmered and the horizon was difficult to see. Poole made a

On 1 October 1937 Courtier *became a victim of the phenomenon 'glassy calm'. As Captain Poole approached Athens, the bay shimmered and the horizon was difficult to see. Poole misjudged his height and struck the sea with great force. Although salvage was started, salt-water corrosion had taken hold before the Short Bros team arrived.* (Newnham)

straight-in approach, misjudged his height and struck the sea with great force, having failed to check the descent.

Nine of the passengers, Wing Commander W. R. Dyke Acland, Officer Commanding No. 70 Squadron RAF Iraq and former RNAS deck-landing pioneer, an American – Mr Raymond Henderson, and Mr Alexandre Elefterakis – a Greek, were drowned in their cabin. Four passengers were slightly injured and were treated in the Red Cross Hospital. The injured were Squadron Leader J. Bussey, 70 Squadron, Mrs Greir, Mr M. S. Croonist and Mr J. Dagg. Two passengers, one unnamed, the other the Reverend Richard Lees, RAF chaplain, were unhurt. Captain Poole and his four crewmen, First Officer Jack 'Ginger' Hall, Wireless Operator Dunk, Flight Clerk Boughton and Steward McQuarrie, were also comparatively unscathed. The subsequent rescue was hampered as the propellers continued to turn.

Peter Newnham was on the Shorts' salvage team and he was despatched to Athens. An attempt was made to salvage the wings and tailplane. Although these pieces of the airframe were removed from *Courtier,* by the time inspection ashore could take place, the onset of corrosion had occurred.

In Parliament, it was noted that of Captain Poole's total of 4,000 flying hours, only 200 were on flying-boats, 180 hours as supernumerary captain and 20 as commander. The Under-Secretary of State for Air stated regulations did not require 'B'-class pilots to fly as co-pilots before their licences could be endorsed for type. Colonel Ropner MP asked the Under-Secretary why no more than small hatches were provided in the roof. Soon, there was legislation requiring lap straps for all

passengers, and, if ten or more passengers were carried, two emergency exits were stipulated. The remainder of the fleet were modified, 'push-out' windows and enlarged exits on the top-side of the 'boats being fitted.

Another accident resulted in the loss of *Cygnus* at Brindisi. She had first flown at the beginning of March 1937 and was delivered to Imperial Airways the following day. Within the week, she commenced operations on the route to Alexandria and in mid-June 1937 paid the first of two visits to Durban. In November and December she made scheduled flights to Karachi, and it was whilst returning from Karachi, during the morning of Sunday 5 December 1937, that she suffered a take-off accident.

Captain Roger Mollard had under his command First Officer (Acting Captain) F. U. Hollins, Second Officer Ralph Mountain, Wireless Operator E. C. Barnes, Flight Clerk F. J. Hanscombe and Steward Fredrick Lawrence Stoppani. On board were eight passengers and mails from India and Australia.

On the morning of 5 December, a strong wind blew at Brindisi and its direction precluded an into-wind departure within the confines of the inner harbour. Captain Mollard taxied *Cygnus* into the outer harbour at nine o'clock. Although the weather was fair, in addition to the wind there was a long, deep swell upon the water. To reduce the take-off run, the flaps were lowered, but by intention or mistake full-flap was run-out. It was usual to use only a quarter-flap for take-off as this would give increased lift but only a minimal increase in drag. As *Cygnus* lifted up onto the step, but before she had accelerated to flying-speed, she was thrown into the air, possibly by the rolling swell. The nose fell and hit the water, and by a combination of bouncing and

Attempting take-off from Brindisi on 5 December 1937, Cygnus *briefly became airborne before slamming back into the sea. Among the casualties was Government Director of Imperial Airways, Air Marshal Sir John Salmond.* (Newnham)

over-control, *Cygnus* porpoised, ever more steeply, until she smashed into the sea. The mooring compartment, forward cabin, galley and toilets were stove in.

An eye-witness to the accident recounted:

'The boat took an unusually long run into the strong wind and then began to rise but did not clear wholly successive waves. She was thrown high into the air, at the first time she touched and still higher when she [next] made contact with the water. The third time she struck, the bows were stove in and the boat began to sink nose first.'

Among the passengers was Government Director of

Imperial Airways, Air Marshal Sir John Salmond. Sir John had, ostensibly, been on a fact-finding tour for Imperial Airways, having flown out to Singapore on the *Cordelia*. Nearer the truth, he had been examining Imperial Defences and the needs of the RAF. Sir John had met Sir Arthur Tedder, the RAF Air Commander in Singapore, and Shenton Thomas, the Governor. They were in unison about the real state of Singapore's defences and agreed to allow the Governor to enlighten the Cabinet, but this he failed to do. Salmond departed Singapore with *Cordelia* and stayed a few days at Karachi, from where he boarded *Cygnus* for the return to England. He suffered a fractured collar bone and injuries to his knee. One of the other passengers was Mr Robert Lutyens, architect son of Sir Edwin Lutyens.

Mr Lutyens sustained a cut down one cheek, another to his nose and a slight injury to his shin. He gave a graphic account several days later when he arrived in Rome:

'I was sitting in the smoking room talking to Sir John. The sea was calm and smooth; there seemed a nice take-off wind, enough to stir the flags on the vessel to port. The throttle was opened and the stick was back. We had gone some two hundred yards perhaps, when our head went up. One felt the first lift, as one always does when a plane takes-off. And then, instead of feeling the second lift, the machine bounced onto the water and thrown up, bounced again, twenty or thirty feet. The water came in at once, and before one realized it, one was fighting to reach the air.

There was only about three foot from the water to the top of the cabin. Fortunately the hatch way was open and I got out. I swam to a motor launch that was rushing to meet us. An awful moment, I felt the weight of my overcoat dragging me down into the water, I am a good swimmer but it pulled me down. In the end I got it off and was helped into the launch.

I saw Sir John struggling in the water behind me, he escaped by the same hatch way.'

Cygnus was severely holed and started to sink by the nose. A motor launch quickly put out from the harbour and was upon the scene in seconds. *Cygnus* remained afloat for a few minutes and Second Officer Mountain, who had been flung through the windscreen, relatively unscathed, managed to swim back to the rear cabin and rescue three passengers. For this, he was awarded the Royal Humane Society's Hope Medal. (When a 'C-class' crashed, the nose tended to split down the centreline, thus allowing the crew to be thrown clear of the wreckage.)

Neither he nor the other rescuers were able to save Steward Stoppani or Captain William MacDonald Farquhar, Australian Army. Their bodies were recovered later by divers. More fortunate were Mrs Ritchie, who sustained a broken collar bone, Mrs Queenie Falconer, the sister of the late Captain MacDonald Farquhar, James Charles Patrick, Lieutenant John H. Barringer and an Indian, Sharma Prabhur Dutt, all of whom were saved. Later the 'boat was raised and towed ashore, but only part of the luggage and mail was salvaged.

That evening, Lady Salmond left London to be with her husband and took him to the Anglo-American Nursing Home in Rome the following morning. Their stay in Rome was brief. The Air Marshal was continually pestered by fascist Italian officers trying to impress Mussolini's ways upon him. As soon as he was able, he journeyed home to England.

The crash was the first to be investigated by the Accident Investigation Board. By 9 December, the inquiry had completed their preliminary findings and had forwarded them to London. Although they found no fault with the structure of the machine, Imperial Airways was censured for a lack of escape hatches in the roof. In fairness, enlarged 'push-out' windows were being retro-fitted and the escape hatches enlarged.

As a result of trials flown in *Cooee*, Lankester Parker demonstrated full-flap take-offs could produce porpoising, and if this divergence was not caught immediately, the 'boat would go out of control. Further trials revealed that although a 'safe' departure from rough water could be made if full-flap were selected, the same was not so in conditions of smooth water, with a long rolling swell. In such conditions, Lankester Parker almost lost control of the 'boat.

The Air Ministry's Chief Inspector of Accidents published his report in August 1938. He stated the accident had resulted from the attempted take-off with full-flap. No fault was found with the aircraft or its controls, it was operating below its maximum weight and the load was correctly distributed. He concluded that the cause was an improper selection of the flap which was not rectified, as correct pre-take-off checks were not followed. The crew were, however, exonerated, as possibly the understanding of the effects of flap was still limited. The Inspector did, however, comment favourably upon the prompt rescue and salvage operations carried out by the authorities at Brindisi, and added that Second Officer Mountain showed particular courage by entering the rear cabin and saving three passengers. He concluded by noting that since the accident Imperial Airways had reviewed their pre-take-off procedures.

Ralph Mountain was one of eight flying-boat crewmen lost when Sunderland G-AGIB crashed 130 miles south of Tobruk on 5/6 November 1943.

THE NORTH ATLANTIC
Early studies, brave attempts – Political manoeuvres – Aeronautical answers – Gentlemen's Agreement – Trial crossings of Caledonia *and* Cambria.

Whilst, during the 1920s and early 1930s, Imperial Airways surveyed and operated an expanding route structure throughout the Old World, the way to the New World remained barred by the North Atlantic. In 1919, Sir Frederick Sykes, Controller-General of Civil Aviation, had proposed that a fleet of modified First World War flying-boats could run a transatlantic service, via the Azores and Bermuda – the southern crossing. This route, although longer than the northern route, benefited from better weather. Sykes even approached the Portuguese Government and obtained permission to survey the Azores, with a view to establishing a flying-boat base. However, the Treasury agreed to allot only a mere £5,000 and the project was abandoned.

Some years later, encouraged by Lindbergh's flight, Imperial Airways decided to endorse an experimental transatlantic flight. One of their senior pilots, Lieutenant-Colonel Freddie 'Dan' Minchin, was given leave of absence to fly Princess Anne Lowenstein-Wertheim across the Atlantic. She was funding an east to west crossing and had purchased a Fokker monoplane, G-EBTQ, and co-opted the services of the reluctant Captain Leslie Hamilton as second-pilot. Their aircraft was christened *St Raphael* by the Bishop of Cardiff. Early in the morning of 31 August 1927, they staggered aloft from RAF Upavon. That evening, they were spotted in mid-Atlantic by the tanker *Josiah Macy*; they were never seen again.

The following year, Captain W. G. R. Hinchcliffe and the Hon. Elsie Mackay died in similar mysterious circumstances. Imperial Airways distanced themselves from the Atlantic. It was to be another decade before the 'C-class' boats and the 'Clippers' would face this wild ocean.

The main problems associated with crossing the North Atlantic were the distance, the prevailing westerly winds and the atrocious weather, especially in the winter. Some ingenious solutions were formulated throughout the next decade. Floating islands, to act as either aerodromes for sea and land planes or docks for ocean liners, were studied by two Americans, Williams and Armstrong, and the Australian Heiser. Estimates for these mid-ocean platforms varied from £3 million to £6 million. The French went one stage further and proposed to moor their island in the mid-Atlantic shallows around the lost Atlantis. Although not believing in Atlantis, Imperial Airways and Shorts did believe in Newfoundland and Bermuda, and, in order to make best use of the islands, developed in-flight refuelling and pick-a-back aircraft. The Germans worked with their catapult ships.

The Post Office tendered little help, as they wished not to risk capital on any transatlantic scheme until it had been proved viable. The British Government continued with their policy of minimum interference, whilst encouraging the maximum of co-operation from the Royal Air Force. That being said, the Government were pro-airship and, by 1930, had spent £2 million on the Burney Airship Development scheme.

Between 13 and 16 August 1930, R.100 completed the twelfth safe crossing of the North Atlantic by lighter-than-air craft. This was compared with thirteen failures in twenty-four attempts by heavier-than-air craft. Also in August, between the 18th and 26th, the first east–west crossing of the Atlantic by flying-boat was made. Germans, Wolfgang von Gronau and three crewmen, flew their Dornier Wal in stages from Sylt to New York. The first non-stop east–west crossing of the Atlantic had also been made by Germany. On 12–13 April 1928, the Junkers W 33 land plane *Bremen* had flown from Baldonnel, Ireland, to Labrador.

France and America were also active. As there were problems finding year-round bases for flying-boats and as existing land planes lacked the range for non-stop crossings, various land-hopping routes were examined. France's Aéropostal obtained exclusive landing rights in the Azores and then went broke. Juan Trippe, of Pan American Airways (Pan Am), employed Charles Lindbergh to survey an Arctic route. However, Trippe was confronted by the Newfoundland Government, which took an objectionist stand towards Pan Am. As a result, Trippe bought out Trans-American Airlines and their 75-year concession to land on Iceland, thus bypassing Newfoundland. Lindbergh was then employed to survey a route through Greenland and Iceland. By 1935, Pan Am considered they were ready to commence a North Atlantic service.

British progress was, as usual, marred by Governmental indifference and supposed minimal interference. However, the Royal Geographic Society and the Air Ministry did sponsor an expedition to Greenland. The expedition took two de Havilland Gipsy Moths, fitted with special Short-designed ski/float undercarriages. Flight Lieutenant N. H. D'Aeth RAF, officer-in-charge of flying, operated 74 sorties, totalling 86 hours, the majority of which were flown off the ice during winter. It was shown that, apart from the few weeks a year when the ice melted, it would be possible to cross Greenland with currently available aircraft. Notwithstanding D'Aeth's report, neither the British nor the Americans pursued this Arctic route. They preferred the climatically more acceptable Azores to Bermuda crossing. Moreover, Imperial were more interested in developing their Empire Routes to Africa and India and, whereas a 500-mile range was adequate for the Arctic route, a 2,000-mile range was required for the Azores to Bermuda leg. Such a range was beyond the capability of the day.

Imperial Airways were acutely aware they suffered from a lack of long-range aircraft to overfly the great oceans and the politically difficult countries along the Empire Route. Mutual assistance from Pan Am was sought. Woods Humphery discussed transatlantic crossings with Trippe, but the depression and the Air Ministry's cancellation of the Vickers Supermarine Model 179, a six-engined monoplane flying-boat, dashed hopes for the next few years. Undaunted, and having dismissed aircraft carrier combinations, Imperial examined high-altitude flying, load weight-reduction by micro-filming the airmail, diesel engines, in-flight refuelling and composite aircraft. Between 1932 and 1935, Imperial Airways lobbied the Air Ministry to provide financial support towards half the costs of the composite prototype. It was 1937 before the Air Ministry agreed.

As well as aircraft, radio and meteorological services were wanting. To these ends, Woods Humphery had already requested that 'at the earliest possible moment'

the Air Ministry establish such facilities in Newfoundland and Bermuda. Great Britain, Canada and Newfoundland discussed possible transatlantic routes out of Newfoundland. Subsequently, Newfoundland's Prime Minister announced a joint agreement had been reached giving Imperial Airways a fifty-year monopoly on landing rights in Newfoundland. Pan Am seemed interested only in the Azores route. At the 1933 Imperial Airways stockholders' meeting, Geddes promised a Bermuda to New York service later that year! They waited until 1937, but throughout 1934 rumours abounded about designs for Imperial Airways' transatlantic aircraft.

The Secretary of State for Air, Lord Londonderry, was moved by the lack of progress and, on 21 November 1934, he stated, in the House of Lords, the United States' postal service subsidy for 1933 had been in excess of £4 million. He continued:

'The United States Government expenditure on civil aviation in the seven years from 1927 to 1933, inclusive, revealed a staggering total of £25 million.'

In comparison, the Imperial Airways' subsidy had been negligible. He demanded a special arrangement be made with aircraft manufacturers to build aircraft suitable for the Atlantic.

Possibly as a result of Londonderry, on 13 February 1935, Sir Francis Shelmerdine, Director-General Civil Aviation, met with Woods Humphery and Mayo, in the Air Ministry. They were attempting 'to clarify the situation in regard to aircraft for the North Atlantic.' Without being blatantly biased, the Air Ministry technical staff admitted readily that the Americans, particularly Sikorsky and Martin, were ahead of the British in the realm of flying-boat design. Whereas Woods Humphery requested urgently a specification based upon Martin's Model 130 flying-boat and Shelmerdine proposed that a mail-only aircraft should be pursued, the Air Ministry staff sought not to dismiss passenger-carrying aircraft or land-plane designs for the moment. Two days later, Woods Humphery wrote to Shelmerdine advising him that a new Shorts' design, the 'C-class', was 'right up-to-date' and exceeded any American designs then available.

Fourteen, soon increased to twenty-eight, 'C-class' were ordered, primarily for the short sectors of the Empire Route. The 'C-class' may have been modern but it could not cross the Atlantic. In comparison, the Sikorsky S.42, although showing its age, did a have a range 500 miles greater than that of Shorts' 'boat. De Havilland proposed to enter the fray with their four-engined D.H.91 Albatross, the first of which flew at the end of May 1937. The transatlantic version would sacrifice internal seating for a fuel tank to give sufficient range. The Albatross never flew the Atlantic.

Looking ahead, any modernity that the S.23 possessed was soon overshadowed by the Boeing 314, six of which were ordered by Pan Am in July 1936. To regain the British lead, Shelmerdine promised £10,000 towards the design of three forthcoming transatlantic boats, the Short 'G-class'. In addition, he suggested to Woods Humphery that negotiations ought to be opened, possibly with Shorts, to design and construct the 130-ton flying-boat proposed by Gouge at a recent lecture. However, it would be the mid-1940s before powerful enough engines became available. Gouge pursued his giant flying-boat through the Shetland, but only to see his dream dashed. Despite becoming Vice-Chairman of Saunders-Roe, the 150-ton Saro Princesses were finally broken up in 1967, having lain cocooned for 14 years.

For many years, Woods Humphery and Trippe strove to secure a mutually exclusive transatlantic service. Thanks to Martin, Consolidated and Sikorsky, Trippe was in a better position than Woods Humphery with respect to long-range aircraft. As Imperial would be unable to provide a service for some years, Woods Humphery and Trippe had agreed neither would start a service until the other was ready. This pact was known as the 'Gentlemen's Agreement'. By 1935, Pan Am had the flying-boats to operate a service via Bermuda and the Azores but there was no base in Bermuda and the Portuguese had not granted Pan Am landing rights in the Azores.

Lord Londonderry requested that Imperial Airways develop the Atlantic route with all haste. Imperial replied that lack of subsidies and long-range aircraft were against them. Imperial suggested that some routes could be given to Pan Am, but that would have broken the 'Gentlemen's Agreement' and allowed Pan Am to operate immediately. Perhaps to appease their critics, Imperial Airways had two of the S.23 'boats, *Caledonia* and *Cambria*, modified to long-range standard. In support, in June 1935, the British Government formed the Sassoon Committee, to counter the progress Pan Am were making towards the inauguration of a transatlantic service. The Committee saw potential in the composite but erred on the side of the large flying-boat. They recognized the concern, that if a land plane were employed, the risk of forced landing at sea would restrict the service to mail only. However, they did recommend the building of an experimental land plane. There followed much Government and airline discussion.

During summer 1936, as the first S.23 was making her early flights, the public became aware of the negotiations between Imperial Airways and Pan Am. It was announced in Washington that agreement had been reached for a flying-boat service between England and the United States. Two routes were contemplated, the southern route via Bermuda and the northern via Canada, Newfoundland and Ireland. Pan Am declared:

'It is probable that the service will begin within six weeks – we shall employ the large four-engine Clipper type, now used on the services across the Pacific.'

Pan Am were negotiating only on their own behalf, but Imperial had the British Government and others to contend with. The proposed North Atlantic route joined Great Britain, the Irish Free State (Eire as from June 1937), and Canada, by way of Newfoundland (then governed by Great Britain). Hence three governments sought a share of the transatlantic business.

Later that July, Sir Philip Sassoon announced the transatlantic service. He told the House that discussions, which had taken place in Ottawa the previous November, had led to the United Kingdom, Canada, Irish Free State and Newfoundland agreeing that survey flights should be undertaken and an experimental service established as soon as possible. Eventually, a mail and passenger service, scheduled at two flights a week in each direction, would be operated. Further discussions with the United States had also occurred. It was understood that a transatlantic service, employing the principle of full reciprocity, would connect both countries. The governments of the United Kingdom, Irish Free State and Canada would set up a joint operating company incorporating three companies nominated by the respective governments. The company nominated by the British Government would be Imperial Airways. The stock of the joint company would be split, 51% held by the United Kingdom, 24.5% by Canada and 24.5% by Ireland.

Later, three sites, Botwood in Newfoundland, Boucherville near Montreal and Foynes, on the Shannon in the Irish Republic, were chosen, and by the close of 1936, communications and direction-finding equipment was being installed. On the Atlantic, British meteorological observers spent many months crossing and recrossing the ocean in SS *Manchester Port*, taking observations. Slowly, an understanding of Atlantic weather systems was being gained.

Meanwhile, the 100th return crossing of the, albeit, southern Atlantic had just been made by an Air France flying-boat, the Latécoère 301. Although the first 301 had been lost in February 1936, the second and third continued to serve in the South Atlantic between Dakar and Port Natal. Moreover, the French had reached the United States, but admittedly by way of the South Atlantic, with the Latécoère 521, which duly sank at Pensacola. At the close of 1937, the Deutsche Lufthansa (DLH) announced their plans for a regular trans-North Atlantic service in 1938. They had already made 22 successful trial crossings and were in a position to proceed with a service. They planned, ultimately, to offer a combined service with American Airlines. If the Americans were unable to assist in a mail service in 1938, then the Germans would fly an interim service alone. DLH were preparing to replace their four catapult-launched seaplanes and support ships on the South Atlantic with four-engined land planes and move the catapult operations into the North Atlantic. However, the Germans were only carrying out trial flights without payloads and still lacked permission to land in the USA. Trippe and Woods Humphery could see their mutual lead being eroded. They had to cross the Atlantic. Trippe summoned the old but trusted Sikorsky S.42B, and Woods Humphery had *Caledonia* and *Cambria* lightened and prepared for the Atlantic.

Canopus *at Rochester, most likely during February 1937, having been ferried home 'on three' by Captain Bailey.* (Short Bros plc)

When the original order for fourteen 'boats was increased to twenty-eight, it was intended that twenty-six would be 'standard'. The other two, *Caledonia* and *Cambria*, would be constructed as 'long-range' 'boats, with Atlantic survey flights in mind. Whereas the standard fuel capacity of the S.23 was 650 gallons, *Caledonia* and *Cambria* had an additional six fuel tanks located between the engine nacelles and across the top of the cabin, aft of the flight deck. These gave them a fuel capacity of 2,320 gallons, a range of 3,300 miles. Their all-up weight was increased to 45,000 lb.

Following certification, *Caledonia*'s preparation for the transatlantic flights to Botwood was delayed whilst she was pressed into Christmas mail service. On 11 January 1937, *Cambria* was launched, and delivered to Imperial Airways on the 20th. She made a proving flight to Marseilles before joining *Caledonia* at Hythe on 30 January. On her flight from Marseilles, she escorted *Canopus*, in which Captain Bailey had lost an engine and was now ferrying home on 'three'.

Long-range proving flights for *Caledonia* started in earnest on 9 February. In showery weather, she left Southampton Water early in the morning and at maximum weight of 45,000 lb was airborne after about 30 seconds. On that day she was airborne for six hours, over the south-west approaches and off Ireland. The objective of the sortie was to practise operating with, and homing onto, the new wireless station at Foynes.

The next long-range flight was delayed 24 hours,

until 18 February. *Caledonia*, loaded with 600 lb of ballast, in addition to her fuel, flew non-stop from Southampton to Alexandria in 13 hours and 35 minutes. Captains Cumming and Wilcockson, First Officer 'Geordie' Garner and Wireless Operators Stocker and Burden made up the crew. On 4 March, she left the Alexandria flare-path at 00:30 GMT and alighted at Southampton at 15:45 GMT, having flown 2,222 miles, a distance 400 miles greater than that from Ireland to Newfoundland. They had left Egypt in fine weather but, as they progressed across the Mediterranean, a steady headwind confronted them until they reached southern Italy. From thereafter the weather deteriorated and they crossed Corsica sandwiched between the mountain tops and low cloud. They forged across France and the Channel through heavy rain storms. After this flight, *Caledonia* joined *Cambria* at Foynes for the transatlantic trials.

Whilst *Caledonia* was being prepared for her flight to Alexandria, *Cambria* had flown 1,200 miles around Great Britain on 21 February, to test the Foynes wireless facilities. *Cambria* departed Southampton, early in the morning, with a crew of seven, Squadron Leader E. H. D. Spence, Department of Civil Aviation of the Air Ministry, Captain 'Taffy' Powell, First Officer E. M. Gurney, engineer E. J. Crowsen and three wireless operators. At 08:30 the weather over England was fine, and before crossing London and the Thames at 2,500 feet, they circled Croydon. They continued up the east coast to Scotland, and although they were able to see Edinburgh, Glasgow was shrouded in fog. Throughout the flight, they were in constant touch with Foynes. Captain Powell later remarked that it was the longest flight he had ever made without being called upon to use his passport.

A few days later, on 25 February, *Cambria* flew to Foynes to use the newly constructed seadrome in preparation for transatlantic services. For about three hours, in rain and hail, they flew up and down the west coast between Valentia and Aran, testing the wireless facilities and taking radio bearings. By 1 March they were back in Southampton.

Internationally, difficulties remained. Canada and USA fell out over the choice of the western terminus. Canada and the United Kingdom naturally preferred Montreal, as it would help link Vancouver and Hong Kong, but the United States saw New York as a better choice, possibly because they did not like the idea of a British service across the Pacific. On the southern route, the Portuguese now allowed the United States landing rights at Madeira and the Azores.

All was now ready for the first commercial survey. In America, *Clipper III*, a Sikorsky S.42B, previously *The Alaskan Clipper* (NC16736), and Captain Harold E. Gray, a pilot with considerable experience of long overseas flights, were being prepared.

Caledonia was the chosen 'boat and Captain A. S. Wilcockson, First Officer C. H. Bowes, the two wireless operators, T. E. Hobbs and, seconded from Marconi, T. A. Vallette, were her crew. They had little experience of trans-oceanic flight. The 'boat had been stripped bare, so as to save weight. She was a shell. They departed Hythe on 4 July and arrived on the River Shannon that afternoon. For an hour before alighting, Wilcockson

orbited Rineanna taking and receiving radio bearings, so a comparison could be made once they had alighted. Once *Caledonia* had touched down, they paid compliments by flying the flag of the Irish Free State. Then, symbolizing the joint nature of this venture, they flew the flags of Great Britain and Canada, in addition to the British Civil Air Ensign. There was much local interest and a large crowd had gathered to welcome the crew as they stepped ashore from the Airport Officer's launch.

Once ashore, the Officer of the Watch from the radio station accompanied *Caledonia*'s crew to Foynes, 40 miles away. There, a conference was held with Major Brackley. The meeting would either declare *Caledonia* ready for the flight the following evening or state further radio tests, this time out to 500 miles off-shore, were required. They decided to depart on the morrow.

President De Valera bade them farewell and upon departure, Wilcockson said of the weather, 'Not at all the sort of night that one would choose for a jaunt of this description.'

Loaded with 2,320 gallons of fuel, they slipped moorings at 18:42 GMT, on 5 July 1937. A fresh westerly wind, of about 30 mph, gave the river a rough chop. Having taxied around the western end of Foynes Island, they took off diagonally across the river into a rain-strewn sky, full of low cloud. Airborne at 18:57 GMT, they turned immediately onto track for Loop Head, the Atlantic and Botwood. They coasted out from Loop Head at 19:14 GMT. Five hundred feet below them the Atlantic stretched ahead. Of the crossing of Loop Head, Wilcockson observed:

'It was to be our last sight of land for two thousand miles, but I can honestly say that we all experienced a certain sense of relief to see it disappear in the rain, and

Imperial Airways and Pan Am had agreed not to compete on the Atlantic – The Gentlemen's Agreement – and while Caledonia *flew to the 'States, Captain Harold E. Gray brought the Sikorsky S.42B,* Clipper III, *to Southampton, arriving at noon on 8 July 1937. They stayed for almost a week. (Peek)*

know we had finished with the waiting and preparations.'

For meteorological forecasts, the route was divided into two zones: the western zone, Newfoundland, and the eastern zone, Foynes. For the Clipper, the western agency had forecast moderate westerly winds at 10,000 feet, and the Foynes agency had furnished Wilcockson with warnings of low cloud and strong headwinds.

For the first couple of hours *Caledonia* ploughed along at less than 1,000 feet through moderate rain and into a 25 mph wind. The route selected was a Rhumb line, which although easier to navigate using radio aids was about 30 miles longer than the great circle route. An hour and a half after take-off, they contacted SS *New York City* and obtained a position. Forty-five minutes later they called SS *Atlantic,* two hours later SS *Beaverdale,* then SS *Black Hawk* and the *Empress of Britain.* Of these ships and others, they saw only two and they both failed to respond to the radio. Heavy cloud prevented them from obtaining star shots and it was not until 03:26 GMT, 6 July, that they saw their first stars. They achieved a fix from Jupiter and Arcturus which placed them 33 miles south of track, 1,000 miles out into an Atlantic night.

The Clipper was airborne at about 21:00 GMT, 5 July, and climbed to 10,000 feet. She had arrived at Botwood on 3 July after an eight-hour flight from Port Washington and an *en route* stop at Shediac, New Brunswick. For dinner that night, the Americans chose from shrimp cocktail, soup, filet mignon and mushroom sauce, salad, ice cream, cake and demitasse.

Shortly after 03:00 GMT, 6 July, the Clipper and *Caledonia* passed abeam by about 60 miles.

From 08:40 GMT, Wilcockson used radio bearings from Botwood to effect the final landfall. Wilcockson and crew obtained their first sight of land at 09:15 GMT, and landfall, at Cobbler's Island, was made at 09:27 GMT. They were only six miles south of their plotted track. They arrived at Botwood at 10:03 GMT and alighted upon the Bay of Exploits at 10:08 GMT, 15 hours and 26 minutes after they had slipped moorings.

Whilst Wilcockson and his crew were being met by the Governor of Newfoundland and Lady Walwyn, *Clipper III* was already in Foynes. Assisted by tailwinds she had alighted at 09:47 GMT, 6 July. Her crossing took 12 hours 30 minutes. The Clipper continued to Southampton, arriving at noon on the 8th. She was met by a large and enthusiastic crowd of spectators. Captain Gray said that the Clipper would remain at Southampton for several days, for the engines to be serviced. Later, that evening, Woods Humphery entertained the crew to dinner in London.

In Botwood, *Caledonia* was refuelled and the crews had a rest day. They continued westwards on 8 July and circled Quebec at 18:40 GMT and were overhead Montreal by 20:00 GMT. They finally touched down in Canada, at Boucherville on the St Lawerence, at 20:08 GMT. They were met, this time, by Mackenzie King, the Premier of Canada. The flight from Botwood had taken

5 hours 30 minutes. On the river, all the ships were dressed overall and sounded their sirens in salute. *Caledonia's* crew were driven in style to the Town Hall, where they were welcomed by the Mayor. The following day, 9 July, they departed Montreal for the two-hour run to New York and Port Washington. A reception was held in the Pan Am offices in the heart of New York.

Wilcockson and his crew spent the weekend in New York, which, incidently, was enjoying a heatwave. *Caledonia* left Port Washington at noon on Monday 12 July and spent the night at Boucherville. The following morning, they left for Botwood which was reached in fine weather. A day, the 14th, was spent at Botwood before leaving at 21:25 GMT on the 15th and alighting at Foynes at 09:30 GMT on the 16th. The eastbound crossing took 12 hours 5 minutes. Wilcockson described his eastbound crossing as 'Quite good', and continued, 'We flew under cloud for 400 or 500 miles and then climbed to 8,000 feet over full cloud, which lasted for about two-thirds of the journey.' He also said that they had used the automatic pilot for most of the way, as it steered a better course than they could. Radio contact with Foynes had been established almost immediately they became airborne. He regarded the flight as a triumph and thanked the ground organization, but concluded he 'quite sympathized' with those before him who had flown the Atlantic without ground assistance.

The Secretary of State for Air, Lord Swinton, sent telegrams of congratulations to Wilcockson and Gray. *Clipper III* started her reciprocal crossing from Southampton on the morning of 14 July, and on 15 July, at 18:25 GMT, a crowd of several hundred saw her rise smoothly from Irish waters on her journey back to America. Prepared to spend up to 20 hours in the air, they carried an additional 250 gallons of fuel and, to reduce weight, had left some baggage and rations in Ireland.

Meanwhile, between 6 and 11 July, Powell and his crew, Madge, Woods, Scott and Butterfield, had taken *Cambria* non-stop to Lisbon. As a precursor to a southern route crossing to the United States of America, they had continued their survey to the Azores. On departure from Horta, they flew a brief survey of the local area.

Following *Caledonia's* exemplary crossing, the second experimental flight was made by Captain Powell in *Cambria,* at the end of July. Powell's crew were First Officer Elder and Wireless Operators Woods and Lewis. (In addition to Powell's log, this account is based upon Lewis's *Advancing Backwards in The Boats That Flew.*)

This flight was:

'... part of the first properly organised Atlantic flights, with full weather information and radio control all the way ...'

and showed the fickle, unconquered nature of the Atlantic. Despite the crew's thorough and professional preparation, events did not follow Powell's flight plan.

Powell positioned *Cambria* at Foynes on 27 July and the following day was spent preparing the meticulous

Between 5 July and 16 July 1937, Captain Wilcockson and crew made the return crossing of the Atlantic in Caledonia. *Meanwhile, 'Taffy' Powell had taken* Cambria *non-stop to Lisbon and on to the Azores, as a precursor to a possible southern route crossing.*

flight plan. Powell calculated the crossing would take sixteen and a quarter hours and, as always on the Atlantic, fuel would be critical. Excess weight was of such a concern that the crew's baggage allowance had been cut from 14 kilograms to one pair of spare shoes. Clean clothing was to be purchased on arrival. Apart from clean clothes, they would be leaving behind a team of meteorologists and wireless operators who would be able to provide them with information once they were in flight. A cloudy and showery crossing with generally fair visibility was forecast. Apart from a tailwind for the first couple of hundred miles, they would face a north-westerly of 20 to 25 mph. The crew completed their preparations in good time but were slightly unnerved by the last minute adjustments the radio engineers were making to the additional, and brand-new, radio they were fitting. This radio was purported to be extremely powerful and would enable them to 'remain in radio control' throughout the crossing. Final pre-flight checks found everything, including the new radio, fit for the Atlantic crossing.

Their all-up weight for departure was 45,000 lb, of which over 19,000 lb was fuel and oil. Once the mooring was slipped, they taxied to the fairway and began a long take-off run. They were heavy. At 18:01 GMT, on 29 July, *Cambria* set course for Botwood.

After an hour and a half, they lost sight of the sea due to low cloud beneath them. The tailwind dropped and they descended in search of the surface, breaking cloud at 500 feet. Powell remained at low level to avoid headwinds until darkness forced a climb up to 1,500 feet and into a 25 mph headwind. Navigation was made difficult as they were unable to obtain star shots until they climbed through the cloud two hours later.

They managed to 'shoot' Arcturus and Polaris and plotted their 23:30 GMT position as North 51 degrees 22 minutes, West 024 degrees 22 minutes. Radio communications were difficult, possibly as a result of atmospheric interference caused by the Northern Lights. At midnight their groundspeed was down to 100 knots and they had used 710 gallons of fuel. They had sufficient fuel for another 14 hours of flight.

It was after they climbed into the dark, cold night air, high above the Atlantic, that the brand-new radio failed. The cause of the failure was quite simple – the radio fell to pieces. The radio's chassis was constructed from a new, man-made insulation material. Whereas this material may well have performed satisfactorily in the workshop or on brief test flights, once subjected to cold and vibration it simply disintegrated. Woods and Lewis, somewhat relieved that the monstrosity of the new radio had been reduced to a 'box of bits', turned to the trusted standard equipment.

Having been tested by the new radio, the crew calculated the groundspeed was down a few knots and the fuel consumption was up a few gallons per hour. *Cambria* was thundering westwards, at around 2,000 feet in thick cloud, when the Sperry autopilot pitched them to port and seaward. Powell quickly disengaged the autopilot and climbed *Cambria* up to 2,300 feet, where he re-engaged the Sperry. At 02:00 GMT he radioed Foynes asking for the latest position of shipping in the area. Powell was none too confident of his position, as apart from the single astro position at 23:30 GMT, he had depended upon dead reckoning and forecast winds. The autopilot was not behaving itself and

Summer 1937, the crew of Cambria *(L to R) Wireless Operators Lewis and Woods, Captain Powell and (ex-RAF sergeant pilot) First Officer Elder.* (Woods)

Powell and Elder struggled with the controls to battle *Cambria* through the Atlantic night. A series of bearings from Botwood, Foynes and the *Sea Venture* established, at 02:28 GMT, 30 July, they were slightly north of track.

The weather was not as expected; breaks in the cloud were few, the stars remained hidden and navigation was primarily by dead reckoning. The anticipated stream of weather reports and forecasts never arrived. Lewis and Woods began to suspect their main radio. The indications were that the aerial had trailed correctly but there were symptoms that it was earthing somewhere. The transmitting circuit and the aerial switch box were stripped down and examined. Nothing untoward was found. In Foynes, and unbeknown to *Cambria*, the wireless operators were desperately trying to contact the flying-boat. Power to the transmitters was increased to the point where fire was feared. From *Cambria*, came silence. On board, they concluded the trailing aerial had failed them. Remaining, there was the short-range fixed aerial, but it would be some time before they were in range of Newfoundland to use that.

Through the night, they battled against continuous rain, heavy at times. Fearful of icing, the engine cooling gills were closed and warm air was selected to the carburettor. At 06:10 GMT they established they were now slightly south of track. The rain and low cloud kept the longed-for dawn at bay. Approaching land, they could now use their loop aerial to take radio bearings from shore stations.

Nature now played them a poor hand. It is a known effect that as the sun rises there is a brief period of poor radio reception. The effect, 'dawn effect' as it is known, is especially disruptive of the low frequencies then in use. On this particular dawn, the disruption was most marked. With the sun rising directly behind them, they could only take bearings from those stations on their beam. To the north, there was nothing, and to the south, those stations received were deep in the southern States and beyond the coverage of their charts. A loop bearing from a Boston-bound boat confirmed they were south of track, but Powell, devoid of bearings from Botwood, was unable to fix his position. A series of four bearings from Cape Race and a couple of ships were of no help, as they bore no relation to even their most pessimistic of tracks made good. The bearings were erratic, almost senseless and Woods and Lewis began to doubt the reliability of the direction-finding loop aerial. They tried to retract the loop for inspection but the retraction mechanism was frozen solid.

Woods was an ex-RAF wireless operator but Lewis had received his training in the Merchant Marine and it was his experience, 'my justification for being there at all', Lewis later wrote, that dictated the next move. Lewis tapped-out a distress call on the marine frequency in hope of raising one of the ocean liners below. There was no response.

Then suddenly, there below them, to port, 'wallowing in a typical Atlantic swell' was a small ungainly tramp steamer, the SS *Roxborough*. Lewis told Powell to circle the ship and flash the letters WT, in morse, on *Cambria*'s landing lights. Hopefully, the watchkeeper would rouse the wireless operator. *Cambria* signalled:

'SHIP BELOW ? QTH? ?hr GADUV Urgent QTH? SHIP BELOW Ship below – what is your present position? This is Imperial Airways flying-boat *CAMBRIA* Urgent.'

But *Cambria* was short of fuel and they could not circle the ship for too long; they turned away. 'My present position is ...', started the response. Lewis took down the position, passed it to Elder and a course to Botwood was plotted.

As Lewis sent his thanks to the 'ship below' the ship interjected, 'Your signals are very weak, sorry can no longer read you.' Weak signals? They could still see the ship!

Just two hours later, at 09:40 GMT, they touched down at Botwood, on the morning of 30 July. They had been in the air for 17 hours and 40 minutes. All four were exhausted and Lewis fell asleep in the mooring compartment. Upon the wings, the engineers dipped the fuel tanks – empty! A small civic reception hosted by the Mayor of St Johns followed but the crew were too exhausted to enjoy it.

Regarding the radios, the brand-new radio was never heard of again and the fault with the trailing aerial was soon rectified. Once *Cambria* was moored and Lewis and Woods were sufficiently recovered to inspect the trailing aerial, they rowed out and examined the underside of the chine, where the trailing aerial entered the 'boat. They discovered that the insulation of the 'Dexine' tube had broken down, thus earthing the aerial.

Powell logged a number of lessons learnt from that crossing, including:

'Never leave Foynes without a complete Botwood forecast.
Leave Foynes as late in the evening as possible to get max daylight going into Newfoundland.
Do not accept radio bearings from Botwood until about 300 miles out.'

Lewis later wrote of Powell and his leadership during that flight:

'Through it all the man who sat in the left-hand pilot's seat, the aircraft captain, the man burdened with responsibility for all that did or could happen, never lost his poise. Always calm, always agreeable and understanding, he set a classic example of just exactly

how the man in command should behave when for hour upon hour prospects never seemed to improve, only worsen.
The title "Commander" was never better earned.'

On 1 August they departed Botwood for Boucherville, Montreal, and the following day they flew on to New York, arriving at 16:00 GMT. They eventually departed Port Washington, New York, and returned to Montreal on 6 August; most of the flight was spent at 5,000 feet. At the close of 7 August they were back at Botwood, facing the Atlantic.

On 8 August they departed Botwood at 21:30 GMT with a forecast 20-knot tailwind. For the first six hours the wind was favourable and they cruised at 10,000 feet, well above the cloud tops; visibility was good. In comparison to the outbound flight they made many star shots and obtained bearings and positions from several ships. They altered course slightly to the north-east, to avoid lightning they could see ahead, and entered high cloud, which they ran through for about an hour. During the latter part of the crossing, *Cambria* asked Foynes if there were any ships closer than the *Empress of Britain*. Foynes replied that contact might be established with the SS *New York*. As dawn broke, they saw the eastern sky was overcast with high cirrus. For the next couple of hours, and with assistance from Foynes, they wove their way between storm clouds. At 06:20 GMT, they climbed to 11,700 feet. By 08:00 GMT, they were through the worst of the cloud and were catching glimpses of the sea far below them. They commenced descent from 10,000 feet at 08:45 GMT and touched down at Foynes on 9 August at 09:27 GMT.

After a mere four hours they went on to Hythe.

The second crossing in *Caledonia* was on 15 August. The flight to Botwood was in daylight so radio performance checks could be made. They returned on the night of 20/21 August, arriving at Foynes at 09:09 GMT, Saturday 21 August. A tailwind helped them to achieve an average speed of about 170 mph and it took 11 hours 33 minutes, 3 minutes greater than the record. At times they had to climb to 16,000 feet to get above the cloud.

Whilst stopping at Botwood on one of his subsequent flights, Wilcockson met the captain of the SS *Geraldine May* and arranged to rendezvous with him mid-Atlantic on his return journey. Although the ship's captain was somewhat sceptical, he kept his side of the agreement and was rewarded by sight of *Caledonia* in mid-Atlantic only 22 miles from their planned meeting point. As she flew past, *Caledonia* flashed her lights and *Geraldine May* answered with a white flare.

Powell's next transatlantic flight was dogged. On 24 August, he flight-tested *Cambria* and found all was in order. However, during the morning of the 25th, a severe oil leak from the port-outer was spotted. The engine and the oil pump were changed. A further flight test would be required but the engine change was not finished until after dark so an engine run had to suffice.

All was set for an early departure from Hythe when a second leak was discovered. Yet another engine was fitted to the port-outer position. After a seven-hour delay, *Cambria* started engines at 14:50 GMT on 26 August and fifteen minutes later left Hythe for Foynes.

At 04:20 GMT the following morning they started engines. Take-off was delayed. The weather was fine, but facing into the light westerly breeze, towards the remnants of night, there was no horizon to effect a safe take-off. Powell turned the 'boat to the east and, with a slight tailwind, took off guided by the horizon dawn was offering. Accompanying Captain Powell were Elder, Woods and Dangerfield. (Powell's log records Murray and Audel being aboard from New York to Montreal on 2 September; possibly they too were aboard from Foynes.) At 07:30 GMT, crossing eighteen and a half West, the starboard-inner engine started to sound very rough but all must have been well for Powell did not mention the engine again in his log. For the first four hours, there was little cloud and the visibility was good. *Cambria* cruised at 1,000 feet. Thereafter, under a 1,200-foot cloud base, the weather remained fine and the wind, although north-westerly, was only of 15 or 20 mph. Towards the end of the day, the cloud lowered and it started to rain. They were forced down to 500 feet with the cloud base only 100 feet above them. The next hour was spent on instruments, but by 18:30 GMT, they had made their landfall and the weather had improved. In good visibility and a 10 mph southerly wind they touched down at Botwood at 19:00 GMT. Having completed the flight in 14 hours 26 minutes, it had been the fastest east–west to date.

Botwood was slipped early on the morning of 29 August and a course was set for Montreal. They had just over an hour in Canada before getting airborne for New York, arriving at 21:04 GMT.

New York was departed on the morning of 2 September and they alighted in Montreal before lunch. On 3 September, they visited Ottawa and, as part of the annual Canadian Exhibition, continued to Belleville, Toronto, where they stayed the night. It was planned that the following day they would fly to Windsor and return to Toronto before setting out, on 5 September, for Hamilton *en route* to Montreal.

But, alighting back at Toronto on 4 September, disaster struck. The 'boat heeled to port as though it were about to capsize. A float had been lost. Only the prompt action of the crew, who scrambled out of the top-side hatch and took up position upon the higher wing-tip, kept the 'craft on an even keel. It transpired the float might well have been punctured when they took off from Ottawa.

Damage was more extensive than first thought. In addition to the port float, the port aileron and tailplane were in need of replacement. During their enforced stay in Toronto, the crew were guests at several dinners and on 9 September they visited the Niagara Falls. Meanwhile, replacement parts were shipped across the Atlantic in the *Queen Mary*. To oversee the repair, Imperial Airways despatched Mr Ernie Arrol. Once in Toronto, he was assisted by a Mr Rowland Doyle. With the float, aileron and tailplane all replaced, a successful test flight was flown during the morning of 22 September. On the 23rd, *Cambria* returned to Botwood.

Her eventual return was the fastest yet of the series of trial crossings. Having departed Botwood at 20:37 GMT on Monday 27 September, she arrived at Foynes at 07:14 GMT on Tuesday 28 September. The crossing lasted 10 hours and 36 minutes, the average speed being 190 mph. Rough weather had been the characteristic of this crossing. At one stage they climbed to get above the weather, but finding themselves in icing conditions they descended to 13,500 feet. During a 90-minute stopover in Foynes, the crew breakfasted whilst the 'boat was refuelled, and then aloft again, and 2 hours 25 minutes later, home at Hythe.

The Secretary of State for Air congratulated them by telegram:

'Heartiest congratulations on your record crossing. A good ending to a very successful series of experimental flights.'

Taffy Powell made his own gesture of congratulation to his crew and presented each of them with a pewter tankard inscribed:

CAMBRIA'S EXPERIMENTAL FLIGHTS 1937
In appreciation of untiring and successful efforts.

Following the transatlantic flights, arrangements were made with the Air Ministry for Wilcockson to fly *Caledonia* on a three-day 'Round Britain' journey. *Caledonia* would overfly all the seaside resorts, allowing as many people as possible to see her. They departed Hythe on Monday 30 August and flew anti-clockwise around England, making Felixstowe their night stop. The following day they continued around the coast as far as Brough, on the Humber Estuary. The third day was devoted to the west coast and the night was spent at Pembroke Dock.

Although departure on the third transatlantic flight commanded by Wilcockson was planned for 10 September, it was delayed by the sickness of First Officer Bowes. However, at the time the press were led to believe the delay was due to poor weather. Finally *Caledonia* departed Foynes on the evening of 13 September. She crossed for the last of the trial flights and returned on 23 September. The crossing was made in 11 hours 38 minutes. In order to gain 26 mph from a tailwind the first six hours of the crossing were made at 13,000 feet. They were able to obtain good star shots in the early part of the crossing and, towards the end, when they descended to find favourable winds, they contacted several ships. After a short stay at Foynes, they continued to Hythe.

Having completed five round trips, *Caledonia* three and *Cambria* two, the trial was complete. During that period the Americans had flown three crossings, one of which had been via the southern route, through Bermuda and the Azores. Wilcockson acknowledged that in some areas Pan Am was better prepared than

In September 1937, whilst touring Canada, Cambria *lost a float at Toronto. Only the prompt action of the crew saved* Cambria.
In addition to the float, an aileron and the port tailplane needed replacement. A successful test-flight was flown on 22 September. (Doyle)

Imperial and he suggested some of Pan Am's procedures should be followed by Imperial. Particularly problematical were the inaccurate weather forecasts and the poor radio reception around Newfoundland. However, overall Pan Am and Imperial Airways were encouraged by the trial flights and hoped to start a passenger service in 1939. Before that, mail flights were proposed for the summer of 1938.

Caledonia continued to make survey flights into the Atlantic and Powell flew the Lisbon to Azores route. New York via Bermuda was not attempted. Again Powell was crewed with Elder, Woods and Dangerfield, and accompanied by Scott. An air test was flown on 5 October 1937 and at 08:11 GMT on 6 October they slipped mooring. Little cloud, a following wind and good visibility sped them to their Lisbon mooring, reached at 14:16 GMT. Powell noted, for his final report, there was a need to get the cabin heating system to work for 15-hour flights.

After a night at the Tivoli Hotel, Avenidà, they woke to find excellent conditions for their impending crossing to Horta, in the Azores. Although the starboard-outer engine developed a slight oil leak, navigation was perfect and the cloud-bedecked islands appeared on time.

On 9 October a local sortie of 45 minutes was flown from Horta. At a weight of 42,000 lb they were airborne in 24 seconds, but immediately after take-off it was necessary to make a steep right-hand turn. The semi-sheltered waters of the inner harbour offered little space for safe take-off, and outside the harbour there was a heavy swell.

The flight on 10 October, from Horta to Lisbon, was difficult. Mindful of the previous day's confined take-off, Powell taxied *Caledonia* to the outer harbour, only to find an impossible swell. He decided to return to the inner harbour and risk the confines of the high ground. Now beyond the breakwater, Powell almost lost *Caledonia* as he turned her across the swell to return to the inner harbour. Once airborne, they commenced what was to be a very rough and uncomfortable flight. Frontal storms and thunderous showers had to be avoided. After seven and a quarter hours they thankfully moored at Lisbon. Despite the fog covering the Tagus on the morning of 11 October, they taxied to a clear area and, after a thirteen-second run, they set course for Finisterre and Hythe. They moored at 14:15 GMT, the Atlantic trials were complete and the Azores were declared unsuitable for Empire 'Boats.

It was announced in November that *Caledonia* and *Cambria* would be employed to carry the 1937 Christmas mail. Each aircraft would carry five tons of mail and no passengers. It was planned that they would make one or two journeys respectively to Durban. After Christmas, *Cambria* carried out flight refuelling trials with the prototype Armstrong Whitworth bomber/transport, the AW 23 (K3585). By the spring of 1938, *Cambria, Caledonia* and *Centaurus* were returned to Hythe for scheduled use. It is reported that the long-range tanks were removed from *Cambria* and presumably *Caledonia*, but *Centaurus* is believed to have retained her tanks.

UNREST – IMPERIAL DIFFICULTIES

Empire Airmail Scheme – 1937 Turbulent times – Death of Geddes – Perkins and the Cadman Committee.

After considerable Parliamentary discussion, it was stated the Empire Airmail Scheme (EAMS) would commence in 1937 and the airmail-handling facility at Croydon would be closed in favour of Hythe, the temporary flying-boat base. On 4 March 1937, the last Imperial Airways' Empire Service land plane carrying mail from Africa landed at Croydon. From then on, Imperial Airways used Croydon only for its European services. The new passenger terminal and mail-handling facilities at Hythe were opened the following day. All first-class mail, letters and postcards between Britain and the Commonwealth – Canada excluded – would from then go by air. The governments of Australia, India, New Zealand and South Africa agreed to assist with Empire route infrastructure. It was initially proposed there would be a comprehensive service of nine aircraft a week to Egypt, five to India, three to Malaya and Australia and a pair to South Africa.

Before the introduction of mail-carrying Empire 'Boats, mail was flown to Paris and hauled by train to Brindisi, where it re-took to the air for Alexandria. However, even following the introduction of EAMS, those mails for Africa and from India continued to use this rail-augmented route. To ensure two airmails a week, a complex routine remained in force until additional flying-boats became available.

This complex arrangement ensured the 'boat which departed Southampton on Saturday, with the mail bound for India, would arrive at Alexandria by Monday, in time to be turned around to bring the mail from Africa on Tuesday. Meanwhile, the 'boat which departed Alexandria on Saturday, carrying mail from Africa, would be at Southampton by Monday and then readied for Wednesday's departure to India.

The White Paper laying out the *modus operandi* for Imperial Airways and the Post Office was issued on 25 May 1937. It laid out a progressive expansion of air transport on the Empire's air routes and detailed the intended scheme.

The Empire Airmail Scheme was eventually inaugurated on 29 June 1937 when *Centurion*, commanded by Captain Bailey, departed Hythe for the Sudan, Northern Rhodesia, Nyasaland and South Africa. On board were 3,500 lb of unsurcharged airmail. A half-ounce letter was charged 1½d and a card 1d. For the meantime surcharges for mail to Australia would remain, 5d for a half ounce outward. It was expected that the cost of the service would exceed the £700,000 revenue by £200,000 per annum. Before departure, the Secretary of State for Air, Lord Swinton, and the Post Master General, Rt. Hon. G. C. Tryon, attended a small ceremony on board Cunard's Motor Vessel *Medina*, on Southampton Water. Other dignitaries present included Sir Alan Cobham, Colonel Charles Lindbergh and Sir George Beharrell.

Overseas, progress was being made on a political level. On 24 September 1937, Lieutenant-Colonel A. J. Muirhead, the Under-Secretary for Air, arrived back from a tour of the Middle East and Africa. He reported the chances of co-operation and co-ordination of civil air routes with South Africa and other countries was good. At home it was the contrary. The formation of British Airways, in 1936, had coincided with much criticism of Imperial Airways, some of which was founded and some not. Although the Government wanted to encourage the aggressive development of European traffic and British Airways appeared an ideal candidate, Government hands were tied as they had already selected Imperial Airways as the 'chosen instrument' for civil aviation development. In an attempt to reallocate routes, Lord Swinton approached Geddes over lunch and suggested that Imperial Airways might wish to relinquish its monopoly on routes north of Cologne to Budapest. He also suggested the Government might wish to offer support to other companies operating north of a line between these cities.

Geddes noted afterwards that he felt:

'We were drifting from the position from being their [the Government's] *principal chosen civil aviation agent and were becoming one of a lot of competing operating companies.'*

He was correct; the Government and the country were expressing an increased dissatisfaction with Imperial Airways, especially their European routes.

A new aircraft, new routes and a new rôle were about to spawn further unrest at Imperial. Just as the airline had been born during a strike, in April 1924, so another crisis was being driven by the pilots, the press and the politicians. Added to this, no sooner had the 'C-class' been introduced than *Capricornus*, *Courtier* and *Cygnus* were lost. The air safety and operations of Imperial Airways were also being called into question. With regard to the strike, there were three main areas of unrest: firstly, the obsolescence of the fleet as a whole, secondly, pilots' conditions of service and thirdly, the rumoured 9% dividend that was about to be paid to shareholders. The dismissal of those pilots unsuitable for flying-boats and the proposed pay-cut, coincident with the rumoured 9% dividend, particularly galled the pilots.

Three months after the loss of *Capricornus*, Imperial were dealt a further blow with the sudden death of their Chairman, Sir Eric Geddes. His guidance had been pivotal to the development of Imperial Airways. He was succeeded by Sir John George Beharrell DSO, then aged 63. He had been Geddes' Financial Assistant at both Dunlop and Imperial Airways.

Matters came to a head. In response to rumours, the pilots, using their recently formed union – British Airline Pilots' Association (BALPA) – attempted to consult with Imperial Airways, but Imperial were far from helpful.

On 28 October 1937, Mr Robert Perkins, Conservative MP for Stroud, launched a calm and organized attack upon the airline. Perkins, who was a pilot and long-time critic of Imperial Airways, was also the founder, Vice-President and spokesman for BALPA. He drew attention to the gross dissatisfaction felt by the pilots of Imperial and other British airlines. In the four months since BALPA was formed, its Chairman and Vice-Chairman had been dismissed from Imperial Airways, despite eight years' service between them. The attack continued. Some pilots had been sacked for merely criticizing Imperial Airways and others had had peculiar dismissals. Captain Wilson, pilot of the Calcutta *City of Khartoum* which ran out of fuel and had crashed off Alexandria two years earlier, was dismissed with minimal notice, notwithstanding his seven years' experience and his 'Master's Ticket'. It is possible that he was dismissed as a result of evidence he gave at the *City of Khartoum* inquiry, the findings of which proved detrimental to Imperial Airways. The Under-Secretary of State for Air, Colonel Muirhead, replying to Perkins on behalf of the Air Minister, said the recent dismissal of ten pilots from Imperial Airways was, as a matter of staff employment and dismissal, 'within the commercial discretion of the company'.

The land-plane services were not without criticism as the company had received a letter, from two Imperial Airways captains, which suggested the service to Budapest should cease during the winter months, the route being considered unsafe. As further evidence, Perkins divulged other letters stating the aircraft used on the European routes were unsuited to the task. They were obsolete and without de-icing equipment. [At the time, aircraft icing was still an unsolved problem.] Although the Budapest service was duly stopped, the two pilots were peremptorily dismissed. Perkins continued, Imperial had made every attempt to break BALPA, and refused discussions. The pilots wanted only to discuss such subjects as rates of pay, unfair dismissal and unfit route structure. Overall, Imperial Airways had, as far as its service in Europe was concerned, become the 'laughing stock of the world'. Perkins requested Government intervention to call a conference between BALPA and the Imperial Airways' management. Although his call for an official enquiry was supported by the Labour opposition, the Under-Secretary refused an inquiry on behalf of the Government.

Some of Perkins's criticisms were poorly founded and a number of dismissals seemed just. One captain was rude to passengers, insubordinate and would not retrain to fly the Avro 652. A second was well qualified but refused to take instructions, and a third, a first officer, was slovenly, issued invalid cheques and contracted venereal disease. A fourth was declared temperamentally unsuitable, as he was nervous. The probationary pilots, too, were scrutinized. One performed poorly under training, was sullen and drank too much, so his services were dispensed with.

Woods Humphery replied radically, on 29 October. He defended the modernity of the fleet and terms of employment, stating that all of their aircraft had Airworthiness Certificates, that the Government had delayed the procurement of equipment and that the pilots' wages were fair. He said of EAMS:

'It is unquestionably the greatest step forward in postal development since the introduction of the penny-post and will give immense benefit to the Empire and promote its consolidation and unity. To carry out this programme, Imperial Airways needs the support of the press and people of this country and the Empire.'

Perkins responded on 1 November, stating that of the allegations he had made in the House, Imperial had admitted a few but denied most. Imperial admitted they would prefer their pilots not to join BALPA, an organization only four months old and unrecognized by any airline, but would willingly deal with the long-established Guild of Air Pilots and Navigators (GAPAN). Moreover, a new pay formula had been established and it was true that some pilots had suffered pay cuts, despite the higher dividend about to be offered to shareholders. In defence, the airline's machines were not equipped with de-icing equipment as the de-icing equipment available was not absolutely reliable – a view not shared by other British airlines. Imperial declared, as not all destination fields had appropriate ground facilities installed (not strictly true), it was sufficient that only two of their fleet were equipped with full blind-flying equipment. As for radios, the present air radios were, quoted Imperial, '99.35% efficient', and so there was no need to install a second set in their aircraft. Perkins countered with the fact that two radios were required in ships at sea, so why not in aircraft?

Sir Alan Cobham, although agreeing with part of Perkins's argument, entered the fray. Of Perkins, he said on 4 November, '… but I hope he [Perkins] will use his talents and position in Parliament to better advantage than merely continuing attacks on Imperial Airways'.

In turn, Perkins reiterated, BALPA were simply attempting to arrange discussions of matters of mutual interest with the Imperial Airways' management but Imperial would not entertain them. He suggested that Cobham was biased, 'What exactly have your relations with Imperial Airways been in the past?' There appeared little affection between the two of them. Resolution was achieved thanks to GAPAN, who acted as mediators between Perkins and BALPA on one hand and Imperial Airways on the other.

Amidst the turmoil, and quelling some of the rumours, the 13th AGM of Imperial Airways was held on 10 November 1937. To begin, Chairman Sir George Beharrell paid tribute to the late Sir Eric Geddes. Sir George's report regretted the delayed delivery of the fast land planes (Armstrong Whitworth Ensign) that Geddes had ordered, but recent progress with the long-range flying-boat, composites and in-flight refuelling made better news. Nevertheless, obstacles, political and otherwise, were still being encountered at the Empire marine airport, Langstone harbour, Portsmouth. Fortunately, the operation of the temporary base at Southampton was being made easier thanks to help from Vickers Supermarine. The financial statement showed £17,000 had been set aside for directors' fees and a 9% dividend, at a cost to the company of £42,100, was to be paid, despite a lower pay scale for aircrew and some other personnel.

Perkins persisted, and on 17 November a public inquiry into British civil aviation was called for by him. The main points of his speech were:

> 'State subsidies give Imperial Airways an unfair advantage over British Airways. Even so, Imperial Airways' safety record has declined, their image is poor and it is thought they ought to have a full-time Chairman. Of the Government, they have neither fostered the design of a medium sized airliner, to compete with the Americans, nor provided funding for a new London airport. On a human scale, pilots' pay has been cut and the airlines have unfair control over pilots' employment prospects.'

Perkins was seconded by Lieutenant-Colonel J. T. C. Moore-Brabazon, saying, 'That nothing short of a public inquiry would shake the Air Ministry up to the seriousness of the present position.' The scene was set for a deep and searching inquiry into British civil aviation and Imperial Airways in particular.

In response, a committee, chaired by the Rt Hon. Lord Cadman, was to inquire into and investigate the alleged shortcomings of British civil aviation. Lord Cadman was a leading figure in the Anglo-Iranian Oil Company, an expert in the oil industry, not civil aviation. Other members of the committee were Sir Warren Fisher, Permanent Secretary to the Treasury, and Sir William Brown, Permanent Secretary to the Board of Trade. Air Minister Swinton proposed not to lay down formal terms of reference but allow the committee to cover all points raised in earlier debates, except matters of Government policy. The Labour opposition contended this was a ruse, and Mr Attlee strongly opposed the composition, saying, 'It did not correspond to the promise of an independent inquiry.'

The Prime Minister bowed to the opposition suggestion and agreed to confer with Swinton. However, a further complication was that the Air Minister lacked popular Parliamentary support. He was a member of the House of Lords and the commissioning of this inquiry was based upon events as reported to him by Muirhead, his Under-Secretary. The opposition declared that Lord Swinton had not been correctly informed as to the feeling of Parliament. Furthermore, the opposition's shadow Air Minister, Lieutenant-Commander Fletcher, suggested that the Air Minister ought be a member of the Commons.

Sittings began on 2 December 1937, and following public outcry, the Government reconstituted the committee and widened their terms of reference. The committee's new members were Sir Fredrick Marquis (later

Lord Walton), Mr T. Harrison Hughes and J. W. Bowan (then, recently General Secretary of the Union of Postal Workers). They were tasked to investigate all of Perkins's charges except those of the pilots' pay and conditions.

THE EMPIRE AIRMAIL SCHEME MATURES
Christmas 1937 – Services are expanded and accelerated – Londonderry's letters – Christmas 1938.

In addition to the political moves at Whitehall, Christmas, with its extra burden of mail, awaited Imperial. Drawing upon their experience of 1936, extra flights, *Caledonia* and *Cambria* included, were arranged. As always, political points were there to be scored. On Monday 20 December, Mr Banfield (Labour) asked the Postmaster General (PMG) to state what amount of mail was being carried to Africa and whether or not the available facilities were adequate to meet the task without delay. The PMG replied that during November, Imperial Airways had carried forty-five tons of mail to South and East Africa, this being double the normal load. The PMG concluded that provisions would be found to be adequate, and they were.

After the event, the mail loads of 1936 were compared to those of 1937. It was found that 14,590 lb of mail had been sent to Australia and India in 1936 but 16,300 lb was dispatched in 1937. On the Africa route the increase was more outstanding, at 8,000 lb for 1936 against 67,300 lb for 1937. This phenomenal increase was due primarily to the introduction, earlier that year, of the EAMS for African destinations.

For 1938, Imperial Airways was awarded a mail contract worth £900,000 and a subsidy of £600,000. However, costs varied along the routes. South Africa found it necessary to charge twice the standard Empire rate and Australia required a subsidy of £20,000 to equal the Empire rate.

The New Year brought expansion. As Empire 'Boats became available, new routes came into being. On 12 January it was announced that, as from 23 February 1938, all first-class mail from Great Britain to Egypt, the Middle East, India, Seychelles, Tibet, Burma and the Federated Malay States would be carried by air. In the meantime, the Malay authorities were developing Glugor Bay, on Penang island, as the north Malaya terminal. They agreed to equip it with buildings, hangars, piers and approach beacons. Duly on 23 February, *Coolangatta*, accompanied by Captain 'Scotty' Allen in *Centurion*, loaded with 5,000 lb of mail, left Southampton for Karachi and Singapore.

As the 'boats continued their journey across the subcontinent, indigenous airlines distributed the mail around India. On arrival at Gwalior, *en route* to the Malay States, the crew of *Centurion* were met by the Maharajah Scindia. The State Priest blessed the 'boat and the crew were presented with a gold-hilted sword bearing the Scindia crest.

Although delivery times could not be guaranteed, the public were urged to post as early as possible. It was envisaged that mail would take three or four days to

The waters around Salisbury Island, Durban Harbour, were initially the landing area for the flying-boats. The wooded hill in the background is 'The Bluff'. In April 1940, the less congested Congella Basin site was officially opened. (Author, via Inggs)

reach Alexandria, a week to reach Calcutta and ten days to arrive in Singapore. This compared with the four to six days to Alexandria, sixteen days to Calcutta and twenty-two days to Singapore as achieved by the fast mail-ships. With the introduction of more 'boats and as a result of the efficiencies gained by the benefit of experience, even faster than anticipated services came into being. An accelerated service was announced on 18 March 1938. The accelerated service to Africa and India would commence on 10 April. Flight-time to Africa would be reduced from six and a half to four and a half days and India from four to two and a half days. Once the new schedules were introduced, the journey times became three and a half days to Calcutta, four and a half days to Bangkok, five and a half days to Hong Kong or Singapore and nine days to Brisbane. On the Africa route, it now took only one and a half days to reach Cairo, three days to get to Kisumu, another half day to Mozambique and a total of four and a half days to Durban.

The first accelerated flight to Singapore was made by *Centaurus*, commanded by the bluff, larger than life Irishman, Captain J. 'Paddy' Sheppard. They departed Hythe on 10 April. These new schedules had been achieved by the introduction of new overnight stops. On the African route these were Athens, Wadi Halfa, Kisumu and Mozambique. On the Australian route passengers would sleep at Athens, Basra, Karachi, Calcutta, Bangkok, Singapore, Rambang, Darwin and Longreach. The rescheduled routes proved to be almost as rapid as those originally envisaged employing night flying.

Not only were the flights faster but they were more plentiful, there being seven flights a week to Egypt, four to India and two to South Africa, Malaya, Hong Kong and Australia. On the route to Australia 'boats were changed at Alexandria, and at Singapore the QANTAS crews took over for the legs to Sydney. Hong Kong was reached via Bangkok, where passengers changed to a D.H.86.

On 22 July 1938, the Postmaster General (PMG) announced a further expansion of the EAMS as, from then on, all first-class mail to Australia, Oceania and New Zealand would be included. As a consequence, on 21 July the last surface dispatch to Australia sailed from England, the last to New Zealand casting off two days later. Such was the demand for mail, that passengers were ousted in its favour.

Other than an official ceremony planned to take place on board the MV *Medina*, there had been little fuss. Lord Londonderry, in an attempt to put the scheme into perspective, succeeded in ruffling a few feathers, on 23 July. Whilst referring to recent announcements in the press and on the radio, he expressed the opinion that the EAMS had now been completed without undue ceremony:

'Thus quietly and in a characteristically British way, unheralded, comes into operation a scheme of infinite hope for the future of the Empire and civilization in general ...'

Londonderry went on to applaud those who had had the foresight to conceive this scheme and the temerity to pursue its conclusion. However, it was debatable to

Centurion *becoming airborne from Gladstone, Australia, late 1930s.* (Mears)

whom he accredited the original idea. Emphasis was given to Christopher Bullock, once Permanent Under-Secretary to the Air Minister, and Mr F. G. L. Bertram, who had carried out some of the original discussions with the governments of the Empire Colonies.

Four days later, 27 July, Sir George Beharrell replied to Londonderry:

'It was not the Air Ministry that conceived EAMS but Imperial Airways. Under the guidance of Sir Eric Geddes and Woods Humphery, Imperial Airways presented the Ministry with a serious practical proposal and not some nebulous idea as suggested by Londonderry.'

The Empire Airmail Scheme, as originally envisaged, was finally, and officially, completed on 28 July 1938, the date the first eastbound mail rose from Southampton Water to fly the new extended route. Beyond Australia, the Empire's airmail was delivered to New Zealand, Tasmania, Fiji, Papua, Norfolk Island, Lord Howe Island, Nauru, the Mandated Territories of Western Samoa and the Territories under the jurisdiction of the Commissioner for the Western Pacific. The future seemed assured. From now, and for the next three years, Imperial Airways would receive a subsidy of £750,000 per annum. Thereafter, the subsidy would be reduced gradually as the projected mail loads rose to over 2,000 tons per year.

Honour for the first flight went to *Calypso*. Yet again the quarterdeck of the MV *Medina* was the scene of the departure ceremony, which, this time, was chaired by Sir John Reith, Imperial Airways' new Chairman. Attending were the Secretary of State for Air, Kingsley Wood; the Postmaster General, Major Tryon and representatives from the Australian and New Zealand Governments. Accompanying them were many other dignitaries, who had taken the special train from London on the morning of 28 July. The Air Minister handed the PMG letters from King George VI to the Acting Governor-General of Australia and the Governor-General of New Zealand. The letters were franked personally by the PMG, using a commemorative silver die. He then placed the letters into silk bags and handed them in turn to Sir George Beharrell, who placed them in the charge of the Commander of *Calypso*, the diminutive Captain E. H. 'Tich' Attwood. (Attwood was so short he had to sit on a cushion to see over the cockpit coaming.) Shortly after 11:00 *Calypso* ascended into the cloud-straggled blue sky, circled once and set off on her 13,000-mile journey to Australia – thence to New Zealand. In her hold were 68 mail bags, amounting to two tons of unsurcharged airmail. She arrived in Sydney on 6 August and returned on the 9th. Although the New Zealand mail was flown only to Australia and then crossed the Tasman Sea by ship, the scheme was heralded a triumph. On the practical side there were hiccups. Due to the still inadequate arrangements at Darwin, the first mail into Australia was a day late arriving at Sydney. Fortunately, the old land planes were still available and the mail was further distributed on time. The second service was also delayed, when the aircraft broke down between Rangoon and Singapore.

Further to Londonderry's letter, Christopher Bullock presented his view of the conception on 29 July. He reminded readers of the historic origins of EAMS as examined, after the Great War, by Sefton Brancker and Holt-Thomas. He reasoned that they were defeated by the technical difficulties of their day. However, he did accredit Londonderry, ably assisted by Sir Donald Banks, for rendering considerable aid in easing the matter through the House. Also, when negotiations became turgid, Londonderry had deputized Bullock to negotiate with the Union Government of South Africa and the Government of Australia. Similarly India, represented by Sir Joseph Bhore, was party to Bullock's diplomacy. Such was the extent of Bullock's involvement, that for some time the arrangements for regulations governing air transport across India were known as 'The Bullock–Bhore Agreement'. However, Bullock's prime reason for writing was to emphasize the Empire character of the scheme and to pay tribute to all those who built up the EAMS.

Gladstone, Australia, was typical of the many refuelling stops between Hythe and Sydney. (L to R) Roy Haack (Skipper), Bill Smyth (Customs), Clive 'Starry' Night (bending) and Ernie Martin, on the Shell boat Reliance, *late 1930s. (Mears)*

At the close of July, Londonderry again wrote. He explained he had no wish to cause controversy and, allying himself with the Bullock letter, he reiterated Bullock's sympathies that EAMS was a team effort.

The first return mail from Australia was pre-empted by *Carpentaria's* departure on 2 August 1938. The official first EAM out of Australia was on 4 August in *Camilla*, under the command of Lester Brain. The symbolic restraining ribbon was cut by Lord Huntingfield, the Acting Governor-General. Eight passengers, 120 kilograms of freight and 95 kilograms of airmail were aboard. Following these inaugural passages, the schedule was increased to three flights a week.

Further services were added to EAMS on 2 September 1938 by means of a land-plane spur from Bangkok to Hong Kong, thus connecting the Empire of the Orient with Australia. On average, 19 tons of mail per week were being dispatched from Southampton, an almost three-fold increase since the facility was opened in March 1937. Moreover, the amount of airmail to South Africa had increased ten-fold since the introduction of the subsidies. During the past year,

Canopus *taking off from the Salisbury Island fairway, Durban. The promontory in the background is called 'The Bluff'. (Author via Inggs)*

Imperial had flown nearly nine million miles.

Notwithstanding the Post Office's excellent planning, no account could be taken of human habit. Traditionally, overseas surface-post was dispatched at the end of the week and, despite the Post Office's efforts to inform the public otherwise, there was still a surge of posting as the week closed. At times, this surge overwhelmed the capacity of the outbound services. In resolution, the Post Office ceased publishing scheduled posting times and artificially controlled the flow by restricting the amount of mail they sent down to Southampton. Even so, it was a regular occurrence that at least two 'boats a week were so overloaded with mail, they could carry only four passengers. Yet, the carriage of airmail was the expressed purpose of the Empire Flying-Boats.

By mid-September, routes, including the recently opened Far East one, were being over-subscribed to such an extent that extra 'boats had to be scheduled. Imperial Airways rapidly became a victim of their own success. Of the passengers arriving at Calcutta, Imperial Airways carried three times as many as their combined competitors. The future seemed to hold no respite. Even the 25 'boats Imperial had in service were insufficient, and the six larger ones (S.30) on order were already allocated to the expanded service and the North Atlantic route. Adverse publicity resulted from passengers being ousted, and many sought passages on other airlines. This lack of capacity was most marked on the initial outbound legs from England. Here, the mail load was high, as little had been dropped off along the route. The problem was a symptom of an airline funded by mail revenue but scheduled by the pace at which passengers were willing to travel. Inbound, there was simply less mail, hence the problem did not occur. The possibility of special mail-carrying planes was mooted. Perhaps the composite had a future after all.

The London Chamber of Commerce (Civil Aviation Section) wrote to the Secretary of State for Air, suggesting passengers and mails ought to be separated. The Chamber highlighted that it was possible to move mails continuously, in weathers that would be unsuitable for passengers, and it seemed feasible to employ Vickers Wellington bombers to fly long-range, mail-only sorties. The Chamber concluded by suggesting that to alleviate this conflict of interests the Government ought to issue a specification for a twin-engined, land-plane mail-carrier, capable of cruising at 250 mph.

As the summer of 1938 mellowed into autumn, the schedule to Singapore and beyond settled into a routine. With apparent disregard to their lack of passenger capacity, in September Imperial Airways reduced the London to Singapore fare from £156 to £130. A passage from London to Sydney return cost £274.

The challenge of the year, Christmas airmail, came around again. As stated, about 19 tons of airmail were carried each week. Although Imperial expected to carry a greater amount during the Christmas period, they had no precise figures to work towards: 100 tons a week had been forecast. In early November, plans to use almost 70 aircraft were announced. Every available aircraft was to be pressed into service, the *Maia* and *Mercury* composite included. It was proposed that *Mercury* would carry mails to Alexandria and perhaps Karachi, whilst *Maia* would take mails out to the Mediterranean. The H.P.42s and *Scylla* class were to be fitted with extra fuel tanks, to give them the range to reach Marseilles. Some routes were to be denuded of their aircraft. In particular those serving the continent out of Croydon would have their places taken by the newly delivered Ensigns and Albatrosses. Additionally, the company decided to limit the passenger loads still further, in order to carry extra mail. Apart from the complete Imperial Airways' fleet, the Royal Air Force and assorted charter flights of Olley Air Services, Wrightways and Swissair would be employed to carry the mail to Alexandria, where further sorting would take place.

Each evening, Imperial Airways received from the Post Office mail destined for overseas. The airline staff, working in conjunction with the Post Office, selected appropriate mail loads according to capacity of the aircraft waiting at Southampton or Croydon. Care was taken to ensure the bags were dispatched in chronological order.

The sundry deliveries to Alexandria brought their own problem. Because of the dissimilar speeds and various delays of the aircraft, mail arrived at Alexandria in an order different from that in which it had left London. The task was even made more difficult as mails were continually arriving, having taken between three and ten days to make the flight. Details of each aircraft load were cabled ahead to Alexandria, so that the Officer-in-Charge, Mr R. Stapleton, could attempt to re-establish the chronological precedent for onward shipment.

Once Christmas was behind them, Imperial Airways declared that the total distance flown had been 1,158,000 miles. Scheduled services had flown 695,000 miles, including 123,000 miles by QANTAS on the Singapore to Sydney sector. A further 463,000 miles had been flown on non-scheduled flights. Of these, Imperial Airways had flown 282,000 miles, the RAF 29,000 miles and chartered aircraft 152,000 miles. Imperial's new D.H.91 Albatross, the Frobisher class, had operated between Croydon and Alexandria, whilst the Ensigns went to Calcutta and the H.P.42 flew on routes to Kisumu and Calcutta. The Atalantas plied between Karachi and Penang and the D.H.86s flew from Karachi to Darwin. Between Bangkok and Hong Kong, a DC-3 was chartered to complement the D.H.86s. The RAF had flown one service from Plymouth to Penang, two return services between Alexandria and Kisumu and seven return services between Alexandria and Lake Habbaniyah. Chartered aircraft had made 20 return flights between Croydon and Alexandria. This vast effort managed to move 197 tons of airmail – 200 had been forecast – from England, in the lead-up to Christmas 1938. Of the 197 tons, 65 tons went to Australia and New Zealand, 46 tons to India, 10 tons to Egypt, 35 tons to South Africa, 6 tons to both Rhodesia and Nyasaland, a similar amount to Kenya, Tanganyika and Zanzibar, a ton and a half

One of many tenders employed throughout the route. At most staging posts passengers were ferried to their flying-boat by launch. This launch is pictured at Laropi, Africa, around 1946. (Baldwin and Bigby)

Fuel and oil were arranged by the Shell Agent and taken out to the 'boats, either in bulk or in four-gallon cans. (Baldwin and Bigby)

was despatched to Sudan, a ton for the west coast of Africa and 7 tons went to Hong Kong. Returning aircraft bore a lesser, but still significant, amount.

The Empire Airmail Scheme was one of the great milestones in British aviation history. Although the War intervened before Christmas 1939, the principle of moving mail by air was now well established.

REORGANIZATION
Cadman Report – Arrival of Reith.

The Cadman Report was published on 8 March 1938. It was described as 'the most sensible document yet issued of civil aviation'. In summary, its findings were:

> 'Notwithstanding that the Government's priority of Rearmament was correct and blame for earlier friction should be shared between them and Imperial Airways, the Government could have been more helpful to civil aviation.
>
> The Government needed greater control of civil aviation and a department with its own Under-Secretary ought to be established. Meanwhile, Imperial Airways should concentrate on the Empire routes whilst British

Airways, using British aircraft, should service the principal European cities. In addition, British Airways should immediately seek Government subsidies for routes to South America, the Pacific and the Caribbean.

> There should have been greater correlation between civil and military aviation and more research, especially on the subject of anti-icing equipment, was required. The lack of progress with building a dedicated flying-boat base was disappointing.
>
> Imperial Airways suffered a poor relationship with their staff.'

The Committee commented that since the company's inception, thirteen years previously, a dividend had not been paid. However, it was accepted the amount of dividend ought to be limited, as the company was subsidized. They found the Imperial fleet airworthy and 90% of their services were operated by flying-boats. Armstrong Whitworth Ensign land planes, ordered in 1934, were not yet available as the manufacturers were concentrating on the production of Whitley bombers. Moreover, Government indecision had caused procurement delays.

Although the Committee credited Imperial for the comfort and safety of their service, they considered the airline had expanded greatly and a full-time Chairman, to replace the harshly criticized Managing Director, Woods Humphery, was now required:

> 'We are profoundly dissatisfied with them [Imperial Airways' relations with company staff]. *Although the carriage of air-passengers in safety and comfort and conveyance of mail and freight have been achieved with considerable efficiency, we cannot avoid the conclusion that management has been defective in other respects. We consider that the responsibilities confronting the company can no longer be borne, for practical purposes, by a Managing Director. The Chairman should give his whole time to the direction of the business and should personally control the management of the company, aided by one or more full-time directors.'*

In reply, Imperial Airways said they were not pre-warned of the detailed criticisms in the findings. Thus, Woods Humphery had been condemned before he was able to defend himself. Further criticism was levelled at him. Even though he had the Board's approval, he was charged with taking a blinkered, commercial view of his responsibilities. In defence, the question of profit or prestige should be for the Government to decide and not the Managing Director. Woods Humphery became the scapegoat for the reorganization that followed.

Debate upon Cadman's findings opened, on 16 March, with the statement:

> 'Except on the Empire routes, this country is backward on civil air-transport. We consider that there is reason for more than apprehension, indeed we view with extreme disquiet the position disclosed by our enquiry.'

The Government maintained that the interests of the Empire were paramount and, overall, Imperial Airways' route structure served that end. The Government strongly desired continued investment in Empire routes and additional funds were sought. Shrewdly, they wished to invest in apparently lucrative aspects of aviation, airmail for instance. The House further found civil and military aviation could not be wholly separated and co-operation and co-ordination between the departments were essential. More Governmental help with research and development and aircraft construction was promised. Prime Minister Chamberlain announced that, in order to expand civil aviation, he sought approval for Imperial's annual subsidy to be increased from one and a half million to £3 million. It was proposed to grant Imperial the higher subsidy until 1944.

The Government disagreed with Cadman's recommendation to establish a separate Under-Secretary for Civil Aviation. Instead, the Rt Hon. Earl Winterton, MP, agreed to act as Deputy to the Under-Secretary of State for Air, and would handle all military air questions. Alas, as was to be proved, Winterton's appointment was as much due to Lord Swinton's inability to defend himself in the Commons as to Winterton's abilities. Winterton misjudged the mood of the House on matters of military aircraft production and was forced to resign only two months after his appointment.

Debate on Cadman's report continued, and a measure of its criticisms lodged upon Swinton, and considering Winterton's poor 'military' performance, Swinton resigned in spring 1938. He understood the difficulties of being a Minister confined to the Lords. Prime Minister Chamberlain acknowledged Swinton's achievements in ensuring that rearmament had been so successful, and announced that Sir Kingsley Wood would become Secretary of State for Air. As he had previously been Postmaster-General and Minister of Health, he was admirably qualified. The new Air Minister was no champion of his predecessor and he accused Swinton of paying too much attention to detail in policy, rather than maintaining an overview.

Chamberlain thanked Cadman, saying that the members of the Committee had performed their task without fear or favour. He emphasized their impartiality, as he recalled the derogatory and unworthy reflections that were cast upon them from the Opposition front bench. Most of Cadman's findings were accepted by the Government but little favour was found with Imperial's acting Chairman, Beharrell.

Even before the acceptance of Cadman, influential powers were at work. Kingsley Wood (not then Air Minister) had spoken with Sir John Reith, suggesting he should quit the post of Director-General of the BBC and hinting a further position might be in the offing.

John Charles Walsham Reith, the fifth son of the Rev. D. George Reith, was a stern, punctilious, yet fair man, who was publicly applauded. Among his friends and admirers was Woods Humphery. Their friendship reached back to when they worked as apprentice engineers in the North British Locomotive Company. Reith had even been best man at Woods Humphery's wedding, where Reith's father officiated. Their friendship had continued throughout the intervening years but their ideals differed. Whereas Woods Humphery had a strong sense of duty towards the shareholder, Reith was driven by an overwhelming sense of public service.

In November 1937, about the time of the Perkins row, Reith, aware of the criticism being levelled at Imperial, met Woods Humphery. Reith received the impression that Woods Humphery knew the chairmanship of Imperial Airways would soon be available. Moreover, inference that Woods Humphery considered himself a likely contender for the chair was given to Reith. However, like Cadman, Reith believed that the post ought to be filled by a full-time managing director. In the past, Geddes had confided in Reith that Woods Humphery was one of the dozen best executives in England. This contrasted with the opinion of many, who thought Woods Humphery was overawed by Geddes. Reith expressed to Woods Humphery the opinion that Imperial Airways were too dividend motivated and they ought to employ staff of greater capability, in larger numbers, and reward them accordingly. Although Woods Humphery agreed Imperial Airways needed a good public relations man, he thought the company could not afford to pay additional executives.

Reith was not enamoured with the prospect of joining Imperial, which he had previously avoided. In the previous May, Reith had been offered something with far more appeal, the reorganization of the War Office, but that had gone elsewhere. It was suggested Reith might as well get Imperial Airways instead. The chairmanship had been offered to Sir John Salmond, one-time Chief of Air Staff and Government Director of Imperial, but he refused it.

On 3 June 1938, Reith was summoned. It transpired that Chamberlain and Sir Kingsley Wood desired Reith to chair Imperial Airways from 4 June 1938, the following day! Reith was not in favour, as he had no wish to leave the BBC and, having seen the Cadman Report, relished Imperial Airways even less. Kingsley Wood suggested that Woods Humphery would be asked to resign from Imperial Airways. Reith's previous public silence on the whole subject had been taken as acceptance of the post but this was not the case. Reith insisted upon hearing the request from the PM's own lips. That being done, Reith accepted reluctantly on the condition that Woods Humphery resigned and the company be nationalized.

With the exception of Woods Humphery, Imperial Airways agreed with Cadman that a full-time chairman was required. As Reith thought, Woods Humphery expected to be offered the post, which was understandable, as he had been Managing Director since 1925. Following the PM's offer, Reith discussed Imperial Airways with Woods Humphery, who, now seemingly aware the chairmanship had been offered to Reith, considered resignation. However, whilst explaining the responsibilities and duties, Reith thought Woods Humphery was deliberately seeking to dissuade him from acceptance.

Reith's first meeting with Beharrell produced friction. Beharrell wanted Woods Humphery to stay, but Reith insisted only he could be full-time Chairman and Managing Director. He wanted no power sharing. It was, however, agreed that Woods Humphery could remain until Reith was comfortably ensconced. Reith's desire for Woods Humphery's departure is surprising considering their previous friendship and the telegram Reith sent Woods Humphery:

'My first act on joining the great organization which owes so much to you, is to send this signal of greeting and goodwill. I am glad you are standing by.'

Eventually, on 4 July 1938, Reith went to the shabby offices, an old furniture depository, behind Victoria Station. This was the headquarters of Imperial Airways. His initial impression was of a company seemingly totally lacking in any organization. The whole concern had been run through Woods Humphery, who had dealt with a myriad of trivia. Reith's first task, left by Woods Humphery, was to concur to the construction of new toilets at Croydon Airport – cost £238.

Only slowly was Reith able to win round Woods Humphery, who, in later years, bitterly accused Reith of 'smashing the Imperial Airways organization'. Finally, Woods Humphery resigned; his departure was degrading. Reith was now free to champion the amalgamation of Imperial Airways and British Airways into one Government-owned State airline.

HOME BASE
Hythe, a temporary arrangement – Langstone harbour.

Mr Scott-Paine represented the British Marine Air Navigation Company, during the founding of Imperial Airways in 1924. His company operated two Supermarine Sea Eagle flying-boats on a seasonal Southampton to Channel Isles service. The company shared the Hythe facilities of Supermarine and British Power Boats Ltd. Imperial Airways inherited the Sea Eagles, one of which was rammed and lost at Guernsey in 1927 and the other was withdrawn in 1929. Meanwhile, Imperial ordered the Short Calcutta for the trans-Mediterranean service. For a week, in September 1928, one Calcutta flew a daily Belfast–Liverpool schedule, soon to be followed by a brief period of flying Southampton to Jersey. In April 1929, the Calcuttas entered Mediterranean service.

That was the total of Imperial's experience of operating flying-boats out of England. This was of no immediate concern as, initially, the first Empire 'Boat route was across the Mediterranean and servicing facilities were established at Alexandria, in the old coaling yard. The existing Kent and Calcutta flying-boat facilities around the Mediterranean would be adequate for the Empires.

With an Empire Route terminus in mind, Imperial, recalling their early days operating the Sea Eagles, approached Vickers Supermarine and made 'temporary' arrangements with them to share their hangar at Hythe. A separate company, Imperial Airways (Repair Works) Ltd, was set up to maintain the Empire 'Boats. This 'temporary' arrangement was to last for some time.

Initially, passengers boarded a Southern Railway Pullman Car at Waterloo, London. This carriage, complete with 'Imperial Airways Empire Service' running boards and a guard's van, in which the flight clerk processed the luggage, steamed out of London as part of the 08:30 down train.

At Southampton Dock, Berth 50, the passengers embarked upon launches which ferried them across to the flying-boats moored at Hythe. Passengers had to step either from the launch into the flying-boat or from the launch onto a raft secured to the flying-boat's port side. From September 1937, passengers boarded launches at Berth 9.

It had been forecast that the Southampton to Sydney service would take ten and a quarter days, soon shortening to seven and a quarter, once the ground facilities were complete. However, one of the problems affecting departure time was the inability of Imperial Airways to get their passengers, who checked in at London, down to Southampton before mid-morning. This was eventually circumvented by getting the passengers to Southampton the night before. Although it increased the overall journey time, nobody seemed to object.

Once it was decided the passengers would overnight in Southampton, they departed Waterloo at 07:30. Following the 6 June 1939 opening of *Airways House*, the new Buckingham Palace Road terminal, Platform 17 at Victoria Station was used. Despite the claimed one-hour journey time, the trip took about ninety minutes, during which time dinner was served.

Throughout this period, there was much debate as to where the purpose-built Empire Flying-Boat base should be. The Portsmouth Corporation considered constructing a combined marine and land aerodrome at Langstone, to the east of Portsmouth. At the end of July 1936, the Portsmouth Corporation applied for the substantial grant that was available for such a project. Portsmouth planned an alighting channel six feet deep, 200 yards wide and a mile in length. They hoped flying operations could start in January 1937, but the Corporation's timetable was grossly optimistic.

There were two studies: one a tidal landing area and the other a non-tidal barraged seadrome. It was thought a tidal landing area was not as safe as a barraged seadrome and operations would be less efficient. On the other hand, a barraged seadrome would be more expensive. The Docks and Airports Committee's recommendation to build a non-tidal, barraged seadrome for over £1 million was accepted by the Council, on 24 February 1937, by two votes. The Government offered a 50% grant, up to a maximum of £600,000, and a further 15-year guaranteed annual income of £30,000.

Notwithstanding the success of the Corporation's negotiations and the advantages of a non-tidal barrage, the City Council reconsidered the project. A substantial

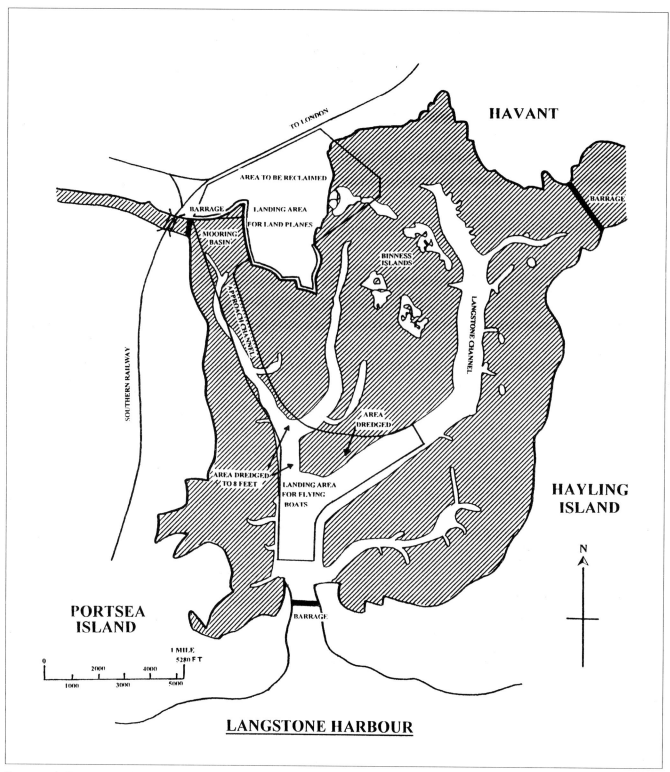

Portsmouth Corporation, the City Council and the Docks and Airports Committee were in favour of developing Langstone harbour as the Empire seadrome, but the level of support from the Air Ministry and objections from the Admiralty sowed the seeds of the project's downfall. (Author)

saving could be achieved if the tidal seadrome was built instead. By a majority, on this occasion, of three votes, they turned against the non-tidal seadrome. Now it was thought, if part of the reduced cost was borne by the ratepayers, the project could be financed with the help of a thirty-year loan. There were dissenters, as Imperial Airways already received a Government subsidy in excess of £500,000 per annum and some ratepayers

thought it unfair they should subsidize the airline further. The Council agreed to contact the Air Ministry, who, spurred by the rejection of the barrage, did offer to reopen negotiations with a view to a tidal seadrome. Despite a tidal seadrome being contrary to the desires of Imperial Airways, and airmen in general, and aware of criticism that the Air Ministry was jeopardizing the safety and future of British Empire Aviation solely on the ground of cost, the Air Ministry seemed to support a tidal seadrome. Imperial Airways agreed reluctantly.

Meanwhile, from April 1938, in parallel with the Langstone debate, the Air Ministry, Southampton Harbour Board and the Board of Trade discussed operating a seadrome at Southampton. Possibly pre-empting any decision, Imperial Airways started to build terminal buildings, covered walkways and two aircraft boarding jetties, within the new Southampton Liner Dock.

It was being realized that Southampton might well become the marine base. A requirement for a regulated, one-mile-long strip of water, reserved for flying-boats and equipped with a flare-path, was submitted. In June, Captain H. H. Balfour, the Under-Secretary of State for Air, was quoted as saying, 'The matter was under consideration with the port authorities for some time.'

The Air Ministry and Imperial Airways were in no doubt that Southampton's first concern should be towards its ocean-going liner traffic. However, the airline's practice of boarding passengers adjacent to the New Docks, along the River Test, rather than on Southampton Water, was cause for concern as to the safety of mixing liner, launches and flying-boats. Probably mindful of this hazard, Imperial built their terminal within the liner dock and passengers were boarded first at Berth 101 and, from August, at Berth 108.

In contrast, a year after the sumptuous land and seadrome at Singapore and four months after the Shatt-al-Arab airport at Basra were opened, Imperial Airways opened their terminal at Lake Bracciano, 80 miles from Rome. General Pelligrini, Italy's Chief of Civil Aviation, officiated at the ceremony on Saturday 9 July.

As a result of discussions during the previous months, it was announced, on 28 July, Southampton was to become the permanent Empire air base. The Air Ministry's proposal for establishing facilities in the port of Southampton Water had been accepted by the Harbour Board. A stretch of water, one mile long and 1,200 feet wide, situated to the east of the main channel, would be reserved for flying-boats. The Air Ministry would be responsible for dredging but the Harbour Board would be responsible for the provision of launches. The Air Ministry did admit that Langstone, which would have prohibited all shipping, was a better location than Southampton. Approaches to the Southampton fairways were often masked by shipping, especially so in poor visibility or low cloud. On 13 September, Captain Alger, fearful of striking a ship whilst making a shallow approach in fog, put *Camilla* down in the English Channel, two miles off Foreland, Isle of Wight, before taxiing to his mooring.

The all 'Red Route' Empire Service had expanded considerably during the past eighteen months and it became necessary to make dawn take-offs and dusk arrivals. An electric flare-path was developed, naked lights not being permitted upon Southampton Water. In May of 1938, a demonstration installation was laid opposite Netley Hospital, a grossly unsuitable site that was receiving Air Ministry backing. On 24 September, *Canopus* and *Corinthian* became the first two flying-boats

to make a scheduled night departure from Southampton.

The flare-path consisted of lines of six flares, mounted upon anchored buoys aligned into wind. Each flare was made up of two bulbs suspended from a slender pole atop of the buoy. The buoys contained twelve-volt batteries, and the 18-watt light shone through an amber lens. The flares were set 200 yards apart, thus the total length was just over 3,000 feet. A launch was positioned at the end of the flare-path. After take-off the launch and flare-path remained in position, until it was certain the flying-boat would not be returning. Then the flare-path could be hauled aboard the launch.

The Netley flare-path was used 'in anger' in mid-November, allowing Captain Kelly Rogers to bring *Camilla* to rest after an arduous, 60-hour-long Christmas mail flight to Alexandria and return. Several days later, poor weather forced *Corinthian* to divert to Rochester, on her return from India, and delayed the departures of *Centaurus* and *Cordelia*.

Along the route, Imperial Airways were able to use paraffin lamps in the flare-path. A conical buoy, fitted with a detachable lamp, was developed. A line of five buoys was laid at 200 yards spacing from the rear of a launch. At the over-run end a sixth buoy was moored to show the width of the strip. Once trimmed, the lamps would burn for four or five hours. About 50 seadromes were equipped with the new oil-burning flare-path.

Possibly spurred by events at Southampton, in September 1938, the Portsmouth City Council proposed to operate Langstone as a private-enterprise Empire 'Boat terminal. The promoters of this scheme were seeking to acquire the existing Corporation aerodrome and adjoining land. Once the Admiralty became aware of this private venture, they reiterated their 1936 reservations about the premier naval base in the Empire operating within the close proximity of a seadrome. However, in the greater interest of Empire, they were willing to acquiesce. The proposal came to nought as the whole scheme was rejected by the Council.

At the close of 1938, the Southampton Harbour Board Works' Committee were informed the Government were about to introduce a Bill setting up an Empire Flying-Boat base at Southampton. The Bill would enable the Board to reserve a portion of the harbour for the exclusive use of flying-boats and charge landing fees. However, it was probable neither the Bill would be passed before July 1939 nor the facilities ready before late 1940. The Board was sceptical, but the Air Ministry's proposal to spend up to £300,000 upon the scheme was hardly an indication they lacked commitment to see the project completed. The Bill was submitted to the House of Lords' Committee for Unopposed Bills on 3 May 1939.

As a result of the apparent indecision over siting the Empire seadrome, a move started to develop an artificial lake somewhere on the Sussex or Kent shore. Unofficially, sites were examined by a firm of harbour and dock engineers. It was suggested a site could be excavated, dykes could be built and the 'pond' could then be filled with sea-water, which would not freeze. Such a site would have clear, flat approaches and would be free from conflicting naval or air force activity. It seemed the disadvantages of the cost of dredging and maintaining a channel at Southampton, the risks of operating flying-boats amidst shipping lanes and the overall expense of Langstone harbour could be circumvented if the 'Round Pond' was adopted.

Another suggestion was the old Pagham harbour, between Selsey Bill and Bognor Regis. Having a constant depth of nine or ten feet, it could be used as a tidal lake. Following dredging, a one-mile take-off run would be available and the surrounding land, which had been reclaimed in 1874, would offer clear unobstructed approaches or, alternatively, could be used as an adjacent aerodrome for land planes. Moreover, there were adequate rail connections to Chichester and the area was well served with trunk-roads.

If the Irish could build the base at Foynes and the Italians a seadrome at Bracciano, surely the British could achieve something similar? After all, four years had elapsed since Imperial Airways had first approached the Ministry and sought such a facility. In fact, all that had been achieved was in the best of British tradition: do nothing and compromise.

A question in the House, posed by Mr Murray Sueter on 11 May, finally laid Langstone harbour to rest:

'Were any alternative sites to Langstone Harbour and Southampton considered when making this decision?'

Captain Balfour replied:

'A total of nine suggested sites had been examined. However once account had been taken of cost, operational convenience, construction and the future of the Empire 'Boats and Empire Airmail Scheme, it had been decided that in the present circumstances the base would remain at Southampton.'

Where Imperial controlled matters, they made greater progress. In November 1937, it was revealed that their new terminal building and headquarters was under construction in London. Designed by Mr A. Lakeman, this edifice was to become the starting point for all Imperial Airways' passenger flights in Europe and throughout the Empire. There would be an entrance from Buckingham Palace Road in addition to direct access from Victoria Station. Although it was hoped the building would be complete by the end of 1938, it was not until Friday, 2 June 1939 that Imperial Airways took over their new headquarters, *Airways House*. The following Monday, at 08:00, the first coach, full of passengers for Croydon and the continent, departed. At 14:30, the first 'Empire Special' train from Southampton arrived at Imperial's Platform 17 on Victoria Station. Outbound passengers departed on the 20:05 that evening and spent the night at Southampton, before their pre-breakfast take-off.

No sooner had the building been opened than observation as to its unsuitability as a headquarters following the proposed amalgamation with British Airways was made. However, bearing in mind the requirement to have ready access to the Victoria to Southampton railway and the limited availability of building land at the time, no one could have foreseen this shortfall. Nevertheless, extensions were being planned before the building came into use.

Southampton may have become the terminus and a new headquarters was being built in London, but maintenance of the Empire 'Boats continued to be done across Southampton Water, at Hythe. Even throughout the forthcoming war, the home maintenance base remained at Hythe.

MAINTENANCE
Beaching – Turnaround – Night staging posts – Daily servicing – Engine starting.

Before the advent of the Empire Flying-Boats, Imperial Airways had operated a variety of aircraft, each designed with a specific area of operation in mind. Captains tended to be allocated a particular aircraft and the flying task of individual machines was not high. Aircraft spent ample time on the ground for maintenance and punctuality was not expected. Introduction of the Empire Airmail Scheme called for regular, scheduled flights, adhering to a strict timetable. Should Imperial fail to deliver the mail on time, the Post Office could invoke the financial penalties within the contract.

By June 1938, the airline had a fleet of 59 aircraft. By far the greatest part of the productive fleet were the Empire 'Boats. For the first time, Imperial Airways had an aircraft capable of tirelessly operating throughout the length of their route structure. Schedules were written to keep the mail moving and minimize the time the 'boats were not available for flight.

Throughout the life of the Empires, the main servicing facility in England remained at Hythe but all engines were overhauled at Croydon. Routine servicing, for a two-day turnaround, was carried out at Hythe but deeper maintenance and repair could be done at the Imperial Airways (Repair Works) Ltd site across the water, in the Folland hangar near Hamble. The Hythe hangar was shared with Supermarine until May 1938, when Imperial took it over completely. From then on, three 'boats could be housed but parking was on a 'first in, last out basis'. Hence much of the maintenance was done on the apron, between the slipway and the hangar. Normally there would be no more than five 'boats at Hythe, two of which would be moored.

A laden 'boat drew about four and half feet and beaching, always a fraught task, was best done at high water. A particular hazard at Hythe was the wash of passing ocean liners. To beach a 'boat it was first moored by the head, close to the slipway, and then the main beaching gear was floated out and attached. The 'boat was next towed, tail-first, towards the slipway. Here, a man, donned in waders, attached the tail trolley, which was used to support and steer the 'boat once ashore. A tail line was attached to a winch or tractor and the 'boat

Looking forward from the aft cabin, through the promenade deck and into the 'mid' or 'spar' cabin. The dark corridor has the pantry to the right and the lavatories to the left. Beyond, lies the forward cabin, which, early in life, was converted to mail carriage. Between schedules, the 'boats were thoroughly cleaned, with the interior furnishings being removed for cleaning and inspection. (Peek)

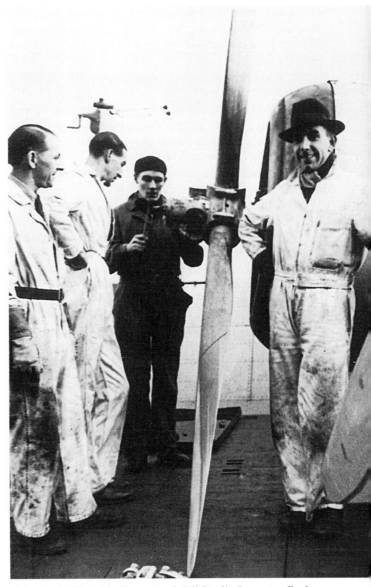

(L to R) MacDougall, Charge-hand; Bill Brodie, Inspector; Fred Smith, Fitter and Sid Goldsmith, Inspector. It was Mac (far left) who fell from the working platform and broke both legs. Bill Peek was promoted to Charge-hand. The port-inner engine is receiving attention. The mast bearing the pitot head, the radio aerial and the ensign jack-staff appear in the background. (Peek)

was gingerly pulled up the slip'. This manoeuvre was best done in calm water to ensure an even transference of weight onto the beaching chassis. Once the 'boat was clear of the water, the salt and slime were hosed off.

The engineers at Hythe worked two eight-hour shifts, and during the two days the 'boats were beached, the interiors were given thorough attention. Chairs, carpets, linen and life-jackets were all removed for cleaning and inspection. The CofA maintenance requirement did not naturally dovetail into Imperial's schedule, so a rolling inspection was carried out, with part being done each time the 'boat was at Hythe. As a rule, engines were changed after 250 hours and propellers overhauled every 270 hours. At far shorter intervals, the airframe, electrical system, fuel system and engines were inspected, lubricated and adjusted, as laid down in the maintenance schedule.

Regular, through-the-night, night-flying did not become a feature of the Empire Route, so the staging posts and refuelling stops designated early in the aircraft's career continued to be used. At the designated night halts, modest engineering facilities were established and turnarounds, the infrequent engine change or other small repairs, were within the means of the

staff. Should circumstances and unscheduled arrivals dictate, the engineering staff could find themselves with four or five 'boats to service, let alone the occasional engine change.

Such was the pressure upon Imperial Airways to keep the mail on schedule, that often the engineers toiled late into the night. Alf Cowling recalled one night at Basra, when they had eight 'boats to turn around. At Basra, simple routines had added hazards. One of the fitters, having finished his task upon the oily Pegasus engine, walked across the wing and wiped his hands upon the Iraqi ensign, flying from the masthead. This act was unfortunately seen by one of the local staff. Only the most diplomatic of approaches by the Station Superintendent kept the fitter from jail.

After a night upon the water, the bilges in the hull and floats would be checked, a little seepage being acceptable. Should the wing-floats have taken water, the hand-held bilge pump could be used. Captains expected to find a serviceable aircraft on their dawn visit to the mooring.

On another occasion, as recalled by Alf Cowling, some adjustments had been made to an engine and the engine cowling rested upon the wing. The engine was started and, not too surprisingly, the cowling blew off into the murky depths of the Shatt-al-Arab. Hythe was duly signalled, 'Cowling lost overboard, send replacement.' Hythe's reply was, 'Request Cowling's next-of-kin.'

Accidents did happen as aircraft were slippery and, particularly at Hythe, the waters could be cold. But the apron was always hard. Bill Peek earned unexpected promotion at Hythe when 'Mac' MacDougall, the white-overalled charge-hand, slipped from the wing of a 'boat, fell twelve or so feet and broke both legs. The foreman came to the accident and told the workers to remove 'Mac's' overalls. Still warm, they were passed to Bill Peek, instantly promoted and resplendent in his coloured collar and cuffs, the insignia of a charge-hand.

Every evening along the route, the 'boats came to rest and similar scenes were re-enacted. As the engines were closed down, the propellers were inched around on the starter motor so as to stand one blade vertical.

This left space beneath for the launch to pass. To prevent rain from entering the vertical exhaust stacks, and draining down towards the lower cylinders, bungs were available to place in the exhausts. Also, it was practice to ensure the inlet and exhaust valves on those lower cylinders were closed. This was achieved by marking one blade of the propeller and ensuring that it was the one parked vertically. Equally harmful was the accumulation of engine oil in the lower cylinders. This was prevented by the removal of those lower sparking plugs, thus allowing the oil to drain.

Daily servicing was done with the 'boat moored, victim to the swell. A dropped spanner was a lost spanner and lines with cork floats were attached to the tools. In clearer waters, the mechanics could 'fish' for dropped tools using a battery-powered electro-magnet. To attend to the prop and the front of the engine, it was possible to sit astride the propeller, having climbed onto it from the nacelle, but one had to apply one's weight against the compression rather than with it or else the blade would rotate and deposit the unfortunate into the water. Thus moored, the magnetos were checked, the coarse oil-sump filters cleaned and the valve clearances adjusted. The exhaust collector rings were another source of minor irritation and small holes would be welded closed.

In the hangar at Hythe. Jack Cruddace, engine fitter, is repairing the air-intake flange. The intakes were often damaged by poorly fitted bottom cowlings. The exhaust collector ring is propped behind the suspended propeller. The leading-edge working platform/access hatch has been opened. (Peek)

Following an engine change, a short ten-minute air test was usually flown, but if time was pressing, a ground run could suffice. The engines were normally started by use of an electric starter motor, powered from internal or external batteries. On the starboard side of the hull, adjacent to the single-point refuelling connection, was a socket for external power. The external batteries were carried by tender and it was not unknown for flying-boats to commence taxiing with the tender still attached by way of the battery cable.

The engines had a magneto ignition system, and additional high-tension, or booster, coils were fitted to provide a spark for starting. Should the starter motor fail, or the battery be down, it was possible to insert a

A dropped spanner was a lost spanner. In murky waters the tools were fitted with lines attached to floats. In clearer waters they could be fished from the bottom using an electro-magnet. Alternatively one of 'the local boys' could be encouraged to dive for the tool. Here, in Auckland, Jim Slater (at rear), seaman i/c ropes and marine gear, steadies the dinghy whilst launch-hand Cyril Hendren 'fishes'. The electro-magnet had been made by S. J. Bradshaw. (Peek)

Perseus sleeve-valve engines were fitted to the S.30 'boats. A working platform has been suspended from the leading edge access and the cowling removed. (Peek)

The cowling has been removed and the leading-edge work platform has been lowered. The engine starting handle is visible. The collar aft of the cylinder heads is the mount for the cooling gills. (Turnill)

hand-crank into the nacelle and start the engines by hand. However, to do this it was necessary to lower the pull-down, leading-edge maintenance platforms. These platforms, when open, operated a micro-switch which, for safety during routine maintenance, disabled the booster coils. Thus if the engine was to be started whilst the maintenance platforms were down, someone had to lean into the recess and depress the micro-switch. If the booster coils gave trouble, a hand-wound magneto could be attached to the high-tension circuit.

There were those mechanics who had the knack of rotating the engine to just that point before top dead centre (where the plug would fire), priming the engine with directly injected fuel and then turning on the ignition. The explosive mixture in the primed cylinder would fire and the engine would catch.

Working conditions were harsh, and after the comforts of Croydon, the waters of Hythe or some 'fly-blown' overseas staging post were often seen as a punishment posting.

The inspector (in white) checks on Dick Freemantle fitting the propeller. Engine fitter Archie Pitt stands above the nacelle, and a visitor from Imperial Airways is learning the ropes before his posting to Africa. The cooling gills are open and the fish-tail exhaust is visible. (Peek)

CHAPTER FIVE

Alternative Developments

DEVELOPMENTS ELSEWHERE
Italy – France – Germany – America and Pan Am.

Elsewhere, the aircraft industries of Italy, France, Germany and America were developing aircraft with trans-oceanic capability. The collective achievements of these nations placed flying-boats and float-planes in the forefront of airliner development. It seemed many of the problems confronting the development of large land planes could be circumvented if flying-boats were employed as an alternative. The runways of increased length and strength required for future heavier aircraft could be done away with, as unlimited take-off distance was available to seaplanes. Moreover, seadromes were not surrounded by obstacles and, should engine failure occur, the 'boat could alight on water, or in the case of the Martin M-130, on grass – the hull being especially strengthened. An additional saving could be achieved by not carrying a heavy, non-revenue-earning, undercarriage. However, other problems did exist: it was difficult for passengers to board in poor weather and, although limited night alighting facilities were available, night operations were never popular with the aircrews.

Great hope had been vested in the airship, but after the disasters in Great Britain and America, Germany alone continued development. Following the May 1937 *Hindenburg* disaster, commercial airship operation ceased, despite the *Graf Zeppelin* remaining airworthy.

Amongst the noteworthy flying-boats which preceded the Empires were those built by the Italians. From somewhere, the Caproni organization received the inspiration and funding to build the first 100-seat, transatlantic airliner. The Caproni Ca 60 was a nine-winged, eight 400 hp Liberty-engined, 24¹/₂-ton monstrosity. Although apparently owing its lineage to the successful Ca 4 series of tri-motor bombers and passenger liners, the Ca 60 looked like a houseboat with three sets of triplane wings. Five of the engines, two pairs in tandem and a single tractor, were mounted upon the forward wings, and upon the rear wings were two tractor and one pusher engine. Taxiing trials commenced on 21 February 1921. Surprisingly, on 2 March 1921, this contraption flew. Predictably, on 4 March 1921, it crashed. On this second flight, it entered an uncontrollable descent and struck the water. The design was inherently lacking in effective pitch control, the only 'elevators' being small surfaces mounted between the hull and the floats, below the centre set of triplanes. Mounted amidships, they had no moment arm about which to operate. The Ca 60 was an uncontrollable, aerodynamic disaster. Although salvaged, it caught fire during repairs and was lost. The wing floats and bow of this leviathan are preserved in the Museo Caproni, Milan.

A greater success was the Savoia-Marchetti SM 55 designed by the Italian engineer Alessandro Marchetti. He joined the Savoia Company and built the twin-hulled SM 55 torpedo-bomber which was later developed into a ten-seater airliner. SM 55s served in the Mediterranean until 1937. Italy's greatest pre-war flying-boat feat was achieved by General Italo Balbo (Regia Aeronautica). In 1931 and 1933, he led large formations of flying-boats on transatlantic flights from Rome to South and North America. Such was the impact of these flights that the word 'Balbo' is now synonymous with large formations of aircraft. These flights were of great political importance for the emergent *Duce*, Benito Mussolini. The successful SM 55 was further developed into the trimotor SM 66 which was to continue in service until 1943.

The French were far from idle and they developed routes through North Africa and across the South Atlantic between Dakar and Natal (Brazil). As early as 1930, they achieved the first commercial crossing of the South Atlantic, using a Latécoère 28, singled-engined float-plane. Although a schedule, as such, was not established until 1934, by the end of that year eight crossings had been made. For several years Latécoère '300'-series 'boats crossed the South Atlantic. However, the *Croix du Sud* was lost with all hands on 7 December 1936, and two further 'boats were also lost. Despite their untimely ends, they had done much useful work.

Latécoère next constructed the Laté 521, a giant, powered by six Hispano-Suiza 860 hp V-12 engines. She was designed to seat 70 passengers for the trans-Mediterranean haul or 30 on the longer trans-South Atlantic routes and first flew on 17 January 1935. The 521 was registered F-NORD and christened *Paris Lieutenant de Vaisseau*. She departed Biscarosse for New York, via the South Atlantic, on 8 December 1935. In early January she had reached Pensacola (Florida) but sank at her mooring during a hurricane. Salvaged, and

The Laté 522, christened Ville de Saint Pierre, made her first flight in April 1939 and departed Biscarosse on 16 June to cross the Atlantic. During her subsequent July/August crossing she moored adjacent to Caribou in Newfoundland. (Lawford)

shipped to France, she flew again in June 1937 and made another experimental transatlantic flight in September. The following year, on 23 August, the Laté 521 again departed Biscarosse for New York via Lisbon and the Azores. Another successful experimental crossing was flown in May 1939, and her final return crossing was non-stop, New York to Biscarosse, in the summer of 1939.

The more refined Laté 522 made its first flight on 20 April 1939. Christened *Ville de Saint Pierre* and registered F-ARAP, she was similar to the 523 which was a military development of the 521. *Ville de Saint Pierre* left Biscarosse on June 16 to cross the Atlantic. A second crossing, returning via the northern route, was made during July and August. She stayed for a few days at Newfoundland and moored adjacent to *Caribou*, which was opening the in-flight-refuelled, transatlantic, air-mail route. During the war, the civil 521 and 522 joined the military 523, flying for French and German forces. By late 1944 they had all been lost.

German efforts may have lacked practicality but they did provide spectacle. A most remarkable aircraft was the Dornier Do X, 12-engined, 130-foot-long, three-decked flying-boat. On one test flight she carried 169 people: crew, passengers and nine stowaways. Regretfully she was terribly underpowered and rarely managed to climb much above 1,500 feet. Much of her flying was done within surface effect. (When an aircraft

flies very low, about fifty feet, it tends to ride on a bubble of high-pressure air, thus allowing it to lift a greater weight than could be taken to more acceptable heights.) During 1931 and the early part of 1932, the Do X flew the Atlantic to South America, continued to New York and returned to Germany: a not uneventful journey that involved fires, modifications and disappointing performance, hence the 17 months required for the round trip. After returning to Europe in 1932, she flew little and, along with the Berlin museum in which she was housed, was destroyed during the war. Two further Do Xs were built for Italy. They were fitted with Fiat engines but proved unsuccessful in both civil and military guise.

In the early 1930s, the German transatlantic liners *Bremen* and *Europa* were fitted with catapults to handle single-engined, mail-carrying float-planes. These were launched when the liners had about 600 miles to run to New York, Bordeaux or Southampton, so that the post arrived ashore one day ahead of the liner. More successful was the operation of Dornier flying-boats in conjunction with catapult ships in mid-South Atlantic. The Dornier Wal, a tandem-engined, high-wing monoplane 'boat, was catapulted from the *Westfalen*, a steamer chartered by Deutsche Lufthansa (DLH). On early experimental flights, the Wal flew from Bathurst, British Gambia, and alighted in mid-Atlantic next to *Westfalen*. Although fitted with radio direction-finding equipment, these flights must have been a feat of navigation. Once down, the Wal taxied to the rear of the steamer, from where a large bamboo and canvas apron, or *stausegel*, was trailed to calm the waters. The Wal taxied onto the comparatively smooth waters and was hoisted aboard, refuelled and then shot-off towards Pernambuco in Brazil. Experimental runs commenced in May 1933 and soon a weekly service was in operation. The operation was modified and the Wal and *Westfalen* steamed westwards for 36 hours before a launch at the South American mainland was made. In 1934, a second support ship, *Schwabenland*, was obtained. *Westfalen* kept station off Gambia and *Schwabenland* lay off the Brazilian coast, near Fernando de Noronha. By March 1935, night-flying cut the journey time between Berlin and Rio de Janeiro to three days. In all, 328 mail flights were made by this method.

In the autumn of 1936 the Dornier Do 18s, *Zephir* and *Aeolus*, were launched towards New York from *Schwabenland*, as she lay off the Azores. A series of four round trips was flown, the flights being of 20 to 25 hours' duration.

During 1937 and 1938, a further seven return flights between the Azores and New York were made, this time using the four-engined float-plane, Blohm und Voss Ha 139. The catapult boats *Schwabenland* and *Friesenland* were employed. Following the success of these flights, DLH announced plans for a regular trans-North Atlantic service the following year. Ultimately, a combined German / American operation was proposed, but DLH were prepared to operate a mail-only service alone. The Azores to New York service, with Ha 139s, would be fed by Do 18s, operating from Lisbon. As it was, these plans came to nought.

The potential for commercial development of any catapult-launch system was limited. An inherent weakness in the system was the $4^1/_2$ 'G' acceleration, inflicted upon passengers and mail alike. Moreover, once the German aircraft was aloft, much of the flight was carried out at ultra-low level, within surface-effect. None of this was conducive to passenger ease.

However, DLH had already identified these weaknesses and were preparing to replace their catapult-launched seaplanes on the South Atlantic crossing with four-engined land planes. They were carrying out some successful trial flights with land planes but lacked permission to land in the USA. In mid-August 1938, the Focke-Wolf FW 200 Condor V1, for propaganda purposes re-designated S1, reregistered D-ACON and renamed *Brandenburg*, left Berlin for New York. She arrived after a 25-hour, non-stop flight. The return to Tempelhof took only 20 hours and a leaflet drop was used to summon the Berlin public to turn out in their dutiful, welcoming masses.

It had originally been intended to fly around the world but propaganda value had been stolen by Howard Hughes and his recent record-breaking flight. As a consolation, *Flugkapitäne* Henke and von Moreau did become the first pilots of a four-engined land plane to cross the Atlantic. The only modification to the Condor was the installation of additional petrol tanks.

The American flying-boat story is enshrined in the success of Pan American Airways (Pan Am) and its founder, Juan Trippe. In 1927, Trippe won a contract to fly mail from Florida to Cuba, then in American hands. Trippe leased from Sikorsky one of their S.36 twin-engined, biplane flying-boats. Trippe and Sikorsky formed a bond that served the Caribbean, the Atlantic and the Pacific until the Second World War. In August 1930, Trippe bought out the rival New York, Rio and Buenos Aires Line Inc. and acquired a fleet of Consolidated Commodore flying-boats. He now had 97 aircraft and was serving routes down to Argentina. The Sikorsky S.40 was added to the fleet, the first being christened by President Hoover's wife on 12 October 1930, the name chosen, *American Clipper*. The word clipper was long associated with all flying-boats and then lived on as the collective callsign for Pan Am's airliners.

After the Caribbean and South America, thought was given to developing a route to China, by way of the Pacific islands. A 'boat with a 2,500-mile range was required, as was a string of refuelling, accommodation, engineering and meteorology facilities across the Pacific. Sikorsky tendered the S.42 and Martin the M-130. The construction of three of each went ahead. Routes were surveyed, facilities built and the S.42 made its maiden flight in March 1932. Although the four-engined high-wing monoplane never met the range specification, it entered service on the shorter San Francisco to Hawaii leg in April 1935. The Martin 'boat was delivered in October 1935 and served on the longer legs. Trippe ordered ten S.42s but only three Martins, christened *China Clipper, Philippine Clipper* and *Hawaii Clipper*. The type became better known as the *China Clipper*. The aircraft had a range of 3,200 miles and was well suited to Pacific operations. But for the Pan Am/Imperial Airways 'Gentlemen's Agreement', the Martin M-130 might well have appeared on the Atlantic. Trans-Pacific schedules were flown by the Clippers from November 1935 until December 1941, America's entry into the Second World War.

The account of the Atlantic challenge is elsewhere (Chapter 7) but in summer 1939, Pan Am commenced an Atlantic service with Boeing's entry into the intercontinental market, the four-engined Boeing Model 314 flying-boat. The 314 had a range of 3,500 miles and could carry 77 passengers. Six aircraft were ordered, of which the first replaced the lost Martin M-130 *Hawaii Clipper* and the second, *Yankee Clipper*, entered service on the Atlantic.

MAIA AND MERCURY, 'THE PICK-A-BACK 'PLANE'
Early flights – The Atlantic – South Africa – The war and the end of composite.

The story of the Empire Flying-Boats cannot be told without reference to the Short–Mayo composite, *Maia* and *Mercury*. Major Mayo, a shy and mild-mannered man, was Imperial Airways' Technical General Manager. In the struggle to increase the useful range of

The composite. Mercury *being craned upon* Maia *at Rochester, 1 November 1937. (Short Bros BBC H.1056(4), via R. T. Jackson)*

aircraft, Mayo broached the subject of composites in a memo dated 1932. Therein, he laid out the idea of using a large, lightly laden aircraft to lift a smaller, overladen aircraft to a height, from which it would be released for onward flight. The design of the smaller aircraft would be optimized for long range. Crossing the Atlantic was the goal. At the time, the composite was competing with catapult launch and in-flight refuelling as methods of achieving a transatlantic capability.

The composite design, being more practical than catapult launching and further advanced than in-flight refuelling, found favour with Imperial Airways and the Air Ministry. Imperial specified a seaplane layout for the long-range upper component, so the Azores and Bermuda, which lacked suitable airfields, could be used as staging posts. A contract, based upon Specification 13/33, was placed with Short Bros and funded by the Treasury and Imperial Airways. The upper component was designated S.20 and the lower S.21. Construction of the two craft took place at Rochester, during 1936 and 1937. Originally, it was envisaged that the composites would supplement the in-flight-refuelled S.30s on the North Atlantic service, which was to commence in 1938. As it was, the composite became available before the S.30s as difficulties with the in-flight refuelling system were being experienced.

The apparent layout of the bottom, or carrier, component, *Maia*, was similar to that of the 'C-class'. However, her designed preceded the S.23 and there were several differences. Most noticeable was the tumblehome sides which gave *Maia* a wider beam and greater lateral stability, so necessary with a high centre of gravity as a result of bearing *Mercury*, the upper component. The Pegasus engines were installed further outboard, thus avoiding the float structure of *Mercury*. One factor of the concept was that the control surfaces of the upper component were locked until release; hence the control surfaces of *Maia* were larger than those of the S.23. Also, the tail was upswept, positioning the tailplane and rudder in a compromise position for control of the 'mated pair' biplane and the solo *Maia*. To lift this load, the wing area was a little greater than that of the S.23.

The upper component, *Mercury*, was a twin-float, all-metal monoplane, powered by four Napier Rapier air-cooled H-engines of 340 hp. She carried a crew of two, pilot and radio operator. The 1,000 lb payload of mail was carried part in the fuselage and part in the floats. Twelve hundred gallons of fuel, carried in a span-wise, cylindrical fuel tank, gave *Mercury* a still-air range of 3,800 miles.

Maia, G-ADHK – c/n S.797, was first flown on 27

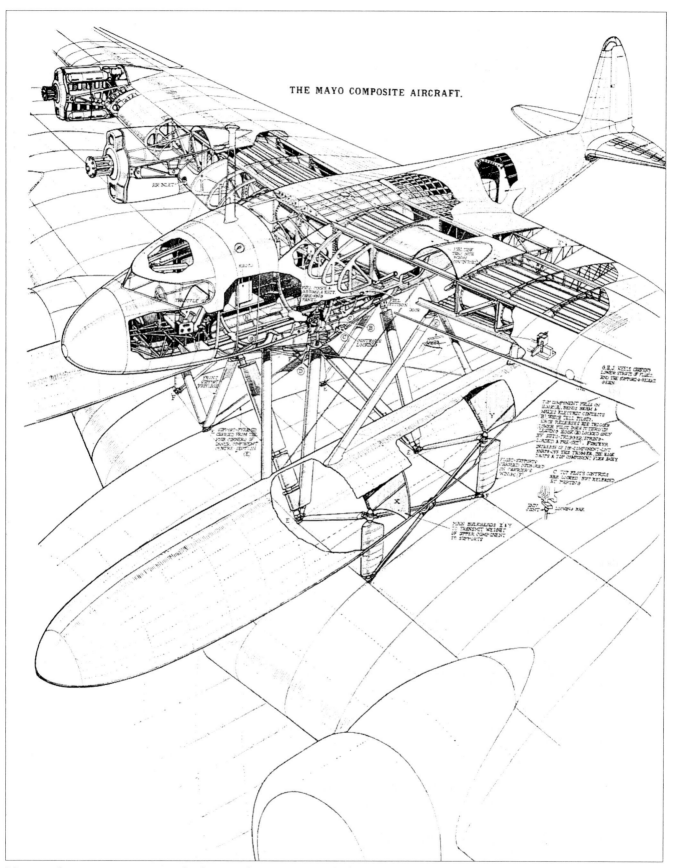

THE MAYO COMPOSITE AIRCRAFT.

Mercury, *the upper component, was fixed on top of* Maia, *a purpose-built carrier evolved from the S.23. The aim of this device was to get* Mercury *airborne and then to release the float-plane to continue on its way.* (The Aeroplane)

July 1937, with Lankester Parker at the helm. For the first flight, *Maia* was fitted with four-bladed, fixed-pitch, wooden propellers and was devoid of the composite mounting gantry. By mid-August, three-bladed propellers and the gantry had been fitted. *Mercury*, G-ADHJ – c/n S.796, was launched the following month, on the 25th, and first flew, again under the hand of Lankester Parker, on 5 September 1937. The first 'official' flight of *Mercury* was the following day. In a mere 19 seconds, Lankester Parker was airborne. The landing was a little less assuring. *Mercury* possessed such clean lines and, not being fitted with flaps, she 'floated' above the surface for a full half-mile before finally touching down.

After an extended period of 'solo' flying by Parker in *Maia* and his assistant, New Zealander Harold Piper, in *Mercury*, the pair were mated on 13 October 1937. On a frosty New Year's Day, Lankester Parker took the composite onto the Medway. Harold Piper sat at the locked controls of *Mercury*. A third member of crew, Bill Hambrook, stood on top of *Maia* and, despite the icy slipstream, observed the release mechanism under aerodynamic load. Powered solely by *Maia*'s engines, first tests found the craft handled satisfactorily on the water. Frustratingly, further tests were delayed as winter gales ravaged southern England. The composite rode them out safely. On the 19 January 1938, the pair started high-speed runs and on one they briefly became airborne.

Yet again, a first flight had been completed without fuss, but this was very much in character with John Lankester Parker. The 'official' first flight of the composite pair occurred on 20 January. They were cheered into the air by several hundred onlookers standing upon the banks of the Medway. Lankester Parker had intended to carry out only further taxi tests. The weather was perfect, the previous day's hop had given Parker confidence and, as all was going so well, after a run of only 500 yards, he eased the pair off the water. Lankester Parker and Piper climbed to 1,000 feet, circled Rochester for ten minutes and then landed.

Once ashore the pilots were congratulated by Mayo, and Lankester Parker was quoted as having said, 'Everything went satisfactorily, there was no intention on this flight to attempt separation.'

There was some concern in uninformed circles that the design would fail in actual trials. Major Mayo's patented separation system was ingenious. Quite simply, *Mercury* rested upon six spigots on *Maia*'s back and was connected firmly by three latches, one of which was under the control of each pilot and the third released automatically. As the pair became airborne, the majority of the lift came from *Maia*, but as they accelerated to cruising speed, *Maia*'s lift reduced whereas *Mercury*'s lift increased. Thus at height, rather than *Maia* lifting up *Mercury*, *Mercury* was holding up *Maia*. When all was ready for separation, both pilots pulled their respective releases but the aircraft would remain joined. As the pair accelerated further, the lift differential would increase towards a predetermined load (5,000 lb). At this point the third release would operate and, so the theory said, *Mercury* with the excess of lift would rise and *Maia*,

generating insufficient lift to support herself, would descend. Thus safe separation would be achieved.

During take-off, all eight engines would be at full throttle but, because of the excess power available, *Mercury*'s engines would be only lightly loaded. As *Mercury*'s propellers were fixed in pitch to suit economical cruising, under her own power her take-off performance was not outstanding. A solo take-off was all the more difficult as *Mercury*'s wing gave its best lift at the higher speeds. Once the 'Siamesed' pair was airborne, the composite would be climbed to 4–5,000 feet, the proposed separation altitude. The elevator position of both aircraft was indicated to the pilots by a system of lights, and other indicators showed whether or not *Mercury* was lifting evenly. Apart from radio, the two pilots could speak to each other by telephone link. This link did cause a few problems and may have delayed the flight trials. Following mutual agreement, both pilots would operate their respective releases and wait as the craft accelerated further, increasing the lift differential. Eventually, at 140 mph to 150 mph, with the aircraft straining to be separated, the automatic, lift differential release would trigger and the aircraft spring apart. As they sprang apart the controls of the upper aircraft automatically unlocked and *Mercury*'s pilot took control. Should they not separate, each pilot could 'rebolt' the two aircraft back together and the rigid structure could alight as one.

The first separation was made on 6 February 1938. When the composite took-off, separation had not been planned. Lankester Parker had reservations about the possible imbalance of trim between the aircraft, it having been incorrectly set on an earlier test. Once aloft, Piper, in *Mercury*, was able to 'feel' the fore and aft control within the limits of the mountings. Apart from the amount of lift being sensed by the latching device, fore and aft trim was also indicated. The pitch up or down following release had to be within tight limits to ensure clean separation. As soon as they became airborne, the indicator lights, showing trim was within the three degree limit, glowed reassuringly. Lankester Parker mentioned this to Piper, 'What about it?'

Piper replied in agreement and they climbed in search of smooth air, which was first found at 700 feet. However, Lankester Parker continued up to 900 feet but found only rougher air and decided to slip back down to 700 feet. Afterwards Lankester Parker said, 'I thought it better to lose my parachute chance than to take another sort of risk in bumpy conditions.'

Lankester Parker steadied the pair on a perfectly even keel and indicated to Piper that in *Maia* all was well. Piper, in *Mercury*, operated his release, followed by Lankester Parker. A moment later, the final restraint was overcome by the lift differential. As soon as the aircraft were apart, *Mercury* adopted a tail-down attitude whilst the nose of *Maia* fell. This ensured separation. Although safely apart, there were a few moments of mutual concern as neither pilot could see the other aircraft. Lankester Parker first saw *Mercury* some 50 yards ahead of him and 20 feet above. Whether this longitudinal displacement was a factor of the lift differential, or due to Parker throttling back and easing *Maia* down, is debatable. The problem of trim was quintessential to the success of this trial.

After only seven minutes of flight *Maia*, or the 'porter aircraft' as contemporary sources referred to her, was back on the water, her work being done. Lankester Parker later said, 'The indicator lights were indispensable, I would never have dared pull the plug without them.'

The principle had been proved to work in practice and aerodynamic forces had sprung the final latch. *Mercury* stayed aloft for 40 minutes, in order to burn the fuel down to a lower weight for alighting. Lankester Parker and Harold Piper were satisfied with the separation and were prepared to repeat the operation.

The second separation occurred on the afternoon of Wednesday 23 February, at 800 feet over the Medway. Amidst the host of reporters were the official guests of Mayo, senior officials of the Air Ministry and Mr H. Scott-Paine, a director of Imperial Airways. *Corinna*, flown by Captain Powell, was made available for those members of the press who wished 'to take to the air'. Perhaps slightly staged, the Shorts workmen were summoned at the run by the factory hooter, so that they could cheer the 'planes apart. Imperial's Captain Wilcockson accompanied Parker in *Maia* and Harold Piper was in *Mercury*. A Very fired from *Maia* was the signal for Powell to bring *Corinna* alongside to allow photographers a view of the parting.

Separation was smooth and decisive. Piper operated his separation lever first, followed by Parker. The aerodynamic forces took over and the third catch was withdrawn. *Maia* fell clear, as *Mercury*, gently but positively, climbed away. Immediately following separation, the pilots were able to see each other. Within a few minutes, *Maia* was back at her mooring. Lightly loaded *Mercury* cruised around for about half-an-hour, showing a fine turn of speed to the residents of Rochester. After the flight, Lankester Parker said, with a smile, 'I think the chief thing we discovered, was it weren't a fluke the first time.'

On 17 March 1938, Parker and Piper flew the two aircraft separately to the Marine Aircraft Experimental Establishment (MAEE), Felixstowe, for trials that would precede the award of a CofA. The possibility of a long-range trial-flight was aired and speculation abounded that eventually the composite would become an integral part of the Empire Airmail Service. Captain Wilcockson, who had earlier crossed the Atlantic in *Caledonia*, was expected to be one of the Mercury pilots for future transatlantic flights. The project's shortfall was the lack of launch aircraft on the western side of the Atlantic, and *Mercury's* configuration for cruising (wooden propellers of a relatively coarse fixed pitch, no flaps and engines producing a total of only 1,380 hp). *Mercury* was hardly suited to making her own way across the Atlantic but it was hoped that the prevailing westerly winds would assist.

On 9 May, maximum weight separation was achieved successfully by Lankester Parker and Piper. On the following day, Squadron Leaders L. Martin and M. C.

Fred Ellen, an engine fitter from Canada, stands amongst the cable-controlled release gear on Maia. *In the foreground are the supports for* Mercury's *floats. (Peek)*

Collins, in *Maia*, and Squadron Leader K. F. T. Pickles, in *Mercury*, repeated the procedure. The separations were achieved smoothly from launch heights of below 3,000 feet. *Mercury* was loaded with 1,180 gallons of petrol and weighed 20,800 lb; this gave her a wing-loading of 34 lb per sq ft. *Maia*, at her normal operating weight, had a wing-loading of 16 lb per sq ft. The wing-loading of the composite was 29 lb per sq ft. On both occasions, in almost still air, take-off was achieved in seventeen or eighteen seconds. At separation, *Mercury* carried sufficient fuel for twenty hours of flight, enough to reach New York in still air. Once separated, the opportunity was taken to demonstrate the fuel-jettison system. The span-wise fuel tank was fitted with a fuel-jettison pipe, which led down one of the float legs to the rear of the float. The system was so arranged that 900 gallons of the fuel-load could be dumped in fifteen minutes. Before fuel dumping, *Mercury* climbed to 12,000 feet and flew for several hours. Mayo and Wilcockson returned to Felixstowe for the last complete day of testing and on 19 May the composite was handed to Imperial Airways.

As early as 8 February 1938, the possibility of *Mercury* making a transatlantic flight that coming summer was announced. Confirmation came from Imperial, when they took delivery of the composite. They also announced that a round-Britain trial would be flown, and also before the Atlantic crossing, new engines would be fitted. The possibility of a non-stop trial flight to Alexandria was mooted but the lack of a porter boat, for the return journey, would force *Mercury* to hop back in easy stages.

Mr and Mrs Bennett look on as Mercury *is prepared for one of her record-breaking flights.* (Munro)

MAEE tests showed that the aircraft was down on range. This was odd, as the aircraft had returned speeds 20 mph higher than forecast. However, the results were in error, as the MAEE were not familiar with the Exactor hydraulic engine-control system and had flown the fuel-consumption tests in rich mixture! It was a CofA requirement for civil aircraft to have inter-connected throttles and mixture controls, in order to automatically return the fuel mixture to rich when the throttles were closed. The design of *Mercury's* linkage was not ideal and it was difficult to 'lean off' the mixture. Later, con-trary to regulations, Captain D. C. T. Bennett (then assigned to *Mercury* and the North Atlantic Division) had the linkage disconnected.

On 28 May, Empire Day, and as part of the MAEE open day, *Maia* and *Mercury* returned to be amongst the varied selection of flying-boats on display.

The Germans, however, were making their mark in the seaplane record books, with their Dornier Do 18. In March, a crew already experienced at Atlantic crossing covered over 5,000 miles from Start Bay, Devon, where they had been catapulted aloft, to Caravellas, near Rio de Janeiro, South America. During the forty-three-hour flight, they never went above 4,000 feet and were often skimming within surface-effect, in order to break the

Italian record of 4,200 miles.

At the end of May, Imperial Airways announced Captains Wilcockson and D. C. T. Bennett were to be assigned to special duty on the Short-Mayo composite aircraft as part of the Imperial Airways Atlantic Division. Wilcockson was already Manager of the Atlantic Division, having crossed the Atlantic in the summer of 1937 in *Caledonia*. Don Munro, ground engi-neer, was posted to the Atlantic Division and attached to the composite that May. Despite doubts expressed by the Air Ministry, Imperial Airways and Bennett were confident that *Mercury* could fly the Atlantic.

CofAs were not issued to *Maia* and *Mercury* until 1 June and 7 July 1938 respectively. *Mercury's* had been delayed until the more powerful Napier Rapier V engines had been fitted.

A series of long-range test flights was flown. Before one, engineering staff toiled throughout the night, preparing the composite for flight. Over 1,000 gallons of fuel had been pumped aboard *Mercury*. The Sperry autopilot had been serviced, spilling a little hydraulic oil upon the aircraft. That night there was a heavy dew and the top of *Maia*, at the foot of the ladder up to *Mercury*, was slippery. Bennett arrived around dawn and was warned of the hazardous surface. The handling crew offered to help him with his maps, chronometers and sextant but he declined the offer, preferring to carry them himself. Clutching his wares he entered *Maia*, climbed out of the top hatch and walked towards the ladder up to *Mercury*. Below, Don Munro and others heard a thud and a splash. Looking out, they saw Captain Bennett surface, still clutching his maps and navigational instruments.

'Here, take these,' he said, clambering out of the water, 'My, that is slippery up there.' There was neither further word nor comment about the incident. He changed into a dry pair of overalls and flew the trial flight.

On 14 July, with Bennett in command, *Mercury* separated from *Maia* over Southampton and flew 2,040 miles, past Foynes and out into the Atlantic. Twelve hours later, Bennett returned *Mercury* to Southampton, having made wireless contact with Botwood and Foynes. All was set for the first commercial air crossing of the North Atlantic.

Early morning mist on 19 July delayed the departure of the two seaplanes from Southampton. *Mercury* was eventually airborne first and *Maia* followed one minute later. Shortly after noon, both machines alighted at Foynes. Departure for America, planned initially for the following day, was delayed until 21 July. At Foynes, *Mercury* was craned on top of *Maia*. Thereupon she was loaded with newspapers, mail and the latest newsreels, including that of the Royal visit to Paris. *Mercury* would follow the northern route to New York, via Botwood and Montreal.

As light lingered during the evening of 21 July 1938, the final engine runs were completed before the pair took-off. Following a crisp separation, Wilcockson slid *Maia* back onto the Shannon. *Mercury*, laden to approximately 20,650 lb, dropped down from the separation height of 2,000 feet to 200 feet, and once over the water to 50 feet. The weather was fair and the full penalty of the forecast headwinds could be avoided close to the surface.

Bennett considered *Mercury* to be one of the finest navigational platforms he had ever flown. Aided by an excellent autopilot, chart on knee and sextant safely lodged, Bennett navigated his way across the ocean below. His crewman was Radio Officer A. J. Coster (Faithful Coster – his regular radio officer). As darkness fell, they climbed to a safer 500 feet. Later, a turbulent warm front gave them heavy rain. Every hour, Coster passed position reports, and between reports he attempted to contact shipping. His midnight message reported them 560 miles out and climbing a little, as the wind stiffened. All was going well, as they followed the great-circle route. By three-quarter distance, they were able to climb to a more economical height, without the penalty of the earlier head winds. Now in skies unhampered by the front, Bennett was able to use his sextant. Their Newfoundland landfall was at Cape Baulewn on the Straits of Belle Isle. Thirteen and a half hours after separation, Bennett, Master Navigator, was dead on track. It was now daylight and they had sufficient fuel

to overfly Botwood direct for Montreal. At 12:20, Eastern Daylight Time, with only 80 gallons of fuel remaining, they alighted at Boucherville, Montreal. They had completed the quickest east–west crossing of the Atlantic to date, 2,930 miles in 20 hours 20 minutes.

Despite a tumultuous press reception, they off-loaded some of the newspapers and newsreels, refuelled and sped on. They alighted at Manhasset Bay, Port Washington, on New York's Long Island, two hours later, 16:08 Eastern Daylight Time 22 July. Bennett cleared customs, whilst attached to a buoy, and then taxied to a pier for mooring. The remaining papers and newsreels was rushed to New York by fast car. Bennett and Coster were exhausted. Only after the formalities had been completed with the port authorities, did Bennett acknowledge the waiting hordes of pressmen. As they stepped ashore, Bennett said they had had little or no sleep and the crossing had been rough in places but the rain and head winds had been light and the auto-pilot functioned well. However the newspapers they carried did not fare so well. By the end of the first hour of sales only one copy of *The Times* had been sold. But the following New York editions had full-page pictures of Bennett and *Mercury*.

Amongst the fellow guests at a dinner in their honour, were the crew of the German seaplane which had just flown in, having been catapult-launched from a point off the Azores. Bennett recalled that six months earlier, the Germans had gained the world record for long-range seaplane flights, at 5,000 miles. Bennett decided to better that.

The return flight, without the boost of *Maia*, was made in short hops, carrying no payload and only one-third of the normal fuel-load. They departed New York, staged through Boucherville, and stayed overnight at Botwood. Following an early start on 26 July, and 7 hours and 38 minutes of flight, *Mercury* touched down in the wide, unsheltered bay of Horta in the Azores. Fortunately, there was little swell. The following morning, they continued to Lisbon and made good time, for by noon they had covered more than one-third of the distance. Their Lisbon turnaround was brisk and by mid-afternoon they were airborne again. They were not expected back in England until the 28th but Bennett was anxious to return to his wife. At seven that evening a message was received in England, reporting that *Mercury* was 22 miles off the Casquets (Alderney) at low level and in heavy rain. *Mercury* touched down on Southampton Water at 20:12 BST. A crowd of two turned out to meet them. Composite theory was proved and, at a lecture in Cambridge on 8 August, Major Mayo revealed plans for a land plane composite, that would cruise at almost 300 mph.

Imperial hoped that by autumn they would be in receipt of a Government order for a fleet of composites to carry airmail across the Atlantic. The mail would be in the form of 'Airgraphs'. The airgraphs technique of microfilming letters had been perfected in 1935 by Charles Chase of Kodak, Imperial Airways and Pan Am. Initially it came to nought, as the Post Office declared the procedure a breach of privacy. However, the technique was employed, greatly expanded, during the 1939–45 war. The airgraphs scheme was finally disbanded in 1946, having made a large profit. The Air Ministry finally ruled against the composite. They argued that it would soon be outclassed by the competition, it was not sufficiently advanced, its usefulness was impaired as it did not carry passengers and production would affect other contracts being fulfilled by Short Bros.

In dismay, Imperial approached the Director of Civil Aviation, suggesting that the project would be viable if four Mercury-type aircraft were built and Ensigns were modified to carry them. They suggested a three-day service to Australia could be flown and, in the event of war, a high-speed long-range service would be available. All to no avail.

Bennett, supported by Mayo and Woods Humphery, sought personal approval for the long-distance record attempt from the Secretary of State for Air, Sir Kingsley Wood. Bennett wanted to fly from Southampton to Cape Town. However, notwithstanding the Royal Air Force's intention to capture the absolute distance record with an impending flight by Vickers Wellesleys from Ismailia to Darwin, it was decided *Mercury* too would make an attempt on the absolute distance record. To this end, it was decided to launch *Mercury* from the River Tay, Dundee. Approval for the flight was forthcoming and another transatlantic flight, planned for 17 August, was postponed.

The goal was feasible, especially as the recent transatlantic flight had shown the Napier Rapier engines to be more economical than first supposed. As to the aircraft's maximum permissible all-up weight, that was debatable. The CofA allowed the float-plane to be loaded to a weight of 14,200 lb as a separate aircraft, yet up to 20,800 lb when mated with *Maia*. Moreover, the aircraft had a large margin of in-built strength, to cater for any unforeseen over-weight landing. It was likely that *Mercury* could be modified to carry a payload greater than the certificated 10,000 lb, and a 7,000-mile flight seemed possible.

During the summer, *Mercury*'s fuel capacity was doubled. Short Bros installed additional tanks inside the floats and fitted electric pumps to feed fuel up to the main wing-tanks. In the event of electric pump failure, a small hand-pump was fitted.

To handle engineering matters in South Africa, Don Munro was despatched to Cape Town on 26 August. His journey was not without incident. *Cassiopeia*, commanded by Captain Loraine, lost an engine at Malakal. A spare was flown in by 'Paddy' Shepherd, and Munro assisted with the engine change, before continuing to Durban. At Durban, Munro reported to Garth Trace, Imperial Airways Manager South Africa. Munro next proceeded to Cape Town, where he contacted the Shell Manager, who would be able to assist.

With the aid of the harbour-master and the Shell manager, Munro checked the alighting area and the mooring in Table Bay. Although the area was satisfacto-

Don Munro at work on one of Mercury's *H-24 cylinder air-cooled Napier Rapier engine at Hythe.* (Munro)

ry, the mooring buoy was best suited to an ocean liner. Munro suggested a Shorts' buoy could be obtained from Durban but the Shell manager believed the Royal Navy had some float-plane buoys at Simonstown. The Navy agreed to lay a mooring the following day. Whilst at Simonstown, Munro noticed that HMS *Amphion* (later HMAS *Perth*) carried Napier-Rapier-powered Fairey Seafoxes. It was whilst lunching the following day, overlooking Table Bay, Munro was somewhat amazed to see HMS *Amphion* steam around the point and lay 'his' mooring. There now followed a five-week wait.

Before they departed Hythe, Bennett, and his engineer, Geoff Wells, carried out the pre-flight inspection. All appeared well, until Bennett saw fluid dripping from a wing; he sampled the fluid but only Wells could see one of the handling party relieving himself from the cockpit. A few days later, on 21 September 1938, *Mercury* and *Maia* touched down at Dundee, *Mercury* alighting at 14:00, closely followed by *Maia*. They were moored at the RAF Marine Craft Establishment. The following morning, one of the harbour cranes hoisted *Mercury* aboard *Maia*. A world record was not the avowed intention of the flight, according to Imperial. However, three records were vulnerable: the Russian-held all-aircraft long-distance record, the Italian-held seaplane long-distance record and the fastest time between London and Cape Town. Had departure been from Southampton, the distance to Cape Town would have been 390 miles less or only 74 miles greater than the existing Russian-held record, and as a record had to be exceeded by at least 100 kilometres (62 miles), a departure from Southampton would allow only a very small margin for error.

Departure was dogged. A minor fault in *Mercury* had already been rectified, when the forecast of the evening of the 22nd predicted head winds for the first 2,000 miles. Completion of the refuelling was not pressed and departure would have to await more favourable weather. In ideal conditions it was expected the flight could be completed in 40 hours, but 45 hours was a more realistic time. To add to their difficulties, the departure time had to be calculated to ensure a Cape Town arrival in daylight.

Whilst preparations were being made, Mayo confessed that an attempt was to be made on the world absolute distance record, and two sealed barographs for submission to the International Aeronautical Federation had been fitted. On 23 September, Wing Commander E. B. Baker, Commanding Officer of RAF Leuchars, was nominated as official observer of the start. *Maia* would be flown by Wilcockson with B. C. Frost as first officer, and Bennett would be accompanied by Ian Harvey, a qualified pilot and radio operator. The two-day flight would call for the services of two pilots.

The meteorological forecast remained disappointing. With the Munich Crisis brewing, preparation of *Mercury* continued. As the loathsome 'Peace for our time' (often misquoted as 'Peace in our time') echoed from the wireless, Bennett expressed his disgust at appeasement and the all-clear for the record attempt was given. Dismally, on 3 October, the winds were still not favourable, and despite a brief westerly gale, the wind backed to blow from the south, where it had lain for the last two weeks. Doubts were now being raised as to whether or not the flight would ever take place. There were added difficulties. The high state of the River Tay estuary made getting the launch alongside *Maia* hazardous, and attempts to relieve Jock Bell, the watchman, were abandoned. Many local workers were given the day off work to watch the take-off but, despite the fine post-storm weather, the sea state was unsuitable and a disappointed crowd was called upon to disperse by the police.

The weather worsened. Gales! Mayo, Wilcockson and Bennett watched anxiously the pitch, roll and buck of the composite. On the 4th, winds exceeded 60 mph and gusted to 80 mph. Such was the strength of the winds that *Mercury*'s propellers were turned but the gusts failed to displace her. The two aircraft were lashed, as well as locked, together but there was concern that a wing-tip float might be damaged or the two-inch mooring rope might snap. If the composite could have been moved to the more sheltered waters of the Perthshire bank of the Tay, it would have been, but they were all at the mercy of the winds. Another fear was that one of the RAF Sunderlands, moored upwind, might break free and drift into *Maia* and *Mercury*. Bennett availed himself of an RAF launch, inspected the composite moorings and threw rations to Jock Bell, marooned upon *Maia*. By now the majority of the watchmen, and their reliefs, were severely sea-sick and those in the launch were sorely drenched. Apart from the Sunderlands, small boats were a risk to *Maia*. One of the RAF dinghies broke free and started towards her. Bennett secured a line and took it in tow to the jetty. This was a wasted effort, for when the Tay ferry-boat came to dock, she overshot her mooring and crushed the dinghy against the jetty wall.

The gales diminished, the wind along the route became fair, and although the Tay remained choppy, it was decided to launch on Thursday 6 October. At a weight far in excess of anything tried before, *Maia* and *Mercury* became airborne for the twelfth separation. They powered their way up to 4,700 feet, a greater altitude to allow for the unexpected during this heavier-than-usual separation. Bennett took the feel of the controls within the leeway allowed on the locking spigots; all was well. With correct light indications glowing, Bennett unlocked *Mercury*. Wilcockson reported over the intercom that all was in order aboard *Maia* and he too was releasing. The pair sprang apart and Wilcockson eased *Maia* positively away from the laden *Mercury*. At 13:19 GMT, Wilcockson wished Bennett good luck, and watched him wheel over Angus, on the outskirts of Dundee, and set course for Cape Town. As *Mercury* struggled aloft, every horsepower pulled a 20 lb load and every square foot of wing supported a 45 lb weight. Never before had such a low-powered, high-wing-loaded aircraft become airborne. *Mercury* was one-third heavier than she had been for the transatlantic flight. Five minutes later, she was seen over the Tay, climbing slowly away on her southerly course.

Albeit unknown at the time, due to the higher than normal speed required for the separation, part of a streamlined engine cowling had detached. Once the additional drag had been discovered, Bennett calculated their range would be reduced by a few per cent. They had few options: they could land and fit a new cowl, but landing could not be attempted for at least 12 hours if all possible fuel was jettisoned, or 24 hours if it was burnt off; moreover, there were those who would probably never authorize a second attempt on this record. Bennett decided to proceed and see what happened. The drag-eroded climb performance caused them to run into icing conditions that they had hoped to fly above. Valuable height was lost as they descended into warmer air at 3,000 feet over Hatfield. Once over the coast, and clear of the icing, they climbed again to 5,000 feet. Avoiding the ice had cost them fuel but they were compensated by a westerly beam-wind that made good their ground speed.

The flight over France was uneventful but as they crossed the Mediterranean, and Africa loomed into view, the wind backed to oppose them. The peaks of the Atlas Mountains were barely cleared. At 23:30, Thursday, their position was North 34 degrees 20 minutes East 006 degrees 20 minutes, altitude 10,000 feet. They were slightly north of Chott (Lake) Melrhir, having crossed Algeria a little after 10 hours and 1,635 miles of flight. At the end of the first 12 hours, fuel and position checks gave Bennett reassurance, but by 03:00 their ground speed was less than 130 mph. Prospects brightened as the sun rose to port for the first time on this arduous flight. The sun beat down relentlessly upon the Sahara Desert below but by midday Friday the average ground speed was back up to 146 mph. Bennett found the float-plane easier to fly as the weight decreased and the aircraft entered the realms of known performance. Bennett estimated that they could remain in the air for 47 hours; there was every chance that they would achieve the seaplane record but the absolute distance record was beginning to appear a little less certain.

There was, however, a minor problem. They had discovered that first evening that the electric fuel pump in the floats had failed. The small hand-pump was hardly suitable for other than emergencies. Despite every effort of Harvey to rectify the fault, they were faced with the mammoth task of hand-pumping 1,400 gallons of fuel up the 10–12 feet from the float to the wing-tanks. Although Bennett managed to get a visual fix from the railway at Kano, the fuel problem was his main concern. Hand-pumping would have to be done at 13,000 feet or so, without oxygen. In addition to navigation, the routine radio reports had to be sent as these were used as the basis of the newspaper reports that tracked Bennett's progress southwards. A message from Lagos was received in London on the Friday night and gave Bennett's and Harvey's position at 15:32 as just past the Equator at Makokou – French Equatorial Africa. They had by now covered 4,000 miles. Throughout the flight, Imperial Airways' signals staff, Harry Pusey included, remained on duty tracking the flight by way of the position reports.

Ahead, in the Hotel Metropole, Cape Town, Don Munro had received a telegram during the evening of the 6th:

'MERCURY LEFT DUNDEE 1325 GMT TODAY STOP TRACE UNABLE TO ATTEND ARRIVAL CAPETOWN STOP'

Throughout the 7th, rumour was rife and there were many reports of sightings. Later that evening there was a report of *Mercury* being within 1,000 miles. Although slightly wary of this report, Don erred on the side of safety and arranged for the Navy to lay a flare-path.

On board *Mercury*, the second dusk fell rapidly. The thunderstorms, heavy turbulence and torrential rain of the late afternoon were replaced by darkness. Harvey soon became exhausted and he rested by taking a spell at the controls, whilst Bennett went aft to take over the pumping. Regular fuel checks revealed they had pumped insufficient fuel into the wing-tanks to remain airborne through the night. The thought of a night forced-landing did not appeal to Bennett. However, by pumping at every free moment, it would just be possible to stave off the inevitable fuel starvation. Harvey became more and more exhausted and was even unable to rest at the controls. He became victim of hallucinations and for a while was convinced there was a third person on the aircraft. Thanks to Bennett's determination and trust in the excellent autopilot, he was able to pump the fuel himself. Their second dawn saw them still airborne. Bennett calculated that although they had broken the seaplane record, the goal of Cape Town and the absolute distance record had eluded them. Harvey signalled, 'May be unable to reach Cape Town. Bennett.' Munro received this message after daybreak.

Bennett had decided to press on as far as possible before alighting at a suitable site, but seaplane bases were sparse in South West Africa in 1938. Stretching their luck to the limit, they reached South Africa and touched down at Alexander Bay on the Orange River. It was 09:25 Saturday. At the end of 42 hours and 26 minutes, a track distance of 6,045 miles, later ratified as a straight-line distance of 5,995.5 miles, had been flown. This seaplane record still stands.

They were 325 miles short of Cape Town. *Mercury* touched down within the security area of a diamond mine. Apart from stirring a cloud of flamingoes, they roused the mine's guard force. Bennett and Harvey were soon surrounded by a band of wild-looking men in small boats. The guards knew of the record attempt and were delighted that it should have ended there.

News of the alighting reached Munro, and mindful of the lack of compressed air for engine-starting and the other difficulties *Mercury* might experience, Don set off to Alexander Bay in the Shell aircraft, taking a couple of air cylinders.

Bennett, never to be thwarted, received 200 gallons of fuel and assistance from the guards. Although the normal starting procedure was to use bottled compressed air to start number three engine and then use the compressor on three to start the other engines, number three did have a hand crank facility. It was by cranking that Bennett was able to get *Mercury* under way. At 15:25, local time, *Mercury* threaded her way amongst uncharted sand banks and made a hazardous take-off. In his book, *Pathfinder*, Bennett comments upon an aeroplane carrying reporters appearing overhead. It was in fact Don Munro arriving. Munro landed and was met by the fearsome security guards. They were not particularly welcoming. Munro left for Cape Town.

Mercury arrived overhead Cape Town at 18:35 local time. Reports of their landing at Alexander Bay preceded them and flares had been lit on Table Mountain to guide them in. Although disappointed that they had not left from Southampton, the record was a proud achievement. Bennett said:

'We are very sorry to disappoint everyone. We had a little bit of everything on the way down: ice over Scotland, headwind in Algeria, thunderstorms over west Africa. The headwinds were mostly responsible for the fuel shrinking. Bad luck – but all in the game.'

It was ironic that probably less than another 100 gallons of fuel would have carried them on to Cape Town. The floats could have carried an additional 250 gallons but Major Mayo ordered them not to be filled for fear of marring the heavy-weight separation. Had they reached Cape Town, they would have held the absolute distance record, but only for a short while. In November, RAF Wellesleys flew over 7,000 miles non-stop, from Ismailia to Darwin.

Once Don Munro caught up with his charge, inspection revealed that part of the aluminium cowling from the starboard-inner engine was missing, as was a fuel-tank filler-cap fairing. With assistance from Shell, replacement parts were manufactured and a departure for Durban was planned for the morning of 11 October. On boarding, they found the two 'Nife' aircraft batteries

Mercury *at Durban, on her way home from her record-breaking, non-stop flight to South Africa.* (Stephen)

had discharged. Ian Harvey thought he had left the radio on overnight. Munro, highly improperly, borrowed a couple of 'lead acids' from the harbour-master's launch and managed to get *Mercury* started. Five and a half hours later Bennett, Harvey and Munro were in Durban.

The following day they commenced preparation for the return flight, which would be in easy stages. Working from two suspended servicing platforms, all the cowlings were removed and the 128 spark plugs were changed. It was whilst removing the Tecalemit oil filter, that mechanic John Duplesis dropped the filter cover into twenty feet or so of Durban harbour. One of the other mechanics, Mick Foster, repeatedly dived for it and the Section Engineer, Mr McMillan, called for a deep-sea diver. The cover was not found. Munro recalled *Amphion* and her Seafoxes. Imperial Airways, Durban, telegrammed Shell, Cape Town, and requested loan of a cover from the Royal Navy. The cover was delivered the following morning and the servicing was completed.

But now another difficulty appeared – repeated magneto drops on several of the engines. This drop in engine revolutions was caused by an inherent fault in the Rapier spark plugs. It was all too easy to over-tighten the plugs and cause them to short. Eventually, all the plugs were correctly set and they departed early the following morning. They had been airborne but ten minutes, when Bennett carried out an in-flight magneto check, only to find the port-outer and starboard-inner engines were down. He consulted Munro, and bearing

in mind the limited facilities at Beira, their intended night stop, they returned to Durban. More plug changing, more mag' drops. Finally, with darkness falling, Munro, McMillan and a Zulu seaman managed to get all four Rapiers running sweetly. It was only by observing whether or not flames were spouting from the exhaust stacks that Munro was able to discover which cylinders were firing. Midnight and the cowlings were all secured. Munro had his luggage with him so he settled down for the night on *Mercury,* as she bobbed upon the Congella Basin.

On 16 October, Bennett, Harvey and Munro reached Beira without further ado and the remainder of the return flight, which followed Imperial's route, was a leisurely affair. The outward flight to Cape Town had taken 42½ hours, the return flight from Durban took six days. *Mercury* was a two-seat aircraft and the only place for Don Munro to sit upon was the Elsan toilet.

They carried home a letter from the Mayor of Cape Town for the Lord Provost of Dundee which read:

'Your letter has been brought to me by Captain Bennett and his co-pilot First Officer Harvey. Their attempt on the non-stop record was a gallant failure which aroused in us all the most heart felt sympathy and we all unite in wishing them better luck next time.'

On arrival in Southampton on 20 October, they were greeted by the Mayor and Mayoress, Wilcockson and

Clive Adams, the Imperial Airways Station Superintendent at Southampton. Bennett said it was the most interesting trip he had ever made and it was nice to know that one was getting into an aircraft and was going to stay there for two days. It felt like a job of work and he was quite willing to do the flight again. He continued that naturally they were disappointed they did not get to Cape Town non-stop but he had the satisfaction of knowing that they had put up the world record long-range flight for seaplanes by a significant margin. Again, Bennett gave the wind as the reason for their failure, but from a technical point the flight was a total success. In the best British understated traditions of those times, Bennett, Harvey and Munro received no formal recognition from Napiers, Shorts, Imperial or the Government.

Mercury was returned to her more normal trim as a freight carrier. By the end of November she was tasked with the delivery of the 1938 Christmas mail. As the scheduled Empire 'Boats tended to drop more mail than they picked up, the first leg out of Southampton was a bottleneck. To circumvent this restriction, *Mercury* would assist by carrying mail to Egypt.

The first of these mail specials lifted out of Southampton shortly before 16:00 on 29 November. *Maia* was piloted by Wilcockson, with Frost as first officer and Major Mayo as observer. At 800 feet, another uneventful separation occurred. At 16:05, 1,000 gallons of petrol and more than a ton of mail set course into the night towards Alexandria, 14 hours away. On this occasion a crew of three was carried: Captain Bennett, Radio Officer Coster and Engineer Munro. Barely eight minutes elapsed between *Maia* getting airborne and her mooring. *Mercury*'s flight was the first non-stop commercial flight to Egypt and the first night flight along that route.

At about 22:00, they had crossed Marseilles outbound and the weather deteriorated. Their route took them towards Corsica and then south-eastward to Malta, passing a little to the west of Sicily. They were unable to climb above the weather, and at midnight, Coster reported their altitude as 9,000 feet. Inside the unheated aircraft, Coster and Munro were bitterly cold, but such discomforts did not bother Bennett. The weather improved and by 04:00 they were half-way across the Mediterranean. The weather had not hampered navigation, as several radio aids were available in the Mediterranean. Rome and Naples had provided radio bearings and the RAF at Malta and Alexandria had also provided weather reports.

As they neared their destination, the sun rose ahead of them. Don Bennett turned to Don Munro, who had come up front to observe the sunrise, and said: 'When war comes, accurate bombing of the targets in Germany will depend upon precise navigation. I have navigated this flight with this in mind and should we now release a bomb it would target Ras-el-Tin immediately ahead and below.' Bennett closed the throttles, banked to the left and descended through the unbroken cloud. As they emerged, the Imperial Airways flying-boat base at

Ras-el-Tin lay immediately below.

The return trip was made in stages, without payload, as there was no launch-aircraft at the eastern end of the route. The flight had taken 14 hours and 33 minutes, most of it by night, much of it on instruments and all of it in the intense cold of the unheated cockpit.

Separation was becoming routine, and on the fourteenth occasion, Major Mayo gave up his observation station in *Maia* in favour of the aeronautical correspondent of *The Times*. The second Christmas mail flight, on 12 December, was duly reported. *Maia* stayed aloft for almost an hour during the launch. Wilcockson's first officer was Joe Shakespeare and he operated the compressed air starters for *Mercury*'s engines, as they taxied to an area clear of shipping for take-off. They left a choppy Southampton Water and climbed 1,000 feet into the grey light of a stormy dawn. Flying down Southampton Water, in search of some clear, smooth air for separation, the lights showing that aerodynamic forces were pulling the composite apart soon illuminated. Bennett and Wilcockson discussed power settings and Wilcockson allowed Bennett to check *Mercury*'s trim.

'If you are ready, release your latch', said Wilcockson. Bennett replied that he had already released, and with Wilcockson's departing call, 'I am releasing mine', the two machines sprang apart. It was 07:50 and *Mercury* set course. Although 40 mph head winds were forecast until Sardinia and they estimated Alexandria at 01:00 GMT on the 13th, they made good time and arrived at 22:30 GMT on the 12th. On the afternoon of the 14th *Mercury* arrived back in Southampton, having left Alexandria the previous day.

Of interest was a libel case which Major Mayo brought against *The Sunday Referee*, one of the tabloids of the day, which wrote thus of the composite:

> *'Britain's £100,000 pick-a-back aeroplane, the* Mercury, *the upper machine, which took four years of inventive genius to develop and which only last Thursday made its successful debut at Rochester may be scrapped. It will never be allowed to carry any passengers. The machine embodies one of the most brilliant discoveries in aviation but in the opinion of many experts it is already out of date. It will only be used for occasional flights, an entirely new pair of pick-a-back airplanes will have to be built before the practical value of the principle can be judged. Major Mayo has prepared plans for another effort.'*

Mayo complained that reference to the project being scrapped implied that Shorts had wasted £100,000 in design costs on an aircraft which would be unsafe and unreliable for the purpose for which it was intended and that they were incompetent to conduct their business. This *The Sunday Referee* denied. Although Shorts' and Mayo's case was upheld it was judged that *The Sunday Referee* was not libellous.

The Sunday Referee did carry some truth. At the end of March 1939, the Director of Civil Aviation wrote to Shorts, stating that unless the segregation of mail from passengers became policy, there seemed little future for the composite. Such a policy change was not envisaged. The Director was, however, content that Imperial should make best use of the pair for commercial purposes. As it was, *Mercury* flew very little during the last year of peace, although she may have been used for de-icing equipment trials and spent some time in Folland's hangar at Hamble. *Maia* had ten seats fitted so she could operate as an unscheduled passenger-carrying craft or mobile workshop, when required by Imperial or Short Bros. Hugh Gordon recalls being flown to St Nazaire for one of his salvage missions in *Maia*. A row of seats had been installed upon the duck-boards and Hugh was given a hamper containing his in-flight meals.

Hangar space became a premium and *Mercury* was moored off Hythe. One day, early in the summer of 1939, it was noticed that *Mercury* had taken on a severe list. One wing was under water and the out-board engine was at risk of being doused. Fortunately the tide was out and only the grounding of the wing tip upon the muddy bottom prevented *Mercury* from turning turtle. Due to the interest and priority being afforded to the in-flight-refuelled *Cabot* and *Caribou*, *Mercury* had been neglected and regular inspections of the float bilges had been overlooked. Water, which had washed over the mail hatches in the floats, had seeped into the bilges. This had produced a slight list which was accentuated by fuel in the span-wise tank seeping past the anti-surge baffles. The 'upper' wing was weighted with sand-bags and *Mercury* was towed ashore, but not without comedy. Some sandbags slipped from the 'upper' wing, struck the bow of a dinghy below and catapulted the crew into the murky Southampton Water. *Mercury* was beached upon the slipway and de-fuelled. As the tide rose, she floated off on an even keel. The only repair called for was the replacement of the fabric on the sodden aileron.

Both aircraft had a brief service career, but that only delayed their ignominious ends. Very early in the war, just after Bennett had returned from America in *Cabot*, he was tasked to fly a covert mission in *Mercury*. Although ostensibly they were carrying out fuel-consumption trials, Bennett and Mitchell were ordered to search for German submarines which were believed to be in the coastal waters of Eire. This was the only occasion on which Mitchell flew as radio operator in *Mercury*. Finally, on 18 June 1940, Bennett delivered *Mercury* from Hythe to Felixstowe and the RAF further dispatched her to Pembroke Dock. Here she was operated in the reconnaissance training role by No. 320 Squadron, Royal Netherlands Air Force. They had a mix of Fokkers, in which they had escaped, Ansons and Hudsons. When 320 re-equipped with Hudsons, *Mercury* was returned to Felixstowe, in October 1940. In July 1941, instructions were received to return *Mercury* to Rochester; this was done on 9 August 1941, and on the 21st, wearing camouflage, she was scrapped.

Meanwhile, *Maia* had operated out of Poole as a training machine and passenger carrier on the shuttle to Foynes. In early 1941, she was overhauled, had her pylons removed and Pegasus XC engines fitted. However, her career ceased in the early hours of 11 May 1941. Whilst moored at Salterne Pier, she was destroyed in an air raid. A Heinkel He 111 was returning from an aborted raid on RAF Bicester and was seeking a target of opportunity before coasting out. Poole Harbour presented that target. Although the Heinkel was subsequently shot down, *Maia* was hit and, despite the valiant rescue attempts of some stevedores, her watchman, 'Bunko' Heath, died in the ensuing fire.

CHAPTER SIX

Eastward and Southward

THE MIDDLE EAST AND INDIA

Ceres in India – Corio in the Persian Gulf – Calpurnia at Habbaniyah – Centurion in Calcutta – Calypso at Bahrain.

The service had settled down. Africa and India were being traversed regularly but passage was not without mishap and adventure. In mid-June 1938, Captain Gurney, in *Ceres*, was forced down by poor weather and subsequently ran aground on Lake Dingari, in the State of Tonk (about fifty miles south of Jaipur, India). *Ceres* became inaccessibly stuck in the mud. The nearest telephone was twenty miles away and, presumably, a runner was dispatched to raise the alarm. There was little else the crew and passengers could do. Stoically, as crocodiles rubbed their backs upon the thin hull, dinner was served. The passengers settled for an early night but sleep was fitful in the sultry air as thoughts turned to the crocodiles beneath. The following morning, after the passengers had been despatched to Gwalior, a multitude of local labourers was assembled and, fearlessly, they entered the waters to pull *Ceres* free. Although the passengers were sped on their way (possibly in *Capella*), the crew awaited a favourable wind for take-off and remained at Tonk until 20 June. They were sustained with food and water parachuted from passing 'boats.

Of an incident to *Corio*, in the Persian Gulf and probably at Sharjah, little has yet come to light. At the time she wore the QANTAS registration VH-ABD: this would place the incident between July 1938 and September 1939. On 16 July she did arrive in Dubai but it was not until 26 August 1938 that she was next in service. Peter Newnham, of Shorts, was part of the *Corio* repair party, but from March 1939 he was involved with *Corsair*. It would thus seem likely that the incident occurred in July 1938. Photographic evidence shows that *Corio* lost her starboard float and severely damaged the leading edge of her port wing.

The following November, there occurred the only 'C-class' loss of 1938 – *Calpurnia*. She left Southampton on Friday 25 November, loaded solely with mail, and was expected to spend the night of Sunday, 27 November, at Habbaniyah. The crew slipped at Alexandria but Captain Ernest Henry 'Tich' Attwood carried on to Tiberias, Sea of Galilee. Here they refuelled, and at 12:18 GMT were airborne again, appearing to make good progress. At 15:32 GMT, the expected time of arrival, they called for a radio bearing and were found to be 'on course'. That was the last communication from the fated aircraft. *Calpurnia* circled Lake Ramedi, twelve miles north of Habbaniyah, a couple of times at very low altitude. The aircraft levelled its wings and on a even keel, with the engines at cruise power, she struck the eight-foot-deep waters of the lake. 'Tich' Attwood and First Officer Alexander N. Spottiswood were killed instantly. The survivors, Radio Officer Bayne-Rees, Steward Anderson and Station Officer Harrison, a staff passenger, sheltered the night upon the port wing. During the night, Radio Officer Bayne-Rees died.

Meanwhile on Lake Habbaniyah, Imperial Airways' staff, having laid the flare-path for the night arrival, awaited the captain's request for permission to alight. The launch was on station and its searchlight swept the fairway in anticipation of the touchdown. It became apparent that something untoward had occurred; at 17:00 GMT *Calpurnia* was declared missing and the launch went off in search. Nothing could be found. Unbeknown to them, *Calpurnia* lay twelve miles to the

Corio lost her starboard float and severely damaged the leading edge of her port wing. This accident most likely occurred in July 1938, and probably at Sharjah. Peter Newnham, of Shorts, was part of the salvage party. The port float is laden with sand-bags to prevent her from toppling. (Newnham)

north. Their safe arrival was, meanwhile, unfortunately announced in *The Times*.

It was not until the following morning when, with the assistance of RAF aircraft, the hulk of *Calpurnia* was found. She lay partially submerged in the waters of Lake Ramadi. Steward Anderson and his fellow survivor suffered from shock and exposure in addition to their injuries. One body, presumably Bayne-Rees, was found, but those of the captain, first officer and Flight Clerk F. G. Ubee were initially declared missing, believed drowned. It was felt fortunate the flight had been for mail only and fare-paying passengers were not being carried.

Why they should have crashed, when so near to their destination, remains a mystery, but visibility was poor owing to a sandstorm that extended to 20,000 feet and it was getting dark. Possibly of greater significance, the radio station for Habbaniyah was at Lake Ramadi. Despite the station's callsign 'Lake Ramadi', it is conceivable Attwood and his crew were unaware the radio station was not adjacent to the Habbaniyah alighting area. Having fixed their position as 'overhead' the radio facility, they may have thought they were over the deeper waters of Habbaniyah. After all, they had received radio bearings and they were on time. Possibly they saw the water through the dust and dusk and decided to let down. Had the water been deeper, they might have survived. Alternatively, they may simply have struck the water flying too low, in poor visibility.

The Christmas mail, which was scattered across the lake, was salvaged by the RAF, and the rescuers expected the grim discovery of the remaining bodies. To assist with the salvage, Imperial Airways staff came out from Basra; they were accompanied by some GPO personnel who were not pleased to find the RAF drying out the mail in an irregular manner. By 30 November, eighteen mailbags had been recovered but the bodies of Spottiswood and Ubee were still missing; Steward Anderson was making progress but was still critically ill.

Minor accidents seem to have been fairly common. There are several incidents of flying-boats being struck and damaged by marine vessels. On 9 March 1939, *Carpentaria,* under the command of Captain Esmonde, with Bill Morgan as purser, was rammed and damaged by a junk at Bangkok.

A year after *Ceres* ran aground on Lake Dingari, there was another accident in India. On 12 June 1939, *Centurion* was approaching the Hooghly River alighting area at Bally, outside Calcutta. There, Imperial Airways staff were awaiting the arrival of Captain Loraine homebound from Sydney. Storms were approaching. The sky was black and, nearby, thunder and lightning were present. In the distance rain was marching towards them. The Hooghly was treacherous at the best of times. The fairway, always full of debris, was surrounded by small craft, fringed with large dockside cranes and bounded by the Willingdon Bridge. As Loraine turned the 'boat onto final approach, a squally wind blew. Touchdown seemed normal, but as she slowed, a gust of wind

caught *Centurion* under the tail. The tail rose alarmingly and swung *Centurion* viciously to port. The 'boat, still with considerable forward speed, dug her nose into the river and crabbed towards the shore. The sideways loading was too much for the hull and it was stove in, causing the 'boat to roll and sink.

Of the five crew, Captain Loraine, First Officer E. A. T. Murray and Steward A. Carter were injured. Radio Officer E. B. Brown and Flight Clerk L. R. Smith escaped serious injury, but the same was not so for Mr Kinlock, a passenger from Singapore, as he broke a leg. On shore, the station staff, Reg Moss included, summoned an ambulance. On the waters, both launches were patrolling and they sped to assist. Mr Kinlock was whisked away to hospital in the ambulance and the other passengers and crew were dispatched in the Imperial Airways passenger coach. From the time of the crash until the last person was ashore a mere 16 minutes had elapsed. An attempt to salvage the aircraft was made later but the strong currents had done much damage to the hulk. The aft section was beached and after a prolonged search the tailplane, fin, rudder, engines and fuel and oil tanks were recovered. The wings and forward fuselage had been damaged beyond repair. Although three engines were recovered, the main body of the 'boat broke in two, whilst attempts to lift her with chains were being made. Further repairs were not attempted. The wreck, which now lay in twelve feet of water at low tide, was a hazard to shipping and she was demolished with explosives.

Of the accident, Imperial Airways announced:

'The Centurion, operating the airmail service from Sydney to Southampton, was damaged on alighting at Calcutta today, owing to a sudden north-wester lifting her tail and causing the aircraft to nose into the water; the passengers and crew were all saved without serious injury. The aircraft is partly submerged. The mails are being salved with the assistance of the port authorities.'

The following month, July, *Calypso* was eastbound and Tommy Rose was first officer. They left Basra on 14 July, and as they alighted at Bahrain, *Calypso*'s keel and afterstep were damaged slightly on coral. There were no injuries and they were able to make a test flight later that day. *Cooee*, which was lying at Karachi, was rescheduled to pick up the mail and passengers from Bahrain and take them on to their destinations. A few days later, 17 July, *Calypso* continued from Bahrain to Dubai and on to Karachi.

To the east, the Rising Sun cast a shadow over Imperial's operation. There were several instances of Imperial's D.H.86s being harassed by Japanese fighters, and in November 1939 *Dardanus*, routing from Bangkok to Hong Kong, was fired upon. Although 92 bullet holes were counted, the passengers and crew were unhurt. There was no apology. The Japanese stated the aircraft had come too close to their base at Wai Chao Island and requested that Imperial abandon the route. The view of Imperial, however, was that there was no need to abandon the route. On the contrary, as Imperial's aircraft were clearly marked, it was up to the Japanese to avoid such incidents. As a precaution, Imperial decided to divert their route but publicly maintained the right to fly wherever they liked.

CAMBRIA FORCE-LANDS
The rescue of Brigadier-General Lewin – Alcock and the forced landing of Cambria.

In the last year or so of peace, the Empire-'Boats' scheduled service became a matter of routine, although the Atlantic, *Maia* and *Mercury* and in-flight refuelling still attracted attention. That being said, records were being made. On 15 April 1938, *Calpurnia* (before her loss) arrived in Southampton having completed the fastest journey yet from Durban by 'C-class'. *Calpurnia* had carried one and a half tons of mail and ten passengers. She had taken four and a half days. At that time, the Cape to London record stood at 57 hours and 23 minutes, held by Mrs Kirby-Green and Flying Officer Coulston.

The following month, having returned to Southampton from Karachi three days previously, *Calpurnia* gave a display of flying at the Royal Aeronautical Society Garden Party held at Richard Fairey's aerodrome, now part of Heathrow, on Sunday 8 May 1938. Of the event, it was described:

> 'An Empire flying-boat, which came unexpectedly out of the mist, was the highlight on the civil side.'

Lankester Parker's display:

> '... cut capers in the way of vertically banked turns which showed that even the hard working matron of the airways of the Empire could feel the spring ...'

Down the route, and in Africa in particular, aviation was not so genteel. Six months earlier, October 1937, *Cassiopeia*, commanded by Captain Casperuthus, with John Locke as first officer and Bill Morgan purser, was instrumental in the rescue of 63-year-old Brigadier Lewin and his wife. On 10 October, the Lewins were flying to their Kenya homestead when, short of fuel, they force-landed their Miles Whitney Straight somewhere in the Nile sud, having overshot Malakal. *Cassiopeia,* on service DS 30, had followed the schedule down as far as Malakal when they were asked to keep a look-out for Brigadier and Mrs Lewin. *Cassiopeia* departed Malakal on the morning of 12 October and at 10:10 am they spotted the stricken machine, which had lain in the swamp, upside down, for four days. For the next two hours they circled overhead and dropped some food and messages to the mosquito-plagued couple. They stayed with the Lewins until lack of fuel forced them to return to Malakal. The following day, 13 October, *Cassiopeia* led eight machines of 47 Squadron RAF to the crash site. The RAF aircraft dropped further supplies, including a message-picking-up apparatus. The Brigadier and his wife spent five further days in the swamp until they were rescued by a party of Dinka tribesmen that had

travelled overland. It then took several days for the party to reach 'civilization' as Mrs Lewin had to be stretchered out.

The forced alighting of *Cambria* is incredible, but Radio Officer 'Paddy' Cussans was on the aircraft and Captain E. S. 'John' Alcock published his account in the *Evening Standard* of 10 July 1956. The radio report made by 'Paddy' Cussans and an eye-witness account by Mr Steve Stephen (traffic officer) support the Alcock tale.

On the east coast of Africa, in the mouth of the five-mile-diameter Mosuril Bay, lies Mozambique island, Portuguese East Africa, the last night-stop before Durban. Imperial's staff lived at Lumbo, the adjacent mainland town which had once been a slave port. Five or six miles inland, on the site of Lumbo Radio, stood a 300-foot-high, unlit radio mast. It had been erected by colonialists towards the close of the First World War but never used. Warning lamps had not been fitted during construction and now was too late to make amends. Imperial's staff feared the mast was hazardous to descending aircraft, as they passed low over the station whilst making approaches through cloud.

In the spring of 1939, Steve Stephen was one of two traffic officers at Mozambique. Other permanent staff were two engineers, two Portuguese coxswains, ten native seamen, one native cook and one native houseboy. In earlier years, their accommodation, two semi-detached bungalows, was also used for night-stopping crews and passengers. Thus, whenever a flying-boat stopped, the staff had to relinquish their beds to the travellers. Matters were later eased when the staff built an annexe for themselves, complete with 'English' plumbing. Passenger, and staff, accommodation was further improved with the arrival of the houseboat *Richard King*, nick-named 'Wretched Thing'. *Richard King* had been purchased by Imperial as the hulk of an ancient Durban tug. She was converted to accommodation, fitted with a bank of batteries and towed up to Mozambique. It was proposed that during the day, before the passengers arrived, a thunderous generator would charge the batteries to power the accommodation through the night. The *Richard King* was used between about 1939 and 1941. Thereafter the conversion of the earlier slave market, once railway headquarters, into the 'Hotel do Lumbo' brought Mozambique's facilities up to the standard expected of BOAC.

Cambria, commanded by Captain Alcock, with First Officer Shakespeare and Radio Officer Cussans completing the flight-deck crew, departed Southampton on 1 March 1939. On board were airmail and six passengers for Durban. Flight Clerk Parsons and Steward Riddock were the two remaining crewmen. They night-stopped at Alexandria on 2 March 1939 and the following day made a 30-minute test flight before continuing to Khartoum and Kisumu, which they eventually left on 8 March 1939.

At the Dar-es-Salaam refuelling stop, fuel from a temporary refuelling barge was pumped into *Cambria's* tanks. Although never proved, this may have been the cause of their impending downfall. Their next port of call was Lindi, with Mozambique being the last stop of the day. Shortly after leaving Lindi, atmospheric conditions began to affect the radio but Cussans changed frequency to short wave (45 metres) and continued to exchange messages. The Mozambique landing weather report was obtained from Lindi. Lindi later asked *Cambria* for an ETA at Mozambique. The time 14:25 GMT was duly passed and acknowledged by both Lindi and Lumbo Radio, Mozambique.

At 14:09 GMT, forty miles from Mozambique, weather conditions deteriorated rapidly. Ahead, hanging before them like a huge black curtain, stretching from horizon to horizon, was a gigantic dark storm. It was larger and more awesome than any of them had seen before. There was no way around it or over it! To compound matters, the electrical storm was now so severe they lost wireless contact with Lumbo. They later learned that Lumbo Radio had closed down, it being in the storm's centre.

About 220 gallons of fuel remained, enough for another one hour and fifty minutes of flying time, but in one and a half hours' time it would be dark. Moreover, they had insufficient fuel to return to Lindi. The passengers were asked to remain in their seats and fasten their seat belts. Alcock had decided to set course for Lumbo and fly through the storm. There was no alternative, even if it were to be the worst rain ever experienced.

At 14:14 GMT they entered the black curtain of cloud. The next fifteen minutes were sheer nightmare, visibility was absolutely nil. The instruments were useless, 'all boxing the compass', to quote Alcock. In appalling conditions, Alcock stayed in the air, on course, on a reasonably even keel and hoped. The electrical interference worsened and they were still unable to contact Lumbo Radio but they could work Lindi.

Cussans broadcast to all stations:

'Flying in a storm and heavy rain. Reception impossible. Request all stations wait and keep listening.'

The message was timed at 14:18 GMT.

At 14:25 GMT they started their descent. Down to 100 feet. Suddenly! The top of the unused Lumbo radio mast sprang into sight, piercing the cloud which covered the station. In the gale-force conditions it would be folly to penetrate the cloud and attempt an alighting. They climbed, altered course east, over the sea, and tried to escape the storm. A mile or so out, salvation came none too soon, as Alcock's limbs felt as if they had been stretched on the rack during those last frightful fifteen minutes.

Below *Cambria*, in Mozambique, Steve Stephen and his staff had heard the engines, as the 'boat circled the Lumbo mast before moving eastward. More frantic calls on the antiquated telephone followed and they were told at 14:26 of Cussans' call of 14:18, 'Flying in a storm and heavy rain… .' At 14:29, Lumbo contacted *Cambria* which replied with their position and situation *vis-à-vis* the storm. As reception was poor, 'Paddy' asked Lumbo to acknowledge his message with a long dash. Lumbo

gave the OK and followed up with the Lumbo surface wind. (The meteorological observation station was at the Lumbo Radio Station and not down at the Mosuril Bay fairway. Usually Steve Stephen made his own observations and had them transmitted to the 'boats.)

The crew of *Cambria* had little option other than to wait until the storm passed inland. Alcock handed control to First Officer Shakespeare and descended from the flight deck into the pantry and out into the passenger cabins. Here he consulted Colonel Garth Trace, Manager of the South African Division, Imperial Airways and a former pilot. Returning to the flight-deck they weighed up the situation and decided it best to alight in sheltered waters and wait out the storm. Soon, it would be dark and an emergency alighting would then be impossible.

Cussans signalled Lumbo, informing them they were still flying but now along the edge of the storm. Again he asked for the latest weather report, two attempts being required to get the message through. They continued up the coast, parallel to the storm front, and counted seven water spouts, spaced about 100 yards apart and all reaching a height of 200 feet.

There were a number of bays along the coast, and, as they emerged from the storm, Colonel Trace had seen one that might be suitable. Although squally airstreams still buffeted them, Alcock instructed Shakespeare to turn back towards the bay. Meanwhile, 'Paddy' Cussans was still working under the transmitter's waterproof cover, as the rain continued to come in through the port-side cockpit window which Alcock had opened in order to see the vestige of a horizon.

At 14:42 GMT, all four engines faded.

Shakespeare was at the controls when that deathly hush descended as they were half-way through the turn. All four engines faded, completely and rapidly, as though all the throttles had been closed.

Alcock glanced back at the petrol gauges, situated on the rear bulk-head, then rushed to his seat. One hundred and eighty gallons of fuel remained. An air lock? This was no time for conjecture, their height was only 1,000 feet, they were running with a gale-force wind, visibility was minimal, below was a mountainous sea with eight- to ten-foot waves and the four de Havilland variable-pitch propellers were windmilling. (Note: The official record states that between 110 and 165 gallons of fuel remained and most of that was in the starboard tanks. Moreover, the 'Telelevel' contents gauges did not give a continuous reading.)

It would have been difficult to prescribe more hazardous circumstances in which to alight a flying-boat. Alcock was faced with an impossible task. Without power and with insufficient height, a turn into wind would be fatal. They could never complete the turn for, as they neared the waves, with the wind drifting them sideways, the floats would either be knocked off or dig in and cartwheel the whole aircraft.

Cambria was about one and a half miles due east of Kroosi Bay, too far to glide. The entrance was narrow and there was no time to consult the chart to see if rock or coral obstructed the way. Alcock glided down as near to the bay's entrance as possible. He hoped to sail through, after the alighting run was complete. (A flying-boat can be sailed against tide and wind just like a sailing dinghy. It would be a tricky job but, once down, using aileron, rudder and elevator as sails, Alcock hoped to tack towards safer waters.)

Cambria was established in a steep glide at 90 to 100 mph. Alcock again needed all his strength to keep the aircraft under control. Closing with the surface, Alcock, summoning all his skill, experience and an element of luck, chose his moment and eased the control column forward, to push *Cambria's* nose into a wave, between crest and trough. The idea was to ride through the trough and then up the next crest without bouncing or porpoising.

For an age, green water hammered at the cockpit windows, *Cambria* bucked up the next crest and the ship teetered at the top of the wave. Fearing she would topple sideways, Alcock gave a violent kick on the rudder and heaved the control column back as far as it would go. Within seconds, *Cambria* reared to a halt and lay pitching, rolling – dead upon the waters. Alcock proceeded to sail *Cambria* into Kroosi Bay. Cussans and Flight Clerk Parsons went into the bows to 'out anchor'. To help them ride the heavy seas more evenly and prevent *Cambria* drifting out into the Indian Ocean they prepared the drogues for streaming.

Now, comparatively safe, 'Paddy' returned to the flight-deck and, at 14:58 GMT, transmitted a distress signal on the short and medium waves. He sent the automatic alarm signal followed by SOS, and asked all stations to await their position. Interference was awful and reception was near impossible. Although an acknowledgement to their SOS was not heard, with difficulty they did hear Lindi call Lumbo and then Lumbo call *Cambria*, once. 'Paddy' vainly, immediately answered. No reply from either Lindi or Lumbo. He transmitted their position again on the maritime wavelength but thought this futile as the electrical storms were disrupting all wavelengths.

By 15:30 GMT, there was little more to be gained from the radio and Alcock instructed Cussans to cease watch and conserve the batteries. Owing to the violent pitching of the 'boat and rain coming in fast through the open port window, they were unable to start the two-stroke, which could power the radios. When conditions improved, they would try again to raise Lumbo.

With great skill, Captain Alcock had managed to get *Cambria* into the relatively sheltered waters of Kroosi Bay. They made fast for the night and pondered on their further action.

A native boat was sighted, coming from the shore. As always in these circumstances, the crew feared the natives might have been full of good intentions but lacking in seamanship. They did not wish to be rammed. A line was eventually passed from the boat to *Cambria* and a tow attempted. Not surprisingly, the natives did not understand Alcock's instructions, in English, and 'Paddy' Cussans was told to board the native boat and take command. Heavy rain still fell; the sea was

confused, and trying to tow twenty tons behind a native canoe was ineffectual. The canoe came alongside, embarked four passengers and proceeded ashore. They steered for a distant light, as indicated by the natives. It was a trading post, so 'Paddy' was able to make the passengers comfortable before returning to *Cambria*. The remaining passengers – Garth Trace included – and the flight clerk were taken ashore.

Cussans made his way back to Alcock and *Cambria*, and recommenced radio watch. The situation began to look more favourable as they were contacted by a German ship which relayed their plight to Lumbo. Cussans had already arranged that should Colonel Trace have a message for Alcock, Trace would signal it by Morse. Alas, his Morse was none too clear and yet again 'Paddy' had to haul back to the trading post. The tide had receded so he walked. On arrival, he duly signalled the message himself, 'Have despatched runner to Lumbo with message. Colonel Trace.' Alcock and Shakespeare afloat, Cussans and passengers ashore, they spent the remainder of the night in uneasy sleep.

At Mozambique, throughout the late afternoon and evening, garbled messages were received over the telephone link from Lumbo Radio. Possibly, *Cambria* had crashed. From the German liner, the Norddeutscher *Columbus*, 'All four engines failed due to the severity of the rain – forced landing being attempted' was received. Finally:

'Forced down all four engines cut. Position Kroosi Bay.'

The station superintendent, the Portuguese port captain and an engineer boarded the control launch, and with four forty-four-gallon drums of petrol they started up the coast to look for the flying-boat. After about four hours, the launch returned, the seas being too rough to get beyond Mozambique Island. The search would be resumed a few hours before dawn, when the seas calmed. A Portuguese Junkers Ju 52, flown by a friend of Imperial's staff, was chartered to depart Lumbo aerodrome at dawn and make a search of Kroosi Bay.

Early the following morning, Steve Stephen and the rest of the Imperial staff were informed that the Junkers had taken-off. Steve laid out the fairway marker buoys but it was hot work as his lightweight 'whites' had been soaked the previous day and he was forced to wear his heavy gaberdine 'blues'. It was a hot day; moreover Steve did not wish to go ashore, in case a 'boat should suddenly appear.

During the night, First Officer Shakespeare had disembarked to check on the 'boat. He found it high and dry on the soft coral, listing to port; this was fortunate for, in the morning, they were able to inspect the hull. They found it sound.

Just before dawn, as the search was resuming from Mozambique, 'Paddy' Cussans returned to *Cambria* and opened the radio watch. He called all stations and although he received no reply on short wave, he heard Lindi working a ship on 600 metres. Immediately Cussans called – no reply. He urgently asked for a reply from any station. He heard Lindi instruct the ship, the German liner *Columbus,* to listen out. Cussans contacted Columbus. *Columbus* replied they had changed course and were speeding to their rescue.

The liner had been diverted to search for *Cambria* and, as a result, most of the passengers had stayed up all night to witness the event. The Ju 52 communicated with *Cambria;* it was guiding the launch towards them. *Columbus* took bearings from *Cambria* and maintained contact until, almost disappointingly – as far as the passengers were concerned – *Cambria* was able to tell *Columbus* there was an aircraft circling above them and the Imperial launch was almost alongside. They were out of immediate danger; the search was called off and the Ju 52 went upon its way at 06:30. Alcock decided it best if the 'boat were towed until a proper hull inspection was completed.

Once the Imperial Airways' engineers arrived on the launch, they gave *Cambria* a cursory examination and found sand and water in the filters and carburettor wells. Unable to carry out a detailed inspection, or start the engines, the launch took *Cambria* in tow for Mosuril Bay.

At the radio, Cussans signalled Lumbo they had departed Kroosi and then, to comply with Board of Trade regulations, as he considered they were a ship at sea, kept watch on 600 metres. He managed to start the two-stroke and put the batteries on charge. Shortly before midday and very much to Stephen's surprise, the launch, with *Cambria* in tow, appeared at the mouth of the bay.

Once safely moored, the radios were serviced and it was found they had suffered no ill effects from the rain. Deeper inspection of the fuel system, however, found more sand and water in the tank wells and elsewhere. Had they picked it up when they refuelled at Dar-es-Salaam? It was never proved conclusively. As it was, a short test-flight was made on the 10th, and late the following day they arrived in Durban for a night-landing.

With time to reflect, they wondered what would have happened had the engines failed earlier. The skill of Alcock is to be marvelled at. How did he pull off a downwind, glide landing on the open sea during a storm? Many had failed before him and others would fail after him. The official file tells of a vapour lock, a common problem when taking on warm fuel. Moreover, considering the turbulence *Cambria* suffered, vaporization of fuel seems likely. Perhaps sediments had been disturbed. Although heavy rain had been known to douse the ignition systems, the loss of four engines simultaneously indicates a fuel problem. Mismanagement of the fuel system was possible. They may have been burning the fuel from one tank, a wise precaution as they were fuel critical, but a practice that can be fraught should the fuel supply become exhausted or interrupted by vapour or sediment.

With no time for rest, *Cambria* departed Durban on 12 March 1939 for Kisumu. For Alcock and his crew this should have been a routine return to England. Unbeknown to them they were embarking on the most

wondrous Empire adventure yet. The next few days would follow 'Paddy' Cussans for the rest of his life and become the inspiration for this book.

But before that inspirational tale is told, recent research has uncovered an account of another forced landing. Although the weather at the time was more benign, it does show that a glide-landing in a flying-boat was possible. The source of this account is the late Radio Officer John H. A. Lewis, one of 'Taffy' Powell's wireless operators on the transatlantic *Cambria* flights of 1937. I am indebted to his widow, Mrs Peggy Lewis, for allowing me access to his unpublished draft of *Advancing Backwards in The Boats That Flew*, a collection of short stories recalling his time with Imperial Airways. Although I am unable to corroborate this account or attach any date, other than that given by Lewis, I do believe it. As I am unable to add to the account, I have reproduced Lewis's words below:

'There'd been every likelihood that all score of us aboard that particular "C" class flying-boat might have perished, been splattered into the red soil of Uganda. An aircraft of that size, out of fuel and with all four engines stopped, her props merely windmilling, was extremely likely to drop clean out of the sky. The fact that we didn't crash I shall always credit to the lightning reactions and consummate skill of Captain F. J. (Bill) Bailey. Instead, with only inches to spare us from disaster, we glided to safety.

"Fuel contents gauges measure approximately 85 gallons," reported the engineers subsequently, "but a check by dipstick indicated that your tanks are bone dry."

The unbelievable had happened. Despite every precaution, 18 miles from our destination, at an altitude of 7,000 feet and seven miles from the edge of Lake Victoria, we'd run out of fuel. Phew!

I believe "Bill" Bailey held No. 1 flying-boat pilot's licence, certainly he was a No. 1 pilot, a No. 1 gentleman and his exploit that day in 1937 must have ranked No. 1 in the annals of aviation pilotage skill, for his instantaneous reactions proved perfect and no doubt saved all our lives.

I flew with him a lot. Happily. He had the knack of showing that he appreciated his crew, their skills and their needs whatever their status. A fatherly figure with a wealth of experience, a calm man with whom it was extremely pleasant to fly. What more can be said?

Negligence, that we should run out of fuel? No, definitely not. We'd departed from Malakal in the Southern Sudan for Port Bell/Entebbe in Uganda with a warning of strong head winds, information that was reiterated by radio. En route navigation proved that those adverse winds were quite fierce initially but were gradually declining and we were advised that we could expect to find them less severe at an altitude of 7,000 feet.

Naturally every consideration was given to our prospects and long before we reached our critical point the chances of having to divert to an emergency alighting area and there refuel were closely discussed by the

Captain and his First Officer. My job was to supply the route information and in that we had the fullest possible cooperation from the forecasters stationed at Kisumu Aeradio, not far from our intended destination. A decision had to be reached, either divert or proceed, and I noticed that our F/O was checking the fuel remaining every fifteen minutes instead of every half hour.

The emergency stop available to us ranked high in the zone of "bush" alighting areas – bush in every sense. It was late afternoon, we could expect a delay of at least three hours while we refuelled by hand and there were no night take-off facilities. There was no control launch and that stretch of the Nile was liable to be clogged by seasonal weed. There was no rest house, little shelter for the passengers and a sun temperature of about 110 degrees which would doubtless subject us all to great discomfort, thirst and in all probability, heat exhaustion. Altogether a good place to avoid except in dire emergency, which is what it was intended for.

We were the subject of no such emergency but our reason for overflying the place had nothing to do with the major inconveniences it offered. We overflew because we established satisfactorily that we had adequate fuel aboard with which to reach our destination. The decision to proceed was reached only after the most meticulous checking of the amount of petrol remaining in the tanks.

Measuring the contents of each of the four cross-feed petrol tanks located in the wing was effected by means of control wheels which wound down an internal flat plate on to the surface of the petrol, the contents in gallons being indicated by a mechanical gauge, a perfectly satisfactory arrangement providing that the aircraft lay still enough to prevent the fuel from slopping about. Otherwise it was a matter of averaged readings and intelligent guesswork related to the amount of accurately measured fuel previously pumped aboard by the Shell refuelling barge, elapsed time, engine consumption etc, a process hastily improved upon after our experience that day.

Visibility was good and in that area, navigation by map-reading was simplicity itself. Before reaching the critical point, Captain Bailey asked me if I knew how to "read the tanks". I replied that I'd only watched it being done and he explained the procedure in close detail and followed that with an unusual order.

"The First Officer has taken his readings," he told me, showing me a folded slip of paper. "So have I." He showed me his own folded slip. "Now you do the same by exactly the same process. Check each tank contents scale. Wind back and check again. And again. Average the results. Then repeat. Repeat again, average your cumulative findings and give your figuring to me."

I gave him my readings, returned to watch-keeping. He took the trouble a little later to inform me that the nett result of the 324 readings established beyond doubt that we had enough fuel to reach our destination, plus adequate reserve. We all sighed with relief and got on with our jobs. Eventually Lake Victoria came into sight, bang on schedule.

Seven miles from the lake's edge, still flying at 7,000 feet, all four engines suddenly spluttered and stopped. All four. We began to drop …

My immediate reaction was that of the village idiot. Busy copying a passenger uplift signal from Kisumu through the vicious crackle of static radiating from a nearby thunderstorm, the sudden cessation of engine roar made my task so much easier that for a very, very brief moment I actually enjoyed the relative hush. A second later, shocked rigid by the implication, I swung round to fix my feverish eyes upon the Captain.

Already the aircraft had been put into a sharp bank to port. He levelled up, banked her as sharply to starboard, levelled up again and put her into a dive, a cumulative action which resulted in the drainings of petrol in the fuel pipe lines reaching the engines. As they roared into life he used their last atom of thrust to recover and increase height before once again, all four engines stopped. Then he dived the aircraft to gain speed before selecting a glide angle that could so easily have proved to be our last manoeuvre.

There was a tense, eerie silence broken only by the swish of the glide and the ground seemed to rush upwards as he steered for a small ravine. I swung round and watched through my tiny window as both the port float and the port wing tip missed solid earth or rocky outcrop by mere inches. The hull itself sped through the gap formed by the ravine, then we were carving a wake as we made a perfect touch down on the surface of the lake. All our tensions vanished as it became evident that this remote area of the lake had sufficient depth and was free of submerged banks or outcrops. We ploughed to a stop.

With every sincerity the First Officer and I humbly congratulated the man whose perfect reactions had spared us almost certain calamity. Captain Bailey merely exhaled and nodded.

"Check those damned gauges again." And to me, with a finger on the map, "Tell them that we ran out of fuel seven miles north of this spot, are undamaged and need a tow. Then go and drop the anchor."

Disregarding its sharp-fluked hazards, I hurled the anchor overboard as if it was made of wood, such was my relief. We drifted gently onto a taut line, swung idly in a flat calm. The control launch travelled eleven miles to reach us. Ultimately, the cables began flashing to and fro: "Contents gauges measured 85 gallons … dipstick … bone dry." Modifications were initiated and the processes of safer flying took another step forward…'

CORSAIR
The forced landing of Corsair *– Salvaged.*

Whilst the *Cambria*'s forced landing was taking place in Mozambique, events in England were shaping the future of *Corsair*. On 10 March 1939, *Corsair* had departed Southampton for Kisumu and routinely night-stopped at Alexandria on 12 March, before proceeding to Khartoum. She reached her destination on the evening of 13 March. The journey down was uneventful but for the failure of one of the radios. That night, at the Kisumu maintenance base, the radio was changed. The following morning, Alcock and his crew accepted command of *Corsair*, having flown up from Durban.

As Radio Officer 'Paddy' Cussans went about his pre-flight check, he found a note from the previous night's radio fitter, to the effect, 'Have fitted new radio but have not checked Direction Finding Sense Switches wired correctly.' (Incorrectly wired sense switches had in the past caused navigational errors: crews had steered away from radio beacons rather than towards them.) The other crew members were First Officer Shakespeare, Flight Clerk Parsons and Steward Riddock, all of whom had been on *Cambria*. They staged through Port Bell, which they departed at 04:00 GMT.

It must be borne in mind navigation was primarily by hand-held map and the maps were not particularly accurate. Moreover, there was only one navigational aid available to Imperial's crew, direction finding (DF) using either ground-based DF stations or airborne DF equipment. These aids operated in the 'medium' waveband and were prone to interference from electrical storms and other phenomena. However, crews soon became familiar with routes, and dead reckoning, combined with the accurate flying of compass courses, eased by use of autopilot, usually ensured safe navigation. Many of the captains, John Alcock included, had land-plane experience on these African routes.

Corsair departed Port Bell for Juba (Rejaf), a straightforward leg. Captain Alcock handed over command to Shakespeare and went down to the passenger deck to rest. Shakespeare and Cussans were left upon the flight-deck. Having rested, Alcock looked from the cabin and saw that visibility was poor; he returned to the flight-deck, where he found Shakespeare and Cussans in a relaxed mood. The autopilot was engaged and the aircraft was cruising smoothly at 3 or 4,000 feet. That they were uncertain of their position was inferred by the hushed silence that met Alcock's questioning. Alcock asked Cussans to obtain bearings. They attempted to obtain a DF fix; errors and uncertainty were compounded. 'Paddy' Cussans had little confidence in the accuracy of the bearings.

Fuel was running low; Captain Alcock had no option but to put the 'boat down on any suitable water. At 10:00 they saw a straight stretch of river and Alcock descended to alight on the River Dangu, near Faradje in the Belgian Congo, about 150 miles south-west of Juba. How Alcock found himself almost one hour's flying time west of track, after three hours and forty-five minutes of flight on a leg that should have been only two and a quarter hours' length, was never publicly explained. Even if he deviated twenty minutes west to the Murchison Falls, a permitted practice, that would have confirmed his position.

Nearing the surface, Alcock saw a large rock on the port side and successfully skidded the plane and avoided it. The touchdown was successful, but as they slowed, and the flying-boat settled into the water, they crossed a submerged rock. The planing bottom adjacent to the main step was punctured. Instantly recognizing his precarious predicament, Alcock applied power and ran the boat into the shallows. The 'boat settled tail down. The crew and passengers were unable to escape from either the rear or forward entrances as they were awash. The flight-deck escape hatch jammed and it was necessary to use the fire axe to cut through the roof of the flight-deck. Outside, the hull had stove in and the port float was damaged. Although 'Paddy' Cussans had suffered concussion and was soon sent to hospital at Aba, no one else was injured.

Corsair awash on the banks of the River Dangu, near Faradje in the Belgian Congo. In circumstances that are still unclear, Captain Alcock, his crew and a number of passengers were forced down, short of fuel, on this tributary of the River Congo. The events that followed inspired this book. (Pett)

At Rejaf, Mr Geoffrey Pett was station superintendent, and by mid-morning he was growing uneasy about *Corsair*'s absence. He instigated a radio search through Imperial's network. The search took some time as the radios had a range of only about fifty miles. Contact with Port Bell was gained by way of several relays using radio (Wireless Telegraphy) and telephone. It was eventually established that *Corsair* had departed Port Bell with a full fuel load. Nothing could be heard from *Corsair*, despite routine calls every five minutes. Soon, a search, in which *Clio* and a RAF Wellesley assisted, was instigated. At last Rejaf received a call, transferred from Stanleyville, '*Corsair* is down at Faradje.' Pett understood that there were no casualties but the hull was damaged. Using Imperial's Ford V-8 station-wagon and a couple of vehicles borrowed from the Sudan Railways Hotel, Pett sped to the rescue. Ahead lay 150 miles of dirt roads and uncertainty.

Fortunately, the mail and passengers had been picked up and driven to Aba by the Belgian Resident Officer. Late that night, Geoff Pett found the passengers awaiting further help in uncomfortable, sparse shelter provided by the Belgian authorities. Pett, the passengers, some of their hand baggage and all the mail set off to Juba. He had also been given Alcock's handwritten accident report. Sharing the return journey was an American couple on their honeymoon and a female relative of Prime Minister Chamberlain. During the long night-drive up to Juba, they were confronted by a herd of buffalo, which was wandering across the road. Geoff slammed the vehicle to a stop and switched off the lights. He feared that if the buffalo saw the 'eye' of their vehicle lights, there was every chance the herd would charge and stampede over the vehicle.

Still lacking their luggage, the passengers waited a few days at Juba. Here most of their immediate needs were charged to Imperial's account with a local Greek trader, or 'Durkah', – unfortunately, he was unable to supply ladies' underclothes, the natives having little need. Soon they continued their journey with Captain Foy and *Centurion*.

Meanwhile, in England, Hugh Gordon, assistant pilot and engineer, sat in his Rochester office finalizing the report from his previous trip overseas. As a licensed engineer and experienced pilot it was his job to deliver, oversee assembly and when necessary repair and salvage aircraft for Short Bros. Recently he had returned from Habbaniyah and the wrecked *Calpurnia*.

There was a knock at his door and the office boy entered. Mr Kemp would like to see him. Kemp explained Imperial had been in contact earlier that day and relayed the story of *Corsair*'s plight on the Dungu. Imperial Airways had contracted Shorts to repair and re-launch the 'boat whilst Imperial, themselves, would overhaul the engines.

Gordon was instructed to get himself down to Southampton where the Imperial Airways office at the South Western Hotel would know all about him. It was difficult to plan a salvage until the damage had been inspected, so Hugh Gordon usually surveyed the crash site before calling forward his salvage team. He worked with a hard core of men and called for specialists as needed. Peter Newnham regularly led the main workforce and acted as Gordon's second-in-command. Gordon returned to his office and prepared, selecting those drawings he thought he would need. Final arrangements were made. Without knowing when he would return, he packed his kit and took the evening train to Southampton.

At the South Western Hotel, his reservation was in order. That was not always the case. On one occasion, the clerk seemed unaware of him and was adamant that boarding was not allowed without a valid ticket. But to placate Mr Gordon, the clerk allowed him to go down to the berth in Imperial's car. At the berth he was told to wait while the passengers boarded. This was shoddy treatment and not to Imperial's usual standard. Across the water he saw the last of the passengers board via the forward entrance. The launch turned around and powered back to the jetty.

'Jump aboard! Look lively! Captain can't slip without you', shouted the traffic officer. They skimmed across the water towards the waiting flying-boat. 'Seems Captain Esmonde had been told to expect you. Pity they did not tell us.'

As it transpired, on that occasion, Captain Esmonde had been notified not to leave without Hugh Gordon. This time, Gordon soon settled down to a two-and-a-half-day journey to Rejaf.

Throughout this period, Captain Alcock and crew had been waiting at Aba for 'Paddy' Cussans to recover from his concussion and a team of Imperial Airways engineers to arrive overland. Arriving, they found *Corsair* listing to port, the float sunk and the port-outer engine partially submerged. The craft was badly down at the stern, aground. The tailplane was awash and, to starboard, the float was on the water. It would be several weeks before a salvage team arrived and it was necessary to protect the 'boat. Fortunately, the Belgian mining and engineering company, SHUN, had a depot in Aba. Their engineer, Mr Lackovitch, proved himself invaluable during the next months. Lackovitch was a remarkably practical engineer, well practised in the improvised engineering so often resorted to in the Congo. He converted lorries into long-load carriers, and old fuel-bowser tanks into pontoons.

A channel was dug in front of *Corsair*, and whilst the waters were high, she was pulled into the cut. To keep wild animals at bay, a fence was thrown around her. Although minus her port float, she settled onto a relatively even keel when the waters fell.

'Paddy' came out of hospital and waited as plane guard until Hugh Gordon arrived to survey the damage. Gordon walked the last few miles, to find the 'boat like a corralled and stranded whale. The river had fallen again and the 'boat was stuck fast in concrete-like mud. Closer examination found that there was extensive airframe damage below the water line, just forward of the main step. The port float required new struts and

Corsair *being pulled out of the river, assistance coming from a Belgian mining company.* (Pett)

rigging. All these facts were recorded in Gordon's notebook or committed to memory. With an overall idea firmly in mind, Gordon reported back to Rochester. On 21 March 1939, it was decided to repair the 'boat *in situ*, and Gordon assembled his team and returned to the Congo.

Removal of the radio, and associated DF equipment, took place on 1 April, possibly at the behest of Imperial Airways. It was discovered that the DF sensors had been fitted in the reverse sense. This may have exacerbated the crew's navigational difficulties. It would appear that BOAC, as they were becoming, may have considered suing Marconi over the faulty DF. A joint inquiry into *Cambria* and *Corsair* was held, and although with hindsight Alcock admitted that he ought to have suspended his crew after the *Cambria* incident, no fault for either occurrence was attached to the flight crew. It seems the initial enquiry attempted to blame Cussans for obtaining reciprocal bearings. They even attempted to lay some fault upon the Rejaf staff, who should have seen or heard *Corsair* searching for them. The fact that Alcock was unable to see either the Nile or the cone-shaped hill at Rejaf confounded the enquirers.

As scheduled 'boats became available, the salvage team travelled independently, or in small groups, to Faradje; Peter Newnham entered Sudan on 6 April. One afternoon, a few days later, Peter arrived at the Aba Guest House but there were no staff to be found. Looking around, he entered the kitchens and was confronted by a young lion. Peter rapidly shut the door before the beast could attack him. It turned out the

'Paddy' Cussans, the radio officer (R), and two others await the arrival of Hugh Gordon. Imperial Airways surveyed Corsair *and issued instructions to Short Bros to repair the flying-boat. 'Paddy' spent a few days in hospital following the forced landing, returning to flying duties once Hugh Gordon arrived on site.* (Pett)

animal was a pet, if not tame. By 14 April the team, Peter Newnham, his friend Raynor, Blake, Waterman, Cooper, Tomlinson, Spice, Whittaker and recently married Hurn, were assembled at Aba. They were a dedicated and loyal team. Such was Hugh Gordon's leadership, that on the earlier Sharjah task, Hurn had delayed his marriage so that he might accompany the team to the Gulf.

Gordon well understood the 'gamesmanship' of commercial aircraft salvage and comprehended the penalty for late completion of a contract. Imperial wished for the 'boat as soon as possible. Gordon knew that whatever estimate he first gave, Shorts would demand earlier completion. However, he was the man on the spot and the Board always accepted his estimate eventually. Thus he tended to add a little time to his estimate so that he would, apparently, be able to complete the task ahead of schedule. Everything hinged upon Gordon's estimate but on this occasion Imperial probably knew that six weeks, given by Gordon, may have been a little optimistic.

The first task was to free *Corsair* from her concrete-like mud entombment. Gordon decided to excavate around the hull and fit the beaching chassis, which SHUN had brought in by road from Juba. Work, in earnest, commenced with the building of a dam around the damaged areas so the river bed, upon which the 'boat now sat, could be excavated. Beyond the dams, the river rose six feet.

Under Belgian colonial regulations, local labour could be employed, but for only 28 days, as after that time they had to be released to their own devices. This colonial system was more akin to impressment. Occasionally, a blind eye was turned and some of the natives worked willingly for more than their 28 days. Money was not their only reward: the natives borrowed Shorts' fine files to shape their teeth, as was their custom. Engineering assistance was given by Lackovitch. He had already arranged for some of the offending rocks to be blasted to mere remnants of their former size and hazard. Lackovitch, despite his enthusiasm for the salvage, had little social contact with members of the group other than Hugh himself. He was invited to the engineer's bungalow of an evening so they might take their quinine together – with a little whisky.

Pits were sunk either side of the hull, and after much toil and the removal of many cubic yards of mud, the wheelless beaching chassis was attached. Hydraulic jacks were placed under the chassis's stub axles and the hull was jacked clear of her bonds. At least, as far as the salvage plan went, that was the idea. It was difficult to foresee all the obstacles and challenges hidden in such a task and Hugh Gordon was expected to surmount all difficulties whilst out in the field.

Digging and jacking proved an onerous task. A rock was discovered on the port side and many baulks of timber were sunk into the mud in an attempt to steady the jacks. Moreover, the local labourers spoke Bengala

Whilst Corsair *sat in the hardening mud, the level of the river fell. The fence had been thrown around to keep wild game at bay.* (Newnham)

Corsair *stuck fast in the mud.* (Newnham)

and Shorts spoke English. In the best Alan Cobham tradition, much frustration arose and shouting was done trying to convey the task in hand to the workforce. When the natives thought they understood the job, they would sing and chant and work in unison, despite the fact that due to their misunderstanding they were either damaging the 'boat or hazarding themselves. One day, Gordon was toiling and shouting in the pit when to his amazement, the natives started to do exactly what he wanted, although he had not learnt Bengala nor the natives English. He heard a voice giving orders in Bengala. He raised his head to look out of the pit, and shading his eyes against the sun, he saw a large man with rimless glasses and a forever-present beaming smile, towering over him. The figure shouted down, 'Harry Stamm! From the American Church Mission.' He had heard that the 'boat had come down and that the team were having some difficulties. Harry was to become, literally, a godsend to this poor forsaken team.

The Mission and its adjoining hospital were outside Aba; Harry invited the team for prayer or company but they were too busy. However, the Mission assisted Gordon's men by repairing clothes and providing a few comforts at the Aba Hotel. Hugh Gordon went to thank Harry, and his wife Alma, and was invited to share their supper. For the first time Gordon ate corn-on-the-cob; this was followed by ice cream and cake, a pleasant change after the rigours of the river. The following day, Gordon recounted his evening to the men and suggested they attend the Mission, but there was little space for religion in the men's minds. Peter Newnham, who had

The beaching gear sank into the mud. A pit was dug and timber piles were driven in to give a firm foundation. Whilst Gordon was toiling in the pit, Harry Stamm, American missionary, appeared and offered assistance. (Newnham)

been brought up in a strongly Christian family, was the exception; along with Raynor, he visited the Stamms. Subject of much ribbing from his comrades, Newnham and Raynor returned bearing candles.

The toil continued. The heat was unbearable. The pit was frequently flooded by tropical storms, and daily they sheltered as Gordon earthed the stranded plane, as protection against lightning strikes.

On just such a day, Blake turned to Newnham and said, 'You've been up there praying. Can't you get HIM to help us?'

Gordon suggested that Blake went to the mission; he was reluctant but soon became appreciative of the hospital when struck down with malaria. Blake finally felt in need of a change of company and prepared to visit, but Gordon had to chide him for his state of dress, braces and without a jacket and tie. Gordon insisted that his men wore a jacket or bush shirt when going up to the Mission. Mutual support and friendship developed between the Stamms and Shorts. Gordon assisted by driving the Mission's bus on Sundays and Peter Newnham used to accompany Harry Stamm on visits to local schools and churches. Newnham also joined Harry and Dr Klienschmidt in a visit to a leper colony, and although Newnham was a little hesitant at entering, Klienschmidt told him to have faith in God and all would be well. Slowly the Mission began to adopt the young men from Shorts and provide them with spiritual and homely sustenance.

After about a month, they were ready to haul the 'boat from the pit to firm ground, having cleared her of mud, water and many dead toads. Hugh Gordon had long learnt that preparation of a slipway could not be skimped. Too many hours had been lost trying to get beaching trolleys onto firm footings after they had skidded from narrow slipways. The District Officer arranged for plentiful supply of labour from the local prison. Work was always being sought for the many

inmates sentenced to hard labour. The prisoners were employed collecting timber and moving the heavy, waterlogged baulks of ironwood which were used to build the slipway. A pitiful sight of shackled prisoners, harshly treated by native guards, was how the Englishmen saw these men.

Having freed the hull, the 'boat was swung around to face the river and repair commenced. Once the rigging, or alignment, of the 'boat was checked (the craft might have become twisted in the rigours of the alighting and excavation), a slipway, back to the river, was dug and decked with planks.

The damaged panels were drilled off carefully and put aside to be used as patterns. Blistered hands and aching limbs were the norm. Hand-tools were in predominance, the generator being unreliable. Even Lackovitch and a set of piston rings manufactured from sections of cast-iron drain pipe were unable to breath reliability into the machine. Gordon's preparation had been thorough and little had to be ordered from Rochester. Sheet metal and stringers had been taken out, as had the drawings, but they did not always accurately reflect the construction detail of the particular hull under repair and it was up to Hugh Gordon to modify, design or repair where necessary.

The interior was stripped and, supposedly, sent back to Juba, but some fittings found their way to the Mission hospital and the seats were kept at the site. When the generator was working, Hugh would signal the start of tea breaks by switching it off. The men took it in turns to sit in the now removed cabin seats, as there were insufficient for all. Hugh dictated whose turn it was to stand.

Communication with Imperial was limited and formal progress reports were not sent. An Imperial radio operator, Mr Dangerfield, was seconded to the repair team and he worked Juba twice a day but passed only brief messages. The on-board auxiliary generator was

Native forced labour from the local prison was employed to pull Corsair *from the pit.* (Newnham)

Only when Corsair *was free from her bonds could repair commence. Local labour was employed for some of the manual tasks.* (Pett)

used but, as always, that eventually broke down. They had been running it on high octane aviation fuel and they wondered if that had damaged the motor.

On 22 May 1939 Brackley visited the site and reported:

'Short's men are doing magnificent repair work under trying conditions of heat, humidity, flies, mosquitos and hornets. I've had my full share of bites from a small black beetle shaped fly with a sting like a hornet. I've never met this type before and I don't want to again.'

In normal circumstances the repairs would have been straightforward but the same could not be said about the environment. They had tried to rid the area of insects and mosquitos by putting petrol onto the water and firing it, but to little avail. Before arrival, Gordon had thought that some accommodation could be built at Faradje, but that was not possible and they had to travel daily from the somewhat colonial Aba Hotel, about 40 miles away. For lunch, they took sandwiches but it became a race as to whether the ants or the men ate them first. However, the men soon became accustomed to the hardships and privations. A few ants became the least of their problems compared to bilharzia and tropical disease. Their first-aid kit was minimal but to the natives it represented 'white man's medicine'. In reality Shorts' men could offer little real help to the tribesmen, but medicines were in great demand and often administered to stop the natives harrying Gordon's team. Naturally the tribesmen spoke no English. Gordon, in best bedside manner, commented to one, a trustee, that he had not seen him for some time. Raynor replied that was because on his last visit they had given him laxatives. On another occasion, iodine was splashed onto a cut foot and the patient almost fainted. Hugh Gordon rapidly administered a phial of smelling salts and the casualty took off into the bush.

In mid-June, the hull repair was completed and *Corsair* was eased down the wooden slipway and floated upon the river. Hugh Gordon's task was done but it was expected that he, and his team, would see the aircraft off. The engines were to be overhauled *in situ* by Imperial's engine fitters. When the fitting team arrived, they asked Gordon if any of the engines had been in the water. Well, when Gordon arrived, the 'boat was on an even keel so he was unable to say positively whether or not the engines had been immersed. Imperial's man took the easy option and assumed they had not.

Salvage was finally completed at the end of June 1939 and, a few days later in England, Captains Alcock and Bailey flew a series of take-off trials to calculate the run required for the extraction. In the Congo, improvements were made to the fairway. As it was little wider than the wingspan, some of the obstacles were removed and the elephant grass cut down.

'John' Alcock returned to the Congo after the trials. He was aware of the rock he had hit at the end of his initial forced landing but this rock had been blasted and was now below the water's surface. As far as Gordon was concerned, the 'boat would be up on the step and clear of the rock anyway. Alcock suggested that a stake should be driven into the rock and a line stretched to the bank. Attached to the line would be two paper markers, between which Alcock should drive the 'boat to remain clear of the rock during take-off.

The District Commissioner commented that the water was low and possibly still falling. Although damming the river was considered, no action was taken. Alcock was under great pressure from Imperial Airways to return the flying-boat, and a proper planning meeting to discuss the take-off was never held. Hugh Gordon understood the pressures Alcock was under, but felt that with more discussion they might have decided against the flawed departure.

Engine runs were completed. Alcock was only too aware of the hazards of the large rock he had avoided on alighting and the remnants of the other he had struck. Furthermore, the river curved gently. It was agreed that Gordon would stand upon the river bank, just beyond the apex of the curve, and signal to Alcock whether he should steer left or right to follow the safe passage.

Dawn 14 July. The morning was still and cool; Captain Alcock, First Officer 'Geordie' Garner and another crew member boarded the lightly laden 'boat. At 06:05 the attempt was made. The throttles were slowly advanced and the roar of the engines shattered the dawn stillness of the river bank. Peter Newnham was battered by the slipstream as he stood adjacent to the tail-line which held *Corsair* in check. Once Alcock operated the release, the 'boat surged forward, down the narrow strip of water, and Newnham, from his vantage point, saw the boat climb rapidly up onto the step, as she sped away. The whole salvage team, including Blake, who had been released from hospital, looked on at the departing *Corsair*. Another task was coming to a successful end.

From where Gordon was standing, he was unable to

see the start of the take-off run. After a few seconds, the 'boat came into view, but not where expected. Perhaps Alcock was using a different technique? This was not what Alcock and Gordon had discussed! The nose of the aircraft had risen to such as extent that Alcock was unable to see and Gordon watched with amazement as the power was reduced and the boat swung across to starboard, settling back into the water. The starboard float dug into the river, slewing the 'boat further right. There was insufficient water to manoeuvre. What was Alcock doing so close to the bank? Out of control, *Corsair* struck the rock and the starboard side was ripped open.

Dumbfounded silence and speechlessness prevailed, only broken by the ticking of cooling engines and the gentle sobbing of Blake. This was more than any man was expected to stand. The top hatch was flung open and, of this Gordon is certain, the two pilots appeared and commented about the engines and a lack of performance from the starboard motor. There was no suitable reply from the riverside.

The engine-man ran up to Gordon, 'What did they say?'

'Something about the engines', replied a disconsolate Hugh.

'Well, they can't pin this one on me!' came from the 'boat.

Once again *Corsair* settled into the Congo; the starboard wing was over the river bank and the float was crushed.

Imperial Airways, probably somewhat sheepishly, contacted Shorts and explained the current, but hardly new, predicament. 'Hand hull to Gordon!' came the reply.

Morale among the Shorts team was already tried; many men were fearful for their health, working in sun, bush and water, and scant news from Europe did little to comfort them. However, it was soon decided to make another attempt, and Hugh Gordon's men fashioned a temporary patch to effect repair. However, they were unable to fit the patch as the water rose quicker than they could pump the 'boat dry. Again, Lackovitch assisted. He and Gordon went south to Watsa, the gold mining centre, and borrowed some high-capacity water pumps. A diving apparatus was constructed, again with Lackovitch's help. It was ballasted with large iron bars, fitted with a window and covered Gordon's head, shoulders and arms. His foot was in a safety rope so he could be pulled clear, if the crocodiles appeared. They were not the only hazard. To protect himself against bilharzia, he was injected in the stomach, and to ward off the parasite, carbolic soap was used to block all bodily orifices. Underwater, he started to fit the patch, but the diving apparatus collapsed and Gordon was dragged over the reeds and nearly drowned, a harrowing experience which had seemed like a good idea at the time.

European events overtook them; the men were tired, some were sick, so Gordon sent them home, whilst he and Newnham thought about what to do next. After a few days, Gordon offered Peter Newnham a chance to go home. Newnham accepted and departed. Alone, Gordon planned his next salvage. A day or so later, as Gordon secured the 'boat, he saw in the distant fading light a dishevelled figure striding towards him: too far

An engine problem may have led to the aborted take-off. Running out of room to manoeuvre, Alcock breached the hull of Corsair *for a second time.* (Newnham)

to recognize but definitely an Englishman. It was Newnham. He had returned; it was unfair to abandon Gordon in this African hell.

Gordon, near exhaustion, cabled Rochester, 'Returning home for further instructions', and set out for Juba and England. Newnham was left in Faradje. There was little for him to do, other than watch over the 'boat, so he spent much of his time at the Mission.

Once home, Gouge, the General Manager, told Gordon he would not be returning to Africa. He was deeply disappointed, as it was the one job he had been unable to finish. Although he was aware that his men had had enough, he knew that if asked, they would follow him back to the Congo. They too were disappointed that Corsair had been left undone. Newnham was recalled, and after a fraught passage arrived home as war broke out. Corsair was abandoned.

With the repair of Corsair seemingly impossible, Imperial Airways despatched a party from Alexandria to inspect the wreck. They left on 9 September 1939, night-stopped at Khartoum and Juba, and arrived in Faradje on the 11th. The intention was to salvage engines, propellers, radios, instruments and easily detached parts of the airframe from Corsair. Shorts had already removed the cabin interior fittings. The hulk of Corsair would be left to rot.

The team was led by Jock Halliday, Imperial Airways' engineer-in-charge at Alexandria. Accompanying him were Roy Sisson, aircraft engineer, and Harry Hawkins and Cyril Burl, airframe riggers. The fifth member of the team, another engineer, was Alf Cowling. He had the foresight to document and photograph the salvage and repair, thus enabling this record to be made.

Cursory inspection of Corsair, as she lay with her starboard wing and outer engine over the river bank, revealed that beneath the starboard-inner engine was the large rock that had ripped her open, during Alcock's aborted departure. She rested slightly nose down with the forward door below the level of the river. Corsair was aground on the Aba side of the river, the slipway, however, being on the far bank. Alcock's aborted take-off from the slipway had moved the 'boat five to six hundred yards along the river and across it. Inspection complete, the Imperial Airways' team returned to the Aba Hotel.

The next few days were spent preparing the aircraft for stripping; Roy Sisson and Alf Cowling prepared the port engines for dropping, while Harry Hawkins and Cyril Burl removed the starboard float, which had been damaged. As far as Jock Halliday was concerned, the machine would have to be scrapped, and he left for Juba to report his findings. Removal of the port propellers was delayed by a lack of the correct spanner and they discovered the two engine stands were of the wrong type.

As they worked, the waters receded and the true state of the damage became visible. It was becoming apparent that complete salvage was possible. They decided to await Halliday's return with the final decision to scrap. Regardless of Imperial's decision, the flaps were removed; they were salvageable and if it was decided to repair Corsair their absence would make the forthcoming lifting of the 'boat easier.

Contact with Alexandria was via telegraph from Aba to Imperial's Juba office, and then further telegraph to Khartoum, which in turn was in radio contact with Alexandria. That weekend the salvage crew rested, as they had been telegraphed that Halliday was returning with tools and spares; another attempt was to be made to rescue the downed craft – every aircraft was valuable now that Britain was at war. Ominously, their rest was disturbed when the bungalows of the Aba Hotel were struck by lightning.

With the decision to save Corsair, salvage recommenced. Halliday had brought Ken Wycherley, a radio operator, from Alexandria. Using Corsair's W/T, Wycherley was able to communicate with Alexandria, via Juba, and demand spares. Fortunately, the aircraft's batteries, at the rear of the flight deck and easily accessed through the flight-deck loading hatch, were still in good working order. Yet again SHUN offered engineering assistance and charged their batteries.

Time, or at least the Congo waters, were against them. The river rose two feet. They tried to raise the 'boat using pontoons made by SHUN taken from the tanks off disused petrol bowsers. The tanks were sunk adjacent to the 'boat and lashed to it. Then they were pumped dry in the hope that, as they rose, Corsair would float higher in the water. This was not successful and, relentlessly, the water rose towards the rear door. It was thought the 'boat might float higher if lightened. The tanks were hastily converted into a floating work area and the port engines were lowered onto this platform. To act as a counterweight, several locally employed labourers sat on the opposite end of the platform. The starboard, or overland, engines were also removed and all four were taken back to SHUN's garage at Aba. Here Sisson and Cowling would overhaul them. It rained, the water rose and washed into the rear freight door.

By the second week, the effects of hard toil in the Congo basin were being felt and Harry Hawkins was taken sick with heat stroke. In the battle against the rising river, some headway was made and water was emptied from the rear bilges. The pontoons had been modified yet again and now, surmounted by jacks, they were placed under the wings and an attempt to lift the craft was made. Although success at lifting was slow in coming, by the end of the week Sisson and Cowling had started to overhaul the engines, but only just in time. Already, some of the valves were seized and corrosion was becoming established.

The inhabitants of the bush, used to the presence of the 'mad' Englishmen following Shorts' attempt, regularly came to watch. Some were employed and others coerced. The natives nicknamed Alf Cowling 'M'Bigadie', which means short and energetic. Cowling was always telling the boys, 'Do this – get cracking', and generally hastening them. Ken Wycherley, the radio operator, got the name 'Mokoto' (the King), as he never

Imperial Airways initially decided to strip Corsair *and leave the hulk to rot. However, in England the 'phoney war' was coming to an end and every airframe was valuable. The team from Imperial realised they could rebuild* Corsair. *(Cowling)*

appeared to do any physical work. Moreover, he spoke to people far away.

Towards the end of September, Mr McMeekin, the Imperial Airways' Engineer Inspector of Outstations, accompanied by the Belgian District Officer, arrived for a few days. On his return he was able to report that the salvage party was beginning to have some success. The machine had been lifted about a foot and Sisson and Cowling had completed 'top end' overhauls on the four engines; moreover, the propellers, which had had their pitch change mechanism inspected, were declared serviceable. Rescue seemed probable.

Work now concentrated on raising and drying the 'boat, but in daily rainstorms, and whilst the gash remained in her side, water flowed in as quickly as they could pump it out. They were further hindered by the inadequate performance of SHUN's water pump. Nevertheless, over the next few days, with constant packing and jacking, they managed to lift *Corsair* another foot or so. The swollen river, now carrying numbers of poisonous snakes from the upper reaches, continued to enter the 'boat, despite a tarpaulin tied under the keel and the nose having been raised a little. Progress remained desperately slow. It became necessary to pump the bilges throughout the night, 'local boys' being employed to work the bilge pumps. The Imperial team decided to attempt repair of the hole whilst it was still below the water line. Instead of a tarpaulin, a more robust temporary repair was made using thin aluminium sheet, secured from the outside with small brass screws. Waist deep in rising water, confronted by

tropical heat and poisonous snakes, harassed by pressing demands to recover the aircraft to help the war effort, they managed to repair practically all of the large hole.

Triumph! On 5 October, for the first time since Alcock's aborted departure, almost three months previously, *Corsair* was upon the river. The starboard wing, still over the bank, awaited its float, which had been repaired.

With *Corsair* floating, a return to the slipway and a start on the permanent repair could be effected. Following a great struggle, they managed to secure the 'boat in midstream, and in preparation for the five to six-hundred-yard tow back to the slipway, lines were slung from the tail release hook to the river banks. There, gangs of 'local boys' awaited the order to heave. The operation was steered by Wycherley, who, with both drogues at the ready, stood upon the broad flat back of the 'boat as she was manhandled to the slip. On nearing the slip, the beaching chassis was fitted.

Now in their fifth week at Faradje, they faced one of the more strenuous tasks, that of hauling the 'boat ashore. *Corsair* rested in soft mud, tail facing the slip. For two days, they dug into the mud attempting to fit the tail trolley, whilst a runway of planks for the main beaching gear was being laid. Although minor jobs like distributor overhauls were completed successfully, it was to take another four days to get the 'boat onto the slipway. They were assisted by 75 convicts, conscripted by the Belgian District Commissioner, and, more effectively, by Lackovitch, who brought a 60-ton winch and some 75-ton cables to attack the task. Still difficulties. After moving but a foot, the tail trolley came off the planks and sank into three feet of mud. Having dug out the trolley, they had to fill the resultant hole before they were able to jack up the tail unit and refit the trolley. A bigger and wider runway was laid; their lesson had been painfully learnt. Finally, on 16 October 1939, *Corsair* was secured upon the slipway.

To assist with the repair, Ernie Arrol, Imperial Airways' chargehand (two years previously he had sailed to Canada to repair *Cambria*), Bert Owens, a sheet-metal worker, the sheet-metallist's Greek mate, Stavro, and Jock Love, an aircraft electrician, all arrived from Alexandria. A rare day off was taken.

Whilst Bert Owens, with Stavro's help, started to drill off the damaged panels, Alf Cowling and Roy Sisson began cleaning the fuel system. Jock Love began an examination of the electrics and Harry Hawkins rigged the starboard float. By the start of the seventh week, they were ready to reinstall the engines. However, *Corsair* was now across the river from Aba, where the engines had been overhauled. Yet again, SHUN's petrol tanks came into service, this time as a raft to ferry the engines. The first crossing was almost a disaster. They had decided to trust two engines to the raft. With one person to punt the raft across the river, the craft was slightly top heavy. Only by a frantic, almost comical, balancing act was disaster averted and the engines saved from toppling into the river. The two remaining engines were ferried across one at a time. By the end of the seventh week, engine installation was

almost complete. Their old enemy, the river, was beginning to rise, so a low dam was built across the slipway, but to little benefit. They arrived on site on the morning of 25 October to find the dam broken and the slipway and working area flooded. The rising waters had bought unexpected visitors, hippopotamuses.

By the end of October, they had been in the bush for almost two months and the exertion was beginning to affect their health. Bert Owens went sick. A few days later, Sisson was silenced with laryngitis and Jock Love, the electrician, had contracted malaria. Between bouts of sickness they completed the engine installation, fitted the propellers and reinstalled the flaps.

The ancillary work on the engines' exhaust extensions, carburettors and distributors was attended to during the close of October and the first week of November. As usual, the Exactor hydraulic throttle controls were difficult to set up and the port-outer's carburettor accelerator pump had suffered severe corrosion. It was the port-outer which had been partially submerged following the original forced landing. The engine overhaul was completed and the cowlings refitted on 5 November. The following day, Bill Drane, Airframe and Engine Inspector, arrived to examine and countersign that work already completed.

The second crash had damaged the frames that formed the chine angle, and replacement pieces of frame were despatched from Alexandria. Alf and Roy fitted the new pieces of frame and started to replace the metal sheeting which formed the keel. Love, meanwhile, was so sick he was sent to hospital at Juba.

Once the engines had been overhauled, it was necessary to ferry them back to the temporary slipway. Control of the top-heavy raft was as comical as it was near disastrous. The remaining two engines were ferried back one at a time. (Cowling)

Eventually, Corsair *was dragged ashore for a second time; then repair commenced.* (Cowling)

Although they still awaited fresh oil and petrol and new booster coils (necessary to ensure engine start), the generators had been reconnected and all was set for engine runs.

Once the fuel arrived, they tried to run the port-inner engine, but only a new coil overcame its reluctance to start. The rhythmic beat of the Pegasus at tick-over attracted the natives from the bush and they stared in wonderment at the machine. They were not quite so complacent when the engine was opened up, and were soon scattering back fearfully into the bush. Sickness and injury continued to dog the team. Harry Hawkins developed septic poisoning of the hand, possibly from a splinter of aluminium alloy, and was ordered to bed for a few days. His hand soon worsened and he was admitted to hospital. Love was discharged.

Re-launch of *Corsair* was scheduled for 13 November, but Bert Owens pointed out the portent of the date and the launch was delayed. Again the river struck and flooded the slipway. This had to be dried with beam pumps and convict help before the plank runway for the beaching gear could be laid. They planned to move the 'boat down the slipway behind the coffer dam and then breach the dam to allow the rising waters to lift *Corsair*. Finally, in mid-November, with their difficulties seemingly behind them, they rolled *Corsair* forward. Two of the native labourers had their hands crushed as they fought to prevent the 'boat's beaching gear breaking through the plank runway into the deep, soft mud.

To regain the runway and allow the aircraft to continue down the slip, the starboard side was jacked up, new planking laid and an obstructing rock was chipped away. Sickness continued. Roy Sisson, with malaria, went back to Aba to accompany Ernie Arrol, already there suffering a bad throat. *Corsair* was almost back upon the river and the convicts cleared the barrage. The engines were started. Only slowly did they edge uncertainly forward, as the river receded before them. Again

progress was slow, a mere seven feet being the achievement for one day's hardship. The following day, Sunday 19 November 1939, *Corsair* finally floated free. But only on the third attempt, with engines advanced abusively to full power, did *Corsair,* so long a prisoner of the bush, finally shake, shudder and thunder herself free.

By now it was the third week of November. The 'boat had been afloat overnight, secured by a tail line, and as a testament to their craftsmanship, there were no leaks. The beaching gear was removed. During the last week of November the few outstanding tasks were completed. A fault with the starboard fuel contents indicator transpired to be a defective gauge; slats were laid down for the floor and the remaining petrol and oil was put into the aircraft. There was good news about Roy Sisson: he was up and about. After almost three months' hard work they accepted gratefully an invitation to a Thanksgiving Dinner at Harry Stamm's Mission.

What remained was more a matter of tidying up, fixing minor problems with the flying-boat and preparing for the final departure. They dragged the beaching gear those six hundred yards back to the rock in order to return it to SHUN's garage, where it could be stripped. But they were unable to dismantle it because of corrosion, and the beaching gear went from Aba to Juba in one rusted piece. As December approached, they positioned the 'boat for departure, carried out final engine runs, permanently wire-locked all the necessary nuts and fasteners and awaited the arrival of the pilot.

Captain Jack Kelly Rogers arrived on 1 December. He was accompanied by First Officer 'Geordie' Garner, returning for yet another attempt to fly *Corsair* out. Accompanying them was the new East Africa Area Manager, Mr Bilborough, who would pay-off the native staff. 'Geordie' was an amateur magician; with his tricks he used to amuse, and sometimes frighten, the local children, especially when he made coins disappear by sleight of hand. Kelly Rogers gained from the experience of Alcock's aborted take-off and, before leaving England, he too had done low-weight take-off trials.

Having prepared *Corsair* for departure, they now turned their attention to the river. Alf Cowling and Cyril Burl waded down the river towards the rapids and took soundings. There was insufficient depth for a safe take-off. The only answer, as they did not have enough time to await the next year's rains, was to dam the river. This proposal was forwarded to London. Whilst they awaited a reply, there was time for a little entertainment, and the District Commissioner invited them to his house to see native dancing. The break from their arduous toil was much appreciated.

They returned to work and a routine run of all engines revealed that still the port-outer was giving trouble, as at 1,800 rpm it faded. Even the recently arrived Kelly Rogers was unable to avoid medical problems, as he had toothache. Ernie Arrol meanwhile took his turn to suffer from malaria.

By the second week of December, it had been decided to proceed with the barrage. This would be built by Lackovitch and his men. Using mud, stones and wood,

(L to R) Radio Officer Ken Wycherly, Roy Sisson, Jock Love, Ernie Arrol and Alf Cowling, the Imperial Airways repair team. (Cowling)

Corsair *ready to fly out: at last! (Cowling)*

which had to be hauled thirty miles, a double-buttressed palisade was constructed, damming the river. The site of the dam was some distance down stream, so a road there had to be built. The natives also constructed themselves a small settlement – 'Corsairville'. Imperial's men continued to survey the river bed, marking the shallows with stakes and charting the position of the rocks which lay beneath the surface. On the bank of the river, they erected markers indicating the length of take-off run.

Harry Hawkins returned from Juba, his hand much improved, and with their tremendous task almost complete they took a few days' break and visited the Elephant Farm at Gangalla Na Bodio. As they completed odd jobs around the aircraft and continued with the survey of the river, the natives made steady progress with the dam. There were some distractions. One evening, as they returned by car from a further survey of the river, they knocked down a wild pig. With true resourcefulness they ate well that night.

Cowling's final job on *Corsair* was to fit two new Exactor controls, and on 18 December, as Captain Kelly Rogers arrived back from Juba, Cowling received orders to return to Alexandria. A few days before Christmas 1939, Cowling paid his final visit to *Corsair*, where she had lain for the past ten months. Had it not been for him and the others in the team she might have remained there – that might have been a more fitting final resting place. However, she had many more miles yet to fly. As for Cowling, his part in the epic story of the 'C-class' flying-boat was not complete. We shall meet him again before the scrapman's axe and melting pot devoured the remaining Empire 'boats.

Dawn broke over *Corsair* for one last time as she lay on the Dangu on 6 January 1940. Captain Kelly Rogers, First Officer Garner and Radio Officer 'Ginger' Dangerfield boarded the 'boat and went about their

routine. This time careful preparation and professionalism paid dividends and *Corsair* was lifted away safely from her temporary berth. They flew the short leg to Rejaf, where she was refuelled, and then on to Alexandria. At Alexandria she had a two-day refit, but there was little in need of urgent attention, such had been the standard of work in the Congo. The engineers in Alexandria commented upon how clean and oil free were the engines. Refit complete, *Corsair* was flown back to England and was soon pounding the routes.

THE LOSS OF *CHALLENGER*
Mozambique, 1 May 1939.

Mozambique harbour is formed by a large, shallow, tidal bay, Mosuril Bay. Across its mouth lies a narrow island, upon which stands the old fortified town of Mozambique. On the mainland, at the village of Lumbo, is a long jetty, reaching deep into the bay.

Challenger, commanded by Captain Upton, with Tommy Rose as first officer, left Southampton for Durban on 26 April 1939. Bad weather delayed them in the Mediterranean and on 29 April, at Kampala, an exhaust needed repair. The following day they left for Kisumu. Here, Captain Upton relinquished command to Captain Smith. Smith, knowing he was expected to make up lost time, had departed Dar-es-Salaam early (01:35 GMT – 04:15 local) on 1 May. As the morning mist cleared to give a clear, calm day, Captain Smith, First Officer Saunders and First Officer Gavshon arrived over Mozambique.

Contemporary official reports state Captain Smith made a straight-in approach, aiming to complete his alighting run adjacent to the jetty, thus saving time. This he judged poorly, and during the ensuing overshoot, he crashed into the shallows with all engines churning the waters. The 'boat came to rest. The flight deck had crashed down into the forward compartment and the

Mosuril Bay. Looking down the jetty across the bay from Lumbo. (Baldwin and Bigby)

front of the flying-boat was pushed back towards the leading edge of the wing. Flight Clerk George Knight died at his post in the rear of the forward cabin and the radio officer, Tom Webb, was missing. No explanation was given as to why two first officers were being carried.

Captain Smith and the two first officers were thrown from the flight deck by the force of the deceleration. One of the first officers, Saunders, punctured a lung as he struck the windscreen framing; Captain Smith damaged his spine and First Officer Gavshon sustained a minor gash to his thigh.

The accident investigator's report was published in August 1939. Amongst its findings, the Inquiry stated that although the commander was in current flying practice and was competent to fly the aircraft, he had made grave errors of airmanship in attempting to make a straight-in approach in the opposite direction to that he had previously alighted. They attributed the cause to pilot error. During the approach, it was purported that Captain Smith had handled the throttles himself and called for the first officer to select the propellers to fine pitch and to extend half-flap. Once over the bay, he committed himself to an alighting and ordered the first officer to select full-flap. He misjudged the approach, and realizing there was insufficient water ahead of him and

that collision with the jetty and a dinghy which now drifted across the fairway seemed inevitable, he decided to go around. As he raised the nose, to avoid the end of the jetty, he called for 'flaps in' and applied full power. Too low, too slow, the nose dropped and, although the engines roared in response, *Challenger* struck the water, about 200 yards north of the jetty. With full power still applied, the 'boat bounced, staggered ten feet into the air, stalled and plummeted into two feet of water, crashing to a halt, wiping away the keel. The engines thrashed away uselessly at full power, the tips of the props throwing up clouds of spray, or so accounts of the day said.

The Inquiry was, however, pleased to record that the rescue operations were carried out with efficiency and speed.

Among those responsible for the efficient and speedy rescue was Traffic Officer A. H. 'Steve' Stephen. He saw the approaches, all three of them. The first approach was made in the usual direction, low over Mozambique Island and onto the bay. The second, from the mainland, passed close overhead Lumbo. The third and final approach was towards Lumbo and the jetty. Other contemporary accounts record more than one approach but put the aborted alightings down to Captain Smith's inexperience and state he was trying to

The wreck of Challenger. *Contemporary reports attribute the cause of the accident to an error of judgement by Captain Smith. Two crew members died and the flight-deck presence of a visiting first officer was never explained.* (Stephen)

alight adjacent to his mooring and the jetty – saving time.

Usually, after an approach over the narrow spit of Mozambique Island, 'boats taxied across to their moorings. The final approach by Captain Smith was not onto the standard alighting area. Instead, it was a long, low, into-wind approach, from the seaward side of the island. Furthermore, he delayed his touchdown, once clear of the island, in the hope of finishing the touchdown run at the jetty. The final resting place is not disputed. Steve Stephen recalls the third approach being made from the north, towards the jetty.

On impact, as was the characteristic of the 'C-class', the nose split in two, either side of the centre-line. The three pilots were thrown, relatively uninjured, through the aperture. (Seat belts were provided for the pilots but they were seldom worn.)

Fortune smiled upon the steward and the three passengers, as they had been in the rear cabin and were unhurt. Steve took the auxiliary launch towards Challenger, stepped out and waded across to the rear passenger door. The launch came alongside and Steve helped the passengers disembark. Last to leave the rear cabin was Steward Millard; he looked at Mr Stephen and in disbelief said, 'Christ you're standing!'

Mr Stephen was still unaware of the 'boat's full complement. Steward Millard told him there were five other crew members. As the launch took the steward and the passengers to the security of the jetty, Steve waded to the front of the 'boat. Here he was told that the three pilots had been thrown clear and taken ashore by the control launch but the flight clerk and the radio officer were missing. The hull forward of the wing was severely crushed, and the force of the impact may have ripped the reduction gear, complete with propeller, from the port-outer engine.

Steve could see the three pilots on the jetty. Captain Smith and First Officer Saunders were taken to hospital in Mozambique, where they stayed until they could be flown south, but Gavshon, once over his initial shock, attempted to assume command of the situation. This was until he was forcibly put in his place by the Imperial staff and Lieutenant-Colonel Kisch, one of the passengers. Lieutenant-Colonel F. H. Kisch was the Chairman of the Palestine Zionist Executive. On his return flight, Lieutenant-Colonel Kisch presented the four Mozambique staff with inscribed cigarette cases, in recognition of their toil during the rescue.

The search for the missing crewmen commenced. With the help of local native labour, Steve removed the wrecked remnants of the nose cone, revealing a grim scene. The body of Flight Clerk George Knight was entangled in the flight-deck equipment; there was no trace of the radio officer. The search was called off in the face of the rising tide. This was fortuitous, as Imperial Airways' orders stipulated that in the event of a crash, the removal of the airline's insignia from the wreckage was to be given the utmost priority. Within four hours of the crash, all but the tailplane was below the water. There was little official thought given to the dead or the

survivors in the barrage of coded signals that came from Durban, Nairobi and London.

That night, two coxswains and their sailors guarded the wreckage. The dawn ebb-tide uncovered the macabre body of the radio officer; one of the guards was dispatched to Steve's rest-house. In the early morning light, it appeared that at the moment of impact, the radio officer had been with the flight clerk in the forward cabin. He would have been waiting to enter the mooring compartment in preparation for picking up their buoy. His body, stripped naked by the passage of two tides, was suspended by its legs.

Later that morning, natives from the far side of the bay paddled their dugouts to Lumbo with several mail bags in tow. Once the story broke, Imperial quickly announced that the mails had been recovered and had been sent on their way in Canopus.

The truth will probably never be known. However, at Kisumu, Gavshon, a first officer from land planes, scrounged a lift down to Durban. On the leg to Mozambique, Gavshon occupied the right-hand seat and First Officer Saunders squatted between the pilots. It has been known for 'visiting' pilots to be given an opportunity to make a landing in a strange aircraft. This may have occurred on the 1st May.

For various reasons the aircraft fell uncontrollably and seemingly porpoised or bounced.

The term 'porpoise' had been coined in 1913, and research into the phenomenon, using a Short Singapore, had been done by the MAEE Felixstowe during the autumn of 1934. The drill to recover from an incipient porpoise was full power to inboard engines, which would restore elevator authority, then gently ease back on the control column.

In Challenger's case, full flap was being retracted, a process that took in excess of a minute. It is likely the elevators were severely blanked by the flaps, thus reducing the effect of full power. Photographs taken soon after the crash show Challenger to be devoid of the outboard propellers. Whether they had already been salvaged or had been shed during impact is uncertain; however, the port-outer engine is believed to have lost its prop during the crash. The Pegasus reduction gear casings were prone to failure and, during impact, if the propellers plunged into the denser medium, water, they could have been pulled from the reduction gear. Photographic evidence shows the propeller blades bent forward, an indication they were producing thrust at impact, possibly in a forlorn attempt to recover from the porpoise.

The subsequent Board of Inquiry was met with a vow of silence from the crew, and Smith, whose [quote] 'normal flying ability was not doubted', took most of the blame.

Following the crash, Station Superintendent Brian Palmer and his traffic staff assisted Reg Barton, head of engineering, to remove the wings from Challenger and drag the fuselage ashore. It was expected that Captain Smith would soon be passing through Mozambique as a passenger, and to save his feelings, Reg Barton decided that the hulk should be disposed of by burning. This was not particularly successful and a large section of wreckage remained upon the beach. When the dis-favoured Captain Smith arrived, Steve Stephen escorted him from the flying-boat down that long jetty to the rest-house. Throughout the walk, Smith was unable to avert his haunted eyes from the shattered carcase that had once been his command.

Although Captain Smith remained in the employ of Imperial Airways, he never flew for them again. He was a maligned man; he had never sought command, yet, as Captain, he understood he was ultimately responsible.

CHAPTER SEVEN

Bermuda and the Atlantic Conquered

BERMUDA
The forced landing of Calypso – Cavalier, Bermuda and the
Atlantic miracle.

Despite the success of the Christmas airmails of 1938,
some embarrassment was caused by the precau-
tionary alighting of *Calypso*, in the English Channel.
Calypso had departed Durban on Christmas Day, and by
late in the afternoon of New Year's Eve, she was out of
St Nazaire for Southampton. On board were a crew of
six, two passengers and the ubiquitous one and a half
tons of mail. At St Nazaire, they had encountered
Canopus, commanded by Captain Burgess. One of
Burgess's passengers was Don Munro, returning from
Alexandria after his mail-delivery flight in *Mercury*.
Also at St Nazaire was Captain John Lock (probably) in
Corio. *Canopus* was the last 'boat to arrive at St Nazaire
and thus the last to continue to Southampton.

As *Calypso* crossed Jersey, she met low cloud. Icing
was forecast above 3,000 feet. Wishing to keep the surface in sight, Captain 'Bonzo' Brown descended to 150
feet. The forecast for Southampton was poor, cloud

lowered further, visibility reduced, the light started to
fail and ice began to form upon the wings of *Calypso*.
Captain Brown had no option other than to attempt
alighting in the open Channel and, hopefully, taxi the
sixty-four miles to Cherbourg. As dusk settled upon the
waters, the steward approached the two passengers,
Lieutenant-Colonel W. S. Brayne, a tea planter from
Kenya, and a Mr K. T. Clarke, offered them complimen-
tary whisky and sodas, and asked them to put on their
life-jackets. There was no need to worry but they were
about to alight in the open sea. *Calypso* successfully executed the landing about fifteen miles north of Alderney.
The sea was calm and the wind light. For the next three
hours Brown's skilful handling of the engines kept the
'boat under control in the strong currents. SOS messages
brought several boats to their rescue, one being the
steamship *Regal*. SS *Regal* took on the passengers and,
throughout New Year's Eve, towed the flying-boat
towards Cherbourg. They docked early on New Year's
Day, 1939. Later that day, Colonel Brayne and Mr Clarke
were flown on to Croydon.

The reason for the alighting was not immediately
made public. Following the incident, the Captain stated
one of the ailerons was damaged, but he did not make
clear whether the damage occurred during the alighting, beforehand or afterwards. Meanwhile, *Canopus*, the
last to depart St Nazaire, also entered the atrocious
Channel weather and received the alarming weather
report from Southampton. Burgess, however, had
obtained some reliable radio bearings, and certain of his
position he descended towards the surface. Burgess felt
his way shoreward until he could see the Bournemouth
lights, climbed over the New Forest and swung east to
Netley, where he alighted. Whilst clearing Customs,
Burgess asked after *Corio* and *Calypso*. There was great
concern, as Lock, in *Corio*, was safely in but Brown and
Calypso were overdue and (at that time) believed down
in the Channel. It transpired that the alarming weather
report obtained by Burgess had also been received by
Brown, but rather than being a report from coastal,
Southampton/Hythe, it was the weather report from
inland, Southampton/Eastleigh. Believing it to be
Hythe weather, Brown had taken a prudent course of
action but Burgess and Lock had both been a little
courageous.

The *Calypso* incident reinforced the premise: flying-
boats were safer than land planes.

'Bonzo' Brown, about 1943. (Brown)

The wings were detached and Cavalier *was put into giant crates for the transatlantic voyage as deck cargo on the SS* Loch Katrine. *(Turnill)*

The giant crate was lifted from SS Loch Katrine *by the RN crane at Somerset, Bermuda.* Cavalier *then had ancillary floats fitted before being towed across the Great Sound to Darrell's Island.*

In 1934, the British Government and Bermudan authorities granted permission for Imperial Airways to run an airmail and passenger service between Bermuda and New York. Pan American Airways (Pan Am), fearful of foreign progress, had coerced Imperial Airways into joint action upon this route. The venture received subsidies, in the form of a £34,500 grant from the Colonial Development Fund, a £3,200 grant from Bermuda and annual awards of £48,000 and £54,000 in 1937 and 1938 respectively.

Two 'boats, *Centaurus* and *Cavalier,* were ordered with the Bermuda to New York run in mind. Although similar to the Mk.I S.23, these Mk.II 'boats were fitted with an additional fuel tank in each wing, giving a total fuel capacity of 1,010 gallons, hence a still-air range of 1,078 nm. Imperial Airways was under great commercial pressure from both their own Empire and Mediterranean routes and Pan Am's readiness to operate a Bermuda–New York schedule. In response, all Imperial Airways could spare for the Bermuda–New York route was *Cavalier*.

Cavalier came off the slipway on 21 November 1936, a month behind *Centaurus.* Hurriedly, she was test-flown before being dismantled later that day and crated for shipping to Bermuda. The main components were placed into three giant, waterproof crates; 18 other packing cases held the remaining parts. The crates were put aboard barges and towed up the Thames to London Docks where, joined by a team of engineers from Shorts and Imperial (Len Turnill included), *Cavalier* was put aboard the SS *Loch Katrine.* The crates containing the wings overhung the sides of the ship and that carrying the fuselage was almost lost when lifting gear attached to the crate collapsed.

They arrived at Bermuda on 30 December 1936. The hull, in its 100-foot crate, and wings were offloaded at the Royal Naval Dockyard at Somerset, where the only crane strong enough to lift them was to be found.

Stabilizing floats, shipped from England, were rigged either side of the fuselage when free of its crate. The wings, still in their waterproof cases, and the wingless hull were towed the five miles to Darrell's Island.

Small and rocky, Darrell's Island lies in the Great Sound, which is at the western end of Bermuda. The isle, close to Hamilton and accessible only by water, had formerly been a fever quarantine and Boer prisoner-of-war camp. The flying-boat station would officially be opened on 12 June 1937 but it already boasted a hangar, large enough to shelter both the Imperial and Pan Am 'boats, and a terminal. Throughout early 1937, engineers of Shorts and Imperial toiled to reassemble *Cavalier.*

The Imperial and Pan Am joint venture called for the route to be shared and passenger and aircraft handling services to be mutually provided. Imperial agreed to be responsible for the Bermuda terminal whilst Pan Am provided assistance in the States. During winter, November to April, New York became ice-bound, and it was arranged to relocate the terminal to Baltimore. Even before the aircraft was ready, 405 passengers had paid the required fare of £20 single or £36 return for the six-hour flight.

Cavalier was test-flown after only six weeks, on 19 February 1937. Captain Armstrong, Area Manager and reserve pilot, was assisted during the flight by First

Cavalier *being reassembled in Bermuda.* (Turnill)

Officer Richardson. Further test-flights culminated in Captain W. N. Cumming, senior pilot, commanding a proving flight out to New York on 25 May and back on 26 May. Cumming's crew comprised First Officer Richardson, two wireless operators, J. Howard and H. W. Chapman, an engineer, F. A. Hine, Purser H. W. Watson and R. J. 'Bobby' Spence the steward. Also aboard were Mr Bell of Shorts and Mr Hayden of the Air Ministry's Inspection Directorate (AID). Pan Am proved the route with Captain H. E. Gray in the Sikorsky S.42 *Bermuda Clipper*, registered NC 16735. Down at 1,000 feet avoiding headwinds, *Cavalier* took five hours and fifty-five minutes to make the crossing but Howard and Chapman were able to establish wireless contact with Imperial Airways, London. The lightly loaded *Bermuda Clipper* benefited from a following wind and took ten minutes less.

Mid-morning on Wednesday, 16 June 1937, *Cavalier* departed Bermuda on the inaugural flight. She arrived in New York's Port Washington half an hour late (15:00 New York time) having taken the fourteen passengers on a city sightseeing diversion. Throughout the day, radio announcements, relayed from the aircraft, had been clearly heard on public broadcasts. That evening, Captain Cumming was guest-of-honour at a Pan Am dinner in the 'Cloud Room' of the Chrysler Building.

The more capacious *Bermuda Clipper* carried twenty-eight passengers, including some press and radio men, when she left New York for Bermuda the following Friday, 18 June.

At the outset, it was scheduled that each airline would make a weekly return journey. Imperial would depart Bermuda on Wednesdays, returning Saturdays, whilst Pan Am would depart New York on Sundays and return on Thursdays. By August 1937, however, the schedule was doubled, and *Cavalier* departed Bermuda on Mondays and Fridays to return the following days.

In 1938 Imperial Airways found it necessary to confer upon Captain M. R. 'Roly' Alderson the post of Senior Pilot, replacing Captain Cumming, who was temperamental and not universally popular. Captain 'Taffy' Powell had already been promoted to Area Manager and relief pilot, succeeding Captain Armstrong in 1937. Mr Robinson was the station superintendent.

For eighteen months, *Cavalier* was to ply between the United States and Grand Sound, Bermuda. In May 1938, she was acclaimed in the influential journal *American Aviation*, in which the editor compared *Cavalier* to the *Clipper*. Such was his praise, and alarm, as to the standards achieved by Shorts and Imperial, that he exhorted the American airline executives to hold their next air transport operators' meeting in Bermuda and sample the two services for themselves. The Port Washington Chamber of Commerce noted the advice and they took to the air for a short flight in *Cavalier*, on 1 June 1938.

Notwithstanding American praise and *Cavalier*'s faithful service, the winter of 1938/9 brought icing. Although the hazards of airframe icing were understood and the phenomenon was visible, carburettor icing was an insidious, unseen and poorly understood danger which plagued aviators.

The Claudel Hobson carburettors fitted to the Pegasus engines had three anti-icing devices. Firstly, under the control of the crew, the engine air-intakes could be selected to one of two positions, 'hot' or 'cold'. Ambient 'cold' air was drawn into the carburettor by an intake in front of numbers five and six cylinders. A selection to 'hot' air shuttered off the supply of cold out-side-air and allowed air, warmed by its passage around numbers five and six cylinders, to enter the intake. Secondly, the area of the butterfly throttles was jacketed in hot engine-oil. Thirdly, a seasonally set, wire-locked valve allowed exhaust gases to be routed adjacent to the top of the carburettors. However, these anti-icing devices lacked effectiveness. If icing struck and an engine faltered, the choking ice could sometimes be blown clear by manipulating the throttles and switching the ignition off and on, to backfire the engine, but more effective was flight into warmer air. Alderson had reported carburettor icing on several flights but Captain Powell never suffered the same.

Icing, when encountered, rarely left a trace. Be that as it may, on 8 October 1938, Alderson experienced engine fading, believed due to carburettor icing. Manipulation of the throttle failed to clear the blockage. On shutdown in Bermuda, Alderson closed the throttle and found the engine continued to run at high speed. The carburettor was stripped by Len Turnill and he discovered the butterfly operating shaft had been twisted. This had presumably happened when Alderson slammed the throttles during his attempt to clear the iced-up carburettor chokes. As a precaution against further problems, the seasonally set, exhaust routings were positioned at their winter setting.

The offending carburettor was shipped back to England. Imperial reported the damage was probably due to badly set throttle stops; however, they acknowledged the fading could be due to icing. After seeing Imperial's reply to his report, Captain Alderson said he was: 'Disturbed that the gravity of the situation was not more fully realised.' On 17 December he reported icing again, as did pilots in Europe on Christmas Eve and 30 December. Finally, on 20 January, Alderson wrote an engineering report specifying how icing around the carburettor butterfly valves had given much trouble and caused damage. His engineering report was to be quoted in full during a subsequent accident inquiry.

On Saturday 21 January 1939, the 290th flight was due out of Port Washington under the command of Captain Alderson. The weather forecast was poor; two cold fronts had to be crossed and sleet and snow were expected at the outset of the transit. The freezing level was at sea level but it was expected to rise to 12,000 feet by the midway point. Conditions were typical for the time of year and Alderson had no hesitation in making the flight. His four crewmen were First Officer Neil Richardson, Radio Officer Patrick Chapman, who had recently wed, Senior Steward David Williams and Steward 'Bobby' Spence. The crew were very experienced and had flown the route many times. 'Bobby' Spence, however, had decided to give up flying, as he was often airsick. In the crew's care were eight passengers: Mr and Mrs Donald Miller of Lincoln Nebraska, Mr and Mrs J. Gordon Noakes of Melba New York, Mrs Edna Watson of Paget Bermuda, Mrs George 'Honey' Ingham of Pembroke Bermuda, Miss Nellie Tucker Smith, also of Pembroke, and Mr Charles Talbot of Brookline Massachusetts.

Once the passengers were boarded, the engines were started. Radio Officer Chapman took post at the flight-deck escape hatch, Pyrene fire-extinguisher in hand. Satisfied all engines were running smoothly, Chapman moved down to the bow mooring hatch and readied the drogues, should Alderson's whistle call for them to aid manoeuvring. The tail line was slipped and *Cavalier* eased forward. The engines warmed, Alderson carried out the engine checks and Richardson set the cooling gills for take-off. Richardson and Chapman returned to their seats; all was secure for departure. With a skilful blend of asymmetric power, aileron and rudder Captain Alderson allowed the mighty Pegasus engines to thrust *Cavalier* straight across Port Washington's waters. The bow wave rose, gently spraying the cabin windows. As speed increased, the passengers sensed the flying-boat seeming to sink lower into the water as the bow wave washed along the side of the flying-boat. Like an aquatic Phoenix, *Cavalier* lifted onto the step and raised herself above the waters. Skimming, the floats were clear of the water. Wavelets battered the keel with a flapping sound. The sound stopped as *Cavalier* skipped into the air, only to sink back down to allow the keel to receive a more rapid pounding. Again the sound from below ceased, drowned by the roar of the engines, and *Cavalier* was aloft. Alderson called Richardson to reduce power and bring the flaps up. In the cabin, passengers heard the Rotax electric motor wind in the flaps.

They were airborne from Port Washington at 10:38 (New York local time), and just before entering the overcast at 10:45, they selected carburettor air to 'hot'. A thin covering of ice formed upon the nose of the floats, the bracing wires and the mainplane's leading edge. The amount was less than Alderson had anticipated. For the next two hours the flight was uneventful. When *Cavalier* had levelled off above the cloud, the sun had melted the ice accumulation. Lunch was prepared. At 12:25, to escape turbulent air, Captain Alderson climbed the 'boat up through a layer of cumulus cloud which lay ahead.

When they entered the cloud, they had experienced radio interference and the wireless operator was reported to have transmitted, at 12:23, the message: 'Running into bad weather. May have to earth [wind in the trailing radio aerial and stop transmitting].' This message was erroneously rendered to the press and accepted literally as: 'Running into bad weather – May have to land.' At 12:27 (N Y time) a second message: 'Still in bad weather. Severe static.'

Ten minutes into the climb, at about 11,000 feet, the engines went out of synchronization and began to fade. Within a minute, the inboards were giving less than 1,000 rpm. Opening and closing of the throttles failed to clear the engines and the Captain decided to turn back to the cloud-free layer below, at 9,000 feet. Steward Spence told the passengers that they were about to descend, but the flying-boat suddenly plunged. Alderson, losing height quickly, realised he would be unable to regain the clear patch, so he turned about again and resumed course southwards. The outboards picked up but the inboard engines stubbornly refused to respond to the throttle. They passed 6,000 feet and it was noticed the oil temperatures had fallen to 40 to 45 degrees centigrade. There was still insufficient power to maintain height.

As *Cavalier* continued to descend, now passing 3,000 feet, she emerged into warmer air – there was a little rain. 'Cold' air was selected for the inboards; they gave a momentary burst of power and then fell back. The outer engines gave only partial power so a forced descent seemed unavoidable and an SOS was transmitted. During this period, Port Washington had fruitlessly attempted to raise the stricken plane. At 12:50 Alderson ordered Chapman to transmit a distress message and First Officer Richardson told Spence to collect the life-preservers from the unoccupied rear cabin without causing undue alarm. In desperation, Richardson pumped fuel directly into the cylinders using the priming pumps, but this had no effect.

An SOS was transmitted at 12:57, 'All engines failing through ice. Altitude 1,500 feet. Force landing in a few minutes.' Port Washington acknowledged. Bermuda received the SOS, but eight or nine minutes later, and still in the air, *Cavalier* called again saying she had two engines running and was attempting to restart the others. On board, Mrs Edna Watson recalled that the aircraft had flown through several snow and hail squalls but there had been no alarm until the engines began to slow down. The pulsating rhythm of the engines seemed not to have registered with Miss Smith but Mr Talbot noted the 'boat was skimming the surface with the inboard engines stopped.

Captain Alderson was to be censured in some quarters for continuing south for almost fifty minutes after sending his first message. The official accident report, however, endorsed Captain Alderson's actions, as the water temperature increased by three degrees centigrade for every 100 miles flown towards Bermuda, a crucial fact. Although it was normal practice for one pilot to concentrate upon the flying and for the other to act as navigator, their preoccupation with the engines had been at the expense of the navigational log. They were unable to give an accurate position in their distress message.

The battle was soon to be lost. Alderson was in an unenviable position: he could not trust the engines yet he had to make headway towards the warmer currents. Rather than await, suicidally, total engine failure, he prepared for a precautionary alighting. From height, Captain Alderson saw a sea smoother than he had ever seen previously. All boded well. Miss Smith was enjoying a fairly good brandy and water with her fellow passengers, when 'Bobby' Spence told them lunch would be served once they had alighted: this was the first warning that some recalled. Quickly and quietly, Spence instructed the passengers to hang on as fast as they could as a landing was possible. Steward Williams helped Miss Smith into her life-jacket. The other passengers, according to Miss Smith, were similarly jacketed, as they, and the crew, stoically awaited their fate. The inboards were practically useless and the outboards gave only 1,800 rpm.

The crew estimated there was a very light breeze, 8 mph from the south-east, and Alderson picked his spot upon which to put down. As he made his final approach, aghast, he realized there was a moderate sea and a confused swell. He thought there was a chance of getting down, yet he knew damage was a possibility, but – he was committed to a landing. The two inner engines were useless, another was faltering; approach and landing speeds were higher than ideal. At 110 mph *Cavalier* descended the last few feet. Holding-off, the keel sliced through the top of one swell and she bounced onto a second. The nose reared up and the 'boat slammed into the third ridge. The planing bottom stove in, just behind the main step.

Up on the flight-deck, Alderson and Richardson were thrown gently forward in their seats. An abnormal deceleration followed and Alderson sensed the hull was breached. None of the passengers in the forward cabin were hurt and they were not unduly alarmed. In the cabin, Mrs George 'Honey' Ingham felt the jar of the crash. As she gathered her thoughts, Spence was assisting the passengers into their life-jackets. Williams had been at the rear of the promenade deck; he was thrown to the floor by the impact, picked up by a torrent of water and washed into the aft cabin. Mr and Mrs Noakes were the sole passengers of the aft cabin. Mr Noakes had attempted to stand up for the impact but, unable to hold fast, he too was thrown to the floor. He sustained awful head injuries, became unconscious and was never fully aware of his predicament again. Williams struggled forward with the Noakeses.

Pat Chapman, radio officer, stayed at his post; 'Landed OK. Switches Off. Standby' was received in Bermuda at 13:12. Alderson went to the rear of the flight-deck and opened the top escape hatch. He descended the ladder into the pantry, entered the cabins and personally ordered abandonment. He knew *Cavalier* would fill quickly and sink.

Williams opened the forward door and Mr Donald Miller, clutching his life-jacket, slipped as he stepped out and was struck by a huge wave that pushed him up into the sinking wing, rendering him semi-conscious.

Mrs Miller, her life-jacket improperly fitted, was next into the water.

Mrs Ingham and Miss Smith had been sitting together and, with Spence's help, escaped by the forward door. Water spouted through the floor as 'Honey' Ingham, life-jacket bundled in arms, leapt into the sea; Miss Smith followed, dropping into the ocean. 'Honey' looked back to the wreckage, as she swam away, fearful of being drawn down with the craft. She saw Miss Smith enter the water and called out to her. Shoeless, both women strove away. By now the 'boat was settling.

Mrs Watson recalled later, 'When the aeroplane struck the water, I was almost immediately taken by the steward to the emergency door in the pantry. By the time the steward had the door open, the water was already pouring in. I literally had to step out onto the ocean.'

Spence continued to collect the lifebelts from their stowage, but water cascaded into the cabin. Mr Talbot and Spence, without lifebelts themselves, were the last to leave. Spence swam to Miller's aid. A second wave struck the pair, again Miller was pummelled against the wing. Once the water subsided, Miller was gone. Still at post was Chapman, transmitting the crucial Mayday. An unknown operator acknowledged him but, without pause, the sea rose, erupted through the open pantry hatchway onto the flight-deck and flooded the adjacent battery. The radio went silent. It was a quarter past one.

At 13:13 the ominous message: 'Sinking!' This was not received in Bermuda and, outwardly, Imperial remained optimistic. After all, Alderson had had ample time to prepare for a precautionary alighting, which was thought to be within the 'boat's capability, and, south of the fronts, the weather was believed to be fair. What is more, there would have been ample time to warn the passengers. Once *Cavalier* had landed safely, she would, anyway, be unable to communicate directly with Bermuda, as the range of the radio was limited when lacking the trailing aerial and powered only by the standby generator or battery. Officially, only the most guarded of statements were made by Captain Powell.

After the initial scramble out of the cabin, most of the passengers clambered on top of the hull. Richardson and Chapman helped Mrs Watson and the Noakeses, who, without life-jackets, had come up through the flight-deck hatch. The more able helped the less fortunate. For a few moments they sat upon the hull, but it was now in two pieces and settling slowly. Part of the cargo was three hundred baby chickens, 'They kept chirping to the very end', said Senior Steward Williams.

About fifteen minutes after the alighting, gently, *Cavalier* was swallowed by the Atlantic. The wretched people hung onto the lifebelts; there were about half a dozen belts between the twelve of them. 'Honey' and Nellie Smith swam back to the main group.

As soon as the plight of *Cavalier* was reported to Bermuda, Captain Powell calculated where the stricken 'boat likely lay: North 37 degrees 17 minutes, West 069 degrees 45 minutes. Powell's estimate was at variance with that of Pan Am but sense prevailed and Powell's calculations were accepted. Captain Powell next requested Pan Am's S.42 get airborne from Darrell's Island and fly to the crash site in order to commence a search for *Cavalier*. Hastily, the Clipper was fuelled. At 14:00, Captain C. A. Lorber lifted the Sikorsky into a greying sky. Captain Powell and his staff could now do little other than wait.

A massive search and rescue operation was being instigated. In the United States, Coast Guards were alerted and a flying-boat from Long Island was despatched over the Atlantic. She remained on station for only ninety minutes, then darkness forced her to withdraw. The United States Army Air Corps assisted with one of the new B-17 Flying Fortresses, which dropped flares, until she too was forced to retire by worsening weather. At Lakehurst, a dirigible was on standby. These and other aircraft went to the search area but no sightings were made. On the surface, Coast Guard cutters and US Naval vessels, in addition to ships diverted from their routes, fared no better.

Earlier, about 15:30, Lorber, in the Clipper, had faced severe head winds, and it became obvious that darkness would overtake them before they arrived at the crash site. They returned to Bermuda, intent on a resumption of the search at dawn. Hope began to fade. The Canadian destroyer *Saguenay,* having raised steam in forty-five minutes and slipped her Bermuda mooring at 16:30, finally left the colony late Saturday night. At 30 knots, she ploughed through heavy seas towards *Cavalier*'s last position.

Once *Cavalier* had sunk, the survivors struggled to form a compact group, with arms and legs intertwined. Few, if any, had put on their lifebelts correctly. Charles Talbot, with his arm in plaster – the result of a recent skiing accident – was further hampered. Fortunately, they had reached the warmer waters of the Gulf Stream and, for the early part of the afternoon, the water was not choppy but there was a considerable swell. As the sun lowered, waves occasionally broke over them. One of the cushion-type life-preservers floated up from the wreck and was given to Mr and Mrs Noakes. This easily supported them. Although there were no life-jackets for the injured Captain Alderson, Steward Spence and Mr Talbot, there was sufficient flotation equipment for the huddled group.

With the exception of Mr and Mrs Noakes, the remaining passengers seemed in fair condition. Mr Noakes's head injury was, however, most severe and he was barely conscious. Mrs Watson thought he never regained consciousness, but he was attended, as well as possible, by First Officer Richardson and Steward Spence. When they were not attending Noakes, they circled the group, raising morale and assisting where possible. Steward 'Bobby' Spence heroically continued to attend his passengers, but this was to be his downfall. From time to time, they suffered the odd rain shower, but their ordeal was only just beginning. Sadly, about an hour after darkness, Noakes succumbed to his injuries. He was released from the group. The others began to feel cold, very cold.

The first vessel into the area was a Coast Guard 'plane, V166. It had left Floyd Bennett Field, New York, and whilst *en route* had signalled, at 18:00, 'Will keep a sharp lookout for flares. There is unlimited ceiling and clear visibility for 10 miles.' Despite the crew's assurances, the sun had set and darkness relentlessly engulfed the survivors before V166 arrived. V166 or another aeroplane may, however, have been briefly sighted by the survivors.

Physically, the group owed their life, so far, to the warm waters of the Gulf Stream. But ultimate survival of the human frame is dependent upon mental wellbeing. Mrs Edna Watson, Canadian born but a resident of Bermuda, spiritually bonded the unfortunates. Holding the weaker members above the waves, which were becoming very rough, Edna Watson boosted their dampened morale with song, gossip and jokes. There was no panic or open despair. As the eleven survivors floundered in the water, First Officer Richardson saw his trousers float by; however, he rescued his pipe from them.

Another fear raised was the thought of sharks. Richardson circled the group so as to ward off any predators but, as the time-blurring blanket of darkness descended, he rejoined the pack. 'Bobby' Spence, another Bermudan resident but of Irish stock, became most restless. He started swimming away from the group, wasting his energy. The remaining survivors repeatedly called on him to return until on one excursion he started to thrash wildly in the water. He was dragged back to the mutual support of the group, but support and comfort from the first officer and Mrs Watson were of no help. He quickly became delirious and died. Vain attempts were made to massage him back to life, but he too was released to the deep. Ten remained.

The night darkened and the waves rose. Twice, in the distance, they saw passing lights and rockets from searching ships, but their cries were lost upon the Atlantic's swirl and potential deliverance steamed away. Mournfully, a pitiful song issued from one of the crew members. Time lost all purpose and, inwardly dejected, sodden despair enveloped the party.

A miraculous rescue was at hand. Rockets were seen and a ship's light appeared through the heaving waters; the survivors cried out, louder than ever, their hopes raised. The boat remained steadfast on her track – away. Almost in desperation, Richardson and Chapman struck out towards the ship. The others followed feebly: cold was slowly killing them and, again, the lights seemed to be passing. They could see the boat, lights twinkling, rockets soaring, a spectacle of salvation slowly slipping behind the inky waves. Weakly, Richardson and Chapman made their way to a wan pool of light thrown from a porthole. Relief! They were seen from the bridge and two deck hands called out to them. In New York it was 23:25.

The *Esso Baytown*, commanded by Captain Spurr, had steamed to Powell's position. Spurr, navigating through the poor weather of a January Atlantic night, had achieved the exact spot Captain Powell had

deemed. The *Baytown* was slowed and hands were positioned on deck. Spurr called, 'Stop Engines', and listened. Providence and skill were rewarded with the cries from the survivors. The searchlights ran across the surface; Chapman and Richardson were bathed in light. It was 23:25 New York time. *Baytown* immediately signalled she had sighted wreckage and launched a lifeboat towards the survivors. Only their cries could guide the lifeboat through the high seas of the stormy, starless night. For thirty minutes, the six men vainly searched for the huddled group, encouraged, yet at the same time frustrated, by their cries.

Stanley Taylor stood in the bow of the lifeboat. With flashlight in hand he speared the darkness. Behind him, commanded by Chief Officer Anderson, were the four strongest oarsmen *Baytown* could muster. From somewhere in the distance a song struggled to pierce the wind. The boat hove to for Richardson and Chapman to be dragged aboard; they slumped into the bottom of the whaler. Again the song was heard, this time closer. Taylor swung his torch, lancing the night. They continued to row. Then, about two hundred yards from where they had saved Richardson and Chapman, Taylor saw the soaked bundle of the remaining eight. They had only four life-jackets between them. The thankful survivors were plucked from the increasing swell and dragged across the gunwales!

Considering their prolonged ordeal, they were in fine spirits as a breeches buoy hoisted them aboard *Baytown*. Gently, the unconscious Captain Alderson was lifted aboard. The night had almost claimed him. He was at the end of his tether. Injured only slightly, but exhausted, he too owed his life to Mrs Watson who had kept him afloat, and alive. By now a fifteen-foot swell ran and recovery of the whaler was impossible. One and a half hours after Captain Spurr had put out his lifeboat, he was under way.

At 00:20, on Sunday 22 January, the *Baytown* signalled, 'We have picked up ten survivors. These survivors feel that the other three are lost. We need a doctor badly.' The gunboat *Erie* responded. Surgeon Lieutenant-Commander S. H. White USN and the Pharmacist's Mate were put aboard, despite the now heaving seas. Coast Guard cutter *Champlain* provided additional medical supplies. *Champlain* and seven other Coast Guard vessels continued the search for the remaining three. Neither bodies nor survivors were to be found but flotsam from the crash was strewn across the water.

With the rescue accomplished, the search was terminated and the vast armada that was being prepared was stood down. *Baytown* steamed out of the area towards New York and made a further signal, 'Survivors in good condition.'

The immediate tragedy was past and, in order to meet *Baytown*, Captain Powell flew to New York in the Sikorsky. He was accompanied by Mrs Richardson and Mrs Chapman, the radio operator's bride of two weeks. 'Honey' Ingham's husband flew to New York a few days later. They flew over the spot where *Cavalier* now rested and Captain Powell later said to a reporter, 'I am astonished that anyone was rescued at all. It was some kind of miracle.'

On Monday morning, Captain Powell, Mrs Richardson and Mrs Chapman boarded a Coast Guard cutter and rendezvoused with *Baytown*. Later that afternoon, the *Esso Baytown*, escorted by five tugs and two cutters, docked at Manhattan's Pier 9. Ships' sirens, whistles and hooters sounded a welcome; overhead, aircraft circled. The rescued passengers came out on deck: some waved, one danced and others just stood. Mrs Noakes was in a state of collapse, and the widow of Donald Miller fainted when confronted with the crush of people at the pier.

Once in New York's Beekman Hotel, Mrs Nellie Smith was interviewed over radio-telephone for the *Bermudan Royal Gazette*. She said she had suffered no ill effects from the ordeal. On the contrary, she closed the interview, 'I never experienced anything more wonderful than the *esprit de corps* that was shown after we found ourselves in the water.'

An investigation was convened in the Chrysler Building and was attended by Group Captain G. C. Pirie, Air Attaché to the British Embassy, Washington, on behalf of the British authorities. His provisional report was forwarded to Wing Commander Vernon S. Brown, Chief Inspector of Accidents for the Air Ministry. Brown was due to arrive in America in February and, with the co-operation of the United States Civil Aeronautics Authority, was expected to finalize the report.

It was initially stated by Imperial that Captain Alderson was unable to confirm that the 'boat was forced down because of carburettor icing. However, Imperial Airways failed to provide any rational alternative explanation. Captain Alderson, probably directed by Imperial, was quoted as saying, 'The whole thing is a mystery to me.'

The accident report was published on 25 March 1939. The Air Ministry Inspector found the accident was as a result of icing in the carburettors of all four engines. It was also noted that Alderson had alerted Imperial Airways to the problem of carburettor icing, which also occurred on the European routes, on several occasions since the previous October.

Icing occurred despite existing air-intake heaters. Alderson had suggested the installation of an American barometric/thermostatic device that regulated the amount of air entering the intake and maintained the air temperature at 90 degrees Fahrenheit (32 degrees C). Overall, the Inspector of Accidents agreed, suggesting that to prevent icing, the engines should be run at a higher oil temperature and, to prevent unheated air leaking into the intake, a more airtight hot-air intake shutter ought to be fitted. Moreover, these modifications should be incorporated into the Empire 'boats before they were permitted to operate the New York to Bermuda sector again. Fault was also found with the Exactor hydraulic engine control system, favoured by some designers for its ease of installation and pipe routing.

The report found Imperial wanting in the use of life-jackets and escape drills. It recommended passengers be instructed in the fastening of life-jackets and the location of emergency exits. Although there were twenty-two seat-type and six crew-type life-preservers on board, only four of each could be used. Provision of extra survival equipment was also recommended, such as survival rations, life-rafts and distress flares. Moreover, airlines were urged to compel passengers to fasten seat belts for take-off and landing: Noakes sustained head injuries as he attempted to stand during the crash landing. Additional modifications to the top escape hatch, further to those called for following the *Cygnus* accident in Brindisi, were also recommended.

Imperial commented that they were generally in favour with the report; however, they contended that the weather was more severe than forecast, more severe than ever previously experienced, and the three separate carburettor heating devices had been overcome.

April 1939. In reply to a Parliamentary question by Mr Perkins MP, Captain Balfour, Under-Secretary of State for Air, said:

> 'It would appear that Imperial Airways were not remiss in the way that they had handled the situation. In the meantime, Imperial Airways had issued instructions to their pilots to avoid flying through severe icing conditions and if necessary delay departures. In the circumstances it was not proposed to suspend the Certificates of Airworthiness of the Empire flying-boats in Europe.'

Mrs Donald Miller was demanding Reith's appearance in court to face allegations of wilful negligence and misconduct on the part of Imperial Airways Bermuda Limited. She also claimed $200,000 damages. The case was to be heard in the Admiralty section of the United States District court as they had jurisdiction over Admiralty matters. Mr Iserman, attorney to the widowed Mrs Miller, served Sir John with a subpoena as he toured the British Pavilion of the World's Fair on Monday 7 August 1939. He had earlier arrived from Southampton in the *Queen Mary*.

An alternative account tells of how Reith was in his hotel room when the subpoena was served. Bailiffs called at the door for 'Sir Reith'. Reith instructed a companion to tell the bailiffs that, 'He is not in'. Such gentlemanly etiquette held no sway in America and the bailiffs entered and gave Sir John the document, saying, 'The subpoena is duly served.' Settlement was made out of court.

The chosen replacement craft for *Cavalier* was *Champion,* the first S.30 to be built. Unlike her sister 'boats, *Cabot, Caribou* and *Connemara, Champion* was not fitted with in-flight refuelling equipment. The S.30 was powered by Perseus XII C sleeve-valve engines, and being stronger than the S.23, was allowed an all-up weight for take-off of 46,000 lb. This gave her a range of 1,500 miles. Lankester Parker took *Champion* for her

Cassiopeia *undergoing a carburettor de-icing trial. The port-inner carburettor intake has been modified. There is non-standard connection between the exhaust collector ring and the air intake. The propellers are fitted with spinners.* (Hackett)

maiden flight on 28 September 1938. Between 17 and 21 October, *Champion* was fitted with wooden fixed-pitch propellers for a trial, but on 26 October, these were replaced with de Havilland variable-pitch propellers. She next plied the Empire Routes from 8 November 1938 until 2 September 1939.

Throughout the year, Imperial Airways had been experiencing difficulty in meeting the demand for mail and passengers and had found themselves unable to release *Champion* to the Bermuda route. Moreover, following the *Cavalier* accident report, she was being used for a 400-hour icing trial.

Carburettor icing was to plague aviation for some years to come. However, Imperial were stirred into action by the events of winter 1938/39 and tried several experiments. One system involved spraying de-icer into the carburettor intake. On flight-tests this proved to be of little use.

In July 1939, the Bermuda Chamber of Commerce voiced their anxiety that *Champion* had not arrived. They were informed this was due partly to the icing trial and partly to the fact that the route 'Taffy' Powell was to

fly *Champion* out to Bermuda (via West Africa and South America) had yet to be surveyed.

During the summer of 1939, Captain Powell returned to England via South America and West Africa, laying moorings at the *en route* sites. As it transpired, Powell arrived in England on 3 September 1939: world events overtook Imperial Airways and the North Atlantic. There being no aircraft available for the New York to Bermuda route, Imperial Airways withdrew. Meantime Pan Am introduced the Boeing Model 314.

Postscript:

'The late Captain Powell acknowledged, in 1993, that providence was at hand that night and congratulates Captain Spurr, master of the Esso Baytown, on his navigation. He also said Alderson later confided, that with hindsight, had the true sea state been known, he perhaps should have risked his continuing struggle to remain aloft whilst he sought warmer air.'

AIR-TO-AIR REFUELLING AND THE ATLANTIC

Early trial – Cobham joins research – Cobham to India – 'C-class' system works – Pan Am looks at the Atlantic – 'The Gentlemen's Agreement' laid to rest – The Clippers cross – 'G-class', and others – Cabot, Caribou, Connemara and Clyde equipped – Harrows to Botwood – Perseus trial – Pan Am and the Boeing 314 mail service – Connemara trials and loss – The S.30 system, final demonstration – Cabot's and Caribou's crossings of summer '39 – Impressed.

The examination of the potential for in-flight refuelling started during the First World War. In 1917, the Royal Naval Air Service investigated the possibility of passing fuel down a hose connecting two aircraft. Similar trials were taking place elsewhere, and one of the earliest successes was by Smith and Ritcher, on 27 June 1923, at San Diego. Their technique was crude, simple but effective. A hose, attached along its length to a steel cable, was winched down from the tanker to the rear-seat passenger in the receiver aircraft below. The receiver passenger stood up in the slipstream, grabbed the hose and stuck the nozzle into the fuel tank. By the end of the decade, the US Army using two Douglas aircraft as tankers kept a Fokker receiver aircraft airborne for 151 hours – a week.

The Air Ministry instructed our Air Attaché in Washington, Flight Lieutenant David Atcherly, to monitor progress. Meanwhile, a private trial was being carried out in England under the leadership of the Hon. Mrs Victor Bruce. She had acquired a Saro Windover amphibian – with RAF crew – and an RAF Bristol fighter to act as tanker. They managed to stay aloft for 54 hours and 13 minutes during August 1932. Probably as a result of the Hon. Bruce and Atcherly's further research in Amman, the Air Ministry formed an RAF In-flight Refuelling Trials Unit. They used Atcherly's patented technique, almost identical to the earlier Smith Ritcher, a Vickers Virginia tanker and a Westland Wapiti receiver.

Sir Alan Cobham had discovered the unruly aerodynamics of a trailing and flailing hose as early as 1931. This respect for the flailing hose, already identified by Smith and Ritcher, led Cobham to develop the 'looped hose method', whereby initial contact was made by a light line. In 1933, Cobham flew trials formating upon weighted lines, suspended from a D.H.4 flown by Squadron Leader Helmore. The looped hose, or variations thereof, was to be the basis of Cobham's technique for the next decade or more.

Cobham's research was on behalf of Imperial Airways, which was subsidized by the Government. The Air Ministry realised that, effectively, the RAF In-flight Refuelling Trials Unit was competing with Imperial Airways and, as a consequence, the RAF trials unit was disbanded. Atcherly's patents remained under the control of the Air Ministry but they assisted Cobham with the offer of a few aircraft and sanctions to continue research.

Cobham, also a director of Airspeed Aviation, used the new Airspeed Courier as receiver and a Handley Page W10 transporter as tanker. For the trials the interi- or of the W10 had been stripped and tracks laid the length of the cabin. Along these tracks, standard fuel drums were rolled aft, where they were connected to the 'tanker' end of the refuelling hose. The nozzle end was attached to a trail rope. Cobham flew the Courier, and on a few occasions Mr Nevil Shute Norway, the aircraft designer and author, acted as co-pilot. Contact was established as the Courier formated 50 to 100 feet below and astern the W10. Helmore, or Shute, would then open the Courier's top hatch and stand up in the 90 mph slipstream. Armed with their special equipment – a shepherd's crook – they captured a weighted light line which had been lowered from the W10. Once the light line had been secured, a heavier rope was attached to the hose, which had a trigger nozzle. Then, the hose was lowered and connections to the receiver's tank were made. Fuel flowed under gravity assistance. One problem was that the W10 had to be in a shallow dive in order for the Courier to fly with a safe margin of speed above the stall. This operation called for great skill on the part of both pilots: it worked but was hazardous.

The weight at the end of the line was a small football, filled with lead shot. Cobham was worried that the Courier's prop might strike the weight and shatter. As a result, the football was replaced, initially, with a water-filled condom, but more successfully with a water-filled rubber bag manufactured by Dunlop. Their troubles were not over: on one occasion, the weighted line jammed the Courier's aileron. The Courier was thrown out of control and entered a spiral dive. After six turns and thoroughly shaken, Cobham and Helmore managed to recover the aircraft, directly above Chichester Cathedral.

For a man who publicly announced that he would fly from Rochester, Kent, to the Houses of Parliament, via Melbourne, Australia, in 1926 and achieved just that, the dream to fly non-stop to Australia seemed quite reasonable, and for several years, this had been Cobham's declared goal. Despite his enthusiastic support for himself, he was unable to convince the Air Ministry that they should lend him half a dozen or so aircraft, crews and all the necessary paraphernalia to mount the attempt. He did, however, sway Air Marshal Dowding, then an Air Staff officer with responsibilities for research and development, to provide the required assistance to attempt a non-stop flight to Karachi. At the end of September 1934, Cobham and Helmore commenced their pioneering flight to India in the Courier. The first in-flight refuelling, to top off the tanks over Portsmouth, was successful, as was the second over Malta: his other W10 had been positioned at Hal Far. Subsequent refuellings, using RAF tankers, were planned for Alexandria (Aboukir) and Basra.

As Malta slipped beneath their wing, 3,000 feet below, they broke contact for the second time. Cobham applied power to climb back to cruising height, and although the engine continued to run it was no longer under his control. The throttle linkage had broken. In such circumstances the return spring automatically, and slowly, throttled back the engine. A forced landing was inevitable but the aircraft was laden with almost two tons of petrol. The engine was gradually giving less and less power and Cobham was unable to maintain height. He turned towards Hal Far and made a successful but hazardous forced landing, grossly overweight. He decided to leave the wheels retracted and only narrowly succeeded in reaching the field. Despite a full fuel load little damage was done to the aircraft other than a bent propeller.

Inspection revealed a cotter pin that held the throttle linkage together had not been secured by a split pin. It was apparent that the split pin had never been inserted and the linkage could have collapsed at any time. Having extricated himself from disaster, he learnt the W10, which had refuelled him over Portsmouth, had also crashed. It had left Ford, for Coventry, but over Aston Clinton, Buckinghamshire, a tailplane bracing wire failed; in the ensuing crash and fire, Flight Lieutenant Brembridge and his crew of three perished. The aircraft had carried 100,000 fare-paying passengers for Cobham without injury. Thoroughly disappointed, the expedition to India was abandoned.

Despite these setbacks, Cobham continued working on in-flight refuelling. His new company, Flight Refuelling Ltd, was drawn up on 29 October 1934 and formed in association with Airspeed, at Ford on the Sussex coast.

Although he had yet to produce a practical system, Cobham entered into an agreement, in 1936, with Imperial Airways to develop his system for use with the Empire Flying-Boats. Imperial wanted to give the 'boat a transatlantic capability. Continuing his work at Ford, he received additional Government support: two Virginias, an HP 51 (Harrow forerunner), a Boulton and Paul Overstrand and the Vickers B 9/27 bomber/transport.

The weighted bag and shepherd's crook, as used for the ill-fated record run to India, remained the mainstay of Cobham's system. Following difficulties in hauling in the lines onto the Virginia, a simple hand-winch was fitted. The receiving aircraft was fitted with a pair of long poles that extended from the nose, with a view to catching the trailed line. Called the 'Horns Method', it was not favoured.

Cobham realised the Atcherly patents possibly held the way ahead. He managed to get Air Ministry approval and was awarded a development contract in 1937, to evaluate the Atcherly 'Inter-Air' or 'Crossed Lines' system and improve both his own system and that of Atcherly. Soon, shepherd's crooks and weighted bags were replaced by parachutes, pulleys and grapples. The principle, as before, was that the aircraft would be joined by a flexible pipe, 300 feet long in this case. Again, initial contact would be made by light line, but there was to be more automation and the really skilled flying was entrusted to the tanker crew – they were more practised.

The procedure commenced with the receiver streaming a 400-foot cable with a grapple upon its end. The tanker reeled out a similar line. Then, flying across and above the receiver, the tanker trawled its grapple to snag the receiver's line. Once the line was snagged, the tanker's grapple would run down the line and finally connect with the receiver's grapple. Having captured the receiver, the tanker formated above and hauled in the joined lines. Once the receiver's line was in the tanker, it was connected to the delivery nozzle of the fuel hose. Completion of this action was then signalled to the receiver, a series of coded flags being used to communicate.

The receiver now had to pull the hose, from the drum in the tanker, across the space between the two aircraft and towards its own refuelling coupling. The motive force for this was a trailed parachute. The receiver's end of the light line was looped over a pulley, attached to a small parachute and then trailed into the slipstream. The parachute thus pulled the light line over the pulley, and in turn, pulled the hose from the tanker to the receiver. Once the refuelling nozzle entered the receiver, it was automatically guided into the coupling and held in position by the drag force exerted by the parachute on the light line. After a signal to the tanker, a 10hp wind-driven pump supplied fuel to the receiver at 80 gallons a minute.

Once refuelling was completed, the aircraft pulled away. The hose, still attached to the light line, disconnected, the parting force of the aircraft being greater than the drag of the parachute. The line was then pulled back across the pulley, dragging the parachute towards the receiver. As the parachute approached the receiver an increase in line thickness was sensed and a guillotine severed the line and thus jettisoned the parachute. The tanker, now trailing the hose with the remnants of the light line attached, was free and the two aircraft could go their own way.

By 1937, Cobham had designed a workable system for Imperial's flying-boats, but certain aspects, especially the initial contact system had yet to be perfected. At this time, in-flight refuelling, as a range enhancement technique, was having to compete with the *Maia* and *Mercury* composite. In addition to his arrangement with Imperial Airways, Cobham undertook a partnership with the Shell Oil Company, who were already heavily involved with aircraft fuels, lubricants and fuel bowsers. Cobham envisaged that his company would soon be running a fleet of airborne tankers throughout the world, and a fuel company was the obvious partner.

Cobham's in-flight refuelling was not the only contestant on the North Atlantic. In America, great progress was being made. On 22 September 1936, Pan Am announced that as from 21 October they would be offering a transpacific passenger service. Back to cooler waters, on 15 February 1937, Washington announced, Pan Am and Imperial Airways proposed a transatlantic mail service from November 1937, but a passenger service was still some way off. Moreover, there was still no decision as to where the western terminus of the transatlantic service would be sited. North Beach, Long Island, had been suggested but first the City needed to raise £300,000 to purchase the site. The US Government, so it was reported, had set aside £700,000 for development, and several east-coast towns were vying for the honours, Boston, Newark, Baltimore and Charleston being favoured.

Although Pan Am were operating the Martin Clipper in the Pacific, they had yet to choose an aircraft for the Atlantic. In December 1937 they tasked Lindbergh to scout around the European manufacturers to see if any one could meet a new Pan Am specification. Their requirement was for an aircraft, fitted with dining saloons and sleeping quarters, capable of carrying 100 passengers and a large load of mail and freight for 5,000 miles at 200 mph. Pan Am would finance this project and they hoped to offer a service between New York and the European capitals.

The November 1937 mail service came to nought and in Washington, the Secretary of Air Commerce announced, on 8 June 1938, a transatlantic airmail service would now probably start during the forthcoming September. It had been planned to commence a service, in conjunction with Imperial Airways, in August, but this too was delayed, probably as a result the difficulties Boeing were having with their 314.

The French were progressing: on 13 June 1938, they revealed that verbal assurances had been received from the Portuguese, permitting French landing rights in the Azores for an experimental South Atlantic survey route. This arrangement evened the state of affairs, as Germany, Great Britain and the USA already had landing rights in the Azores. Previously, requests from the French had fallen upon stony ground.

Britain was reported to be lining-up contenders for the Atlantic, and in July 1938 the Under-Secretary of State for Air, Capt H. H. Balfour, presented the intended programme for British Atlantic crossings for the remainder of 1938. Another fifteen crossings were planned and the aircraft involved would be *Cabot, Mercury* and the new de Havilland Albatross. The provisional programme was:

July 15 – 20	*Mercury* Southampton to New York.
July 21 – 28	*Mercury* return via Azores.
August 15 – 20	*Mercury* to New York.
August 21 – 28	*Mercury* return.
September 1 – 10	Albatross to New York.
September 11 – 16	Albatross return.
September 20 – 25	*Cabot* to New York.
September 26 – 30	*Cabot* return.
October 1 – 5	Albatross 1 to New York.
October 5 – 10	Albatross 2 to Canada.
October 6 – 11	Albatross 1 return.
October 10 – 15	*Cabot* to New York.
October 15 – 20	*Mercury* to New York.
October 16 – 21	*Cabot* return.
October 21 – 26	*Mercury* return.

It was assumed Albatross 2 would winter in Canada.

As it turned out, *Mercury* made only the one Atlantic return crossing. Of the seven Albatrosses built, only the first two were completed as long-range mail planes. Development was delayed by a wheels-up landing of the first aircraft and a structural failure of the second. Although the Atlantic continued to be a goal for the Albatross, the two aircraft were soon being used as crew trainers before joining the European schedules. They never flew the Atlantic. *Cabot* and in-flight refuelling were also delayed. Balfour's 1938 Atlantic programme was not realized.

Once the Germans, previously seen to be strong in float-planes, revealed their four-engined monoplane, the Focke-Wulf Condor, pressure truly mounted upon Pan Am and Imperial to commence a service.

In November 1938, the Air Ministry declared the transatlantic mail service would now commence in the spring of 1939, once the ice at Botwood was clear. The Ministry tempered their intention by stating introduction would be subject to the successful completion of in-flight refuelling trials, being carried out by *Cabot,* and a trial crossing of the Atlantic, which had been planned for autumn of 1938 but delayed because of the Munich Crisis. Moreover, extensive long-range flight-testing of the new Perseus sleeve-valve engines and crew training would take place.

Details followed in January 1939. The flights would be operated by the North Atlantic Division of Imperial Airways, headed by Captain Wilcockson. Selection for the North Atlantic Division had commenced in August 1938 when land-plane pilots, Captains E. R. B. White and A. C. P. Johnstone, were nominated. Bennett, J. W. G. James and Kelly Rogers from 'boats soon followed, as did A. C. 'Tony' Loraine, A. Gordon Store and S. G. 'Sammy' Long, their selection being announced in January.

With commercial pressures mounting upon Pan Am and Imperial, the 'Gentlemen's Agreement' was finally laid to rest on 2 February 1939. The State Department, Washington, announced that on 1 June 1939 an American transatlantic, seasonal air service would commence. The British Government had waived the restrictions of the 'Gentlemen's Agreement' of 1935.

Talk became deeds the following month. On 26 March, Pan Am's Boeing 314, *Yankee Clipper,* commanded by Captain Harold Gray, left Baltimore harbour at 14:34 New York time. Lifting from a calm sea, in about 30 seconds, she carried 21 people: 12 crew and 9 representatives from the US Government and Boeing. At that time it was a record number of people in one aircraft on an Atlantic crossing and gave a foretaste of Pan Am's and Boeing's transatlantic capabilities. The flight's task was to prove the *en route* facilities. The *Clipper* would spend a few days at each staging post, in order to familiarize the air- and ground-crews with servicing and mooring procedures.

Clipper alighted at Horta at 08:06, New York time, 13:06 GMT, thus completing the leg from Baltimore in 17 hours and 32 minutes, at an average speed of 165 mph. Pan Am took the opportunity to announce that a sister ship of the *Yankee Clipper* would, from Wednesday 29 March 1939, replace the Sikorsky S.42 on the

The Boeing Model 314 flying-boat, in the guise of Yankee Clipper, *first appeared at Southampton in April 1939. (Peek)*

Bermuda–Baltimore schedule.

From Horta, *Yankee Clipper* continued to Lisbon where she alighted upon the Tagus on Thursday 30 March. She departed two days later for Marseilles. Bordeaux was reached on the afternoon of 2 April when the *Clipper* alighted upon Lake Bicarosse. Finally, on to Southampton. On Wednesday, 5 April, *Yankee Clipper* attempted to reach Foynes, but 48 minutes out of Southampton, bad weather forced Captain Gray to return. Another attempt to reach Foynes, early the following week, was successful and in fine weather conditions *Yankee Clipper* alighted smoothly upon the Shannon. The following day, 12 April, *Yankee Clipper* returned to Southampton, at the start of her voyage home. The same route, with a possible additional call at Bermuda, was planned for her return. The northern route could not be used as the harbour at Botwood was still frozen.

Yankee Clipper staged through Lisbon and on to Horta on 14 April and called at Bermuda on the 15th. She departed Horta at 23:10 New York time and arrived overhead Bermuda before light at 03:13 on the 15th. She then held off until 04:40, when it was light enough to land. After a brief two-hour stop she was airborne again

on the final leg. *Yankee Clipper* eventually alighted at Baltimore at 12:41 New York time, thus completing the transatlantic survey flight. It was noted by the pro-Empire lobby that whereas the Empire 'boats got airborne in about 25 seconds, the 314 took almost a minute. Although the 314 was twice the weight of an Empire, she had only one and a half times the power. This was acceptable if the waters were long enough, but Southampton Water received some criticism from the American crew.

Despite the transatlantic achievements of Imperial Airways with *Cambria* and *Caledonia* and the expected success of in-flight refuelling, the airline knew they did not have a commercially viable means of crossing the ocean until the three new 'G-class' 'boats were in operation. The 'G-class' were of a similar layout as the 'C-class' but larger and more powerful. Their loaded weight would be 72,000 lb, their span 134 feet and length 101 feet. Power would come from four Bristol Hercules sleeve-valve radial engines, giving 1,380 hp each and driving three-bladed constant-speed airscrews of 14 feet 6 inches diameter. Without recourse to in-flight refuelling, the 'G-class' could carry a 3,700 lb payload across the Atlantic.

The Short G-class Flying-boat

Four 1,375 h.p. Bristol Hercules Motors

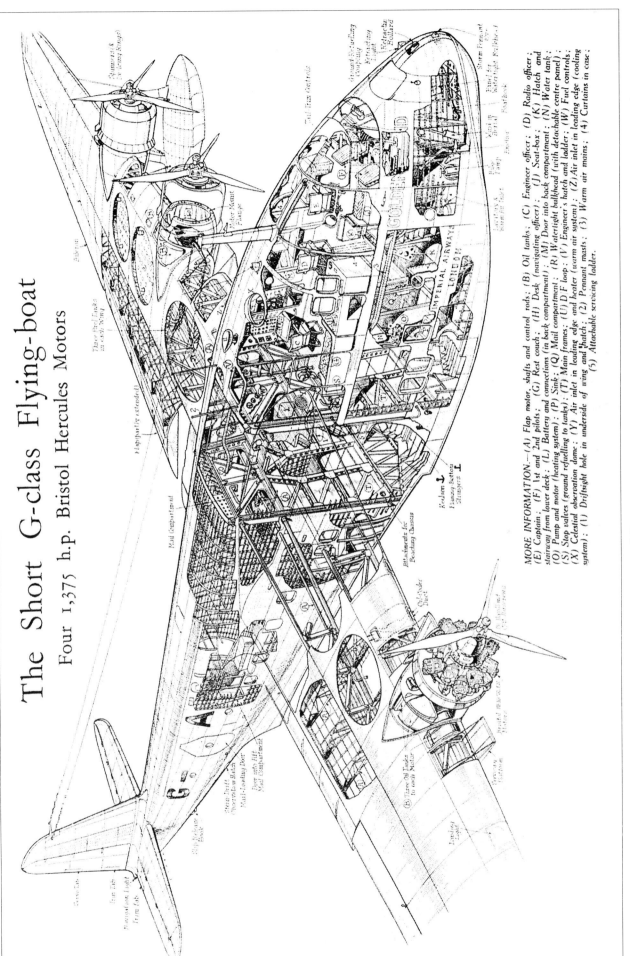

MORE INFORMATION.—(A) Flap motor, shafts and control rods; (B) Oil tanks; (C) Engineer officer; (D) Radio officer; (E) Captain; (F) 1st and 2nd pilots; (G) Rest couch; (H) Desk (navigating officer); (J) Seat-box; (K) Hatch and stairway from lower deck; (L) Battery and connections (in back compartment); (M) Door into back compartment; (N) Water tank; (O) Pump and motor (heating system); (P) Sink; (Q) Mail compartment; (R) Watertight bulkhead (with detachable centre panel); (S) Stop valves (ground refuelling to tanks); (T) Main frames; (U) D.F loop; (V) Engineer's hatch and ladder; (W) Fuel controls; (X) Celestial observation dome; (Y) Air inlet in leading edge and heater (warm air system); (Z) Air inlet in leading edge (cooling system); (1) Driftsight hole in underside of wing and hatch; (2) Pennant masts; (3) Warm air mains; (4) Curtains in case; (5) Attachable servicing ladder.

The S.26 'G-class' was an enlargement of the 'C-class' with supposed transatlantic capability. (The Aeroplane)

It would appear that at sometime before the war, it was intended to complete the 'G' boats in three different fits. One would carry mail only, the second would carry six passengers and a mix of mail and freight and the third would carry twenty-four passengers; their fuel capacity would also vary.

Any substance in the 'three-fit proposal' was quashed a little later with the announcement the 'boats would operate a mail-only service across the Atlantic. A range of 3,200 miles at 180 mph was expected from them and launchings were due in April, May and June of 1939. Funding had been provided by the RAF, on the understanding that the 'boats would enter military service if war was declared. It was proposed that a joint Canadian, Irish and British operating company would operate the new 'G' 'boats.

In addition to the 'G-class', there were three other contenders for the Atlantic, all land planes: the de Havilland Albatross, the Fairey Long-Range Airliner and the Short S.32. The de Havilland Albatross was built with an Atlantic option in mind. An additional fuel tank was carried in the fuselage, at the expense of passenger capacity. The Fairey Long-Range Airliner was to be pressurized so it could cruise at 15,000 feet. Fairey already had considerable experience building water-tight aircraft for the Navy: it was thus analogous that they could build airtight aircraft for high-altitude operation. Pressurization would be achieved by compressors fitted to two of the four Bristol Taurus engines. Each compressor would be capable of providing twice the amount of air required, and thus the loss of one engine would not be critical to the pressurization. Before the war, Richard Fairey had a contract to build fourteen of his airliners for the Air Ministry. They were to have a top speed of 275 mph and cruise at 220 mph, carrying thirty passengers, a crew of six and a load of mail. Only a mock-up was built.

Shorts, on the other hand, made a little more progress. Following the Cadman Committee's report of February 1938 and the merger of Imperial Airways and British Airways, the Air Ministry issued two specifications, 14/38 and 15/38, for airliners for the Empire and European routes respectively. Specification 14/38 could be met by Shorts with a land plane based upon the 'G' boat. To Shorts' surprise they were awarded a contract to build three of these aircraft under the type number S.32. One of these was to be pressurized, at 6 lb per sq in differential. Manufacturer's numbers S.1022 to S.1024 and registrations G-AFMK to G-AFMM were allotted. They were designed to cruise at 240 to 280 mph, weigh more than 73,000 lb and have a range in excess of 3,000 miles, carrying a payload of 7,500 lb. It was intended that two of them would fly at 'normal' height (5,000 ft) with a top speed of 280 mph and the other would cruise at 25,000 ft at 330 mph. Powered by four turbo-super-charged Bristol Hercules VI C engines, the monoplanes, in their low-altitude version, would carry twelve passengers with day/night accommodation or twenty-four passengers with day only seating. The high-altitude version would carry six passengers, mail and freight. There

was to be a crew of seven. The aircraft had a mid-wing layout, similar to the Stirling bomber, a circular cross-section fuselage and twin fins and rudders. The partially completed fuselages were shown to the King and Queen when they visited on 14 March 1939. The project was finally abandoned in May 1940, along with the last S.33 'boat.

The 'chosen instrument' for the Atlantic was the S.30, 'C-class', nine of which were built, two eventually going to Tasman Empire Airways Ltd (TEAL) (see Chapter Ten). Of the seven which remained in Imperial Airways' fleet, four, *Cabot*, *Caribou*, *Clyde* and *Connemara*, were fitted with in-flight refuelling equipment for the Atlantic route. Other modifications included strengthening the structure and installing tankage for 2,500 gallons. The in-flight-refuelled S.30s could carry a payload of 4,270 lb, as opposed to 6,250 lb for the non-in-flight-refuelled 'boats. Their cleared maximum weight for take-off (and landing) was 46,000 lb but, once airborne, they could be refuelled up to a gross weight of 53,000 lb. With in-flight refuelling they had a range in excess of 2,500 nm and an endurance of 15 hours. Their engines were the Bristol Perseus XIIC sleeve-valve radial of 890 hp. The Perseus was slightly less powerful than the Pegasus but, being devoid of overhead valve gear, it had a smaller frontal area. The improved fuel consumption of the S.30 was due as much to the lower drag of the engine installation as it was to the greater efficiency of the sleeve-valve. However, Kelly Rogers, in his lecture to the Royal Aeronautical Society, in January 1939, stated that take-off runs tended to be about thirty seconds' duration rather than the normal twenty seconds, a factor that could be attributed to the lower power of the Perseus.

Although there was much publicity as to future use of S.30s on the promised transatlantic airmail service,

Although the sleeve-valve Perseus engine was less powerful than the Pegasus, being devoid of overhead-valve gear, it offered less drag. Thus there was a resultant improvement in fuel consumption.
(Peek)

the Air Ministry had yet to show their hand as far as tanker aircraft were concerned. Short-lived speculation stated Harrow bombers, now being used as tankers in the trials, were not suitable: Ennis airport, adjacent to Foynes, was not expected to be completed until August 1939. The only alternative land-plane aerodrome in Eire capable of supporting the weight of a heavily laden tanker was at Dublin, 100 miles away from Foynes. Things were not quite as bad in Newfoundland as Hatties' Camp (Gander) was suitable for Harrows. It seemed that the only suitable tanker for the Irish end would be another flying-boat, but the Air Ministry had made no provision for such a craft. Speculation ceased when it was announced from Ennis that progress with the runway was faster than expected. A strip 1,200 yards long was ready for use by heavy aircraft and if land drainage continued apace, the complete surface would be available by the end of May. The Air Ministry's stand, 'Sunderland aircraft would not be used as tankers, their use would have been excessively expensive', was accompanied by reiteration that their plans had always assumed land planes and suitable facilities would be available.

Despite the Air Ministry's confidence in Cobham, he was not comfortable with the thought of two uncontrolled grapples flailing around before contact was properly established. As a result, the wing-tip hook technique, which had been developed in secret over the past two years, was announced in spring 1939. For a while, the wing-tip hook technique became the preferred contact method and Imperial Airways' crews commenced training at Ford in early March.

As for the technique: once the receiver was at height, an operator in the tail paid out a weighted contact line. The line routed through the in-flight refuelling cup fitted in the extreme tail of the aircraft. The tanker approached from below, and to one side, and positioned so as to allow the drooping contact line to fall across the leading edge of the tanker's wing. Aerodynamic forces, assisted by a brisk turn away, slid the line outwards, towards the tanker's wing-tip. At the wing-tip, the contact line engaged a latched hook. The hook then pulled clear of the wing-tip but was attached to the tanker's winch by a line. As the wing-tip hook became free, the tanker operator winched in the contact line, which, thanks to the 'tip hook' was now connected to the receiver.

During this hauling in, the tanker moved from below to a position about sixty feet above and slightly to the side of the receiver. When the receiver's contact line entered the tanker, the operator attached the receiver's line to the drum-mounted fuel-transfer hose. Once the hose was connected, the tanker's winch was released and the hose paid out. At the same time in the receiver, the contact line (which routed through the refuelling cup) was hauled in. On the end of the transfer hose there was a bayonet coupling which automatically engaged the refuelling socket at the base of the receiver's refuelling cup. The socket and bayonet coupling were designed so as to release at a predetermined pull force.

This new method of contact was significantly safer than the older methods and far removed from weighted lines and grappling hooks.

When both aircraft were ready to commence transfer, the tanker positioned with its nose over the tail of the receiver. In this way the hose formed a 'C'-shape loop and entered the receiver from directly behind. Hence the only force that the hose exerted upon the receiver was one of drag; it did not affect the control or handling of the receiver and the pilot of the receiver had little feeling of being connected to another aircraft. Similarly, there was little effect upon the handling of the tanker, as the hose drum sat on the tanker's centre of gravity. In order to achieve 70 or 80 feet of separation, 180 feet of hose was payed out. Although the hose tended to slow the tanker, trials had shown that at the refuelling speed of 120 to 130 mph there was an adequate safety margin above the aircraft's stalling speeds.

The Under-Secretary of State for Air, Sir Harold Balfour, announced that before the S.30s were unleashed upon the Atlantic, they would fly a series of long-range flights around Great Britain. Although Imperial Airways would provide the crews, the trial would be managed jointly by Imperial and the Air Ministry. Of the North Atlantic route Balfour said: 'It is the most important advance in the history of civil aviation since the beginning of the Empire services twelve years previous.'

That being said, the introduction of a British in-flight-refuelled service was further deferred until 1 June 1939. The trial Atlantic crossing had still not been flown. In early March, the postal authorities of Great Britain, Canada and the United States discussed the surcharge rate that would be applied to make the service viable. It was hoped that once the service became well established the surcharge would cease. The route would be Southampton to New York via Shannon, Botwood and Montreal, and Cobham had won the contract to in-flight-refuel Imperial's Empire Boats, *Cabot*, *Caribou*, *Connemara* and *Clyde*.

Still there were delays. Imperial Airways explained the service was now thwarted by difficulties with the refuelling equipment, static electricity, fuel leaks and the fuel jettison system. The design of the flying-boat's six wing fuel tanks had been altered and, as the wing-tip hook method of contact had flaws, a new method of initial contact was being perfected. The difficulties were soon overcome and fuel could be delivered in any weather that was suitable for the flying-boat to get airborne.

It was known that the electrical potential of adjacent aircraft differed, and a spark, which might ignite any fumes present, could result as the aircraft made contact. However, with the wing-tip hook method, any potential charge was dispersed as contact with the wing-tip hook was made. Moreover, the steel armour of the refuelling hose acted as a continuous bond between the two aircraft. Despite differentials as large as 40,000 volts having been detected in three years of trials, there had been no reports of sparks at the moment of initial contact.

Another appreciated hazard: static electricity could be generated by the flowing of fuel down the rubber refuelling hose. Here, possible sparks, which might ignite the petrol/air mixture in the hose, were rendered harmless by flushing the hose with the inert gas nitrogen. There remained the risk of generating static electricity as petrol splashed into the tanks. This danger was met by a redesign of the fuel tanks. Whereas, earlier, the fuel had been introduced into the top of the tanks, it was now fed in from beneath the level of the fuel. This stopped sloshing and foaming of the fuel, which had previously prevented the tanks from filling completely and in the correct sequence. The nitrogen purging gases were allowed to vent from the hose into the tanks, thus ensuring that the tanks were free of explosive vapour before the fuel entered them.

As it was intended to refuel the 'boats to 53,000 lb, 7,000 lb above the maximum take-off weight, a fuel jettison system was required to allow emergency landing immediately after refuelling. The system had to route the jettisoned fuel well clear of the outside of the aircraft and the engines' hot exhausts. Disasters had occurred. Pan Am's Sikorsky, *Samoan Clipper,* was most likely lost as the result of a fire or explosion whilst she was jettisoning fuel before a precautionary landing.

Cobham's early jettison trials resulted in filling the 'boat with petrol fumes. Shorts took over the research themselves. As part of their investigation, the rear quarter and undersurface of the 'boat was coated with a special, petrol-sensitive, red paint. By examining the streaks on the paint, the flow of petrol could be determined. Success was finally achieved by increasing the length of the jettison pipe to about six feet. At that length, it protruded well into the undisturbed airstream below the 'boat. Held in place by a strut, it could be retracted when not required.

Fumes further filled the fuselage from the leaking couplings. The receiver coupling was redesigned and fitted with a shroud to contain any spillage. As the coupling parted, as expected when an excessive pull was exerted upon it, a small amount of fuel would spill, before the automatic valves ceased the flow. This spillage would be contained and, along with the coupling, doused automatically with methyl-bromide (a fire-extinguishing compound).

Finally, the somewhat hazardous wing-tip hook was replaced. Another aircraft joined Cobham's fleet, as in April 1939, after a period of storage at Bagington, the Air Ministry lent Cobham the AW 23 (Whitley forerunner). Modifications to allow the AW 23 to act as tanker, or receiver, included: the fitting of a hose drum over a hole in the floor, fuselage fuel tanks, and a large Perspex viewing panel in the side of the fuselage. For fuel reception, winches, receiving cup and piping were fitted. The AW 23 system employed, not a wing-tip hook, but a rocket-propelled grapple, fired from the side of the tanker. Yet again the Cobham touch was applied. The grapple projectile, similar to that used by lifeboat men, was fired from an Army surplus rifle, a Greener gun of 1880 vintage. Cobham managed to buy up a stock of these Victorian short-barrelled cavalry rifles. Suitably modified, they were now blessed with a vicious recoil.

In order to prove his system and silence his critics, Cobham demonstrated his revised procedures at Rochester in April 1939. Cobham had mounted an AC fuel pump on the back of a car chassis and, by means of a length of hose, proceeded to pump petrol into the rear in-flight-refuelling coupling of *Cabot*, as she rested upon the slipway. The ever confident Cobham orchestrated the trial, whilst staff from Shorts and Imperial looked on in horror, for petrol spouted and leaked from various joints and couplings. Success was achieved finally at the third attempt. An operational system had been achieved – but only in Cobham's eyes.

The AW 23 was replaced by three Handley Page Harrows on loan from the RAF. They were placed on the civil register as G-AFRG K 6933, G-AFRH K 7029 and G-AFRL K 7027. Cobham had contrived to get the letters 'FR' – Flight Refuelling – into all their registrations. The now standard modifications for refuelling, including the fitting of 1,000-gallon fuel tanks and large transparencies in the forward nose, were made.

In preparation for the weekly transatlantic mail service, it was necessary to ship the first two Harrows to Montreal. The wings were taken by road from Hamble to Surrey Docks, London, and stowed below deck on the SS *Beaverford*. She first sailed for Southampton, where the fuselages, which had been towed down a ramp at Hamble and put onto a barge, were craned on board as deck cargo. The decks had already been cleared of ventilators and similar obstructions. *Beaverford* sailed on 14 April and docked in Montreal on the 30 April. In Montreal the Harrows were reassembled and flown to Hatties' Camp. Flight Lieutenants Johnson and Atkinson were Flight Refuelling Ltd's pilots in Canada. They sailed from Liverpool on 8 April. During the war, the Harrows were impressed into the Royal Canadian Air Force at Rockliffe, Ottawa.

Having been decided suddenly that the S.30's sleeve-valve engines were not sufficiently well proved for transatlantic use, one aircraft was to be extensively flown for 400 hours and then have its engines stripped and examined. *Connemara*, first flown in December 1938 by Harold Piper, was selected and she arrived at Hythe in March 1939. The test-flying was a burdensome schedule of 12-hour flights around the British Isles; the crews, Bennett's and Kelly Rogers's, were slipped when the aircraft landed for refuelling. Shortly after *Connemara* arrived, *Clyde* was delivered, but the appearance of *Cabot* and *Caribou* was awaited. Meanwhile, on 4 April the Boeing 314, *Yankee Clipper,* captained by Captain Harold Gray, arrived on a survey flight. *Connemara* acted as escort for the last few miles.

All was not well with Imperial: on 11 May 1939, they announced yet another delay for the long awaited transatlantic service. The service had been due to start on 1 June but late delivery of flying-boats was being quoted:

'It will not be possible to start the Atlantic service on 1

June as arranged. For various reasons unavoidable delay has occurred in the delivery of flying-boats allocated for the service. The delay has deprived Imperial of the opportunity of obtaining, during the winter and spring months, experience which is necessary before the aircraft be put into operation. Certain modifications, which have been shown to be necessary during the initial trials of in-flight refuelling, are now being incorporated. On completion of these modifications, further trials and experience will be required before the aircraft can be used for the actual service of in-flight refuelling. Considerable delay must be necessary before a start can be made. Consequently, it is not yet possible to give an approximate starting date.'

Scheduled crossing of the Atlantic finally came into being with *Yankee Clipper,* commanded by Captain La Porte. Symbolically coinciding with the twelfth anniversary of Lindbergh's flight, the Boeing left New York for Lisbon, via the Azores, on Saturday 20 May 1939. She arrived in Lisbon on the evening of the 21st, the flight having taken 26 hours and 42 minutes. The *Clipper* carried 180,000 pieces of mail from the United States and another 3,000 from the Azores. All available airmail stamps on the Azores were used up in this inaugural flight. Under the conditions of their licence, Pan Am had to make five return journeys before fare-paying passengers could be taken. It was hoped to complete these five crossings before the end of June. Once scheduled fare-paying crossings commenced, Pan Am was then limited to two landings a week on the eastern side of the Atlantic.

From Lisbon, *Yankee Clipper* continued to Marignane, Marseilles, on the afternoon of 22 May 1939. The flight was a 7 hours 10 minutes battle against head winds. Ironically, the return journey to Lisbon, on 25 May, was also against the wind. *Yankee Clipper* carried 800 lb of mail and finally reached home base, New York, on the afternoon of Saturday 27 May. An unplanned stop had to be made at Bermuda, to pick up fuel, replacing that burnt by a southerly diversion to avoid ever-present head winds. As *Yankee Clipper* touched down in New York, her sister 'plane, *Atlantic Clipper,* departed for Europe. The crews exchanged pleasantries; *Atlantic Clipper* lifted and set course for the old world on Pan Am's second mail-only scheduled flight across the Atlantic. Just ten minutes was spent in the Azores, and *Atlantic Clipper* finally arrived in Marseilles on the afternoon of Monday 29 May.

Not all the crossings were completely uneventful. *Yankee Clipper* had to turn back to America, when only 95 miles out, on 3 June as she was suffering from an autopilot fault. Having returned to Baltimore for repairs, she finally left with her mail a day late. The following week, *Yankee Clipper* arrived at Marseilles, on the Monday evening, carrying the latest cinema newsreels of the Royal visit to the United States. The films were rushed on to London, where some stills had to be processed before they could be screened on the Tuesday evening.

A party, which included sixteen journalists, crossed in *Atlantic Clipper* on 19 and 20 June. As recorded below, they were able to sample the luxuries that awaited the fare-paying passengers:

'They slept in comfortable bunks and were able to shave more easily than if they had been in a Pullman Car and were excellently fed, though they renounced the eggs at breakfast time on learning that the altitude would have made 25 minutes cooking necessary.'

The trial the Air Ministry and Imperial Airways were conducting into the Perseus engine continued. On Monday 19 June, at about 21:25, Bennett, accompanied by Francis Chichester, was waiting to board *Connemara,* which was moored about a quarter-mile offshore, upon the calm Southampton Water. Chichester, then an employee of Henry Hughes and Sons, manufacturers of bubble sextants and other navigational instruments, was carrying out flight-trials of these instruments. He considered Bennett to be one of the finest navigators in the world.

The heavily laden Shell-Mex refuelling barge, commanded by Mr George Henry Summers and crewed by deckhand Parram Edwin Augustus Barker and relief pumpman Mr Headly Newton Vincent, was positioned beneath *Connemara's* starboard wing. Refuelling was being overseen by Imperial's Mr Don Munro and he had gone out to *Connemara* accompanied by Ground Engineer Marsden, Imperial Airways Refueller Henry Thomas John Fosse, Coxswain Oliver and a seaman. Oliver and his seaman returned to the jetty to pick up Bennett.

To ensure that an accurate measurement of the amount of fuel delivered could be made, it was standard practice to charge the refuelling hoses before delivery. Pressure refuelling, via the single point, was not being used, and Mr Fosse climbed onto the starboard wing and prepared to hoist the refuelling hose up from the barge. Meanwhile, Don Munro spoke with Summers, the commander of the barge, and explained the importance of exact fuel measurement and hose charging. To charge the hose, a little fuel was pumped into a bucket. Although never proved significant, the bucket was accidentally knocked over and the fuel spilt upon the deck of the barge. Once Munro had seen the fuel mopped up, none was believed to have entered the barge, he resumed the refuelling and took up his position on board *Connemara.*

As Mr Fosse hoisted up the hose and placed the refuelling nozzle into the filler, the delivery hose for the engine oil was run from the barge, in through the starboard hatch, out through the flight-deck escape hatch and along the wing's top surface to the engines, thus tying the flying-boat to the barge. Vincent, in the barge's engine room, started the engine. Immediately it was heard to race away and, at the same time, there was a laboured sound and a loud hydraulic banging emanating from the refuelling hose. Refueller Fosse was about to shout a warning when Mr Summers was seen to leap into the engine room in order to shut down the fuel pump. Simultaneously – a flash and a dull explosion. Summers screamed! The rear of the barge was engulfed. Nobody saw Vincent jumping or being blown from the stern of the barge.

Munro, aboard the flight-deck of *Connemara*, thought at the time the noise came from the engine, but upon reflection he decided it came from the pump. As Summers screamed, Munro rushed to the rear of the deck and peered down from the starboard loading hatch. The rear of the barge, beneath the wing, was a mass of flames. He grabbed an extinguisher, jumped down onto the blazing barge and attempted to fight the fire. Unable to quell the flames, he ran to the bow of the barge and untied the forward mooring ropes, hoping the fire would burn through those aft. But the barge remained connected by way of the oil-delivery hose, which was routed through *Connemara*. Such was the intensity of the heat, the lines could not be disconnected. Don Munro, in a desperate attempt to save the aircraft, re-entered via the bow mooring hatch.

Fosse, still on the wing, saw Summers jump into the water; Fosse too slipped into Southampton Water. From the shore, figures were seen to leap from *Connemara* and the refuelling barge. Bennett grabbed a launch and rushed to the rescue, as did Captain S. G. Oatley, commander of the Trinity House pilot cutter *Jessica*. With Oatley were a Captain A. E. Gadd and Albert B. Hurst, cook. Gadd and Hurst leapt into an adjacent launch and they too sped to the conflagration.

Mr Summers was picked up by the *Jessica* but he had been badly burnt. Deckhand Barker shouted he was unable to swim and *Jessica* was manoeuvred beneath the starboard wing-tip, so he could drop into the boat. Fosse was picked up, as was Marsden, who had stripped and dived from the starboard wing. Oatley sped *Jessica* shorewards and the injured were taken to hospital by the hastily summoned ambulances. Summers was accompanied to hospital by Fosse. Despite his injuries, Summers's concern was for Vincent, the missing man. It had been Vincent's first day on the refuelling barge.

The fire travelled along the fuelling hose and, fanned by a fresh north-westerly, it spread rapidly and engulfed the starboard wing. Flames leapt fifty feet into the air from the open fuel tanks! Munro, the last to leave the blazing *Connemara*, was forced to abandon her from

Connemara was destroyed in June 1939, following an explosion in the refuelling barge. Sadly, the fire took the life of relief pumpman Mr Headly Newton Vincent. Don Munro was lauded for his great courage during the rescue attempts. (Peek)

the port wing. Immediately he was picked up by Coxswain Ray White, in the Imperial launch.

The starboard wingspar broke; the fuel tanks ruptured; soon the decks of the barge were six inches deep in blazing fuel. Within a few minutes the wing burnt through and fell off. Moments later, the other wing collapsed. Bennett, seeing there was little more he could do to assist in the rescue, moved one of two other Empire 'boats which were moored perilously close. Within twenty minutes from the start of the blaze, *Connemara* turned turtle and sank in ten to twelve feet of water. As soon as the flames upon the refuelling barge died down, Harry Pusey went aboard and secured a grapple so the still burning hulk could be beached.

The following day it was announced that Mr Summers was satisfactory, considering the very serious nature of his injuries. Also that day, a diver was sent down to examine the wreckage. Later, the engines and propellers were salvaged, stripped and found to be all right.

A week later, 26 June, the sea gave up the body of Vincent. A post-mortem was inconclusive but it seemed probable that Vincent, badly burnt, had either jumped or been blown overboard, only to subsequently drown.

The preliminary Home Office report by the coroner was inconclusive as to the cause of the accident, but no negligence was attached to any party and Don Munro was singled out for his display of great courage in assisting in the rescue and trying to save *Connemara*. There was, however, some doubt as to whether or not a serviceable automatic pressure-relief valve was fitted to the refuelling system, but as the inquiry was investigating the death of Vincent, such matters were outside its jurisdiction. The Court awaited the technical report. The jury offered their fees to Vincent's widow.

Following the loss of *Connemara*, *Ao-Tea-Roa*, one of the TEAL 'boats, was earmarked by Imperial Airways for the long-range trial, but her place was soon to be taken by *Australia*, being rebuilt and renamed *Clare*, following the Basra incident. Thereafter, *Ao-Tea-Roa*, no longer required for the long-range trial, was released to New Zealand. Refuelling trials continued and, on 3 July 1939, *Caribou* was refuelled in flight, over the Hamble estuary. On 12 July the maximum weights of 50,500 lb for take-off and 48,000 lb for landing were cleared.

Pan Am's transatlantic airmail service had so far been via the southern route. Maiden use of the northern route was further delayed as *Yankee Clipper*, Juan Trippe and five Pan Am officials found themselves fogbound at Shediac, New Brunswick. *Yankee Clipper* finally slipped away after a couple of days, refuelled at Botwood and Foynes and arrived at Southampton on the evening of 28 June. Amongst those greeting the 'Clipper on her arrival was Sir Francis Shelmerdine, Director-General of Civil Aviation.

Pan Am announced the passenger service was about to start. The airline, and Trippe in particular, had remained patient, but 'The Gentlemen's Agreement' had been dissolved in February and American Export Airlines were seeking licences with a

view to a competitive Atlantic service with their recently ordered Vought-Sikorsky VS-44A. The first fare-paying passengers crossed the Atlantic, via the southern route, in *Dixie Clipper*, on 28 and 29 June. Captain R. O. D. Sullivan commanded a crew of ten to cater for the twenty-two passengers. They stopped for one hour to refuel at Horta, night-stopped in Lisbon and arrived in Marseilles during the afternoon of Friday 30 June. Transatlantic passenger flight soon became 'old hat' and it was not long before the 'man bites dog' stories emerged. There was a report, on 19 July, that 90-year-old Mr Russell Frost claimed to be the oldest person to fly the Atlantic, when he disembarked from *Atlantic Clipper* at Marseilles.

In response, the British declared, on 17 July, their weekly service would start on 5 August and the first return would be on 9 August. The delay in opening the British service was attributed to the recent difficulties with the flight refuelling system. The Postmaster-General gave official confirmation on 27 July. With the companion American service there would be two crossings a week. Later that day, *Cabot* was delivered from Rochester to Southampton by Captain S. G. Long. The opportunity was taken to allow the people of London a

One of Flight Refuelling Ltd's Harrows refuelling an Empire Flying-Boat over the Solent. Despite Sir Alan Cobham's pre-war success with in-flight refuelling, little development was done during the war. (Photograph courtesy of Cobham plc)

sight of the transatlantic airliner. Flying low, her markings plainly visible, she followed the course of the Thames before setting heading once over the City.

The revised refuelling procedures, using the rocket grapples, were demonstrated to the press and public alike two days later. The receiver *Cabot*, commanded by Bennett, and the Harrow tanker were joined in the air by *Cameronian*, carrying a party of 'ringside' journalists. Conditions for the demonstration were far from ideal: there was a lot of summer turbulence at 500 feet, the height at which Bennett decided to make this most impressive demonstration. All the various safety devices and procedures were demonstrated and many people saw the refuelling from the ground, as the tanker circled tightly overhead.

The first officer and the radio officer worked the manual winch and wound out the weighted cable with the grapple upon its end. The Harrow formated to starboard of the flying-boat and fired the Schermuly rocket-cable projectile. The line was aimed into the parabolic arc formed by the receiver's trailing weighted line. As the ejected line lost forward momentum it would fall back and snag the receiver's arced trailing line. On some occasions the fired line failed to snag the receiver's trail and had to be rewound and fired again. Final positioning of the line could be achieved by rapidly climbing or diving the tanker.

As with the earlier contact systems, the receiver's line was wound into the tanker, attached to the refuelling hose and then winched into the receiver, automatically coupling with the receiving cup. If contact was broken, as was demonstrated on this blustery July day, the nozzle would disconnect and fuel would be vented, until the delivery cocks shut. The hose, still attached to the receiver by means of the line, was gently wound back into contact and delivery resumed.

Once refuelling was complete, the refuelling hose was wound out into the slipstream, purged with nitrogen and then reeled out until the hose was about thirty feet behind the receiver. Then, the trail line was severed and the tanker, its hose with a short length of receiver's trail line still attached, was free of the receiver.

At the close of July, the transatlantic crews at Hythe were visited by Reith, who was about to sail to America in the *Queen Mary*. Just before sailing Reith was asked when a transatlantic passenger service would be started. He replied, 'The answer is unknown and unknowable.'

When further questioned about the impending North Atlantic mail service and whether it would be diverted to the southern crossing for the winter, he said, 'I do not think that there is much chance of our being able to maintain a service by that route owing to the shortage of aircraft on the Empire Services, unless something happens and our fleet is unexpectedly increased and the chances of such a project are highly problematical.'

On the night of the second, Kelly Rogers commanded *Caribou* for a fourteen-hour test flight. Part of this flight, which started and ended at Southampton, was deliberately flown into atrocious weather. On 3 August, Imperial Airways announced that they had sold all the special airmail envelopes for use on their first transatlantic service. Some 20,000 had been issued, and a further 5,000 were later made available.

It was decided to carry a second master navigator on transatlantic flights, thus the full crew for this inaugural in-flight refuelled crossing comprised Captain J. C. Kelly Rogers in command; Captain S. G. Long, chief officer and master navigator; First Officer B. C. Frost and Radio Officers A. J. Coster and C. E. Wilcockson. They departed Southampton on 5 August at 14:13 BST and landed at Foynes around 16:40 BST, having covered the 355 miles at 156 mph. Kelly Rogers was met by Mr de Valera, the Prime Minister of Eire, and Lord Monteagle, who headed a delegation of the Foynes Regatta, Kelly Rogers being a member. The delegation presented him with an inscribed silver tray. *Caribou* was refuelled. The navigation plan showed them to be facing a sixteen-hour crossing. The aircraft would lift-off with fuel for sixteen hours and then take another seven hours' worth from the tanker.

A deputation comprising Sir Francis Shelmerdine, Director-General of Civil Aviation; Air Marshal Sir John Salmond and Mr Leslie Runciman, directors of Imperial Airways; Major McCrindle, Chairman of British Airways; Mr J. Dulanty, High Commissioner for Eire in London, and Captain Wilcockson, Manager Atlantic Division Imperial Airways had flown from Southampton aboard *Maia*, which had departed shortly before *Caribou*. After *Caribou* finally departed, Shelmerdine, Runciman and Wilcockson returned to Southampton in Pan Am's *American Clipper*, which was making her maiden passenger flight on the northern route.

Kelly Rogers had planned to set course as soon as he was airborne, but as the Prime Minister was present it was decided to formate with the Harrow (G-AFRL) and overfly the official party. *Caribou* took off at 18:10 BST and turned inland to meet up with Tyson, in the Harrow, which was airborne from the recently upgraded *Rineanna*. As the two aircraft approached the well-wishing onlookers, connection was still not complete. Tyson had to apply full throttle and dive to keep pace with *Caribou*. Once connected, the drag of the hose caused Tyson to drift back. The pull between the two 'craft was sufficient to part the connection; as a result, there was a spectacular spray of fuel and a smoky wisp of methyl-bromide from behind the flying-boat. Although the coupling was remade and fuelling continued, *Caribou* left a sparkling trail, as she powered down the Shannon towards the sinking sun and an Atlantic crossing. Sir Alan Cobham, standing next to Mr de Valera, had observed the drama unfold above him but the transfer was successful and in the eyes of the press without incident.

Although they ran into cloud almost as soon as they were airborne, the crossing was uneventful. During the passage, Kelly Rogers signalled Reith, crossing the

Atlantic below them in the *Queen Mary,* and advised him of *Caribou*'s progress. Despite severe weather just before Botwood, they had fortunately been able to obtain a star fix and were confident of their position. The head winds were stronger than forecast and Kelly Rogers landed at Botwood at 14:30 BST, 6 August, 3 hours 22 minutes late, having spent 19 hours 22 minutes aloft. They had averaged 102.5 mph for the 1,980 miles.

Refuelling took 2 hours 20 minutes; they then continued to Boucherville, seven miles from Montreal on the St Lawrence. An hour was made up on this leg by routing directly overland, rather than following the St Lawrence, and they arrived in Canada mid-afternoon. Once ashore, they were met by Mr G. D. Howe, the Canadian Minister of Transport.

They re-boarded within the hour and took off for New York. As the sun set ahead of them, the sky became overcast and Kelly Rogers contemplated that his first ever alighting in New York would be at night. *Caribou* radioed the Pan Am officials at Port Washington and Kelly Rogers was signalled full instructions. At 21:30 New York time (on the night of 6 August), Kelly Rogers placed *Caribou* upon the smooth waters of Port Washington. To eager pressmen, Kelly Rogers later said he was able to make 'a normal landing'. The thresholds of the landing area were marked with red and white lights and the edges were delineated with further white lights. The complete surface was bathed by a powerful search light. Kelly Rogers concluded his statement by saying the majority of the crossing had been made in cloud but they had put their trust in the automatic pilot to relieve themselves of some of the strain.

Caribou had carried 1,055 lb of mail but burnt twenty times that weight of fuel to lug it across the Atlantic. And this had only been achieved after one-third of the fuel load had been delivered to the aircraft once airborne.

Reith called upon *Caribou* in New York, where there was concern that she might be impounded as a result of litigation, following the crash of *Cavalier* in January. Although Reith hastened his departure from the States as a result of the impending legal action, *Caribou* left without hindrance for Montreal on 9 August. They stayed at Montreal overnight and continued to Botwood, which they left at about midnight. Thanks to favourable winds, the eastbound crossing was made in 12 hours and 5 minutes and in-flight refuelling was not required. After a brief stop at Foynes, no fuel was taken on there, *Caribou* went on to Southampton.

The other S.30, *Cabot,* commanded by Bennett, left Southampton early on Saturday afternoon, 12 August. Tony Loraine was chief officer and 'Tommy' Farnsworth was first officer; the radio officers were Martin and Cheeseman. For President Roosevelt, they carried some grouse, shot in Yorkshire that 'glorious' morning, flown to London and then put on a train to Southampton. After breaking contact with the Harrow tanker, a fairly uneventful 16½ hours saw them in Botwood and on to Montreal. They too were visited by Reith. On her return, *Cabot* carried beaver skins that had been presented to

Caribou being refuelled in Newfoundland following her in-flight-refuelled crossing of the Atlantic during the August/September 1939 service. (Lawford)

the King on an earlier Royal visit, moccasins, newsreels, a live insect intended for medical research in Palestine and gifts of flowers for the Lord Mayor of London and the Canadian High Commission.

The remainder of the trial passed without fuss, but the events of September 1939 were soon to be witnessed by the Empires. On 3 September, *Cabot*, again commanded by Bennett, was 24 hours late out of Southampton, having been delayed by weather. In darkness above the Atlantic, the distress calls of the SS *Athenia* were picked up by Radio Officer Mitchell. The experimental schedule ended as *Cabot* arrived in Poole on 30 September, under the command of Captain Store. The full programme of sixteen flights had been completed on the date which had been allotted before the outbreak of the war. This was despite radio silence and minimal weather information. Other crewmen who took part in this trial were Captains J. W. G. James, S. G. Long, First Officer G. H. Bowes and Radio Officers Brent, Hillier and Hobbs.

Diversion seadromes suitable for a passenger service were sparse. At the Newfoundland end, the only alternative to Botwood was Moncton, 500 miles further west. The refuellings had not always gone smoothly. Usually carried out at 1,000 feet, on one occasion low cloud forced them down to the treetop height. Five times fuel had been forced into the hull, and once it ran into the bilges and had to be mopped up and secured until they arrived at Botwood. Passenger flights were still some way off.

However, for those six or seven weeks of the summer of 1939, there were two airmail services leaving New York for Europe on a Wednesday. Customers were encouraged to mark their envelopes with their choice of service, Pan Am or Imperial. Letters not so marked would be flown by Imperial Airways, if their destination was the United Kingdom, or Pan Am, if it was elsewhere in Europe. It had been agreed that mail from the United Kingdom would be carried free of additional charge once it arrived in America or Canada, and, similarly, mail from Newfoundland and Canada would be forwarded throughout the Empire without additional charge.

In reality, Pan Am, and the Boeings had beaten the Empire 'Boats well into second place on this transatlantic race. But other routes were being explored. Preempting the findings of Cadman, on 17 November 1937, British Airways and the Air Ministry despatched a joint team to survey the Lisbon to Bathurst route. They investigated the possibility of an extended service to South America, via West Africa, and searched the African coastal areas for likely landing places. Both land planes and seaplanes were being considered. The survey returned on 28 January 1938, not being impressed with the flying-boat facilities discovered on the west coast of Africa. It appeared the waters at Sierra Leone, Gambia and other parts of the coast were not of sufficient quality to support flying-boat operations. The option of using land planes on a route to Lisbon, Casablanca and, finally, Dakar seemed favourite. That being said, the following year, 1939, it was announced British Airways would operate a service to South America. Possibly they would use the 'C-class' 'boats during the northern hemisphere's winter, when the North Atlantic was ice-bound. In addition, Fairey's new long-range airliner was expected to be available in 1940.

Whilst attention had been upon the Atlantic, the first 'G' or *Grenadier*-class boat, *Golden Hind*, (G-AFCI) was floated upon the Medway on 17 June 1939 – two months late – and she was then towed to another slipway for engine trials. *Golden Hind*'s first flight, by Lankester Parker, was on Friday 21 July 1939 and was watched by Major Mayo, Arthur Gouge and Oswald Short: it lasted sixteen minutes. The other two 'boats, *Golden Fleece* (G-AFCJ) and *Golden Horn* (G-AFCK), laid down as *Grenville* and *Grenadier* respectively, were to be renamed on launching. *'Hind* flew her manufacturer's trials on 29 August and 5 September before being handed over to Imperial at Hythe on 24 September 1939 for crew training.

Too late, the war intervened and the three 'G' 'boats, in addition to *Cabot* and *Caribou*, were impressed into the RAF, which was short of long-range aircraft.

As for the future of the Atlantic, on 11 November 1939, Reith wrote to Woods Humphery saying the new 'G-class' flying-boats were all that was practically available for the Atlantic, and they lacked really useful capabilities. Of other projects, the Short S.32 and the Fairey long-range land plane, were soon to be shelved by a hard-pressed Government, but three Boeing 314As, purchased by Balfour, were to prove invaluable on the west coast of Africa and across the Atlantic.

The first Grenadier-class boat, Golden Hind, *was launched on 17 June 1939. The other two 'boats,* Golden Fleece *and* Golden Horn, *were completed in RAF colours and followed three months later. (RAF Museum AC94/40/6 Page 1)*

CHAPTER EIGHT

To Australia and Beyond

QANTAS receive the 'boats – Camilla to Singapore – Challenger and the Darwin débâcle – From a journalist's viewpoint – EAMS, Australia to England – Salvage of Coorong – Damage to Capella.

To return to those 'boats pounding the Empire Routes: by early 1938, the Empire 'Boats had been in service for a year and Australia had ordered *Coogee, Corio, Coorong, Carpentaria, Coolangatta* and *Cooee*. New Zealand too was expected to purchase 'boats, and between December 1937 and February 1938, Captain Burgess flew *Centaurus* to New Zealand and back on a survey flight. This flight is detailed in Chapter Ten, but the journey, which was via Australia, allowed the Australian public a glimpse of their future.

On 17 February 1938, the Empire Airmail Scheme was extended to Malaya. The first flight, made by Captain 'Scotty' Allan in *Centurion*, arrived in Karachi at dusk on 27 February, being accompanied by *Coolangatta*. *Centurion* carried 5,000 lb of mail, consisting of 181 mail bags and 40 packages. *Centurion* continued her journey across the subcontinent whilst indigenous airlines further distributed the India mail. Meanwhile, *Coolangatta* flew on to Singapore, arriving on 2 March, several days before *Centurion*. On 9 March, 'Scotty' Allan departed Singapore, in *Centurion,* for Southampton but his stay in England was brief and he was soon Australia-bound again.

In preparation for their flying-boat service, QANTAS arranged for their captains to attend dinghy-sailing classes and Lester Brain purchased a 12-foot dinghy. The RAAF and the RAF in Singapore, however, were unable to offer training in flying-boats but the Singapore Flying Club did allow QANTAS use of their D.H. Moth, which had been fitted with floats. Later, QANTAS purchased a Saro A.17 Cutty Sark (probably VH-UNV) and used her as a trainer, until it was landed wheels-down in the Brisbane River. Although a date to start the service had not been agreed, *Coolangatta* arrived in early April. She had departed Southampton on 18 March 1938, under the command of 'Scotty' Allan. His crew was First Officer Bill Purton, Radio Officer A. S. Patterson, Steward Drury and Engineers Eric Kydd and G. J. Aldous. *Cooee* was the second 'boat to be delivered and she arrived commanded by Captain Lynch-Blosse.

Construction of support facilities was continuing apace and, in accordance with an earlier decision, arrangements were made to transfer QANTAS's headquarters from Brisbane to the Shell Building, Sydney. On 22 April, the Prime Minister of New Zealand, Mr Savage, announced that within the week the Governments of the three countries would be announcing their nominated companies for the proposed Tasman Sea crossings. The previous day, the Australian Prime Minister, Mr Lyons, announced that as of July there would be three return services per week to England, two with flying-boats and one with land planes. By August, all three services would be filled by flying-boats.

Over the weekend of 28 May, QANTAS staff made the move from Brisbane to Shell House, Sydney, and the following month, on the 10th, *Coolangatta* and *Cooee* flew into Rose Bay. With the introduction of the new service to Australia, there was a great demand for the inaugural flight. On 20 June 1938 it was announced that two 'boats would depart Southampton; one would drop off passengers *en route* and the other would fly all the way to Singapore, where through-passengers would transfer to one of the QEA 'boats. They were expected at Sydney on 5 July 1938.

It was announced that *Camilla*, commanded by Captain Alcock, and *Cordelia*, commanded by Captain C. E. Madge, would leave Southampton, soon after dawn on Sunday 26 June, carrying twenty passengers and over three tons of mail. Eleven of the passengers

Carpentaria bearing the QEA Brisbane logo. (Author from Moss)

and much of the mail were booked through to Australia. Although there were three passengers bound for Brisbane, the remaining tickets had been paid for by QANTAS and issued to one Australian and seven British journalists who would go through to Sydney. They were to provide their newspapers with regular reports from along the route. *Camilla* would proceed to Karachi and there the passengers and mail would transfer to *Cordelia*. The expected transit times were Alexandria one day three hours, Karachi two days nine hours, Calcutta three days six hours, Bangkok four days seven hours, Singapore five days two hours, Darwin seven days two hours, Brisbane eight days twenty-two hours and Sydney nine days two hours.

The experiences gained by the journalists must have been similar to those shared by the many hundreds of passengers who were to follow …

Most of the passengers for the flight had travelled from Waterloo Station on Saturday evening, sampling Imperial's Pullman coach. At 04:30, as a cold steel-blue summer dawn was breaking, the passengers were roused from their Southampton hotel and taken by coach to Hythe, where they boarded *Cordelia*. Funnels of ocean liners peeped through the mist, as the harbour awoke. Shadowy figures busied themselves around the silver flying-boat as, waiting, she lay moored. The crew, dressed in blue serge, busied themselves with the final preparations. They awaited the Air Ministry meteorological forecast, brought down from Calshot by launch. If the forecast was late, the captain knew nasty weather lay ahead. The flight clerk oversaw the loading of nets of mailbags, swung across the jetty by a huge crane. Mail was stowed and trim sheets were completed.

Inside, the stark electric lights showed the steward checking provisions. Bleary-eyed passengers stumbled to their seats at 05:30.

The captain boarded and the trim sheet was presented for his signature. He checked the flight-deck notice board to see if any pertinent message had been left by the previous commander. The first officer had already checked over the 'boat and primed the Exactor throttle and mixture controls. The radio officer had checked his equipment and gone into the bow compartment, ready to slip the mooring.

Meanwhile, in the cabins, the steward seated the passengers, explained the safety procedures and warned them not to be alarmed by the spray, the whine of the flap motor or the flames from the exhaust. The flight clerk ensured all doors and hatches were secured.

'All clear for starting', and the 'boat was warped forward from the Braby pontoon. The shore party disconnected the external batteries, and to the captain's blast of 'L' in Morse upon his whistle, the radio operator reported, 'All clear forward', and switched the 'riding' light for the 'steaming' light. He turned around, gave the windscreen a last wipe before securing the bow hatch and returned either to his radios or to the top hatch, from whence he watched for engine-fires on start-up.

At last, the engines were started and warmed and the launch towed *Cordelia* to the take-off area. The first officer monitored the cylinder head and oil temperatures as we proceeded to the fairway. Each control surface was held at full deflection for one minute to bleed any air out of the autopilot. For the past few minutes, each engine had been running on its individual supply to ensure that each fuel pump was working. Common

Coolangatta being loaded at Hythe. The mail is being craned onto the jetty adjacent to the starboard rear freight door, in preparation for loading. (Peek)

supply was then selected and all the balance cocks opened. The control launch then swept ahead of us picking up debris and, if necessary, ruffling the water surface, to allow our 'boat to get up onto the step more easily. At the far end of the flare-path, the launch awaited the captain's Aldis, 'OKTO' (Is it OK to Take-off?). The launch replied with a 'steady white'. Flaps were run out to a quarter, the mixture being set fully-rich, so as to override the automatic boost control, the trim tabs were set for take-off and pitch checked to be fine. Captain Madge turned *Cordelia* into wind – about 100 yards short of the first flare – and walked the throttles forward. The first officer reported all engines responding and monitored the boost gauges and engine revolutions. After a run of about twenty seconds, we were airborne over Southampton Water.

Once safely aloft, the boost override was deselected, the propellers were set to coarse pitch and the flaps were run in. Below, the Shell wharves, Calshot and then the Isle of Wight slipped by. In the cabins, the passengers dozed, only to be stirred by the tinkling of crockery and cutlery from the pantry. Breakfast was taken as Mont Blanc towered above them to port and mists swirled in the Rhône Valley below. As *Cordelia* began her descent to Étang de Berre, with the village of Marignane nestling upon the lakeside, they avoided the restricted military area of Marseilles. The flight clerk busied himself sorting the papers and manifests to ensure a brisk turnaround and the steward stowed the pantry and asked the passengers to return to their seats. During the last couple of hundred feet of the descent, the Mistral playfully buffeted the flying-boat.

After a rapid refuelling, Marseilles lay behind them and soon Corsica rose grimly from the sea. A little turbulence reminded *Cordelia* they had crossed the spine of hills. The blueness of the Mediterranean, the brilliant white of the villas below, the green pines, the burnt earth – all passed beneath. To Bracciano, Italy, where Flight Clerk Claridge had slipped from the wing during engine start and drowned, almost a year earlier. Another refuelling ... and so the pattern was to be repeated with only the view from the promenade changing slowly as they flew east.

That first Sunday, with the sun setting behind her, *Cordelia* flew low over the Gulf of Corinth before alighting at Athens. She followed in the wake of *Camilla*, who had left Southampton earlier in order to take on supplies from Marseilles, Rome and Brindisi. At each staging point *Camilla* had arisen almost as *Cordelia* touched down. There was a great feeling of impending British achievement in this venture, for they were soon to enter Australia with the largest number of air passengers ever to enter on one flight. Justifiable British pride was expressed in the reports as to the capabilities, size and comfort of these 'boats. Moreover, the view was expressed that the Australians ought to be proud that they too would soon be able to operate the Empire 'Boats.

Their night at the Grande Bretagne Hotel was agreeable but cut short by a dawn awakening. The second day's flying was faultless. By evening both 'boats had touched down at Basra, having completed the longest day planned for the journey. At Alexandria, the crew of *Cordelia* were slipped in favour of Captain 'Tich' Attwood, assisted by First Officer Reece. For the new

Cordelia at Karachi. The propellers have been 'dressed' to allow the launch bearing the traffic officer and the customs officer room for manoeuvre beneath the leading edge. Approaches were made from the leading edge: the trailing edge tended to drip oil. (Hartle)

crew, their first stage was across more than 500 miles of searing Syrian desert. On the ground, at noon when they stopped at Lake Habbaniyah, the temperature reached 106 degrees Fahrenheit in the shade. Throughout the day *Cordelia* led *Camilla* by fifteen minutes. Basra, surrounded by vast date-palm plantations, was their resting place at the completion of a perfectly run day. There had been no hold-ups at any of the three staging posts along the 1,724 miles, which took a full 12 hours 20 minutes. On the morrow they could expect a half-past-four-in-the-morning departure for Karachi.

After a third dawn take-off, breakfast was followed by another hour or two of sleep. In the aft cabin, the air was thick with tobacco. Elsewhere a few rubbers of bridge were being played and, at intervals, the captain came down to discuss the flight's progress with the passengers. It was an idyllic way to fly. Outside, to port, the forbidding Cathedral Rocks rose 1,300 feet direct from the Gulf of Oman and marked the shores of Baluchistan. The wind favoured them that day: the 1,400 miles from Basra to Karachi was spanned at an average speed of 164 mph. Fine weather was unlikely to prevail as the flight continued across the tropics, where the weather was, and still is, invariably fraught. The forecast looked grim. For the next three days they would be in the monsoon area.

Ahead, in Australia on 29 June, the Australian Minister of Defence, Mr Thorby, was presenting the Empire Airmail Bill to the Australian House. Introducing the Bill, he explained that following inauguration in July, all airmail would enter Australia through Darwin. From there, mails for Brisbane and Sydney would remain in the flying-boat. Land planes would continue down to Melbourne, then Adelaide and across to Hobart. The empty tracts to Central Australia and, along the barren west coast, to Perth would also be traversed by land planes. Thus all airmail would reach Australia's capital cities within one day of arriving in the country. A couple of days later, 1 July, the Commonwealth Parliament passed the 1938 Empire Air Services Act. Agreement between the Australian and British Governments and a separate agreement between the Commonwealth and QEA had been achieved. Australia retained the Darwin to Singapore sector and was to have six 'boats at her disposal at any one time. To ease operational complexity, a free interchange of aircraft between the various companies would take place. Moreover, QEA would be responsible for its own maintenance. There would be three schedules a week, and the 11-day journey time would be cut to seven, once night-flying facilities were established. The agreement was to stand for fifteen years.

According to plan, *Camilla* did not venture beyond Karachi, 'The Gateway to India', and the remaining mail and passengers continued eastward in *Cordelia*. On 29 June, *Cordelia* kissed the Hooghly, another 1,200 miles behind her. Two days ahead lay Singapore, where their load would be transferred to the QEA 'boat, *Challenger*, commanded by 'Scotty' Allan.

Crossing the Bay of Bengal, the monsoon broke.

Thoughts went out to Kingsford Smith and Tommy Pethyridge, lost three years before in such a storm. The flying-boat, tossed and buffeted by the heavy winds, fought her way through to a calmer Bangkok. Since leaving Calcutta she had averaged 152 mph. They were fortunate in that they were able to climb above much of the weather, but being unpressurized, climbing would always be an option with limited potential.

Before Singapore they had staged through Koh Samui, 'as yet untrammelled by modern civilization and tourists'. Here the correspondents were greatly impressed with the slick immigration and refuelling but noted that the crews had had two years' experience. They were down for only 26 minutes, taking on 300 gallons of fuel in that short time. They praised the comfort of the seating, especially as they often needed to get back to sleep following the pre-breakfast, dawn starts. Finally, they wondered what the next few days would bring as they approached the new East Indies staging posts, which had yet to see a scheduled boat.

Glugor Bay, Penang, was followed by Singapore, for so long the crossroads of the Orient. As dusk descended on 1 July, *Cordelia* alighted at Kallang airport. The mail and passengers bound for Australia were assigned to *Challenger*. By using two operating companies to service the route, both companies avoided the difficulties associated with extended lines of communication and supply.

In Singapore one journalist had time to reflect:

'Was it only yesterday that we visited a temple in Bangkok. Or surely it was more than four days ago that we paid an evening visit to the Acropolis in Athens.'

Despite their apprehension, *Challenger*'s passengers had little cause for concern, as they departed Singapore and overflew the East Indies on 2 July. The improvised arrangements worked well and their captain was the legendary G. U. 'Scotty' Allan. Admittedly, refuelling at Kupang had been from a clumsy native barge and at other places passenger launches were not available but, in general, the crossing of the Timor Sea was satisfactory. In order to get above the thick tropical clouds, they climbed to 15,000 feet. It was not the lack of pressurization or oxygen that generated comment from the journalists but the extreme cold. Calls were made at Batavia, Surabaya, Bima and Kupang. The longest refuelling stop was only 50 minutes and regular weather reports and upper wind forecast were available, even from Bima.

The débâcle at Darwin – according to Fysh, 'a lazy and difficult port' – began shortly after *Challenger* alighted on the evening of 3 July, having journeyed for 7 days 3 hours and 45 minutes. Other than the laying of a few mooring buoys, little other preparation seemed to have been completed. To add to the frustrations, there was a strong south-easterly wind and a choppy sea.

Once *Challenger* finally picked up her mooring, the officious immigration officials entered the 'boat to proceed doggedly with their formalities. During the examination of vaccination certificates, it transpired that three passengers and three crew were not adequately vaccinated. The immigration officers insisted that they be ministered to there and then, whilst still on board the flying-boat. By now, no short time had elapsed, and the light was failing. Refuelling, difficult enough in wind and wave, now hampered by poor light, was made all the more exacting as the petrol tender was proving troublesome. Dragging her anchor, she drifted perilously close to the starboard wing-tip float. Once refuelling on one side was complete, the tender was swung around to the port side and refuelling continued. After an hour, again the tender broke her moorings and this time she did come into contact with the 'boat and struck the port float. Although it was difficult to carry out a thorough inspection, it was now dark, damage appeared to be minimal and the float seemed watertight. As a result of the incident, the late hour and the roughening sea, refuelling was curtailed, as was the engine servicing. It was then announced an early start the following day would be impossible. Furthermore, the consequential late departure from Darwin would mean that only Groote Island or Karumba could be reached, but there was no overnight accommodation at those staging posts. Hence it was decided to delay departure for Townsville until the Tuesday. And still the passengers had not disembarked, despite having landed two hours previously. A small boat was then made available and in three parties the crew, customs officers, health officials and passengers disembarked across the choppy sea. The short crossing was not enjoyable and one of the customs officers was seasick. Dampened, dispirited and probably a little annoyed, they were herded into the small and inadequate customs shed at the end of the jetty.

As if any final offence was needed, the following day a Dutch airliner called at Darwin. She carried only five passengers and they were met by the Administrator of the Northern Territories. There had been no such welcome for *Challenger*. After only 35 minutes the Dutch aircraft was speeding on its way, all formalities complete. *Challenger* had taken two hours and was only partially processed. In yet greater contrast, the Dutch passengers were motored to a restaurant, so the customs facilities could be attended to in comfort.

Whilst the Dutch were being pampered, the British complained and examined *Challenger*'s float. It was not damaged. With greater efficiency the refuelling was completed and an early start on the fifth was forecast. Events at Darwin caused political repercussions. Minister of Defence Thorby demanded an urgent explanation from officials at Darwin regarding the allegations about inadequate facilities.

On 5 July, Captain Lynch-Blosse took *Cooee* off from Rose Bay for the first through flying-boat service back to the old country. Also on board were Captain Crowther, First Officers Gurney and Horner, Radio Officers Patterson and Lander and Stewards Drury and Jones. At Singapore, command was given to an Imperial Airways' crew and they eventually arrived at Southampton on 18 July.

Meanwhile, on Wednesday 6 July, the first Empire flight to Sydney was completed. The flight was described by *The Times* correspondent on 7 July 1938:

'The journey was marred by an almost complete lack of adventure and a whole crowd of experiences and impressions. Unlike a ship, an aeroplane shows the passengers sights and scenes changing continuously at such high speeds and in such a perfusion that would defy immediate digestion. Half a world to pass in a view in ten days. It seems full of contrast yet strangely empty of human beings. Only two days apart were the deserts of Iraq, dry and deserted, and the flooded paddy-fields of Burma, where oxen ploughed drainage furrows to get the water away. Northern Australia, where a farmer must cross hundreds of miles of bush to the nearest road. Isolated bits of civilisation were equally surprising, for example, the huge white marble dam, the palace and the temples at Raj Samand, the alighting place in India.

Contrasts were found in the least expected places, even in matters of accommodation and comfort. We're still remarking on the differences between the cheerful conditions of Bangkok and the grubby shambles of Darwin, only three days away. We're still recalling lovely scenes and sights like the sunset over the great mountains, the pink flush of dawn reflected on the underside of the wing, glowing full in the sunshine as the aeroplane climbed apparently faster than the sun, or the snowy top of Carmel seen from the sweltering heat of the Sea of Galilee, some hundreds of feet below sea level. We are still marvelling at the belt of fine weather found half way round the world. Bumps over mountains are unavoidable without oxygen apparatus for high flying and over the desert they are still found at up to 10,000 feet owing to the huge columns of rising air. We have discovered how this side of Singapore how much our comfort on the new route is dependent upon the weather sense of the captain. The meteorological service is developing with the air service. Captain Allan has studied the weather on this route and in this trip invariably found a helpful, or at any rate least awkward, wind by his observations. On one section of the route today, he chose his height on the strength of cloud tops curling backwards in the direction of the lower winds concluding that the top of the cloud was travelling faster than the base. He flew high and we reached Brisbane ahead of schedule. Much depends upon the captains east of Singapore, for on the early part of the route, progression is far more certain and a more easier operation. A small example of this was the fact the flying-boat's windows were cleaned outside at every small port between Southampton and Singapore but from that point they were not cleaned, even at night halts. However, the spirits of the crews and ground staff promises equal efficiency throughout the route shortly, but Darwin presents a problem which defies solution without the building of a breakwater and a hotel which will have to install its own water and drainage systems.

The experience of the flight was worth even the discomfort and depression of Darwin and many short nights of sleep. The joy of flying alongside Buddhist shrines gleaming like golden convolvulus in Burma and of skimming over the thousand islands of the Java Seas all crowded together all free of cloud and all fringed alike with yellow sands! One readily exchanged a cool bed at Surabaya for the sight of craters, smoking and dead, or Bali at eye level and two miles range. One rejoiced in the untouched tropic loveliness of Koh Samui and the genuine sense of being off the track in bargaining in dumb shows for a kris with a native in a dug-out canoe at Bima. These delights all come to one in the luxury of a boat within which one may walk about, smoke, drink and eat from the ease of the pneumatic chair. The quiet is such to enable discussions with passengers at the opposite ends of the saloon.'

Improved procedures were quickly adopted at Darwin. They were favourably commented upon when the second 'boat came through on 9 July. The officials had the passengers ashore within nine minutes of mooring and all the passengers' luggage was taken to the Don Hotel for customs examination. These interim procedures would be followed until a new terminal building was completed. For now, officials, armed with stop watches, monitored the passengers' treatment.

But that second flight had been marred by an engine failure in Bima that necessitated a delay while they awaited the arrival of a spare engine from Sydney. Thanks to a reciprocal arrangement with the Dutch, the airmail was not delayed.

On their return, the journalists came home in *Castor*. Of the whole venture, *The Times* correspondent wrote on 23 July 1938:

'The flat rainbow seen on the cloud surface of Burma, the forest right up to the mountain summits of Siam looking like carpets of tree-tops. The boat-hook made of a bamboo pole and a sawn-off stag horn with which a native in a petrol launch was equipped belong more to the story book than the crowded doings on a long voyage. Just a few of the incidents stand out in the stark reality and help to redeem the whole. One might pick first the surprise of the Dutch agent in Bima at our polite refusal to sleep three or even two in a bed at the local rest house. The strange idiosyncrasy of the British who will share a room but not a bed must have been met by borrowing the beds of the staff that night.'

Sometimes departures were unscheduled, as at Singapore:

'The night porter of the hotel, appraised suddenly at one after midnight that the flying-boat passengers due to be called at a quarter past four needed not be aroused until 8 am, promptly rang round all our rooms to advise the guests of their good fortune. When consulting with one's fellows next morning [we discovered] to our joy that one of our more distinguished companions, housed in a suite so magnificent that he could not discern the telephone had taken his bath and got dressed before he learnt the purport of the message.

By the end of the journey we have become practised in the routine of early morning starts and the overnight shave has become an unashamed common place. The darkness of early morning is a less oppressive cloak than it was three weeks ago. One has become used to crawling out from beneath the net to find the mosquitoes at their liveliest and most ruthless. A new habit of awakening just long enough for dawn take-off and climb and then resuming the broken sleep in the most comfortable of chairs until breakfast is placed on a table before one's recumbent form has been formed and may not be too easily broken. The early mornings were generally among the most real of the sensations. Necessity brought passengers fully awake at the first summons, though on two occasions that came as early as 2:30 am and on two others at 3:15 am. Cases had to be packed and ready for the porters within 45 minutes and sometimes less. Passengers were expected soon afterwards and taken by car to the airport and thence by launch to the flying-boat. Sometimes when the launch was delayed delivering a big load of luggage, a passenger grumbled sleepily. More often his sleepiness took him dumb until he might roll into the dawn couch and resume the silent business of the night. Before the first alighting breakfast had come to restore the ways of civilized life.*

The windows at one's elbow and the row of windows on the promenade deck ought to be shunned. Sunglasses may religiously be worn and the eyes restrained from peering at the more distant scenes sometimes sixty or seventy miles away, but the eyes are tired when the day is done. Would it have been better to miss the sight of basking sharks and of the naked pearl divers coming up from the sea bottom on their harness in the Persian Gulf. Would one have been content to miss the smoking craters of Bali in the dawn or the band of pink mist set like a girdle about the mountains of Java.'

However, flight at this low and leisurely pace had its drawbacks when the weather was bad. Although the weather out to Australia had been good, the journalist experienced 2,000 miles of rain on his return:

'The passengers were thankful for the safety and comfort being kept beneath the storms. We were delayed in Allahabad for eight hours because of storms. We had to delay our take-off until the next alighting place, Gwalior, should be clear enough to find. And then on our way to it we took a path around the blacker patches of the storms often only three hundred feet above the ground.

Only in fair weather could the passenger attempt distractions which might keep him away from the window. I found I read two novels in the course of about 200 hours of flying. If I had not slept a little I might have read two more. On two days a card school established itself among the members sitting like urchins on the broad step between the promenade deck and the after saloon. One passenger disciplined himself daily with games of patience. We took our meals gratefully and brought to them good appetites partly in response to their excellence. Sometimes we took refreshments between meals and often the whole complement of passengers was assembled and smoking in the saloon allotted to that diversion. If our gathering momentarily upset the trim of the boat, the officers never complained, better still, the Captain, at intervals, looked us over, answered our questions and joined our discussions. But the talks led most often to the examination of flying maps and the identification of places of interest below. The lure of the window is still irresistible and perhaps none but the most stern disciplinarians would have it otherwise.

On Wednesday at Basra we were called at 2:30 am and were in the air just before dawn. We alighted after nightfall at Athens and were called on Thursday morning at 2:15. Calls were made at Brindisi, Rome, Marseilles and Macon and a journey of 1,685 miles ended that evening at Southampton at 19:30. Two such long days impress upon the traveller the fact that this is primarily a mail service and that passengers must make their contributions in endurance to the cause of the mails. It is in the mail service that the routes are subsidized. Mail loads form the most regular and important source of revenue. And it is as a mail service that the work of the flying-boats will be judged.'

Castor arrived back in England on 15 July. The route to Australia was now established by the 'C-class' 'boats of QANTAS operating to Singapore and those of Imperial Airways covering the remainder of the journey to Southampton. *Cooee, Camilla, Carpentaria, Cordelia* and *Challenger* were employed upon the route. Further significant improvements in the speed of the service would have to await the introduction of night-flying equipment at the various staging posts.

On 23 July, the Commonwealth of Australia awarded QEA the contract to operate the Singapore–Sydney route. This was seen as a victory by the Australian authorities, as the United Kingdom Government had proposed QEA should sign with Imperial Airways. To the Australians, that was interpreted as England attempting to take control of the complete Southampton to Sydney route. The contract would run for fifteen years and was inaugurated on 28 July with 'Tich' Attwood's flight of *Calypso* to Sydney.

Although, on 2 August, Captain O. D. Denny left Sydney with the first Empire Airmail for England, in *Carpentaria*, the service was officially opened on 4 August by *Camilla*, captained by Lester Brain. The Acting Governor, Lord Huntingfield, in front of dignitaries and a crowd of 5,000 people declared the thrice-weekly mail and passenger service to the United Kingdom to be open. This was signified by cutting a ribbon joining *Camilla*'s wing-tip to the jetty at Rose Bay. The Australian Premier and Postmaster General were also dispatching letters to their opposite numbers in England. Escort to *Camilla* was provided by a machine of the local aeroclub.

Efforts to improve facilities south of Singapore and get the route fully opened were being made. Australia's Premier Lyons told his Parliament, at the end of November, that the Commonwealth were making every

effort to instigate the Empire Service. In particular, the feasibility of erecting temporary facilities in north-west Australia was being examined with a view to them being available in the New Year. Already QEA had agreed to provide temporary fuelling facilities, if the Commonwealth provided radio and meteorological services.

The Australian Government had not shared the British Government's enthusiasm over EAMS. For three years they had quite successfully operated the landplane service and now found themselves subsidizing two routes, the Empire route and their own interior schedule, vital for the development of the outback. On top of that, flying-boat bases were required at Sydney Harbour, Brisbane, Gladstone, Townsville, Groote Island and Darwin. The Australian Government had already stated that they were unwilling to fund the air service *in toto* and the British Air Ministry agreed to pay any outstanding sum after the Australians had made a modest initial payment. That limit was soon breached and facilities were not always quite as expected.

There were other inadequacies as to the landing places, particularly two in India. The journalist aboard *Castor* witnessed one hazardous departure from Raj Samand. They had arrived and alighted easily enough, having skirted the monsoon and the surrounding hills, but once laden with fuel, passengers and mail take-off was not so easy. As the lake was surrounded by hills, the initial climbout had to be towards the lower of the summits. This necessitated a crosswind take-off. On two occasions the wind blew the 'boat off course and take-off was aborted. Only on the third attempt, with the judicious balancing of the flying-controls and throttles was a safe departure achieved. Had it not been for the skill of the pilot or had the monsoon wind been more severe they could have been delayed at Raj Samand awaiting a break in the weather. Poor visibility also affected approaches to the River Hooghly at Calcutta, where it was necessary to make a steep approach across the Willingdon Bridge. Alternatively there was the Bennett method: on one occasion he is reported to have flown under the bridge.

Similar problems were found throughout the route. At Rangoon, the Irrawaddy River was attended by an aerial farm and in Singapore the new seadrome at Kallang was close to the busy Singapore roads. The port of Kupang was just as hazardous, as flying-boats had to alight in the open roadstead amongst tropical flotsam and jetsam. Having survived the landing they then faced a unwieldy and dangerous Shell barge. If the waters were suitable, often the approaches were obscured. At Bima, the sheltered waters were surrounded by high mountains; conversely, at Darwin, where the adjacent terrain was flat, the waters were unsheltered. *Coorong* was to become a victim of Darwin's waters.

On 12 December 1938, Lester Brain had landed *Coorong* at Darwin, without incident in a choppy sea and rising wind. The 'boat was fuelled and secured for the night. As the wind grew stronger, the station engineer, Norm Roberts, became concerned. He boarded

Coorong and ran her engines to ease the strain upon the moorings. The wind appeared to abate, so he went ashore. At about eight o'clock that evening, the now increasing winds, which coincided with a very high tide, caused *Coorong* to break free. She was driven ashore and forced between the breakwater and jetty. Lester Brain took charge of the salvage. The starboard side of the 'boat sustained the injury, as did the underside of the rear fuselage and the starboard tailplane. In addition, the starboard wing and float were damaged when the 'boat rode up onto the jetty. The forward fuselage was also wedged against the jetty. Fortunately, due to the great tidal range she was high and dry on the breakwater. The sea went down and with judicious sandbagging of the wings and many ropes they were able to secure *Coorong* before the next high tide. Salt water, however, had entered the punctured hull and damage was beyond QANTAS's resources. During the next few days she was dismantled and shipped to Rochester for repair and eventual return to Imperial Airways. In October 1939 she was re-registered as G-AEUI. Salvage proved a most costly exercise and such an extensive recovery and repair was never repeated.

In December 1938, Hudson Fysh flew in *Coolangatta* to England to meet Reith. In his diary, Fysh noted at Singapore, 'The route as a whole is vastly improved since my trip three months ago and we have much to be proud of.'

But Dutch port facilities continued to plague Hudson Fysh. On 13 February 1939, Fysh had agreed to meet a party of Dutch journalists. They were to board *Challenger* and interview Fysh while he staged through Batavia. The press noticed that Fysh had not been impressed by the poor seamanship being displayed by the launch, which nearly collided with *Challenger*'s float.

Once on board, the journalists were given the quote, '... from Southampton to Sydney, the worst landing facilities were at Batavia ...'

There was some good to be said of the Dutch facilities. At Tandjoeng Perak, Surabaya, a most attractive administration and passenger-handling facility had been built behind the jetty – the best on the route. Eventually QANTAS, rather than the Australian civil aviation authorities, were given the responsibility to liaise with the Dutch, and events proceeded smoothly.

However, Batavia did claim a victim. On 12 March 1939, Captain Hussey was taxiing *Capella* into Prick's Harbour at the end of a QANTAS scheduled flight from Darwin. He came too close to the shore and struck the submerged uncharted wreck of a frigate. Hussey quickly drove the 'boat ashore, where she lay in the shallows and filled with water. Although there were no casualties and everyone disembarked, there was sea-water damage to the hull's interior. Moreover, during salvage operations, the tail was badly damaged. *Capella* was then dismantled and shipped back to Shorts; she was not repaired, however, but scrapped in England.

Any significant improvements in the speed of the service would have to await the introduction of night-flying. It was not prudent to rush ahead until proper facilities for flying-boats were available, and the Australian and Netherlands authorities were, in the opinion of QANTAS, most tardy in the provision of such facilities. Through 1938 and 1939, QANTAS fought bitterly for improved facilities. The slipway and hangar at Rose Bay were essential for the success of the operation. Of greater concern to QANTAS was, with war looming in Europe, the establishment of an engine-repair facility in Australia.

CHAPTER NINE

Reith

British Overseas Airways Corporation – Reith leaves.

To follow the story behind the formation of the British Overseas Airways Corporation (BOAC), it is necessary to return to the wider canvas of politics. In addition to introducing the Air Navigation (Financial Provisions) Bill, on 11 November 1938, the Secretary of State for Air, Sir Kingsley Wood, also announced that Imperial Airways and British Airways would be amalgamated. He declared the Government felt the most satisfactory instrument for the development of overseas civil aviation would be provided by the association of the two 'chosen instruments' into a single public corporation.

The name, British Overseas Airways Corporation, was suggested by Reith. He had envisaged a Commonwealth Corporation, and although Eire, India, Australia, New Zealand and Southern Rhodesia welcomed his ideas, and Canada agreed to change existing treaties in favour of Britain, South Africa was doubtful. Reith eventually came to a compromise with the South African Minister of Transport.

The nationalization of the airline was seen by many as a reversal of the earlier 'Fly by itself' policy. Nationalization would, however, answer the criticisms of the past two years that part of the Government subsidy was being used to provide shareholders with dividends. Imperial were aggrieved their prestige continental routes were being handed to another company. However, they would now, as the new national airline, be able to concentrate on providing an efficient service, at the forefront of the aviation industry, and not be hamstrung by the constant need to make a profit.

At the annual shareholders' meeting of 14 November 1938, Reith stated strongly his disapproval of the 'Buy British' policy and warned he might have to procure aircraft from overseas. In tune with Cadman, he urged, that if the aim of British air leadership was to be met, then the idea of a 'self-supporting' civil aviation ought to be abandoned. He continued his report with the latest news on the deadlock over the much needed combined, co-located Empire Air Base for land- and seaplanes, at Langstone harbour – or elsewhere – and told of how he found the Imperial Airways' organization lacking direction and structure. Regarding the equipment, the late delivery of Ensign and Frobisher aircraft compounded the difficulties faced competing with foreign and other British airlines, who were equipped with newer, better and not necessarily British machines. Unfortunately, the Armstrong Whitworth Ensign had been withdrawn from service, because of engine trouble. Reith made Armstrong Whitworth pay £42,500 compensation. That surprised Armstrong Whitworth. As a result of the Ensign delays, Imperial Airways had been unable to expand their European services as expected but they had managed to carry the same number of passengers as in the previous year. In addition, there was some trouble with the engines for the Empire Flying-Boats. Although Reith had requested the loan of six Harrows from the RAF, Kingsley Wood had advised him that some services might have to be abandoned.

On 28 November 1938, the Directors of Imperial Airways and British Airways invited Mr Walter Leslie Runciman, AFC, to 'associate' himself with the workings of Imperial Airways and British Airways as the first Chief Executive. The 38-year-old Leslie Runciman was an expert on surface transport and had commanded a Royal Auxiliary Air Force squadron; he agreed to accept the appointment from 1 December 1938. Negotiations to bring the amalgamation into fruition were handled by Reith, Runciman and Pearson and, for British Airways, by McCrindle.

Although the amalgamation was taking longer than envisaged, some of the appointments, in addition to Reith as Chairman, were made public in May 1939. At the same time, Kingsley Wood announced the Government would sanction the purchase of Imperial Airways shares for the sum of 32/6d (163 pence) in the pound, and British Airways shares for 15/9d (79 pence). The Imperial Airways' shareholders had earlier been quoted 29/-d (145 pence) plus 40% of the purchase price as a dividend; they were more than satisfied. In the Bill was provision for an increased subsidy for the development of overseas service, up to £4 million per year could be paid until 1953.

The first reading of the British Overseas Airways Bill was presented by Under-Secretary of State for Air, Captain Balfour, on 10 June 1939. Its task was:

'To facilitate the acquisition by that corporation of certain air transport undertakings and to make further and better provision for the operation of air transport services.'

Of the Bill, C. G. Grey wrote:

'The word Imperial has been dropped in accord with the new principles of government afflicting this country for the past twenty years. A series of politicians, afraid to call a spade even an agricultural implement have demonstrated in Ireland and Palestine, and elsewhere, that they are afraid to govern a couple of million people let alone an Empire of hundreds of millions.'

The Bill had its second reading on 10 July.

Perkins said, 'The present situation in Civil Aviation is so bad that any change will be better than no change.'

On the whole the airline had improved since Sir John Reith took over and the spirit of the staff was much improved. As for the price of the shares, it was monstrous that one company, run by a board of incompetent directors who had succeeded in dragging British prestige in Europe down to zero, was being offered 32/6d, whereas another company, which had a live board of directors, and had upheld British prestige in Europe, was to receive only 15/9d per share:

'There should be a fairer distribution of the swag.'

Kingsley Wood stated:

'The main reason for the Government's proposal was the real necessity for advancing our position in reference to civil aviation overseas ... there was great possibility of progress particularly in the development of far sighted long range policy of British aircraft production.'

He continued that under the new corporation, national interests and national advancements would come first.

One of the problems that had been examined by Cadman was that of the pilots' rights to collective bargaining. The British Airline Pilots' Association (BALPA) stated in July they were content with the current arrangements between themselves and Imperial Airways, whilst Reith was at the helm. However, they would be the first to admit that Reith would not always be there and perhaps the inclusion of a collective bargaining clause in the Bill might be prudent. The views of BALPA were shared by a Select Committee of the House of Commons, who stressed the importance of collective bargaining, superannuation and compensation for any person made redundant as a result of the amalgamation.

BOAC was created by Act of Parliament on 24 November 1939, the Bill having received Royal Assent on 4 August. Six months later, 1 April 1940, the facilities and routes of British Airways and Imperial Airways were officially taken over by BOAC; however, the two companies commenced operations as a single entity, following the outbreak of war.

Reith accepted the chair of BOAC, but as far as he was concerned, his job was complete. Before leaving, he laid a marker to see the Corporation through the forthcoming dark years:

'You will agree that we should do what we can to minimize loss of ground during the war and to ensure that British civil aviation gets the best possible start thereafter.'

Unfortunately, BOAC was ill positioned, lacking land planes and flying-boats to service Middle East, African and North American air links.

The third of January 1940 was Reith's last day with the airline before becoming Minister of Information. He chaired a meeting in Bristol, to discuss the loss of an aircraft at Malta, and afterwards, he and Runciman discussed the idea of a chairman's visit along the route.

On 5 January, Reith received a telegram:

'Congratulations on your appointment as a Minister of the Crown although it entails a great loss to us. The very best wishes for the future from all of us.
Imperial and British Airways'

Reith was saddened by his departure; the staff seemed to share the same feelings. Reith's two years of dynamic rule, which had seen the greatest changes to civil aviation since its birth, had drawn to a close. Clive Pearson, who had been Reith's deputy, was elevated to Chairman and Runciman became Director-General BOAC.

Imperial Airways, born in a pilots' strike, almost smothered by poor management and equipment, saw its golden days curtailed by amalgamation and war. Despite the difficulties, the spirit of the aircraft, airline and people that made the Empire Class Flying-Boat survived. Mail and passengers had been carried around the world in a state of luxury that would never be surpassed. The next 'C-class' saga unfurled with nine aircraft already lost; others were to follow.

BOAC took up the reins but the Second World War was to throw all of their plans into confusion.

CHAPTER TEN

Tasman Empire Airways Limited (TEAL)

Kingsford Smith's Tasman dream – Tri-national talks – 1937 the
Centaurus flight – Samoan Clipper – Recruiting for TEAL –
Delivery of Australia – Aotearoa – Awarua in Imperial colours –
Aotearoa to New Zealand – Training and survey – Awarua to
New Zealand – Inauguration.

Through the achievements of QANTAS, QEA, Imperial and now BOAC, the 'Red Route' forged eastward. The final sector, across the Tasman, led to the formation of Tasman Empire Airways Limited (TEAL).

The Tasman was first flown in 1928 by Kingsford Smith and Charles Ulm. During the next eight years, the crossing was made another dozen or so times by Kingsford Smith or his associates. Ulm and Kingsford Smith wished to start a trans-Tasman service. Such a dream was later pursued by Kingsford Smith's widow, but the dreams of Smith and Ulm failed to receive support. In 1935 Geddes commissioned Mr A. E. Rudder to investigate the extension of the Empire Route towards New Zealand. From New Zealand, Colonel Norrie Falla, Chairman of the Union Steamship Company, approached Imperial with the idea of setting up a joint company to operate across the Tasman. In June of that year, Rudder submitted a plan for a tri-national company; ownership was to be shared between Imperial Airways, QEA and the Union Steamship Company of New Zealand. QANTAS, with an eye on the Tasman, ordered three S.30s, naming them *Captain Cook, Canterbury* and *Cumberland.*

A tri-national conference to formulate a commercial trans-Tasman service was held in Wellington, between 29 September and 1 October 1936. The Government of the United Kingdom was represented by Mr F. G. L. Bertram, CBE, who had been Deputy Director of Civil Aviation and was recalled from recent retirement, and Mr P. Liesching, CMG, Secretary to the High Commissioner for the United Kingdom in Australia. The Commonwealth of Australia sent the Hon. Sir Archdale Parkhill, KCMG, Minister of Defence; Mr M. L. Shepherd, CMG, ISO, Secretary of Defence; Mr H. P. Brown, CMG, MBE, Director-General of Post and Telegraph Department; Captain E. C. Johnson, DFC, Controller-General Civil Aviation and Mr M. B. Harry, Chief Inspector (Postal Services). Hosting the conference, the New Zealand delegation included the Hon. P. Fraser, Minister of Marine; the Hon. Walter Nash,

Minister of Finance; the Hon. R. Semple, Minister of Transport and the Hon. F. Jones, Postmaster General and Minister of Defence.

The conference declared that a joint company, to operate a trans-Tasman service, would be formed. Each country would nominate three directors and should they not be in agreement, the decision of any two would be binding. The company would be registered in New Zealand, licensed to operate the service by the three Governments and granted contracts for the carriage of mail across the Tasman. For the first three years, the Governments would contribute annual payments in the ratio of Australia 23%, United Kingdom 38% and New Zealand 39%.

Despite the conference's declaration, tri-national attempts to resolve matters of detail resulted in an impasse. The British Government postulated that Imperial Airways ought to be granted the Australia to New Zealand airmail service, thus linking all the capital cities in the Empire, in accordance with the ethos of the 'Empire Route'. As a counter, Australia and New Zealand ventured that the service should be operated jointly by their national airlines. It had been expected that Australia and New Zealand would form a joint carrier, but Imperial Airways argued it would more economic if they operated the route by themselves. The truth was that Imperial were probably motivated by the desire to complete the 'Empire Route' alone.

Eyes were being cast even further afield, and HMS *Achilles* landed a party of meteorologists on Canton Island, in the Pacific. There, much to the displeasure of the USA, the Union Jack was raised. HMS *Leander* assisted Imperial Airways with a secret survey of Pacific islands. The survey, led by Bob Wimbush, made use of the newly invented echo-sounding gear. HMS *Achilles* also aided Eric Smart, an engineer with New Zealand's Aerodrome Services Branch. Also searching for suitable flying-boat alighting areas was E. A. 'Gibby' Gibson, of the New Zealand Pacific Aviation Survey.

The possibility of resolution before the forthcoming Imperial Conference seemed remote. Yet time was not on the side of Imperial Airways, and further dithering would most likely delay the start of a through-service to New Zealand until January 1938. It was hoped that the 'Empire Route' would connect with the American trans-Pacific service (there was no 'Gentlemen's Agreement' in the Orient), allowing air passage across the Empire and on to America.

Whilst the Commonwealth wrangled, America pioneered. A Sikorsky S.42B flying-boat (NC16734 *Clipper II*), flown by Pan Am's Captain Ed Musick, landed at Auckland, late on the afternoon of 30 March 1937. They had departed Pago Pago (across the International Date Line) at 05:00, 29 March. In total, it had taken 49 hours and 20 minutes to fly from the United States to New Zealand. The British, Australian and New Zealand Governments announced, on 2 April 1937, that agreement had been reached on a joint operating principle for the trans-Tasman service under the name Tasman Empire Airways Limited (TEAL). The agreement was forced by the British statement:

'If no agreement is achieved, Imperial Airways will be authorised to operate the service by itself.'

The details would be worked out at the forthcoming Imperial Conference.

The complete route to New Zealand was surveyed by Empire 'Boat, between December 1937 and February 1938. *Centaurus,* commanded by New Zealander Captain John W. Burgess, and sister 'boat to *Cavalier* – then safely plying the Bermuda–New York route – was the chosen aircraft. Albeit the sister 'boat to *Cavalier,* there are some indications that *Centaurus* had a fuel capacity of 1,300 gallons as opposed to the 1,010 gallons of *Cavalier.* These indications are substantiated by the fact the 1,370-mile Tasman crossing would most likely consume at least 1,050 gallons of fuel.

Although Burgess was experienced on the Africa route, he had had little opportunity to fly the 'C-class' across such vast expanses of water as the Tasman Sea. The remainder of the crew were First Officer C. F. Elder, Mr F. Murray, engineer; two wireless operators, A. Low and H. Dangerfield, and Steward H. J. Bingham. This survey would lend an opportunity to the people of Australia and New Zealand to see the Empire 'Boat at first-hand, before it entered service with QEA, in summer 1938.

After a delay of two hours, rough weather hampering loading, *Centaurus* departed Southampton, at dawn on Friday 3 December 1937, to become the first commercial flying-boat to fly to New Zealand. As a result of the delayed departure, and the absence of night-landing facilities at Lake Bracciano, Burgess was forced to cut short the first day's flight and divert to Marseilles. After the night stop, an uneventful journey followed. In mid-December, they were through Singapore, and on to Klabat Bay, which was followed by a day's break at Batavia and several courtesy flights for Dutch officials. Thereafter, Surabaya, Bima and finally to Kupang and Darwin. The crew were allowed further rest, with stays at Darwin and Brisbane. At Darwin, Lester Brain, Chief Pilot QANTAS, and Squadron Leader Hemple, Royal Australian Air Force, joined the flight. Hemple had accompanied Brackley and Fysh during the May 1937 survey of the Australian sector, and although he did not

share Brackley and Fysh's enthusiasm for 'boats, Burgess found him 'a delightful fellow'. The final days' stages through Australia followed the approved route across the Gulf of Carpentaria and down the coast to Townsville, Gladstone, Brisbane and then Sydney.

They arrived in Brisbane on 21 December; Lester Brain commented upon Darwin, '... had a good alighting area but a twenty-seven-foot fall and rise of tide ... one of the great needs of Darwin is a modern, first class hotel... .'

Sydney was reached on Christmas Eve and the crew received an enthusiastic welcome from A. E. Rudder, the representative of Imperial Airways and instigator of TEAL. *Centaurus* was the first Empire 'Boat to enter Australia and many people turned out to see her, but Imperial Airways, and the British authorities, missed a golden opportunity to present the Empire 'Boat to the Australian public. There had been little advance publicity, an in-flight radio broadcast from *Centaurus* was botched and the press were given scant chance to fly in the 'boat. Arrangements, if there had been any, for selected guests collapsed and invitations for flights were cancelled at the last moment. As for the public, they could view only from afar. Moreover, QANTAS, who had ordered six S.23s, felt slighted by *Centaurus*'s tour, which pre-empted the arrival of their 'boats. Imperial Airways seemed blissfully unaware of the ill-feeling towards them.

For the crossing of the Tasman, QANTAS argued that an Australian pilot ought to be aboard, and it was suggested that Lester Brain should remain. There was perhaps a secret 'political agenda' in trying to keep Brain aboard, but Captain Burgess pleaded difficulties with payload for the Tasman crossing and Brain disembarked at Sydney.

A north-easterly surface wind blew at Force Five and *Centaurus* climbed to 6,000 feet, where the wind was more favourable for the crossing. *Centaurus* arrived on schedule and, in brilliant sunshine, she crossed Auckland's Waitemata harbour at 15:06, on 27 December. Her crossing time from Rose Bay was 9 hours 10 minutes, an average speed of 133 mph, and broke Jean Batten's record by 1 hour 20 minutes. Apart from a wireless conversation that Captain Burgess held with his father, 100 miles ahead in New Zealand, the flight had been uneventful.

Mr Savage, the Premier of New Zealand, accompanied by the Mayor of Auckland, offered a cordial greeting to the 'boat, as did the large crowd that had turned out to witness her arrival. Captain Burgess was especially congratulated by his countrymen for being selected to command the first 'boat into New Zealand. Also offering congratulations was Pan Am's Captain Ed Musick, commander of the *Samoan Clipper*, which now lay alongside *Centaurus*. The captains shook hands over a Union-Jack-covered table. *Samoan Clipper* (previously *Clipper II*), one of the four Sikorsky S.42Bs, had recently completed a second survey flight from Honolulu. Ed Musick had 24 years' experience of route surveying; he had surveyed every Pan Am route since the inception of

Centaurus, *moored at Lyttleton, Christmas week 1937. Photo taken on a Kodak Box Brownie by Bill Peek's brother.* (Peek)

the airline. The clipper was due to leave the following Wednesday, 29 December, and commence a fortnightly express parcel and mail service between Honolulu and Auckland. Despite Musick's renowned ability and reputation as a careful pilot, all was not to go the clipper's way!

Centaurus stayed in Auckland until New Year's Eve, before continuing south to Wellington. On 3 January, they made an hour-and-a-half flight to Lyttleton, where a dinner was held in their honour, but that day's flight was marred by poor visibility. On 4 January, fog continued to plague them, but despite difficult conditions they managed to reach Dunedin. Rather than continue south to Invercargill, Burgess returned direct to Wellington, and in winds gusting to 60 mph and torrential rain, it was only thanks to his local knowledge that they were able to descend safely into Wellington Harbour. There, Centaurus was moored in Evans Bay, in front of the home of Captain J. Burgess, Senior. Once refuelled, she returned to Auckland. Great interest was displayed during the fortnight's tour of New Zealand and many people came out to see Centaurus, but there was disappointment, as members of the public were not allowed aboard. However, local dignitaries and Lord Galway,

Governor-General of New Zealand, were given conducted tours or taken on flights.

Burgess flew back to Sydney on Monday 10 January 1938. On board, as the first trans-Tasman air passenger, was Colonel T. W. White, Australian Minister for Customs. As was the fashion of the day, he took the opportunity during the crossing to speak to Sydney on the wireless telephone. So as to be seen upholding his objection to carrying Lester Brain out to New Zealand, Burgess had Steward Bingham make the return crossing to Sydney by sea, offsetting the burden of Colonel White. A large crowd saw Centaurus touch down on Sydney harbour, at one o'clock in the afternoon. The crossing had taken ten hours. Burgess, hero of the day, was mobbed by women admirers. To the awaiting pressmen, he stated there was no reason why the trip could not be made twice a week, or even more frequently if circumstances demanded, and that subject to radio installations, a commercial service to New Zealand was feasible.

Heady from the success of their New Zealand venture, yet mindful of Pan Am's sombre news then breaking, Centaurus was flown from Sydney to Melbourne. Their noon arrival on 13 January, after a flight of 4 hours and 8 minutes, was one hour early. That afternoon, two trips over the bay, carrying a number of guests, were made. Included were the Governor, Lord and Lady Huntingfield; the Federal Attorney-General, Mr Menzies; the State Minister for Transport, Mr Bassau; the Lord Mayor of Melbourne and Mr Casey, the Federal Treasurer. From Melbourne on to Adelaide, where, on 18 January, a crowd of 2,000 saw *Centaurus* leave for Hobart, Tasmania. At the close of the six-hour flight, *Centaurus* arrived in Hobart 40 minutes ahead of schedule. Mr Ogilvie, Premier of Tasmania, crossed to Sydney on the return flight, the following day. *Centaurus*'s return to Sydney allowed a week to prepare for the flight back to England.

Burgess departed Sydney for Southampton on 27 January and, until 18 February, the flight was uneventful. Whilst in transit from Lake Habbaniyah to Tiberias, the engine oil pressure fell and the temperature rose on one of *Centaurus*'s starboard engines. Burgess shut down the engine, as well as was possible with a non-feathering propeller, and alighted upon the Sea of Galilee. Changing an engine on the Sea of Galilee was not recommended owing to the perverse and unpredictable nature of local storms. Burgess obtained permission to proceed to Alexandria on three engines. Without too much difficulty, the failed engine's propeller was dropped and stowed in the aft hold.

Late that afternoon, in flat calm, Burgess attempted the three-engine take-off but *Centaurus* dragged a float and swung to starboard. Dusk descended. That night, in preparation of a further attempt the following morning, they defuelled the starboard tanks by almost sixty gallons and put a similar amount into the port side. In addition, they pumped fifteen gallons of water into the port float. At daybreak another unsuccessful attempt was made. A more drastic technique was required, one which Burgess had learnt during his RAF days on 203 Squadron Rangoons. All the crew were summoned to the flight-deck. Take-off commenced, and upon Burgess's command the flaps were run out to a quarter and the crew ran aft. This sudden increase in lift, allied with the pitch-up resulting from the rapid rearward movement of the centre of gravity, allowed *Centaurus* to rise from the waters. After a 2 minutes and 47 seconds run, she was airborne.

The offending engine was changed at Imperial Airways' maintenance depot, in the old Royal Navy coaling yard at Alexandria. After almost three months away, *Centaurus* berthed at Southampton, having landed at 15:41 on 23 February 1938. Nobody met them. For half an hour Burgess waited patiently for the tender to arrive. Finally he called for several white Very lights to be fired. These were noticed by the shore staff and Line Manager 'Slack-arse Charlie' (Mr Charlie Cross). The tender ambled out, mooring was completed and the crew went ashore. Burgess was summoned to the Line Manager's office to explain the display of pyrotechnics – hardly a fitting welcome on return from the other side of the world.

Despite the success of the survey to New Zealand, it was blatantly apparent that the S.23 was unsuited for commercial Tasman crossings. A heavier 'boat with an extended range was on the stocks, the S.30.

The achievements of *Centaurus* over Christmas and New Year were overshadowed by the loss Pan Am reported on 12 January 1938. The euphoric speculation of those who foresaw a trans-Pacific service was dashed. *Samoan Clipper* had been lost. With her payload of mail and parcels, she had departed Pago Pago, *en route* to Auckland, early on 11 January. Captain Ed Musick commanded the crew of seven. An engine oil leak had forced them to return to Pago Pago, and Musick radioed that in preparation for landing upon the land-locked harbour, he was dumping fuel. That was the clipper's final message.

At the time, the truth behind this loss was not given due publicity. The probable cause of the accident may be traced to *Clipper II*'s pioneering flight of March 1937. Midway, on that first leg from Alameda, California, to Honolulu, number one engine started to overheat. Musick shut down the engine and started to dump fuel. To the crew's alarm, petrol washed into the cabin, spewing across the chart table. In an instant, Flight Engineer Vic Wright switched off all the electrical services whilst Junior Officer William Holsenbrook opened the windows and ports to vent the cabin and then flooded the bilges with the fire extinguishers. Providence smiled, there was no fire and they made Honolulu on three engines. On arrival in Auckland on 30 March, there was no mention of the incident.

Alarmed by the nature of this near disaster, fuel jettison trials were carried out at San Francisco. It was shown that dumped fuel had a tendency to adhere to the wing's lower surface and, by virtue of the airflow's boundary layer, travel forward and enter the wing's leading edge. Once the fuel had entered the wing it flowed towards the engine nacelles and exhausts and the central wing-mount, which led to the cabin.

Following Ed Musick's final call that he was returning to Pago Pago, a US Navy aircraft spotted an oil slick fourteen miles north-west of Pago Pago, and the minesweeper USS *Avocet* was sent to investigate. A pair of trousers, a drawer full of navigational equipment and other charred wreckage were silent witnesses to the horror that must have unfolded.

The informed press in England speculated that the fuel jettison ports were unreasonably close to the engines' exhaust and, in America, the alarming results of the fuel jettison trials were cited. As a result of the trials, the US Bureau of Commerce had already prohibited the jettisoning of fuel from passenger-carrying S.42s. The loss of Musick and the *Samoan Clipper* was a great shock to New Zealand, and in tribute the Auckland station was named Musick Point. Pan Am and Trippe were pilloried for alleged negligence and Pan Am did not return to New Zealand until the more suitable Boeing Model 314 became available in 1939.

The announcement that Australia and New Zealand had reached an accord on draft proposals for a trans-Tasman service, and the anticipated rapid progress, fuelled speculation. British airliners had reached New Zealand from the west and, notwithstanding their recent loss, the Americans had arrived from the east. It would only be a matter of time before a global scheduled service was established around the Empire. Supposition and rumour were rife. Imperial Airways might co-operate with Pan Am and introduce a trans-Pacific service. It would be of advantage to the Americans as their refuelling stops of Kingman Reef and Pago Pago had certain disadvantages, though the same could not be said of the British possessions of Suava, Phoenix Island and Christmas Island. It was further speculated that once the trans-Pacific service was in operation, Imperial Airways would then offer a trans-America service through Canada, running just to the north of the US border.

Such whimsical hypothesising was supported by reports from Vancouver in mid-January 1938 that Captain F. Entwistle, of the Overseas Branch of the Air Ministry, had arrived from New Zealand. He was reported to have said:

'… it was all but certain that Vancouver would be used as the Pacific terminus for future Imperial Airways services. A site at Lulu Island in the Fraser estuary was favoured but dredging at a cost of £200,000 would be required to make the site suitable.'

The wrangling over the Tasman came to an end on 16 February 1938, with the announcement in Canberra that the Commonwealth Governments were drafting agreements for Empire Airmail operations to New Zealand. The proposal was similar to that for the England to Australia service. A tri-national company, not under the sole control of any one Government, was to be formed. Tasman Empire Air Lines (TEAL), head office Wellington, with a nominal capital of £2 million, was proposed. TEAL would be 30% Australian, 50% New Zealand and 20% British owned. The Directors were to be Colonel N. S. Falla, the Managing Director of the Union Steam Ship Co. and Chairman of New Zealand's Union Airways, Sir Fergus McMaster, KB, Chairman of QANTAS, Mr Hudson Fysh, KBE, DFC, of QANTAS, Mr A. E. Rudder of Imperial Airways, Mr C. G. White, OBE, Director of Union Airways and Mr Tom Barrow, the New Zealand Air Secretary.

The need for a tri-national agreement was complex. Imperial Airways were unable to operate a service to New Zealand without the tacit agreement of Australia and New Zealand. New Zealand lacked the financial and operational wherewithal for a solo operation and Australia lacked Government determination to pursue such a venture alone. Australia and New Zealand did not share mutual trust; neither did they wish to allow a commercial force to enter the project and possibly deprive them of their potential revenue. The final agreement split the company 38% to Imperial Airways, 23% to QEA, 20% to the New Zealand Government and 19% to Union Airways.

Two months later, in June 1938, Mr Savage, the Premier of New Zealand, announced near-completion of the trans-Tasman airmail agreement and that no difficulties were foreseen. He stated:

'The outstanding problems of the trans-Tasman service have been settled and the detailed requirements will be drafted at the London Conference. By Christmas there will be a biweekly service between Auckland and Sydney. The new mark of 'boat, with a 2,000 mile range, will be used as this is more suited to the 1,200 mile ocean crossing.'

A fortnight later, on 7 July, Savage announced that, commencing on 26 July, all letters and postcards from New Zealand for the Commonwealth would be carried on from Australia as airmail. The Empire Airmail Project was complete. (The fact that mail would travel between Australia and New Zealand by ocean liner was quietly ignored.) Savage continued, saying that Empire 'Boat passengers were already out of Southampton for Australia, having left on 5 July, and the first arrivals on Empire 'Boats should disembark in England on 15 July. (Those passengers had transferred from QANTAS land planes at Singapore.)

Once the air service to Australia was established, attention was refocused upon TEAL. Discussions in August 1938 seemed to indicate that a service starting before the end of that year was feasible but a trans-Tasman airmail contract had yet to be awarded. As if to underline their preparedness, Imperial Airways declared they would employ the S.30 Empire 'Boats, if they received the contract. Seemingly, almost by default, Union Airways, which was nurturing the still unborn TEAL, did not suggest any alternative aircraft should TEAL be awarded the contract.

The medium-range S.30s, fitted with the more economic Bristol Perseus engines of 890 hp and built with the Tasman in mind, had a fuel capacity of 1,770 gallons. However, until successful fuel-jettison trials had been completed with *Cabot*, their fuel load had been limited to 1,500 gallons. Following the trials, the maximum all-up weight was raised to 48,000 lb but the maximum landing weight was restricted to 46,000 lb.

During 1938, Colonel Falla, accompanied by Maurice Clarke, General Manager of Union Airways, came to England to recruit staff for their airline. Oscar Garden was seconded from Imperial Airways and expected to deliver TEAL's second 'boat, in September 1939; he would be number two to John Burgess. Captain Cyril Butler was also seconded, and he was expected to fly the first 'boat, *Australia*, out to New Zealand in August. Further secondments were First Officers Bill Craig and Christopher Griffiths, Chief Engineer Owen Houchen and Engineers S. R. 'Bill' Peek and Geoffrey Wells. During their stay in England, Falla and Clarke inspected *Champion*. In addition to seconding staff, Maurice Clarke negotiated with Imperial for Oscar Garden to gain flying-boat experience on the Empire 'Boats. Falla, however, found himself beset with negotiating difficulties. Whereas three years earlier, Imperial Airways,

Braby pontoons were available only here at Mechanics Bay, Auckland, and Hythe. Elsewhere, passenger boarding facilities varied enormously. (Turnill)

Floating flare-path, as used at Mechanics Bay, New Zealand. (Turnill)

under the hand of Geddes and Woods Humphery, had striven to further the all 'Red Route', Reith now had the greater challenge of BOAC in mind, and the setting up of a small airline the other side of the world was not his highest priority.

To help TEAL establish servicing and docking facilities, Imperial loaned the Auckland Harbour Board some engineering staff, Len Turnill included. Turnill recruited some additional staff locally, installed the Braby pontoon and fitted out the engine test shed. However, they were devoid of a slipway and once the 'boats arrived, all work would have to be done either at the mooring or in the Braby pontoon. Should they wish to get the 'boat out of the water, she would have to be taken to Hobsonville, about seven miles by water and twenty miles by road. Part of the TEAL agreement was that the New Zealand Government would provide, at no cost to TEAL, engineering, wireless and marine support as necessary. The Australians agreed to provide those facilities necessary at Rose Bay and Lord Howe Island.

As May closed, it was announced the first TEAL 'boat was expected to leave the United Kingdom at the end of June, but a regular twice-weekly service was unlikely before the end of September. At the same time, *Ao-tea-roa* had made her maiden flight for Imperial. During the flight, piloted by Captain Burgess, she flew from Southampton to Brighton and return. On board were fifteen representatives of New Zealand and Australia.

The formation of TEAL was losing impetus, and possibly the whole affair might be deferred until the crisis in Europe was resolved. Meanwhile the S.30s were in use but to trace their ownership calls for a little patience. *Captain Cook, Canterbury* and *Cumberland* were ordered by QANTAS, potentially for the Tasman, but, in March 1939, they were taken over on the stocks by Imperial Airways. Falla agreed that Imperial, or BOAC as they became, held the S.30s, until TEAL were in a position to receive them. They would be worked out to

Australia and then across the Tasman by the end of 1939. As it transpired, it was not until August that delivery of the first aircraft took place. The three 'boats entered the British register as *Ao-Tea-Roa*, G-AFCY (S.884), *Australia*, G-AFCZ (S.885) and *Awarua*, G-AFDA (S.886). They could not carry their New Zealand registrations as they were now British-registered. That being said, *Ao-Tea-Roa* was launched as ZK-AMA, but by 18 April 1939 she had become G-AFCY and was delivered to Imperial Airways. Imperial retained the 'boats to make good their shortage following the delayed delivery of the Ensigns. Moreover, following the loss of *Connemara*, *Ao-Tea-Roa* was required for the long-range flight trials. *Australia*, G-AFCZ (S.885), delivered to Imperial Airways on 6 July, and *Awarua*, G-AFDA (S.886), delivered on 4 April, were pressed into schedule service. Disaster soon struck *Australia*.

On 7 August 1939, *Australia*, G-AFCZ (S.885), left Hythe for Karachi, having already flown previous services to Alexandria and Karachi. The night of 8 August was spent in the Margil Airport Hotel on the Shatt-el-Arab, Basra. As was the custom, Captain Butler, his crew and probably some of the passengers spent a pleasant evening in the bar. The crew and passengers were given their usual dawn call and they and their luggage were taken down to the 'boat. First Officer Harris, however, failed to turn up and a passenger was dispatched back to the hotel to find him. With Harris finally aboard, Captain Butler taxied down the narrow fairway to the take-off position. He mishandled the turn at the end of the channel and ran smack into the river bank. It was reported, however, that they had collided with part of the flare-path during the take-off run and, having lost power, to prevent her sinking, Butler ran her aground in the shallows. The crew and passengers were taken off. Whilst being towed back to the dock side for repairs, *Australia* sank and sustained serious water-damage. Imperial's engineers at Basra managed to get her ashore, strip out the interior and rebuild the lower nose section. The damage was so great that a locally made jig was employed.

The name of Captain Butler fades from the story of the Empires after his incident at Basra.

Australia remained at Basra until her repair was completed in February 1940. Meanwhile, in November 1939, notwithstanding an Air Staff decision initially to the contrary, it was decided Imperial would retain *Australia*, as a replacement for *Connemara,* and rename her *Clare.* Between 17 and 21 February 1940, Oscar Garden and Christopher Griffiths ferried the repaired *Australia* back to England. At Hythe, an astonished team of engineers found it hard to believe the 'boat had survived the return flight. The next three months were spent reworking the repair and modifying the 'boat to the same 'long-range' standard as *Clyde:* able to take off at 53,000 lb, but without in-flight refuelling equipment.

Political pressure was brought to bear, the Ensigns were becoming available and it was agreed that S.886 as *Awarua* would be delivered in August 1939. The crews were alerted and *Awarua* was returned to Shorts for a brief overhaul. She soon appeared upon their slipway registered ZK-AMC. New Zealand's Union Airways protested. The first flying-boat had to be named *Aotearoa* and registered ZK-AMA. S.886, G-AFDA was thus named *Aotearoa* and registered ZK-AMA. Meanwhile, as S.884, G-AFCY, *Ao-Tea-Roa* was no longer required for the long-range trials, it was decided to make her the second 'boat. She was duly renamed *Awarua* and with registration G-AFCY continued to serve Imperial Airways.

Hence, by August 1939, preparations were well under way for S.886 (built as *Cumberland;* launched as ZK-AMC *Awarua;* first flown, on 9 May 1939, as *Awarua,* G-AFDA; rechristened *Aotearoa*, ZK-AMA) to make her delivery flight to New Zealand. As part of the preparations, the outboard sections of her upper wings were painted, possibly Day-Glo orange. On 15 August, *Aotearoa* carried out two test-flights, one at light weight and the other heavy. After the flights, she was hauled ashore at Hythe. Whilst final preparations were being made, she was inspected by representatives of the Australian and New Zealand Governments, Messrs Maxwell and Drew, and a party from the press. Speculation of her imminent departure had abounded for weeks, but hopes had been dashed repeatedly by delays. Now, it seemed they would be off the next day.

It was a dark drizzly evening, on 15 August, that most of the crew missed, as they were taking an early night in the South Western Hotel, Southampton. At 3 o'clock in the morning on 16 August, the night porter

Following her Basra accident, Australia *sank whilst being towed for repair. Despite the water damage,* Australia *flew again but was renamed* Clare. *(Cowling)*

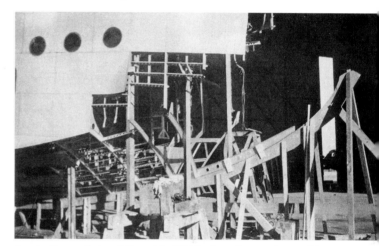

Australia *was being delivered to TEAL when she was damaged in a manoeuvring accident at Basra in 1939. Extensive repairs were made locally – much to the astonishment of the Hythe engineers once they inspected her. (Cowling)*

roused them. Attending an early breakfast with Gerald Brown, of Smiths Instruments, was Russell 'Bill' Peek, who would be the flight's engineer. He was being seen off by his bride of a few days, Peggy. Bob McNamara was the other Imperial Airways' engineer on loan to TEAL, and Bradshaw and Knee were also contracted to TEAL as instrument engineer and engine inspector respectively. The flight crew comprised Captain Burgess, First Officer Bill Craig, Radio Officer 'Paddy' Cussans and Flight Clerk Phillips. In addition, Supernumerary First Officer Kerr would be travelling, but only as far as Singapore.

The drizzle settled upon them as they boarded the bus and launch in turn. From Southampton's Berth 108, the launch motored out into the dawn mist towards the Hythe moorings, where *Aotearoa* lay in the early gloom. The baggage was loaded and farewells were said. Peggy Peek had come out on the launch; it would be some months before she saw Russell again.

The call, 'All doors and hatches closed', rang out. The interior lights dimmed as the electric starter turned the first Perseus. The propeller rotated smoothly, gave a jump, a cloud of white smoke was coughed quietly from the engine and then with a bark the mighty radial caught, and spun the blades to invisibility. The second engine was started and the mooring slipped.

Aotearoa departed Southampton for Auckland at 04:43. Within minutes they were aloft and the autopilot was engaged. Below them, France emerged from the early morning mist, and aloft, breakfast was served. Marseilles was the first refuelling stop and before noon they were airborne again. Just ahead of them was *Carpentaria,* flying the schedule service to Sydney. The two 'boats would jockey for position as they sped to the Far East. Onwards and across Italy, but as the Apennines approached, the crew were experiencing some difficulty with the Exactor hydraulic engine controls. Bert Knee assisted the two pilots and managed to trim the engines to give optimum performance to see them safely across the mountains. Late that afternoon, *Aotearoa* drifted onto Athenian waters. A brief leg-stretch was all there was time for, as John Burgess wanted to press on to Alexandria. Refuelling took fifteen minutes and they were away. After only 100 miles or so they were turned back by the authorities at Alexandria. Apparently the RAF were doing air raid practice over the port and the presence of an Empire 'Boat in their midst was not required. They returned to Athens, and as they stepped ashore, *Carpentaria* touched down at the end of her day.

A night in the Hotel Grande Bretagne was followed by a dawn take-off for Alexandria. The crossing was uneventful and they touched down amongst the British Fleet. After Alexandria, Tiberias on the Sea of Galilee. From here, Captain Burgess took a bottle of water for his son's forthcoming christening. As always, the next sector, across the desert, was bumpy, and before finally landing upon the Shatt-el-Arab at Basra, they refuelled at Habbaniyah. Whilst at Basra, Brown took the chance to inspect the autopilot of *Australia,* which was being repaired after Captain Butler's mishap. *Carpentaria* arrived.

On the morning of the 18th, they left an hour after *Carpentaria.* Gerald Brown spent some time in the bow compartment, a noisy and draughty place, attending to the autopilot, that was behaving none too well. Some time later it was engaged and to the pleasure of all, it held. Following a stage through Jiwani, the night was spent at Karachi, and during the after-flight inspection, they discovered that the starboard-outer engine's rear (long-range) oil tank had split. 'Bill' Peek was able to isolate the tank; they would be able to continue the following day. *Carpentaria* arrived.

An early start on 19 August and they cruised across India, between 500 and 1,000 feet. Because of the shape of the 'boat's nose, if the direct-vision (DV) panel was open, there was a definite 'draught' from the flight-deck, out through the window. First Officer Kerr was sitting in the right-hand seat when he had to bend forward to retrieve a message. As he bent in front of the DV panel, the draught sucked his brand-new hat from his head and out of the window, much to everyone else's amusement. Mirth soon changed to alarm, as an

almighty crash against the canopy brought the demise of a very large bird. Fortunately, it ricocheted off and did not break the windscreen.

Refuelling at Gwalior was completed in steady rain. Aloft in the monsoon on that day's final leg, the view below was desolate. There had been severe flooding and many houses had only their roofs above the waters. The weather forced them lower, navigation was difficult as the landmarks were flooded, but upon ETA, Calcutta loomed upon the nose. Once ashore, Mr Kerr, not content with losing his hat, locked himself out of his bedroom. During dinner, *Aotearoa's* crew learnt that *Carpentaria* too had struggled through the weather to arrive.

At 2 o'clock the following morning, the crew, with the exception of Radio Officer 'Paddy' Cussans, assembled in the hotel foyer. Burgess was all for departing without Cussans, when, half dressed, he tumbled into the lobby. Thirty minutes later, they were over the Bay of Bengal. Rangoon and next Bangkok, where a swollen river made the take-off very difficult, the first attempt being aborted. A speedy refuel at Penang was followed by the last sector to Singapore. Two thousand miles had to be covered that day. Burgess was in a hurry; he had been beaten to New Zealand by Musick in the S.42B and did not wish to come second to Pan Am's Boeing 314, *Californian Clipper.* Almost mesmerized by the myriad of lights that made up Singapore City, the crew searched for their faint orange flare-path off the Kallang airport. Looking too small to be of use, they spotted it, circled and landed. It was the end of 15 hours in the air. Goodbyes were said to First Officer Kerr, for he was to return to England in a day or so. *Carpentaria* spent the night in Penang and was not due in Singapore until the morrow.

At Kallang, Taffy Brownborough, Imperial's resident engineer, assisted in beaching *Aotearoa* so the ruptured oil tank could be repaired. First it was necessary to 'drop' the engine to get at the oil tanks behind, but the resident mechanics were unfamiliar with the Perseus installation and they awaited the arrival of 'Bill' Peek and Bob McNamara from the hotel. However, Captain Burgess was at Kallang and was not pleased with the late arrival of his engineers. In no uncertain way he showed his displeasure and threatened to have Peek returned to England on the next flight. Peek would at least have been reunited with his bride of a few days. Tempers subsided and the oil tank was repaired, but Peek had trouble reseating the cooling-gill ring and it would not close flush. There was no time for perfection as Burgess was adamant he would arrive in New Zealand before the Boeing clipper.

On 23 August, Singapore to Surabaya was only a six-hour hop and the crew had time to relax a little before the next day's crossing of the Timor Sea, *en route* to the mosquito-plagued shanty town of Darwin. By the following dawn, they were crossing Arnhem Land for the Gulf of Carpentaria, crossing mile after mile of empty desert. At Groote Eylandt, whilst refuelling, they chatted to the sparse population, a collection of

Aotearoa *on the slip at Kallang, Singapore, in August 1939. Kallang was a purpose-built combined land- and seaplane aerodrome. Kallang's pill-box-shaped control tower is visible beneath* Aotearoa's *wing.* (Peek)

rough-looking and well-tanned men. They crossed the Gulf of Carpentaria and then the base of the Cape York Peninsula to Townsville, their next night-stop.

Leaving Townsville on 26 August, they flew on to Brisbane and Sydney. The strain was possibly beginning to tell, as Burgess was suffering from a touch of fever, and once airborne, he handed control to Bill Craig and went below for a rest. The flight was uneventful until they reached Mackay. The previous evening the town's authorities had telegrammed Captain Burgess, at Townsville, and, explaining that Mackay was celebrating the opening of a new harbour facility, requested that *Aotearoa* make a fly-past. And so Bill Craig duly exhibited *Aotearoa* and made a low pass over an official-looking and smartly dressed ship at anchor. They also made a low pass up the main street, much to the astonishment of a cyclist, who is reported to have fallen from his bicycle. The show over, they continued on course.

At Brisbane, Burgess was able to deliver a letter from Don Bennett to his mother. It was only a brief stay and soon they were on their way to Sydney. A stiff wind blew across Rose Bay, and once *Aotearoa* had alighted, Captain Burgess was able to manoeuvre her without use of the drogues. Again, a large crowd was present to greet them. The 27th was spent in preparation for a dawn departure the following day.

Burgess, now feeling better, said a few words to radio audiences in Australia and New Zealand but the crew were anxious to get under way. With the lights of Sydney glowing behind them, they set course across the Tasman. By dawn, they were at 6,000 feet over unbroken cloud, but the forecast tailwind had not materialized. Lunch followed breakfast as they droned on above the cloud with only the occasional glimpse of the Tasman below.

At 2 o'clock, the dark smudge of distant land appeared upon the horizon. The sighting enlivened the crew and they busied themselves preparing for arrival. A fix showed they were slightly south of track, and ahead cloud was beginning to obscure the coastline. The cloud forced them lower over the green lush country below, but, with the cloud lowering still more, they climbed to 3,000 feet and proceeded towards Auckland. Once over Auckland, the clouds broke and *Aotearoa* was

Somewhere south of Singapore, and the starboard-outer cooling ring does not seat. Aotearoa, *23 August 1939.* (Peek)

able to announce her arrival with a spirited pass over the airbase, followed by a circuit of the harbour before alighting. Outside it was raining but as always crowds had gathered to witness the arrival. Once down, they taxied smartly to the mooring which 'Paddy' Cussans deftly picked up. The four Perseus engines were closed down, the propellers trimmed and after almost eight hours, silence. The shore party took control and pulled them back into the Braby pontoon. As they set foot upon New Zealand, the sun broke through and the crowd cheered. Burgess was met by his wife and young son. Amidst the cheers, handshakes, photographers and relatives, they noticed *California Clipper* had yet to arrive.

The crew of Aotearoa *following their arrival at Mechanics Bay, Auckland. (L to R) Engineer Russell 'Bill' Peek, Engineer Bob McNamara, Bert Knee – Engine Inspector, Sid Bradshaw – Instrument Engineer, Gerald Brown – Autopilot expert on loan from Smiths, Captain John Burgess, First Officer 'Bill' Craig, Radio Officer 'Paddy' Cussans and Flight Steward Ray Phillips.* (Whites Aviation, neg. 11211)

Pan Am's *California Clipper* arrived on a survey flight a few days later; a proving flight in November preceded the commencement of a weekly service to America from July 1940.

Following *Aotearoa*'s delivery, Peek and McNamara were looked upon as the two engineering experts, Len Turnill's excellent preparations being complete. There followed a period of crew training. On 7 September, *Aotearoa* made her first commercial flight to Fiji; Holden and Wimbush were aboard. They were in the final stages of their vast and prolonged survey of Pacific anchorages. On 24 September, *Aotearoa* made a survey flight from Auckland to Sydney, in 8 hours 25 minutes. Once at Rose Bay, she was hauled ashore and thoroughly inspected. She flew the return in 9 hours 10 minutes on the first of October, having departed Rose Bay at 04:14, and was more than 100 miles out to sea by the time the sun rose. There were light head winds from the east. A landfall was made at Kaipuru Heads. The passengers were Maurice Clark, Len Turnill, Squadron Leader A. G. Gerrand – Service Manager of Union Airways, Mr L. N. Larsen – Officer-in-Charge of the Government Meteorological station at Auckland, Mr J. Paul – Chief Accountant of Union Airways and Messrs F. L. Whillans and E. D. Nicholl – radio operators from Auckland.

A fortnight later, on 13 October, *Aotearoa* flew to Sydney, taking the New Zealand delegation on the first leg of their journey to the Empire Conference on War Measures, being held in London. Prime Minister Savage had fallen sick and his seat at the Conference was being taken by Deputy Prime Minister Fraser. Accompanying Fraser were Cabinet Ministers Walter Nash and Bob Semple. *Aotearoa* returned on the 15th and was soon away on yet another survey flight, this time to Suva, on 18 October. From there they continued to Nuku'alofa, Tonga. Burgess decided they could make a direct flight back to Auckland from Nuku'alofa. This they did on 23 October, and during the crossing, they diverted to

Bill Craig, Len Turnill and John Burgess – New Zealand (1939 to 1940). (Turnill)

Raoul Island and dropped a message to a survey and construction party led by D. O. Haskell. With peace potentially ebbing from The Far East, many airfields in the Pacific were surveyed, and the bases of Lauthala Bay, Suva and Lautoka were prepared for use by Empire 'Boats. *Aotearoa* was worked hard following her arrival in New Zealand, and as the winch on the Hobsonville slip needed resiting, it was to be mid-December before her barnacle-encrusted hull was drawn out of the water.

S.884 as *Ao-tea-roa* G-AFCY, now *Awarua*, was still on Imperial's inventory. Imperial awaited delivery of *Cathay* and was loath to release *Awarua* to TEAL. It had been decided that formation of TEAL would be deferred until the second 'boat arrived and the route was ready.

Whilst in London, Fraser took the opportunity to press for delivery of the second 'boat. Possibly, he reminded the British Government that New Zealand had seconded their squadron of Wellington bombers to the RAF for the duration. *Awarua* was released, but as she had suffered considerable corrosion, she was at Hythe being re-skinned, re-engined and having her control surfaces recovered. Fraser travelled down from London, and having inspected the work he tried his hand at replacing a few rivets. Geoff Wells oversaw

Aotearoa *photograph signed by delivery crew.* (Peek)

Aotearoa *on the only available slipway: RNZAF Hobsonville, about seven miles by water and twenty miles by road from Mechanics Bay.* (Whites Aviation, neg. 11559)

Awarua's overhaul, which commenced late in 1939 and was finished in March 1940. Once complete, *Awarua* was test-flown by Oscar Garden.

In New Zealand, meanwhile, Air Secretary Tom Barrow had been appointed a founding director of TEAL, but time was slipping for the unborn airline. On 24 November, Pan Am's Boeing 314 *Honolulu Clipper* arrived at Auckland from San Francisco on a crew familiarization flight.

Aotearoa continued her round of survey, training and VIP flights. Lord Willingdon, representing Great Britain at the New Zealand Centennial celebrations in January 1940, flew from Sydney to Wellington on the 19th and landed in Evans Bay. They returned to Sydney from Auckland, on 8 February.

Finally, in early March 1940, the Air Ministry announced that the Governments of Great Britain, Australia and New Zealand had agreed to a trans-Tasman service, commencing on a weekly return schedule, starting in April. *Aotearoa* would fly the first schedule; the second boat was expected in New Zealand in the very near future.

At 07:10, on a bitterly cold March day, *Awarua* slipped moorings at Hythe. Captain Oscar Garden and First Officer Christopher Griffiths were at the controls. Behind them were Radio Officer 'Paddy' Cussans, Engineer Geoff Wells, Flight Clerk George Angell and Steward Eldridge. Angell and Eldridge would travel only as far as Singapore, where they were to be replaced by QANTAS staff, Kirkwood and Drury. Three-quarters of a hour later, *Awarua* touched down at Poole, to pick up her six passengers. There were three women. One, Miss Anne Harrison, was flying to New Zealand to marry Petty Officer Squire, serving on HMS *Achilles*. She was the first fare-paying air passenger from England to New Zealand. The wives of First Officer Griffiths and Geoff Wells were also aboard.

Awarua *(Constructor's No. S.884) being re-skinned before delivery to Tasman Empire Airways Limited (TEAL). S.884 as Ao-Tea-Roa G-AFCY served with Imperial Airways before being renamed* Awarua *and prepared for delivery.* (Wells)

Awarua *undergoing engine runs before her March 1940 flight to New Zealand. International recognition stripes have been applied to* Awarua *and the hangars camouflaged.* Coorong *sits in the background.* (Wells)

'Paddy' Cussans in his TEAL radio officer days. (Peek)

In accordance with wartime regulations, *Awarua* had red, white and blue national insignia stripes painted under her registration and upon her tail surfaces. Having taken on freight and passengers for Calcutta, she departed Poole at 09:05 on 15 March. Security dictated that to prevent passengers seeing out, the cabin windows were whitewashed. Over the Channel the weather was clear but low cloud forced them down low over France. They refuelled at Biscarosse before continuing to Marseilles, for a night-stop. During their crossing of France, they were bounced by three Potez fighters of the French Air Force.

Their second night saw them in Brindisi, before carrying on to Alexandria via Athens. Now on board was a party of American date-buyers, destined for Lake Habbaniyah, but *Awarua* was unable to call at Habbaniyah on 18 March, as pro-German activists were at large. They diverted to Tiberias, but accommodation was not available so they retraced their steps further west to Haifa. The weather here was poor and the sea choppy; many vessels were moored near to *Awarua* and, as a precaution, Garden and Cussans spent the night on board as watchmen. Poor weather delayed them a further day.

On 20 March, they gained permission to overfly Habbaniyah direct to Basra, refuelling at Tiberias *en route*. At Basra they stayed at the Margil Airport Hotel on the Shatt-el-Arab. There followed a night-stop at Karachi, and then Calcutta. Here they alighted on the Hooghly River at Bally Beach Marine Airport, having come in low across the Willingdon Bridge. Misfortune struck with the discovery that a magneto drive shaft had sheared. However, they were able to remove the drive shaft fitted to the spare engine carried in the aft hold and effect a repair.

Following the Habbaniyah troubles and the magne-

to shaft they were two days behind schedule. In order to catch up, they made a night take-off from Calcutta, skipped Akyab and stopped briefly to refuel at Rangoon and then Penang. The final leg, for that day, was to Singapore, where *Awarua* was beached for the first time since leaving Hythe. They gained another day *en route* to Darwin. As all the available moorings at Townsville, their next night-stop, were occupied by S.23s, Captain Garden decided to make direct for Brisbane. This they could do once they refuelled at Karumba. Finally, on 28 March, it should have been a short uneventful hop down to Sydney, but the port-outer engine experienced an oil leak. The leak was found to be due to a six-inch crack in the oil tank. Further delays resulted in Sydney as a mark of respect for New Zealand's Prime Minister Savage, who had recently passed away. On 2 April, they flew a short test-flight to iron out some minor snags, and eventually departed Sydney on 3 April at 04:00.

Once established on track, dark endless banks of clouds lay beneath them: above them, the stars. They strained their eyes searching for the first vestige of a pink dawn. Charging towards the sunrise at 150 mph, the dawn suddenly broke: rapidly the colours changed. Streaks of purple, red, then orange rushed towards them. The flight-deck was bathed in gold and light danced upon the swirling steel propeller blades. A crystal sky revealed herself to them. Finally, far away, a faint smudge on the horizon matured into a long, white cloud.

Captain Garden said, 'There you are – Aotearoa, the land of the long, white cloud. New Zealand is hiding underneath it.'

Awarua was at last in Aotearoa. The inner engines were shut down to ease manoeuvring in the brisk south-south-westerly wind and 'Paddy' Cussans deployed the drogues. At the rear, a cable was attached to the towing eye and the 'boat was pulled into the Braby pontoon. A welcoming party of about fifty, which included Captain Garden's mother and his sister Violet, greeted their disembarkation. Also present were Mr Houchen, the TEAL Chief Engineer, Senior Captain Burgess and Captain Bill Craig. During the afternoon of 4 April, Miss Harrison became Mrs R. J. Squire.

With *Awarua*'s arrival, TEAL could be formally established. Representatives of Union Airways, BOAC and QEA met with Minister of Finance Nash, at Wellington, on 9 April. For New Zealand's air interests, Brigadier Norrie Falla took firm control, whilst BOAC was represented by A. E. Rudder, who sought a ten per cent dividend. Nash, however, was most insistent that during TEAL's early years, shareholders' dividends should be severely limited. Barrow, however, sided with Nash, stating that as a national asset, TEAL should not be lining the pockets of shareholders. A period of hard bargaining ensued, finally resolving itself on 25 April. It was agreed that TEAL would aim for a three per cent profit for the first year and eight per cent thereafter.

As the phoney war in Europe came to an end, TEAL was established, on 26 April 1940. The Head Office was

Refuelling over the top. The fuel is being strained through a chamois leather to remove any traces of water. (Peek)

Topping-up the engine oil. (Peek)

in Wellington and ownership was split four ways: 20% to New Zealand Government, 19% to Union Airways, 23% to Australia, and 39% to BOAC. The Directors were Chairman, Brigadier Norrie S. Falla, who was also Managing Director of the Union Steam Ship Co. and Chairman of New Zealand's Union Airways; Deputy Chairman, Mr A. E. Rudder; Directors, Sir Fergus McMaster, KB; Hudson Fysh, KBE, DFC; Mr C. G. White, OBE, Director of Union Airways; and Mr Barrow, the New Zealand Air Secretary. To complicate matters further, all decisions made by the board of TEAL were subject to the approval of the Tasman Air Commission, a body which reported directly to the Governments of New Zealand, Australia and Great Britain. The commission consisted of Sir Harry Batterbee, Britain's High Commissioner, Captain E. C. Johnson, Australian Assistant Director-General of Civil Aviation and J. G. Young of New Zealand's Post and Telegraph Department. TEAL's staff were based in Auckland but the commission sat in Wellington.

Before dawn on the 30th, the New Zealand Postmaster General, Mr Fred Jones, cut the ribbon barring passage along the gangway for the nine passengers. The £30 single fare was probably waived. Entering *Aotearoa* were Hudson Fysh, Rudder, Johnston, C. G. Whyte, T. C. Webster, H. O. Browne, Harvey Turner, Miss Patty Dromgool and Miss Joan Hewitt, a journalist. Some 41,000 letters had already been stowed. Captain Burgess was in command, and the remainder of the crew were First Officer Craig, Second Officer C. A. MacDonald, Radio Officer Williams, Engineer Peek, Flight Clerk R. A. Phillips and Flight Steward Jack Bury.

'Bill' Peek perched upon the prop whilst attending to the front of the engine. As long as one placed one's weight on the prop against the compression of the engine, all was well. The uninitiated who placed their weight upon the 'wrong' blade would be pitched into the water. (Peek)

They were airborne by 06:15, whereupon Fysh paid Rudder the small bet he had taken out that TEAL would not start on time. They arrived at Sydney at 15:30, New Zealand time.

The placing of the final link of the Empire Airmail Scheme, as envisaged in 1919, had, as Rudder said on arrival at Sydney, 'been a slow, exasperating process to achieve'. Unbeknown to those present, the through-service from Southampton would be severed in six weeks' time. As was foreseen by Prime Minister Frazer, such was the demand for tickets across the Tasman, that it was necessary to allocate them by Government rota.

On 2 May, the Sydney to Auckland service was inaugurated by Burgess returning in *Aotearoa; Awarua* made the second Auckland to Sydney scheduled flight on 6 May 1940. The initial schedule of one journey a week rose to three a fortnight, once the Pan Am clipper service commenced in June 1940.

The pre-flight servicing and certification to carry civilian passengers was valid for only twenty-four hours. At Sydney, the engineer chosen to certificate the S.30s was having a little trouble getting his licence endorsed for Perseus engines. Thus 'Bill' Peek and Geoff Wells were the only engineers permitted to service the Perseus engines and hence it was necessary for one of them to be aboard to certificate the 'boat for the return journey from Australia. In the end, 'Bill' Peek flew all

the crossings until a licensed engineer became available at Rose Bay. This requirement for an 'airborne' ground engineer became a feature of much of the 'C-class' operation during the looming conflict.

Although the crossing was usually flown in daylight, *Aotearoa* with Captain Burgess made the first night crossing of the Tasman on 16 May 1940. The crossing from Sydney had been delayed, thus forcing a midnight departure and a dawn arrival in Auckland. Two months later, 18 July, the Pan Am Boeing 314, *American Clipper*, arrived in Auckland at end of the first flight of regular service from San Francisco, stops at Honolulu, Canton Isle and Noumea having been made. However, the first passenger clipper to link up with the Empire 'boats was *American Clipper*. She arrived in Auckland on 16 September carrying a load of seventeen passengers from San Francisco.

After eighteen months of service, Pan Am's trans-Pacific clipper service closed following Pearl Harbor, and NC18609, *Pacific Clipper,* commanded by Captain Ford, found herself stranded on the wrong side of the Pacific war zone. *Pacific Clipper* left Auckland on 15 December 1941 and routed to New York via Australia, Oman, the Red Sea, the Nile, the Congo, Lagos and Brazil to dock finally at La Guardia, on 6 January 1942. Pan Am did not reappear at Auckland until June 1946.

CHAPTER ELEVEN

Imperial at War

ENGLAND 1940
The reserve routes – The Phoney War – Fall of France – Cabot, Caribou *and Norway –* Cathay *to France and Sikorsky – The Horseshoe conceived –* Clare *and* Clyde *to America.*

During the last years of peace, as the rearmament programme accelerated, some thought was given to the effect future conflict might have upon the all 'Red Route.' Indian Ocean Air Services Ltd, based in Perth, Australia, published a pamphlet, possibly inspired by a 1934 article in *The Aeroplane*. Within this pamphlet, they drew attention to the potentially threatening stance of various belligerent countries aligned against the route to Australia. War with Germany would threaten safe passage of European airspace, and if France were to be lost, overflight of the Mediterranean and West Africa would be difficult. Italy, on the other hand, influenced the eastern Mediterranean and East Africa. Conflict with communist Russia could close the Middle East and Persian Gulf, and Indian Nationalist uprisings could affect flights across India. Finally, Japan's sphere of influence could preclude safe air travel over Indo-China, the Malay States, the Dutch East Indies and northern Australia. To counter the denial of our routes, use of allied Portuguese airspace, our small colonies in West Africa and a passage across the Belgian Congo would give us air access to South Africa. From there it was thought possible to stage across the Indian Ocean via the Seychelles, Diego Garcia and the Cocos Islands to Western Australia. In early 1938, C. G. Grey, the outspoken editor of *The Aeroplane*, implored private exploitation of the trans-Indian Ocean route because of its potential, both commercial and military.

Although not all the pamphlet's portents came to be realized and a trans-Indian Ocean schedule was never established, its forecast did lie uncomfortably close to the truth. However, a trans-Indian Ocean survey flight, from Western Australia to Mombasa, was flown. During June 1939, the Commonwealth Government charted the American Consolidated PBY *Guba*. The aircraft, the second to bear the name *Guba,* was privately owned by Dr Richard Archbold. The first *Guba* had been sold to the Russians. Dr Archbold had employed Russell Rogers to command an earlier trans-Pacific and Indonesia expedition. Now, Rogers was acting as chief pilot to Captain P. G. Taylor. The expedition was funded by the Australian

and British Governments. They departed Port Hedland on 4 June and intended to stage through the Cocos Islands, Diego Garcia and Seychelles before finally landing at Mombasa. They were unable to find the Cocos, due to poor weather, and diverted to Batavia. Continuing westward they overflew the Cocos and finally completed the survey flight on 21 June.

Guba continued across Africa and the Atlantic back to America. She was later acquired by the British Purchasing Commission and, as G-AGBJ, served in BOAC colours before going to the RAF and then the Ministry of Aircraft Production. *Guba* was disposed of by sinking at sea in 1944.

News during the summer of 1939 belied events of the pending September. And still the Empire 'Boats set records. On 30 July, *Awarua* arrived in Southampton, having departed Basra only 39 hours previously. The overall flying time had been a mere 23 hours for the distance of 3,469 miles. Ordinarily, two and a half days were required for this journey.

When not breaking its own records, Imperial Airways were offering a comprehensive flying-boat service. There were two schedules a week to Durban, taking five days, and an additional three-day run to Kisumu. The route to Sydney was flown three times a week, and that took ten days, and Singapore was reached in five and a half days. There was a twice-weekly service to India and, during August, the experimental in-flight-refuelled, mail-only service to America started. As for Bermuda, Griffith Powell was preparing to return, with *Champion,* by way of South America, but events would soon overtake that plan.

On 29 August, as the truth of 1939 dawned, Imperial Airways announced the cancellation of their London-Paris service until further notice. As of midnight on the first of September, eastern United Kingdom (defined as a line drawn Poole, Salisbury, Kingsbury, Oxford, Pershore, west of Birmingham, Cannock and Skipton) was closed to civil aircraft. As a result, Imperial Airways' services from Croydon to the Continent were suspended.

Routes into and out of the United Kingdom were specified and regulations were laid down in the Air Navigation (Emergency Restrictions) Order, issued by the Air Ministry. It was ruled that all land planes would enter the United Kingdom at either Shoreham, Belfast Harbour, Bristol, Liverpool or Perth. Seaplanes would enter at Pembroke Dock or Poole. Within the restrictions, flight between sunset and sunrise was prohibited, all aircraft had to fly within sight of the ground and aircraft were not to fly above 3,000 feet or below 1,000 feet, unless forced down by weather. Moreover, every aircraft was required to carry documentation showing the name, permanent address and nationality of each crewman and passenger. Passengers' destinations and particulars of the cargo were also to be documented.

On Saturday 2 September 1939, *The Times* did not publish the aircraft movements. There were no daily papers on Sunday, and the following day – Monday 4 September 1939 – the Second World War began its second day. The halcyon days of flying-boats had been snuffed out. On 3 September, the flying of privately owned aircraft ceased. Control was vested into the hands of National Air Communications, which, under Gerard d'Erlanger, set up the Air Transport Auxiliary, to ferry aircraft. Imperial Airways land planes were moved to Whitchurch, near Bristol, and the 'boats moved to Poole, but their servicing facilities remained at Hythe. Griffith Powell, who had returned from Bermuda on 3 September in preparation for delivering *Champion* to Bermuda, was given the task of moving the fleet to Poole from Hythe. Poole Harbour had been surveyed by Station Superintendent Clive Adams, assisted by John Lee, the previous month and the operations staff moved down to Poole on 1 September. They were accommodated in two boats moored at Poole Quay and their only communication with the outside world was a shared telephone in the harbour-master's office.

Mail censorship commenced on 5 September when the Controller of Postal and Telegraph Censorship issued restrictions upon the content, addressing and posting of mails. Furthermore, airmail services were suspended, but later reinstated on 6 October.

With some restrictions already taking effect, Imperial planned for the worst. *Awarua* (one of the TEAL S.30s), commanded by Captain Harrington and crewed by First Officer Stone, Engineer Johnson, Radio Officer Robbie and Bill Morgan acting as flight clerk and steward, left Hythe on 13 September for Poole, Marseilles and the Mediterranean. *Awarua* had been specially chartered by the Air Ministry and was bound for Egypt, surveying a route that avoided Italy. Also aboard were Major Brackley, Commander Foley and a Mr Lloyd Taylor. Apart from Marseilles, their flight took them to Ajaccio and Bizerte, where they spent the night of the 15th, before going on to Malta, Navarino (south-west Greece), Suda Bay and Athens. The following days saw them at Corfu, returning to Malta, Bizerte and Marseilles. They arrived home at Poole on the 20th and returned the 'boat to Hythe that evening.

Despite *Awarua*'s survey, Imperial Airways, or BOAC, as they were becoming known, were not prepared for war. BOAC offered assistance to the war effort where they thought fit but little attention or guidance was given to them by the war leaders. BOAC's story was a tale of courageous, independent individuals.

Once it was established the war was 'phoney', the earlier curtailed routes were reinstated and operations were transferred back to Berth 108, Southampton. First-class mail that was destined for the French Colonies could be carried again by the French carrier, if the envelopes were marked 'via French Airmail'. For the Empire 'Boats, modified schedules continued throughout the eastbound route structure. On the Atlantic, Pan Am was not faring so well. By the end of October 1939, fear of war was affecting the number of passengers wishing to cross from the States. Pan Am announced that for the first time since the service started, there were no passengers on the eastbound *Dixie Clipper*, other than one who was bound solely for Bermuda.

The New Year brought a reappraisal of the war situation and the 'boats were moved back to Poole, just in time for the winter weather of January 1940, which was especially harsh. Flying-boats froze at their moorings. Ice was even reported at St Nazaire and Marseilles. On 15 January, Bill Morgan in *Calypso*, under the command of Captain Parker, was delayed overnight at Biscarosse, eventually arriving at Poole on 16 January. For the next eight days, services out of England were suspended due to the weather.

In mid-February, it was announced plans were well advanced for the trans-North Atlantic freight and airmail service to resume in June, the month by which Botwood was expected to be ice free. *Cabot, Caribou,* and possibly *Clyde,* using in-flight refuelling, would be employed. This service would be the only direct air link between America and Allied Europe, as the United States considered Eire to be in a war zone and thus inaccessible to American commerce.

Although at war, politics continued. In March, Air Minister Sir Kingsley Wood presented the 1940 Air Estimates to the House. He stated that, briefly, first things must come first and the progress of civil aviation would have to be retarded. However, despite war, the Empire Services of Imperial Airways would be continued. He explained that although arrangements for a weekly service across the Tasman had been made with New Zealand and Australia, resumption of the North Atlantic service would depend upon the inexorable demands of the military. Regular services in Europe would, however, continue. Looking ahead, to safeguard civil aviation after the war, a committee would be set up to keep abreast of developments throughout the world.

The phoney war continued and a semblance of normality returned, but some of the 'boats were painted with red, white and blue recognition stripes: vertically and horizontally upon the tail surface, horizontally on the fuselage sides under the registration and span-wise across the wings. On 1 April 1940, Clive Pearson, now Chairman of BOAC, announced services to Kisumu and Durban would resume their pre-war frequency. In contrast, on 24 April, the Air Minister announced that the transatlantic flying-boat service could not be operated as *Caribou* and *Cabot* were being retained 'for those military duties for which they were particularly suited'.

The military service of the Empire Flying-Boats started in October 1939. Following their in-flight-refuelled crossings of the Atlantic, *Cabot* and *Caribou* were impressed into RAF service, along with their civilian crews. Captain Gordon Store commanded *Cabot* and S. G. Long had *Caribou*. The 'boats were attached to a special duties flight at Invergordon, and seven Vickers K machine-guns were installed: two forward firing to port and starboard, two side guns, an upper gun in the promenade deck and an upper and lower gun in the rear cabin. A dummy gun, protruding from the rear refuelling cup, was also fitted. *Cabot* and *Caribou* amassed 400 hours of trials flying, during which *Caribou*, with her early air to surface vessel radar (ASV), managed to detect an enemy ship.

As agreed between the Air Ministry and Imperial Airways before hostilities, the three 'G-class' flying-boats were impressed into military service. *Golden Hind* had already been completed before the outbreak of war, but the other two 'boats were retained at Rochester for completion to 'military' standard. Their allocated serial numbers were *Golden Hind*, X8275, *Golden Fleece*, X8274 and *Golden Horn*, X8273. Work done at Rochester to militarize the 'G-class' included the installation of two dorsal and one tail Boulton and Paul electrically powered gun turrets and the fitting of underwing racks for 8×500 lb bombs and stowage, as well as launching facilities for flares and flame floats. Armour plating, to protect the crew and inner fuel tanks, was also added. Lankester Parker test-flew *Golden Horn*, still wearing G-AFCK, on 24 February and 9 March 1940. Thereafter conversion work took place and Lankaster Parker next flew her on 13 May, to check the effects of the three gun turrets – the pulpit-like rear turret in particular. *Golden Horn* wore her military serial from July and *Golden Fleece* was launched as X8274 and first flown by Lankaster Parker on 8 July. During this flight, turbulence around the tail turret was found to be causing directional instability. Fitting a fairing ahead of the turret did alleviate the problem, but it was necessary to crop the rudder. On 13 August 1940, *'Fleece* flew again and along with *'Horn* was declared fit for delivery to Blackburn Aircraft Ltd at Dumbarton for the installation of additional military equipment, including radar. They were followed on 17 September 1940 by *Golden Hind*, which since September 1939 had been undergoing acceptance trials at the Maritime Aircraft Experimental Establishment, Helensburgh. At Dumbarton, Blackburns carried out the complete militarization of *Golden Hind*.

Despite BOAC's wishes of March 1940 for return of their two long-range 'boats for the forthcoming transatlantic season, *Cabot* and *Caribou* were sent to Calshot and prepared for a special rôle. BOAC had been under the impression the 'boats were released to them but, following a War Cabinet decision, *Cabot* and *Caribou* were retained by Coastal Command.

Captains Store and Long were commissioned in the RAF as flight lieutenants, and whilst at Hythe, on the evening of 2 May, a dispatch rider handed them orders. The two aircraft were to ferry radar equipment and operating staff to Norway, in support of RAF operations in that theatre.

Golden Fleece fitted with rear turret. Power-operated rear turrets were fitted to the 'G-class' 'boats and some of the 'C-class'.
(RAF Museum H250B)

According to the HMSO-published *History of the RAF in World War II*, Wing Commander R. L. R. Atcherly flew by 'Sunderland' to Harstad between 27 April and 4 May. His brief was to prepare radar sites and reconnoitre for potential fighter landing grounds. When comparing the fragmented accounts of Atcherly's movements with those of *Cabot* and *Caribou,* considerable similarities may be found.

Cabot departed Hythe during the morning of Friday 3 May, and landed at Helensburgh. There, a Lieutenant B. Jaeger Nilsen, Royal Norwegian Navy, was taken aboard. Later that afternoon, they continued to Invergordon, where Flying Officers Clarke and Jukes and Corporal Levity, all ground radar staff, joined them. A senior RAF officer, possibly Wing Commander Atcherly, also came aboard.

Caribou followed from Hythe on 4 May, having flight-tested her recently changed starboard-inner engine during the morning. They arrived at Invergordon that evening. Here, three gunners were added to the crew, as were passengers Admiral Lumley, Flag Officer Narvik, and his staff of four. As this additional payload made them overweight, 200 gallons of fuel was offloaded. The remaining passengers were Flight Lieutenant Carter, Corporal West, a Leading Aircraftman, and Mr Johansen, a translator. Flight Lieutenant Carter's mission was to locate suitable sites to set up the air defence radar.

Cabot left Invergordon for Harstad on 4 May. On reaching Norway, before landing upon Harstad's crowded harbour, *Cabot* made a reconnaissance of the west coast of the Lofoten Islands. Ashore, that afternoon, the crew found the streets thronged with troops, whilst on the hills, oblivious Norwegian civilians skied. Captain Store and crew spent the night upon *Cabot* and early the following morning departed Harstad for Bodö.

Meanwhile, shortly after midnight, Captain Long took *Caribou* off the Cromarty Forth at Invergordon and eventually put her down alongside *Cabot*, at Bodö. However, before *Caribou* arrived, the church bells pealed an air raid warning. Unaware of the hazard, *Caribou* duly ran up the Norwegian national ensign and Long and his crew watched the local policeman row towards them. The policeman came aboard and it was discovered that his waves had not been in welcome but in warning as there were four German bombers in the area.

The enemy planes passed and the church bells rang the all-clear. It was intended that *Cabot* would remain at Bodö for ten days, surveying potential sites for fighter aerodromes and assisting with the radar. *Caribou* was to return to Scotland immediately. Cargoes of weapons and arctic rations were unloaded.

The captains went ashore to confer and were soon informed that local defences were sparse. They had barely completed offloading *Cabot*, when another air raid was warned. A pair of Dornier Do 17s, of 1(F)/120, spotted the two Empire 'Boats and spiralled down to attack. Captains Store and Long scrambled for the dinghies and sped to their 'boats. Store managed to reach *Cabot* but, as he started to taxi, he came under attack from a Dornier skimming across the fjord. Store's crew manned their guns and attempted to stave off the eight attacks developing against them. One of *Cabot's* crew, the airgunner-cook, was absent, for he had rowed across to *Caribou* to borrow some gravy salt to season the steaks he was preparing. In the words of Captain Store:

'Jerry now came in for his first attack, very low, just as *Cabot* was passing the lighthouse at the harbour mouth. Frost acted as Fire Control Officer in the astrodome, and as the Heinkel [sic] approached we opened up to full throttle at right angles to his line of flight, at the same time giving him all we had with what guns could be brought to bear. His burst spattered the water clear of us so these tactics seemed to have rattled him and we repeated them again and again. Our Jerry seemed a plucky and determined fighter, and well protected evidently, as we drilled him full of holes every time he passed over – oil streamed below his wings and fuselage. I think about eight attacks were made. To take-off and continue the battle in flight seemed senseless as this formidable opponent could have attacked from below and astern, out of the field of fire of our guns.*

Long had meanwhile been having some trouble getting Caribou's engines started, but now he was taxying across the harbour. Taking stock of Cabot's position, I had stopped a bullet in the left foot which was feeling wet, warm and crunchy inside the flying boot, but everyone else was OK, although several had had narrow escapes with one crew member having his belt shot away and Frost's steel helmet deflecting a bullet. Smoke was coming out of the wing-roots and the starboard-outer engine refused to answer to the throttle. The bow mooring hatch was shattered. I expected the

*bottom to have suffered several bullet holes, so considered the sensible thing to do was to run *Cabot* gently on to the mud at the north end of the harbour. As we did this Jerry put in a parting burst at *Caribou*, replied to by a long and accurate one from Williams, Long's waist gunner. Jerry's last burst had been an unfortunate one, as four members of *Caribou's* crew were wounded. George Bowes had a bullet in his thigh bone, young Buck got one that made a nasty hole in the calf of his leg, Dupe had been drilled across his back clear of the shoulder blades and Williams had a clean hole through the fleshy part of one arm. Fuel was gushing from the centre section tanks, down to the bilges.*

We got ashore by the simple, though chilly, process of wading and a girl with a Morris Eight on the shore road, who at first had been frightened and had hidden as she thought us Germans, until we hailed her, offered in perfect English to run those who were hurt up to the hospital, which was only about three miles distant.'

During the attack, the Do 17s dropped two bombs. As a result, *Cabot's* starboard-outer engine and one wing were thought to be severely damaged and both 'boats suffered minor damage. Long and Store succeeded in beaching their 'boats at the east-north-east end of Bodö harbour. They then removed the aircraft's machine-guns and the secret Identification Friend or Foe (IFF) equipment, which they sank. The wounded were despatched to the local hospital. As to why the attack caught Long and Store unawares, it is thought the *Luftwaffe* may have shadowed *Caribou* as she approached Norway. On the other side of the engagement, one of the German aircraft was reported to have been holed and crashed thirty miles away.

As there was no onshore accommodation for the sixteen remaining crewmen, it was decided they would sleep on board the 'boats, which now lay stranded by the receding tide. *Cabot* had already been unloaded, and the crews were wading out to *Caribou*, when the Germans struck again. Another couple of bombs were dropped. *Cabot* was missed by 300 yards but the other bomb exploded close to *Caribou* and the fuel that was leaking following that morning's attack ignited. More bombs and machine-gun fire scattered the British crewmen as fire took hold of the Empire 'Boat. *Caribou* was burnt-out. The crew retired to the Bodö Grand Hotel to make plans for the recovery of the surviving *Cabot*.

That northern summer night, the three uninjured officers hired two motor boats and at 23:30 slipped *Cabot* out of Bodö. They towed her into the open sea, in search of safety. Expecting attack at any moment, they found a place hidden under a steep cliff at Mauren, three and a half miles north of Bodö. Because of the rapidly shelving bottom, they had great difficulty mooring *Cabot*. Once secured, she was crudely camouflaged and could be seen only from above. In order to provide *Cabot* with some protection against air attack, it was decided to site the machine-guns upon the cliff top. In the early hours of 6 May, some of the crew returned to Bodö to arrange for the manufacture of gun mounts, whilst aboard *Cabot* the only significant damage that could be found was to the electrical wiring. All equipment was stripped from *Cabot* and stored in the schoolhouse, where the crew were now being billeted.

The *Luftwaffe* returned to Bodö in search of *Cabot* but she had gone. Bodö, itself, was attacked several times on the morning of 6 May, and a Norwegian seaplane was sunk. The attack on Bodö may not have been seen from *Cabot* but the immense column of smoke on the horizon told its own story. Inexorably the *Luftwaffe* searched, and at 10:00, a low-flying Do 17 spotted *Cabot,* tipped in and despatched her with a string of incendaries. BOAC's potential 1940 transatlantic service lay in a Norwegian fjord, consumed by fire.

On 7 May, the Royal Navy evacuated the remnants of the crews to Harstad; from there, another ship took them home to Britain. Those badly wounded spent three weeks in Bodö hospital, during which time, in the skies above them, they watched the gallant struggle of the RAF Gladiators against the marauding *Luftwaffe* and, on a radio salvaged from *Cabot,* they listened to the grim news from Europe.

The *Blitzkrieg,* May 1940, was followed by Mussolini's posturing. It was feared the Mediterranean would be closed to civil traffic, and the Empire 'Boats sought friendlier home skies. Some 'special' preparations were being made and several 'special' missions, some private charter, were flown. *Carpentaria,* with Captain Taylor in command (Bill Morgan, purser), was diverted at the behest of the Foreign Office into Athens. There, a Mr Lilburn of MI3 and his 'special' baggage were disembarked.

Carpentaria's outward journey had not been without incident. The first day's flying was curtailed. They stopped the night of 1 June at Biscarosse, as Marseilles was being bombed. The following day, they called at Marseilles, arriving just after a noon air raid. Oil tanks were ablaze. After an hour on the surface, they hurried on to Ajaccio. On the 3rd, they flew to Malta, via Bizerte, and on the 4th, via Corfu to Athens, where they stayed for 45 minutes before going on to Alexandria.

On 5 June, Bill Morgan returned from Alexandria in *Cassiopeia,* commanded by Captain Taylor. They staged through Suda, Athens, Brindisi, Rome and landed at Ajaccio. Sensing this would probably be their last crossing of the Mediterranean, they said farewell to the staff at Brindisi and Rome. At Ajaccio, they night-stopped, not one of their usual resting places. Here, French facilities were sparse and the arrival of two more passenger-laden craft did little to alleviate the shortages of food, accommodation and fuel. Fortunately, Bill Morgan spoke French and he stayed at the quay side until late that night helping the other crews turn their aircraft around. On the 7th, they overflew France for Hythe.

France fell on 10 June and evacuation was the order of the day. *Caledonia* was staging through Corfu for Alexandria, via Athens and Navarino, when she was called upon to turn about and evacuate the BOAC staff from Brindisi. She was the last east-bound boat from Italy. *Caledonia* continued south, through Africa, to

Durban, to become one of the founder 'boats of what was soon to be coined 'The Horseshoe Route'.

Until the fall of France, the Empire 'Boats had followed their pre-war routes but carried only Government officials, freight and mail. France fell, Italy joined the Axis and the Empire 'Boats fled to safety, *Cathay* scurrying westward for home, calling at Ajaccio. *Clyde* (a long-range S.30), under the command of Kelly Rogers, was in Malta on 11 June. Her passengers included Air Chief Marshal Sir Robert Brooke-Popham and his staff, who were returning urgently to England. The aircraft was down on power on one engine, so Kelly Rogers decided to make a take-off run from the rougher sea towards the calmer waters of Kalafrana Bay. He just cleared the shore by 200 feet. Homeward-bound, they spotted two Italian torpedo-boats off Pantelleria and two submarines. They continued non-stop across France and, with some difficulty, landed at Biscarosse to refuel.

The BOAC staff at St Nazaire were told to evacuate in mid-June. Bordeaux was bombed on the 20th. Maurice Monteux, one of BOAC's officials, left Biscarosse with Captain Loraine, who had arrived the previous day, specially chartered to a Mr Monnet. Monnet agreed that Monteux and his family could travel back to England with them.

The most audacious evacuation was that flown by, who else but, D. C. T. Bennett. An impossible task was set before BOAC, the rescue of the Polish general staff from under the noses of the Germans. General Sikorski had left his Paris headquarters as France fell and, having managed to reach England, he now sought assistance rescuing his staff. With his apologetic smile, Bennett volunteered for the flight. Bennett bumped into Morgan in the corridor and asked him to join the crew of First Officer Tommy Farnsworth, Radio Officer Jimmy Armitage and Steward W. 'Dinty' Moore. On 20 June 1940, carrying General Sikorski and his party in addition to a French general who was in search of his family, they departed Hythe in *Cathay.*

Cathay departed Poole at 09:30 and arrived outside Biscarosse four hours later. Bennett told Sikorski they would have to leave before dark. A shocked Sikorski took Bennett aside and showed him a letter, believed to have been written by Churchill. A somewhat humbled Bennett disembarked his passengers and said he would see them the following dawn. Aware how vulnerable they were as they lay offshore, Bennett taxied in search of sheltered mooring, but an air raid developed and for fifty minutes they skulked beneath trees and in shadows. They were overflown by German aircraft, but being under the cover of trees they were not seen. Once the raid had passed, Bennett and Morgan, in the dinghy, towed *Cathay* to a sheltered mooring on a sandy beach, under the cover of some larger trees. During the tow, one of them 'caught a crab' and lost his oar. (For years afterwards both Morgan and Bennett swore it was the other who lost the oar.) They spun her around and, facing out to sea, were prepared for a rapid escape. They waited. Biscarosse was surrounded by

German troops and an attack was taking place upon a nearby wood.

Morgan found a telephone and rang the hotel from which they usually obtained supplies. He was warned that the Germans were in the village. That afternoon, two of the crew searched the woods and adjacent villages and managed to buy some provisions. They were, however, shot at during their jaunt. That night they could hear the rumble of German tanks and through the trees saw them being refuelled.

Early the next morning, the general with four carloads of people, including his daughter and staff, appeared. They departed Biscarosse at 04:47 on 21 June and arrived at Poole at 09:32. During the take-off they passed over the tanks of the advancing German Army. One of the escape hatches was knocked open so the Poles could bring their small arms to bear, should they be attacked. Although apparently spotted by German fighters, they were not intercepted. Possibly, the Germans mistook them for a well-defended Sunderland. On the return journey they had to evade German fighters by flying through the smoke of a burning oil refinery. They saw several abandoned boats and crossed a blood-bespattered lifeboat with a body in its bilges. It was not only the Axis they should have been avoiding; whilst making the crossing, they were fired upon by a British cruiser lying off the Biscarosse estuary. Shortly after this flight, Bennett left BOAC to set up the Atlantic Ferry Organization.

Not all the special flights were quite so fraught. On 25 June 1940, *Clyde*, commanded by Captain Kelly Rogers, with Bill Morgan as purser, was tasked to Portugal. They flew first from Poole to Mountbatten, Plymouth. Here, they embarked the Duke of Kent, who, with his entourage, was to attend celebrations marking 800 years of Portugese independence. Although the Duke's valet missed his train and the whereabouts of some of the baggage was uncertain, the RAF stepped in to offer all assistance and *Clyde* departed on schedule. With Lord Auckland aboard, *Clyde* returned to Poole on 26 June.

At the end of the month, Captain Kelly Rogers and Bill Morgan again flew to Lisbon, but this time in *Cathay*. They returned a few days later, 5 July. Amongst their passengers were Ms van Zeeland, the Belgian Prime Minister, Mr Edgar Mowrer, Dorothy Thompson, and a Major Phillips, Comptroller to the Duke of Windsor.

Following the fall of France, Great Britain was cut off from her Empire Routes. In 1939, Brackley had surveyed a connecting route which avoided the Mediterranean, but he had assumed the availability of French airspace, both European and African. Now, alas, this was being denied. A reserve route, using a mix of ex-Imperial and ex-British Airways de Havilland Albatross and Lockheed Electra land planes, was planned to link with the trans-African, sub-Saharan land-plane route. In mid-June, an Electra did fly this reserve route from England to Durban and at least one flight was made from Kano to England. The sub-Saharan, trans-African route terminated at Lagos, but additional land planes,

or flying-boats, could extend it to Bathurst, West Africa. Moreover, the four S.30s *Cathay*, *Clyde*, *Clare* and *Champion* had the range to reach Bathurst via Lisbon and thus link up with the Empire Route. Fortuitously, at Lisbon, a connection could be made with Pan Am's transatlantic clippers, and on 28 June, *Champion* and *Cathay* started a twice-weekly service from Poole to Lisbon.

At the eastern end of the Mediterranean, Italy's entry into the war was having a more direct bearing. The Imperial Airways facilities in the old coal yard at Alexandria were moved hastily to Rod-el-Farag, Cairo. This was in good time, as on 12 June a blackout had been imposed upon Alexandria. Not without reason: on 22 June, Alexandria was bombed and air raid sirens were sounded farther south in Cairo. In Alexandria, two people were killed and another twenty injured. There were further sporadic attacks against Alexandria in August, but little damage was caused. Facilities at Rod-el-Farag were sparse. For office and crew accommodation, a number of houseboats were obtained and, from these, the view across the river was a mix of Orient and Occident. To the west was an iron railway bridge, and beyond, a huge water tower squatted upon concrete legs; two factory chimneys and a mosque added to the view. Towering palms lined the river, upon which the lateen-sailed feluccas plied their ancient trade. Many of the 'boats were south or east of Alexandria when the Italians effectively closed the Mediterranean. As will be detailed later, it was decided at BOAC's Victoria headquarters to base the flying-boat service at Durban. The route up Africa would link with the Egypt to New Zealand route. By virtue of its shape on the map, the 'Horseshoe Route' was born.

Following the Basra incident, *Australia* was restored to the British register in October 1939 and renamed *Clare*. She was returned to Hythe in early 1940 but it was not until summer 1940 that she was available for service. During this intervening period, she was modified to the same 'long-range' standard as *Cabot*, able to take off at 53,000 lb, but without in-flight refuelling equipment. In a similar fit was *Clyde*; she had been earmarked for in-flight refuelling but the fuel-receiving equipment was never installed completely. Despite the loss of *Cabot* and *Caribou*, BOAC now possessed two aircraft capable of spanning the Atlantic – just. Between 3 August and 11 October 1940, five round journeys to New York, for VIP and propaganda purposes, are reported to have been made, four by *Clare* and one by *Clyde*.

For the first crossing, on 3 August, *Clare* departed Poole with a crew of Captains Kelly Rogers and E. R. B. White, First Officer Ernie Rotherham and Radio Officers J. L. Burgess and C. E. Wilkinson. Bidding farewell were Sir Archibald Sinclair, Secretary of State for Air; Sir Francis Shelmerdine, Director-General of Civil Aviation; Clive Pearson, Chairman of BOAC and Director-General W. L. Runciman. *Clare* refuelled at Foynes and departed secretly the following morning, landing at Botwood sixteen hours and six minutes later. On board were three passengers, C. R. Fairey (Fairey was taking up leadership of the Air Section of the British Purchasing Mission to the USA), a Government official and a representative of the Secretary of the United States Navy. They were BOAC's first transatlantic passengers.

Clare proceeded to New York, via Montreal, and created much excitement when she arrived at dusk on 6 August, bedecked with camouflaged wing and hull. News of her arrival countered Nazi propaganda that England was near defeat, and the US press made much of this unescorted flight by an unarmed aircraft from besieged England. *Clare* had brought across airmail, parcels and copies of Saturday's *Times* for delivery to prominent people in America and Canada, Roosevelt and Wendel Wilkey included. The return flight from New York commenced mid-afternoon on 8 August. Her six passengers were Sir Frederick Phillips and Mr T. K. Bewley, Treasury officials, and four American pilots (A. A. Crane, L. S. King, S. W. Morgan and F. W. O'Hanlon) who boarded in Montreal. The pilots had been engaged by the Ministry of Aircraft Production to join the Air Transport Auxiliary. *Clare* also carried a goodwill message from Mayor La Guardia of New York to the Lord Mayor of London. Captain Kelly Rogers returned *Clare* to Poole at lunchtime on 10 August.

Four days later, on 14 August, Captain J. T. Kirton made his first crossing of the Atlantic. Joe Shakespeare was his first officer and Tommy Farnsworth acted as navigator. Between them, they lifted *Clare* from Poole on the start of her second crossing. On board were four 'very important passengers'. Possibly, later events of the war were brought forward as a result of the task facing *Clare*'s passengers. Sir Henry Tizard, Scientific Adviser to the Chief of Air Staff, an albeit unofficial title, was travelling to the United States as head of the British Technical and Scientific Mission to the USA. Group Captain Pearce was one of several serving officers, all with recent combat experience, who were accompanying him. The remainder of his mission and several trunks of secret papers and examples of some of the latest top secret inventions of war were already out of Liverpool bound for the States. Tizard and his mission were to offer the United States the most closely guarded of all British scientific secrets: the cavity magnetron, the proximity fuse for anti-aircraft shells and details of chemical and conventional weapons. In return, it was intended that American industry would develop and produce these devices.

In addition to Tizard and Pearce were the Permanent Under-Secretary of State for Air, Captain Harold H. Balfour, and his Parliamentary Private Secretary, Wavell Wakefield. It was during this visit to the United States that Balfour, without Treasury approval, purchased the three Boeing Model 314s.

On the day of the flight, Tizard left London on an early morning train from Waterloo and, suffering a bleak breakfast, journeyed down to Poole. Around noon, he arrived and lunched with his fellow passengers. Afterwards, the launch took them across the sheltered waters and shortly after 14:00 they were airborne. Once aloft, and having skirted the balloon barrage, they were joined by a fighter escort that saw them to Ireland. Balfour and Tizard later recalled the spartan interior of *Clare*, stripped of all earlier luxury – four seats were 'lashed' to the floor between additional fuel tanks.

At Foynes, Tizard noted:

> '*A magnificent tea which we all ate copiously. Lucky I did because we had no dinner on the* Clare *and I had not been warned. Then back to the* Clare *after a stroll, and got off again, fully loaded, at 7.30 p.m.*'

They had a rough gale-lashed crossing of 16 hours and 35 minutes; this gave Tizard ample time to reflect upon an earlier warning that *Clare* was not as comfortable as the clipper service. Coffee, sandwiches and a few hands of bridge under a single naked light bulb did little to relieve the austerity, and the breakfast of Bovril, biscuits and fruit mocked the former grandeur of Imperial Airways. Before landing at Botwood, they passed over Tizard Harbour, named after Sir Henry's father, in recognition of his naval survey of the nineteen century. The outcome of the Tizard Mission and Tizard's further movements are beyond the scope of this narrative – suffice to say Tizard took the Pan Am clipper back to Lisbon in early October.

On 16 August, as *Clare* lay moored in Marine Terminal La Guardia, New York, she was almost involved in a fire which broke out on the wing of *Yankee Clipper*, moored only a few feet away. The prompt action of a young Pan Am mechanic probably saved both 'boats from destruction. He placed his hands over a fuel vent which was spouting flames. He suffered painful burns, before an extinguisher was brought to bear. The New York Police declared the incident an accident. A couple of days were spent in New York before *Clare* returned to England, arriving at Foynes around noon on 20 August.

The third crossing is believed to have departed Poole on 30 August, but, as yet, nothing more has come to light. Alternatively, these were dark days and the *Luftwaffe*'s planned destruction of the RAF seemed to be going to plan. Measures were taken to evacuate the Royal Family, and it would appear that preparations were made to fly the Monarch from either the Welsh Harp, a north London reservoir, or a lake in Wales. Presumably one, or both, of the S.30s may have been on standby for the evacuation flight during the August/September period.

Over London, the Battle of Britain raged, but at Poole on 13 September, Kirton, Shakespeare and Farnsworth departed for Botwood in *Clare*. This was the fourth crossing and proved to be *Clare*'s last. However, bad weather delayed them at Foynes. Finally, on the evening of 15 September, *Clare* continued to Newfoundland. Botwood is on the shores of the Bay of Exploits and behind are hills, rising to a height of several hundred feet. When *Clare* arrived, low cloud and fog were in abundance and she was forced to circle, anticipating a clearance. Once down, they stayed for less than an hour before continuing to Montreal, where two radio

Cordelia/Clio *conversion, showing the dorsal turret and the ASV radar aerials. Forward of the dorsal turret, the astrodome/escape hatch is open. The astrodrome was not large enough for practical use.* (RAF Museum AC 94/40/6 Page 25)

engineers and two members of the Ministry of Aircraft Production disembarked. Another passenger, also a member of the Ministry of Aircraft Production, continued to New York.

On arrival in New York, they cruised low across the waterfront, amongst the skyscrapers, before landing at La Guardia. This crossing gave a new feeling of confidence to Great Britain and the United States. The load of newspapers were contrary proof to the latest Nazi propaganda that Fleet Street was no more. *The New York Post* wrote:

> 'Bombs are dropping in or near Fleet Street every night, and the plants of two great London newspapers have already been damaged.... . This copy reached New York yesterday aboard the flying-boat Clare, only three days after it had rolled off the presses around the corner from Fleet Street.'

On her return flight, Clare carried the Canadian First World War fighter ace 'Billy' Bishop, who was now holding a post with responsibilities for aircrew training, and on 26 September, Bishop met Churchill.

The fifth, and final crossing, was flown by Clyde. She departed Poole on 4 October and arrived back on the eleventh. Clyde was the last Empire Flying-Boat to cross the Atlantic. Winter had closed the route. Fifty passengers, in addition to two tons of urgent mail and freight, had been carried across the Atlantic. Yet, by far the greatest achievement of the Empire Flying-Boats was about to be embarked upon. But, before the story of the 'Horseshoe Route' is told, other RAF impressments must be dealt with.

CORDELIA, CLIO AND THE 'G' BOATS
Cordelia *and* Clio *impressed into the RAF – RAF service of the 'G-class' 'boats.*

As a consequence of the loss of Cabot and Caribou at

Bodö in May, Clio and Cordelia were impressed into RAF service as AX659 and AX660 respectively, on 9 July 1940. Clio was delivered to the RAF at Pembroke Dock on 17 July and flown to Shorts, now at Queen's Island, Belfast, on 31 August. Cordelia followed on 26 September. Between September 1940 and March 1941 the two 'boats were modified to S.23M standard. The work included the installation of two Boulton and Paul power-operated turrets, both housing 4 × .303 inch machine-guns. One turret was mounted in the tail; this called for an enlarged tail fairing and a reduction of fin and rudder area. The other turret, an A type, was mounted in the dorsal position, being offset to starboard. Armour, flare chutes and additional internal fuel tanks were also fitted. The S.23M was given an offensive capability with the addition of 6 × 430 lb depth charges, carried internally in the mid- or spar cabin. The three rectangular windows of the cabin were removed and replaced with a hatch for the ejection of the depth charges. Air to surface vessel radar (ASV) was also fitted and a dorsal and beam aerial array was mounted upon the aft section of the hull.

Clio was relaunched and sent to the MAEE, Helensburgh, for testing. On 27 March 1941 she became operational, making her first convoy patrol. She patrolled between Islay and Iceland and transported supplies to the Hebrides, Shetlands and Orkneys. In mid-April, for a few days, she was attached to 119 Sqn RAF, operating out of Loch Indaal, Bowmore, Isle of Islay. She soon returned to Helensburgh for two days of depth charge trials and was back with 119 Sqn at Bowmore on 19 April.

At the beginning of May, Clio was flown across to Invergordon to collect a party of passengers for Iceland. By the middle of the month, she was back at Bowmore but was there only a few days before going to Calshot for a major inspection, to be carried out by BOAC at Hythe. Clio returned to Bowmore on 20 June 1941. Although 119 Sqn was then transferred south to Pembroke Dock, on 25 July, Clio remained at Bowmore for an engine change, and was nominally on charge to 201 Sqn. This allotment was cancelled on 26 July and 413 Sqn RCAF was substituted.

The engine was changed but flight-testing was delayed several weeks as good weather was awaited. Flying Officer S. J. Rawlins (RAF) would fly the air-test. Eventually on the evening of 22 August 1941 they got airborne into a north-westerly wind. The next few minutes were witnessed by Mr James McColl, then a young man. No sooner were they airborne, when the starboard-outer engine failed. It is possible that the rear turret modification, which necessitated a reduction in rudder surface area, may have adversely affected the asymmetric handling of the 'craft. It is a fact the ensuing crash was attributed to the starboard wing stalling as a result of the excessive drag from the dead engine. The resultant loss of control may have been exacerbated by the apparent turn towards the failed engine. Clio crashed into a quarry, on the north-west side of Loch Indaal, but fortunately without fatalities.

The RAF service of *Cordelia* was similar to that of *Clio,* being delivered to 119 Sqn on 20 April 1941. She too operated between Islay and Iceland and around the Scottish Isles. Following her major inspection at Hythe, she went to Greenock in early June and was equipped with special equipment for depth charge trials. On 4 June, during these trials, *Cordelia* lost her starboard float whilst landing. The loss was attributed to the breaking of a bracing wire due to corrosion or faulty manufacture. *Cordelia* returned to 119 Sqn, now at Pembroke Dock, on 6 August, but was transferred to 413 Sqn RCAF on 9 August. She returned to Scotland and joined the squadron at Stranraer. Her time with the Canadians was brief, for on 19 September she was back with BOAC at Hythe, and on 5 December 1941 she was restored to the British register.

The RAF careers of the 'G' 'boats mirrored those of the two S.23Ms. The conversion work on *'Fleece, 'Hind* and *'Horn* was completed upon 19 November and 13 December 1940 and 22 February 1941 respectively. *'Fleece* and *'Hind* were assigned to Stanraer and commenced operational ASV training. On Christmas Eve 1940, *'Fleece* became 'G' Flight Bowmore, and she was joined on 5 February 1941 by *'Hind*. Together, in mid-March, they became No 119 Sqn and were joined by *'Horn* on 10 April. *Golden Horn* had recently completed heavy-weight trials at MAEE, Helensburgh, and sprung a leak, so she was flown to Rochester for repair. Following repair, she joined the other two 'boats, now attached to No. 10 Sqn RAAF at Mountbatten. On 11 June, long-range transport missions commenced in support of 272 Sqn Beaufighters, based in Egypt and Malta.

On 20 June, Captain S. G. Long and First Officer G. H. Bowes, both now recovered from their ordeal in *Caribou*, were outward bound for Gibraltar in *Golden Fleece*. They were about three hours out of Mountbatten when they broke radio silence to report engine failure and their intention to return to England. About thirty minutes later another message was received, this time saying they were now continuing to Lisbon. After that, silence.

It would appear that trouble with a second engine forced them down, and during the ensuing alighting in rough waters off Cape Finisterre, the hull caved in and eight crew and one passenger were drowned. The remaining passenger and four crewmen, Long and Bowes included, spent three and a half days in a life-raft, before being rescued by a *Luftwaffe* He 115 float-plane and imprisoned.

The two remaining 'G-class' 'boats were returned to Hythe for overhaul and repair by BOAC. *'Horn* went back to the RAF at Calshot, on 30 August, and then to Bowmore on 13 September. She next moved to Oban, where she was accidentally rammed at her moorings on 29 October by a 210 Sqn Catalina, and had to be hauled ashore. Thereafter, following 119 Sqn's move to Pembroke Dock and disbandment, *'Horn* and *'Hind* were returned to Hythe, BOAC and the British register.

THE HORSESHOE ROUTE
Horseshoe activated – Clyde *and the Free French* – Cassiopeia, Corinthian *and* Cooee – *Loss of* Clyde – Habbaniyah – Coorong *and* Cambria *at* Suda – *Across Africa to Lagos* – Aqaba – *Japanese influence in India* – *Loss of* Cassiopeia – Cordelia's *dash to the Horseshoe* – *Captain Alger rescues Catalina crew* – *The loss of* Clare – *'G-class' and Lake Kogella* – *Lock and the loss of* Golden Horn – *Some passengers and freight* – Reid, Cameronian *and* The City of Canton – *Peace looms.*

Since June 1937, when *Canopus* first arrived in Durban harbour, moorings adjacent to Salisbury Island had been used. A more suitable location, closer to the city, was required. Use was made of reclaimed land at Congella Basin, to the east. There, a hangar and slipway, in addition to a large servicing facility, were built. The new terminus was officially opened on 5 April 1940, and the proceedings were broadcast on the BBC. Hauled up onto the slipway, *Camilla* stood resplendent. The next day, Captain Alger and crew, Bill Morgan included, departed for Alexandria, but only a month later Durban was cut off by severe storms and 70 mph winds.

Although the fall of France may not have been foreseen, the closure of the Mediterranean was, and alternative, or reserve, routes had been surveyed. The proposed 'Horseshoe Route', connecting Durban with New Zealand, would maintain some cohesion within the Empire.

Advance parties were already *en route* by air and sea to Durban, before the Mediterranean was closed on 10 June. Those 'boats south or east of Cairo easily made Durban their home base, those in the Mediterranean scuttled to safety, east or west, and a handful were in Great Britain at the time. *Corio*, the first Horseshoe flight for Sydney, departed Durban on 19 June. It would appear that seventeen of BOAC's 'boats were in a position to reach Durban without too much difficulty following the Mediterranean's closure.

The 'boats were *Canopus, Caledonia, Castor, Cambria, Cassiopeia, Corsair, Coriolanus, Ceres, Circe, Camilla, Corinna, Cameronian, Corio, Coorong, Carpentaria, Clifton* and *Cleopatra*.

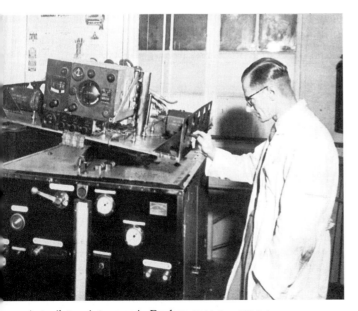

Autopilot maintenance in Durban. (Baldwin and Bigby)

From Singapore, *Corio* continued to Sydney under the command of Captain Tapp. The first westbound Horseshoe 'boat departed Sydney on 19 June. By way of sixteen countries, Durban was linked with Sydney. The route followed the 'All Red' Empire Route: Durban, Lourenço Marques, Beira, Lumbo, Mozambique, night stop. Day two: Lindi, Dar-es-Salaam, Mombasa, Kisumu, Port Bell and the second night stop. On the third day, up the Nile: Laropi, Juba, Malakal and Khartoum, where the third night was spent. Wadi Halfa, Luxor and Cairo were the fourth day's legs. Asia was entered on day five, routing to Habbaniyah, Basra and Bahrain, for the night. To India on the sixth via Sharjah, Jiwani and Karachi, where another night was spent. Onwards across India to Calcutta, where the seventh night was spent, before continuing to Rangoon, Bangkok, for the final night stop before Singapore. As in more peaceful times, QANTAS flew the route after Singapore, but homebound mail from the Empire travelled from Durban to the United Kingdom by sea.

For the next seven years, the Empire 'Boats were to pound this route, which in places was cut by enemy action and in others expanded to meet new demands.

The main party of Imperial Airways' Staff embarked upon the *Capetown Castle* at Liverpool on 27 July 1940, Bill Morgan amongst them. Such was the pride of the Imperial staff that, for the next seven years, those based at Durban considered themselves to be Imperial Airways and not BOAC. The crews continued to wear Imperial Airways insignia and, contrary to instructions from London, the Imperial Airways logos remained painted upon the 'boats for many months. The move was not without hardship, as, initially, BOAC refused to pay dependants' fares to South Africa. Captain John Locke's wife was forced to sell her engagement ring to pay for her passage.

Briefly, before the French were defeated, they had allowed land planes to route to Khartoum by way of Bordeaux, Lezigan, Oran, Goa and Fort Lamy. Once the Mediterranean was closed and France forbade overflights of the Sahara, as of 28 June, this route to Africa via Bordeaux was lost.

Although neutral, Belgium prepared her African colonies for a five-year war and stockpiled many luxury goods as an insurance against disruption of supplies. Their airline, SABENA, operated routes across central Africa, as did the French, but French Equatorial Africa had sided with the pro-German Vichy Government. For Allied aircraft to operate across Africa, the assistance of the Belgian and French authorities would be a benefit. Turning the Vichy sympathizers in central Africa towards the Allied cause would ease operations across Africa linking with the Horseshoe. Flying-boats could connect West Africa with Poole, via Lisbon, and an albeit tenuous route to the Empire could be re-established. In preparation, the Poole–Foynes–Lisbon shuttle was opened on 16 June, by *Cathay*. On her return from the first service, she was fired upon by a British merchantman and thirty-odd bullet holes were counted. It has been reported that on one occasion she was attacked by German aircraft but escaped.

Cathay, *Clare*, *Champion* and *Clyde* commenced flying the Poole–Foynes–Lisbon shuttle from the summer of 1940 and continued until autumn 1941. For a few months thereafter, the Mediterranean situation allowed direct flights to Cairo. However, before *Clyde* became established on the schedule to Lisbon, she flew another key mission. The route to the west coast of Africa had been surveyed by British Airways in preparation of a trans-South Atlantic schedule, but that was with land planes in mind. Now, long-range land planes were not available and flying-boats would have to suffice. Genial Captain Tony Loraine was given a dual task, to survey the route to the west coast of Africa and assist in swaying the Vichy to the Allied cause.

In the evening of 5 August, Tony Loraine was preparing for his forthcoming transatlantic flight in *Clyde*. *Clare* was already *en route*. Whilst still at Poole, he received orders that he was to fly to Lagos, via Lisbon and Bathurst. The 1,650-mile route from Lisbon to Bathurst had not been flown previously by Empire 'Boat, neither had the 1,600-mile Bathurst–Freetown–Lagos sector. Accompanying Loraine were Captain May, as co-pilot, and Radio Officer Cheeseman. Their passengers were Colonel de Larminat, Free French Army, and eight members of his staff. Their mission was to contact the French Equatorial African authorities, in Brazzaville, and sway them to the Gaullist cause. The voyage would have to be made with little ground support, and contact with the Vichy French was to be avoided until central Africa was reached. Possibly, this cancelled Atlantic crossing could account for the lack of evidence for the so-called third crossing.

The following morning, Loraine departed Poole for neutral Lisbon. Here, Engineering Officer Rogers joined them. *Clyde* was the first Empire 'Boat to stage through Lisbon and, initially, the Portuguese authorities were a little reluctant to allow the military passengers to proceed. The difficulties were resolved and Loraine decided to depart as soon as possible, as their movements were being watched by the Lufthansa agents. In order to slip out of Lisbon, *Clyde* departed after dusk. The 'boat was laden to capacity with fuel and their mission almost ended in Lisbon. Of their take-off Captain May wrote:

'I saw what I took to be a thin searchlight, of the kind we have for testing cloud at night, on the hills across the harbour ahead of us. Suddenly, I realized that this searchlight was on the water immediately in our path, that a small ship, probably a fishing vessel, lay directly in front of us and what I saw was our own light shining on a sail furled around her mast. I shouted to Loraine but he was concentrating on take-off and I was not sure whether he had heard me, for the ship was slightly my side, placed so that he could not easily see it. Just then we became airborne, flying only a few feet above the water straight at the vessel. It seemed impossible to miss it, I shouted again.'

May seized the controls and both pilots flung *Clyde*

hard to port. The mast barely missed the flying-boat; the port wing was within inches of the water. Recovered, they set course for Africa. Loraine and May maintained track by following the African coast and monitored their progress by use of cross-track astro-navigation. Next morning, as May was chatting to the passengers, he noticed a V-shape tear beneath the starboard wing, just below the number four engine. A whole section of aileron had been torn out.

At Bathurst, they moored on the small quay at Half Die, an early and aptly named white settlement. After a fetid night's sleep, bedraggled, hot, miserable and feeling forgotten, they set about repairing *Clyde*. They were fortunate in that they found a marine engineer. Using some heavy brass nuts and bolts and a sheet of duralumin, left by Deutsche Lufthansa, who had abandoned their small airfield some eight miles up the Gambia river, the engineer was able to patch the aileron.

Onwards they flew, to Freetown to refuel, their troubles far from over. Once they had moored, a large steel refuelling barge bore down upon them. Fearful they might be rammed, frantic waving by Loraine kept the barge at bay. That night the passengers were accommodated in an Army mess. The following day, 9 August, they attempted again to refuel. It was decided to taxi to more sheltered waters and take on fuel there. Whilst Loraine was surveying the anchorage from a dinghy, he accepted use of a proffered launch. Unfortunately, the launch approached at too high a speed and Loraine's dinghy was struck and sunk. Loraine received a ducking and refuelling was delayed another day. At dawn on 10 August, just as the rain started, they commenced refuelling from four-gallon cans, brought to the sheltered mooring by the refuelling barge. Each can had to be manhandled up onto the wing, before being poured through a funnel into the tanks. The torrential rain was kept out of the fuel by Loraine's mackintosh. It took all day to load the 1,000 gallons.

In a heavy swell, they took-off from Freetown early on the morning of 11 August, with a view to arriving at Lagos that evening. It was intended that Larminat and his staff would disembark at Lagos, but a boat was not available to take them up river. With assistance from the British Consul-General, Loraine signalled London and was ordered to fly the colonel up the Congo, towards Brazzaville, the Vichy capital. French Equatorial Africa bordered the Belgian Congo along the Congo river, and the towns of Leopoldville (Belgian Congo) and Brazzaville (Vichy) were on opposite banks.

On 19 August, *Clyde* flew to Leopoldville. Flying-boats had never landed there before, but a few weeks earlier, the BOAC Regional Director in Nairobi, Mr Vernon Crudge, had travelled across Africa by boat and car to survey a possible route. There were three S.23s in England and plans were being made to fly them out to Durban, by way of West Africa and the Congo. Crudge left his assistant, Ian Scott-Hill, in Leopoldville to await developments. Scott-Hill was surprised to be ordered by the Consul-General to lay a mooring, and advised him of the unsuitability of the waters, but Scott-Hill was informed of the gravity of the task and told to proceed. The mooring was prepared but had yet to be laid when *Clyde* arrived. Captain Loraine circled overhead whilst Scott-Hill laid the mooring and arranged a few other facilities.

The Governor of the Vichy colony was suspicious of the Free French cause and many of the colonialists were ignorant of their existence. A Colonel Carretier was leader of the Vichy French Air Force in Africa and, on 19 August, by way of a ruse he was invited onto *Clyde* by Scott-Hill. On board he met Larminat. Carretier and Larminat, between them, planned the successful *coup d'état* which brought French Equatorial Africa into the war alongside the Allies. Thus a safe air-route to the Middle East was secured.

Clyde was overdue a service, there was a fuel leak and one of the engine oil coolers was giving trouble. They effected repairs at Lagos and continued homeward. The autopilot failed and Loraine contracted malaria, but despite their difficulties they arrived back in England within seven days. Loraine went straight into hospital. Larminat, now appointed Chief of the General Staff, French Near East Army, arrived in London on 26 August.

Whilst negotiations were taking place on *Clyde*, the Horseshoe route was settling down to its arduous slog. Initially, a weekly service was operated, but once the main party of personnel arrived by ship and another three S.23s arrived from Poole, the schedule doubled to twice weekly.

In the midst of the Battle of Britain, *Cassiopeia*, *Corinthian* and *Cooee* were being prepared for their ferry flight to Durban. On 29 August, *Corinthian* and *Cassiopeia* (and presumably *Cooee*) were granted short-term CofAs to operate at a take-off weight of 45,000 lb. Their interiors were fitted with additional fuel tanks and transfer pumps, to enable them to self-refuel on landing.

At the end of September *Corinthian*, *Cassiopeia*, and *Cooee*, captained by Harrington, Davys and Bailey respectively, departed Poole. Harrington, first to leave, on 19 September, was followed at intervals of a few days by Davys and Bailey. All three were to route from Lisbon to Las Palmas (the Canaries) and, in *Clyde*'s footsteps, to Leopoldville.

Harrington left the Canaries for Bathurst, where they picked up an Army officer who 'apparently knew the way'. This was providential as the intended alighting site at Freetown was a shallow salt creek. The Army knew better; the proper mooring had been laid for them in the harbour only the previous week. On to Lagos, where they were able to relax, until, that is, the Governor of Lagos tried to impound the 'boat as transport. Harrington secured the 'boat and forged on to Leopoldville. He gave Libreville a wide berth, for there the remnants of Vichy were still resisting Larminat's *coup d'état*.

With guns and dinghies at the ready they flew on up into the Congo, which they entered at a place called Banana. The flight followed the river through

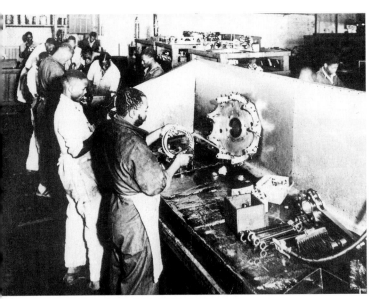

Durban: the engine bay. Pegasus engines being stripped and cleaned. (Baldwin and Bigby)

Engine maintenance at Kisumu. (Baldwin and Bigby)

Fire-boat, Kisumu 1946. (Baldwin and Bigby)

mountainous gorges and they searched for the 'village' of Leopoldville. To their astonishment, Leopoldville turned out to be a major town and a mooring awaited them. *Corinthian* landed, as *Clyde* had done before.

Once moored, Harrington was assured that higher up the Congo, rudimentary moorings and basic support had been prepared by Mr J. P. Ryan, an Imperial's man from Egypt. Harrington continued deeper into the

Congo, further than any other 'boat had been. Airborne, they turned towards the jungle and Stanleyville, leaving the Congo to loop away from them. Several hours later, they regained the river. Mr Ryan was waiting at Stanleyville for *Corinthian*. For two hours he patrolled the river and kept the fairway clear of floating debris. During the afternoon, *Corinthian* arrived. The buoy was a massive steel structure and suited the task admirably. The launch, on the other hand, was noteworthy. The Belgian authorities had mounted a Model T Ford onto an old boat and connected the drive to a propeller. Ryan commandeered this elderly 'boat' and from it he had laid the moorings, erected a wind sock, and now acted as a refuelling barge. Well into the night, Ryan, with Harrington and crew, toiled to complete the refuelling. When at last they came ashore, three naked boys marched ceremoniously towards them and prostrated themselves in the mud. A token of deference, thought Ryan, to the position of station superintendent.

However, despite their ingenuity, the 'launch' failed to work the following morning. With a crocodile-infested raging torrent between them and *Corinthian*, the crew were forced to make the crossing in a dubious-looking native canoe before they could fly on towards Lake Victoria.

Corinthian continued and Ryan awaited the landings of *Cassiopeia* and *Cooee*, as did much of the local population in their canoes. The locals, having got wind of the impending arrival, set off to meet the 'great bird'. Fortunately they paddled off on the wrong day and the 'boats were able to land safely a few days later.

But the journey of the following Empire 'Boat was not without problems. At Leopoldville, for their night stop, Captain Bailey had moored *Cooee* mid-river and left one crewman aboard as watchman, this being standard practice for 'boat operations. A torrential storm arose and the watchman, using white Very cartridges, summoned help from the shore. The shore party rowed through the tropical storm to find a 60-foot-long tree jammed against the mooring rope. Either the rope would snap and the 'boat would drift away or the tree would damage the 'boat. They started the engines and tried to pull the tree clear, but to no avail. They managed to get a steam tug and that vainly tried all night to pull the tree clear. At dawn, and in desperation, they cut the mooring rope in the hope that the 'boat would drift faster than the tree. By the barest of margins, the 'boat drifted clear. Eventually all three 'boats arrived safely in Durban.

By October 1940, the ground staff and reinforcement aircraft were established and operating from Durban. In England, on 19 October 1940, *Clyde* joined *Clare* flying the route from Poole to Lagos, via Lisbon, Bathurst and Freetown. Priority passengers, urgent freight and mail were carried on the flights, which left at intervals of ten days. The route from England to the Empire, by way of the land plane link across Africa, had been re-established.

However, the link was not without cost or hazard. On the night of 14/15 February 1941, Lisbon was struck by a hurricane, and moored upon the River Tagus lay

Clyde. The storm, the worst for 87 years, threw up great waves and winds of up to 100 mph ravaged the moorings. Damage was later costed at £10 million. *Clyde's* crew hurried to the mooring, and finding her riding well, they attempted to board but were forced back by the storm. That she continued to ride the storm for several hours was a testament to her great strength, but eventually a piece of wreckage hit the port wing and punctured the float. A fierce gust lifted the starboard wing and over she went. Tragically, the Portuguese watchman on board was drowned.

The following morning, *Clyde* was found upside down, only a short distance from the river bank. She was dragged towards the shore at Cabo Rivuo but her now inverted fin fouled the river bed and she could be brought no closer. Len Turnill, who was passing through, and Bill Kelly, station engineer, did manage to salvage the engines, propellers and some other pieces from the inverted hulk. The salvaged items were washed and despatched to Hythe on subsequent flights. The hulk of *Clyde* was disposed of locally to a scrapman, who was sworn to secrecy as to the source of the alloy.

Clyde was replaced by the Catalina *Guba*, which was, coincidentally, placed upon the route the following day. *Guba* made two flights between Poole and Lagos but proved unreliable due to engine problems. During the following months, *Cathay* and *Champion* were prepared and joined the West Africa shuttle, as did another Catalina and the three Boeing 314As that had been acquired by Balfour and delivered in July 1941.

As the war in Africa and the Middle East ebbed and flowed, so the Horseshoe was rerouted, expanded or curtailed to match events. In a similar manner, the aircraft were modified to suite changing demands. Records of the modifications done are scant, but the major changes made were to increase the flying-boats' capacity and range. By the spring of 1941, 'boats were being converted to Austerity Standard. The S.23 Austerity had its seating capacity increased to thirty at the expense of luxury fittings and the incorporation of bench seats in the promenade and spar cabins. Additional freight could also be carried. Later in the war, more powerful (1,010 hp) Pegasus XXII engines were fitted and the maximum take-off weight was increased to 52,500 lb. It is certain that QANTAS removed the pantry from their 'boats, and a similar, or partially similar, modification may have been carried out on the BOAC 'boats, at Durban. What is more certain is that QANTAS shipped additional fuel tanks to Durban, around 1941, and these were fitted to some, if not all, of the 'boats.

Nazi strategy dictated a quest for Middle Eastern oil. To further this strategy, an uprising in Iraq was supported. On 1 April 1941, the pro-German Raschid Ali, leader of The Golden Square, led an uprising and deposed the regent, Emir Abdul Ilah, and named the six-year-old King Faisal II as regent. On 30 April, Raschid Ali's forces laid seige to Ramadi and the RAF station at Habbaniyah. The siege caused all BOAC flights through Habbaniyah to be suspended. However, using those 'boats fitted with additional fuel tanks, a

Len Turnill (R) and Bill Kelly (L), Station Engineer Lisbon, salvaged the engines and propellers from Clyde *(turned turtle in background) after she was victim to a horrendous storm. (Turnill)*

twice-weekly service was operated between Tiberias and Basra, Kuwait or Bahrain, depending upon circumstances.

The BOAC traffic superintendent at Habbaniyah, Mr Alistair Thompson, had managed to evacuate the women and children on one of the last through-flying-boats, but he and his remaining staff became virtual house prisoners. On 2 May, the RAF, operating out of RAF Habbaniyah, bombed the besieging forces. Two days later, a 'boat landed and Thompson despatched a launch, but before contact was made, the flying-boat took-off. The Iraqi rebels entered the BOAC compound and Thompson and staff were marched out under armed guard, searched, threatened and interrogated. Finally, they were incarcerated in Baghdad. At the end of May, they were released, as British ground forces intervened and Habbaniyah was reopened. Germany was unable to offer additional support to Iraq as she was getting tied up in Greece and Crete.

In spring 1941, Britain and the Commonwealth stood alone. Empire 'Boats plied the Horseshoe, as the Desert War unfolded. In the Balkans, Italy, with German assistance, had invaded Greece in October 1940, and the following month, the Italian Navy was mauled at Taranto. Activity in the Mediterranean increased and shortly after noon on 28 March 1941, Sunderland N9029, NM-V of No. 230 Sqn spotted the Italian Fleet. The ensuing engagement, the Battle of Cape Matapan (Southern Greece), saw the defeat of a considerable Italian force. Thereafter, Italy needed Axis support, and Germany invaded Greece on 6 April 1941. British Forces, already supporting their Greek allies, became embroiled in a Balkan war for which they were ill prepared. The outcome was inevitable and on 17 April, General Wavell telegraphed London, 'We are making preparations for the evacuation [of Greece] and the holding of Crete.' The next day, 18 April, RAF Sunderlands evacuated King Peter and members of Yugoslavian Royal Family, along with the general staff, to Alexandria.

Whilst the Navy were preparing to evacuate the Army from the beaches of the Peloponnese, the RAF's Middle-East squadrons began a long series of evacuation flights from Greece. The Sunderlands of Nos 228 and 230 Sqn were joined by the Bombays and Lodestars of No. 267 (Communication) Sqn. However, No. 267 Sqn made only five evacuation flights into Greece before it was judged too dangerous to operate; similarly, the Blenheim force was withdrawn from Greece in the third week of April. The evacuation continued with 230 Sqn and 228 Sqn flying from the bay at Kalamata, southern Greece, and other sites. Key personnel were airlifted from Scaramanga, just to the west of Athens, to the comparative safety of Suda Bay, Crete. On one flight, No. 230 Sqn carried but two passengers: the wife of Air Officer Commanding Greece, Air Vice-Marshal J. H. D'Albiac, and her pet canary. As the gravity of the situation worsened, the Greek Royal Family was evacuated.

Crete is a primitive isle with a strategic location. On her north-west shore, surrounded by hills, was Suda Bay, the finest natural harbour in the Mediterranean. However, Suda Bay was as primitive as the rest of Crete. There was a single jetty, a single transit shed, but that took up all the useful space, and no crane.

Across the Mediterranean, in Cairo, the Air Officer Commander-in-Chief RAF Middle East summoned Mr R. D. Nee, the Acting Superintendent for BOAC, to Air HQ on the morning of 22 April. BOAC was asked if they could assist in the evacuation of Crete and it was agreed to divert 'boats off the Horseshoe, as they staged through Cairo. By using crews and 'boats from the standby pool, the Horseshoe schedule would scarcely be disrupted. Fortuitously, *Coorong* had arrived in Cairo from Durban, on 21 April, and her commander, Captain J. L. M. Davys, recorded the tasking:

> '... we on the Horseshoe route had no idea that anything was going seriously wrong until one day when I was on stand off at Cairo, I was called into the office and told in great secrecy that I was to take a "C" class 'boat to Crete and bring back various personnel. Still not realizing that anything much was wrong but impressed by the secrecy, I went down to our Nile base, where I found that everyone else knew about it as the aircraft was being loaded with packing cases marked Crete!'

An alarming brief followed and Davys was told that Greece was collapsing and *Luftwaffe* fighters were everywhere. The RAF required BOAC to fly two sorties, and fighter cover would probably be provided. Their task was to pick up the RAF personnel that had been evacuated from Greece to Suda Bay and bring them back to Egypt. In an attempt to dupe the *Luftwaffe* into thinking the unarmed 'C-class' were Sunderlands, the Empire 'Boats were given a coat of green and brown camouflage paint, applied only to the hull above the waterline and to the top surface. To turn the aircraft around at Suda and rectify any faults, a licensed engineer was carried. One of these engineers was Alf Cowling, who flew with *Coorong*.

In the afternoon of 22 April, *Coorong* departed for Suda Bay. There was no fighter escort. The plan was to

Coorong, or Cambria, makes for Suda Bay to evacuate British troops. Private photography was forbidden during the war – but not everybody followed orders. Camouflage had been applied only above the water line. One float and the mooring hatch remain unpainted.
(Withheld)

arrive at Crete at last light, refuel, load and then take off for Egypt before dawn, avoiding *Luftwaffe* attention. Meanwhile, shipping in Suda Bay, and all around Crete, was regularly under attack from Axis aircraft operating from Rhodes and Greece. The crossing was made at low-level and in the company of an RAF Sunderland. *Coorong*'s crew, unable to see behind, took chilling comfort from the Sunderland tail gunner who pointed things out with his guns. They were fired upon by the Royal Navy, as seemed the norm, and after landfall on southern Crete, threaded their way through the mountain passes, dodged an unidentified aircraft and landed at Suda Bay, after three hours and forty-two minutes. They tied up against a tanker and, with some difficulty, refuelled in the darkness.

The crew went ashore in search of the hot meal the RAF had promised, but all they found were some dirty plates and a few bottles of beer. The beer went back to the 'boat. At four the following morning, 35 airmen appeared and boarded. With the mountain tops visible in dawn's grey light, *Coorong* departed. Captain Davys later commented:

> *'We had only twenty seats but nobody seemed to mind though we were a bit horrified – no seats – no weights – no load sheet, no paper work – not at all the things we were used to.'*

For the return, they were possibly accompanied by 230 Sqn Sunderland T9050 *York*; she carried 63 passengers and 4,600 lb of Hurricane ammunition: *York* was grossly overloaded. *Coorong* arrived back in Alexandria at a quarter-past eight.

After *Coorong* had left Cairo on that first mission, there had been a frantic search for another 'boat that could be used without disrupting the schedule. *Cambria* had arrived on the afternoon of the 22nd, but as her crew was exhausted, Captain F. V. W. Foy's replaced them. Foy took *Cambria* to Crete on 23 April and, on landing, found the tanker crew sweeping up shell splinters. Foy spent the night at Crete and returned early the following day escorted by a Sunderland.

Although the evacuation plan called for minimal disruption to the Horseshoe, the number of evacuees in Crete was greater than anticipated and additional flights were required. Relief crews, arriving from Durban, were driven to Alexandria, from whence they flew to Crete before returning to Cairo to take over the next Horseshoe schedule to Singapore.

For the next week, *Coorong* and *Cambria* repeated the mission, sometimes escorted, other times not. Often there were air raid alerts. On one occasion, as they were tied to the tanker, the alarm sounded and the tanker crew abandoned their posts and took shelter ashore. Davys and *Coorong* felt very vulnerable. At night the guards would patrol and shoot out any lights that were shown. Every morning, another load of airmen would appear, and by the week's end, they were carrying almost fifty airmen at a time.

Throughout the shuttle, the RAF Sunderlands continued to operate between Greece and Egypt, often calling at Suda Bay. Their flights were not without incident. On 23 April, Sunderland *Peter* attempted a three-engine departure from Suda. It was too heavy, carrying 1,000 gallons of fuel, and returned to moorings. *Peter* was caught in the open by seven Stukas and subsequently destroyed. Fortunately, the crew managed to escape unhurt and brought down one Stuka with their machine-guns. On 24 April, 230 Sqn *York*, with Flying Officer D. K. Bednall in command, limped into Suda Bay from Alexandria. He had lost an engine *en route*, probably a consequence of the brutal demands put upon the engines during the overweight take-off the previous morning. An engine change was out of the question, so the crew lashed the non-feathering propeller to the wing, in order to prevent the windmilling propeller causing drag and damage. Bednall departed for Alexandria on three, but no sooner had they crossed Crete when the propeller's lashings became loose. They force-landed south of Crete. All the coxswain could find to re-lash the propeller was the anchor chain. It was adequate and the four-and-a-half-foot swell did not impede their second three-engine take-off of the day too much.

Greece was surrendered to the Axis on 24 April and Sunderland *Uncle* flew Air Officer Commanding Greece, D'Albiac, and General Blamey, with their staffs, to Suda. *Victor*, meanwhile, with 37 passengers escorted *Coorong* and *Cambria*, each with 45 passengers, back to Alexandria. *Coorong* was crewed by Captain Davys, First Officer Bicknall and Ground Engineer Alf Cowling.

On the evening of 25 April, 5,000 troops were landed at Suda by the Royal Navy and Merchant Navy. Once ashore, the men had no tents, warm clothing or cooking materials. Desertion was a problem and the higher levels of command lacked cohesion. Between then and the 28th, a further 20,000 troops arrived from Greece. Suda was under continual threat of air attack, and on the 24th the 10,000-ton tanker *Eleanora Maersk* was bombed and set on fire. She, and several other ships, burnt for days. Bodies floated in the bay.

The evacuation flights by the Empire 'Boats continued. On 25 April, *Coorong* carried 47 passengers to Alexandria while *Cambria* was fired upon as she neared the Egyptian port. On the 26th, Flying Officer Bednall, commanding *York*, escorted *Cambria* and *Coorong* from Suda Bay to Alexandria. They evacuated four tons of Hurricane spares, ammunition and men. On 27 April, both 'boats were escorted back to Suda, *Coorong* commanded by Captain Upton with First Officer Staples, and *Cambria* commanded by Captain Bellin. The RAF meanwhile evacuated the Prime Minister of Greece, a Greek prince and Generals Wilson and Rankin from Greece to the relative safety of Suda Bay.

Departure from Suda on the 28th was recorded by Davys:

> *'Coorong, on that last morning, the starter on our No.3 engine seized up – so we tried to wind it to start but could hardly move it. We all had a go, still with no success, the morning raid was about due. Suddenly the*

sirens went and the First Officer, Ernie Bicknell – one of the strongest little men I know – said, "Let me get at it," and seizing the handle wound it at a terrific rate – bang! – the engine was away, and so were we like a flash, hugging the valleys across the island and down to the wave tops the other side all on our own and, of course, it would be the morning we met our only Jerry. We met almost head-on at nought feet, took one look at each other and bolted in opposite directions.'

Coorong reached safety, and on 1 May, Captain 'P. G.' Woodhouse flew her from Alexandria to Cairo. *Cambria*, on the other hand, was entrusted to Captain 'John' Alcock with Purser Bill Morgan, both recently flown up from Durban, and they flew *Cambria* on return flights to Crete on both the 1 and 2 May.

The final evacuation flight was recorded on 5 May, and a total of thirteen round trips, *Coorong* seven and *Cambria* six, carrying a total of 469 passengers, had been made. On average, 36 passengers were carried on each journey, 47 being crammed in on one occasion. There are reports that the airmen were marched on board until there was no freeboard left at the entrance door.

Amongst the crews who flew these hazardous flights were Captains Davys, Upton, Foy, Alcock, Woodhouse, Mountain and Bellin; First Officers Bicknell, Staples, Rudd and Reynolds; Radio Officers Wilson, Smith, Macpherson, Cosgrave and Neves; and Engineers Alf Cowling, Cyril Burle, Tute and Wright. Despite inadequate rest but thanks to the willingness of the aircrew, only two Horseshoe schedules were delayed 24 hours.

On 20 May the Germans invaded Crete, and finally, on 1 June, Sunderland *Victor*, commanded by Flight Lieutenant Lywood, evacuated eighteen people from Crete to Aboukir, General Wavell, the commander of the Allied Forces Crete, being included.

Axis aircraft bombed Alexandria on 6 June 1941 and killed about a hundred people. However, despite bombing and the fall of Crete, the desert war situation remained relatively stable. Taking advantage of the lack of enemy air activity and in an attempt to make better use of Allied air transport, Air Chief Marshal Tedder, AOCinC Middle East, suggest an integrated air-transport plan – the Tedder Plan. The resources of both the RAF and BOAC would be utilized, and managed by BOAC. Although the operation was never as comprehensive as Tedder had envisaged and was constantly plagued by a lack of aero engines, the service was invaluable and made best use of scant resources. The existing land-plane route across Africa was under much pressure, as war materials built up in West Africa and the stream of ferry pilots returning to Takoradi increased. Although additional land planes were made available, it was decided to augment the trans-Africa land plane service with Empire 'Boats. They would route along a spur from Kisumu to Lagos, following the route across the Congo, blazed by *Corinthian*, *Cassiopeia* and *Cooee* in September 1940. The first 'boat to fly the Kisumu–Lagos shuttle was *Cassiopeia*, on 4 July 1941. She was commanded by Captain 'On Time Dudley'

Travers; the purser was Bill Morgan. They departed Cairo and after Khartoum they turned west for Port Bell, Stanleyville, Cocquilhatville, Leopoldville, Pointe Noire, Libreville and finally Lagos. Throughout the early days of this service, the support facilities gradually improved, but for some time the motley collection of vessels that serviced and refuelled the 'boats did include a number of native dugout canoes. The Horseshoe service, which now incorporated this trans-Congo spur, meant crews were away from their home base of Durban for up to six weeks at a time. It was a punishing schedule which sapped at the health of many of BOAC's pilots, many of whom were flying over 1,500 hours a year. On their return to Durban they usually had about a week stood down from route flying, but there were still air-tests and training flights, often in *Cathay,* to be carried out.

To arrest Axis influence, the Allies occupied Vichy Syria and, during the campaign, BOAC's 'boats lost the use of Tiberias as a staging post. A number of S.23s had been fitted with additional fuel tanks, so that they could overfly Tiberias, but the shorter-range 'boats were forced to route via Aqaba, Jordan's Red Sea port. Here, in the summer of 1941, a refuelling post was set up; Alf Cowling was site manager and resident engineer. The meagre facilities were similar to those at the many isolated outstations established to support the Horseshoe. Refuelling was carried out from a converted twelve-foot sailing boat, fitted with six 40-gallon fuel drums and, in the forward part of the boat, a fuel pump. Engine oil was supplied in four-gallon tins. When Cowling arrived on the site, he found the Shell representatives were paying insufficient attention to the cleanliness of the petrol; moreover, they had no experience in working with flying-boats. Cowling dispatched them back to Shell, and he took over the refuelling and maintenance of the equipment himself. The six fuel drums were removed and cleaned, up to half a pint of water and sludge being found in each. Clean petrol was then poured into the drums and a single-point pressure refuelling coupling was attached to the hose. Previously, refuelling had been done 'over the top'.

Cowling was in Aqaba from 11 June to 6 August 1941. He was assisted by a traffic officer, a wireless operator, a handful of Jordanian guards and several levies. Radio facilities were provided by the radio ship *Imperia*, which had been sailed across from Crete after BOAC pulled out of Mirabella, following Italy's entry into the war. Their tents, the fuel dump and a small brick oven were all enclosed in a barbed wire compound fronting the sea. Only a handful of 'boats called at Aqaba and there was little diversion from the work. Swimming was not advisable because of the sharks and it was dangerous to wander into the silent hills, for as soon as sight of the sea was lost, disorientation struck. All rocky sand dunes looked alike.

Although the United States of America had yet to enter the war, they were providing materials. In addition to the aircraft being shipped to the air ferry head at Takoradi, the Americans established a depot at Asmara,

Alf Cowling upon the wing, somewhere in Africa. The cooling gills were removed from the engines to prevent engine overheating.
(Author)

in Eritrea, for the construction and repair of aircraft and other war materials. In August 1941, a crew under the command of Alcock, with Tommy Rose as first officer, had routed Khartoum to Cairo and, on 19 August, back to Wadi Halfa and Port Sudan. Their passengers were a party of American aircraft engineers bound for the Asmara base. Alf Cowling remembered this trip in particular, not so much because of the American passengers but because he burnt his knees when he knelt down upon the wing surface during refuelling.

As stated, in summer/autumn 1941, *Cathay* joined *Champion* and *Clare* flying to Bathurst, and occasionally on to Lagos. However, before *Cathay*, the last S.30 built, and *Champion*, the first, could join the west-coast schedule they must have had additional fuel tanks fitted. This is supported by 'Bonzo' Brown's flight (Satchwell first officer) at the end of August 1941 in *Champion*. Then, routing Foynes to Poole, they were forced to return to Foynes, following the seizure of the starboard-outer engine. During the return to Ireland, they jettisoned 320 gallons of fuel. In September 1941, Brown made a series of take-offs and landings at 48,000 lb. Moreover, a few days later he flew a consumption test between Hythe, Poole, and Lundy. Their all-up weight for take-off was 50,500 lb. The extended range was put to use with a flight to Cairo, via Gibraltar and Malta in November

1941, the Polish leader, General Sikorski, being one of the passengers.

In autumn 1941, the war situation in the Mediterranean eased and, despite having to cross the German lines of communication and contend with sporadic Italian bombing attacks upon Malta, the Empire 'Boats inaugurated a Lisbon–Gibraltar–Malta–Cairo service on 12 October. The schedule, flown at night, was once a week. The first trip was made by Captain May, in *Clare*. Having left Foynes, he arrived at Lisbon at midnight and waited until the following day before continuing to Gibraltar. Departure from Gibraltar was planned to allow a pre-dawn, twilight landing at Malta. As it was, they had to circle for an hour until it was light enough to touch down. Although the island was not under heavy attack, there were many alarms and, on later flights, the 'boats often had to hold off, or land in the busy harbour whilst air raids were in progress. *Clare* left Malta at dusk bound for Cairo, routing midway between Libya and Crete. Despite bad weather and thunderstorms, which often delayed flights, they reached Rod-el-Farag, Cairo, and three days later returned to Gibraltar via Malta. In addition to bad weather, a confliction of 'parking' sometimes delayed the crossing. The RAF commanders in Malta did not wish to have Sunderlands and Empire 'Boats on the Marsa Scirrocco, Kalafrana Bay, at the same time, as they presented too tempting a target. Whenever possible the Empire 'Boat was pulled out of the water and hangared before daylight and arrival of the first enemy reconnaissance aircraft. The prevailing winds often allowed Gibraltar to be overflown, but on the occasion of May's first return to Gibraltar, the wind and weather were adverse. Once they arrived overhead Gibraltar, Captain May asked for a searchlight to be shone vertically so he could spiral down to a safe landing. Amongst the passengers was a person who held a very senior position inside Number Ten. The flight nevertheless proved that a route across the enemy's lines of communication could be held. *Clare* was withdrawn from the Foynes–West Africa route, as were *Champion* and *Cathay*. All three were positioned for the Lisbon–Cairo route.

During winter 1941/2 BOAC's 'boats were the only civil aircraft to reach Malta. *Clare*'s flight in from Gibraltar on 2/3 February had been blessed by poor weather to protect her, but following her arrival the sky cleared. For some reason she had not been put under cover at Kalafrana and a lone Junkers Ju 88 straddled her with a stick of incendiaries. One of the bombs struck *Clare*. The bomb burnt through the hull and started a fire in one of the cabins. Before the fire took hold, the resident BOAC engineer, G. F. Soler, and the station manager, P. C. Armour, were able to quench the flames. David Brice was first officer on that flight. Following the repair, whilst awaiting departure, they witnessed a flight of Me 109s bring down a Maryland.

The intensity of German bombing increased and it was considered too dangerous to route so close to Libya. On 26 February *Clare*, *Champion* and *Cathay* were transferred back to the West Africa route, but Catalinas continued to make the hazardous Gibraltar–Malta crossing.

Axis action was being felt elsewhere on the Horseshoe. On 27 December 1941 Captain Crowther had to turn back to Calcutta, as Akyab was under attack. Across the Indian Ocean, on the Durban seafront, walked petite Rosamund Madge. She felt ill at ease. Something was amiss. However, a thought cheered her, it would soon be New Year, and although her husband Carlos had been away for Christmas, he was due to return from the Far East in a day or so. That evening, BOAC staff called upon Rosamund. There had been an accident but Carlos was unhurt.

On 22 December 1941, Carlos Madge, in *Cassiopeia*, departed Cairo for Singapore. He ferried ammunition into Singapore, having followed a reserve route, which led down the west coast of Sumatra. Madge took *Cassiopeia* on to Batavia and returned through Singapore on 28 December. Out of Singapore were First Officer N. A. Blount, Radio Officer J. MacPherson and Purser Evans. The passengers were the wives and children of BOAC's Singapore staff and the freight has been described as aircraft parts and 'steel components', possibly gun barrels. On the evening of 28 December, they arrived at Sabang.

They refuelled. The take-off run commenced; *Cassiopeia* covered 1,500 yards through the darkness and reached 78 knots, before she struck heavy swell. Deceleration was smooth but rapid. She hit a second line of swell and the planing bottom was ripped asunder. The 'boat filled rapidly and broke in two, the forward section plunging nose first. Carlos managed to escape from the direct-vision window; the remainder of the crew, the first officer included, fled via the top escape hatch and climbed onto *Cassiopeia*'s broad, flat hull. Appreciating the situation in the cabins, First Officer Blount slid into the water and forced open the promenade-deck escape window. He entered the pitch black, water-filled promenade and spar cabins and extricated one of the women passengers, before exiting via the rent in the floor of the cabin. Alas, once out of the wreck, the woman died.

Purser Evans went along the top surface to the rear cabin escape hatch but, unable to open it, he returned to the mainplane, where the survivors had gathered. The launch surged in out of the darkness, Engineer Cooper at the helm. The tail section of *Cassiopeia* stood vertical; passengers could have been trapped inside and Blount and Cooper struggled vainly to right it, before it sank. Another search of the wreckage revealed another body. Radio Officer MacPherson and the passengers were taken back to the jetty while Captain Madge, Blount and Cooper tried to salvage what they could, but little other than a suitcase or two was found. Three boats made a further search but there were no more survivors. Among the dead were Station Engineer Macmillan's wife, his 17-day-old daughter and two other people.

Macmillan served QANTAS and the Allied effort with great determination and resolve during the forthcoming years, and after the war he returned to London.

Alas, the loss of his family and the horrors of war proved too much for this fine Scotsman. He took his own life in the spring of 1946.

Captain Ambrose, in the next 'boat through Sabang, picked up the survivors and took them on to Durban.

In the next few weeks Singapore and Rangoon fell. Just before Rangoon was lost, Captain Bellin, First Officer Pascoe, Radio Officer Brown and Purser Aldridge took *Coorong* into Rangoon on 21 February and evacuated company stores and personnel. Two days later, they were safe in Basra.

By early spring 1942, *Cordelia* had been returned to her civilian fit, and it was decided she would augment the Durban fleet. Although the S.23M modifications included the provision of additional fuel tanks, the extra capacity was insufficient to allow *Cordelia* to follow the Lisbon–Bathurst route to Durban. *Cordelia* would have to transit the Mediterranean. Uneventfully, they arrived at Gibraltar on 7 May 1942. The complete crew is unknown but the first officer was David Brice and the captain was 'Jackie' (presumably Harrington). Along with a radio operator, they carried an engineer, his task being to manage the auxiliary fuel tanks, one in the spar cabin and two in the centre section.

Luftwaffe long-range fighters roamed the Mediterranean, especially near Malta, and regular Axis supply missions were flown into Libya from Greece and Crete. A route which took advantage of the patrol limits of the fighters and the darkness of night was planned. It was essential to arrive, refuel and depart Malta in the dark and then to be east of 25 degrees East (abeam Crete) before first light.

Strong head winds were forecast and they calculated the flight to Malta would take just over eleven hours. It was already late morning and time was pressing to make their noon departure. They intended to cross the Iles de la Galite (south of Sardinia) around sunset and pass abeam Cape Bon in darkness. The Levanter was blowing and the ever-present plume of cloud was attached to the Rock of Gibraltar. After a few bounces they were aloft and heading east. On the starboard beam, Oran and the Algerian coast passed according to plan, but map reading of the coast was difficult from a distance. Below, the sea foamed white under the influence of the head wind. After about three hours, the sea beneath seemed calm, the wind had dropped and their ground speed had increased significantly. It was now plain they would reach the Galites in daylight. Their fix at Iles de la Galite showed they had 85 miles to run to Cape Bon and 90 minutes of daylight remaining. They had no option but to retrace their steps. Jackie disengaged the autopilot and wheeled *Cordelia* into the setting sun. Maintaining a westerly track, the crew watched the sun set before them. With a start, they heard the monotonous boom of the engines falter, the tachometer for the starboard-outer fell, picked up and then fell again. All tanks were selected and the Pegasus revived, but meanwhile Jackie had turned towards the coast, just in case they had to put *Cordelia* down. It must have been an airlock, for the engine soon settled down to her rhythmic beat and thoughts of French internment camps slipped from their minds.

The sun set, they turned east, and comforting darkness engulfed them. Once around Cape Bon, the track was due south, giving Italian-held Pantelleria as wide a berth as possible. Outside the stars shone and the exhaust rings glowed a dull cherry-red. They passed between the islands of Lampedusa and Linosa.

As if in defiance the Malta radio beacon beckoned all and sundry. *Cordelia* turned towards it and, maintaining their own radio silence, they homed onto the fortress island. Brice stood in the astrodome searching ahead. A pencil of light pierced the black, then another and soon a score. Lights to guide them in? This illusion was shattered by the radio officer, who handed Jackie a message, 'Air Raid!' They flew on; white and yellow tracer arced up and tumbled towards them. Perhaps they had been mistaken for the intruder. And then below, a line of white explosions illuminated the runways. The *Luftwaffe* were finding their mark. A searchlight caught the intruder briefly but he jinked into darkness. *Cordelia* crossed Kalafrana and blipped her recognition lights to the waiting launch. Unbelieving, they held off and watched the raid continue. In the bay, the flare-path unfurled itself. A green Aldis summoned them down. Jackie watched the flare-path and the other three pairs of eyes peered into the impenetrable darkness, searching for the night-fighter stalking their flare-path. Propellers to fine pitch, throttles back and the rich blue exhaust flame changed to a weak white flame. The flying-boat flattened out and the flares passed beneath the wing. With a ripple and then a slap they alighted. Behind them the flare-path was extinguished. A launch led them to their mooring which, despite the blackout, they picked up. After eleven hours of four roaring Pegasuses, the bark of an adjacent 3.7-inch anti-aircraft gun seemed like silence.

The launch took Jackie and his crew to Operations, and amongst brick dust and rubble a meal was served. Refuelling was delayed as the fuel launch was empty. For a while it seemed they might not get away at all. Ninety minutes before sunrise, they took off from Kalafrana and turned to Egypt. Daylight would find them 250 miles inside the range of German fighters. They streaked to safety at 145 mph – did not the pre-war literature boast of 200 mph? thought Brice. As the sun came up, they went as low as they dared to reduce the chance of being spotted. Not a cloud to hide in and not a fighter to hide from. They flew on, the sun getting ever higher. Finally, they were able to get a loop bearing from Marsa Matruh, and it was not too long before they coasted in and were bearing down upon Cairo and a longed-for cold beer in Shepheard's. From Cairo, *Cordelia* turned south for Khartoum, Kisumu and Congella, her new home.

The route structure bent to meet the demands of war. Following the April 1942 campaign to evict the Vichy from the Levant, the Dead Sea port of Kallia became a staging post, reportedly after a 'boat force-landed there. In July 1942, Egypt was under threat from the rapidly advancing Rommel, and Bill Morgan, Captain Travers's purser, stood by with *Ceres,* in Khartoum, ready to evacuate the headquarters BOAC staff from Cairo. Finally, in the autumn of 1942, the headquarters was evacuated to Khartoum. *Imperia* was stationed at Hurghada, on the Red Sea, as another insurance against German advances in the Western Desert.

Further south, the RAF patrolled from Mombasa and Durban, and in October 1942, Flight Lieutenant J. M. Inglis of 209 Sqn left Mombasa for Durban in Catalina 'S' AH543. They stopped at Pamanzi and departed at dusk. Ahead, they saw the birth of an electrical storm which they soon entered. The rain, wind and hail battered the aircraft. They were lofted to 13,000 feet and plunged to 2,000 feet. With the coming of dawn, the storm abated but the compasses were spinning uselessly. They managed to obtain a bearing and finally made landfall, but fuel was short. They saw a small lake and put down upon it. Inglis and his crew were in neutral Portuguese East Africa, about seventy miles south of Lourenço Marques. They were in danger of being interned. Providentially, *Caledonia,* commanded by Captain J. Alger, was passing overhead. He carried no passengers, and albeit against regulations, he decided to put down on the lake and rescue the crew. Of the Catalina, it is believed to have been repaired and taken back to Portugal. Of Captain Alger, it is thought he was grounded for three weeks.

Not all aircraft losses were so straightforward. The story of *Clare*'s loss, off the west coast of Africa, was subject to many inconsistencies.

Clare, carrying thirteen passengers and crew, was lost at sea on 24 September 1942 when, out of Lagos, she failed to reach Bathurst. She had radioed she was in

Cordelia, *probably in Africa in 1943. The leading-edge work platform has been lowered and the cowling removed so that the engine may be attended to.* (Brown)

difficulty, but then there was silence. A search revealed nothing. The crew were Captain G. B. Musson, First Officer A. D. C. Jenkins, Navigator/Second Officer A. O. Grundy and Radio Officers E. F. G. Brent and J. A. Wycherly (*Corsair* rescue). After this loss the 'C-class' 'boats were withdrawn from the Poole–Lagos route.

At least that is what contemporary reports indicated. It would appear that *Clare* was the victim of an engine fire. The previously popularly accepted facts follow:

On 14 September 1942, *Clare* departed Lagos for Bathurst. Thirteen passengers were on board. A message when the aircraft was sixty minutes out of Lagos indicated an engine failure and the 'boat would be returning. Eighteen minutes later, a request for flares was received (it was then dark) and thirteen minutes after that, the last message – 'SOS fire'.

On 15 September all available aircraft at Bathurst (not Lagos) took part in a search. Visibility was poor. A Catalina spotted wreckage some thirty miles west of the estimated crash position. The wreckage was picked up by an unknown naval vessel which had been directed to the site by the Catalina. The vessel also recovered six bodies, one crew member and five passengers, three of whom could be identified. The recovered bodies were buried in Bathurst cemetery on 17 September.

Delving into the various published accounts reveals many discrepancies and inconsistencies. Recent research and a reappraisal of those original accounts led the author to the following hypothesis as to the loss of *Clare* off Bathurst, in September 1942: *Clare* left Lagos early in morning of 14 September 1942. A Mr Hillard and his companion had been trying to return to England for some weeks. The engines were running and Mr Hillard was looking forward to the close of an English summer. To his annoyance, the engines were shut down again and officials boarded the aircraft, instructing Mr Hillard and his companion, both low-priority passengers, to give up their seats to two VIPs. Dawn had yet to break, as they made their way back up the slipway to find some accommodation. The following day (15th), Mr Hillard was told that *Clare* had crashed. He assumed, and to an extent it was published, that *Clare* had never arrived at Bathurst.

That was not quite true: *Clare* arrived in Bathurst, having refuelled at Freetown, on the afternoon of 14 September. At Bathurst, the 'boat was refuelled, the passengers, presumably, fed and the crew, it is assumed, slipped. Later that evening, *Clare*, with Captain Musson, First Officer Jenkins, Second Officer/Navigator Grundy, Radio Officers Brent and Wycherly and thirteen passengers left for Lisbon.

It was standard practice to avoid the Vichy French at Dakar by twenty miles. Captain Musson, however, preferred to draw a sixty-mile arc around Dakar and fly tangents until he was *en route* to Lisbon. One hour out of Bathurst, he announced they were returning, having lost an engine. Eighteen minutes later, in a second radio message, 'Flares' were requested. It was by then dark and presumably a flare-path at Bathurst was being called for. Another thirteen minutes (i.e. now only

thirty to forty minutes from Bathurst) they called 'SOS Fire!' *Clare* crashed thirty to forty minutes' flying-time away from Bathurst, during the late evening of 14 September.

The following day (15th) visibility was poor, but all available aircraft took part in the search. They failed to locate *Clare*. It had been assumed that *Clare* had flown a 'standard' (avoid Dakar by twenty miles) departure and was farther down the route when she turned back. On the 16th a Catalina, commanded by Captain J. C. Parker, with Second Officer Talbot and Navigator Donald McGregor aboard, joined the search. McGregor had flown with Captain Musson and knew of his penchant for non-standard avoidance of Dakar. Accordingly, McGregor searched thirty miles west of the expected, 'official' crash position, farther out to sea. They found six bodies and some wreckage. They circled the wreckage for several hours until relieved by *Champion,* which in turn marked the spot, until late on 16 September, when a small, unnamed, naval vessel picked up the bodies and the wreckage. Parts of upper-deck flooring and one of the toilet doors were found, together with an unopened inflatable life-raft. The life-raft, which had received a severe blow, opened spontaneously as it was being dragged aboard.

There were indications of a fire on the flight-deck and that, on impact, *Clare* had broken in half close to the front spar. The bodies, one crew member and five passengers, were attended to by the Officer of Public Health. Three of the bodies were identified: Sergeant J. E. Hardiman, Sergeant A. C. Aubery and Free French officer Lieutenant-Colonel M. Abilliot. Identification was difficult and the Officer of Public Health later said (around 1952 to A. J. Brown) the bodies should never have been brought ashore. They were buried, communally, on 17 September 1942 at the Clifford Road English Cemetery, Bathurst.

Many accounts say *Clare* did not reach Bathurst. This is true in that she did not regain Bathurst, once she turned back. It would appear that earlier researchers assumed she did not reach Bathurst from Lagos and thus crashed only 30 minutes from Lagos. This gives rise to the inconsistencies of bodies being sent a thousand miles (Lagos to Bathurst) for burial, search aircraft needing ten hours to get on task (from Bathurst), and how the small unnamed naval vessel could have sped back (Lagos to Bathurst) at 30 knots plus is anyone's guess.

The story does not end in 1942. In 1952, or thereabouts, A. J. Brown was station superintendent at Bathurst. Amongst his duties was the regular inspection of English graves, *Clare*'s included. During this period there was correspondence from BOAC, as one of the relatives of the dead from *Clare* wished to have their relation's remains exhumed and re-interred. Apparently a Catholic body had been buried in a Protestant communal grave.

As to what happened in the air, we can only surmise. The fire damage to the cabin could have resulted from a fire after the precautionary landing. But, the seemingly distraught message 'SOS Fire!' implies to the author a fire in the air. The propellers were of the non-feathering type. Thus, a failed engine continued to 'windmill' until either it 'internally junked' itself then seized, and possibly fell off, or generated so much frictional heat that it caught fire. Engine fire extinguishers were not fitted! Such a fire could rage unchecked and engulf the wing fuel tanks.

As previously stated, during her rebuild, *Clare's* fuel system was brought up to the standard of the in-flight-refuelled aircraft, but without the receiving equipment. Whether *Clare* was fitted with fuel jettison equipment or not is uncertain, but *Champion* was – 'Bonzo' Brown was forced to jettison 320 gallons from her in August 1941. Hence it is quite likely that *Clare* was so fitted.

Be that as it may, if she was not equipped to jettison fuel, it is probable that at high weight on a warm evening she would have been unable to maintain height on three engines. A continuous slow descent made a precautionary landing, at night, inevitable. The moon set at about 21:00 local time that evening and they would have had to illuminate the landing area themselves. Although military Sunderlands carried flares, with which they could lay their own flare-path, there appears no direct evidence that Empire 'Boats, as a whole, had a similar capability. However, there are references to some Empire 'Boats being modified to drop smoke-floats, from the flight-deck, to assist in drift assessment on long over-sea flights. As *Clare* was a 'boat with such a navigational task, is it not fair to assume she was so modified? Moreover, as much of the route was flown at night, the carriage of flame-floats would have been more suitable. Alternatively, and possibly a little far fetched – but Musson faced extreme circumstances – could they have been attempting a landing illuminated by Very-pistol flares fired from the cockpit? There was no purpose-built Very-pistol discharge port, and they were fired out of the side windows. Could there have been an accident with a flare on board the aircraft?

Alternatively, and at the time there was a rumour to support this, *Clare* was jettisoning fuel and the vapours ignited. It had happened to Captain Musik and the *Samoan Clipper*. Another factor to be considered is the age and usage of the 'boats. Although their operation did comply with CofA regulations, the 'boats were in constant use. Moreover, Captain Musson confided to his wife, he did not expect to survive the war because the flying-boats were worn out and, under wartime conditions, they were not properly serviced.

Following the loss of *Clare*, the 'C-class' 'boats were finally withdrawn from the Lagos–Freetown–Bathurst–Lisbon–Foynes route. However, the route was not denuded of flying-boats, for the three Boeing 314As and the two 'G-class' 'boats, *Golden Hind* and *Golden Horn*, had been flying the route for some time. The Boeings, purchased from Pan Am and delivered in May, June and July 1941, had been registered G-AGBZ *Bristol*, G-AGCA *Berwick* and G-AGCB *Bangor*. Part of the deal struck between Balfour and Trippe was that should Pan Am lose one of their 314s, and BOAC would relinquish

one of theirs to make up the shortfall. The 314s entered service in August 1941. As all major servicing was done in Baltimore, the 'boats had to make regular crossings of the Atlantic, hence Britain obtained a transatlantic schedule, of sorts, by default.

The 'G-class' 'boats remaining, '*Hind* and '*Horn*, had been restored to the civil register in December 1941, converted to carry 40 passengers in an 'austerity' fit and awarded CofA in January 1942. As their original tail cones could not be located, the rear turrets were faired over and the rudder remained cropped. The 'boats retained camouflage and were adorned with a large Union Jack painted upon the nose and red, white and blue recognition flashes were applied to the fin and to underline the international registration. The 'G-class' 'boats entered service between Poole and Lagos, via Foynes, Lisbon, Bathurst and Accra, on 18 July 1942.

The greater range of the 'G-class' was exploited by *Golden Hind* in a 11 November 1942 survey routing Kisumu – Mombasa – Seychelles – Maldives and finally Lake Cogella (Ceylon). Although this route was flown

The Golden Hind's *flight-deck. Behind the starboard seat is the access to the lower deck. Three pilots, a flight engineer and a radio officer made up the flight-deck crew. (McKenny)*

several times, it did not receive schedule status.

The loss of *Golden Horn*, on 9 January 1943, was tragic as there was needless loss of life. Regulations were breached. The truth behind the loss of *Golden Horn* may never be found, and the following account could be hearsay. The aircraft was in need of an engine air-test following an engine change, and Captain John H. Lock was her commander. Lock was an experienced pilot, having flown in his earlier days for the Hon. Mrs Victor Bruce, during her in-flight refuelling trials, and Hillman Airways. Moreover, Lock was well respected and much liked by all the Lisbon staff, and in recognition of the help the Lisbon staff had given John in the past, he offered to treat them to a flight. He was cautioned against this, as were some of the staff, and someone informed London of what was to happen. Lock was ordered by London not to carry unauthorized passengers. Notwithstanding these instructions, Lock went ahead with the test-flight, and on board he had a mix of marine staff, customs officers, loaders, mechanics and some wives. Because of the nature of the flight, a passenger list was not compiled.

Lock got airborne and set to with his engine air-test. There are accounts that John Lock tended to have his own ideas about cooling gill and oil-cooler settings, and it is feasible that during this flight he may have put his theories to the test. It is not disputed, however, that *Golden Horn* experienced an engine fire. As with the 'C-class', the Hercules engines of the 'G-class' were not fitted with fire extinguishers, nor could the propellers be feathered. The engine fire became uncontained and the tail surfaces suffered damage. Also, as with the 'C-class', there was a natural flow of air from the inside of the wing, forward through the flight-deck and out of the windscreen side panels. That was the path taken by the thick acrid smoke that came from the burning engine and its oil tank.

Lock was unable to see out during the landing he was attempting. They crashed into the Tagus. There were two survivors, Radio Officer Uttley, who only by chance had been selected for the flight, and a Portugese operations officer. The remaining passengers and crew, possibly more than the dozen commonly accepted, perished, uninsured and unrecorded. Soon after, *Golden Hind* was withdrawn to the ignominy of the Poole–Foynes shuttle.

An earlier loss at Durban had taken place on 1 December 1942. *Ceres* was in the BOAC hangar at Congella Basin being serviced when an explosion occurred and fire broke out. The ground staff managed to tow the burning aircraft out of the hangar and extinguish the fire. Although it was never proved, sabotage was suspected. Regretfully one man, Horace Albert Butland Vincent, succumbed to his burns. Two other men, P. D. Wiseman and L. J. Horingold, were injured. Damage had been confined to the fuselage and for some time there was thought of mating *Ceres'* wings with the partially complete S.33 (S.1027, G-AFRB) which languished in a crate at Rochester, following the abandonment of her construction in 1940.

At the other end of the Horseshoe, now foreshortened by Japanese action, the first air raid on Calcutta occurred on 20 December 1942, followed by two more over the succeeding days. The warnings were sounded in good time and, during these short raids, few bombs were dropped, the only significant damage being to a cinema and some dwellings. Those fires which were started were soon brought under control. The size of the attacking force diminished as the days passed; on the third attack, only three enemy aircraft were involved and two of them were claimed as damaged. Throughout the three raids, twenty-five people were killed and fewer than a hundred were injured. There was no evacuation and civilian businesses and shops functioned as normal.

In mid-1942, Madagascar had been occupied by the Allies, and the following December, *Champion* carried out a survey flight, routing Mombasa, Lindi, Diego Suarez. In the New Year, on 25 January 1943, a regular Horseshoe service between Pamanzi and Dar-es-Salaam was started by *Champion*. The 'boat proved to be the one regular link with the outside world. Mail, passengers, equipment and, to one island, fresh vegetables were carried.

The passengers and freight carried along the Horseshoe Route varied. The cricketer Wally Hammond, then a squadron leader in the RAF, was a regular passenger of Bill Morgan's, as was the actress Phyllis Robbins. John Pascoe recalls carrying Lady Dundas, wife of the Governor of Uganda, in June 1944. They were in *Corsair,* out of Kisumu and bound for Beira. Fog, often encountered at Beira, prevented a landing and it was decided to alight upon the calm sea several miles out and await the fog lifting. The motion caused by the gentle swell and the constant lap, lap, lap of the waves proved too much for poor Lady Dundas. She spent most of those two hours on the surface at the forward door being seasick. Tedder, Brooke-Popham and Wavell were regular passengers, and many of the senior officers and VIPs became regular acquaintances with the crews and pursers in particular.

Aircraft spares, ammunition, oxygen and other priority items, in addition to loads of gold bullion, kept the war machine turning. But not all freight was above board and a little customs evasion was often practised. In Durban, life was comparatively idyllic but some commodities, car spares for instance, were in short supply. Captain 'Paddy' Sheppard ran a small car and he was able to acquire his spares from sources in the colonies of neutral Portugal and Belgium. On one occasion, Paddy managed to pass off a set of brand-new tyres as fenders when the customs launch came alongside. Not every one shared Paddy's tastes. The M1D fuel tank fit had left some 'boats, *Coorong* being one, with two tanks in the hull which were permanently wire-locked shut and not used for carrying fuel. Paddy is alleged to have filled one of these tanks with whisky. However, when it was time to drain the contents, someone had opened the cock and bled the whisky into the engines!

The myth of being able to land in the open sea had

been truly exposed. Apart from *Cavalier*, lost off Bermuda, *Calypso* was lost off New Guinea, when an RAAF crew tried to rescue shipwrecked survivors. However, Alcock did manage to put *Cambria* down, off the Mozambique coast, so open sea landings were possible – even if against regulations.

In the summer of 1943, the Merchant Marine operating off the east coast of Africa, between Durban and Suez, were shaken by reports of the torpedoing of *The City of Canton*. It was known that some submarines were in the area, but Captain E. Scrymgeour, commander of 'Canton, thought that coast hugging and zig-zagging would keep him safe. In fact he was stalked by U-178 and, after an abortive attack, struck by several torpedoes, shortly after midnight on 17 July.

Unbeknown to the Allies, however, several lifeboats got away and one made a landfall at the Pinta lighthouse. The U-boat surfaced. In accordance with German High Command policy of capturing Allied Merchant Navy officers, thus weakening the Allied war effort, they took on board Second Officer Broadbent, the only officer they could find. Later, as a PoW, he was handed to the Japanese at Penang and survived the war. The captain and his engine room storekeeper spent six days adrift before they were rescued by a Vichy French cruiser. Others were found by a Portuguese merchantman.

To the Allies, of immediate importance was the search for survivors from *The City of Canton*. The ship may have been in neutral waters, the weather was forecast to deteriorate and there was a shortage of allied search vessels, so the Empire 'Boat crews were asked to keep a lookout. On the afternoon of 19 July, *Cameronian* – Captain Dick Reid, First Officer Johnny Hackett, Radio Officer Bob Hitchins and Purser Alan McGilivray – called at Dar-es-Salaam to refuel *en route* to Lumbo for their night stop. The station officer told them of the loss and search.

They departed Dar-es-Salaam, refuelled at Lindi and entered the territorial waters of neutral Mozambique. Routing some twenty miles further out to sea, they flew at 3,000 feet. It was a cloudless day, the visibility was excellent and the wind about 10 knots. On the surface a swell of two or three feet ran. As they cruised south, searching, the sun was in their rear starboard quarter. First Officer Hackett made the first sighting, five miles off the starboard bow. It turned out to be an empty lifeboat. They continued south, and this time Captain Reid spotted something. They turned port towards the object. It was a lifeboat, full of men. Reid disconnected the autopilot, throttled back, descended and ran out half flap. From about a hundred feet they saw a dejected sight. The boat contained about twenty men, six of whom were standing arms linked, down the length of the boat. The remainder lay at the feet of those standing. A few had the strength to wave. Some were dressed in blues, others in only scant clothing. It appeared that their ship must have sunk rapidly and little time had been available to abandon.

Reid and Hackett contemplated the sight below and wondered why six of the men stood in the boat. 'They look like a living wall', said Hackett. They continued to circle, and then the reason struck: those standing were providing shade to the others. For two days they had been adrift under the searing sun, and the limited shade provided by mutual protection was all that had saved them so far.

Meanwhile, Radio Officer Hitchins had received a message saying that it would be dark in three hours' time, there were no ships or Sunderlands available before dark and storms were forecast for the following day. Having agreed that it seemed unlikely the survivors could last another couple of days while the weather abated and a ship arrived, Reid and Hackett decided to drop what food and water they could. At Reid's instruction, Purser McGilivray put some food and water into a waterproof mailbag and attached a line to it. Reid explained to Hackett how he wanted Hackett to make an approach to the lifeboat, as though he was going to land next to it, and Reid would drop the mailbag and line, as they overflew the lifeboat. Hopefully the line would straddle the boat. Reid would make the drop from the forward door; it would be quite safe as Alan McGilivray would hang onto his ankles.

As Reid and McGilivray made ready, Johnny Hackett continued to circle *Cameronian* above the wretched seamen. He saw a most selfless act. The six who had been standing lowered themselves to the floor of the boat and were replaced by another half-dozen who staggered to their feet. The men who had just dropped to their knees then doused those standing with sea-water, in an attempt to keep the full force of the sun from them.

Dick Reid called up to Hackett that they were ready below. Hackett turned the flying-boat away and set up for his approach. After a run-out of about a mile, he turned around and lined the lifeboat up just to port. Flap to full – propellers, fine pitch selected – mixture fully rich. Hackett trickled the speed back and made a steady approach, slowly easing the 'boat down. With 100 yards to run he was fifteen feet above the gentle swell. As *Cameronian* was about to settle, they flew close abeam the lifeboat. Reid threw out the provisions and Hackett walked the throttles forward to full power, gently easing the control wheel forward as the 'boat accelerated to 95 knots, a minimum safe climbing speed. As he climbed away, the flaps were brought in and Reid and McGilivray came up onto the flight-deck. They looked down upon the pitiful scene. Their drop had been a success. The line straddled the boat but no one had the strength to pull the mailbag aboard.

In the air, they had only two options, either to leave the scene and the survivors to whatever fate held or alight and pick them up. Captain Reid, ultimately responsible for the safety and well-being of his passengers, crew and aircraft, was the only person empowered to make that decision.

Reid decided to risk all and Hackett agreed. The landing was uneventful and they taxied across to the lifeboat. Reid asked Purser McGilivray to instruct the passengers to remain seated and they would be kept informed. Reid went to the forward door; one of the passengers, a bearded gentlemen dressed in civilian clothes, came forward to where Reid stood. Reid impressed upon the passenger that instructions had been given and his return to his cabin would be appreciated. The passenger duly beetled off.

As the engines idled, Reid climbed through the top hatch and with a megaphone hailed the lifeboat, but he was unable to make himself heard against the clamour of the idling engines. To stop engines in the open sea was placing an awful amount of trust in the batteries. Reid called out, 'Stop engines Mr Hackett!' Johnny complied. The engines chuffed, clunked to a stop and then ticked as they cooled; the Indian Ocean lapped against the thin metal hull. *Cameronian* gave the occasional lurch, as the wing-tip floats were jarred by the swell. The sun beat down. Reid hailed and Hitchins reminded all that in just over one hours' time the sun would set.

They prepared to make the rescue. But, they could not go alongside the lifeboat for fear of puncturing their own skin or of breaking a float. Moreover, none of the survivors had the strength to swim across and a few would have barely survived being towed across by line. Reid's dilemma was eased by *The City of Canton*'s chief engineer, Mr Potter, the senior survivor. He decided that the fittest three men should be transferred and the remainder could be rescued the following day when there would be more time. Reid ordered that all food, water, distress rockets and a Very pistol and cartridges should be put aboard the lifeboat. There was little else they could do; boats were on the way and a Sunderland might be available before the weather closed.

Mr Potter and two others were dragged aboard and, with relief, all four Pegasuses started. Once airborne, Bob Hitchins tapped out the latest distress message and gave Lumbo their revised ETA. Partially revived, Potter told Reid his captain and engine room storeman had been seen on a raft and another four men were in the other lifeboat. As Hackett and Reid had thought, the boat had sunk rapidly. Mosuril Bay was reached at dusk and somehow they explained the extra passengers not on the manifest. That evening, as Captain Reid was supping a cool beer with the station superintendent, a visitor was announced. The visitor entered the room, that same bearded gentleman from the afternoon. The gentleman came to offer profuse apologies for going against instructions issued by the captain of a vessel. After all, as a naval man, he understood the responsibilities of command. He was Commander-in-Chief South Atlantic Fleet and would have taken the same action as Reid. A few more beers were opened. (The C-in-C was travelling in civilian clothes, as did all military personnel when travelling through neutral territory.)

The following morning, as *Cameronian* was being prepared for the last leg to Durban, they heard ships had sighted both life-rafts and the men were being plucked from the ocean.

About a week or so later, after Captain Scrymgeour and the storekeeper were fit, Johnny Hackett received an invitation to dinner from Scrymgeour and his crew.

They drank to absent friends, Broadbent – believed lost to the sharks or drowned – included. Many years later, when Johnny Hackett met Arthur Banks, who was researching the Indian Ocean U-Boat activity, Banks learnt that some survivors of *The City of Canton* were airlifted out but, more amazingly, Hackett learnt that Broadbent had survived and returned to Liverpool.

Bearing in mind the success of Reid and the earlier rescue of the Catalina crew by Alger in *Caledonia,* along with Pascoe's landing with the unfortunate Lady Dundas in 1944, Alcock's landing of *Cambria* seems more likely. Moreover, Alcock did publish his account in the *Evening Standard* in July 1956. Open sea landings in good conditions certainly seemed to have been possible, but Alcock's feat with *Cambria* displays that 'John' Alcock was a pilot in a different league.

By summer 1943 the war's outcome seemed to be settling in the Allies' favour, and on 5 August 1943 the camouflage paint was removed from 'boats, *Caledonia* being the first so treated. Amongst the backdrop of world events were small yet deep-reaching tragedies. In October 1943 Bill Morgan and Captain Harris flew out of Dubai for Karachi in *Cambria.* On this flight a five-day-old infant was being transferred to hospital at Karachi for surgery. Sadly the child died; this touched Bill, as some years previously his first son had died at a very tender age.

THE POOLE–FOYNES SHUTTLE
The Poole–Foynes shuttle – Victory in Europe.

In January 1940, the flying-boat service was again transferred to Poole Harbour from Berth 108 at Southampton. A selection of buildings were commandeered, the Mission to Seamen, the Antelope Hotel and the Poole Pottery included. Initially operations off the Wareham Channel were controlled from a vessel moored off Brownsea Island, but more suitable facilities ashore were gained when the Poole Harbour Yacht Club was requisitioned. Maintenance continued to be done at Hythe; although some minor rectification was attended to at the moorings on the north side of Brownsea Island.

Immigration was first located in a greengrocer's in Poole High Street but later moved to the Antelope Hotel. All inbound passengers were subjected to strict immigration procedures. A British immigration officer of the time described the facilities at Poole thus:

> '[Immigration Control] *was at first in the billiard room of the Antelope Hotel in the High Street, after being moved from Sandbanks, and the wooden staircase creaked to an incredible assortment of VIPs, escapers, suspects and "government officials". In mid-1942 the staff moved into better quarters in the Poole Pottery, where there were four cubicles suited to Immigration examination and a main showroom which served as the Customs Hall.'*

As may be imagined, the examination of these flying-boat loads was an extremely protracted business. The immigration officers might take six hours to clear a flight.

On two occasions operations from Poole were temporarily moved elsewhere. In the autumn of 1942, services were transferred back to Hythe. This was, depending upon your source, either in preparation for the Dieppe landings (August 1942) or as part of a contingency plan to mount a diversionary attack upon the Normandy coast should the landings in North Africa (Operation 'Torch', November 1942) run into difficulty. During this period, Immigration and Customs took place in the greenhouse of a Hythe hotel. Later in the war, 30 April to 2 September 1944, the terminus was transferred to Pembroke Dock, thus making Poole harbour available for the D-Day landings.

The Poole–Foynes shuttle was established to link up with the flying-boat services being operated between neutral Eire and Portugal. Various 'boats took part, including *Maia, Cordelia, Cathay, Champion* and *Golden Hind*, which joined in late May 1943. In addition to BOAC, by November 1943 Pan Am and American Export Airlines were operating out of Foynes. During the previous year, August '42–July '43, more than 1,400 'boats and 15,000 passengers passed through Foynes, and the facilities were being expanded, with additional alighting areas being prepared at Queenstown and Blacksod Bay. With the Allies' progress in Africa allowing access to the Mediterranean, on 29 April 1944 the Boeing 314s were withdrawn from the United Kingdom–West Africa route and used entirely on the North Atlantic.

Along the route the schedules progressed, chasing the war. In late 1943, the yacht *Imperia* was positioned at Djerba to act as refuelling station for Sunderlands G-AGET and G-AGEV, which were carrying Field Marshal Lord Wavell and BOAC Director-General, Air Commodore Critchley. BOAC's civilianized Sunderlands also flew the West Africa route from March 1943.

In lighter vein, on 13 April 1944 *Castor* landed in Persian Gulf to rescue a Walrus crew. With the route now rebounding eastward as the Japanese fell back, *Golden Hind* was given a third conversion at Hythe in 1944. It was probably during this conversion that she was fitted with de Havilland fully feathering hydromatic airscrews and a Graviner fire extinguisher system. Her interior was fitted out for thirty-eight passengers and seven crew. She was returned to Durban by Captain Mollard, accompanied by Flight Engineer Everest. Mollard relinquished command to Dudley Travers, and, on 24 September 1944, *Golden Hind* commenced a fortnightly service between Kisumu and the Seychelles, via Mombasa, Pamanzi and Madagascar. During November 1944, another survey flight to Ceylon was made and for a month a service was flown to Ceylon, via the Maldives. The Kisumu–Madagascar service closed in August 1945, and once again *Golden Hind* was returned to Poole. Throughout this period, operation of the sole remaining example of the S.26 was a costly and difficult business.

All through the war BOAC struggled for autonomy and recognition from within the Cabinet, but in 1943, following a threat of subjugation to the newly formed RAF Transport Command, Pearson and Runciman resigned. For a while, the airline was without a chairman, but Sir Harold Howitt took the post for a few months, to be followed by Lord Knollys. Sir Harold became Deputy Chairman and Air Commodore Critchley was appointed as Director-General.

The war in Europe ended but the 'boats continued to ply their way between Durban and Calcutta. However, although their days were numbered, across the Indian Ocean QANTAS had achieved equally great feats and carved more wondrous tales.

CHAPTER TWELVE

The Far East and Australia

RAAF commandeers Centaurus, Calypso, *and others – Special to Manila – The Phases – 7 December 1941 – RAAF early 'C-class' operations – Loss of* Corio *– Fall of Singapore – Darwin attacked – Tjilatjap shuttle –* Circe *lost –* Coogee *– 3 March, Broome – Loss of* Corinthian *–* New Guinea and many rescues *–* Calypso *and* Camilla *are lost –* Clifton *and* Coolangatta *follow –* Coriolanus *the sole survivor.*

In response to events in Europe, a State of Emergency was declared in Australia, on 25 August 1939. On 2 September, the Royal Australian Air Force (RAAF) told QEA to cease service, and Captain Crowther was ordered to return *Champion* to Sydney from Townsville. However, on 6 September, as it was judged that Italy and Japan would not be entering the war, the scheduled services were resumed, but at a twice-, rather than thrice-weekly rate. To reduce the volume of airmail, both the United Kingdom and Australian Governments reinstated surcharges.

Australia's War Plan, should Italy and Japan join the Axis, called for the formation of an RAAF flying-boat squadron. It was stipulated, under the Commonwealth Government's carriage of subsidized airmail scheme, that five QANTAS 'boats and crews should always be south of Singapore. Despite the lack of warlike declarations from Italy and Japan, two 'boats were required. On 20 September, the BOAC 'boats *Centaurus* and *Calypso*, fortuitously at Rose Bay, were impressed into RAAF service, as A18-10 and A18-11 respectively.

On 21 September, the 'boats were allocated to No. 11 Sqn RAAF, being formed at Richmond, New South Wales. Its commanding officer was Flight Lieutenant James Alexander. The squadron personnel included three QANTAS officers, Gurney, Sims and the wit and artist Purton, in addition to eleven ex-QEA men, who made up the shore party. On 25 September, laden with stores and twenty-three personnel, *Centaurus* and *Calypso* left Rose Bay for their new base at Port Moresby, (then) British New Guinea. Meanwhile, in exchange for the commandeered BOAC 'boats, the QANTAS flying-boats *Coorong* and *Corio* were placed upon the British register.

The RAAF were to make great use of the Empire 'Boats, which, despite their limited range, were able to operate as self-contained reconnaissance units, away from a support base for many weeks on end. One 'boat was to spend nine months on patrol before, barnacle encrusted, she returned to Rose Bay. No. 11 Sqn was tasked with 'the rapid investigation of reports received through intelligence sources, combined with periodical but irregular reconnaissance flights'. Their area of operation was New Guinea, the Solomon Islands and the New Hebrides. From its inception, to mid-1941, No. 11 Sqn, known as 'Alexander's Rag Time Band', struggled against a lack of personnel to meet its task. Even the issue of uniforms and pay books was not completed until March 1940.

On 8 June 1940, *Coogee* was commandeered by the RAAF, as was *Coolangatta* on the 26th. They too were allocated to No. 11 Sqn, as A18-12 and A18-13 respectively. An early taste of action came when Captain Sims was tasked to search for the Italian liner *Romolo*. Sims proceeded to Tulagi but was unable to locate the liner. HMAS *Manoora* did manage to intercept *Romolo*, but only as she was being scuttled. Australia's prize was lifeboats full of Italian prisoners-of-war. On Christmas Day 1940, 11 Sqn's 'boats rescued the marooned victims of German surface raiders. The victims had been put ashore on Emira Island, at the northern end of the Bismark Archipelago.

Calypso, Coogee and *Coolangatta* were fitted with three 220-gallon fuel tanks, in addition to the two 325-gallon tanks already in place. *Centaurus* retained the long-range tanks used during the pioneering flight to New Zealand. Bomb racks, capable of carrying either 250 or 500 lb bombs, were fitted beneath the wing, and mounts for Lewis guns were installed either side of the rear freight compartment. The bow mooring hatch was replaced by a strange-looking visual bombing cupola, sufficiently spacious for an observer's head and shoulders. Re-equipping brought re-tasking, and 11 Sqn found themselves searching for German surface raiders and doing much to support the establishment of Advanced Operation Bases and refuelling facilities. The 11 Sqn support infrastructure remained shambolic until the latter half of 1940. Until then, fuel had been scarce, contaminated or both, bombs were in short supply and sound moorings were few.

The Commonwealth Government was concerned about the undue influence Japan was inflicting upon Timor, then a Portuguese colony. It was thought a regular Australian air service to Timor could counter Japan's activities. On 19 January 1941, *Coriolanus*, commanded by Captain Hussey in the company of Hudson Fysh, left

Calypso *A-18-11 in service with the RAF, being refuelled at Suda. The modified bow-position observation hatch is open. In 1941, as the RNZAF prepared for a maritime reconnaissance capability, one Flying Officer Stewart, was detached to No. 11 Squadron, RAAF, at Port Moresby, to investigate maritime operations. This photograph accompanied his report. (RNZAF Museum)*

Sydney to start a fortnightly service to Dili, Timor's capital. On arrival in the quaint, dilapidated, colonial harbour they tied up alongside a mooring laid earlier by the Japanese. Hudson Fysh went ashore to finalize arrangements with the Portuguese Governor. As the meeting progressed, a sodden note, carried by a wet and bedraggled runner, was handed to Fysh. The note explained the refuelling barge had broken down (the 'runner' had swam ashore), and assistance was sought. Fysh returned to Australia in *Cambria* with Captain Russell Tapp, on 21 January. In April 1941, the five-year agreement to link Portuguese Timor to Australia was made public.

In preparation for the potential conflict, and to quote Fysh, 'overcome the wretchedly short range', QANTAS followed the RAAF example and manufactured and installed a number of 220-gallon fuel tanks. A batch of these tanks was shipped to Durban for fitting to the remainder of the BOAC fleet, as and when. However, it proved impossible to completely fit both fleets with long-range tanks before Japan's entry into the war.

QANTAS and Australia were not alone in preparing for war. One little-known Empire Flying-Boat voyage was that of *Cleopatra*, when she took Air Chief Marshal, Sir Robert Brooke-Popham, C-in-C Far East, on a tour of inspection, calling at Manila and Hong Kong. The Air Chief Marshal's entourage comprised Colonel W. L. Fawcett, Squadron Leader F. T. Cox and Sergeant Brewer. Roger Mollard was captain and the remainder of the crew were First Officer Jones, Radio Officer Henshaw, Steward Humphreys and Station Engineer Macmillan. Bill Morgan was their purser.

They departed Singapore on the morning of 31 March 1941 and spent the night at Miri. Leaving there on the morning of 1 April, they refuelled at Labuan and

continued to Sandakan, to arrive at lunch time. They stayed the night, and then flew the final sector to Manila, arriving around noon on 2 April. *Cleopatra* was the first, and last, British flying-boat to enter Manila before the war. It was probably on 3 April that Brooke-Popham met General MacArthur, then military adviser to the Philippines' Government.

In the middle of the morning on 4 April, *Cleopatra* departed Manila for Hong Kong, arriving in the early afternoon. She returned to Manila early on 9 April, having taken on board a Lieutenant-Commander Reid and Mr Gill, the Area Accountant. For the return to Singapore, a Lieutenant-Commander Burnett joined them, and they departed Manila in the early hours of 10 April. Having staged through Labuan, where a Mr Pepys joined them, they finally made Singapore, and, at the close of a long day, alighted with the sun setting over Kallang.

Although 'on the record' Air Chief Marshal Brooke-Popham expressed satisfaction as to what he had seen, he confided in private to Bill Morgan that all was not well.

The tremendous task facing the Empire 'Boats of No. 11 Sqn, RAAF, eased in mid-1941, following the delivery to Australia of PBY Catalinas. Respite was short-lived, as the Catalinas were soon detached to form No. 20 Sqn, RAAF. As peace drained from the Pacific, 11 Sqn's Empire 'Boats made longer and longer flights deeper into their area of responsibility.

Readying itself for the wider conflict, the Australian Civil Aviation Authority (CAA) decreed that in the event of hostilities with Japan, those 'boats to the west of Darwin were to be recalled to Darwin and those between Sydney and Darwin were to return to Sydney. However, the service to Singapore was to be maintained for as long as possible. The Australian CAA later modified their instructions, stating that 'boats at Singapore should continue upon their route if at all possible. Moreover, they criticised QANTAS for allowing the interior fittings to be stripped from at least one 'boat. QANTAS replied, they had stripped several, and the saving of 600 lb weight was 'a worthwhile contribution to the war effort'.

On 18 November, *Centaurus* and *Calypso* were detached to No. 20 Sqn RAAF, to form a transport flight, which existed until February 1942. Overloading was the norm and although 47,500 lb may have been the normal maximum take-off weight, many flights were operated at 52,000 lb.

Through the summer of 1941, BOAC continued upon the Horseshoe but the route was overstretching its resources. To ease the burden, it was agreed that, as of 16 October, QEA's sector would be extended westward from Singapore to Karachi. The first eastbound QEA aircraft departed Karachi on 24 October. Rescheduling stretched the QANTAS crews in turn, and the three who had been seconded to the RAAF were returned. Providentially, QEA had insisted upon their own engine overhaul shop, and this was established at Sydney.

The Japanese had interfered with the Imperial

Airways' routes as early as 1938. Then, a Japanese aircraft had shot at a D.H.86 routing from Bangkok to Hong Kong. The Japanese authorities apologised, stating their pilots had mistaken the biplane for a Chinese 'craft, and suggested Imperial Airways ought to abandon the route. The view of Imperial was to the contrary, for as Imperial's aircraft were clearly marked, it was up to the Japanese to avoid such incidents, and they were not going to be intimidated. There had been similar incidents. Imperial Airways' aircraft, descending into Hong Kong had, allegedly, been fired upon by Japanese ships.

Despite Imperial Airways' earlier show of bravado, four reserve routes between India and Australia were planned, and were known as Phases. In August 1941, the four Phases were surveyed by QEA and preparations were made to centre operations upon Batavia or Surabaya.

Phase I was the omission of Bangkok as a night-stop. Phase II avoided Thailand, and routing from Rangoon to Penang was via Mergui, in southern Burma. Phase III avoided southern Burma and staged through Port Blair, in the Andamans, and Sabang (northern Sumatra), before turning east for Penang. Phase IV steered clear of the Malay peninsula and hopped down the west coast of Sumatra to Batavia, from where a shuttle to Singapore would be operated. In November, BOAC headquarters at Durban, in consultation with RAF (Far East) Headquarters in Singapore, planned the implementation of the Phases.

Dark days for the Empire 'Boats approached.

Singapore, as well as Penang, was first attacked on 8 December and, although serious damage was not done to the city, the Naval Base and Seletar aerodrome were mauled. Many thought it was a realistic training exercise. Mr Malcolm Millar, of Mansfield & Co – the QANTAS agents – and member of the voluntary forces, slept throughout the raid, but at a quarter past four in the morning, Hudson Fysh was woken by the attack. Fysh had arrived in Singapore on 2 December for talks with Walter Runciman, who, with John Brancker (son of Sir Sefton), was on a tour of inspection of the Horseshoe. Fysh and Millar called at the RAFHQ and Millar was appointed Civil Aviation Liaison Officer to Wing Commander Frew. They ascertained *Ceres* had departed westbound that morning, following a short delay, and Captain Aubrey A. Koch, her commander, had been warned to avoid Bangkok and refuel at Mergui.

To the north, in Rangoon, *Castor*'s commander, Ron Adair, had been woken at 23:00 the previous day and told he was to route to Penang via Mergui, instead of via Bangkok. Phase II was coming into operation. Whilst airborne, he was instructed not to proceed to Penang, it being under attack, and Phase III was being introduced immediately. Adair wanted to continue to Belawan, near Medan, on the east coast of Sumatra, but he had insufficient fuel and was forced to return to Mergui. There he met Koch, out of Singapore that morning. They refuelled from a rowing boat laden with 20-gallon cans. Koch needed to uplift only 120 gallons, as he had managed to refuel at Penang, earlier that morning.

Overhead, Japanese fighters circled.

Adair decided to follow Koch up to Rangoon, where they would swap 'boats, there being no instructions to the contrary. By taking *Ceres*, which, unlike *Castor*, had been fitted with the long-range tanks, Adair hoped to reach Singapore by way of Port Blair, Sumatra and Batavia – Phase IV.

Although Adair had charts to see him as far as Port Blair, but no further, he was lacking information about moorings or the availability of fuel at Sabang. The weather over the Bay of Bengal on 9 December was atrocious and only a masterpiece of navigation brought Adair and Port Blair together. Owing to the weather, his arrival was unexpected and Adair had to taxi around looking for the mooring. Refuelling from cans took three hours. Once readied, they flew south to Sabang, where they stayed the night. *Ceres* left Sabang early on 10 December, and during the flight south, the crew twice received radio calls about their well-being. Fearing the transmissions a Japanese ruse, they flew on in radio silence. A few miles out of Singapore, they heeded a broadcast warning of an air raid and held off. Finally, a very relieved QANTAS staff, who had had no word of them for the past two days, welcomed them to Singapore.

As well as passengers, aviation fuel was carried to secret locations. On 13 December, Captain Tapp, in *Corsair*, flew several tons of 100 octane fuel to Sabang, to allow a Blenheim force to reach Singapore. He had to use 48 gallons of the fuel himself for the return flight. The following day, Hudson Fysh left Singapore, for Sydney. He staged through Batavia, where, with the Dutch authorities, he sought how best to face the enemy.

Japanese air activity increased. QANTAS became more aware of the risks and suggested to Air Headquarters that the stop at Medan ought to be omitted. Although this proposal did not find favour with the Air HQ, General HQ accepted it, once an RAF or Dutch shuttle to Singapore could be established. In an attempt to maintain contact between Singapore and India, without recourse to the long detour to Batavia, Captain Tapp surveyed an east–west route across Sumatra to Sibolga. It was not that successful, as the same route had been chosen by Japanese fighters to cross Sumatra.

The night before Carlos Madge lost *Cassiopeia*, 27 December 1941, Captain Crowther turned back to Calcutta, as Akyab was under attack. To the south, the route down the west coast of Sumatra, Phase IV, was not beyond enemy attention. On New Year's Eve, Captain Purton, in *Cleopatra*, saw enemy reconnaissance aircraft circling high above Port Blair. They soon became a regularity, arriving about 11:00 and staying for 45 minutes. There were other difficulties, maintenance facilities were sparse, accommodation was basic, and regarding food, crews soon learnt that roast dog was part of the staple diet.

John Connolly, first officer to Captain Purton, recalled a southbound flight from Sabang:

'Medan radio went off the air. Suspecting the worst, they

*stayed low and kept a good lookout. As they passed
Medan, they saw it was under attack. Trusting that their
camouflage against the backdrop of wooded hills would
save them, they remained low and continued down the
Sumatran coast.'*

As they approached their staging posts, the natives,
wary of all aircraft noise, would scatter to the shelters.
Following arrival, crews invariably had to taxi around
looking for the mooring and generally helping themselves, until the natives emerged.

Japanese punctuality worked to QANTAS's advantage. The enemy tended to raid at the same time each
day, so that rescheduling of the 'boats offered some protection. The timing of some attacks seemed most providential, and fifth columnists were suspected, especially
in Burma. Captain Howard's post-flight report of *Circe*,
18 to 21 January 1942, recorded Rangoon was raided
only an hour after their departure.

Howard's flight south was not without further difficulties. They were unable to establish radio contact with
Port Blair until twenty minutes before landing.
Apparently, Port Blair had not been advised of the
inbound flight and it was only by chance the radio
operator was present. Once down, the Port Blair commander asked Howard to fly a reconnaissance for
Japanese shipping, as enemy aircraft had been seen in
the area. On the 20th, out of Port Blair for Sabang, he
was warned to bypass his destination, as it was under
attack. Fortunately there were strong tail winds and he
had sufficient fuel to carry on down to Sibolga. At
Sibolga, their approach caused panic and the natives
fled to their shelters. This was not surprising, as only an
hour earlier one of the staff had been killed, when the
Japanese strafed and bombed the port. Apart from two
air raid warnings that evening at Sibolga, the remainder
of the flight to Batavia was uneventful.

In common with other cities, the effects of Japanese
air attacks on Rangoon were grim. The native population fled and the authorities were unable to cope with
the number of rotting corpses littering the waters
around the wharves and jetties. The Strand Hotel, used
by QANTAS crews, was adjacent to the jetty, and the
stench of death was overpowering.

QANTAS crews, operating in the face of great adver-
sity, started a shuttle service between Singapore and
Batavia, on 6 January 1942. These unarmed flights, in
skies abounding with enemy aircraft, were some of the
most perilous civil air operations of the war, and called
for a pragmatic approach. It became practice to listen
into the radio for warnings and if necessary wait out the
raid in a sheltered cove or 'funkhole', some of which
were named after their finders. On a practical level,
crew complements were increased to include the carriage of three lookouts to spot Japanese fighters. The
QEA aircraft were modified, having either a hole cut, or
more likely, the escape hatches removed, so that a
capped and goggled observer could keep watch above.

Many times the 'boats spied fighters, and many
landings were made in 'funkholes', whilst the

destinations were under air attack. Schedules were
arranged to avoid the predictable and punctual
Japanese air attacks, but this was not always easy.
Towards the end, in particular, it was necessary to be
airborne by 08:00 and remain aloft until late afternoon,
a period beyond the 'boats' endurance.

Between 6 January and 14 February, when the link to
Calcutta was finally severed, thirty services were flown
through the war zone, down to Australia. The Japanese,
now flying from Kuala Lumpur, only two hundred or so
miles to the north, increased the frequency of attacks
upon Singapore, and it became more and more difficult
to operate in daylight. 'Funkholes' were regularly used
to wait out raids. On 23 January 1942, Captain Thomas
was forced into a 'funkhole' near Port Blair as raids
were in progress at Padang, Sibolga, Port Blair and
Rangoon.

The Singapore schedules were amended to allow
arrivals at dusk and departures at first light the following morning, but with the full moon approaching, the
RAF advised against night-stopping. Considering the
worsening situation, it was decided to position the QEA
standby 'boat at Batavia, rather than Singapore. It flew
down and was secured at the Dutch Naval Base at
Tandjong Priok, Batavia. By mid-January, QANTAS's
engineer in Singapore, Bill Bennett, had dispersed the
QANTAS engineering facilities to India and Batavia.
The relentless Japanese advance continued, and as
Batavia came within range of fighters based in the
Philippines, the standby 'boat was moved to Australia.

Towards the third week of January, the Japanese tar-
geted Kallang airport and John Brancker found himself
there, victim of the bombing. He and Runciman, on
their tour of inspection of the Horseshoe, had earlier
been trapped in Bangkok. QEA had been prohibited
from sending a rescue 'boat into Bangkok for them and
the airline staff, but, fortuitously, they escaped.
Runciman soon managed to get back to London, whilst
Brancker went south to Singapore.

Frying pan to fire – Brancker found himself shelter-
ing with Captain Koch in an ant-infested monsoon
drain. Above, the Japanese attacked. The Kallang terminal building was straddled but damage was only super-
ficial. The passengers, mainly women and children trying to escape, were stoic under attack, the children being
more interested in adding to their shrapnel collections.
Outside, the car park was ablaze and two Brewster
Buffaloes joined the conflagration.

At the close of January, a mooring was laid in the
Inner Road of Singapore's Keppel Harbour. The company operated from Ocean Building and boarded from
Clifford's Pier. This way, passengers were less exposed
to possible air attack. On 26 January, Kallang was
severely damaged and the evacuation of all QEA staff to
Batavia began.

Captain Connolly wrote:

*'Our last run into Singapore was quite hair-raising. We
were about a hundred miles out of Singapore when we
saw two aircraft looming up dead ahead. To be on the safe*

side, we immediately turned and began to retrace our steps in something of a hurry. They altered course and began heading out to sea towards Singkep and it was then that we recognized them as Jap bombers. They made no attempt to chase us however, so we landed at the mouth of a river, gave ourselves half an hour's grace, and then set off once more for Singapore. This time we had arrived within sight of Singapore when the second raid of the morning began. We could see the smoke rising up around Palang.

This time we went in search of a bay nearby, which Captain Thomas had discovered and used under somewhat similar circumstances a few days previously. He had named it "Thomas's Funkhole". In this bay we anchored until Radio Officer Phillips announced the all-clear, then we proceeded to Singapore some miles distant.'

Batavia was not without irritants. As early as 18 December 1941, Captain Gurney had been cut up by a Lockheed, as he attempted to alight at Surabaya. Furthermore, to prevent Japanese flying-boats laden with invasion forces alighting, the Dutch had moored floating, conical, bamboo constructions across Surabaya harbour. The Dutch seemed unaware of the hazard these bamboo pyramids might cause to allied aircraft and, on occasions, Bill Bennett and other QANTAS staff had to assist the flying-boats' captains in moving the obstructions.

As the Empire Route quivered, QANTAS began a Townsville–Cairns–Port Moresby schedule, soon extended to Milne Bay. This commenced on 20 December 1941. To increase range and payload, QANTAS further stripped their 'boats of unnecessary fittings, seats, linings, kitchen equipment and heaters.

On 21 December 1941, *Coolangatta* was returned to Rose Bay for a thorough overhaul. The work included stripping the interior and fitting floor rails to bear cradled aircraft engines. These could be loaded via the starboard hatch and pushed forward (to the navigator's compartment – possibly in the spar compartment). The bombing cupola was removed, the Vickers machine-guns were replaced by more powerful American weapons and she was camouflaged. *Coolangatta* departed Rose Bay, commanded by Flight Lieutenant John Hampshire, on Christmas Eve. They carried a Pratt & Whitney engine for a 13 Sqn Hudson, at Dili. The next day, *Coolangatta* returned with the unserviceable engine, but that was the only occasion upon which she was used to carry aircraft engines. Meanwhile, other 'boats were seeing action. On 26 December, *Calypso* evacuated 42 adults and nine children from Rabaul.

A rearguard action was being fought in 'the island fortress', Singapore. Meanwhile, further south, preparations were being made to repulse the expected attack. On 1 January 1942, *Coolangatta* called at Darwin, whilst operating under orders for the USAAF, taking ammunition on to Surabaya and deeper into the East Indies. This task was completed on 11 January.

Late in the evening on 22 January, the remnants of

No. 24 Sqn, RAAF, were evacuated from Rabaul. With a Japanese invasion imminent, Wing Commander Lerew, commanding officer of the defence force, completed the demolition of the airbase then fled with his men. They trekked down New Britain's southern coast to Sum Sum, the pre-arranged rescue point. One of Lerew's men, a Sergeant Higgs, had radioed Port Moresby, alerting them to the evacuation.

Upon receipt of the radio message, the two 11 Sqn Empires, *Calypso* and *Coogee,* captained by Flight Lieutenants Mike Mather and Len Grey, left Port Moresby to search for the escapers. They diverted to Samari, at the mouth of Milne Bay, and waited whilst an air raid took place at Rabaul. At about 14:00, 23 January, they took off for the rendezvous, intending to arrive off the south coast of New Britain at dusk. They made the crossing at 50 feet and located Lerew's party. Despite the nearness of the enemy and a landing in the open sea, the 'boats squeezed in 50 and 46 persons respectively. At 19:22, the flying-boats departed Sum Sum for Samari, and that night landed with the help of a flare-path that, despite the strong current, had been laid by the commanding officer. The night was still, the waters calm and the crews bedded down. Mather's engineer, Mick Cassimati, was aware of the current, and to wake them should they break free of the mooring, he attached an empty petrol can to the mooring buoy by a line and placed the can upon the flight-deck. In the early hours, when Mike Mather and the first officer returned, they 'tripped' the alarm, roused Cassimati, who immediately started all four engines – believing themselves adrift – and the resultant cacophony awoke the complete mooring.

The small party that remained at Sum Sum found a yacht and sailed it to Tol. On the 24th, Mather in *Calypso* flew 42 of the group to Townsville whilst the remainder went by Catalina to Port Moresby. Meanwhile, Len Grey, in *Coogee,* flew to Tol plantation and rescued the remaining 49 escapers. For these acts, Mather and Grey were awarded the Air Force Cross.

On 17 January, *Coolangatta* evacuated women and children from Kupang and Ambon (north of Timor, in the Molucca Isles). At least three of these ten-hour flights were made, and on one, 60 passengers were carried! *Coolangatta* even flew into Ambon on the same day as the Japanese invaded, 30 January.

Japanese aircraft carriers were probing the Timor Sea, and QEA's game of hide-and-seek could not go on for much longer. On 29 January, Captain Hussey refuelled *Corinthian* at Kupang, between air raids. That same day, Captain Koch in *Corio* returned to Darwin, as Kupang would not reply to his wireless calls. An air raid was presumed: he would try the following day.

On 30 January, a Friday, as the causeway, joining Singapore to Malaya, was being blown, *Corio* made a second attempt to complete a special flight from Darwin to Kupang and then to Surabaya to evacuate women and children. With Koch were his crew, First Officer Victor Lyne, Senior Radio Officer A. S. Patterson, who had accompanied 'Scotty' Allan in *Coolangatta* from

England, Purser W. G. Cruickshank and Steward S. C. Elphick. They carried thirteen passengers, G. A. Farrelly, H. E. Cutfield, J. C. Fisher, F. A. Moore, J. Depinna, J. J. Holiday, W. O. Beckett, W. N. Lee, G. C. Vantereight, E. G. Kerr, J. C. McMillan, Paymaster Lieutenant B. L. Westbrook and D. W. McCulloch.

Before leaving Darwin, Koch was warned that Bima was dangerous but Kupang, although subject to a few recent attacks, was comparatively safe. Koch had arranged with Kupang that they would transmit an 'All-Clear' every thirty minutes. Beneath a 300-foot cloud base, Koch edged his way towards the coast of Timor. Regularly, the reassuring half-hourly broadcasts were received. About thirty miles out, the cloud broke and Radio Officer Patterson reported Kupang had failed to transmit. Koch ordered the radio officer to call Kupang.

As Koch and crew waited, above them, emerging from the high overcast, a flight of Zeros spotted *Corio* against the clear, blue sea. They positioned themselves to run in from astern. Aboard *Corio,* another few minutes would see them in Kupang.

A rattling in the fuselage was heard. The air became tracer-full as seven Mitsubishi A6Ms, Zeros, attacked from behind. Captain Koch dived to wave-top height and headed for the beach, about fifteen miles away, but in the first pass he was wounded in the arm and leg. First Officer Lyne was grazed on the neck but Patterson received serious wounds to his knee. For the passengers, no warning. Tracer fire ripped through the thin skin, the man in front of Westbrook died instantly, the one sitting next to Moore was hit and fell into the aisle. One RAAF man died as he reached for his tin hat, whilst another stirred, only to be struck down. The others grovelled for what little shelter there was on the floor. Noise – bedlam – cabins full of carnage – handling the mighty flying-boat like a fighter – turning in towards the fall of shot, for two or three minutes, Koch coolly evaded the fighters, waiting until their tracer was almost in the cockpit before turning towards his attackers. As a result of the low-level evasion his floats dipped into the sea with each violent manoeuvre. Only minutes from the beach, with two engines set on fire and speed being rapidly lost, Captain Koch was forced to crash-land *Corio* five miles from land, abeam the mouth of the Noelman's River. As he lowered her onto the surface she plunged away from him, both elevators shot away and her bilges ripped open by the cannon fire. Koch was thrown out over the instrument panel, as the nose split before him.

In the cabin, those who had survived the initial onslaught were hurled forward by the impact. Westbrook was jammed under a seat and other debris. Holding his breath, he struggled as the sea poured in and darkened. Almost at his limit, he noticed the light increasing as the hulk settled upon the surface. He struggled upwards to find himself free of the machine, and he was not alone. Moore had swum out through the broken back of *Corio.*

When Koch surfaced, he found *Corio* settling with her wings just above the water. Circling 1,500 feet above, the Japanese fighters admired their handiwork. Koch dodged beneath the wing and the fighters, apparently satisfied or short of fuel, left. Koch swam around the trailing edge to find *Corio* had broken her back and the aft section still floated. Under the wing, he joined Radio Officer Patterson, First Officer Lyne and passengers Moore, Fisher and Westbrook. A desperate passenger, McCulloch, a Navy man, punched out one of the windows and fell into the sea. Koch and the others could see he had dreadful wounds to his chest and head, but he had a lifebelt. Inside the cabin, fire had broken out, but there was no other sign of life. The fire spread rapidly as the fuel tanks spewed over the sea. Fearful of an explosion, the six survivors struggled away from the pyre. Little was said but Mr Fisher thought the 'Japs' were being sporting by not strafing them in the water. Westbrook struck out to a floating mailbag, which proved to be his salvation. *Corio* slipped beneath the sea.

They gathered some wreckage to support themselves. McCulloch was badly wounded in the chest, as was Patterson in the legs. Captain Koch thought he too had been hit in the knee. First Officer Lyne supported himself on a straw basket, but when he saw Patterson, he gave him the basket. Patterson and McCulloch were soon lost. They were about five miles out; Lyne started for help. Moore suggested he and Koch should attempt the swim and seek help from natives. Koch could use only one leg, but his strong overarm stroke made progress. During the swim, he realised he had been wounded in the arm and he worried that the profuse bleeding might attract sharks. Moore offered to tow Koch ashore but the captain was adamant that he would swim until he reached the shore or collapse with exhaustion. After two hours, they reached the breakers. Moore stood up but Captain Koch had to be helped ashore, his leg was useless. Moore dragged Koch clear of the surf and bandaged the wounded pilot's arm and leg as best possible.

Meanwhile, Westbrook was drifting ashore on his mailbag.

Moore set off for help but returned exhausted two hours later, his path having been blocked by a river. Resting and pondering their fate, they saw a figure down the beach. Moore ran down to find Westbrook, who told him two others, First Officer Lyne and Mr Fisher, had made it ashore.

Westbrook and Moore dragged Koch into a crude shelter, whilst First Officer Lyne and Mr Fisher trudged, exhausted, down the beach to join them. Fisher had a couple of broken ribs and he was settled next to Koch, while Moore, Lyne and Westbrook scoured the area for fresh water. They looked inside the mail bag in hope of finding matches and came across medical supplies with which they dressed their wounds. The survivors decided Moore and Westbrook would set out for Kupang that evening, even if it meant them having to swim the 400-yard-wide river, that could well be infested with crocodiles.

Although the river was crossed safely, Moore and

Westbrook's pitiful search proved useless. They huddled together in a small rocky cave as darkness fell. It rained – heavily. They supped rain-water from the leaves. At dawn they continued their search and found a brackish pool that animals had been drinking from. No drink ever tasted so sweet to them. They followed the tracks and, assisted by the sound of crowing cockerels, found some natives who gave them a little food and some water. Retracing their path, they reached the river bank. Here they built a simple raft, and during the afternoon's low water, they floated the food across the river. The natives refused to cross with them, so Moore and Westbrook alone returned to Koch and the others.

Lyne had passed the miserable Saturday in rain showers, tending to Koch and Fisher, but some relief was gained by the return of Westbrook and Moore. Barely rested, Moore, this time with Lyne, again set out to the river, while Westbrook stayed behind. During the crossing, Lyne injured his foot and was in such a poor shape he was unable to go on, so he rested with the natives.

Sunday passed. Koch was now unable to move. The sun set; maybe tomorrow would bring help. Unbeknown to the survivors, once he had crossed the river, Moore had taken a native guide and a pony and, on Monday 2 February, he made contact with the Dutch authorities at Kupang. It was arranged that a steamer, due out that evening, would pick up the party, but as the steamer was about to leave, a Dutch flying-boat arrived and the captain agreed to take the survivors off the beach that evening. A Dr Hecking would accompany them. As the light failed, the note of their engines was heard by Koch. The Dutch Do 24 was sweeping the beach looking for the little group. It circled and, having spotted them, landed outside the surf. It was now dark but Westbrook could hear the crew's voices, as they tried to breach the surf and get ashore in a rubber dinghy.

Dr Hecking treated Koch and Fisher, whilst two of the Dutch crew took the rubber boat across the river in search of the native village and Lyne. Finding him, Lyne was instructed to get down to the beach the following morning and wait to be picked up. That evening there was a very high tide, the river was almost impassable and there were fears for the immobile Koch and Fisher.

The following morning, the waters had receded and, with a desperate struggle through the surf, they managed to get Koch and Fisher onto the flying-boat. Within half an hour of getting airborne, they were all in a tender, being taken ashore at Kupang.

Finally, on 11 February, Flight Lieutenant John Hampshire and *Coolangatta* flew four of the five survivors to Darwin – but not before Captain Koch had had his first experience of Japanese bombing whilst lying in a hospital bed. At Darwin, Koch was sent to hospital but Lyne, Fisher and Moore were allowed to proceed.

The loss of *Corio* was the first crash resulting in injuries to passengers since QANTAS had been in operation. Following the loss, the eastbound service between Batavia and Darwin was suspended, and only two more services from India made it through.

While Captain Koch and crew were fighting for their lives, Bill Morgan, ever willing to take on another flight, stood in for the sick Purser Barron, of QEA. On 30 January, Bill Morgan and Captain Hughes-Jones, *Corsair*, flew out of Karachi for Calcutta. There, Bill slipped to *Centaurus* and Captain Gurney. They followed the Phase IV route to Batavia, arriving on 31 January. Bill then boarded *Corinna*, with Captain Sims, and flew to Singapore, arriving at last light on the 31st. Before dawn on 1 February, they stole away.

Safely returned to Batavia, Bill, now with Captain Adair in *Castor*, headed north. They reached Calcutta on 2 February, but not before they had made many landings on the Palembang–Port Blair sector, avoiding Japanese fighters. As they passed through Rangoon, they evacuated the non-essential staff.

The final Empire 'Boat out of Singapore was flown by Captain W. H. Crowther, on 4 February. He had arrived from Batavia the previous evening and, having skirted the Sumatran mountains to avoid detection, was almost over Singapore before he made radio contact. Singapore replied they were unable to guarantee any facilities on arrival, but Crowther's crew agreed to continue. Departure, at 02:30, was without the aid of a flare-path. Guided through the shipping, minefields and fishing-traps by the Director of Civil Aviation himself, Crowther hauled the heavily laden 'boat into the moon-lit night. There were 40 passengers on board. News of his departure was broadcast by Radio Tokyo the following afternoon. The next day, Japanese guns reached Singapore, and on 6 February, General Headquarters (GHQ) Bandoeng (Java) halted the Singapore–Batavia shuttle.

On 9 February, the Japanese entered Singapore. It would fall on 15 February 1942. Meanwhile, on 8 February, Captain Thomas started a Batavia–Tjilatjap–Australia service, and on the 10th, Captain O. D. Denny departed Sydney, on the reverse.

Captain Tapp took the last through-'boat out of Karachi on 8 February; he routed Calcutta, Akyab and Port Blair. As a precaution whilst on the surface, he had the 'boat unloaded so that, should they be attacked, the freight would not be lost. The availability of fuel at the staging posts was uncertain, so some 'boats were fitted with additional fuel tanks, taken from Wirraway aircraft. The tanks were not connected to the flying-boats' own fuel system and 'boats had to alight in order to transfer the fuel. When Tapp arrived at Port Blair, the daily Japanese aerial surveillance was in progress. Although wary of possible air raids, Tapp was forced to abort take-off from Port Blair due to engine trouble. The temperature was high and the 'boat heavy. They returned to their mooring. Amongst the passengers was BOAC engineer Macmillan, grieving the loss of his wife and child in *Cassiopeia*. He worked upon the trouble-some engine. At midday the reconnaissance aircraft again overflew them; nothing untoward followed. The engine was run successfully that afternoon, and a mid-night departure, allowing a dawn refuelling at Sibolga, was planned. Yet again the take-off was aborted and yet again Macmillan stripped off and set to work on the engine. At 04:00, Tapp and Macmillan carried out a satisfactory engine run, but it was now too late to leave, if they wished to avoid Japanese activity at Sibolga.

They waited until 09:00 before taking off, and initially departed to the west, avoiding any Japanese shipping or aircraft. As dusk approached, they turned east from their southerly track and ran towards Sibolga. Air raid alert was the message they received. Captain Tapp held off. All-clear and they turned in. Another alarm was broadcast, again they held. Fuel and light were limited and Tapp deduced they might have been the cause of the alert. They made another approach towards Sibolga; again a warning, but they ignored it and landed.

The following day, they again first headed out to sea before resuming their track towards Java. To wait out the day's Japanese air activity to the east of Sumatra, they landed on the west coast at South Pagi and moored in Tio Bay. Three hours later, they continued to the Sunda Straits, where they were ineffectually fired upon by a Dutch naval vessel. Finally, Batavia was reached.

Tapp handed the 'boat over for onward flight to Australia; his instructions were to wait and pick up the next westbound returning to Karachi. Whilst waiting, Singapore fell and Tapp was instructed to route through Tjilatjap and across the Timor Sea to Broome and on to Darwin.

Ten 'boats were east of Singapore at the fall on 15 February. The previous day, the Director of Fighter Operations at Bandoeng decreed flying-boat operations between Calcutta and Batavia were to cease as Japanese paratroopers had descended upon Palembang.

The Horseshoe was broken!

The aerodrome at Batavia was strafed regularly by the Japanese, and on 20 February, the QEA operation was transferred across Java from Batavia to Tjilatjap. The last flight from Batavia had been made the day before by Captain Ambrose. The situation in Batavia was now fraught, and QEA staff, Malcolm Miller, Lane, 'Shinty' Colville and others, were making their way from Singapore, across Java to Tjilatjap and then to Australia by whatever means they could find. Desperate searches of the islands were being made for stragglers.

Singapore had fallen; Rangoon would not be long. On 21 February, *Coorong*, crewed by Captain Bellin, First Officer 'Farmer John' Pascoe, Radio Officer Brown and Purser Aldridge, landed in Rangoon and evacuated the company stores and remaining personnel. By 23 February, they were safe in Basra.

The scramble rearwards to Australia was assisted by repeated evacuation flights by the RAAF. *Coolangatta*, with Flight Lieutenant Hampshire, made her final flight to Ambon, already in Japanese hands, on 12 February 1942. They sneaked across the Banda Sea and alighted upon open waters at dusk. Engineer Wylie and the crew refuelled *Coolangatta* from the Wirraway fuel tanks, strapped to the engine transit rails. No signal was seen from the shore. It was too late. The stragglers had

already fallen to the Japanese. To the west of Ambon, on Buru, the rear party from Namlea was rescued on 13 February. *Coolangatta* then returned to Darwin, before commencing the two-day flight south to Rose Bay on 15 February. In recognition of the bravery displayed by himself and his crew, John Hampshire was awarded the Distinguished Flying Cross. *Coolangatta*, meanwhile, was given a major overhaul and she missed events at Darwin. At the end of February, the RAAF Empire 'Boats were transferred to No. 33 Sqn. This transport squadron was commanded by Squadron Leader Gurney, one of the original ex-QANTAS 11 Sqn pilots.

The six remaining Australian Empire 'Boats co-operated with the Dutch, and, with the rout of the Allies continuing, attempts to evacuate civilian personnel and reinforce the servicemen on Java were made. A disastrous period for the Empire 'Boats was about to start. On 19 and 20 February 1942, the Japanese invaded Timor and occupied Dili, which QEA had earlier abandoned on 6 December. Four Japanese aircraft carriers of the 1st Carrier Fleet steamed towards Darwin and land planes of the 21st and 23rd Air Flotillas, based in Celebes and Ambon, prepared. The Japanese commanders, Admiral Nagumo and Commander Fuchida – both veterans of Pearl Harbor, were bringing their forces to bear upon Australia.

In Darwin, the situation was tense. Invasion was feared and the evacuation of Australian nationals from Java was being planned. *Camilla*, a couple of Catalinas and almost fifty ships were moored in the harbour on the morning of 19 February. Warnings from coastwatchers were ignored; then, waves of enemy aircraft appeared over the sparsely defended harbour and attacked systematically.

Less than two hundred yards from the main jetty, *Camilla* was riding her mooring. Captain Bert Hussey was in town, awaiting a shave, when the first bombs fell. Hussey scrambled out through the yard of the Victoria Hotel towards the Hotel Darwin. Above, he saw the bombers and fighters wheeling to attack. Two hundred yards away, the post office received a salvo of bombs. Some struck a trench and nine people were killed, the postmaster, H. C. Bald, his wife and daughter included; eleven others were injured. The air was full of flying wreckage. Out of the maelstrom of debris staggered Captain Bill Crowther. As Hussey dived into a monsoon drain, he was joined by Crowther and Mrs Val Hansen, a QANTAS typist.

They made their way to open ground, away from the target areas. A salvo landed on the post office; drums of telephone cable were lofted into the air by the force of the blast. From above, a flight of Zeros wheeled and dived towards them. Bombs left the aircraft; three exploded close by but one hit the hospital. Inside, Captain Koch was recovering from the *Corio* crash and experiencing his second air raid in a hospital bed. Once the aircraft had passed, Koch staggered out of the ward, intent on reaching the waterfront. After the town, the aerodrome seemed the next target; then it was the harbour. Several aircraft were seen to dive upon *Camilla*.

Bombs could be seen leaving the aircraft, which, once free of their deadly load, turned inland to strafe. The precision attack petered out and Hussey and 'crew' made their way to the Hotel Darwin, in search of a car.

Six of them bundled into a vehicle and Mrs Hansen sped them down to the quayside. The jetty had been severed, and oil and water sprayed from the jagged mess of pipes. Two boats, *Neptuna* and *Barossa*, were burning furiously, clouds of black smoke billowing from them. As if by a miracle, there between the two boats, shielded from Japanese eyes by the smoke, rode *Camilla*!

Crowther and Hussey got out of the car. Mrs Hansen went on to the hospital, to find Koch. Amidst the confusion and trauma, Crowther and Hussey learnt the *Neptuna* carried munitions, including 200 tons of depth-charges. They ran down the ramp to be confronted by a launch landing sodden survivors. Crowther and Hussey rode the launch to the awaiting *Camilla*. There, they let go the storm pennant, and a cursory inspection revealed some minor shrapnel damage to the elevator. The launch sought further survivors. Bert Hussey secured the 'boat and threw the 'dizzie switch', connecting the batteries, before helping Bill Crowther start the engines. Petrol was checked by Hussey as he slid down the ladder to the mooring compartment. He released *Camilla* to the westerly wind and she drifted from *Neptuna*, which blazed crimson, like a vision of hell. A quick check of the bilges revealed the hull was intact. Only three engines were running when Hussey returned to the flight-deck; he looked out and saw they were running into shallow water. The engines were closed down and they considered hiding in the mangrove swamps, but realising they could be left high and dry, they decided they would be better off in the air.

They restarted the engines, this time all four, and as Crowther taxied into deeper water, Hussey brought all the ropes aboard and secured the hatches. Hussey conned from the first officer's hatch and in the distance he saw three explosions. They decided to get airborne and head south at low-level. As they cleared the water and skimmed over the mangrove, there was a loud report from behind them. It was of little consequence as only the pantry window had blown open.

With a tremendous explosion, *Neptuna*, and 45 of her crew, were blown to oblivion only eight minutes after *Camilla* became airborne.

Having collected their thoughts, they made for the Alligator River, 25 miles away. But there communications and fuel supplies could prove difficult, so they turned instead for Groote Eylandt, in the Gulf of Carpentaria. Several hours later they landed and took on 1,400 gallons of fuel.

Darwin could now no longer accept civil aircraft, and further arrivals were prohibited until full communications were restored. Crowther and Hussey signalled Darwin that they would return at sunset, load and depart for Sydney at first light. Their message was acknowledged. In their eyes communications were restored. Unable to find a radio officer, they arranged that a message, indicating that all was clear, should be transmitted by Darwin every half hour. Darwin was reached safely, at dusk.

Nine ships had been sunk and thirteen severely damaged. The jetty was cut and the ill-prepared, adjacent RAAF aerodrome had been mauled, as had the town. Almost thirty aircraft were lost, 243 persons were killed and 330 injured. Despite the bravery of the anti-aircraft gunners and the fighter pilots, American and Australian, the populace, fearful of invasion, left the town and trekked inland. Public order collapsed.

After her narrow escape from Darwin, earlier that day, Engineer Norm Roberts insisted upon giving *Camilla* a thorough check, before allowing her to continue south. Roberts carried out the inspection by the light of a small torch, piercing the total blackout. It was midnight before he was satisfied *Camilla* was undamaged. Only then was the aircraft refuelled and loaded. Awaiting dawn, Captain Koch and other passengers spent three fitful, mosquito-plagued hours trying to sleep in armchairs, in the lobby of the blacked-out Darwin Hotel.

An hour before dawn, they were on the stump of the jetty – no launch – no rowing boats. As the sky lightened they saw an upturned dinghy and beyond – a launch. Having recovered the dinghy, baled it out and then rowed over to the launch, they were unable to start the launch's engine. A Japanese dawn strike was expected. Crowther and Hussey, still on the jetty, ordered the dinghy back, and in desperation they went over to the launch. Dry handkerchiefs attacked the ignition leads and soon the engine was running. With the sun rising and the tide falling, no more time was lost stretchering Captain Koch aboard, and, with the other passengers, they were aloft, Sydney bound.

Several days later, on the evening of 22 February, a 'boat, loaded with evacuees, came in from Broome. She needed to be refuelled and with great difficulty this task was completed. The 'boat departed on the morning of 23 February, amongst her passengers Norm Robert's wife, the last woman to leave Darwin. Those who stayed awaiting the Japanese invasion endured sporadic fighter raids. The invasion came to nought and Darwin settled down, but meanwhile the activity had moved to Broome.

Throughout the past few hectic months, the Australian Department of Civil Aviation had been monitoring events. After the loss of *Corio*, they suggested closing the route through Bima and Kupang, substituting a sector from Western Australia to Java. Events at Darwin forced the pace. The Allied evacuation of Java using land planes had already been thwarted, as the majority of airstrips had fallen to the Japanese. Surabaya, as a marine airbase, had to be discounted as the enemy advance was so swift. A route from Tjilatjap, an isolated port in southern Java, to Broome seemed appropriate. Captain Ambrose took *Corinna* to Tjilatjap and, accompanied by the Dutch Deputy Director of Civil Aviation, surveyed Tjilatjap as a possible evacuation point. Malcolm Millar, late Civil Aviation Liaison Officer, Singapore, now liaised with Air Headquarters

Bandoeng, Java. On 21 February, he was told that Java could not be held and air operations ought to cease by the end of that month.

QANTAS relocated its terminal to the remote pearl-fishing town of Broome. The harbour, subject to a seven-knot, 32-foot tide, was not an ideal site for flying-boat operations. Although it boasted a half-mile-long jetty, at low tide it was necessary to wade out through another half-mile of mud to reach the deep water anchorage. The USAAF Air Defence Commander, Lieutenant-Colonel Richard A. Legg, was in overall command of operations – but he had no resources at his disposal. QANTAS's Captain Lester Brain was despatched to Broome with instructions to assist where possible. Brain arrived on the afternoon of 21 February and was met by Doug Laurie, recently station manager at Darwin. Despite non-existent communications with Sydney, they directed the QANTAS operation.

Broome was a seething mass of evacuees, fever and uncertainty. *Corinthian,* Captain Howard, arrived from Darwin on the 21st or 22nd and joined Ambrose and Purton already at Broome. The shuttle service between Broome and Tjilatjap began on 22 February. Ammunition to bolster Java's defences was flown out and evacuees were brought in. This shuttle followed the flights of Thomas and Denny a week before. The 'boats *Circe, Coriolanus* and *Corinthian* were used and, at this time, *Corinna* was transferred to QANTAS but she retained her British markings. It was 1,200 miles across the Timor Sea, so the payload was reduced to a meagre 1,800 lb as QANTAS was still operating within the peacetime regulations for loadings.

On the 22nd or 23rd, Captain Denny took *Circe* to Tjilatjap. At sea, standing some way off Tjilatjap harbour, lay a Japanese submarine. It took a heavy toll of ships attempting to flee the port's narrow entrance. On one flight, *Circe* and Ambrose stumbled across a Japanese flying-boat but were able to make for cloud before being pursued. Although committed to radio silence, using a pre-arranged code Ambrose warned Broome-bound Captain Purton of the presence of the enemy flying-boat.

On 23 February, *Coriolanus,* carrying three naval officers amongst her passengers, left for Tjilatjap. On the 25th, *Circe* flew a load of machine-guns, but on the 26th, when *Coriolanus* was to take ammunition to Tjilatjap for onward transport to Bandoeng, it was decided that Tjilatjap would be too dangerous and the ammunition was flown direct by the Americans. The re-supply became an evacuation. At crowded Broome, Brain wrote in his diary, 'I shall not be surprised if all this activity brings an enemy raid.'

By 26 February, the position in Tjilatjap became critical, and Millar, advised by Allied Headquarters, Bandoeng, to fly the last shuttle the following day, asked for two 'boats to evacuate the remaining QANTAS staff. Allied Headquarters' instruction to cease flying was carried to Brain by Captain Denny, on the 26th. Brain relayed the message to QANTAS at Sydney. He added the rider that he thought Millar would remain in Tjilatjap until the collapse. Moreover, morale at Broome was excellent, and although he was not in direct contact with Tjilatjap, he would continue to dispatch aircraft to evacuate Java. Brain concluded, although advised by Java Allied Headquarters at Bandoeng to cease operations, the final decision lay with the Department of Civil Aviation at Sydney and he would await their decision.

The following day, Brain dispatched the two requested aircraft to Tjilatjap: *Corinthian,* under the command of Captain Howard, and *Circe,* commanded by Captain Purton, who was to be married when he returned to Australia. First Officers Connolly and Bateman swapped crews, Connolly flying with Howard. The crossing was uneventful. That night, the last of the shipping slipped out of the harbour. The Japanese were close; they had secured Bali and Palembang.

It was intended that *Corinthian* and *Circe,* having spent the night moored at Tjilatjap, would return to Broome with some of the QANTAS staff and stores, early on 28 February. In the meantime, *Coriolanus* was being prepared to make the final evacuation of Millar and the remainder of his staff on 28 February. Once airborne, Captain Denny, commander of *Coriolanus,* settled down for the long crossing to Tjilatjap. Whilst Denny was in the air, the Department of Civil Aviation in Sydney received Brain's relayed warning from Allied Headquarters at Bandoeng. As a result, *Coriolanus* was recalled. Millar, the ground engineer, C. Short, and the Sibolga agent remained at Tjilatjap and were finally airlifted to Broome by a USAAF B-17 on 2 March.

Across the Timor Sea, on the morning of the 28th, *Circe* and *Corinthian* were making ready in the deserted harbour at Tjilatjap. *Corinthian,* with twenty wounded aboard, was away as *Circe* slipped her mooring. In order to distance themselves from the Japanese, Captain Howard and *Corinthian* ran due south, before turning for Broome. On board *Circe,* Captain Purton, First Officer M. W. Bateman, Radio Officer H. G. A. Oates and Purser L. J. Hogan may have had a different plan of escape. Although following *Corinthian*'s arrival at Broome, the pilots did report having seen a couple of submarines; the passengers were emphatic they had seen some aircraft as well and they had insisted the purser report the sighting to Captain Howard. First Officer Connolly thought the sightings to be cloud streaks. Perhaps they were but those on *Circe* were soon to know different. Some two hundred miles out of Java, *Circe* radioed all was well.

Missing, in addition to *Circe*'s crew, were the Dutch Consul-General of Singapore, Mr H. M. J. Fein; his Consul, Mr J. M. Viruley and their wives and daughters; the Vice-Consul, Mr J. H. Crawincle; the Chancellor of the Consulate, Mr F. H. Van Haefen; the Secretary of the Consul-General, Miss Venselaar; the Confidential Secretary of the Consulate, Miss Demaret; and three other Dutch nationals.

It would seem they fell into the path of a flight of Mitsubushi A6Ms which were returning from their successful attack upon the American aircraft carrier USS *Langley.* A four-engined and a twin-engined (probably a

Dutch Catalina) flying-boat were claimed by the Zeros.

About 8,000 evacuees passed through Broome, and accommodation was so scarce that many crews lived aboard their 'boats. This measure saved the crews the discomfort of having to trudge through the mud at low tide. During the last week of February, many women and children were evacuated aboard the SS *Koolinda*, which was subsequently beached following air attack. A series of ten shuttle flights had been flown to Java. In all, seven and a half tons of freight and 88 evacuees, mostly Dutch nationals, had been taken from Tjilatjap.

Aircraft were not only falling to enemy action. *Coogee* had been impressed into RAAF service in June 1940, and on the afternoon of 28 February 1942 she was on a test flight from Townsville. She was commanded by Flying Officer Robert Love, one of her former first officers. On the flight-deck were a number of RAAF passengers, many of them women. With so many people on the flight-deck, the centre of gravity may have moved forward and Love may not have anticipated correctly the large nose-down trim change he would experience when power was reduced. Ernie Aldis, then QANTAS station engineer at Townsville, witnessed the touchdown. *Coogee* passed over the Queen's Hotel, heading for the bay and parallel to the breakwater. From a distance, he seemed to make a normal approach, although he may have been closer to the beach than necessary. However, as the 'boat continued its landing run, it seemed to settle deeper and deeper into the water. Either it had hit something or the impact of alighting had stove in the planing bottom. With no regard to the cause, a torrent of water entered the torn cabin, swept up the crew and passengers upon the flight-deck and swirled them around inside the jagged wreckage. The hulk settled about a half-mile offshore. Eight people, including Love, had died. *Coogee* lay with her nose hidden beneath the waters and her rear fuselage protruding above the waves. It took two days to extricate the mangled bodies from the wreckage. The hulk was beached and taken to a hangar on the nearby Garbutt Air Base, from whence it was eventually scrapped.

On the west coast, evacuees were taken from Broome, south to Port Headland or beyond to Perth, and many a search and rescue mission was flown, in addition to those for *Circe*. On 28 February, Captain Denny in *Coriolanus* was asked to search for the crew of a USAAF DC-3, downed upon a beach north of Broome. The survivors' wireless was still working but their food and water were dwindling rapidly. Denny was unable to find the Americans, but on return, careful study of all the available information revealed they should have been searching further to the north.

On 1 March, Denny, this time in *Corinthian*, was *en route* to Darwin when a flare from the USAAF DC-3 was spotted at Vansittart Bay. They circled and landed outside the surf. A thrilling ride in a rubber boat completed the rescue, albeit made more difficult by the strong currents. Having dropped off the survivors, *Corinthian* and *Coriolanus* left for Sydney on 2 March 1942. Ambrose and Thomas, in *Corinna*, spent ten hours searching for

Circe, but still she could not be found.

Captain Sims was more successful. In *Camilla*, he rescued twenty-five passengers and crew from the damaged SS *Koolinda*, which had left Broome only days before. She had been bombed and, unable to make Wyndham jetty, had been driven aground. From Wyndham, Sims took the survivors to Port Headland. Brain had instructed Sims not to return to Broome before 11:00 on 3 March, thus allowing time to dispatch some flying-boats from Broome.

Although Broome may have been further than Darwin from the Japanese, it was within range of their reconnaissance aircraft, and on the afternoon of 2 March, one appeared over the harbour at 15:00. At height, it circled the town a few times, spied three moored flying-boats, then flew off. Lester Brain was now fearful there would be a raid the following day and he warned the assembled captains. Later that afternoon, the situation was compounded by the arrival of another four 'boats, Dutch Do 24s carrying the crews' families. After sunset, another nine arrived. Their captains were instructed to refuel quickly and fly south. But the harbour could only accommodate three flying-boats at a time. The remainder lay out in the bay, and when the tide receded, they were stranded.

Brain decided that as there was no trace of *Circe*, the search ought be discontinued, and *Corinna*, once refuelled, was to be dispatched to Sydney upon the morning high tide of 3 March. Some captains had tried to get away but had been forced to return, Flight Lieutenant Keith Caldwell RAAF being one. He had sought refuge to the south but aborted and returned with *Centaurus* to Broome, where his crew resigned themselves to another night on the town. Some had not heeded the warning but most had tried vainly to refuel from the sparse facilities. There was one refuelling lighter, *Nicol Bay*. Her master, Captain H. Mathieson, slaved through the night and managed to refuel three of the Dutch Dorniers.

The following morning, Caldwell's crew were worse for wear, whilst others had slept fitfully on their aircraft. And it was that following morning, at about 09:30, that the Japanese attacked. Only one float-plane, the orphaned spotter from the sunken USS *Houston*, had managed to get away before the raid. There was little warning and few defences. The tide was out and many 'boats wallowed in the mud. Captain Ambrose and his twenty-five passengers stood at the end of the half-mile-long jetty, waiting to board *Corinna* for Port Headland. They were among the first to sight the nine or so silver fighters, glinting in the morning sun. Three remained high, top cover, and the remainder, in line astern, dived upon the defenceless flying-boats. A Catalina crew were strafed and killed, as they slept in their bunks.

Centaurus filled the Japanese gunsights. Caldwell and his co-pilot were ashore, as the first cannon shells ripped through her vulnerable skin. From the spar compartment, Corporal Andrew Ireland rushed up to the flight-deck to release the rubber survival dinghy. The remainder of the crew dived from the hatches, as 1,400 gallons of fuel ignited. Dutch evacuees and the crew of

Centaurus, thirteen in total, clung to the five-man dinghy and struggled ashore. For his heroism, Ireland was awarded the British Empire Medal.

On *Corinna,* Engineer G. R. Jenkins was on the wing, refuelling from Mathieson's *Nichol Bay.* Jenkins, hearing the rattle of cannon fire, dived off the wing. As he fought for breath he could hear the shells hitting the water around him. He surfaced, saw *Corinna* – already blazing – and the *Nichol Bay* drifting clear, cut free by Mathieson. Jenkins struck out to safety; he came across a dinghy, being rowed by the Shell representative. Jenkins boarded and went on to rescue several others. At one stage they were attacked by a strafing Zero. They dived overboard, to the sound of more shells striking the water. Mathieson, in *Nichol Bay,* was still carrying 180 drums of petrol and some survivors did not consider themselves rescued when he appeared upon the scene.

Within seconds, many of the flying-boats were ablaze, jets of flaming petrol sprayed over the struggling survivors. Their agonized cries were drowned only by the roar of Japanese engines and the cackle of machine-guns and cannon ravishing the port. Ashore, lone voices answered in defiance. A Dutch pilot, Lieutenant Gus Winkel, unshipped a Lewis gun from an aircraft being repaired. He laid the barrel across his forearm and did not stop firing until the red-hot barrel had burnt into his arm. Small arms and guns on the flying-boats fired back. Although, upon their return, six of the Japanese fighters were found to have sustained damage, only one Zero was destroyed, probably by Gus Winkel.

Lester Brain was aroused from a bout of fever by the sound of gunfire. He dashed to the water's edge; panic had set in among the natives and it was apparent that the Japanese fighters were intent on destroying every aircraft at Broome. Helped by Malcolm Millar, who had arrived from Java only earlier that morning, Brain managed to get a rowing boat onto the water. They pulled into the bay, and once half a mile out, they saw heads bobbing in the water. They succeeded in rescuing a Dutch woman who, in a state of near collapse, was being supported by two Dutch men. A baby was being held above the water by another survivor. Four more Dutch men and a boy were also rescued. The women, baby, boy and the three most exhausted Dutch men were taken aboard, and the others clung to the side of the boat as they struggled towards the mangrove-covered shore. Nearing the shore, Brain saw many of the 'boats destroyed, but the two refuelling luggers were still afloat and committed to rescue.

One of the QANTAS staff suffered the sight of his wife being machine-gunned and his three children drowned. In the chaos and carnage, Captain Ambrose looked out to see a chilling sight, a Liberator, which had left moments before the raid, cartwheeling – an aerial pyre – into the sea. Two, maybe three, survived the crash, but of them only one managed to walk ashore, and that was after thirty-six hours in the sea.

Just as in Darwin, the local people fled, but the heroism displayed by the military and evacuees was commendable. People dived into the blazing harbour to rescue the many Dutch women and children fleeing the flaming flying-boats that only moments before had been their salvation. Some 'boats had only recently arrived, and their complement of wounded had yet to disembark. There were many fatalities by both enemy action and sharks. Rescue was all the more difficult as the attackers had destroyed many of the small craft.

From the end of the jetty, Captain Ambrose directed the search for survivors and the dead. The grim task of transporting the bodies to the shore fell upon one of the QANTAS stewards, J. C. Oram. Seventy dead and dying were laid upon the jetty. The narrow-gauge railway took the bodies and the wounded to the quay side, a pitiful sight. QANTAS were unable to lend men to the army commander for a burial party as the QANTAS staff were needed to turn around the 'planes expected soon. A mass grave was dug by a few civilians and Dutch servicemen. Some of the bodies had been stripped of their clothes by the fires and explosions, and the USAAF supplied surplus flying overalls, in which the dead were buried. The names of twenty-nine were never known, such was the confusion of the evacuation and the ferocity of the fifteen-minute attack. The following day, the hulks were further searched. Found in one was a mother, clutching her two children, all of them burnt.

In total, twenty-four aircraft were destroyed, fifteen of them flying-boats. *Centaurus* was carrying six, 44-gallon fuel drums in her hull, which no doubt added to her destruction, and *Corinna* was struck whilst being refuelled. After the harbour, the airport was attacked, and here, six aircraft were destroyed on the ground. In the air, as well as the Liberator, USS *Houston*'s spotter aircraft and a KLM DC-3 were forced down. Although Captain Ivan Smirnoff, KLM's senior captain and commander of the DC-3, and a number of passengers and crew were eventually rescued by the Beagle Bay Mission, the reported cargo of £1 million worth of diamonds was never traced.

The train carrying the dead clattered down the jetty whilst, in accordance with Brain's schedule, *Camilla,* and the unknowing Captain Sims, steadily made their way inbound from Port Headland. Overseeing the movement of the dead and wounded from the immediate area, Captain Ambrose wanted to alert Sims to the Japanese attack but he was unable to make radio contact. Upon reflection, Brain and Ambrose felt a second attack unlikely, as few targets remained. Moreover, Brain needed *Camilla* to fly the wounded to safety. It was decided to allow *Camilla* to land.

By now, all was relatively quiet. Sims landed, approached the jetty, where the moorings had been sunk, and was met by a launch, dispatched by Captain Ambrose. Sims was instructed to taxi *Camilla* to the more secluded Roebuck Bay. Here, there was a chance that she could be refuelled, but as she manoeuvred close to a lugger, the mast stuck and dented her wing-tip. In the mangroves, Captain Ambrose and Bill Bennett, now out of Singapore and Batavia, set to hand-pump sufficient fuel for the 300-mile flight to Port Headland.

Colonel Legg, the USAAF Air Defence Commander, wanted Brain to use *Camilla* to search for the crew of the B-24 shot down at the beginning of the attack. Brain refused, arguing that movement of the wounded was a better use of their meagre resources than a futile search for unlikely survivors. Legg was not pleased. Brain did, however, agree to take part in a surface search. Flight Lieutenant Smith, an RAAF doctor, Mr Caseldene, a Shell coxswain and Bill Bennett all agreed to accompany Brain in a borrowed American motor launch. Sea conditions were not ideal and several times they were swamped. After twenty-four wasted hours, they returned to Broome.

Once refuelled, the wing-tip being ignored, Captain Sims took *Camilla,* loaded with wounded and evacuees, to Port Headland. On board were nineteen US Navy and seventeen airline people, Malcolm Millar included. There were no proper refuelling facilities at Port Headland and Captain Sims displayed extreme skill and seamanship by bringing *Camilla* nose-on to the jetty, at the height of the 02:00 flood tide. Lashed there, they refuelled over the top from fuel drums rolled down the jetty.

They departed for Broome at 06:15, 4 March, intent on evacuating more wounded. Once at Broome, rather than fly yet another evacuation flight to Port Headland, it was decided that *Camilla* ought to continue south to Perth with the more seriously wounded. With the flight to Perth completed, *Camilla,* Sims and Thomas returned to Broome.

Sims' arrival in Broome, on 7 March, gave rise to one of the lighter moments of this harrowing campaign.

Brain took the QANTAS motor launch, and armed with a Very pistol and some green flares, he set off into the fairway to await *Camilla.* As she hove into sight he loaded a green flare and fired:

'… to my amazement, it turned out to be red, so Sims immediately turned around and disappeared into the blue.'

Not believing his error, Brain extracted the cartridge from the American Very pistol:

'… it was painted green sure enough. I looked at it and the cartridge had on it "Made in Japan".'

Sims, of course, interpreted the red signal as expected and scurried inland, where he thought he would be safe. Eventually, with little fuel remaining, Captain Sims was forced to return to Broome.

On the 8th, *Camilla* flew from Broome to Perth carrying the remaining QANTAS staff and Lester Brain.

From Perth, north again with Captain Thomas, First Officer Howse and Radio Officer Jackson. *En route* they called at Geraldton; they carried a ton and a half of gelignite, a ton and a half of vegetables and medical supplies. They returned with Captain Smirnoff and crew. Engineer Jenkins coaxed the 'boat along. The prolonged operation of *Camilla* was beginning to tell, and

she was taking 200 gallons of water a night in her bilges, there was metal in the engine-oil filters and the damage to the wing-tip remained. Eventually, Bill Bennett called it a day. They were, supposedly, still operating in accordance with civil, peacetime regulations, and Bennett was now unwilling to sign *Camilla* out as airworthy. It befell Captains Sims and Thomas, ably assisted by Bill Bennett, to stage *Camilla* along the southern coast of Australia to Sydney, and home, which they gained on 18 March 1942.

Adding to QANTAS's problems, the RAAF requested another 'boat, to make good the loss of *Coogee*. QANTAS were being stretched into non-existence. It was agreed to release *Clifton*, the first S.33. All that was left of the QEA Empire Flying-Boat fleet were *Camilla, Corinthian* and *Coriolanus*.

Clifton was impressed into RAAF service as A18-14, and on 14 March, Flight Lieutenant Caldwell delivered her from Rose Bay to No. 33 Sqn RAAF. There then followed a period of intense training, with regular day and night flights being made to Port Moresby. Australia stood isolated from the air routes. It was not until American air freighters arrived through the Pacific and the tortuous Perth to Ceylon sector was established by Catalina, that rapid transport out of area was re-established.

For QANTAS the situation worsened. Just after midnight on 22 March, *Corinthian* crashed whilst alighting at Darwin. Although Captain Tapp (first officer) recalled conditions were good, the commander, Captain Ambrose, may have been dazzled by a searchlight. *Corinthian* seemed to fly into the water, short of the flare-path, unchecked. Alternatively she may have struck debris in the unswept area. Nevertheless, the planing bottom broke and the 'boat capsized. The incident was exacerbated by the poorly lashed load of gun barrels, ammunition boxes, tripods and bales of wire which broke free and breached the hull. In addition to the crew, twelve US military personnel were on board.

The rescue launch picked up those survivors at hand but two could not be accounted for. Courageously, Tapp re-entered the dark, sinking hull of *Corinthian* and searched for the two missing men. Their bodies were not located. Nine of the passengers were slightly hurt but Captain Ambrose and two passengers were severely injured.

Shortly before midnight on 25 July 1942, Japanese raiders, believed to be flying-boats, bombed Townsville for the first time. The bombs fell wide and no damage was done. Around this time, Darwin and Port Moresby were also attacked, Port Moresby being struck by over thirty enemy aircraft. Casualties and damage were only slight. Three days after the first Townsville raid, a sole aircraft struck. On this occasion the enemy was driven off by anti-aircraft fire and forced to jettison its bombs. The sporadic air raids continued, and on 1 August 1942, there was a significant attack on Darwin, and for the first time, attacks were made on Port Headland and Horn Island in the Torres Straits. Darwin was attacked twice more, on 24 August and 20 September.

The two remaining QANTAS 'boats, *Camilla* and *Coriolanus*, were chartered to the Department of Civil Aviation and, during March and April, flew fifteen flights between Sydney and Darwin. The 'boats were frequently diverted to Milne Bay, taking in troops, trained bushmen and stores, and bringing out personnel going on leave and wounded. On 15 June 1942, QANTAS began a service to Noumea from Sydney. However, in July and August the 'boats were again chartered and came under the control of RAAF Air Transport Command. The charter was somewhat flexible by nature. At first, eight return flights from Townsville to Port Moresby were planned, the first on 12 August, the second the following day and two more on 14 August. QANTAS were then asked to extend the route to Milne Bay, which would necessitate a night stop at Port Moresby. The route was Townsville–Cairns–Port Moresby–Milne Bay, followed by a direct return to Townsville. Port Moresby had already experienced air raids and the 'boats were to be moored there during the full moon. The crews were apprehensive but luck was with them.

Radio silence, poor charts and atrocious monsoon weather rendered the extension to Milne Bay difficult. Lester Brain had been there a few weeks previously and escaped with a load of fifty passengers, only moments before the first Japanese air raid. Departures from Port Moresby were usually before dawn, thus a relatively early arrival and departure at Milne Bay could be achieved. Often, the load to Milne Bay was 31 fully-equipped soldiers, but for a few days, nothing but 25 lb fragmentation bombs was carried. A more unusual load was a complete B-26 plexiglass nose cone; more welcome was 3,000 lb of mail. Towards the end of the contract, Captain Denny was almost caught upon the surface at Milne Bay, on 25 August, when Japanese invasion forces landed an hour after he had left. After two weeks of fighting at Milne Bay, the Japanese invaders were repulsed and driven back into the sea.

Throughout New Guinea, ground forces maintained a heroic struggle, supported by QANTAS land- and sea-planes. As from 20 December 1942, the charter became a daily schedule for *Camilla* and *Coriolanus* and they were now able to night-stop at Milne Bay. Flights along the Papuan coast were difficult; tropical monsoon weather, few navigational aids and ever-possible enemy aircraft added to the challenge. Flight plans were frequently changed at short notice, as the military situation demanded, and fuel reserves dictated that 'boats regularly operated at the maximum weights. Furthermore, as the servicing facilities were so poor, 'boats still had to return to Sydney for major overhaul. The crossing of the Coral Sea was beneath the weather and around the waterspouts. At Milne Bay, the facilities may have been rudimentary but military hospitality was warm. Crews left the 'comfort' of their 'boats with greatcoats to ward off the rain, mosquito ointment to keep the insects at bay and tin hats in case an air raid should develop.

On New Year's Day 1943, *Camilla* and Captain Crowther were diverted to Milne Bay, owing to poor weather at Port Moresby. As they arrived unexpectedly, the refuelling barge was absent, collecting fruit from outlying plantations. Laboriously, Crowther had to refuel from cans, straining the fuel through a chamois leather. During refuelling, Crowther was asked to fly to the Trobriand Islands to rescue the crew of an American bomber which, returning from a raid against New Britain, had been attacked by fighters and ditched. Friendly natives had taken the survivors ashore and alerted the Allies by radio. Crowther calculated there was sufficient daylight, and with the minimum of fuel he got airborne. Despite the poor charts he found the islands and alighted. Cautiously they taxied, for the sea bottom shelved steeply and it was necessary to get close to the beach for the anchor to bite. The crew waited, and before long, a small native lugger bearing the survivors appeared in the bay. A treacherous current made the transfer of USAAF Major Kuhl's crew, one of whom was dead, difficult. They returned to Milne Bay and touched down with barely sufficient light. On 5 January, *Camilla* and Crowther returned to the Trobriands to rescue another crew, this time from a Liberator.

On 5 January 1943, *Coriolanus* and Captain Hussey were at Port Moresby taking on thirty-three sick and wounded, when an air raid alert was declared and loading stopped. Whilst waiting for the raid to pass, Hussey was asked to rescue the crew of another four-engined bomber; this would mean offloading the wounded. Hussey was persuaded by General Kenney, Commander Fifth Air Force, that the rescue was warranted, and a doctor and medical attendant were put aboard. A fighter escort was provided, and over 6 and 7 January the rescue flight was flown. The initial search centred upon Wamena Island, to the north of Milne Bay, but nothing was found. A party was, however, located at Goodenough Island, about fifty miles west of Wamena Island. Having alighted in the open sea, *Coriolanus* taxied in to the shore, seeking the crew. They had crash landed after losing an engine and suffering a fuel leak during an attack on Rabaul. The crew was whisked back to base at Milne Bay and Hussey continued his schedule.

During these flights, thirty tons of equipment and 260 passengers were carried in and 230 people evacuated. The war was beginning to turn against the Japanese, and by the close of January 1943, southern Papua was free of invaders.

QANTAS received a strange request in April 1943. Their two 'boats were to proceed from Townsville to Cairns and remain on call to the Army, for an indefinite period. Japanese troops, about fifty in number, had been reported in the Nassua River area, ninety miles north of Karumba, overlooking the Gulf of Carpentaria. Tapp, in *Camilla*, went to Karumba and landed troops and equipment. The following day the force was taken up to Staaten River. There was no sign of an enemy invasion and both 'boats were stood down and returned to Townsville.

Whilst, for the past year, QANTAS had achieved valiant service from its Empire 'Boats, the RAAF had been having trials and tribulations with their 'boats. *Calypso*, it will be remembered, had, along with *Centaurus*, been impressed in September 1939. She first served with No. 11 Sqn, until 18 November 1941, and was then transferred to No. 20 Sqn, only to be further transferred to No. 33 Sqn. On 8 August 1942, Flight Lieutenant Mather took part in a search for survivors from the MV *Mamutu*, which had been torpedoed off Daru, to the west of Port Moresby. A lifeboat with eight survivors aboard was spotted, and despite rough weather, Mather attempted an open sea landing. The heavy swell proved too much for the thinly skinned nose and the water poured in. *Calypso* bounced. The second impact tore away the lower hull, and within a minute or two, *Calypso* was slipping beneath the waves, taking a crewman with her. The remaining crew scrambled aboard the two dinghies that broke free from the wreckage. By now the lifeboat was nowhere to be seen, but one of the MV *Mamutu*'s survivors, William Griffin, had left the lifeboat to swim to *Calypso*. He was dragged into one of the dinghies. After two exhausting days trying to keep the dinghies together, the party made a landfall, in the early hours of 10 August, on the shores of the Torres Straits, off the Fly River. Then, assisted by natives, they spent eight days walking the inhospitable coast, before reaching Kikori and eventual passage by lugger to Port Moresby, where they arrived on 28 August.

As more land planes became available to the RAAF, it was decided to transfer the remaining 'boats, *Coolangatta* and *Clifton*, to No. 41 (Sea Transport) Sqn. This was commanded by John Hampshire and was formed with just the two Empire 'Boats on 21 August 1942. They remained with 41 Sqn until 1943 and, during that time, operated between Australia and New Guinea.

On 26 June 1943, *Clifton*, followed three days later by *Coolangatta*, was returned to QANTAS. No sooner had *Clifton* been transferred, than she was sent to Horne Island (Cape York) to complete a freight task to Tanahmerah in New Guinea, about a hundred miles north of Merauke, on the Digoel River. *Clifton* operated as part of 'Torres Force', completing a task which she had started under the 41 Sqn guise.

With the return of the RAAF 'boats potentially bolstering the QANTAS fleet, *Camilla* was flying a regular service to Port Moresby. Less than an hour after noon on 22 April 1943, Captain Koch, survivor of *Corio*, lifted *Camilla* from the waters at Townsville. He set a northerly heading, on the regular run to Port Moresby. The weather forecast was fair although, in April, it can be most treacherous. Sprawled among the cargo were twenty-two RAAF and five US Army personnel. As Koch was leaving Townsville, Ambrose, now recovered from his Darwin crash in *Corinthian*, was departing Port Moresby. If the Port Moresby weather was poor, Ambrose was expected to break radio silence and give Koch a warning. There was no warning and, what is more, the expected tropical front had not materialized. On *Camilla*, twenty minutes before landfall, they took a sunshot. It was at this stage that events took an ominous

turn. Port Moresby reported a cloud base of around 600 feet and visibility of 1,100 yards. Koch contemplated a precautionary landing at his landfall but that was obscured. However, there really was no problem, as the coast ahead of them – the route to Port Moresby – lay clear.

Heartened by an improved weather report from Port Moresby – 1,000 feet cloud base and 2,000 yards visibility in light rain – they routed direct. As Koch approached the Basilisk Lighthouse, outside Port Moresby harbour, he entered the light rain. Ahead of him stood an evil, black cyclonic cloud; he thought of alighting to the north of the Basilisk light and taxiing in, but the shallows were uncharted. Port Moresby now reported, 'Visibility nil. Can *Camilla* hold off? A flare-path is being laid.' Koch held off.

Koch was confident that the local weather would improve once night fell, and instrument flying presented no problem. He circled the Basilisk, but after a few circuits, he decided to explore the coast for an alternative landing site. There was no improvement. He returned to the Basilisk but was now unable to see it. Port Moresby radioed the flare-path was laid but visibility was still nil! Koch continued past the port towards the anchorage at Yule Island. *En route*, he instructed Purser Barley to get the passengers into life-jackets and brief them on the life-raft and emergency exits, as they might be about to make a precautionary landing. The impenetrable weather extended along the coast. Seawards it was clear.

Radio Officer Phillips asked Port Moresby to switch on the radio beacon, for they would home onto it. They climbed to 4,000 feet. Visibility nil. For a couple of hours now, Koch had fought to keep *Camilla* under control, bucked by the tropical storm. He and First Officer Peak waited. But darkness would not wait. Koch knew he had no option. He had insufficient fuel to return to Townsville, and Port Moresby was the only alighting place. He started to search out a likely area for an open sea landing. After several searches he was down to 90 gallons, 45 minutes. At about 19:15, they gave Port Moresby their intentions. They would make an instrument descent on autopilot. They crossed the radio beacon one last time on a southerly heading and flew on for ten minutes, slipping down to 1,500 feet. Descending at 105 miles per hour and 200 feet a minute, it was possible to 'fly' the 'boat onto the water using the autopilot. Hopefully, they would spot the surface at 100 or so feet and ease *Camilla* down the last few feet manually.

The ten-minute outbound leg had been flown, the stopwatch was reset and Purser Barley went below to fetch cool drinks for the labouring pilots. The bow and wing lights failed to pierce the darkness; Peak peered into the silver rain which streaked the windscreen. Carefully Koch caressed *Camilla* through the procedure. A mix of torrential rain, it always found its way in, and tense, humid sweat soaked the two pilots. The altimeter showed less than 100 feet as Peak saw the surface. He called to Koch, who disengaged the autopilot and eased the nose up to lessen the rate of descent.

Peak now announced the sea was still some way below. It was a difficult sea to judge, visibility was horrendous in the rain and dark. Too late, speed was falling as *Camilla* adopted a landing attitude. They stalled. The nose dropped and Koch recalled seeing a 400-feet-a-minute rate of descent and minus 30 feet on the instruments. *Camilla* crashed and broke up; it was about 19:45.

Koch, strapped in, found himself trapped as the stricken *Camilla* settled. He reached down, freed himself and, fighting for breath, struck up to the surface through the remains of the windscreen. In the cabins of *Camilla*, many should have perished as the cargo broke free but by a miracle there were eighteen survivors.

Aubrey Koch came to the surface and called out the names of his crew. There was no response. He swam to the rear door and, noticing that the life-raft had not deployed, tried to get aboard to free it. Koch was met by the army boot of a soldier standing at the jammed door. He was marshalling the survivors into the water. Again Koch tried and again he was repulsed. Possibly the 'doorman' thought Koch was trying to get aboard in a panicked attempt to save his own skin. Men were scrambling through the half-open door and the escape hatch windows. The 'boat was sinking and Koch swam across to the port float, though the struts were broken and the wing was already awash. He climbed up onto the wing, with the idea of freeing the life-raft via the top escape hatch. Once clear of the water, Koch felt a sticky warmness, his right elbow was severely cut. One of the survivors, now on top of *Camilla*, applied a tourniquet. Koch passed out and slipped into the seas. The fresh dousing revived him and once again he clambered onto the wing. *Camilla* shuddered and sank beneath them.

In the water with Koch were three of the passengers, one of them a non-swimmer without a life-jacket. Koch told his fellow survivors that a message had been sent to Port Moresby and they knew exactly where they had crashed. A boat would be upon them soon. The weather cleared and the Basilisk light was visible. They swam towards it. Suddenly a launch appeared, a searchlight swung towards them … and then the light dimmed and the launch turned away.

They swam all night but the Basilisk light seemed to be receding. The current was taking them eastward, out to sea and, by dawn, Koch could see they were nearing Bootless Inlet. The four continued to swim. At around midday, First Officer Peak, who was floating on a kit bag, joined them. Now five, they continued to battle against the current.

Finally, at about three that afternoon they were picked up by a steamer, with a schooner in tow. Another four were brought ashore by the natives and nine were rescued by the 'crash' boat. The warm water and life-jackets saved many. Alas, eleven passengers and two crew, Radio Officer Phillips and Purser Barley, perished.

However, up until the loss of *Camilla*, she and *Coriolanus* had made 564 flights, during which 200 tons of mail and freight and 12,750 passengers were flown in support of the New Guinea campaign.

Clifton, one of the two S.33s, had been impressed into RAAF service in 1942 as A18-14, replacing *Corio*. She was released to QANTAS on 23 June 1943, as VH-CRC. The last RAAF flight by an Empire 'Boat took place on 13 July 1943 when John Hampshire ferried *Coolangatta* from Townsville to Rose Bay. Back with QANTAS, the Empires continued to fare badly.

On 4 August 1943, Captain Nichol was attempting to alight *Coriolanus* at Rose Bay when one of the floats struck an object. The float was pushed backwards and the struts collapsed. Nichol applied full power and managed to get airborne again. Once safely in the air, he flew down to Botany Bay, where the QANTAS staff had been alerted to expect him. He touched down and was immediately surrounded by small craft which disgorged men who scrambled up onto the wing to keep the damaged float from entering the water. She was safely beached, and once repaired, *Coriolanus* was returned to Rose Bay.

On 10 January 1944, *Coolangatta*, now reregistered VH-CRB, entered a storm between Rathmines and Newcastle. She was being flown by Captain F. A. Reeve when, struck by turbulence, she dropped hundreds of feet. The passengers were caught unawares and several were flung against the interior, causing injuries to themselves and damage to the 'boat. *Clifton*'s career came to an end on 18 January that year in Rose Bay. Captain Ashley was receiving night-landing instruction from Captain Hussey. They porpoised, skipped into the air, stalled, hit the bay and sank. One of the crew was slightly hurt.

Coolangatta was soon to follow. On 11 October 1944, she had been airborne only twenty minutes when Captains Brain and Cauldwell, both extremely experienced, decided to return to Rose Bay as they had noticed a loss of oil pressure from the starboard-inner engine. On landing, they stalled in from ten or twelve feet and broke up on impact. One passenger was killed and two passengers and two crew were seriously injured.

At the end was *Coriolanus*, which had been sold to QANTAS in September 1942 and spent most of her life routing between Townsville, Cairns, Port Moresby and Milne Bay. On 27 February 1945, whilst being launched at Rose Bay, she was allowed to collide with a tractor, causing significant damage to her hull. She was repaired.

With the war over, *Coriolanus* found herself back on part of the all 'Red Route'. On 25 September, commanded by Captain Crowther, she returned to Singapore. It was a far call from that dark night on 4 February 1942, when, courageously, Captain Crowther had taken the last Empire Flying-Boat out of Singapore. However, the end of the flying-boats was in sight, and, somewhat ironically on 4 October 1945, Captain Caldwell flew *Coriolanus* off Rose Bay for Singapore in order to survey the proposed land-plane route. They arrived in Singapore on 8 October. Four days later, *Coriolanus* departed Singapore, carrying home 34 Australian ex-PoWs. They arrived in Sydney on 17 October.

There was great demand upon the shipping lines for

passages, as families and friends attempted to reunite themselves after the conflict. At the request of the Governments of Australia and New Zealand, QANTAS commenced a service linking Sydney with Fiji, via Noumea. The first flight was made by Captain Denny in *Coriolanus*, on 17 November. And it was this newly formed service that had the distinction of being the last service to be operated by an Empire Flying-Boat. On 20 December 1947, 'The Grand Old Lady' – *Coriolanus* – touched down at Rose Bay under the deft hand of Captain J. Lower, on return from Noumea. A bare three days later, *Coriolanus* was sold to Sims Metal Co. for scrap and was dismantled at Rose Bay in 1948. All that remained were the log books and nameplate, which were handed to Hudson Fysh by the Operations Manager, Captain Crowther. *Coriolanus*, the most travelled 'boat, had flown 2,523,641 miles in 18,500 hours.

Post-war, QANTAS assisted BOAC in their flying-boat service to Australia, and in the early/mid-1950s operated three second-hand Sandringhams themselves, but overall the airline went the American way with Douglas and Lockheed. Although flying-boats were flown by several smaller operators in Australia, the final operational chapter to this tale is that of TEAL and New Zealand.

CHAPTER THIRTEEN

New Zealand at War

Military use of TEAL 'boats – New Zealand hastens Awarua *– Awarua despatched – Awarua and surface raiders* Orion *and* Komet *– Turakina sunk – Rangitane sunk – Chief of Air Staff's Inquiry – Standing orders – Militarization of the 'boats, bombs, guns and radar – Liaison with No. 11 Sqn RAAF – January '42* Awarua *to Honolulu with Nash – Covert mission – Engine problems – Hamilton Standard propellers – No more specials – 1947 final beaching – After the Empires.*

The training, survey and VIP flights of *Aotearoa*, before the inaugural flight of 2 May 1940, conceal another story. The true nature of many of the flights of the two TEAL 'boats has rarely been publicly acknowledged. At last, there was an air-route connecting New Zealand and Australia, and to maintain this service across the Tasman throughout the war, as the two 'boats did, was quite an achievement. However, there is another story to tell, that of the TEAL flying-boats' military service.

In April 1939, a Defence Conference, which hosted delegations from the United Kingdom, Australia and New Zealand, was held in Wellington. One item discussed was the potential threat posed by Japanese Navy vessels and German commerce raiders. Although the conference identified a requirement for reconnaissance of the waters around Tonga, Fiji, the New Hebrides and eastern New Guinea, the Royal New Zealand Air Force (RNZAF) lacked modern long-range aircraft. To defend New Zealand's coast line, a squadron of Vickers Wellingtons was being formed in England, but they were soon donated to assist in the European conflict and became No. 75 (NZ) Sqn.

The conference realized the potential of the S.30s for long-range reconnaissance, and the New Zealand Government's Secretary of State sought approval from His Majesty's Government (the Governor-General) to use the TEAL 'boats, even if this meant interrupting the Empire Airmail Service. Approval for armed reconnaissance was given in a secret telegram from the Governor-General to the Secretary of Dominion Affairs on 24 May 1939. However, in July, London expressed hopes that the New Zealand Government would consult them regarding the best use of the flying-boats.

With the approval to utilize the 'boats for military service realized, armament was next considered but there seemed little threat. Air attacks upon the flying-boats were not envisaged, and if the flying-boats kept unidentified shipping at bay, they would not be fired upon. Moreover, other than possibly armed merchantmen, no fighting ships were believed to be within the area of operation.

In July 1939, Group Captain Saundby (Department of Research, Air Ministry, London) advised the Headquarters Royal New Zealand Air Force (HQRNZAF), Wellington, that the RAF were examining the possibility of arming the 'C-class' 'boats and he would keep HQRNZAF abreast of progress. HQRAFNZ replied on 12 July, saying air opposition was not expected and 'defensive armament therefore not essential' but a cheap [sic] rear gun would be acceptable. Most desirable however, was a capability to carry the 250 lb General Purpose (GP) and the 540 lb 'B' (buoyant) anti-shipping bomb. To this, the Air Ministry responded that Short Bros had no plans for such modifications, but the Ministry would examine the requirement and if possible despatch modification kits to New Zealand.

Rather than delay delivery of the 'boats, it was decided to modify them in New Zealand, and procurement of Lewis guns, one for an upper mount and two for side mounting, was pursued.

London's reservations regarding use of the 'boats expressed in July became agreement in principle in a secret telegram of 1 September. Following on, in October 1939, the High Commissioner, London, telegrammed New Zealand's Prime Minister, querying if first intentions were to fly reconnaissance flights or to commence the trans-Tasman service. Meanwhile, Australia, although content for the service to go ahead, was equally aware of her lack of long-range aircraft and, bearing in mind the recent impressment of *Centaurus* and *Calypso* into the RAAF, she too thought military use of the TEAL 'boats should be considered.

Wellington's reply, dated 5 October, proposed not to use the 'boats for military work until the necessity arose. More to the point, Wellington reminded London of the lack of suitable aircraft currently in New Zealand and requested the delivery of *Awarua* be hastened. Similarly, the timely delivery of the third 'boat, *Australia,* now lying damaged at Basra, was sought. As a response, Wellington was advised the Air Ministry had deferred the decision on delivery of, and policy for, *Awarua* to the Government, and in turn, the United Kingdom Government could not foresee inauguration before the war's end. New Zealand's Prime Minister replied,

18 October, that the subject would be raised when his deputy, Mr Fraser, arrived in London in November.

Shorts informed the Air Ministry of the headway made in arming the 'boats, on 1 November 1939. They considered the necessary strengthening parts could be manufactured and sent to New Zealand, but had found it impractical to mount the four-position Universal Bomb Carrier behind the outboard engines, as it interfered with the float bracing wires. However, it was possible to mount one carrier outboard and three other carriers inboard. Thus a load of 8 2 250 lb GP Semi-Armour-Piercing or Anti-Submarine bombs or 6 2 'B' bomb and 2 2 250 lb [sic] could be carried. It was, however, commented upon that in order to maintain a safe landing weight whilst carrying the full 2,000 lb armament, the fuel load should not exceed 1,412 gallons. In New Zealand, a less costly proposal to install the armaments locally was set before the Cabinet and accepted.

Deputy Prime Minister Fraser arrived in England and, on 3 November, attended a meeting at the Air Ministry to consider priorities for civil aviation. Fraser's timely reminder of his country's generous loan of the No. 75 (NZ) Sqn Wellingtons towards the British war effort may well have prompted the British Government to release *Awarua*. Moreover, Fraser argued the two remaining S.30s (it was still hoped that *Clare*, née *Australia*, would join TEAL) were still required to join *Aotearoa* in making reconnaissance and training flights to New Zealand's surrounding islands. On a commercial level, if the other 'boats were not delivered, Pan Am could easily become established across the Tasman, before TEAL was ready.

The Air Staff considered the matter carefully and, overall, felt the military aspects were paramount and the requirements for the RAF to patrol the Atlantic, especially now it was known that German capital ships were abroad, ought to be given priority. However, they were mindful of the situation in New Zealand and were aware that only *Aotearoa* and a handful of totally unsuitable aircraft were available to patrol New Zealand's waters. They considered the force inadequate to counter the potential threat that would be imposed should armed merchantmen or surface raiders enter those waters. On balance, it was decided, on 5 November, that the available 'boat, *Awarua*, should be handed to New Zealand without delay and the third 'boat should be repaired and handed to New Zealand as soon as possible.

The availability of the 'boats was being addressed, and in early December 1939 HQRNZAF corresponded with TEAL as to the competence of the TEAL navigators. Burgess replied, writing that they (Craig, Chapman and himself) were RNZAF reservists and were probably better qualified than many RAF navigators, and were well prepared for any reconnaissance tasks.

The subject was raised in greater detail by the Commodore Commanding New Zealand Squadron, Royal Navy, in a letter to the Naval Secretary at Wellington, early in December. Points raised by the Commodore were:

TEAL aircrew should be given training in reconnaissance duties and, as Garden and Craig are reservist officers, it will be more expeditious to train the TEAL crews than calling up a Royal Navy Volunteer Reserve (RNVR) officer and training him to observe from the air. It will however, be necessary to train the radio operator in Naval procedures and codes. The Commodore proposes a two-week training period, spread around the scheduled flights, commencing as soon as possible. He presumes the crews will be seconded temporarily to the RNZAF and uniformed. It is feared the Germans may retaliate and attack civil aircraft in Europe, if it is known that reconnaissance flights against their armed merchantmen are being flown by 'civil' aircraft.

The presence of surface raiders accelerated matters. In June 1940, Allied Naval Intelligence was alerted to reports of German surface activity to the east of New Zealand. On 19 June, SS *Niagara* struck a mine that had been laid by the German Raider *Orion*. The following day, Burgess, in *Awarua*, was asked to keep a look-out for shipping. There was some confusion as to whether or not sightings should be reported in code, in clear or held until they arrived back in Auckland. As it was, no ships were seen.

On 25 June 1940, the Minister of Defence was asked to approve arrangements for *Awarua* to make a search of the Kermadec Islands the following day. Permission for the TEAL crew to be seconded to the RNZAF was also sought. For this flight the crews were given temporary ranks. Captain Burgess became a Flight Lieutenant with three years' seniority; First Officer Craig, a Flight Lieutenant; Second Officer Peak [sic] was appointed Flying Officer, as were Radio Officers E. D. Nicholl and Reid. Flight Clerk R. A. Phillips was appointed Sergeant. Accompanying them would be Wing Commander Grundy and Lieutenant-Commander Lewis. It was also requested that the New Zealand Government accept responsibility for insuring the 'boat and that TEAL be paid 7s10d (39p) per mile.

Awarua and HMS *Achilles* duly arrived on task and *Achilles* intercepted a message from *Awarua* stating she was in the Curtis Island area, and, at 11:15, another message reported nothing found. At 13:45, *Achilles* sighted *Awarua*. Both craft returned to Auckland. Wing Commander Grundy reported, on 29 June, that although the search had taken 12 hours and 40 minutes, covered an area 110 by 150 miles (using Curtis Island as a datum), no enemy shipping had been sighted. Bill Peek recalls that on their first 'military' mission they flew in civilian clothes but thereafter they were sworn in and received temporary commissions. After the flight, all paper-work pertaining to their brief service in the military was destroyed. Towards the end of Bill's time with TEAL, a uniform allowance was made available.

From July 1940, the Australian Government permitted TEAL to make reconnaissance flights at short notice, in the Tonga, Fiji and New Hebrides area, but details of the immediately subsequent military flights are scant.

However, on 15 July 1940, TEAL were advised that the New Zealand Government would require a 'boat for the period 19–26 July and an 06:00 departure was being planned. The flight would proceed to Suva and Captain Burgess and his crew were preferred. In mid-August, a special flight to carry a party of American journalists was arranged.

On 20 August, the steamer *Turakina* was sunk by a German surface vessel whilst midway between Australia and New Zealand. In response, before dawn on 21 August, *Awarua* took off from Auckland to search the area, well to the west of Cape Farewell. At about 08:00, and again during the afternoon, HMS *Achilles* spotted *Awarua*, but as *Achilles* entered the search area, *Awarua* withdrew to Auckland. The culprit vessel was the surface raider *Orion* and she had fled to waters south and west of Australia. However, Naval authorities believed she had remained in New Zealand's waters, and fruitless searches to the north and south of New Zealand were carried out on 22 August. After a few more days chasing spurious reports, the search died down.

Further flights included a reconnaissance around the Chatham Islands (to the south-east of New Zealand) flown by Burgess, and a search of the South Island fjords, with Oscar Garden commanding *Awarua* and Eddie Brooke-Taylor acting as RNZAF pilot-observer. In a different vein, Pan Am wished to fly some personnel to Australia. They had proposed to fly them across the Pacific to Noumea and then give them passage to Sydney on a yacht. New Zealand's Prime Minister suggested they travelled to Auckland, then took the TEAL to Australia.

In November 1940, the German surface raider *Orion*, accompanied by *Komet*, entered the waters to the east of New Zealand and began searching for vessels. Eventually, on 25 November, they chanced upon the *Holmwood*, midway between the Chatham Islands and Wellington. The raiders seized her crew, passengers and part of the cargo of sheep, before sinking the boat with gunfire. *Holmwood* had not transmitted a distress call and New Zealand was unaware of her fate. Less than two days later, in the early hours of 27 November, the New Zealand Shipping Company's motor-liner *Rangitane* was attacked, boarded and sunk about 450 miles to the north of the Chatham Islands. On this occasion, *Rangitane* did manage to get messages through to New Zealand stating they were being attacked. *Rangitane* gave her position as South 36 degrees 58 minutes, West 175 degrees 22 minutes (about 300 miles east of New Zealand). *Rangitane*'s passengers and crew, over 300 in total, were taken aboard *Komet*.

Acting upon the message from *Rangitane*, HMS *Achilles* and the TEAL 'boats were made ready. This first 'scramble' of the TEAL 'boat highlighted weaknesses in liaison along the tortuous chain of command from the Central War Room Wellington, through the Officer Commanding No. 1 (General Reconnaissance) Squadron RNZAF, Whenuapi, to Captain Burgess, Chief Pilot TEAL. In the TEAL Control Office at Mechanics

Bay was one Flight Lieutenant Canavan, control officer. Also present was Pilot Officer Robinson, the TEAL traffic superintendent and liaison officer. Following the operation, the Chief of Air Staff, Group Captain H. W. L. Saunders, convened an inquiry to examine the events surrounding the reconnaissance.

It would appear that before dawn on 27 November, Flight Lieutenant Canavan rang the TEAL Control Office to ascertain the positions of the flying-boats, only to discover the Chief of Air Staff had already contacted TEAL. Presumably Air HQ had been alerted to *Rangitane*'s plight. Canavan then contacted Air HQ and was briefed on the situation. His reaction was to alert Musick Point radio station and the high-speed launches. Canavan then awaited official notification.

One and a half hours later, Flight Lieutenant Canavan received orders from the Naval Base and in turn he contacted the Commanding Officer of No. 1 (GR) Sqn, Squadron Leader (later Air Commodore Sir Geoffrey 'Jumbo') Roberts. Canavan assumed Roberts would board his RNZAF men at Hobsonville, where *Aotearoa* lay. As it was, Roberts decided to board his men at Mechanics Bay. At 07:00, as *Aotearoa*'s crew assembled upon the slip at Hobsonville, Canavan received from Robinson the first indication that 'something might be happening shortly'. Canavan expected *Aotearoa* to be at Mechanics Bay by 08:30. However, it was 09:20 before she arrived, and finally at 11:14 she was airborne. Meanwhile, HMS *Achilles* had steamed out of Lyttleton, towards the scene of the engagement, at 08:00.

In addition to Captain Burgess, *Aotearoa* carried First Officer Brownjohn, Second Officer Higgs, Radio Officer Whillans and Flight Steward Bury. The RNZAF personnel included Sub-Lieutenant Crisp, Flying Officer Parry and Sergeant McDowell. It was assumed the raiders would seek refuge in the waters to the south and east, so *Aotearoa* was set on course to intercept *Komet* and *Orion*. They arrived in their search area at 14:21 and they stayed on task until 17:51. At first the weather was quite good, there being 9/10 cumulus base 2,000 feet, with tops at 4,500 feet, a visibility of 20 miles and a wind speed of 15 knots. With darkness descending, the weather worsened to give an 800-foot cloud base and, in scattered rain showers, the visibility reduced to 500 yards; however, outside the showers, the visibility remained 15 to 20 miles. Eventually, the search was abandoned due to low visibility and poor light. *Aotearoa* turned for home and landed at Auckland just after 22:30.

Whilst *Aotearoa* had been the standby 'boat, *Awarua* was returning from Sydney according to the schedule. Oscar Garden brought *Awarua* into Auckland harbour around 11:00, on 27 November. He proceed directly to the mooring and offloaded his passengers, but *Awarua* was not taken to the refuelling pontoon for almost an hour. It was 14:20 before she too departed for the search area. *Awarua*'s crew were Captain Garden, First Officer C. Griffiths, Second Officer C. A. Macdonald and Radio Officer Nicholl. As did *Aotearoa*, they carried out a search across the expected track of the raiders, this time to the north and west of *Rangitane's* position. Nothing was seen. Apart from the odd shower and some patchy haze, the weather was better than that to the south, but at 19:00 they had reached the end of their search and turned for Auckland. They alighted at 23:31.

Unbeknown to Oscar Garden and crew, Captain Weyer, master of the *Orion*, did log the sighting of an aircraft that evening. He recorded that, whilst 150 miles north-east of the sinking position, *Orion* stopped engines when an aircraft, mis-identified as a Wellington, was seen barely two miles away. Fortunately, for Weyer and possibly for Garden, there was a light haze and the aircraft, most likely *Awarua*, turned away from the ship.

The search continued into the second day, and barely sixteen hours after landing, Captain Burgess, now in *Awarua*, was aloft again. His crew, Bill Craig as first officer, Second Officer Higgs and Radio Officer Reid, were joined by Lieutenant-Commander Gilfillan, RNVR, and Flying Officer King, RNZAF.

Before dawn, they were on track to search the area around *Rangitane's* last position. As they flew into the daylight, the outbound weather was overcast and only one sun sight could be taken. A half-hour short of the search area, they spotted something in the water and turned about to investigate. It was nothing and ten minutes later they were back on course. Despite these difficulties, Bill Craig navigated *Awarua* with precision and at 08:10 they arrived upon the search area. Immediately they located an oil slick, six miles long and two miles wide. Below them, several small objects, similar to loaves of bread, were floating in the water. These were photographed and the report, 'Large oil patch at point of attack. Small wreckage. Continuing search', was signalled to the Central War Room Wellington and received at 08:53.

Awarua commenced a square search of the area. At 10:40, they encountered HMS *Achilles* and, by Aldis lamp, signalled their findings. With a visibility of about five miles, but later increasing to ten, they continued their square search. They retired from the search area at 13:10 and were afloat in Auckland at half past four that afternoon.

That evening, Burgess sent his post-flight reports to Air HQ Wellington. He apologized for the lack of Garden's report, but Garden was now *en route* to Sydney and would submit his account upon return. Burgess commented upon Craig's navigation (*Awarua's* flight of 28 November):

> *'The navigation on this flight was excellent and the Navigator, Flight Lieutenant W.J. Craig, deserves special credit as it should be realized that it is not an easy matter to navigate an aircraft and to locate a position approximately 500 miles from the point of departure.'*

Burgess included a hand-written postscript saying the photographs of the oil slick were being processed and would be forwarded to Air HQ.

The raiders had slipped away to the north, and by morning 29 November they were off the Kermadec Islands. Also on 29 November, the *Holmwood,* of which nothing had been heard all this time, was reported overdue. *Awarua* was tasked to search the Chatham Islands, to the south.

According to Craig's post-flight report he left the mooring only five minutes after receiving his orders and a further two minutes later, at 11:40, he was airborne, with First Officer Griffiths, setting a course for the Chatham Islands. Macdonald was the second officer, Reid the radio operator and L. G. McMillan the steward. Bill Peek recalls this may have been the sortie in which he flew, but neither his name, nor the names of any supernumeraries, appear upon the navigation log.

They sighted the Chatham Islands at 15:50, and using the double drift method, Griffiths calculated the wind. Underneath a layer of broken cumulous cloud they started their search at 16:08. The area to be investigated lay to the south-west of the islands, and from 1,500 feet visibility was good. However, by the end of the fourth leg of the search, a change of wind had blown them eight miles south. Moreover, visibility had reduced to ten miles, so the search tracks were closed to eliminate any unsearched areas between the tracks. At 19:15, they ceased searching as visibility had decreased to two miles. No vessels were sighted throughout the search and they touched down at Auckland at almost midnight, 29 November.

It was imperative the raiders were found, and *Awarua* spent only six hours and twenty-one minutes at her mooring before she was airborne at 07:00, on the 30th. First Officer Griffiths and Radio Officer Reid could only have snatched about five hours' sleep between the two sorties. The flight on the 29th had been almost twelve hours long and the flight in which Griffiths and Reid now found themselves would be in excess of eleven hours. The remainder of the TEAL crew were Captain Burgess, Second Officer Higgs and Flight Clerk Phillips. The supernumeraries were Flying Officer Garrick, Sub-Lieutenant Osmint and Sergeant Millar. They were to search an area midway between the Chatham Islands and South Island. When they commenced their search, at 09:30, there was no low cloud and the visibility was 10 to 20 miles. But thirty minutes later they were forced to descend below the 600–1,000-foot cloud base. A few minutes later, they ran into sea fog and from a height of only 50 feet, they could see barely a mile. Although visibility improved, for the remainder of the search they were unable to climb above 800 feet without losing sight of the surface. The wind increased and, below them, a moderate to rough sea was beginning to run. At 13:18, they completed their search and turned for Auckland. Again they entered fog and at 300 feet they chanced across the SS *Maui Pomare*. If the scrappy navigation log is an indication, a very tiring day's flying ended at 17:05.

It is apparent the Chief of Air Staff was concerned about the apparent delays during the 'scramble' of *Awarua* and *Aotearoa* on the 27th. Flight Lieutenant Canning (Air 2), gave a written account of his conversation of the 27th with Flight Lieutenant Canavan. Dated

28 November, Canning's report to the Chief of Air Staff highlighted the refuelling delays and the slow rate at which Canavan received information. Canning made the observation:

'One very marked feature of the operation was the lack of co-operation between the members of the civil staff, i.e. the Air Department and Tasman Empire Airways. There appears to be altogether too much petty jealousy and bickering.'

Canning further observed:

'It is very strongly recommended that Standing Orders be immediately instituted both at Air Liaison Officers Headquarters and at Central Control Tasman Airways. These Standing Orders should show the procedure necessary for both civil and service staff when the presence of a raider is reported.'

On 6 December, Canning's letter was appended to the effect that the Air Staff had drafted standing orders; moreover, 'everything possible was done to get the 'boats off. (and) Flight Lieutenant Canavan had no idea what work was still to be done.'

The standing orders for the Control and Operation of the TEAL 'boats, by the RNZAF, were drafted in early December but the date of issue is uncertain. It would appear the orders took account of other plans then pending, the arming of the 'boats in particular.

In essence, the orders, which were most detailed, specified in particular:

The Chief of Air Staff may requisition the TEAL 'boats for long-range reconnaissance duties. TEAL crews, who are part of the RNZAF Reserve, and RNZAF personnel will form the crews. The RNZAF will provide radar operators, bomb aimers and gunners, in addition to observers (carried on earlier flights). They will also provide an armourer to be responsible for the defensive armament and the 4 × 250 lb bombs.

TEAL is to ensure that at least one 'boat is available at one hour's notice; the second 'boat should be available whenever possible. When tasked, the 'boats will be under the command of the Central War Room Wellington, through OC No. 1 (GR) Sqn RNZAF, at the RNZAF base of Whenuapi, Hobsonville. There, an operations room is to be manned throughout searches and all radio messages to the 'boat are to be coded and transmitted from Musick Point. The TEAL Traffic Superintendent is to act as Liaison Officer at Mechanics Bay'

On 8 December 1940, the Union Steam Ship Company's motor-vessel *Karitane* sent a 'Raider' report from midway between Tasmania and New Zealand. *Achilles* and *Aotearoa* responded, *Aotearoa* slipping at noon. On board were Captain Burgess, with First Officer Craig, R. A. Phillips (appearing on the manifest as Second Officer), Radio Officer Nicholl, Flight Steward McMillan and RNZAF supernumeraries Flight Lieutenant Wilkes and Sergeant Stratford. Seven

minutes later, they set course for position South 42 degrees 20 minutes, East 158 degrees 53 minutes. *Achilles* had barely left harbour when *Karitane* then signalled it had identified the raider as the Dutch tanker, *Nederland*. *Achilles* and *Aotearoa* were recalled at 13:40 and *Aotearoa* landed at 15:15. At the time, the German raiders were 2,500 miles to the north, in the Naru islands.

The next 'Special Reconnaissance Flight', Number 13, on 29 December 1940, is particularly noteworthy. *Awarua*, crewed by Captains Craig and Burgess, with C. A. MacDonald as navigator, Radio Officer Nicholl and Flight Steward McMillan, flew a trial for the RNZAF. The flight carried Squadron Leader Hunter, Flight Sergeant Kells, Leading Aircraftman J. Parr and a Professor White. They were airborne at 05:00 and for four hours flew up and down the east coast of North Island. The post-flight report, signed by Burgess, records, 'The special tests as requested by Professor White were successfully carried out.'

Although the purpose of the tests is not recorded, Squadron Leader Hunter held the post of 'Air 1' at Wellington Air HQ. He had responsibilities towards the operation of TEAL 'boats and apparently considered this trial to be important. Leading Aircraftman J. Parr appears on the manifests of subsequent flights and may have been a radar operator. The presence of Professor White indicates something out of the ordinary. Surely a professor would not be required for a machine-gun or bombing trial? The navigational log makes repeated reference to passing within a mile of various rocks, or other coastal features, and of circling ships at distances of up to ten miles. This flight could have been the first use of Air to Surface Vessel (ASV) radar by the RNZAF from the TEAL 'boats.

Amidst military flights the schedule continued, and at times additional commercial flights were fitted into the busy routine. In January 1941, Pan Am had 30 passengers booked to Auckland, but wishing to connect with Sydney. Following a flood of telegraphic messages between Australia and New Zealand, a TEAL special was laid on to fly the Americans to Australia.

Rumours abounded and there was speculation that the raiders were being informed of ships' positions from enemy agents ashore. These rumours heightened once survivors who had been marooned by the raiders finally got back to New Zealand. Despite the standing orders and the new equipment being fitted, not all flights were executed proficiently. Special Flight 14 was called to readiness on 23 January 1941. Captain Garden received his orders over the telephone from Squadron Leader Hunter at Air HQ. Garden was instructed to search an area centred upon South 32 degrees 59 minutes, West 177 degrees 52 minutes. The *Maui Pomare* had sighted a suspicious vessel. In addition to *Maui Pomare,* four other friendly ships were believed to be in the area. The search was to continue until darkness.

Garden boarded *Aotearoa* with his crew, First Officer Griffiths, Second Officer Brownjohn, Radio Officer Nicholl, Flight Steward MacMillan and, supernumerary,

Flying Officer Hare. At 11:05 they slipped, were airborne two minutes later and turned immediately onto a heading of 023 degrees, destined for the search area. It was standard practice for the captain to check the navigation being done by the second officer. However, on this flight they suffered a tropical cyclone that reduced visibility to nil, pummelled them with torrential rain and severely buffeted the flying-boat. At 1,000 feet above the sea, it was not a pleasant flight. Oscar Garden was fully occupied keeping *Aotearoa* in the air and on course. Griffiths, working at the navigation table in the flight-deck mail compartment, was similarly distracted by the buffeting. At 13:21, they commenced a square search as instructed. To the north-west of the search area the weather was good, but as they turned to the south-east, they re-entered the cyclone. No ships were sighted. At 16:30 they received a signal from Musick Point ordering them to return.

It was only when the navigation log was handed to the chief pilot, Captain Burgess, that anyone realized they had been searching the wrong area. The chart clearly showed the square search centred upon South 32 degrees 59 minutes, **East** 177 degrees 52 minutes and not South 32 degrees 59 minutes, **West** 177 degrees 52 minutes, as it should have been. They had been 210 miles short of their search area.

In his report to the Chief of Air Staff, Captain Burgess wrote:

> *'It is most unfortunate that two fully qualified Navigators should be confused by the Date Line and the only explanation I can give is the possibility of their being over keen in their anxiety to be successful in their search.'*

Oscar Garden and Griffiths could offer no explanation. Griffiths admitted the error was his but in mitigation the weather had been atrocious. Post-mortem and apologies continued, and Maurice Clarke, General Manager of Union Airways, wrote to the Chief of Air Staff and forwarded a copy of the traffic superintendent's log. Although Pilot Officer Robinson's log reveals nothing of interest about the navigational error, it does refer to Aircraftman Parr fitting special equipment. In all it took ninety minutes to install the special equipment (presumably radar), and following departure, Squadron Leader Hunter and Chief Engineer Houchen discussed the need to keep the special equipment installed in the 'boat when it was on standby.

It is difficult to be accurate as to when modifications to arm the 'boats commenced, but the close of 1940 saw the installation of radar, and during early 1941, equipment was being collected, manufactured and prepared for fitting. From Australia, Bill Peek obtained some drawings showing the installation of the Scarff ring within in the aft escape hatch. Using these, with RNZAF assistance, Bill constructed a cupola and fitted the Scarff ring. In addition, a couple of brackets were fitted dead astern, so as to stop over-enthusiastic gunners firing at the tail plane. Bill also helped to fit a bomb-sight in the mooring

TEAL navigation officer at his chart table in the flight-deck mail compartment. (Peek)

hatch cupola, the bomb-release switches in the cabin and brackets for the radar in the aft freight bay. To ensure engine-start, should they land away from base, two high-capacity batteries were carried in the galley. From there a lead could be routed out through the galley window and into the external power socket on the starboard side.

On 2 and 3 January 1941, Wing Commander Granville (T.Arm HQRNZAF) met Squadron Leader George Bolt, Senior Engineering Officer RNZAF Base at Hobsonville, and Owen Houchen, Chief Engineer TEAL. Granville examined progress in arming the 'boats and reported back to the Chief of Air Staff on 7 January. His report is illuminating: Although Scarff rings had been obtained from the RNZAF Baffin squadron, replacement rings to enable the Baffins to continue their training were required. Also outstanding were a number of fittings and other minor pieces to accommodate the military equipment. Moreover, there seemed to be insufficient space to place the gunner of the upper gun (fitted over the escape hatch of the aft passenger compartment) and the drawings supplied did not reflect the construction of the TEAL 'boats.

Regarding bomb loading, that could be accomplished easily at Mechanics Bay working from the Braby pontoon. At dispersed locations, the seven-foot distance from bomb-carrier to water surface could present problems. In order to meet the readiness times, it would be necessary to store bombs at Mechanics Bay but such storage might be opposed by local authorities.

Although the Experimental W/T (radar) had already been fitted on the starboard side of the aft freight compartment, it could be repositioned further aft thus making space for the gunner. To enable the crew to communicate, a seven-position intercom was being fitted. (On Imperial's 'boats, the captain communicated with his dispersed crew by use of a whistle.) Some thought had been given to additional navigational equipment but following consultation with Craig, in the absence of Burgess, more equipment was considered unnecessary. Of interest, Craig commented he believed the RAAF had installed their navigators in the aft freight hold.

There was still concern at the difficulties arising from holding the 'boats at one hour standby. In the past, the 'boats were taken down the Hobsonville slipway, refuelled and towed, in daylight, to Mechanics Bay. They could not be refuelled upon arrival from Australia, as in a refuelled state, they were too heavy to be taken up the slipway. Neither could they lay at Hobsonville, convenient for the RNZAF mechanics to fit the 'military' equipment, as, in the event of an alert, towing down to Mechanics Bay in darkness could prove hazardous.

Houchen had not been told officially of the extent of the modifications but he agreed to let Bolt know when the 'boats would be hangared at Hobsonville, or moored at Mechanics Bay, and available to the modification teams. Houchen also accepted a list of shortages which, in addition to details of gun mountings, he would attempt to obtain from QANTAS.

Following Granville's discussions, Houchen advised Maurice Clarke, General Manager of Union Airways, who in turn notified the TEAL Board. Clarke's main concern was that modifications might be contrary to Certificate of Airworthiness (CofA) regulations and the weight of the equipment fitted to the 'boats would be commercially detrimental. Moreover, with the requirement to keep one 'boat at one-hour standby, whilst the other was on scheduled service, there was little time available for the routine maintenance necessary to fulfil CofA regulations.

Maurice Clarke was particularly concerned that a military requirement to secure the floorboards by wire, to ease hull repairs, or remove them completely was both contrary to regulations governing the security of passenger seating and impractical. Moreover, the Scarff ring and its windshield would cause excessive drag if left in place. Finally, in order to increase buoyancy in the event of hull leak, it had been suggested that bulkheads, with a height of 20 inches, should be constructed at either end of the central passage. These would greatly inconvenience passenger operation and reduce comfort.

As for the flying-boats' structure, Houchen was most disturbed by the proposal to cut a hole in the side of the rear freight compartment for the mounting of the port beam gun. He felt such work should not be attempted without due consultation of Short Bros. Overall, the military argument was once the 'boats had been modified, the change of rôle could be achieved routinely, but Houchen thought such work could take several days. Finally, Granville's report ended with the ominous observation that the Australian 'boats, similarly modified, had been withdrawn from commercial service. This comment raised fears that a similar fate might await the TEAL 'boats.

At the close of January, the RNZAF liaison officer in Melbourne, Group Captain Wilkes, wrote to the Chief of Air Staff and advised of the conversion done by the Australians. A Mr R. S. Robinson, BSc, Aeronautical Engineer, Department of Civil Aviation, had overseen the work. Wilkes stated that flight trials and detailed stress analysis had been completed before the modification. However, he cautioned that as the TEAL 'boats operated at higher weights, the stresses would be considerably more severe. He recommended the 'boats be restressed before metal was cut – this was imperative if the 'boats were to maintain their CofA.

In early February, permission was given to install the upper gun mounts on both aircraft, but there was uncertainty as to whether or not bomb carriers should be fitted permanently. Following a trial during which the racks were fitted in five minutes, it was decided not to fit the racks permanently. It was also decided that the offensive load would be 8 × 250 lb General Purpose bombs, fused instantaneously, nose and tail. As it would be necessary to load the bombs at Mechanics Bay, storage for the weapons was sought.

A week later, Bolt reported to Air HQ that both machines had been modified to accept the upper gun and bomb gear, but he sought advice as to the permanent fitting of the Scarff ring and windshield. He said it took two men about an hour and a half to fit the gun and rings. These could be modified so that one man could fit them in 45 minutes. Bolt was ready to fit the side doors for the beam guns, but four days would be required to complete this job and he awaited authority. He too expressed uncertainty about cutting into the hull, and further asked if fittings for the carriage of flares should be incorporated in the forward freight compartment.

On 18 February, by way of a letter to be considered as 'MOST SECRET', the Chief of Air Staff advised TEAL that the upper gun mount and shield were to be permanently fitted; however, the gun would not be carried, and bomb carriers would be fitted whilst the 'boat was standing by. Access to the 'boats by armourers was requested. Of the 1,468 lb of military equipment envisaged, only 130 lb of it was to be installed permanently.

Once the military equipment had been fitted to *Aotearoa* and *Awarua*, RNZAF aircrew were required as operators. On 5 March, Squadron Leader Hunter wrote to the CO of 1 (GR) Squadron, tasking him to provide a gunner, in addition to the two observers he normally provided. The squadron was told that a second crew might be called to stand by and that in the near future, bomb aimers, armourers and three gunners would be required. A fortnight later, Aircraftman Cox was posted to Mechanics Bay and he was to be responsible for the maintenance of the armament. By the end of the month, the crews were practised at loading the bombs. This could be done within 20 minutes and, with six magazines of Lewis gun ammunition, the 'boats had some offensive capability at last.

In April, there were further flights to the Chatham Islands. One, flown by *Aotearoa*, departed Auckland early one morning, but an engine oil leak developed and

Captain Burgess was forced to divert to Wellington. They were only upon the surface for a few hours and, by noon 17 April, they were back on track for the Chathams. The weather deteriorated and *Aotearoa* returned again to Wellington, landing just before dusk. The sortie was flown during the following days and the ship *Firethorn* was sighted.

More significant were a series of flights flown to the Chathams at the end of April 1941. During the afternoon of 28 April, the Navy Office in Wellington received reports of aircraft, ships and gunfire in the region of the Chatham Islands. The reports had been relayed by Captain Miller, the Master of the *Port Waikato*, following notification by Constable Spencer of events which had occurred between 24 and 26 April. *Aotearoa* was tasked to depart Auckland at 02:30 on 29 April, proceed to the vicinity of the *Port Waikato* and thence to the Chathams. There, she would carry out a search, land and, as a trial, take on 44 gallons of fuel. Thereafter, she would return to Auckland, via Lyttelton. The crew for this flight were Burgess, Brownjohn and Nicholl. Jackson was radio operator and McNamara, temporarily serving as corporal RNZAF, was the flight engineer. Known to have responsibilities towards the radar and bombs, respectively, were supernumeraries Parr and Cox. Other RNZAF personnel were Flying Officer King, Pilot Officer McDowell, Sergeant Hoffman, Sergeant Jackson, Leading Aircraftman Bury and Corporal Cooper.

After an initial cruise at 8,000 feet, they descended below the cloud to 1,500 feet. Visibility was good and a square search around the Chatham Islands was completed. They set course back to the Chathams, and, after a careful examination of the Te Whanga Lagoon landing area, to the north-east of Waitangi Bay, they set down at 11:20. Despite some minor difficulties securing the fuel couplings, the correct tools not being available, the uplift of 44 gallons was completed successfully. Such was the enthusiasm of the reception prepared by the islanders, that events seems to have overwhelmed Mr Glennie, the control officer, and Captain Day, the harbour-master, orchestrated the brief stay. The islanders had provided lunch for the crew but Burgess was forced to decline the hospitality and continue with the reconnaissance. Within ninety minutes of landing, they were again airborne. They set course for Lyttelton and *en route* they intercepted the *Port Waikato*, which they circled twice.

Although there was fog in the Banks Peninsula area, they alighted at Lyttelton at 16:36. In preparation for a night departure, a flare-path had been laid. However, the weather was poor and the crew struggled for four and a half hours to refuel from a barge which was both poorly fendered and equipped with a low-capacity fuel pump. Taking account of the general lack of organization, it was decided to depart the following day. Some of the crew were accommodated at the Mitre and Canterbury hotels and others stayed on *Aotearoa*, as plane guard. Three of the crew were allowed ashore to Christchurch, on the understanding they would be back at the jetty by 07:30 the following day.

On the morning of 30 April, Squadron Leader Hunter telephoned Captain Burgess and gave him the tasking for their mission out of Lyttleton. They departed at 08:00 without Sergeant Hoffman. He had not returned and was left to find his own way back. *Aotearoa* intercepted the *Port Waikato*, delivering a copy of the Christchurch morning paper by air, and then proceeded north-east before taking a westerly track for Auckland. Landfall at the Coromandel Peninsula was at 15:00. The weather deteriorated, and to obtain loop bearings from Musick Point they climbed from just above the surface to 4,000 feet. Difficulties were encountered getting a weather report and bearings from Musick Point. The operators lacked supervision and seemed more interested in working the Pan Am clipper, with its seemingly interminable messages. Only after Burgess declared a state of emergency did he get the weather report essential to his landing. To compound matters, some of the messages were received in a code not carried by *Aotearoa*.

Following this futile reconnaissance, there was an inquiry. It transpired that planes' engines had not been heard, the reports about lights were contradictory and, as the original report had been made by children, it was doubtful if there had been an aircraft in the vicinity. As for the gunfire – it was probably thunder.

Within his post-flight report, Burgess suggested the refuelling facilities at Lyttleton should be improved, a suitable tool kit made available at the Chatham Islands and, to ease any communication problems during these flights, an RNZAF or TEAL officer ought to be on duty at Musick Point. Finally, it was hoped that Sergeant Hoffman's absence would be investigated.

In the spring of 1941, as part of the RNZAF's preparations for the establishment of maritime reconnaissance facilities in the Pacific, OC RNZAF Fiji was permitted to detach one of his officers, Flying Officer Stewart, to No. 11 Squadron, RAAF, at Port Moresby. There, the RAAF were operating the Empire 'Boats *Centaurus* and *Calypso* in addition to some Catalinas (PBYs). OC RNZAF Fiji had highlighted to Air HQ Wellington the difficulty of building landing strips without considerable cost, but noted that there were many places from which flying-boats could be operated safely. Flying Officer Stewart, in his report which covers the period 7 April to 14 May 1941, recorded many of No. 11 Sqn's operational procedures and gives an insight as to their capability. Although Stewart had had no previous flying-boat experience, he considered that any pilot with reasonable ability should have no difficulty in converting onto Empire 'Boats, although he thought the Catalina easier to handle. He stressed that seamanship and similar skills would be required of all potential flying-boat crews.

Throughout all these military preparations, TEAL had continued to maintain the trans-Tasman service. In June 1941, in order to connect Sydney with Pan Am's trans-Pacific clipper out of Auckland, it was decided to reschedule a Sydney–Auckland flight to a night crossing. The clipper was scheduled to depart Auckland at

10:00 and TEAL intended to depart Sydney at 22:00, the previous evening.

The Controller Civil Aviation was informed of the intended night crossing. Acting Controller Barrow wrote, on 5 June, to Sir Harry Batterbee, Chairman of the Tasman Air Commission, the body which had been set up to approve all TEAL decisions and report directly to the Governments of New Zealand, Australia and Great Britain. Barrow absolved his department from any responsibility as to the safety of the night flight. Barrow also wrote to Maurice Clarke, General Manager Union Airways, seeking prior assurances as to the accomplishment of this flight.

The Commission responded. They had assumed Union Airways (as managing agents for TEAL), having approved the proposed crossing, had gained the concurrence of the Civil Aviation Authority. The Commission refused to accept any responsibility for the safety of the night flight and reminded the Controller of Civil Aviation that the New Zealand Government was responsible for air safety.

Maurice Clarke replied to Acting Controller Barrow, stating regulations had been complied with and, anyway, part of every trip was flown at night, landing in daylight. Moreover, special precautions were always taken regarding the weather, and on this night flight, as with previous ones, Clarke had no doubt the same attention would be applied to weather conditions generally.

During the last half of 1941, with military preparations continuing apace, it became necessary to establish a link between the RNZAF Fiji detachment and New Zealand. TEAL 'boats and RAAF Catalinas were considered but eventually use was made of the Pan Am clipper service.

In August 1941, New Zealand's Acting Prime Minister stressed to the Australian Secretary of State the essential need to continue employing the TEAL 'boats on military reconnaissance missions, until replacement Catalinas became available. After all, that had been the main argument for supplying the Empire 'boats to TEAL during war. The only alternative was to speed up the delivery of Hudsons and Catalinas.

Australia was still awaiting delivery of her Catalinas, and, during August and September of 1941, the need arose to ferry a number of aircrew to the United States, to collect a batch of Catalinas from Consolidated. America, still neutral, was unable to deliver military equipment into a war zone. The Australian Government requested that TEAL put on a special flight to connect with Pan Am's service out of Auckland. There was difficulty meeting this special, and messages were exchanged at Prime Ministerial level. It was finally agreed QANTAS could connect directly with Pan Am at Noumea. To an extent, this was seen by TEAL as poaching, but the urgency of the RAAF was appreciated by TEAL. TEAL did lay on one special flight, and although the QANTAS flight to Noumea was permitted, it was not to be considered a precedent.

TEAL did not restrict themselves to crossing just the Tasman. In November 1941, *Awarua*, commanded by Burgess, started an Auckland–Suva–Lautoka service (Lautoka and Suva are opposite sides of the island of Viti Levu, Fiji). Later, at the close of November, Duff Cooper was provided with a 'boat as part of his special mission for Churchill to resolve problems between military and civil authorities. Following Pearl Harbor and the departure of Pan Am from the south-west Pacific, New Zealand lay isolated, connected to the Allies only by TEAL's trans-Tasman service. However, the previous month, a United States Navy *Coronado* had made a survey flight to New Zealand. Soon others followed, but from 22 December civilian flying was banned unless authorized by the Government. This ruling stayed in force until 24 December 1945.

Returning to the armament fit of *Aotearoa* and *Awarua*, scant evidence has come to light that a gun turret, designed and manufactured by a Corporal Davis based at Hobsonville, was fitted to *Awarua* and test-flown on 16 January 1942. The turret was fitted above the rear escape hatch and some stiffening of the hull had been carried out. Although the test flight, less gun, was most satisfactorily flown by Burgess, the Air Staff thought the comments of the Aeronautical Inspection Division a little vague. It had not been possible to incorporate fire guards, to prevent the gunner hitting the tail, and, as with the Australian 'boats, protection was achieved by the painting of red warning lines on the top of the rear fuselage. Unfortunately, further technical information and photographs of the turret have not come to light.

Fortunately the same cannot be said about what is possibly the greatest myth of TEAL 'boats – the Walter Nash flight.

Following America's entry into the war, the post of New Zealand's Resident Minister to the United States was bestowed upon the Honourable Walter Nash. Accompanied by his wife, he would fly to America. As Pan Am no longer operated west of Hawaii, it befell TEAL to fly Nash to Honolulu, where he would connect with the clipper. An island-hopping route, by way of Fiji, Canton Island and Palmyra, was chosen. Palmyra lagoon is about five miles across, but Canton Island is even smaller, and navigation would be both challenging and critical.

Awarua, commanded by Burgess, with Brownjohn as first officer and Doug Reid as radio operator, was readied for the flight. In their wisdom, someone decided it would be best if *Awarua* flew without any national insignia or identifying marks.

To make best use of astro-navigation, they left Auckland at 22:00 on 18 January 1942. An uneventful flight, through a night ideal for navigation, brought them to Suva at 07:00. They spent the day of the 19th in Suva, Burgess and Nash calling upon His Excellency the Governor and others. The various authorities resident in Fiji were most helpful, almost too helpful, and there was some confusion over the radio frequencies to be used as they flew into the Central Pacific. However, sound advice on the approaches to Canton, Palmyra and

Honolulu was forthcoming from the United States Navy.

Awarua departed Suva for Canton Island on the morning of 20 January. Burgess had chosen Wallis Island, Atafu and Hull Island as *en route* fixes, but squally, heavy rain was encountered and reduced visibility prevented them sighting Atafu. At Hull Island and Canton Island there were wireless stations, and the aircraft's loop aerial was used to good effect to make successful landfalls. When only a short distance out of Canton Island, they crossed the International Date Line and thus arrived late afternoon on 19 January. Their first sighting of Canton brought alarm. In the atoll lay an unidentified warship. It turned out to be American. Ashore, only a small party of Americans were present, as Canton Island was considered too close to the Japanese and vulnerable to attack. *Awarua* moored close to the jetty and was hauled in tail-first towards her berth.

It had been Burgess's intention to depart Canton at midnight 19 January, stage through Palmyra and make Honolulu in one day. However, as a weather front lay across his route, the staff at Canton Island advised Burgess to delay his departure until 07:00 on the 20th and then fly just the single stage to Palmyra. With an unplanned night-stop imposed upon them, the crew and passengers were accommodated in the deserted Pan Am Hotel. Although a blackout was imposed and conditions were difficult, the American Army served a good meal and allowed the passengers to make themselves comfortable where they could.

In fair weather, they departed Canton as suggested, but rain showers persisted throughout the latter part of the six-and-a-half-hour flight. They alighted at Palmyra, made fast and had the passengers taken ashore to the Naval barracks. Burgess and Radio Officer Reid remained aboard *Awarua* for the night, acting as watchmen. It rained – incessantly – and Burgess and Reid suffered a sleepless night with the rain leaking onto Burgess's and Nash's luggage to boot. From Palmyra, they departed on the morning of 21 January, and that afternoon, *Awarua* was met in Pearl Harbor by the Pan Am launch, *Panair*. *Awarua* was the first Commonwealth aircraft to visit Pearl Harbor since that infamous day in December 1941 and the first British commercial service to enter the Pacific. Nash flew on to Washington.

Originally, Burgess intended to stay only one and a half days in Honolulu and leave on the morning of 23 January, but due to the civilian curfew, effective from six in the evenings, they decided to stay an extra day at the Hotel Halekulani and depart on the morning of the 24th.

A pre-dawn departure from Honolulu was essential if Burgess was to make Canton Island in one day. To avoid the danger of taxiing through Pearl Harbor at night, *Awarua* had slipped her Pan Am mooring at 17:00 the previous evening and taxied across to the alighting area at Hickham Field. They took off from Pearl Harbor at 04:25 and by mid-morning were approaching Palmyra. Turnaround was completed two minutes

inside the hour. Before noon, they were airborne again, navigating the critical leg that should end with a landfall at the diminutive Canton Island. Throughout the six-hour flight they maintained communication with Palmyra, but trouble was had raising Canton. Burgess needed Canton to come on the air so they could home onto the island. Messages back to Palmyra and Honolulu, urging them to contact Canton Island to listen out, were to no avail. Without the use of radio aids, Burgess was committed to astro-navigation using the sun. By virtue of his mastery of navigation, Burgess 'ran down' his sun line to find the islands. They landed at Canton 22 minutes before sunset on 24 January. Canton Island had finally come onto the air, but only seven minutes before they alighted and just as they saw the island.

Captain Burgess had additional difficulties locating the mooring. Taxiing with the sun in his eyes, he misidentified the British Resident's house for the building adjacent to the slipway. Moreover, Reid, standing in the open bow compartment, was unable to gauge the depth of the clear Pacific waters beneath them. They found themselves surrounded by coral growths. The step fouled. Burgess cut the inboard engines and called Reid to deploy both drogues to slow their progress. Next, the outboards were stopped and the anchor lowered; attempts were made to sound the depth. Extraction seemed impossible and the 'boat was bearing down upon a large coral reef. By judicious starting and stopping of the outboards, they managed to stay clear of the reef. Relief came when a launch arrived to tow them to the mooring. Once moored, an inspection revealed only a few scratches on the hull and the starboard float.

The coral had been marked by Pan Am, but upon their withdrawal from Canton, they had removed the buoys. The Army had made an attempt at marking but their system seemed most haphazard. As the moon rose, refuelling was being completed, and that night the crew, and their only passenger, a Captain Beasley, slept on board. The next day, 25 January, an early departure for Suva was made and soon the International Date Line was crossed.

The events of 25 January 1942 have spawned many myths. At 08:20 (local time) Burgess, breakfasting below in the spar cabin, was informed of the sighting of a US naval aircraft, now known to be a Douglas Dauntless flown by Lieutenant Kroeger of Air Group 6, from the carrier USS *Enterprise*. The Dauntless came alongside to identify the flying-boat, which, as a result of instructions before departure, was devoid of insignia or registration. Burgess ordered Brownjohn to signal a response by use of the Aldis lamp. The signal was, however, thwarted by the lamp blowing a fuse. A high-powered torch was substituted but, apparently receiving no reply, and mistaking *Awarua* for a Japanese flying-boat, the Dauntless commenced an attack. The Dauntless made three passes, engaging the 'boat with its forward-firing machine-guns. Evasion was impossible, as there was little cloud, and it sounded as every round was striking home, but no damage was apparent. Further attempts were made to identify themselves and Burgess called for the Civil Air Ensign to be flown from the observation hatch. On the third pass the aircraft broke off and formated upon Burgess's wing and signalled, 'Please inspect your hull for damage – have fired on you.' The Dauntless then carried out a visual check of *Awarua*, waved farewell and continued on its patrol.

Since the event the story has been much embellished. In truth, only one bullet struck, and it passed clean through the wing. The attack is believed to have been terminated when the Dauntless's ammunition was exhausted.

Before landing, they lifted all nine bilge covers and inspected the hull. No holes were found, and without further incident they landed at Suva, late in the afternoon of 26 January, refuelled immediately and waited for nightfall. At 22:00, they departed Suva and arrived at Auckland on 27 January at 06:15.

The repair to *Awarua* was overseen by Bill Peek. Beforehand, he ran a cord from the underwing entry hole to the top-surface exit and discovered the single bullet had only just missed the fuel tank. The holes were cut out and the panels patched. The bullet hole itself was given to one of the hangar boys as a souvenir. A little later, when one of the TEAL executives was departing, it was suggested that he be presented with 'the hole'. As the maintenance staff no longer possessed 'the hole', one was fabricated from a piece of scrap metal, suitably modified by use of a centre punch.

The mix of scheduled flights and specials continued, but such was the demand for the aircraft that non-priority passengers were continually moved down the waiting lists. Matters were not improved when, in the face of the oncoming Japanese, a number of New Zealand nationals were evacuated to Australia and now awaited repatriation to New Zealand. After much discussion, they returned home by ship.

Reconnaissance Flight 16 took place on 17–19 April 1942. *Aotearoa* departed Auckland early in the morning of 17 April. The weather, according to the captain's report, was very bad. After a pre-dawn take-off, they climbed through drizzle and cloud to 6,500 feet and set course for a position to the south of the Chatham Islands. About ninety minutes out, whilst abeam Hawke Bay, an oil-leak from the port-outer engine was observed. A considerable amount of oil seemed to be escaping and they diverted to Wellington. Captain Burgess's post-flight report states:

'… *course was altered for Wellington. The Flight Engineer was able to crawl out inside the wing and carry out a temporary repair.*

The aircraft moored at Wellington at 21:13 GMT. At 22:00 the aircraft was again ready for service.'

Whether the above means the engineer, Bob McNamara, crawled out into the wing in flight is unclear. Considering Burgess was commander when Supernumerary First Officer Reid climbed into the wing of *Castor* to make inflight repairs to a leaking oil tank in

June 1937, and, moreover, McNamara's build was similar to that of Reid, it is possible a temporary repair was made in flight.

Aotearoa was soon airborne again, but when only eighty miles short of the Chatham Islands, reports of thick fog forced them to return to Wellington. By now the weather at Wellington had deteriorated and a north-westerly was gusting at over 70 mph. They managed to get *Aotearoa* down but the gales prevented refuelling. A lull on the 18th allowed them to refuel, but the wind was still too strong for take-off. Eventually at 06:30, 19 April, they were able to get away, tasked to make a square search near the Chatham Islands. They had been airborne a little over half an hour when SS *Firethorne* (presumably their quest) was sighted. They returned to Wellington, as they had been unable to raise Musick Point and report their sighting. Once down at Wellington, Air Headquarters ordered them back to Auckland.

An additional route was proved on 25 May 1942 when Burgess took *Aotearoa* from Auckland to Suva, and on 29 May he continued with a proving flight to Tonga. On 1 June, *Aotearoa* made the first commercial flight from Nuku'alofa, Tonga, to Satapuala, Western Samoa, and return. Later that year, in August, Burgess flew the first of five return flights to Noumea, New Caledonia, taking American Army personnel and mail. This operation terminated on 30 November.

Of these flights, one special requires a particular mention. Although Bill Peek was flight engineer and his account follows, the records do not reveal this flight. However, over this period one of the 'boats was declared unavailable.

'On the 11th of that month [August 1942] we started more flights to Noumea in New Caledonia, carrying US Brass plus others, and on two occasions we went further north to Espiritu Santo in the New Hebrides. I was never told how it came about or who gave the orders but we embarked about eight USN men and two officers, together with many cases of provisions and other gear which looked like radio equipment; they also had several big batteries and a charging unit. The last thing to be loaded was a collapsible boat which was made of rubber/fabric and plywood. We left Santo just after midday and flew north; the TEAL crew were Captain Burgess, a radio operator and myself. A USN pilot occupied the 1st officer's seat with his charts and a mystery man, in shorts and a bush shirt, knelt behind him. We flew quite low, island hopping, and finally landed in a large lagoon at a bush covered island which I believe was somewhere near Santa Cruz Island. I believe the civilian was a Planter from the island as he gave us all the directions and also guided us to a sheltered spot to unload. We anchored while the Yanks got the boat assembled; they were experts and everything was ashore in under two hours. We had no trouble getting started and without any load the take-off was short and Burgess used a lot of power until we were well clear of the area. That night we stayed at Santo and arrived back in*

Auckland the next afternoon. This exercise was never talked about but it was hinted that the aircraft the Yanks were to use had engine trouble and we had the only one with a freight door large enough to take their boat. Nothing was entered in the log books and the extra flying time was "lost" in the next two trips to Noumea.'

With only two aircraft, a civil schedule and a number of military missions to fly, the ground staff worked long and hard to maintain the 'boats at readiness. The amount of flying being done was greater than that originally envisaged and consequently engine usage was greater than expected. Additional spares were not readily available and often the air-freight cost of an essential item was greater than the cost of the item itself. During engine overhauls, meticulous inspection of all parts was carried out. Tolerances were checked and re-checked and every item was subject to the most rigorous inspection in order that valuable engine parts could be used safely for as long as possible. Matters were not eased by the loss of two ships from England carrying aircraft spares. There was a ball-bearing shortage and a plea was put out over the radio asking the public to donate any bearings they had. Sufficient were collected to be tested and installed in the Perseus engines, albeit with a reduced overhaul interval.

Despite the hard work of men like Bill Peek and Geoff Wells, the Perseus-engined Tasman 'boats regularly flew for eight or nine hours, unlike the three or four hours flown by the Pegasus-engined S.23s. These longer flights revealed weaknesses in the ignition systems, intake casings and oil-coolers in particular. The engines were being pushed to the limits. So small were the fuel and power reserves that if the forecast head wind was in excess of 15 knots the crossing was cancelled, and on occasions the 'boats turned back.

Bill Peek made many crossings of the Tasman but recalls only one engine failure. As the 'boats were underpowered, the engines were under severe load for the early part of the crossing, until the fuel had been burnt. On one crossing, Captain Burgess and First Officer Griffiths were about three hours out of Auckland, benefiting from a good tail wind. Griffiths was attending to the navigation at the table in the flight-deck mail-hold and Bill Peek was sitting in the right-hand seat, rather than on his tool box.

Griffiths came forward and in his terribly precise manner said, 'There is something not quite right, out through the window on the port-inner.'

Burgess craned his neck around but could see little, so he asked Peek to go back and take a look. To Bill's amazement, one cylinder was missing from the engine. In its place was a blur: the gyrating sleeve-valve, located by the crank-case and the cam drive. More significant was the cowling, slowly opening out and causing a sickening increase in drag. Fuel and ignition to the offending engine were shut off. The propeller could not be feathered and the damaged engine continued to turn. Burgess applied rated power to maintain height, but with several hours to run to Sydney they had to reduce

power. Slowly they descended. With hearts in mouths they watched as the sleeve bobbed up and down. After fifteen minutes or so, the cowling finally tore itself free, and now, with less drag, they were able to maintain height without resorting to rated power. The immediate crisis was over. They soldiered on to Sydney and there the damaged engine was replaced with the spare held at Rose Bay. They had a few beers that night, and oddly, the damaged engine had used no more oil than the other three.

On one occasion it was only a fortuitous change in the weather and Oscar Garden's presence of mind that saved the flying-boat from having to ditch. Garden had almost completed an already fraught crossing from Auckland, and they had been forced to close down an engine, when nearing Australia the three remaining engines started to overheat. As they approached the coast, they ran into a belt of warm air. The three engines were already labouring and the cylinder head and oil temperatures rose as the oil pressures fell. The possibility of a forced landing in the Tasman seemed real. As Garden considered jettisoning baggage to lighten the aircraft, they encountered a cool southerly showery airstream, and Garden steered the 'boat into the cool rain showers, reducing the engine temperatures to within limits.

On another occasion, Captain Brownjohn suffered ignition problems and elected to make a precautionary landing in the difficult waters of Lord Howe island. The Perseus engines suffered repeatedly from ignition problems, and most were traced to a breakdown of the insulation on the 'Callender' (name of manufacturer) ignition harnesses. Geoff Wells finally cured the problem for TEAL by changing the 'Callender' cables for standard automobile ignition cables.

The S.30 was fitted with the British Smith autopilot, unlike the S.23s, which were fitted with the American Sperry. For several months the Smiths gave problems, often launching the aircraft into an undemanded dive. Fortunately the problem was eventually solved. Some problems were beyond the control of man. Oscar Garden had a close call when the aircraft was struck by lightning. The trailing aerial for the wireless entered the aircraft to the left of the captain's seat; it was usual practice to wind in the aerial if there was a risk of thunderstorms. They entered a violent storm and earthed the radio but Radio Officer Doug Williams was not aware that he was expected to wind in the aerial. The resultant strike entered the aircraft just to the left of Oscar Garden, travelled up the back of Garden's seat and scorched his hair. The left-hand wall of the cockpit and much of the wiring was burnt.

The great weakness of the Empire 'boats was the lack of feathering airscrews. Around mid-1942, from somewhere, there arrived at Mechanics Bay about ten triangular crates. Each one contained a Hamilton Standard feathering propeller. There were, however, no installation instructions. With initiative and ingenuity Bill Peek designed an installation kit and made the necessary modifications to the engines to mount feathering pumps and the other paraphernalia. He was, however, a little concerned as to pitch angles. But with the loan of an inclinometer from the RNZAF at Hobsonville he inspected the propeller hubs and decided they had all been set correctly by the manufacturers. The installation went ahead, and from mid-1942 until their final demise, *Aotearoa* and *Awarua* had feathering propellers, the only 'C-class' flying-boats so equipped.

In 1943 there was a great change-over of staff, there being considerable unrest and dissatisfaction. In March, Burgess left TEAL for BOAC and Boeing 314s, and Oscar Garden became chief pilot. Bill Craig went into the Air Force and Bill Peek moved to Baltimore and 314s to find himself reunited with Len Turnill. With the delivery of the first RNZAF Catalinas in mid-1943, there was no longer a requirement for the TEAL 'boats to fly the military missions, and they were able to concentrate on the commercial enterprise. In October 1943, it was announced that during the past year TEAL had flown 192,960 miles, 2,259 passengers, 33,990 lb of freight and 101,737 lb of mail, an almost full load capacity, with 100% reliability. In 1944 frequency of flights increased to three a week. The unrest and dissatisfaction continued, and in January 1944 Houchen departed and George Bolt was appointed chief engineer to TEAL. As Squadron Leader Bolt, he had overseen the militarization of the 'boats at Hobsonville.

The 1,000th crossing was made on 19 June 1945 by Garden in *Awarua*, and around this time *Aotearoa*, and probably *Awarua*, were retrofitted with different engines, possibly the Pegasus XXIIs, to bring them in line with the Sunderlands. Following the war's end there was much debate as to replacement aircraft.

On 24 October 1947, TEAL advised the Director of Civil Aviation that *Aotearoa* would be withdrawn from service by 31 October, the CofA expiry date. *Aotearoa* made the last 'C-class' crossing of the Tasman on 29 October, after 441 previous crossings. It was decided to beach *Aotearoa* at Hobsonville. On 17 November

Propeller being removed from TEAL 'boat. The hand-operated crane has been attached to the top of the nacelle. It could be used to drop the prop or the engine. (Peek)

Aotearoa was permanently withdrawn from service. She had flown 1,250,000 miles in 8,500 hours. By mid-January 1948, *Aotearoa* had been beached and stripped of all useful equipment. Although TEAL had no further use for the aircraft, an Australian company was showing some interest, but the deal fell through and the 'boat was sold to Messrs Carter and Maybee on 25 June 1948, and the CofA was finally cancelled on 5 July.

On 9 June, TEAL submitted tenders for the sale of both 'boats and a quantity of spares. *Awarua* was withdrawn on 16 June, and a seven-day extension to the CofA was granted to allow her to make some training flights. She was broken up in November 1947 at Tamaki Estuary, Auckland, having flown 8,740 hours. Her CofA registration was finally cancelled in January 1948.

Aotearoa won a short reprieve from the executioner when Messrs Carter and Maybee took her to Mission

Aotearoa was taken by Messrs Carter and Maybee and displayed at the Mission Bay site of the Walsh Brothers' Flying School. There, she lay as a seaside attraction, being taken away for scrap in the early 1950s. (The New Zealand Herald)

Bay and displayed her on the site of the Walsh Brothers' Flying School. There, for a short while she lay as a seaside attraction, adjacent to the crazy golf and a coffee-bar. Finally, and various dates between 1950 and 1954 are mentioned, she was taken away for scrap. Truly the end of an era.

The replacement of the 'C-class' by Short Sandringhams, soon to be followed by Short Solents, is a story of politics rather than commercial aircraft operation. The Douglas DC-4 was seen by many to be the ideal 'C-class' replacement but the politics did not fit. On 2 July 1946, the first of four Sandringhams for TEAL was launched at Belfast and entered service the following December. The Sandringhams were not ideal; on 3 December 1947, one narrowly avoided ditching mid-Tasman, following engine failure. An inquiry followed. On 22 February 1948, the Sandringham service was suspended. Ironically, DC-4s provided a temporary service. The first Solent was christened by Princess Elizabeth on 26 May 1949 and entered service at the end of the year. The Solents served TEAL until September 1960 but were withdrawn from the Tasman in 1954. Although flying-boats continued to serve in the Pacific for some years, the departure of 'boats from the Tasman may be considered the demise of mainstream use of flying-boats in what remained of, or had once been, the British Empire.

CHAPTER FOURTEEN

End of Empire

BOAC in turmoil – Empire seadrome again – 'There was a great future' but the 'C-class' scrapped – Land planes! – The Princess – Postscript from Mayo.

The fairway ahead of the flying-boat, after September 1945, was vastly different from the wake it had left behind in September 1939. Although the aircraft industries of France and Germany, both pre-war champions of the flying-boat, lay in tatters, France had managed to keep a vestige of flying-boat development alive. In the United States, Douglas and Lockheed were vying with each other to provide land-plane airliners for America and the world. In Britain, the war economy was being brought to a rapid halt and, unaware of the hardships before them, the people of Britain looked forward. British airlines soldiered on with a motley collection of flying-boats, converted bombers and ex-military transport aircraft; even twelve captured Junkers Ju 52 aircraft came to serve with British European Airways between 1946 and '48.

Of the Empire 'Boats, one remained in Australia, the two TEAL 'boats continued to give sterling service in New Zealand and thirteen 'C-class' stoically operated from Durban. In addition, there were *Golden Hind* and the three Boeing 314s. Much reliance was being put upon converted Sunderlands and their 'Hythe' and 'Sandringham' derivatives. In all, BOAC operated over thirty Sunderlands, most of which were later converted to the less austere Hythe. These were followed by twelve Sandringhams, an even more extensive civilianization of the Sunderland, and finally, eighteen Solents, based upon the more capable Seaford. However, the tale of the demise of the flying-boat, for that is what happened, is a litany of intransigence, lack of foresight, lack of money and, perhaps most importantly, the inevitable outcome of the changes forged by war. It would take a few years for the dust of war to settle and allow all this to become visible.

In addition to the sixteen 'boats which survived the war, mention must be made of the fate of the forty-third 'C-class' S.1027, which, although registered G-AFRB, remained unnamed. Construction had been abandoned in May 1940, along with the Fairey and Short Bros long-range land-plane airliners, and, at the time, the development of the British civil airliner ceased. The hull of S.1027 was stored in a large wooden crate, in the barge yard at Rochester, and there she stayed for several years. Records show that as of 28 February 1942 she had been dismantled and stored, awaiting possible completion after the war. The date of her final 'reduction to produce' is uncertain, but in May 1943 the crate was dismantled and at a later date the hull destroyed.

Around this time, the status of BOAC was questionable. The RAF, lacking an adequate air transport force, increasingly imposed upon BOAC to meet its transport requirements. In America, civil air transport had absorbed its military counterpart, but in Great Britain, it seemed the opposite would happen. As a consequence, the BOAC board of directors resigned in protest at the establishment of RAF Transport Command. In the House of Lords, Viscount Rothermere argued that tasking such a military organization with air transport could only be detrimental to the future of British civil air transport, and would it not have been better to expand BOAC?

Although the Secretary of State for Air, Sinclair, had appointed Harold Howitt as temporary chairman, Sinclair did respond to a written request from BOAC employees, and invited Lord Reith to re-take the chair. Lord Reith commented that the formation of the RAF Transport Command was not the sole, but the culminating, reason for the resignation of the board. Reith deplored resignations and refused to accept the position.

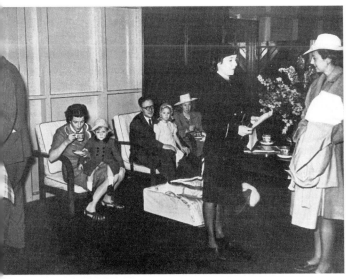

Post-war Durban: BOAC passengers take tea before boarding.
(Baldwin and Bigby)

Reith continued that BOAC had, despite support from Air Minister Kingsley Wood, never functioned as an Empire-wide corporation. Constitutionally, BOAC had not been established until after the outbreak of war, and then it was under the control of the Secretary of State. The directors felt they were never allowed to control the development of the airline without ministerial, and Air Ministry, interference. Moreover, whilst the Civil Aviation Department had done much that had been contrary to the war effort, BOAC had provided valuable service without direction or support from the Government.

Finally, with the revealing clarity brought by hindsight, Reith stated that British civil aviation would be at the mercy of American airliners once the war was over. Likewise, the Dominions would turn to America for the provision of aircraft if Great Britain was unable to provide them.

A similar warning was sounded by Major-General Sir Fredrick Sykes, once Controller of Civil Aviation. He said the Government should lead the advance of civil air transport. He warned of a post-war collision with American interests. Whereas the United Kingdom was, rightly so, building military aircraft, the Americans were building transport aircraft, mapping out the world's air-routes and building expertise on the operation of the said routes. If the war were to end tomorrow, Great Britain would find herself cluttered with super-fluous military aircraft, whilst American civil aviation would be able to progress without competition.

Lord Knollys' appointment as chairman of BOAC in May 1943 may have quietened some voices. Similarly, the setting up of the Brabazon Committee in December 1942, to examine the future requirements of British Civil Air Transport and to keep abreast of developments elsewhere, may have quietened others. However, by late 1943, with an Allied victory seeming probable, thoughts turned towards another facet of post-war civil air operations, the construction of new aerodromes. Gatwick was seen in need of upgrading and Heston (now Heathrow) had potential, but still the flying-boat had to be accommodated. Many of the proposed aerodrome plans incorporated a lagoon for the operation of flying-boats. A design proposed for the Isle of Dogs, east London, was seen as lacking development potential, whereas one submitted by the aircraft designer, F. G. Miles, and earmarked for Cliffe, on the Thames Estuary between Chatham and Rochester, seemed more promising.

In early 1944, Lord Knollys commenced a world tour visiting India, Australia and New Zealand, returning via the Pacific. He discussed the future of BOAC with its associate companies, and, the following November, it was announced that South Africa and Great Britain would operate a joint land-plane service between the two countries.

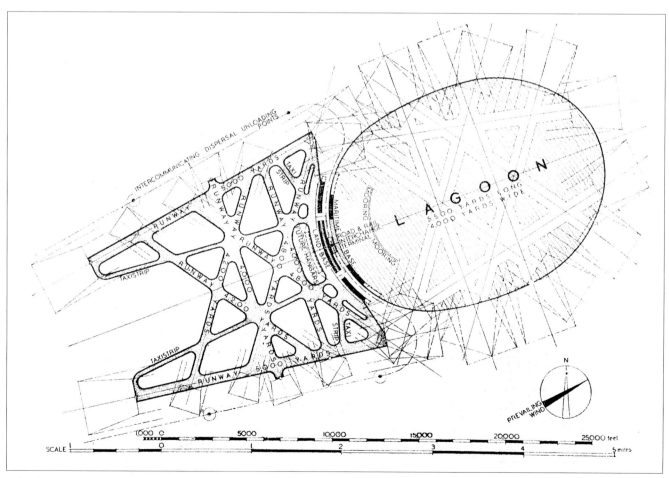

After the war, the Empire seadrome raised its head again. A design for the Isle of Dogs area lacked potential, but various ideas for the Solent and Southampton Water appeared, as did this F. G. Miles plan for Cliffe, between Chatham and Rochester.
(*Quadrant Picture Library*/Flight International)

With regard to new airliners, there was little of immediate promise on the stocks, other than bomber conversions and flying-boats. Short Bros and Saunders-Roe had co-operated to design and build the Shetland, two examples being laid down. The first, in military guise, made its maiden flight in the hands of Lankester Parker and Geoffrey Tyson in December 1944. It was destroyed as a result of a galley fire whilst moored at Felixstowe in January 1946. The second 'boat was completed as a 70-seater civil transport and was flown in September 1947 by Harold Piper and T. Brooke-Smith.

In British circles, a future for the flying-boat was still seen, and a proposal from the American, Glenn Martin, for purpose-built flying-boat terminals was picked up in an advertising campaign by Saunders-Roe. One of Martin's special features was a system of automatic winches and cables to 'capture' and moor the 'boats. Nevertheless, existing equipment was getting old and, on 19 January 1945, the last service by Empire 'Boat between Durban and Vaaldam was flown by *Cameronian*, commanded by Captain Bellin. Meanwhile, Lord Knollys seemed reticent to commit BOAC in positive support of the flying-boat. The Corporation would watch developments and consider employment.

In an uncertain atmosphere, Saunders-Roe revealed the Saro scheme, a proposed hangar-cum-terminal building for flying-boats, situated on the edge of a salt-water-filled tideless lagoon. It was the brainchild of Arthur Gouge, and outwardly shared much with Glenn Martin. In essence, once the flying-boat had landed and taxied towards the hangar, it would automatically be snared by an underwater, endless cable, running between the breakwater and the 'boat's mooring, and then winched into position.

Other voices were again being heard, and in July 1945, Major Mayo made three compelling points:

'... successful trials of the Shetland have revealed that the flying-boat is alive, though suffering neglect.

... and although the flying-boat continued to play a part [in the recent war] *it could not hold its own with the land planes because it was no longer undergoing a comparable amount of development.*

[During the war] *To serve the land planes, long runway aerodromes were built wherever they might be required, regardless of cost. It is this fait accompli – that has done more than anything else to swing opinion in favour of the land plane...'*

Mayo closed with an argument favouring the efficiencies of the large (200,000 lb plus) flying-boat over the similarly sized land plane, and made a plea for the British aircraft industry to re-establish its pre-war eminence as flying-boat builders.

If the aircraft manufacturers need goading, the same could not be said of the Government of Eire. On 21 September 1945, plans to build a flying-boat base at Rineanna, adjacent to the new airport at Shannon, were announced. However, the flying-boat base would take about two years to complete. For the meantime, Foynes would continue in use, despite London-bound passengers having to make a long coach journey to transfer from Foynes to Shannon.

Late in November 1945, the first Short Sandringham was launched from Rochester, and, as if in sympathy, the apparent requirement for a purpose-built flying-boat base, possibly incorporating land-plane runways, gained in popularity. The Portsmouth Council resurrected the Langstone harbour plans of before the war. Most of the original pre-war objections had been proved unfounded by war's experience, and, with sufficient dredging, a combined land and seadrome could be built within the confines of Langstone harbour.

Langstone already possessed limited natural facilities for flying-boats, and if the planned interim move of passenger operations from Poole to Southampton was delayed, then the transfer of the complete operation could be to Langstone, without incurring the expense of the interim move. In response, the Southampton Harbour Board dusted down plans, first drawn up in 1944, to rival Langstone harbour. Their site was at the junction of Southampton Water, the Solent and Spithead, near Gosport. A great disadvantage of pre-war Southampton had been the incursion of shipping and the hazard of floating debris. The new plan envisaged the construction of a lagoon, presumably in the Fareham District. Despite the pro-Southampton claim that the new giant 'boats, such as the Princess, would need runways four or five miles long and such runways could not be accommodated within Langstone harbour, the flying-boat designers explained that take-off distances need not be any greater than those of existing 'boats.

On 24 January 1946, before the first Shetland was destroyed as a result of a galley fire, the Parliamentary Secretary to the Ministry of Civil Aviation, Mr Ivor Thomas, introduced the plan for civil aviation to the House. The following day, Lord Winster, Minister of Civil Aviation, said there was a great future for the flying-boat and Langstone harbour was again under consideration. The Parliamentary agenda of 26 January contained arguments that had been heard before: the flying-boat had a great future – there were many natural marine bases in the British Commonwealth – many 'boats were in service and new 'boats had been ordered. Moreover, the Minister had stimulated research into flying-boat design, an area which had been lacking in research and development during the war.

On 28 January, the Shetland caught fire and sunk.

Emotion was clouding judgment. The success of the pre-war Empire 'Boats was due to the Empire Airmail Scheme. It was so successful it would have probably collapsed under its own success had war not intervened. The volume of mail outweighed the revenue earned. Before the war, Imperial had assumed that the weight of mail would not rise, but post-war negotiations were very much on a weight carried basis, and the Air Ministry reported:

'I can find no friend for a renewal of the pre-war all-up Empire Airmail Scheme.'

As the first of the Hythe-class flying-boats was inaugurating the service to Singapore, there were those, in January 1946, the Parkstone Yacht Club in particular, who wished to return to the pre-war status quo. The yacht club, seen by many as a noisy minority, were advancing arguments for BOAC to hasten its departure from Poole. Although it was BOAC's intention to move from Poole, Lord Knollys said in February that the Sunderlands were still required to service the routes to Singapore and 'C-class' 'boats remained upon the remnants of the Horseshoe, Durban to Calcutta. Moreover, the Sunderlands were soon to be replaced by Solents, and an order for the three, yet unnamed, Princesses was expected soon.

Contrary to Lord Knollys' apparent support for 'boats, BOAC's transatlantic service ceased on 10 March 1946 when the last of the three Boeing 314s, arrived at Baltimore. Almost blind to the fact that the future lay with the land plane, the British continued their love affair with the 'boat. It should be remembered that before the war, air travel was a luxury and those who could afford it wanted the service retained. Whereas BOAC was about to introduce a sleeper service with their transatlantic Constellations, the Americans expected their more egalitarian passengers to sit for the seventeen hours or so of the crossing.

With the future apparently assured by the imminent order of the new generation of luxury, giant flying-boats, the struggle to be chosen as the site of the new seadrome continued. Portsmouth, as a counter to Southampton's Gosport plan, suggested a temporary facility could be built at Southsea, until Langstone harbour was completed. All of the plans which intended to employ Southampton Water suffered a common disadvantage: they were susceptible to rough water. The Solent, or any similar stretch of water, is susceptible to the power and vagaries of the weather. A rolling swell, waves and crosswinds could all preclude the use of the semi-open waters. By using an artificial lagoon or a dredged and enclose natural harbour, such as Langstone, operations would not be prone to disruptions due to weather. Meanwhile, BOAC were advocating the construction of interim facilities, costing £150,000, at Berth 50, Southampton Harbour.

Having replaced the Boeing 314 'boats with Lockheed Constellation land planes, BOAC announced, on 5 April 1946, that for an indefinite period they were discontinuing the use of Foynes for transatlantic services. Some of their staff would be retained, possibly to deal with land planes at the recently commissioned Shannon Airport. Moreover, the decision to use land planes on the Atlantic should not be considered irrevocable. That being said, on 12 April, *The Aeroplane* announced that the 'C-class' 'boats on the Horseshoe were to be withdrawn by the year's end, but, that same month, Lord Winster placed an order for the three Saro Princesses. Hot on the heels of the Princess order, the Ministry of Supply ordered twelve Short Solents, on 3 May 1946, and BOAC extended their Hythe service past Calcutta and on to Sydney. But at the

end of the month, the eastern terminus for the 'C-class' on the Horseshoe service was drawn back from Calcutta to Karachi.

Although Lord Winster's visit to Portsmouth, on 13 April, to discuss flying-boat facilities was seen as further support for Langstone harbour, the following month BOAC moved its Poole headquarters from Poole Pottery, where they had spent the war, to Poole Yacht Club. At the end of May 1946, *Champion* returned to Poole to start a weekly service to Cairo. She would be replaced the following September by *Golden Hind*. As always, when seemingly difficult decisions had to be made, a committee was formed. As May closed, the Minister of Civil Aviation announced the appointment of Lord Pakenham to chair a committee to review the various proposals for a future marine air base. It was hoped the committee would be able to report before the end on June 1946. On the committee were Lord Pakenham; Air Marshal Slater, AOC-in-C Coastal Command; Major Thornton, BOAC, and Arthur Gouge. Ironically, the following day, Heathrow airport opened and a fortnight later, Prime Minister Attlee visited BOAC at Poole harbour.

The beginning of July heralded the start of BOAC's new transatlantic service with Constellations, whilst at the close of the month, with scarcely a murmur, Lord Pakenham submitted his report to the Government. There was no public announcement as to his findings.

Whilst Sir Henry Self, the new Permanent Secretary to the Ministry of Civil Aviation, prepared his treatise, 'The Status of Civil Aviation, 1946', a Hythe flying-boat departed Poole inaugurating the 'Dragon' route to Hong Kong, on 26 August.

In his treatise, presented in September 1946, Sir Henry said:

'It is now recognized that if flying-boats are to be operated on a sound commercial basis, they must be able to demand operational and terminal facilities that are in no sense inferior to those provided for land planes.'

He continued:

'The decision to place an order for three large boats [the Princess] *require that measures should be taken to provide a suitable operating base.'*

Another month passed. On 30 October, BOAC announced that, in the summer of 1947, their Poole terminal would be moved to Southampton, whilst the maintenance facility would remain at Hythe. These would be only temporary measures until the purpose-built marine base was opened. Meanwhile, to improve the maintenance facilities at Hythe, a 1,100-foot pier and additional moorings had been constructed.

Having spent her last summer on the Mediterranean, *Champion* was withdrawn on 21 September 1946. *Golden Hind*, commanded by Dudley Travers, replaced her, and, for a year, Dudley operated what amounted to be his private airline routing via Augusta, Sicily, to Cairo.

After retirement, in September 1947, *Golden Hind* suffered a fairly ignominious end in October 1953.

It was not only the people of Great Britain who had an affinity for the flying-boat. Their love was shared by the people of South Africa. News of BOAC's decision to replace the flying-boat service to Durban with a landplane (Avro York) service to Johannesburg instead, from the end of 1946, brought near public outcry in Durban. The loss of the highly developed, most efficient facility could not be understood. It was felt that if the British gave up their operation at Congella Basin, they would never be able to re-establish themselves, considering the harbour development being planned. The South African Federated Chamber of Industry was implored by its annual convention to make urgent representations, requesting BOAC to reconsider the closure of Durban.

Possibly there was a political motive behind the change to land planes, as earlier, South African Airways

26 August 1946. BOAC Operations, Durban. *(Baldwin and Bigby)*

had accepted responsibility for the provision of the ground services between Nairobi and the Cape. Private enterprise stepped in, and Captain Caspareuthus was asked to front a South African bid to purchase ex-BOAC flying-boats. This enterprise came to nothing. The agreement between BOAC and South African Airways was based upon them both operating the Avro Tudor. However, trials found the Avro Tudor unable to operate south of Nairobi (or east of Calcutta) until the runways were lengthened, and, as it transpired, BOAC's order was eventually cancelled. As the Tudor was no longer available, South African Airways obtained American DC-4s and commenced a service. A similar chain of events characterized BOAC's dealing with QANTAS, and the Australians purchased Constellations.

As winter 1946 approached, the last of the Hythes were being launched, and *Canopus,* lacking engines and registration marks, was towed from Hythe, up Southampton Water, to a final beaching with the scrapman. She was soon followed by *Cleopatra.* They had flown 15,026 and 10,513 hours respectively, and when the time came for the others to fall to the axe, they too had flown similar amounts.

News of the agreement between BOAC and South African Airways leaked out in December 1946. As the Tudors were not available, BOAC's Yorks to Johannesburg would be replaced by South African Airways DC-4s, and Solent flying-boats would eventually be introduced by BOAC on the route to Durban. However, the Durban maintenance facility would close, as the Solents would be based at Hythe. Solents would also be operated out to Karachi, but whereas the comfort and pace of flying-boats would continue, for a while at least, speed came in the form of a DC-4 or a Constellation.

Over Christmas and New Year 1946/7, it became known that the Pakenham Committee had favoured Langstone harbour, but still the Admiralty objected. Their prime objections, this time, centred upon the incompatibility of flying-boat operations with a

GOODBYE

TO AN OLD FRIEND

Canopus *under tow at Hythe on her way to the breakers.* (The Aeroplane)

gunnery school and a radar site. The Air Ministry, the Government and the City Council were all in support of the project. It was argued that both Admiralty installations could be relocated, as the cost of moving naval facilities was small compared with the loss of revenue from the marine base. What was more, Portsmouth had often given way to Admiralty interests and now it was time for the Admiralty to repay its debt to Portsmouth. Announcement of the decision was pressing, especially as BOAC had put the Sandringhams and Solents into service. It was reiterated, Southampton was unsuitable for other than a temporary base because of the shipping.

In January 1947, the Ministry announced Langstone harbour and Cliffe had been selected as potential locations for the new marine air base. Despite Pakenham's preference for Langstone, the Government, taking everything into consideration, found against Langstone, and Lord Nathan, Minister of Civil Aviation, called for a detailed study of the site at Cliffe.

To the east, the Horseshoe Route, once the realm of the 'C-class', continued to shrink, and on 15 January, *Castor* made the last Horseshoe flight from Calcutta to Cairo. She was commanded by 'Farmer' John Pascoe, and once they had left Kallia, on the Dead Sea, the staging post there was closed. *Castor* continued to England, and through late 1946 and early 1947 the remaining

BOAC 'C-class' flying-boats were sold to R. J. Coley and Sons for scrapping. The 'boats, devoid of engines and other useful fittings, were beached at Hythe, had their wings severed by oxy-acetylene torches and, stranded on their beaching trolleys, were then hacked to death by axe men. The pieces were trimmed to size for the melting-down furnace and carted away by lorry. Much of the alloy found its way into the motor vehicle industry and was made into engine sumps. At some stage, some of the alloy was cast into crude ashtrays, depicting a relief of the Speedbird logo. There was a half-hearted attempt to preserve one 'boat, and *Cathay* was offered to the Science Museum, but they had insufficient space, and in March 1947, having flown 6,683 hours, she went down under Coley's axe.

The decade of the adventurous Empires drew to a close with *Caledonia* making the last 'C-class' flight out of Durban on 12 March 1947. Captain Peter Horne and his crew were the last to fly that rump of what had once been the 'Horseshoe Route'. By the end of March, she too had been dismembered by Coley's wreckers. By mid-April, Coley's work was completed with the destruction of *Cordelia*, but although that was the end of the British 'boats, *Awarua* succumbed at the year's end, *Coriolanus* just saw 1948 and *Aotearoa* had a brief, but undignified, existence as a tourist attraction.

Corsair: a forlorn end to a great and adventurous lady. The contract to break the 'boats went to R. J. Coley and Son. (R. J. Coley and Son)

Out of Africa for the last time. Caledonia *was the last C-class scheduled out of Durban on 12 March 1947. (L to R) Station Traffic Assistant De Abrew, Captain Peter Horn, First Officer Roberts, Radio Officer Revelle, Purser Moule and Station Superintendent Hutchins. (Baldwin and Bigby)*

Caledonia *being boarded for one last time. (Baldwin and Bigby)*

The tale of what remained once the Empires had gone is tinged with bitterness and sadness at the loss of the flying-boat. They may have been the passengers' favourite but they were an expensive mode of air transport. The much-talked-about move from Poole to Southampton occurred on 31 March 1947, and there was still hope, as, in May, Sandringhams replaced some Hythes on the route to the Persian Gulf. It was further announced, in the summer of 1947, the new BOAC terminal at Southampton's Berth 50 was expected to be operational by the end of the year, and being closer to the maintenance facility at Hythe, additional efficiencies and savings could be made. Yet again, tagged on to the end: this temporary base would remain in operation until the permanent facility was available.

And just where was that to be? On 24 July 1947, Pakenham announced another set of findings, and this time short-listed three sites, Langstone harbour, Cliffe and the previously unmentioned Brambles Shoal on the Solent. Despite it being the alleged policy of the Poole Corporation to encourage BOAC to remain at Poole, Pakenham did not take evidence from Poole. There were those who wondered if, 'Poole submitted any evidence?' Langstone harbour remained the favourite, but the Admiralty continued to object. At the end of the summer, the Government announced it was firm in its decision not to develop Langstone harbour. These were sad days for flying-boats, and on 21 September 1947 *Golden Hind* made her final flight for BOAC. *Golden Hind* escaped the attention of Coley but languished at Rochester. She was then sold, and it was whilst being towed around Kent to Hamble, for an overhaul, that she foundered in a storm at Harty Ferry in the Swale in October 1953.

The post-war Government of Britain repeatedly suffered economic crises and, in October 1947, fears were expressed that the Comet, the Brabazon and the Princess could all be vulnerable to cancellation on economic grounds. In the April of the next year, during Ministerial discussions about the future of the Princess,

it was noted that only BOAC had a commitment to the flying-boat on any scale, and it befell BOAC to establish seadromes and not simply 'buy in' services with landing fees. With uncertainty looming for the next generation of flying-boats, the 70-seater civil transport version of the Short Shetland completed preliminary trials, having first flown in September 1947. At the end of the trials, dejected, the flying-boat lay at Shorts' Belfast factory, awaiting events.

All seemed not lost, for in May 1948, Solents were introduced onto the Southampton–Vaaldam route, but within a few weeks the 'boats were 'grounded' for three months, whilst wing-tip float modifications were carried out. That same week a reorganization of BOAC was announced. Although much of the future would depend upon the Tudor and Argonaut, the Government were supporting British South American Airways' bid to operate the Saro Princess. The Minister of Civil Aviation trusted 'the S.R.45 (Princess) will maintain the British leadership in flying-boat operation which has been so much a feature of British commercial flying for so many years.' However, on the routes to South Africa and the Middle East, the Handley Page Hermes land plane was earmarked to replace the Solent flying-boats in 1950. Possibly the Solent could remain in service if it proved profitable. Questions were already being asked as to why the Solent was to be withdrawn after only eighteen months of service.

The following year, May 1949, the Solents were employed on the Southampton–Karachi route. In October 1948, Rod-el-Farag, Cairo, was closed in favour of Alexandria, and an alighting area was prepared at Lake Mariut. Reality, however, saw the forties close with the Hythe 'boat gradually being replaced by land planes. By the close of 1949, the only flying-boats left in service were the Solents plying to Vaaldam. Meanwhile, the Princess project was slipping, but, although operation by BOAC was certainly some distance in the future, plans to provide the Princess with servicing facilities at Hythe were being drawn up.

A new decade dawned, and BOAC's Chairman, Sir Miles Thomas, gave a grave New Year warning of financially dire times ahead, but he was pleased to note that where land planes had replaced flying-boats a financial upturn was taking place. Only a few months later, BOAC announced the imminent suspension of the Solent service, and on 7 November 1950, BOAC's last flying-boat service was replaced by a Handley Page Hermes land plane. Thus ended the involvement of British national airlines with passenger-carrying flying-boats. Flying-boats had served Imperial Airways and BOAC since 1924, the past quarter-century. Although the 'big' Shorts' 'boats lingered on around the world, serving with Aquila until September 1958 and TEAL until 1960, their successors never saw operation.

In Britain, the potential successor to the Shorts' 'boats was the Saunders-Roe (Saro) Princess. In the early '50s, the scope of the technical problems besetting the Princess became apparent. Second in size only to Howard Hughes's 'Spruce Goose', she was the culmination of much hard work and many dreams. Since the early 1930s, Arthur Gouge had championed the giant flying-boat. Gouge moved from Shorts to Saro in April 1943, but design studies into the giant flying-boat, under the guidance of Henry Knowler, reach back to pre-war years. In 1945, the Ministry of Supply invited tenders for a giant flying-boat airliner, and Gouge and Knowler worked together. The airliner was to be powered by ten, then new, turbo-prop engines. Construction was authorized in 1946, and BOAC expressed an interest in operating the flying-boat across the Atlantic.

Rumours that BOAC did not want the Princess started in autumn 1947, and during the 1948 reorganization, BOAC declared that both the Princess and the Brabazon were national experiments and the airline would await prototype development before they committed themselves. The project slipped: there were problems with the engines and controls. In 1951, BOAC became committed to land planes, and thoughts of Langstone harbour, Cliffe and other seadromes were quietly forgotten. In Belfast, the Shetland was scrapped.

In response, the Ministry of Supply stated the RAF would operate the Princesses as strategic transports. Finally, in August 1952, Geoffery Tyson took the Princess on her maiden flight. A test-flying programme was authorized and the large and graceful 'boat was displayed at Farnborough in 1952 and '53. The trials were completed successfully, but construction of the second and third aircraft was suspended pending engine development. Soon afterwards, following a General Election in which the Conservatives defeated the Labour Party, development of the Princess was abandoned.

In 1954, the completed Princess was cocooned and stored at Cowes, whilst the second and third airframes, similarly preserved, were stored at Calshot. And there they stayed, supposedly awaiting engine development. In the late 1950s, the United States Navy considered acquiring the hulks as part of their airborne nuclear reactor trial, but that came to nought. Finally, in 1967 the Princesses were scrapped.

Seemingly, in the 1920s and 1930s, the flying-boat would solve the problems designers of long-range aircraft were confronting. The resulting high all-up weights required long concrete runways, but the restrictive size of aerodromes and the exorbitant expense of runway construction prohibited large-scale developments. Aircraft designers promised great economies of scale with large flying-boats, and a speedy, luxurious service, capable of competing with the airship and the ocean liner, seemed possible. Even by 1940, there was still not a flying-boat, other than possibly the Boeing 314, capable of commercial operation across the North Atlantic. The Imperial Airways fleet of Empire Flying-Boats was operated primarily, and commercially, as a mail service, the passengers being of secondary importance. During the war, the commercial aspect was no longer important and many of the pre-war problems were solved. After the war, the world was awash with long runways and powerful engines, and, although there may have been few commercially viable passenger-carrying airframes, there was great potential for the development of the modern airliner as we know it today. The war destroyed many social barriers, and the improving standards of living, generally world-wide, in the '50s and '60s saw a vast increase in demand for cheap, 'no frills' air travel. The flying-boat was never cheap, it had many frills, and it was slow. It may have been popular with the passengers but flying-boat passengers never paid a market price for their seats. They were subsidized by the airmail, the war effort, the tax payer and finally the land plane.

In the summer of 1939, Major Mayo presented a paper examining the specification of a future flying-boat. His paper is enlightening, for it shows that the shortcomings of the 'C-class', and S.23 in particular, had been identified by 1939. It is fitting that the man who was Imperial Airways' Technical Adviser, and had prepared the specification for what became the 'C-class' flying-boat, should summarize the 'boats' achievements and shortfalls.

With hindsight of only a few years, it became apparent that some of the original design assumptions that dictated a flying-boat were erroneous. It had been assumed the cost of aviation fuel would be lower at a seaboard or waterway aerodrome than it would be inland. That may have been true but the cost of providing water-borne refuelling facilities greatly outweighed any savings in fuel cost.

However successful the 'C-class' had then (1939) been, they had shown themselves to be deficient in payload. The problem was exacerbated by the disappointment and delays of the Armstrong Whitworth Ensign. But the fault did not so much lie in the aircraft as in the manner in which she was operated. As an airliner, Imperial's capabilities were never put to the test, as they never truly night flew and the passenger load was always secondary to the mail. The weight of the luxurious fittings, which could never be used if passengers were ousted in favour of mail, contributed much to the 'boats' poor payload performance.

Once in service, the overall 'passenger speed' achieved was far slower than anticipated. This was mainly due to the lack of night-flying facilities which, in turn, were due to a lack of night navigation and landing aids, inadequate weather forecasting and the inherent limited range of the aircraft. Being slower than anticipated, the regularity of the service was not as expected. Many of those original assumptions had been based upon land plane operation and could not necessarily be read directly across to maritime operation. Weather proved to be a far more debilitating factor than expected. More fundamentally, the poor maintenance facilities at the Hythe home base compounded matters as did the restrictively short engine life, the unreliability of the engines and a general shortage of spare engines along the route.

However, some of the engine problems could be attributed to use in a marine environment. The prime cause of engine failures which dictated the 200-hour overhaul cycle was the failure of big end bearings and this was a design fault (which was later corrected). It was thought that lengthy taxiing may have been a cause but a change to taxi procedures brought no reduction to big end failure rates. There was some concern that the long take-off runs, experienced in the 'hot and high' of Africa, may have helped to shorten bearing life.

Experience had shown that the maintenance difficulties faced by flying-boats at marine bases were far greater than those faced by comparable land planes. There were many insignificant and inadequate staging posts along the route, few of them benefited from beaching facilities, and engine changes had to be done with 'boats upon the water. If the waters were rough, maintenance often had to await kinder weather. Some of the staging posts were considered to, at least, delay the schedule, let alone hazard it. As a result of the inadequate facilities, aircraft often spent over twenty per cent of their flying day taxiing or refuelling. Such was the appeal of some staging posts, that captains often overflew them, at the expense of reaching their destination with lower fuel margins. Facilities at home base Hythe were little better and every hour, of the two or three days between schedules, was precious to the maintenance engineers.

Flying-boat operation brought inherent difficulties when loading fuel, freight or passengers. Southampton was (then) the only base equipped with pontoons to assist boarding. Other bases could be fitted (Auckland was) but the mooring process took time, even in calm weather.

On the water and in flight the aircraft handled very well, despite possibly approaching the limit of size for un-servo assisted controls. In rough weather, it often took the strength of both pilots to keep a rein on the 'boat. The S.23's range specification called for a 500-mile range against a 40 mph headwind. This was exceeded by 50 miles and it was not the aircraft that lacked range but the specification which spawned her. The range specification assumed there would always be alternate landing sites in mid-France and at Crete. This was not to be, and the sectors over France and the Mediterranean often proved to be a bottle neck, further restricting the schedule.

Underlining all that had gone before, it had been noted the operating costs exceeded expectations.

Finally, there was the accident record. Initially, the Empire 'Boats suffered a high accident rate which it was thought could, partially, have been attributed to the operation of marine aircraft. The accident rate did most certainly dent general confidence in the safety of the flying-boat. It was not unknown in the early days to lose a float on landing. Many of the losses were attributed to captains having difficulty judging the 'wings level' attitude. This tendency disappeared once a horizontal marker wire was placed across the curved windscreen, giving the pilots a visual reference to the horizon.

The strength of the 'boat was also lacking and although constructed to the accepted standards of the time, there had been little operational experience of large flying-boats to call upon. The hull was always prone to damage during normal operation let alone during poor landings or rough weather. In April 1938, Centaurus made a heavy landing at night at Alexandria and was out of service for some months. Of the losses at the time (Courtier, Cygnus, Calpurnia, Cavalier and Centurion) all the fatalities had resulted from hull failures in conditions which could barely be termed as moderately severe. The hulls should have withstood the landings. Such was Shorts' concern over hull strength that the 'G-class' 'boats were being fitted with hulls twice as strong and similarly strengthened hulls were planned for the S.30 and, as a modification when possible, for all the remaining 'boats.

Another reason for the apparently high attrition was the difficulty in salvaging flying-boats from the waters in which they lay. Many of the total losses seemed to have been the result of over enthusiastic or untrained salvage crews doing more damage to the flying-boat whilst attempting recovery than was caused during the accident. Both Coorong and Capella were returned to Rochester for repair, but only Coorong was returned to service. Corrosion was too far gone in Capella to make repair possible.

Events proved Mayo right, and the difficulties of flying-boat operations persisted, and likewise the enthusiasm shared by Mayo and Gouge was not rewarded by the sight of a truly giant flying-boat in operation. That dream was killed by the war. Be that as it may, it cannot be denied that the Short 'C-class' (to the purist, the only Empire Flying-Boat) was the most successful, most numerous, purpose-built passenger-carrying flying-boat of all time. And yes, I wish I could have journeyed with Hugh Gordon in those magnificent flying machines, in the golden years of aviation, and experienced my own Adventurous Empire.

Bibliography

The publications listed below were consulted during research for *Adventurous Empires*

The Age of the Biplane. Chaz Bowyer – Hamlyn
Annals of British and Commonwealth Air Transport.
    J. Stroud – Pitman
Airline. Driscoll
Air Transport Before WWII. Taylor/Munson – New English
    Library
Air War for Yugoslavia, Greece and Crete 1940–41.
    C. Shores and others
Airliners. Robert Wall – Collins London 1980
Airspeed – The Company and its Aeroplanes. Middleton
Approach March. Autobiography Julian Amery – Hutchinson
Armstrong Whitworth Aircraft Since 1913. Oliver Tapper
Atlantic Air Conquest. Ellis – William Kimber
The Atlantic Bridge. Air Ministry London 1945
Australian Air Force Since 1911. Parnell and Lynch –
    A. H. and A. W. Reid
Australia in Empire Air Transports. W. Hudson Fysh – Journal
    RAes Jan 46
Bloody Shambles. C. Shores and others – Grub Street
Boats Of The Air. David Wragg
Brackles. F. Brackley
Britain's Imperial Air Routes 1918–39. Robin Hingmam – Foulis
British Civil Aircraft Since 1919. A. Jackson – Putnam
British Commercial Aircraft – 60 Years in Pictures. Ellis – Janes
British Flying Boats & Amphibians. Durval – Putnam
Challenging Horizons. John Gunn – University of Queensland
    Press
Cross Country. H. E. Travers
Defeating Distance. John Gunn – University of Queensland
    Press
*Diary of the delivery of the flying-boat ZK-AMA 'Aotearoa' from
    Southampton England to Auckland, New Zealand; August
    16th to August 28th 1939.* Auckland: Gerald W. Brown
    1939
Dice on Regardless. Ken Robinson
Ferryman. Griffith Powell – Airlife Publishing Ltd
Fledging Eagles. Christopher Shores and others –
    Grub Street
Flying Boat. Jablonski
Flying Boat. Kenneth Poolman – William Kimber
The Flying Boat Era. David Lowe – Lodestar Press Auckland
Flying Empires. Brian Cassidy – Queen's Parade Press
From Many Angels. Rt Hon. Maj. Gen Sir F. Sykes – Harrop
    and Co.
Frontline Airline. E. Bennet-Bremner – Angus and Robertson
Giants in the Sky. Taylor and Monday – Janes
The Golden Age of New Zealand Flying Boats. Harrison,
    Lockstaff and Anderson – Random House New Zealand
The Guinness Book of Air Facts and Feats. John W. R. Taylor,
    Michael J. H. Taylor, David Mondey 1973 and onwards –
    Guinness Superlatives Limited
Head In The Clouds. G. N. Wells – Hodder and Stoughton
Illustrated History of Seaplanes & Flying boats. Maurice
Illustrated Encyclopaedia of Aircraft. Orbis
Illustrated Encyclopaedia of Propeller Airliners. Gunston –
    Winwood
Into The Wind. Reith – Hodder
Kangaroo Route. Hooper Meredith – Angus and Robertson
The Log of a Merchant Airman. John Locke and John Creasey
The Lonely Sea and the Sky. Francis Chichester
Merchant Airmen. The Air Ministry Account of British Civil
    Aviation: 1939–1944. HMSO Ministry of Information
Off The Beam. Chandler
Ominous Skies. Penrose – HMSO
Pathfinder Bennett. AVM D.C.T. Bennett
Pathfinder Bennett Airman Extraordinary. A. S. Jackson–Terence
    Dalton
Pictorial History of BOAC & Imperial Airways. Munson – Ian
    Allen
Pride of Unicorns. Biography of the Atcherly Bros
QANTAS Rising. H. Fysh – Angus and Robertson
QANTAS at War. H. Fysh – Angus and Robertson
*Recounting the Operations of RAAF Catalinas May
    1941 to March 1943.* Jack Riddell – Murwillumbah Print
    Spot
The Reith Diaries. C. Stuart – Collins
The Royal Mail. F. George Kay – Rockcliff
Seven Skies. John Pudney – Putnam
Shorts Aircraft Since 1900. Barnes – Putnam
A Short History – The History of Short Bros. 1909–1964
Shorts Planemakers. Michael Taylor – Janes
Slide Rule. Nevil Shute – Pan
Sun On My Wings. Bednall – Paterchurch publications
Swifter than Eagles. John Laffin – W. Blackwood
    and Sons
Test Pilots. Don Middleton – Willow Books London
20,000 Miles in a Flying boat: My flight around Africa. Sir Alan
    Cobham – George G. Harrop and Co. Ltd
Tizard. R. W. Clark – Methuen and Co. Ltd
Unsung Heroes of the Air. A H. Narcott – Muller
The Water Jump. David Beaty – Secker and Warburg
Wings over Dorset. Leslie Dawson – Dorset
    Publishing Co.
Wings over Westminster. Biography of H. H. Balfour
Wingspread. Leo White – Whites Aviation New Zealand
The Royal New Zealand Navy. Sydney D. Waters. 1946
and
Royal New Zealand Air Force. J. M. S. Ross. 1955. Both
    published by Wellington: War History Branch,
    Department of Internal Affairs
Periodicals: *The Aeroplane, Aeroplane Monthly, Air Enthusiast
    Quarterly, Air Pictorial, Flight International, The Times*

APPENDIX 1

The Imperial Airways/BOAC S.23 Flying-Boats

Hull Number	Regist'n	Name	Date of CofA or First Flight	Subsequent Registrations	Final Disposal	Date
S.795	G-ADHL	CANOPUS	20 Oct 36		Scrapped Hythe	Nov 46
S.804	G-ADHM	CALEDONIA	2 Dec 36		Scrapped Hythe	Mar 47
S.811	G-ADUT	CENTAURUS	28 Oct 36	RAAF A18-10 20 Sep 39	Enemy action – bombed Broome	3 Mar 42
S.812	G-ADUU	CAVALIER	25 Nov 36		Crashed Atlantic – precautionary landing – icing – hull breached – sank	2 Jan 39
S.813	G-ADUV	CAMBRIA	15 Jan 37		Scrapped Hythe	Jan 46
S.814	G-ADUW	CASTOR	23 Dec 36		Scrapped Hythe	Feb 47
S.815	G-ADUX	CASSIOPEIA	25 Jan 37		Crashed on take-off Sabang – sank	29 Dec 41
S.816	G-ADUY	CAPELLA	16 Feb 37		Hit uncharted wreck Batavia – sank	12 Mar 39
S.817	G-ADUZ	CYGNUS	1 Mar 37		Attempted full-flap take-off Brindisi – porpoised – sank	5 Dec 37
S.818	G-ADVA	CAPRICORNUS	14 Mar 37		Crashed Macon, France – hit high ground – navigational error	24 Mar 37
S.819	G-ADVB	CORSAIR	3 Apr 37		Scrapped Hythe	Jan 47
S.820	G-ADVC	COURTIER	21 Apr 37		Crashed on landing Athens – glassy calm sea – hull breached	1 Oct 37
S.821	G-ADVD	CHALLENGER	8 May 37		Crashed on landing Mozambique – possible crew error – sank	1 May 39
S.822	G-ADVE	CENTURION	29 May 37		Crashed on landing Calcutta – wind shear – sank	12 Jun 39
S.838	G-AETV	CORIOLANUS	17 Jun 37	QEA VH-ABG Sep 42	Scrapped Rose Bay	Dec 47
S.839	G-AETW	CALPURNIA	28 Jun 37		Crashed Habbaniyah descent in bad weather – landed in shallow water	27 Nov 38
S.840	G-AETX	CERES	16 Jul 37	Written off 28 Feb 43	Hangar fire Durban	1 Dec 42
S.841	G-AETY	CLIO	26 Jul 37	RAF as 23M AX659 Jul 40	Crashed Loch Indaal (Islay) engine failure during air test	22 Aug 41
S.842	G-AETZ	CIRCE	16 Aug 37		Presumed shot down Japanese Java	28 Feb 42
S.843	G-AEUA	CALYPSO	26 Aug 37	RAAF A18-11 20 Sep 39 QEA Apr 42	New Guinea Daru – landed in open sea – hull breached – sank	8 Aug 42
S.844	G-AEUB	CAMILLA	13 Sep 37	QEA VH-ADU 13 Jul 42	Crashed Port Moresby – forced down in poor weather – hull breached – sank	22 Mar 43
S.845	G-AEUC	CORINNA	25 Sep 37	QEA Sep 39 but remain on UK reg	Enemy action – bombed at Broome	3 Mar 42
S.846	G-AEUD	CORDELIA	9 Oct 37	RAF as S.23M AX660 Jul 40 BOAC Dec 41	Scrapped Hythe	Apr 47
S.847	G-AEUE	Laid down as Cairngorm CAMERONIAN	23 Oct 37		Scrapped Hythe	Jan 47
S.848	G-AEUF	Laid down as Cotswold CORINTHIAN	9 Nov 37		Crashed Darwin – night landing – pilot possibly dazzled – sank	21/2 Mar 42

APPENDIX 2
The QANTAS Empire Airways S.23 Flying-Boats

Hull Number	Regist'n	Name	Date of CofA or First Flight	Subsequent Registrations	Final Disposal	Date
S.849	G-AEUG	Laid down as Cheviot COOGEE	8 Jan 38	QEA VH-ABC Jul 38 RAAF A18-12 8 Jun 40	Crashed on landing Townsville -possibly incorrect handling – sank	28 Feb 42
S.850	G-AEUH	Laid down as Coolin CORIO	10 Feb 38	QEA VH-ABD Feb 38	Enemy Action – shot down by Japanese, Timor Kupang	3 Jan 42
S.851	G-AEUI	Laid down as Calpe COORONG	26 Feb 38	QEA VH-ABE Mar 38 Rebuilt Rochester BOAC G-AEUI Nov 40	Scrapped Hythe	Feb 47
S.876	G-AFBJ	CARPENTARIA	25 Nov 37	QEA VH-ABA Jun 38 BOAC G-AFBJ Jun 42	Scrapped Hythe	Jan 47
S.877	G-AFBK	COOLANGATTA	18 Dec 37	QEA VH-ABB Mar 38 RAAF A18-13 26 Jun 40 VH-CRB Jul 43	Crashed Rose Bay – precautionary landing – low oil pressure – stalled – hull breached – sank	11 Oct 44
S.878	G-AFBL	COOEE	30 Mar 38	QEA VH-ABF Mar 38 BOAC Jun 42	Scrapped Hythe	Feb 47

APPENDIX 3
The Imperial Airways/BOAC S.30 Flying-Boats

Hull Number	Regist'n	Name	Date of CofA or First Flight	Subsequent Registrations	Final Disposal	Date
S.879	G-AFCT	CHAMPION	27 Oct 38	(Pegasus-engined S.30)	Scrapped Hythe	Apr 47
S.880	G-AFCU	CABOT	8 Mar 39	RAF V3137 Oct 39	Enemy action bombed at Bodö	6 May 40
S.881	G-AFCV	CARIBOU	7 Jul 39	RAF V3138 Oct 39	Enemy action bombed at Bodö	5 May 40
S.882	G-AFCW	CONNEMARA	25 Mar 39		Refuelling fire burnt out at Hythe	19 Jun 39
S.883	G-AFCX	CLYDE	29 Mar 39		Wrecked in storm at Lisbon	15 Feb 41
S.1003	G-AFKZ	CATHAY	26 Feb 40		Scrapped Hythe	Mar 47

APPENDIX 4
The Tasman Empire Airways Limited Flying-Boats

Hull Number	Regist'n	Name	Date of CofA or First Flight	Subsequent Registrations	Final Disposal	Date
S.884	G-AFCY	QANTAS as Captain Cook AWARUA	24 Apr 39	Loan to Imperial Airways March 1939. Launched as Ao-Tea-Roa ZK-AMA. 8 Apr 39 became AWARUA G-AFCY	Scrapped Auckland	Nov 47
S.885	G-AFCZ	QANTAS as Canterbury AUSTRALIA CLARE	6 Apr 39	Loan to Imperial Airways March 1939.Launched as AUSTRALIA ZK-AMB. Aug 39–Jul 40 rebuilt as CLARE G-AFCZ	Crashed Bathurst presumed engine failure	4 Sep 42
S.886	G-AFDA	QANTAS as Cumberland AOTEAROA	12 May 39	To Imperial Airways March 1939. Launched as AWARUA ZK-AMA. May 1939 became G-AFDA. Briefly Reg ZK-AMC before becoming ZK-AMA AOTEAROA	Taken out of water and displayed at Walsh Brothers' Flying School	Tourist attraction until 195?

APPENDIX 5
Short S.33 Empire Flying-Boats

Date of Hull Number	Regist'n	Name	CofA or First Flight	Subsequent Registrations	Final Disposal	Date
S.1025	G-AFPZ	CLIFTON	18 Nov 40	RAAF A18-14 Mar 42 QEA VH-ACD Jul 43	Crashed Rose Bay – night-landing training – sank	18 Jan 44
S.1026	G-AFRA	CLEOPATRA	8 May 40		Scrapped Hythe	Nov 46
S.1027	G-AFRB		Construction abandoned May 40		Stored – broken up Rochester	After May 43

APPENDIX 6
Short Composite S.20 Maia and S.21 Mercury

Date of Hull Number	Regist'n	Name	CofA or First Flight	Subsequent Registrations	Final Disposal	Date
S.796	G-ADHJ	MERCURY	2 Jul 38	RNLAF 320 Sqn Oct 40	Scrapped Rochester	Aug 41
S.797	G-ADHK	MAIA	1 Jun 38		Enemy action – bombed at Poole	11 May 41

APPENDIX 7
Short S.26 'G-class' Flying-Boats

Date of Hull Number	Regist'n	Name	CofA or First Flight	Subsequent Registrations	Final Disposal	Date
S.871	G-AFCI	GOLDEN HIND	f.f. 21 Jul 39	RAF X8275 Jul 40 BOAC Dec 41	Last flight BOAC Sep 47 – wrecked during storm Harty Ferry	Mar 54
S.872	G-AFCJ	GOLDEN FLEECE	f.f. 8 Jul 40	RAF X8274	Forced down Cape Finisterre – multi-engine failure – hull breached	20 Jun 41
S.873	G-AFCK	GOLDEN HORN	f.f. 24 Feb 40	RAF X8273 Jul 40 BOAC Dec 41	Crashed on landing Lisbon – engine failure on air test – smoke filled cockpit	9 Jan 43

APPENDIX 8

M a p s

Africa

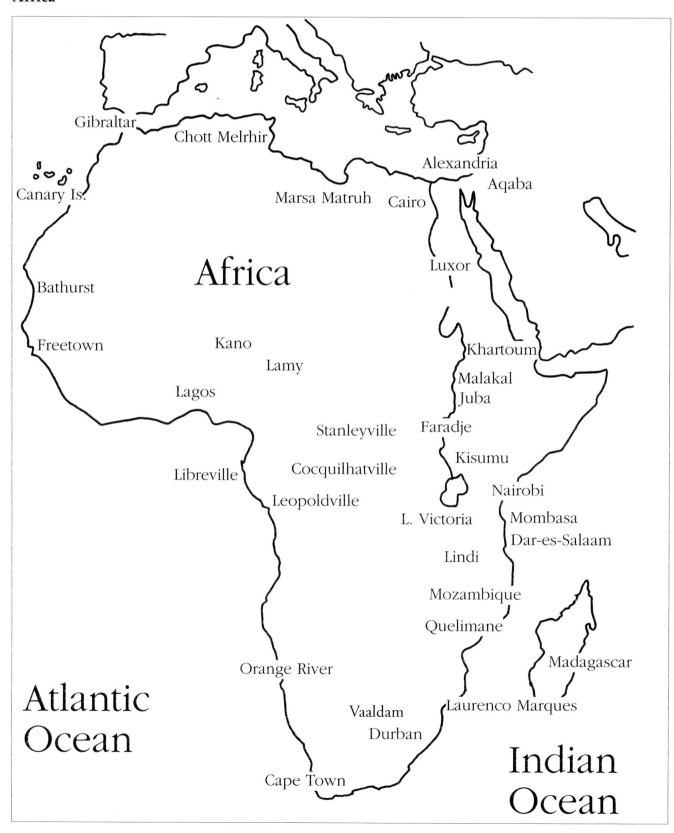

Gibraltar

Chott Melrhir

Alexandria

Aqaba

Canary Is.

Marsa Matruh

Cairo

Africa

Luxor

Bathurst

Freetown

Kano

Khartoum

Lamy

Malakal

Juba

Lagos

Stanleyville

Faradje

Kisumu

Libreville

Cocquilhatville

Nairobi

Leopoldville

Mombasa

L. Victoria

Dar-es-Salaam

Lindi

Mozambique

Quelimane

Orange River

Madagascar

Atlantic
Ocean

Vaaldam

Laurenco Marques

Durban

Indian
Ocean

Cape Town

Europe and the Mediterranean

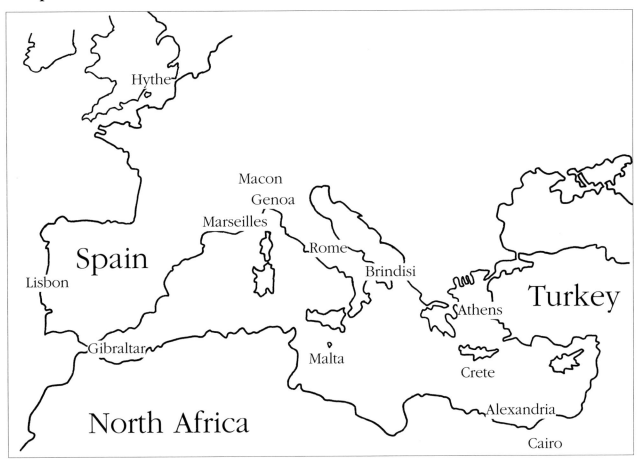

The North Atlantic

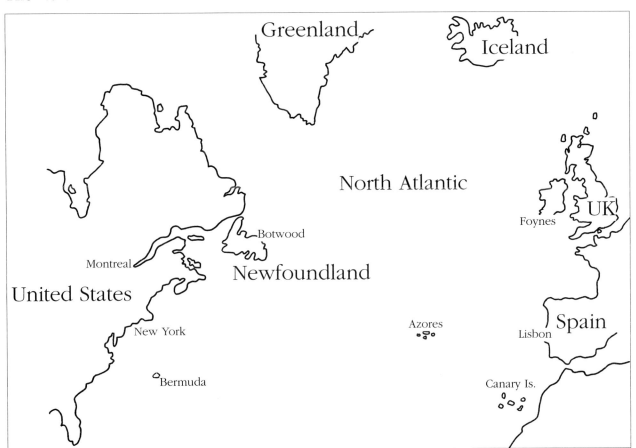

The Indian Ocean

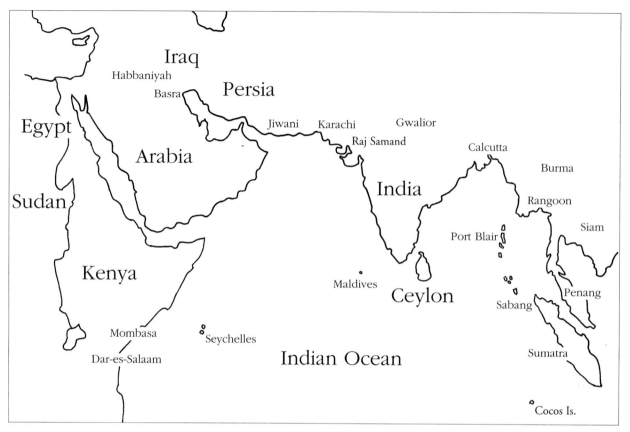

South-east Asia, Australasia and Oceania

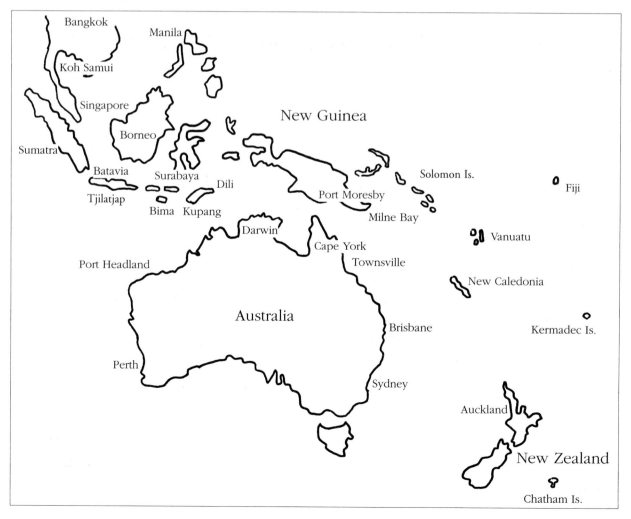

Index

Aircraft
Armstrong Whitworth Argosy 19, 21, 22
Armstrong Whitworth Ensign 16, 25, 73, 81, 86, 106, 167, 174, 175, 246
Atlantic Shirl 13
Avro Tudor 243, 245
Avro York 243
Boeing Model 314 70, 99, 144–148, 152, 158, 172, 176, 179, 182, 189, 195, 203, 207, 237, 239, 242, 246
Bristol Brabazon 245, 246
City of Khartoum 19, 21, 81
D.H.66 18–22
D.H.88 Comet Racer 23
D.H.91 Albatross 25, 70, 75, 86, 147, 150, 188
Dornier Do 17 186
Dornier Do 18 99, 104
Dornier Do 24 218
Dornier Wal 69, 98
Dornier Do X 98
Douglas DC-2 23, 24
Douglas DC-3 60, 86, 218, 219
Douglas DC-4 238, 243
Fairey FC 1 Airliner 150, 158
Handley Page Harrow 145, 146, 151, 152, 156, 157, 167
Handley Page Hermes 245, 246
Handley Page H.P.42 20, 23, 41, 49, 86
Handley Page 0/400 16
Handley Page V/1500 13
Handley Page W10 145, 146
Junkers 20, 53, 70, 116, 199, 239
Lockheed Constellation 242, 243
Martin M-130 Clipper 97, 99, 147
Martinsyde 13
NC-1/NC-3/NC-4 13
Saro Princess 242, 245, 246
Short Calcutta 19, 21, 42, 48, 49, 81, 86, 89
Short Hythe 239, 242, 243, 245
Short Kent 19, 20, 21, 24, 35, 38, 39, 40, 42, 48, 89
Satyrus 19, 21, 38, 42, 43, 48
Scipio 19, 34, 35, 39
Scylla 19, 86
Syrinx 19
Short Rangoon 49, 172
Short Sandringham 224, 238, 239, 241, 244, 245
Short Sarafand 24
Short Seaford 239
Short Shetland 71, 241, 245, 246
Short Shirl *Shamrock* 12, 13
Short Singapore 18, 19, 45, 134
Short Solent 242–246
Short Sunderland 25, 37, 69, 107, 151, 185, 188, 195, 196, 197, 199, 203, 205, 206, 207, 237, 239, 242
Short Valetta 17, 18
Sikorsky S.42 24, 70, 71, 73, 99, 138, 141, 148
Vickers Vernon 14
Vought-Sikorsky VS-44 A 155
Airmail
early airmail 22
Kingsford Smith saves the day 22
Airship
British Zeppelin Syndicate 17
Burney Airship Scheme 17, 69
Cardington 17
Hindenburg 17
R.100 17
R.101 17
Zeppelin 17
Airlines
Aircraft Transport and Travel AT&T 12
American Export Airlines 155, 207

British Air Transport Service 15, 89
British Marine Air Navigation 15, 89
Daimler Airways 15, 17
Imperial Air Transport Company 15
Imperial Air Transport Ltd 15
Imperial Airways, birth of 16
Indian Trans-Continental Airways 20, 23, 45
Pan American Airways PAA (Pan Am) 38, 70, 71, 74, 78, 79, 97, 99, 105, 138, 138, 141, 144–147, 152–158, 170–173, 176, 178, 179, 182, 184, 188, 189, 203, 207, 226, 227, 229, 232–234
QANTAS – Queensland and Northern Territories Aerial Service Company 12, 15, 22, 23, 45, 83, 86, 112, 159, 160, 165, 166, 169, 170, 173, 174, 179, 192, 195, 200, 207–212, 214, 215, 217–224, 231, 233, 243
QANTAS Empire Airways QEA 38, 45, 48, 49, 159, 162, 165, 169, 170, 173, 180, 208, 209, 210, 211, 212, 214, 215, 220
The Atlantic Ocean
Boeing Model 314 70, 144, 145, 147, 148, 152, 158, 189, 195, 203, 207, 242, 246
Caledonia and *Cambria* 38, 69, 71, 72, 79
Clare and *Clyde* to America 150, 152, 183, 187–190
early attempts 12
inflight refuelling *Cabot* and *Caribou* 111, 143, 147, 152, 155–158, 183, 184, 188
Maia and *Mercury* 24, 104

blind-flying 13, 27, 81
Brabazon Committee 240C-Class 16, 24, 25, 33, 35, 40, 48, 49, 68, 69, 70, 80, 145, 158, 182, 202, 225, 237, 239, 242, 246, 247

C-Class scrapped 244
carburettor 21, 60, 76, 117, 129, 139, 143, 144
'Castor' oiled 41
Christmas mail 21, 40, 72, 79, 110, 113
Christmas 1936 airmail 38, 40
Composite (*Maia and Mercury*)
the Atlantic 24, 104
Christmas airmail 110
description 100
early flights 102
long-distance record 105–110
separation 102, 103, 105, 107, 108, 110
war service 111
Curtiss 12, 13
Customs 12, 50, 105, 136, 163, 164, 171, 204, 206, 207

Daily Mail 13
Delhi Flying Club 20
Dunlop 15, 80, 145

Empire Airmail Scheme
accelerated service 83
Christmas 1936 38, 40
Christmas 1937 82
Christmas 1938 82, 86
EAMS announced 23
Empire Air Mail gains support 23
Geddes presents his plan 23
Engines
Armstrong Siddeley Genet Major 49
Armstrong Siddeley Jaguar 17
Bristol Hercules 148, 150, 204
Bristol Pegasus 26, 30, 34, 93, 100, 111, 130, 134, 139, 150, 195, 236, 237
Bristol Perseus 95, 143, 145, 147, 150, 153, 173, 176, 182, 236
Bristol Taurus 150

Engine failure 21, 35, 66, 97, 140, 164, 191, 202, 236, 238, 247
Napier Rapier 100, 104, 106, 109

flare-path 21, 72, 91, 108, 112, 161, 175, 176, 201–203, 212, 214, 222, 232
forced alighting/landing 14, 17, 18, 21, 49, 71, 114, 116-118, 125, 129, 136, 145, 146
France, fall of 183, 187, 188, 191

'G-class' flying-boat
description 148
RAF Service 185, 190, 191
return to BOAC 191
loss of *Golden Fleece* 191
loss of *Golden Horn* 204
demise of *Golden Hind* 185, 190, 243, 245
Gentlemen's Agreement, The 71, 99, 147, 155, 169

Hamilton Standard propellers 225, 236
Horseshoe Route 183, 187, 188, 191–193, 195–198, 200, 204, 210, 211, 215, 242, 244

Inspector of Accidents 21, 69, 143

liaison with No 11 Sqn RAAF 232

maintenance 92, 93, 95, 118, 162, 172, 198, 206, 210, 231, 235, 242, 243, 245, 247
Marsh Arab 18
meteorological 13, 19, 48, 60, 70, 71, 107, 115, 160, 163, 165, 178

night landing 13, 44, 117, 170, 223
Northern Arabia Persian Gulf Route 20

passenger comfort 38, 50, 51, 55–57, 61
People
Alcock & Brown 12,13
Alcock, Captain E.S. 'John' 40, 42, 61, 66, 114, 115, 117, 119–121, 125–128, 130, 159, 198, 199, 205, 206
Arrol, Ernie 78, 129, 130
Baldwin, Prime Minister 15
Barnard, Captain F. L. 18
Beharrell, Sir John George, D.S.O. 15, 38, 80, 81, 84, 88, 89
Bennett, Air Vice-Marshal D. C. T. 44, 51, 64, 104–111, 147, 152–157, 165, 177, 187, 188
Bennett, 'Bill' 211, 212, 219, 220
Benoist 12
Bibby, Alfred E. 33, 34
Bonar, Law Andrew, Prime Minister 14, 15
Brackley, Major Herbert George 12, 13, 16, 17, 23, 25, 36–40, 45–48, 73, 125, 170, 184, 188
Brancker, AVM John 210, 211
Brancker, Sir Sefton 14, 15, 17, 84
Bullock, Sir Christopher 18, 84, 85
Burl, Cyril 127, 130, 198
Cadman, Lord, Rt Hon. 80, 82, 87, 88, 150, 158, 167, 168
Chamberlain, Neville, Prime Minister 19, 88, 120
Chetwynd, Lord 20
Churchill, Winston 13, 14, 187, 190, 233
Cobham, Sir Alan 17, 18, 38, 80, 81, 145, 146, 151, 152, 156
Cowling, Alf 93, 94, 127–130, 196–199
Curtiss, Glenn 12
Cussans, 'Paddy' 114–117, 119–121, 175–177, 179, 180
Dismore, S.A. 23
Elliott, Arthur B. 18

People (cont.)
Emmott, B.W.G. 17, 18
Fabre, Henri 12
Fysh, Hudson 15, 38, 45–47, 162, 166, 170, 173, 181, 182, 208–210, 224
Geddes, Sir Eric Campbell 15, 23, 24, 36, 38, 70, 80, 81, 84, 88, 169, 174
George V, King 18
George VI, King 34, 54, 84
Gordon, Hugh 57, 59, 60, 111, 120–127, 247
Hambling 14–16
Hamel, Gustav 12, 13, 22
Hackett, Johnny 205, 206
Hill, Roderick 14
Hinkler, Bert 15
Hoare, Lady Maude 18, 19
Hoare, Sir Samuel, Secretary of State for Air 14–16, 18–20, 36
Johnston, Squadron Leader E. L. 18
Lankester, Parker, John 13, 24, 26, 34–37, 69, 102, 103, 114, 143, 158, 185, 241
Lewin, Brigadier-General – rescue of 114
Londonderry, Lord 15, 70, 71, 82–85
Marconi 18, 28, 42, 64, 73, 121
McGuinness, Pat 15
McMaster, Fergus 15, 173, 181
Mollard, Captain Roger 22, 67, 207, 209
Munro, Don 104–106, 108–110, 136, 153–155
Peek, Russell, 'Bill' 94, 173, 175, 176, 178, 181, 182, 226, 228, 230, 235–237
Perkins, MP 80–82, 88, 143, 168
Porte, J.C. 12, 13
Powell, Captain Griffith 'Taffy' 40, 49, 54, 63, 66, 73–79, 103, 117, 138, 139, 141–144, 183, 184
Reid, Captain 'Dick' 49, 66, 191, 205, 206, 235
Reith, Sir J.C.W. 36, 84, 87–89, 143, 156–158, 167, 168, 174, 239, 240
Salmond, Sir Geoffrey, (AOC India) 18
Salmond, Sir John, Marshal of the Royal Air Force 48, 68, 88, 156
Salmond, Lady 69
Searle, Colonel 15
Short Brothers
Albert Eustace 24
Francis 33
Horace Leonard 24, 33
Hugh Oswald 24, 33–35, 157
Sykes, Major-General Sir Fredrick 13, 14, 69, 240
Sisson, Roy 127–130
Smith, Ross 15
Swinton, Major–General Ernest 13, 14, 64, 74, 80, 82, 88
Wadhams, George 34
Wakefield, Sir Charles, Lord 18
Wakefield, Wavell 189
Ward, Sergeant 185
Weir 13, 14
Wellman, Walter 13
Wilson, Captain V. G. 21, 81
Wolley Dod, Captain C. F. 18, 19
Woods Humphery 15–17, 23, 24, 50, 71, 74, 81, 84, 87–89, 106, 158, 174

Phases, the 208, 210, 214
phoney war 180, 183, 184
pilots' strike 17, 168

Places
Aboukir 18, 145, 198
Akyab 22, 44, 180, 200, 210, 214
Alexandria 18–21, 35, 39–43, 48, 49, 61, 64, 66, 67, 72, 81, 83, 86, 89, 91, 103, 110, 112, 114, 118, 127, 129, 132, 136, 145, 160, 161, 172, 174, 176, 180, 187, 188, 191, 196–198, 245, 247
Alor Star 23
Amman 14, 145
Amsterdam 23
Aqaba 191, 198
Athens 19, 21, 35, 39, 55, 64, 66, 67, 83, 161, 162, 165, 176, 180, 184, 187, 196
Atlantic City 13
Auckland 170–174, 176–179, 181, 182, 188, 226–229, 231–233, 235–237, 247
Azores 13, 69, 70, 71, 73, 74, 78, 79, 98–100, 105, 147, 153
Baghdad 14, 17, 20, 22, 43, 195

Bahrain 112, 113, 192, 195
Bangkok 83, 85, 86, 113, 160, 162, 163, 176, 192, 210, 211
Basle 19
Basra 18–20, 43, 44, 83, 91, 93, 113, 145, 155, 161, 162, 165, 174–176, 180, 183, 188, 192, 195, 200, 215, 225
Beira 18, 109, 192, 204
Bombay 13, 44
Brindisi 20, 21, 39, 40, 41, 66, 67, 69, 80, 143, 161, 165, 180, 187
Burma 17, 22, 44, 82, 163, 164, 210, 211
Cairo 13, 14, 17–22, 39, 41, 42, 49, 55, 61, 62, 83, 188, 191, 192, 196–201, 242–245
Calcutta 21, 44, 83, 86, 112, 113, 160, 162, 165, 176, 180, 192, 200, 204, 207, 210, 211, 214, 215, 242–244
Cape Town 13, 21, 23, 38, 106–110
Corfu 19, 184, 187
Crete 19, 21, 35, 55, 66, 195–200, 247
Croydon 12, 14, 15, 17–19, 21–23, 49, 50, 72, 80, 86, 89, 92, 96, 136, 183
Darwin 18, 22, 46–48, 83, 84, 86, 106, 108, 160, 162, 165, 166, 170, 176, 180, 209, 212–215, 218–222
Darwin débâcle 159, 162–164
Darwin attacked 208, 215, 216
Delhi 19, 20, 22, 40
Dili 209, 212, 215
Foynes 71–78, 92, 105, 111, 140, 151, 155–157, 188, 189, 192, 199, 203, 204, 206, 207
Genoa 19–21, 36, 37
Gibraltar 18, 191, 199, 200
Habbaniyah 43, 44, 86, 112, 113, 120, 162, 172, 176, 180, 191, 192, 195
Heathrow 12, 114, 240, 242
Hounslow 12
Hythe 40, 43, 48–50, 58, 62, 63, 66, 72, 73, 77–80, 83, 92–94, 106, 111, 136, 152, 156, 158, 160, 174, 175, 178, 180, 184, 185, 187, 188, 190, 191, 195, 206, 207, 242–245, 247
Iraq 14, 18, 20, 22, 43, 44, 93, 163, 195
Ismailia 17
Italy 19, 21, 23, 91, 97, 98, 161, 176, 183, 184, 187, 188, 198, 208
Jask 19
Kallang 38, 44, 45, 162, 165, 176, 209, 211
Karachi 13, 14, 17–20, 22, 23, 38, 41, 43, 44, 48, 67, 68, 82, 86, 113, 114, 145, 159, 160, 162, 174, 176, 180, 192, 206, 209, 214, 215, 242, 243, 245
Karumba 48, 163, 180, 221
Kenya 21, 87, 114, 136
Khartoum 22, 42, 43, 51, 114, 118, 127, 192, 198, 199, 201
Kisumu 42, 43, 66, 83, 86, 114, 117, 118, 132, 134, 183, 184, 192, 198, 201, 203, 204, 207
Koh Samui 162, 164
Kupang 22, 46, 48, 162, 165, 170, 212–214, 216
La Mede 12
Lagos 108, 182, 188, 191–195, 198, 199, 201–203
Lake Kivu 18, 38
Lake Victoria 18, 22, 38, 118, 194
Lakehurst 17, 141
Langstone harbour 44, 82, 89, 90, 91, 92, 167, 241–246
Lisbon 13, 74, 79, 98, 99, 105, 148, 153, 155, 158, 188, 191–194, 199, 200, 202–204
London Airport 82
Luxor 42, 192
Malta 60, 110, 145, 168, 184, 187, 191, 199, 200, 201
Margil 43, 44, 174, 180
Marsa Matruh 19, 66, 201
Marseilles 12, 39–41, 49, 58–64, 66, 72, 86, 110, 148, 153, 155, 161, 165, 170, 176, 180, 184, 187
Mechanics Bay 227, 229–231
Melbourne 18, 23, 145, 162, 171, 172, 231
Milne Bay 212, 221, 223
Mirabella 35, 36, 39, 66
Montreal 17, 71, 73, 74, 77, 78, 105, 151, 152, 157, 189
Mountbatten 188
Naples 19, 110
New Guinea 205, 208, 221–223, 225
Newfoundland 13, 69–72, 74, 76, 77, 79, 98, 105, 151, 157, 189
Pagham harbour 98
Pembroke Dock 78, 111, 184, 190, 191, 207

Penang 82, 86, 162, 176, 180, 205, 210
Persia 18–20
Persian Gulf 19, 20, 43, 112, 164, 183, 207, 245
Poole Harbour 111, 157, 179, 180, 183, 184, 187, 188, 189, 190, 193–195, 199, 202–204, 206, 207, 241, 242, 245
Poro Bay 66
Port Moresby 12, 208, 212, 220–223, 232
Rineanna 73, 156, 241
River Medway 17, 34–36, 39, 40, 102, 103, 158
Rochester 13, 18, 26, 34–40, 91, 100–103, 110, 111, 120, 121, 124, 127, 145, 152, 155, 166, 185, 191, 204, 239–241, 245, 247
Rod–el–Farag 188, 199, 245
Rome 49, 66, 69, 110, 161, 187
St Petersburg 12
Salonika 19
Sharjah 20, 43, 112, 122, 192
Shatt–el–Arab 44, 175, 176, 180
Singapore 20, 21, 23, 24, 38, 44–48, 50, 55, 68, 82–84, 86, 91, 113, 159, 160, 162–166, 170, 173, 175, 176, 179, 180, 183, 192, 197, 200, 209, 216, 217, 219, 223, 242
fall of Singapore 208, 210–212, 214, 215
Suda Bay 19, 184, 191, 196, 197
Tampa 12
Tasman Sea 47, 84, 159, 169–174, 177, 179, 182, 184, 225, 232, 236, 237, 238
Thames River 18, 72, 137, 156, 240
Timor Sea 18, 162, 176, 212, 215, 217
Tjilatjap (shuttle) 208, 214–218
Tobruk 19, 69
Townsville 48, 163, 165, 170, 177, 180, 208, 218, 220–223
Wadi Halfa 42, 83, 192, 199

Politics
1920 Air Conference 13, 14
Air Navigation Act 13
Cadman Committee 80, 82, 87, 88, 150, 167, 168
Controller–General, Civil Aviation 13
'fly by itself' 14, 167
Hambling Committee 15, 16
Versailles Peace Conference 12
Weir Committee 13, 14
ploughed furrow 14

reserve routes 183, 188, 200, 210

Ships
HMS *Achilles* 169, 179, 226–229
HMS *Amphion* 106, 109
HMS *Brilliant* 21
HMS *Leander* 169
SS *Caernarvon Castle* 23
SS *The City of Canton* 191, 205, 206
SS *Trent* 13
Turakina 225, 227
Rangitane 225, 227, 228
surface raiders
Orion 225–228
Komet 225, 227

subsidies 14, 15, 21, 38, 40, 41, 70, 71, 82, 84, 86–88, 90, 137, 167
surcharge 22–24, 80, 84, 151, 208

Surveys
Brackley to Australia in Atalanta 23
Brancker and Cobham 17
Egglesfield to Durban 42, 48
Egglesfield to Singapore 48
Fysh/Brackley Survey 38, 45–47

Tasman Empire Airways Limited (TEAL)
Awarua to Honolulu 233–235
covert mission 235
delivery of *Australia* 169, 173–176
delivery of *Aotearoa* 175–177
delivery of *Awarua* 175, 178–180
inauguration 169, 181, 182, 225
Kingsford Smith's dream 169
military use of TEAL 'boats 225–236
recruiting for TEAL 169, 173, 174
training and survey 169, 178, 226
tri–national talks 169

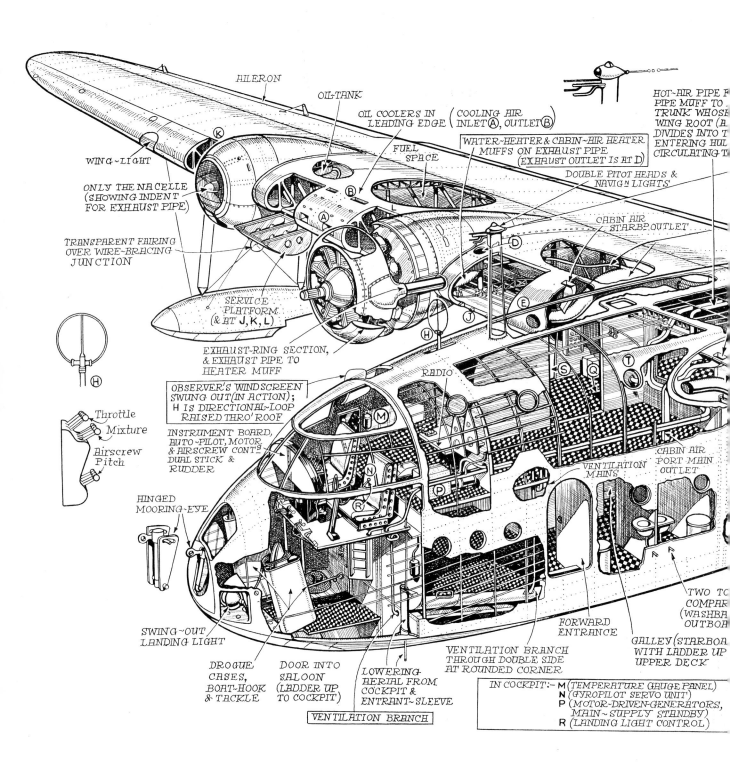

AILERON

OIL-TANK

OIL COOLERS IN
LEADING EDGE (COOLING AIR
INLET Ⓐ, OUTLET Ⓑ)

FUEL
SPACE

WATER~HEATER & CABIN~AIR HEATER
MUFFS ON EXHAUST PIPE
(EXHAUST OUTLET IS AT D)

HOT~AIR PIPE F
PIPE MUFF TO
TRUNK WHOSE
WING ROOT (A
DIVIDES INTO T
ENTERING HUL
CIRCULATING T

DOUBLE PITOT HEADS &
NAVIG~ LIGHTS

WING~LIGHT

ONLY THE NACELLE
(SHOWING INDENT
FOR EXHAUST PIPE)

CABIN AIR
STARB~OUTLET

TRANSPARENT FAIRING
OVER WIRE~BRACING
JUNCTION

SERVICE
PLATFORM
(& AT J, K, L)

EXHAUST-RING SECTION,
& EXHAUST PIPE TO
HEATER MUFF

Throttle

Mixture

Airscrew
Pitch

OBSERVER'S WINDSCREEN
SWUNG OUT (IN ACTION);
H IS DIRECTIONAL~LOOP
RAISED THRO' ROOF

RADIO

VENTILATION
MAINS

CABIN AIR
PORT MAIN
OUTLET

INSTRUMENT BOARD,
AUTO~PILOT, MOTOR
& AIRSCREW CONT~
DUAL STICK &
RUDDER

HINGED
MOORING~EYE

TWO TO
COMPAR
(WASHBA
OUTBOA

SWING~OUT
LANDING LIGHT

FORWARD
ENTRANCE

GALLEY (STARBOA
WITH LADDER UP
UPPER DECK

DROGUE
CASES,
BOAT-HOOK
& TACKLE

DOOR INTO
SALOON
(LADDER UP
TO COCKPIT)

LOWERING~
AERIAL FROM
COCKPIT &
ENTRANT~SLEEVE

VENTILATION BRANCH
THROUGH DOUBLE SIDE
AT ROUNDED CORNER

IN COCKPIT:— M (TEMPERATURE GAUGE PANEL)
N (GYROPILOT SERVO UNIT)
P (MOTOR-DRIVEN-GENERATORS,
MAIN~SUPPLY STANDBY)
R (LANDING LIGHT CONTROL)

VENTILATION BRANCH